On the Edge

NATE SILVER

On the Edge

The Art of Risking Everything

ALLEN LANE
an imprint of
PENGUIN BOOKS

ALLEN LANE

UK | USA | Canada | Ireland | Australia
India | New Zealand | South Africa

Penguin Books is part of the Penguin Random House group of companies
whose addresses can be found at global.penguinrandomhouse.com.

First published in the United States of America by Penguin Random House LLC 2024
First published in Great Britain by Allen Lane 2024
003

Image Credits
Page 19: art by Zach Weinersmith, courtesy of Zach Weinersmith
Page 62: courtesy of Piotr Lopusiewicz
Page 346: courtesy of Jesse Prinz
Page 354: courtesy of xkcd

Printed and bound in Great Britain by Clays Ltd, Elcograf S.p.A.

The authorized representative in the EEA is Penguin Random House Ireland,
Morrison Chambers, 32 Nassau Street, Dublin DO2 YH68

A CIP catalogue record for this book is available from the British Library

HARDBACK ISBN: 978–0–241–55703–7
TRADE PAPERBACK ISBN: 978–0–241–56852–1

www.greenpenguin.co.uk

To Robert Gauldin

CONTENTS

———————

On the Edge

PROLOGUE
Motivation

I'm sure that many of you will know me for my analysis of American elections. But here's something you might not know: in covering politics, I've always felt like a fish out of water.

I played poker professionally before I ever wrote a word about politics or built an election model. I still feel more at home in a casino than at a political convention. I have the numbers of dozens of top poker players in my contacts list—but few people who work in politics or government. In fact, even my decision to start FiveThirtyEight, which I founded in 2008 and worked for until 2023, was an unexpected consequence of a law passed by Congress that ended my three-year tenure as a professional poker player.

So with this book, I'm getting back to my roots. I've spent most of the past three years immersed in a world that I call the River. The River is a sprawling ecosystem of like-minded people that includes everyone from low-stakes poker pros just trying to grind out a living to crypto kings and venture-capital billionaires. It is a way of thinking and a mode of life. People don't know very much about the River, but they should. Most Riverians aren't rich and powerful. But rich and powerful people are disproportionately likely to be Riverians compared to the rest of the population.

Given everything that took place while I was writing this book—poker cheating scandals; Elon Musk's transformation from rocket-launching renegade into X edgelord; the spectacular self-induced implosion of Sam

Bankman-Fried—you'd think the River had a rough few years. But guess what: *the River is winning.* Silicon Valley and Wall Street are still accumulating more and more wealth. Las Vegas is taking in more and more money. In a world forged not by the toil of human hands but by the computations of machines, those of us who understand the algorithms hold the trump cards.

In the course of writing this book, I conducted around two hundred formal interviews—mostly with people I'd describe as residents of the River, but also with outside critics and observers. Then there were countless informal and sometimes off-the-record conversations at poker games, sporting events, or over drinks—the sorts of conversations I've been having my whole life. It became something of a running joke among my friends that I frequently traveled to Las Vegas, South Florida, California, and the Bahamas "for research purposes." But that's where the action is in the River, not in the halls of academia or the rotundas of government buildings.

I also had a lot of hands-on experience. I played in poker games against billionaires and had enough success in poker tournaments to at one point climb into the top three hundred in the Global Poker Index rankings and finish eighty-seventh out of more than ten thousand players in the 2023 World Series of Poker Main Event. I also taught myself to become a moderately proficient sports bettor, making almost $2 million worth of bets. I only turned a modest profit—but I was enough of a threat that DraftKings and several other major U.S. sportsbooks essentially banned me from placing bets with them for any meaningful amount of money, even as their advertisements proliferated across America's sports stadiums and television screens.

My mission is to be a friendly, informative—and occasionally provocative—tour guide to the River. People in the River trust me to tell their stories because—let's be honest—I'm one of them. Their way of thinking, for the most part, is my way of thinking.

But I also hope I can highlight some of the flaws in their thinking. Because if you'll pardon the cliché, the River isn't all fun and games. The activities that everyone agrees are capital-G Gambling—like blackjack and slots and horse racing and lotteries and poker and sports betting—are really just the tip of the iceberg. They are fundamentally not that different from trading stock options or crypto tokens, or investing in new tech startups. The River is full of tributaries and niches, and not all of the people in the River would describe themselves as gamblers. But the various regions of the River have a lot in common, and there are many connections between people in different parts of the environment: hedge-funders who play poker, sports bettors who become entrepreneurs, crypto billionaires who pal around with Oxford philosophers who take a mathematical approach to studying the human condition.

The River also has a canon of influences and ideas, from game theory and Nash equilibria to expected value and marginal utility, that underlie almost all of the activities it undertakes. Most of the ideas are not all that complicated in principle, but they can involve a lot of jargon and inside references. If you hear a Riverian talk about "updating their priors" or "sizing their bets" or making a joke about paper clips, those all refer to parts of the canon. If you didn't bother to learn the lingo—well, sorry, they'll still use it to talk around you like a couple at a dinner party insulting your cooking in a foreign language they know you don't understand. I'll teach you as much of that language as I can.

So buckle up, bring a few bucks to gamble with if you're so inclined—don't tell anyone, but there are poker games in the back of the bus—and let's begin.

0

Introduction

The Seminole Hard Rock Hotel & Casino in Hollywood, Florida, features one nightclub, seven pools, fourteen restaurants, a thirty-foot-high indoor waterfall, dozens of pieces of bedazzled rock-and-roll memorabilia, two hundred gaming tables, 1,275 guest rooms, three thousand slot machines, and a glimmering guitar-shaped hotel that shoots beams of neon blue light twenty thousand feet into the sky.

Like most casinos—and like most things in South Florida—the Hard Rock is designed to overwhelm your senses and undermine your inhibitions. Picture a casino in your head. If you haven't been to a place like the Hard Rock or the Wynn in Las Vegas, you're probably thinking of a dingy "slot barn" full of cigarette smoke and mazelike rows of chirping machines. Indeed, those can be some of the most depressing places on Earth. But at high-end resorts like the Hard Rock, the mood at busy hours is *exuberant*. Few places in American life attract a broader cross section of society. There are adults of all ages, races, classes, ethnic groups, and political orientations. There are senior citizens hoping to hit a slot jackpot; groups of bros and gaggles of girls; and attendees of third-rate trade association conferences compensating for the awkwardness of it all by overindulging in booze and blackjack.

I spent a *lot* of time in casinos over the course of writing this book.

Needless to say, even the most glamorous ones eventually become tiresome. I sometimes had the feeling of being a professional wedding photographer: everyone was having the time of their life, their very *special* day. But I knew all the tropes, all the recurring characters—the dude trying to hide from his buddies at the craps table that he was playing beyond his means; the BFFs from the bachelorette party jockeying for pole position when a hot bachelor walked by; the friendly couple from Nebraska having the night of their life playing blackjack before giving all their winnings back twice over.

It was April 2021. I was in Florida for the Seminole Hard Rock Poker Showdown, the first really big poker tournament in the United States since the pandemic. For better or worse, I'd been pretty careful about avoiding crowded indoor spaces until I got vaccinated for COVID-19. I hadn't even been on a plane since March 11, 2020, when I learned midflight that Tom Hanks had gotten COVID, that the NBA had suspended its season, that President Trump had shut down travel from Europe—and that my fellow passengers and I had landed in a riskier universe.

But it was a year later, and it was time to gamble. Judging by the crowds at the Hard Rock, a lot of other people were in the same frame of mind. Despite their reputation for risk tolerance, casinos mostly did shut down in the early days of COVID. Even the Las Vegas Strip—which I'd always assumed would continue to operate even in the event of a nuclear apocalypse—was closed for two and a half months. During this period, casino gaming revenues across the United States were down by as much as 96 percent from a year earlier.

But they rebounded with a vengeance. Somehow, between the anxiety caused by the unprecedented mass death of COVID and the boredom caused by the unprecedented lack of social interaction, Americans' appetite for YOLO (You Only Live Once) behavior exploded, manifesting itself in everything from illegal fireworks displays to traffic accidents to cryptocurrency bubbles. (Bitcoin prices increased roughly tenfold in the year after the WHO declared COVID-19 to be a pandemic.) And so in April 2021—even as schools remained closed in parts of the country—American casinos won a staggering $4.6 billion in gaming revenues from their patrons, 26 percent *higher* than in the same month two years earlier, before the pandemic.

Poker players came out in a show of force at the Hard Rock. In April 2019, the last time this particular tournament had been held before COVID, it had a respectable 1,360 entrants. The 2021 version drew almost twice as many—2,482 entrants—despite still being in the middle of a pandemic and a travel ban affecting most of the poker-playing world. It could easily have been more: demand was so overwhelming that there were hours-long waits to pony up $3,500 and register for a seat. Still, this was the largest-ever number of entrants for a tournament on the World Poker Tour, which sponsored the event. Appropriately enough, the tournament was eventually won by an ICU nurse from Grand Rapids, Michigan, named Brek Schutten, who had done his time in COVID wards.

We played through unusual conditions. There was a mask mandate, which I'd expected to be an enforcement disaster: poker players are both individualistic and irascible, not the types to quietly follow orders. But most of them were so damn happy to be playing poker again that there were relatively few complaints.* A bigger constraint was that, as a COVID half measure, the poker tables were equipped with kludgy octagonal plexiglass dividers. This made for one entertaining wrinkle: whenever a player got knocked out of the tournament, the floor staff would squeakily eulogize his departure by wiping down his section of the plexiglass, like an NBA towel boy wiping the sweat off the court after some hapless forward had just been dunked on by Giannis Antetokounmpo.

However, the plexiglass had the effect of fun-house mirrors, making it hard to properly view your opponents. Sure, I could see the other players well enough if I concentrated. But contrary to what you might have heard, most poker tells aren't given away by blatantly staring at an opponent and getting a "soul read." Instead, it's subtleties on the boundary of conscious observation: a flick of the wrist here, a quickening of the pulse there; an

---

* This patience would soon evaporate, and by later that year there were constant arguments about mask and vaccine policies at the poker table.

opponent you spy, out of the corner of your eye, looking more erect in her seat after she first peeks at her cards. (She probably has a strong hand.) Poker is *mostly* a mathematical game, but the edges are so thin that you'll take whatever reads you can get.

Between the plexiglass, the masks, and being out of practice being around other people, I felt like I was playing poker underwater. My body betrayed my anxiety. Not only was I feeling my pulse when I made a big decision, but for parts of the tournament, my hands even began trembling when I bet chips, something that's almost never happened to me before or since. When I reviewed a few hands later with my poker coach—yeah, I have a poker coach, like some people have a personal trainer—they nearly all featured me overplaying and overthinking situations as though making up for a year lost during the pandemic. The Hendon Mob Poker Database says I eventually finished in 161st place in the tournament for $7,465, but I actually lost money on the trip.

And yet, it was a great experience. After an isolating election year in 2020—isolating because I was working remotely during the pandemic, and because for reasons I'll explain to you later, I find presidential election years to be alienating—I felt welcome in the poker world. The World Poker Tour even tweeted congratulations to me from their @WPT account, not something they'd usually do for the 161st-place finisher.

I'm not sure I fully recognized it in the moment, but the tournament was the first taste of several realizations I'd have in the course of writing this book. One was that *something important was happening*, something that went beyond poker. That the tournament had drawn a record number of players—that people were so aggressively "returning to normal" in the hyperreal and obviously-not-COVID-safe environment of a casino—that seemed significant. People have always had different risk tolerances, but they're often hidden from public view. If the person standing right in front of me in the grocery line is planning to spend his evening curling up and watching Netflix, and the person right behind me is planning to go on an all-night cocaine bender at a strip club, I don't really have any way to know that and I really don't care.

But COVID made those risk preferences public, worn on our proverbial sleeves and our literal faces. For a lot of folks, COVID was the Wild West, forcing them to confront risk and reward with little precedent to rely upon and expert guidance that changed constantly. My experience in writing this book is that people are becoming more bifurcated in their risk tolerance—and that this affects everything from who we hang out with to how we vote. Maybe Netflix Guy and Strip Club Guy aren't even shopping at the same grocery store anymore; Netflix Guy moved to the country now that he doesn't need to be in the office, and Strip Club Guy moved to Miami—and was probably playing against me in the poker tournament.

I want to be careful here. In any statistical distribution, you'll find some people on either end of the bell curve, and this book often focuses on people on the extreme right tail of risk. But risk-taking is an understudied personality trait, and the academic literature is divided over the extent some people are generally more risk-taking as opposed to taking risks within specific domains. My favorite example of a domain-specific risk-taker is Dr. Ezekiel Emanuel, who served on President Biden's COVID-19 advisory board. In a May 2022 op-ed, Emanuel said that he was avoiding eating indoors at restaurants because he was worried about long COVID, but also bragged about riding a motorcycle. That seems like an insane pair of risk preferences to hold. (Motorcycles are about thirty times as deadly as passenger cars per mile traveled.) With that said, I can think of plenty of areas in my own life in which my risk preferences are hard to defend as being rational or consistent. People are complicated, and even among poker players, there are plenty of degens (degenerate gamblers) and plenty of nits.*

Indeed, most of us seem conflicted about how much risk we want in our lives. One of the truisms in studies of risk is that younger people take on more risk than older ones. That may be changing, however. Teenagers in the United States and other Western countries are undertaking far less risky behavior—drugs, drinking, sex—than they did a generation ago.

---

* A nit is a cautious or tight player, but the term can also refer to risk-aversion or cheapness outside of poker. If you arrive at the airport three hours early for a domestic flight, you're a nit.

And yet, literal gambling is booming. In 2022, Americans lost around $60 billion betting at licensed casinos and online gambling operations—a record even after accounting for inflation. They also lost an estimated $40 billion in unlicensed, gray-market, or black-market gambling—and about $30 billion in state lotteries. To be clear, that's the amount they *lost*, not the amount they *wagered*, which was roughly ten times as much. Between all forms of gambling, Americans are probably making in excess of $1 trillion in bets annually.

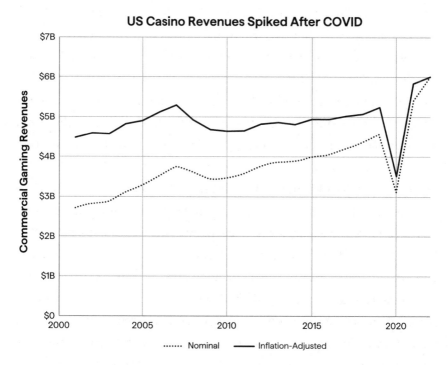

US Casino Revenues Spiked After COVID

And here's something that probably should keep more of us up at night: American life expectancy has stagnated. During the pandemic, in fact, it declined, to 76.4 years in 2021 from 78.8 years in 2019. Life expectancy numbers during a pandemic can be misleading—they essentially assume we'll maintain the same number of COVID deaths going forward when we likely won't—and the numbers have begun rebounding to some extent. Even before COVID, though, American men had lost a tenth of a year of life expectancy between 2014 (76.4 years) and 2019 (76.3).

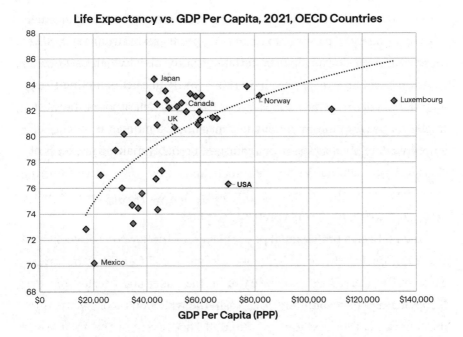

Life Expectancy vs. GDP Per Capita, 2021, OECD Countries

In fact, the United States is now an outlier among highly developed countries. Based on our very high GDP, you'd expect American life expectancy to be about *five years* longer than it is. The reasons for the shortfall are complicated, involving a mix of cultural and political factors as well as the United States' high inequality. But they partly reflect the United States being more risk-taking—we have more driving at freeway speeds, more opioids, more COVID, more firearms—and less willingness to sacrifice freedom or economic growth for longer lifespans.

The other big realization I had on that flight home from Florida was that this world of poker players and poker-playing types—this world of *calculated risk-taking*—was the world where I fit in.

This shouldn't have been a huge surprise. It may even run in my blood. Neither of my parents is much into cards or casinos, but my paternal grandmother, Gladys Silver, was an outstanding gin rummy and bridge player and a notoriously punitive one: if you weren't careful about concealing your cards, she'd take full advantage of that information as a way of teaching you to be more careful next time. My great-grandfather Jacob Silver founded an auto-body shop in Waterbury, Connecticut, which held a poker game on payout day every second Friday—until, according to family legend, the wives of the mechanics forced him to switch payment from cash to checks because too many of their husbands were coming home with empty wallets. *Another* great-grandfather, Ferdinand Thrun, was a notorious arsonist who came up with such innovative ways of committing insurance fraud that there literally weren't laws to charge him with. Ferdinand would have run a pretty good bluff.

And I'd been a professional poker player for three years between 2004 and 2007, during the so-called Poker Boom. The Poker Boom began because of the increasing availability of online poker and because of Chris Moneymaker, an accountant from Nashville who won an online qualifying tournament for a seat at the $10,000 Main Event at the 2003 World Series of Poker and then parlayed that into winning the Main Event for $2.5 million. If you'd asked ChatGPT to design a person who would most increase the amount of interest in poker by winning the WSOP, it might have spat out Moneymaker. An affable, pudgy, late twenty-something dude with a boring corporate job, he was exactly the customer the online poker sites were targeting, an archetype for every office drone who wanted to break out of his cubicle and win the big jackpot. The number of participants in the World Series of Poker Main Event exploded from 839 in Moneymaker's 2003 to 8,773 just three years later in 2006, largely fueled by people who had won their seats online.

I was one of those people who lived the dream. I soon found myself on a nocturnal schedule. Poker games are usually best late at night, when your opponents are some combination of drunk, sleep-deprived, or delirious from winning or losing a bunch of money. So I'd come home from my cubicle, take a nap, and then play poker online, sometimes straight through until the morning, when I'd straggle into work and struggle through the day. Needless to say, this wasn't sustainable, and—making considerably more money as a poker player than as a consultant—I quit my corporate job within about six months to play poker and work for the baseball statistics startup Baseball Prospectus.

It was a good living for a couple of years—but like most edges in gambling, it wouldn't last. Some of this was the natural evolution of the game: the Poker Boom sputtered into more of a poker plateau as losing players either went broke, quit, or got better, removing one sucker from the table at a time.

But it was also partly the doing of the U.S. Congress. In late 2006, the GOP-led Congress, hungry for a victory with "moral majority" voters ahead of the midterms as Republican congressman Mark Foley resigned from office for having sent sexually explicit messages to underage male pages, passed a bill called the Unlawful Internet Gambling Enforcement Act (UIGEA). The UIGEA didn't ban online poker per se, but it established regulations that choked off payment processors: it's hard to play poker if you can't exchange cash for chips. Some sites closed to U.S. players while others remained open, but between the shadow of illegality and the increased friction of getting your money in and out, inexperienced new players avoided the games, making them much tougher to beat.

There was one silver lining: the UIGEA piqued my interest in politics. The bill had been tucked into an unrelated piece of homeland security legislation and passed during the last session before Congress recessed for the midterms. It was a shifty workaround, and having essentially lost my job, I wanted the people responsible for it to lose their jobs, too. And they did: Republicans lost both the House and the Senate, including the seat of Representative Jim Leach of Iowa, the chief sponsor of the UIGEA, whose thirty-year tenure in office ended partly because of poker players who had contributed money to his opponent.

Struggling to win money as the games were drying up, I quit poker about six months later. With my newfound interest in politics and the extra time on my hands, I wound up starting FiveThirtyEight in 2008. There's no way to say this without bragging, but FiveThirtyEight kind of blew up, going from having a few hundred readers per day at the outset to hundreds of thousands by Election Day that year. Then before I knew it, it had *tens of millions* of readers; in 2016, our election forecast page was literally the most engaging piece of content on the internet according to the analytics service Chartbeat.

Expected Value: What Separates the River from the Rest of the World

But here's the thing about having tens of millions of people viewing your forecast: a lot of them aren't going to get it. A probabilistic election forecast—for instance, a forecast that says Democratic senator Mark Kelly has a 66 percent chance of winning re-election in Arizona—is a product of a highly specific way of thinking. It's about the most natural thing in the world to a former professional poker player like me, but will be completely alien to other people.

On November 8, 2016, the statistical model I built for FiveThirtyEight said there was a 71 percent chance that Hillary Clinton would win the presidency and a 29 percent chance that Donald Trump would win. For context, this estimate of Trump's chances was considered high at the time. Other statistical models put Trump's chances at anywhere from 15 percent to less than 1 percent. And betting markets put them at around 1 chance in 6 (17 percent). Trump won, of course, by sweeping several Rust Belt swing states.

The reaction of many people in the political world to this forecast was: "Nate Silver is a fucking idiot." But from *my* standpoint—and from the standpoint of people in the River, the landscape of skilled gamblers and like-minded folks that I introduced in the prologue—this was a *damned good forecast*. It was a good forecast for a simple reason: if you'd bet on it, you would have made a lot of money. If a model says that Trump's chances are 29 percent and the market price is 17 percent, the correct play is to bet on Trump—big. For every $100 you bet on Trump, you'd expect to make a profit of $74.

For the record, I cast my ballot for Clinton. Lots of people are happy to tell you how you should vote. My job is to handicap the race—to tell you how you should *bet*. Or at least dispassionately evaluate the probabilities.

The term we use for this in the River is that my forecast was +EV, meaning "positive expected value"—the result you expect to wind up with *on average* over the long run. In this case, for instance, the EV is calculated thusly:

$$(0.71 \times -\$100) + (0.29 \times +\$500) = +\$74$$

Seventy-one percent of the time, Clinton wins and you lose your $100 stake. But the 29 percent of the time Trump wins, you're paid out at 5:1 odds,* turning your $100 investment into a $500 profit. That's good. *Really* good. Sports bettors are often happy to eke out a 2 to 5 percent expected profit on an individual bet. The stock market has an expected profit of around 8 percent per year after adjusting for inflation. With a bet on Trump, you'd expect to make a 74 percent profit off every dollar you invested.

Expected value is such a foundational concept in the River's way of thinking that 2016 served as a litmus test for who in my life was a member of the tribe and who wasn't. At the same moment a certain type of person was liable to get *very* mad at me, others were *thrilled* that they'd been able to use FiveThirtyEight's forecast to make a winning bet. (I still sometimes get poker players picking up dinner tabs for the money that my forecasts made them in 2016 or other years.)

Maybe this way of thinking seems incredibly foreign to you. That's okay. We're only at the beginning of the tour. And there are some philosophical complications to sort out. What does an "average" outcome mean in the context of a seemingly one-off event like the 2016 election? But I want you to understand that many powerful people and businesses think in expected-value terms—and they win more than they lose in the long run. Businesses like Seminole Gaming, which runs the Hard Rock, make billions of dollars a year, much of it from people who don't understand EV.

As a first step, I'd like to get you thinking probabilistically. The vital point of my first book, *The Signal and the Noise*, is that probabilistic forecasts are a sign of humility, not hubris. The world is a complicated place.

---

* A market price showing a 1-in-6 chance of winning (17 percent) means the odds are 5 to 1 against.

Small perturbations can have outsized effects, from the assassination of Franz Ferdinand to whichever sequence of events in China produced the first version of SARS-CoV-2. Sometimes the entire trajectory of history can turn on nearly random events, like the poorly designed "butterfly ballot" in Palm Beach County, Florida, that caused some Floridians to mistakenly vote for Pat Buchanan and probably cost Al Gore the 2000 presidential election. Play out thousands of poker hands, watch hundreds of sporting events when you have money on the line, or invest in dozens of startups, and you'll quickly learn that between the vagaries of fate and our uncertain state of knowledge about the world, getting things *even somewhat right* is hard enough. Probabilities are usually the best you can do.

But it's more than that. Gamblers, traders, and model builders see the world as complicated, stochastic, and contingent. We scratch and claw for every basis point of value. If our models can be right 53.1 percent of the time instead of 52.7 percent, that counts as a big improvement. We recognize that it's hard to beat the market—not impossible, but hard—and we have the battle scars to prove it.

To be clear, there are plenty of times when ordinary people have an intuitive grasp of probabilities. They'll carry an umbrella if the sky looks menacing. They'll calculate whether it's worth it to go fifteen miles above the speed limit when they're running late to the airport. They'll unconsciously pat their back pockets to check for their phone and wallet in areas known to have a lot of pickpockets. Even when it comes to potentially high-stakes medical decisions, they can play the percentages. For as much controversy as there was over COVID-19 vaccines in the U.S., for instance, 93 percent of seniors—who faced disproportionately higher rates of death and severe disease from COVID—received their initial two doses, including about 85 percent even in extremely red states such as Alabama and Wyoming. Even problem gamblers, according to the experts I spoke with for this book, are not necessarily naïve about the odds they face; they may know they're making a bet with a losing expectation and place it anyway. (I'll have more on this in chapter 3.)

One thing I've found is that people get much less angry at me about my sports forecasts—say, when a team with a 29 percent chance to win the Super Bowl pulls off the upset—than my election forecasts. (At FiveThirtyEight, I also built probabilistic forecasts of sporting events.) This is because of the familiar rhythms of sports: every fan has watched enough penalty kicks sail over the goal or field goals doink off the crossbar to know that the better team doesn't always win. Sports are closer to an everyday, should-I-bring-an-umbrella problem.

Politicians and political parties, by contrast—especially in a highly polarized two-party system like the United States—don't subscribe to this way of thinking and *really* don't want you to think that way about elections either. Instead, they see their victories as being morally righteous—not reflecting contingencies like butterfly ballots or the Electoral College or what the inflation rate happens to be,* but rather as embodying the "right side of history" or even God's will. They see every election as uniquely, existentially important—not drawn from some probability distribution of possible outcomes, as expected value assumes, but its own special snowflake. They also don't want to permit a whole lot of room for nuance or complexity or pluralistic and probabilistic thinking—it's hard enough to keep your coalition together, so you don't want people on your "team" arguing with one another. And they view the whole idea of *betting* on politics as cringey and morally suspect.

I'm wary about using the term "rational" here because it's a word we'll need to define more precisely later in the book. For most philosophers, for instance, "rational" isn't just a synonym for "reasonable." (We'll take this up in chapter 7.) But permit me this one-time informal use of "rational": *people are really fucking irrational about elections.* And that's understandable. Elections are a lot like COVID: high-stakes, high-stress experiences that you don't have a whole lot of control over. Conversely, a probabilistic election forecast is the product of a hyperrationalist intellectual tradition. It makes for a strange cultural clash.

---

* My work suggests that economic conditions such as inflation, the unemployment rate, and the stock market play an important role in whether presidents are re-elected, but presidents themselves often have relatively little to do with these. Exogenous shocks—supply-chain disruptions, weather events, labor disputes, wars breaking out—can potentially have large effects on the American economy.

Welcome to the River

I'm one of those people with a mediocre memory for names—don't bet on me to recall the name of your puppy on the first try—but a good memory for places. When I'm stuck on a knotty problem, I need to get up and take a walk. So in thinking through the material for this book, I've been making a mental map of the landscape of the River.

When I first pitched this project, I had a different name for this metaphorical place: the Pool. I thought this was cute. Poker players and other gamblers love metaphors involving water (a bad player is called a "fish"), and "pool" itself is a gambling term, as in a betting pool.

But the Pool implies some sort of exclusive membership, like a pool at a gym or a country club, when instead gambling is a relatively democratic institution. Imagine that you and your buddies could enter a 3-on-3 basketball tournament, and the first game you played was against LeBron James, Steph Curry, and Luka Dončić. In poker tournaments, that's exactly what you can get. Pay your buy-in, and you can literally play against the best players in the world—or against a celebrity that you'd never have a chance to meet otherwise. At one event at the 2022 World Series of Poker, the player seated one seat to my right was Neymar, the Brazilian great who is one of the best soccer players in the world. (Neymar got much too aggressive with a mediocre hand and I won a big pot off him. He's also scored seventy-nine career goals for the Brazilian national team and I've scored zero.)

So in my mental map, the River is not one discrete place so much as an ecosystem of people and ideas. Residents in different parts of the River don't necessarily know one another, and many don't think of themselves as part of some broader community. But their ties are deeper than I expected when I began working on this project. They speak one another's language with terms such as expected value, Nash equilibriums, and Bayesian priors.

I think of the River as having several subregions. Let's start with the

one that will require the most explanation: **Upriver**. I imagine Upriver as being like Northern California with its major research universities, rolling hills, and ocean views—but also eccentric and aloof, not quite fitting in with the rest of the country. The clearest manifestations of Upriver today are in two related intellectual movements, rationalism and effective altruism. I will define these terms more fully in chapter 7, because they are the subject of a lot of argument—rationalists and EAs (effective altruists) love to argue. Although EA ostensibly has a narrower focus, taking a data-driven approach toward altruism and philanthropy, in practice both EAs and rationalists have a catholic appetite for involving themselves in all sorts of controversies.

Effective altruism came under substantial scrutiny in 2022 following the implosion of the cryptocurrency exchange FTX. Sam Bankman-Fried, FTX's founder—who I spoke with several times for this book both before and after FTX's bankruptcy, and who I cover extensively in chapters 6 through 8—identified as an EA and promised to commit hundreds of millions of dollars to EA-related causes through the FTX Foundation. I saw firsthand that this was not merely an arm's-length relationship. When the Oxford philosopher Will MacAskill, one of the most prominent intellectuals in EA, released his book *What We Owe the Future* in 2022, Bankman-Fried hosted a book launch party for him at Eleven Madison Park, the very expensive vegan restaurant in New York.

Why were Oxford philosophers hanging out with cryptocurrency billionaires at a three-star Michelin restaurant? Well, we're going to get into that. One reason is that EAs are concerned with how to spend money on charitable causes more efficiently—for instance, by donating to purchase anti-malaria bed nets in Africa, thought of as a highly cost-effective intervention—and Bankman-Fried had a lot of money.

But that's hardly a complete answer. The other reason is that there's a lot of like-mindedness between people in different parts of the River, and they naturally get along with one another. One friend calls this type of person an "EV maximizer"—that is, someone who is always trying to calculate the highest expected value in relation to a particular problem, be it how to play a poker hand or how to most effectively donate to charity. The earnest nerdiness of posts on the Effective Altruism Forum—with titles like "Should ChatGPT make us downweight our belief in the consciousness of non-human animals?" and "Does the US public support ultraviolet germicidal irradiation technology for reducing risks from pathogens?"—gives off the same vibes as poker players arguing about the arcane details of poker hands.

EAs and rationalists also have close ties to the tech sector, and many of the leaders of the movement are based in Northern California. And in recent years, some EAs have become less concerned with traditional philanthropy and more interested in the development of artificial intelligence. Many EAs and rationalists believe that AI is an extremely high-stakes problem, one of the most important developments in the history of civilization. Some also believe that AI, if it becomes sufficiently powerful, could end or profoundly harm civilization and pose an existential risk to humanity. So it has been an interesting time to write about these movements. Between their catastrophic association with Sam Bankman-Fried (SBF) on the one hand, and the astonishing progress of AI tools like ChatGPT on the other hand—progress that was well predicted by some EAs—it is vital to understand their mindset.

Further downstream, you'll find what I call **Midriver**, which I picture as having lots of tall, angular buildings, as Manhattan does. This is where people apply the EV maximizer skill set to make lots of money, such as through venture capital and hedge fund investing. There's more in this book on Silicon Valley than on Wall Street, though. The Silicon Valley guys are more of an open book, happier to flaunt their Riverian weirdness and show the middle finger to the East Coast establishment, and more explicitly aligned with movements like rationalism. But make no mistake: Wall Street is making money hand over fist from EV maximization, too.

Then there's **Downriver**, the region we've talked about the most so far. I imagine Downriver as Las Vegas meets New Orleans: lots of tourists and lots of gambling. It's Downriver where the term "edge" comes from (as in the title of this book). "Edge" means having a persistent advantage in gambling—consistently making +EV bets. Against 99.99 percent of customers who set foot on a casino floor and the very large majority in a sportsbook,* the house has the edge, but that doesn't stop Riverians from dreaming of being in the 0.01 percent.

But while games like poker can be fun, they also have an intellectual legacy that's directly downstream from foundational ideas in science, economics, and mathematics. And in some cases, actually, gambling is *upstream* from other scientific developments. Blaise Pascal and Pierre de Fermat developed probability theory in response to a friend's inquiry about the best strategy in a dice game. Signal-processing algorithms at Bell Labs in the 1950s were developed hand in hand with algorithms that told you how much to bet on college football games. And there are more than one hundred references to poker in *Theory of Games and Economic Behavior*, the seminal 1944 book on game theory by John von Neumann and Oskar Morgenstern, published as von Neumann was working with Robert Oppenheimer on the Manhattan Project. As we'll see in chapter 1, through a type of computer program known as a "solver," poker players are quite literally putting game theory into practice.

Finally, there's the **Archipelago,** which I envision as a series of offshore islands adjacent to Downriver where pretty much anything goes. Brick-and-mortar American casinos are more of a prim-and-proper business than you'd think—no longer associated with organized crime, they're heavily regulated and mostly owned by major corporations like MGM and Caesars with ticker symbols on the S&P 500. But the temptations of the Archipelago are never far away if you live in the River, and there is still a lot of gray-market off-the-books gambling activity in online poker, sports betting, and cryptocurrency. Sophisticated gamblers know to avoid the Archipelago—but it lies in wait to pick off the weakest of the herd.

And yet, the people in the River are my tribe—and I wouldn't have it

---

* Excluding poker, where you're playing against other players and not the house. Casinos are still guaranteed to make money from poker because they take a share of the pot called the rake, or charge players an hourly fee to pay. But it's possible to have a big-enough edge over the other players at poker to cover the house's cut.

any other way. Why did my conversations flow so naturally with people in the River, even when they were on subjects I was still learning more about? I think it mostly boils down to two clusters of attributes that are important for success in this environment.

COGNITIVE CLUSTER	PERSONALITY CLUSTER
Analytical	Competitive
Abstract	Critical
Decoupling	Independent-minded (contrarian)
	Risk-tolerant

First, there's what I call the "cognitive cluster." Quite literally: How do people in the River think about the world? It begins with abstract and analytical reasoning. These terms get thrown around a lot, so it's important to consider exactly what they mean. The root words of the term "analysis" mean to break up, loosen, divide, or cut apart—so analysis essentially means to resolve something complex into simpler elements. In regression analysis, for instance—probably the most widely used statistical technique in data science—the goal is to attribute a complex set of observations to relatively simple root causes. A barbecue restaurant in Austin, looking at its sales numbers, could run a regression analysis to adjust for factors like the day of the week, the weather, and if there was a big football game in town.

The natural companion to analytic thinking is abstract thinking—that is, trying to derive general rules or principles from the things you observe in the world. Another way to describe this is "model building." The models can be formal, as in a statistical model or even a philosophical model.* Or they can be informal, as in a mental model, or a set of heuristics (rules of thumb) that adapt well to new situations. In poker, for instance, there are millions of permutations for how a particular hand might play out, and it's impossible to plan for every one. So you need some generalizable rules, e.g., "Don't try to bluff out opponents who have already put a lot of money

---

* Statistical and philosophical models are more alike than you might realize. More about that in chapter 7.

into the pot." Those rules won't be perfect, but as you gain more experience, you can develop more sophisticated ones ("Don't try to bluff out opponents who have already put a lot of money into the pot *unless* it's likely they were on a flush draw and the flush didn't come in").

Analysis and abstraction are the essential steps when trying to draw conclusions from statistical data. The real world is messy, so first you use analysis to strip out the noise and break the problem down into manageable components; then you use abstraction to put the world together again in the form of a model that retains the most essential features and relationships. At the barbecue restaurant, for instance, maybe you raised prices in August and wanted to evaluate the effect this had on sales. To your surprise, sales increased despite the price hike. What happened? Maybe it was your new dry rub? Well, *maybe*. But probably it was that August is when University of Texas students return to town. Statistical analysis on past sales patterns can potentially account for this. It is not as easy as it sounds, and there are many ways it can go wrong (essentially, this is the subject of *The Signal and the Noise*). But nearly all professions in the River, including the more philosophical ones you'll find Upriver, involve some attempt at model building.

The final term in the cognitive cluster, "decoupling," is probably less familiar. It's really just the same thought process as applied to philosophical or political ideas. As Sarah Constantin puts it, decoupling is "the ability to block out context . . . the opposite of holistic thinking. It's the ability to separate, to view things in the abstract, to play devil's advocate." Decoupling has been found by the psychologist Keith Stanovich to correlate with performance on tests of logical and statistical reasoning, a type of intelligence that is valued in the River.

I think of decoupling as the tendency to make "Yes, but . . ." statements. Let me give you a mildly spicy example of a "Yes, but . . ." statement. Imagine someone saying the following:

> *Yes*, I disagree with the Chick-fil-A CEO's position on gay marriage, *but* they make a damned fine chicken sandwich.

This is decoupling. Note that the speaker is not necessarily going to eat at Chick-fil-A. For all you know, she might reveal in the next sentence that she's boycotting them despite their tasty sandwiches. But she's saying the CEO's politics have nothing to do with the quality of the food; she's decoupling them. This type of thinking comes naturally to people in the River. It tends to be highly unnatural when most people discuss politics, however—particularly on the political left in the United States, the tendency is to add context rather than remove it based on the identity of the speaker, the historical provenance of the idea, and so forth. Likewise, the tendency in the media is to contextualize ideas—*The New York Times* is no longer just the facts, but a "juicy collection of great narratives," as Ben Smith described it. This is a big part of why "political types" find people in the River abrasive, and vice versa.

Then there's the "personality cluster." These traits are more self-explanatory. People in the River are trying to beat the market. In sports betting, the average player loses money because the house takes a cut of every bet. So if you follow the consensus, you'll eventually go broke. Investing is more forgiving; just putting your money in index funds still has a positive expected value. Still, professional traders are trying to do better than the market-average return.

So part of the job of people in the River inherently involves being critical of consensus thinking, often to the point of being contrarian. Silicon Valley in particular is proud of its contrarianism—although as we'll see in chapter 5, it's conformist in its own way. Some people in the River can turn these traits off in interpersonal settings, but others can have a hard time.* It's not a coincidence many Riverians like to get in fights about politics on the internet.

Relatedly, people in the River are often intensely competitive. They're so competitive, in fact, that they make decisions that can be irrational, gambling even once they're essentially already set for life (think about Elon Musk's decision to buy Twitter when he was the world's richest

---

* I meekly raise my hand.

person and then one of its most admired). We'll explore this more through-out the book. But if you haven't gambled against other people before, I have to tell you: it can be quite stimulating. Winning money feels good, feeling as though you've outsmarted an opponent feels good, and when the two coincide, your brain is literally flooded with dopamine. It's no surprise that people chase the rush, sometimes to their own demise.

Finally, I put risk tolerance in this cluster because—whether they're degens or nits in other parts of their lives—being willing to break from the herd and go against the consensus is certainly not the safest professional path. Entrepreneurs usually have high levels of openness to experience and low levels of neuroticism, the "Big Five" personality traits that corre-late best with risk tolerance.

The River vs. the Village

There's also another community that competes with the River for power and influence. I call it the Village. I think of the Village as a midsized city, like Washington, D.C., or Boston, the sort of place that's just small enough where everyone knows one another and is a little self-conscious about it. It consists of people who work in government, in much of the media, and in parts of academia (although perhaps excluding some of the more quantita-tive academic fields such as economics). It has distinctly left-of-center politics associated with the Democratic Party.

Part of the rub is the personality clash—remember, Riverians love de-coupling and Villagers hate it—but these communities find themselves in-creasingly at odds. Media coverage is now much more adversarial toward the tech sector and generally skeptical of movements such as EA and ratio-nalism. But the grudge cuts in both directions: people within the River are seeking more political influence. Sam Bankman-Fried had become a ma-jor political player, donating millions of dollars openly to Democrats, but also covertly to Republicans. Meanwhile, Elon Musk's purchase of Twitter in 2022 was treated as a matter of existential importance by people in both the Village and the River. I think that reaction was silly, but it shows the extent to which these communities see themselves as rivals and are ready to go to battle. By 2023, the cold war between these tribes had escalated into open conflict as hedge fund billionaires led the charge to oust Ivy League presidents and *The New York Times* sued OpenAI. Incursions into enemy territory are treated with alarm, like when Google's AI model Gemini was criticized by Riverians for reflecting distinctively Villagey political attitudes.

I have a unique vantage point as someone who passes back and forth between these worlds. To be clear, I am not an unbiased observer. People in the River are—for better or worse—*my kind of people.* Conversely, I've never quite taken to the Village, and I've often felt like media coverage of me and FiveThirtyEight was misinformed, particularly after the 2016 election.

But I do hear a lot of the complaints that these communities have about each other. I don't think they are always articulated well, however. Even as a Riverian myself, I have quite a few criticisms of the River, and I think it could use critiques that hit the target more often. So here's a quick attempt to outline what I think are steelman versions of them. A steelman argument—a favorite technique of EAs and rationalists—is the opposite of a strawman argument. The idea is to build a robust and well-articulated version of the other side's position, even if it's one that you disagree with. Let's begin with the River's critique of the Village since it's the one I'm naturally inclined to sympathize with.

The River's Steelman Critique of the Village

A common complaint among people in the River is that Villagers are "too political."

What does that mean, exactly? It means that Villagers are coupling when they should be decoupling. The River worries that the Village's claims to academic, scientific, and journalistic expertise are becoming increasingly hard to separate from Democratic political partisanship.

Indeed, Riverians inherently distrust political parties, particularly in a two-party system like the United States where they are "big tent" coalitions that couple together positions on dozens of largely unrelated issues. Riverians think that partisan position taking often serves as a shortcut for the more nuanced and rigorous analysis that public intellectuals ought to engage in. They think these problems were particularly apparent during the COVID-19 pandemic and that the Village often adopted nakedly partisan positions—from endorsing public gatherings for the George Floyd protests after weeks of telling people to stay at home, to pushing to discourage Pfizer from making any announcement of the efficacy of its COVID-19 vaccine until after the 2020 presidential election—under the guise of scientific expertise.

Riverians also think that Villagers are too conformist and not aware of the degree to which their views are influenced by confirmation bias and political and social fads within their communities. Having a college degree is almost a prerequisite to the most prestigious Village jobs in academia, government, and media. But as voters sort themselves along political lines and as educational polarization increases, Village communities have become increasingly politically homogenous. In 2020, the twenty-five most-educated counties in the United States voted for Joe Biden over Trump by an average of 44 points, much greater than the 17-point margin by which they voted for Al Gore over George W. Bush in 2000. This shift has happened recently, in other words, and Village institutions like academia and the media—which historically had traditions of nonpartisanship—are struggling to adapt to it.

And remember how competitive Riverians are? Well, Riverians worry that Villagers are stifling competition by increasingly focusing on equity of outcomes rather than equality of opportunity. Riverians usually hold the classic capitalist belief that the free market does a better job than central planners in sorting out winners from losers. Furthermore, they believe that market competition benefits society as a whole by producing technological innovation and economic growth and improvements in the standard of living. And they can cite examples of the Village moving away from meritocracy. For instance, elite colleges and graduate school programs have begun to deemphasize standardized test scores even though most research suggests that standardized tests are less influenced by social upbringing than other ways of evaluating applicants.

And naturally, Riverians think Villagers are too paternalistic, too neurotic, and too risk-averse. The extensive COVID-19 precautions imposed on college, high school, and elementary school students are one prominent example. Riverians viewed these as failing a cost-benefit test, given that young people were much less likely than the general population to have severe outcomes from COVID and the disruptions to education caused huge amounts of learning loss.

Finally, Riverians are fierce advocates for free speech, not just as a constitutional right but as a cultural norm. Remember, Riverians are big into abstraction—they care about principles. They also believe better ideas will win out in the "marketplace of ideas" and that the Village's attempts at speech regulation are hypocritical and often counterproductive. Riverians aren't necessarily "anti-woke"—well, some are, like Elon Musk—but a plurality identify as liberal politically. But they see the culture wars as an annoying Village distraction from the things they really care about.

The Village's Steelman Critique of the River

But the Village can make several strong counter-critiques of the River. One strand of the argument centers around skepticism over unregulated capitalism and the River's conceit of rugged individualism. Sure, Riverians may say they like competition. But the Village, not unreasonably, thinks it's because competitions are often rigged in the River's favor. By any objective measure, Riverians are powerful incumbents rather than the disruptors they sometimes claim to be, and they benefit from existing social hierarchies; you don't have to be super-woke to notice that much of the River is very white, very male, and very wealthy.

Moreover, Villagers are skeptical that Riverians are actually as risk-taking as they claim. Sure, maybe poker players or small-business owners really are putting their own butts on the line. But when it comes to big business like venture capital, founders and investors can fail several times over and still land on their feet. To take one example, Adam Neumann, the cofounder of WeWork who was widely regarded as having mismanaged the company as it lost about 90 percent of its market value, nonetheless received hundreds of millions in venture capital backing for his new company, Flow.

The Village is also concerned about moral hazard. That is, on a variety of questions—from failing to take COVID-19 precautions to making highly leveraged investments—it questions whether people taking on risks bear the consequences of their actions. In the 2007–08 Global Economic Crisis, for instance, excessive risk-taking in the financial sector produced collateral damage to the economy while executives participating in these risky ventures were left relatively unscathed. The Village also questions whether recent technological innovations have in fact benefited society. Silicon Valley may talk a big game about rocket ships to Mars and lifesaving medical technologies, but one of its biggest categories of investment is social media, which has been blamed for everything from the revival of nationalist governments to depression among adolescents. Meanwhile, life expectancy in the United States has stagnated.

The Village also believes that Riverians are naïve about how politics works and about what is happening in the United States. Most pointedly, it sees Donald Trump and the Republican Party as having characteristics of a fascist movement and argues that it is time for moral clarity and unity against these forces. Villagers see themselves as being clearly right on the most important big-picture questions of the day, from climate change to gay and trans rights. So they view the Riverian inclination to poke holes in arguments and "just ask questions" as being a waste of time at best, and as potentially empowering a wake of bad-faith actors and bigots.

And Villagers generally don't share the River's interest in abstract moral philosophy. In the Village's view, some questions can be resolved through common sense, politics is inherently transactional, and not everything needs to be put up for debate or subjected to cost-benefit analysis. They also doubt whether Riverians are really as independent-minded and open to criticism as they claim. From SBF to Elon Musk to AI "accelerationists," the River has developed plenty of cults of personality.

Thank You for Your Purchase!—Here Is Your Itinerary for Flight OTE001

I'm tempted to go over those positions with a red editing pen—to tell you which parts I emphatically agree with, and where I'd push back. I wish it were as simple as just taking the average of Village and River morality. But sometimes the River and the Village bring out the worst in each other. As you're reading this book, keep in mind that both communities consist of a small number of elites that have little in common with the median American voter. For instance, one way to view the phenomenon known as regulatory capture is that the Village creates dumb rules to satisfy its political commitments, which powerful companies in the River then exploit to their advantage. Both groups accomplish their objectives, but the impact falls on everyday citizens and emerging businesses.

But we'll have plenty of time to talk about this later. The rest of this book consists of nine body chapters in two main parts—Gambling and Risk—plus two concluding chapters. The route I've chosen for our tour is upstream, beginning Downriver in the world of gambling proper and then moving upstream toward more abstract ideas.

Part 1: Gambling

- **Chapter 1, Optimization,** is the first of two chapters about poker. There's a lot of poker in this book, both because it was my personal entry point to the River and because it's the River's archetypal activity—a clean application of Riverian reasoning where some messy real-world complications don't apply. Chapter 1 focuses on man vs. machine and the advent of computer solvers, which have revolutionized poker. The basis for these solvers is game theory, which I discuss at length—alongside expected value, game theory is one of the most important concepts in the River.

- However, in **chapter 2, Perception,** we learn that some of those messy real-world complications do apply in poker after all. An explosive allegation of cheating blew up the high-stakes poker world as I was writing this book, and I'll investigate it thoroughly. I'll also introduce you to some of the world's best poker players, help you understand what makes them tick, and use them to guide us through subjects like what risk-taking does to your body and how to spot a bluffer—or a con artist.

- **Chapter 3, Consumption,** is a deeply reported look at the modern casino business, and how Las Vegas evolved from a desert backwater to the epicenter of a massive industry that reflects American capitalism in its most undistilled form. You'll meet a couple of gamblers who beat Vegas—but the vast majority of people don't. In the casino business, instead, the Riverian mindset is coming from *inside the house*, as casinos increasingly use algorithmic exploits to get their customers to gamble even more.

- **Chapter 4, Competition,** is about sports betting, including the inside scoop on how it suddenly came to be so ubiquitous in the United States. Sports betting is the River's ultimate cat-and-mouse game, with both bettors and the sportsbooks using a combination of statistical savvy and street smarts to outflank one another—that is, if the books will let you bet at all. You'll meet some world-class bookmakers and some world-class bettors, who revealed details to me that it might not have been in their best interest to share. This is also the most hands-on chapter—I learned the ropes of the industry the hard way, in an experiment where I bet almost $2 million on the NBA in the 2022–23 season.

Halftime

- **Chapter 13, Inspiration,** is this book's equivalent to a Super Bowl Halftime Show. No, the chapter number is not a misprint—instead, it refers to what I call the Thirteen Habits of Highly Effective Risk-Takers. These habits reflect the overlap between the quantitative risk-takers of the River and people who instead take physical risks: you'll meet an astronaut, an explorer, and an NFL player, among others. I found commonalities that I wouldn't have expected, furthering my view that there is something hardwired in people who seek out risk and wrangle it successfully.

Part 2: Risk

- **Chapter 5, Acceleration,** is about the venture capital industry. Despite its many self-evident flaws, Silicon Valley is remarkably successful on its own terms. From conversations with some of the world's most successful VCs as well as some of their harshest critics, you'll learn what makes founders like Elon Musk behave like they do, why venture capital and the Village are natural enemies, and how the top VC firms can essentially guarantee themselves an excess profit *without* necessarily taking on all that much risk.

- **Chapter 6, Illusion,** is the first of three chapters that can be thought of as a book within a book, structured as a play in five acts. Nominally, the subject of the play is Sam Bankman-Fried. I met with SBF many times, as well as with many people close to him. As a Riverian myself, I see SBF on his own terms—and perhaps see better through his lies and his bullshit. However, SBF was a focal point for many strands of the River, from VC to crypto to effective altruism. As you'll see, the River's ideas can become more dangerous as we traverse from narrow domains like poker to broader and more open-ended problems. The playbill is as follows:
  - *Act 1: New Providence Island, the Bahamas, December 2022.* I meet with SBF shortly after FTX has imploded and probe his mindset in a darkening penthouse just as he's gone from ostensibly being worth $26.5 billion to potentially facing years in prison.

- *Act 2: Miami, Florida, November–December 2021.* A flashback to a party weekend in happier times in the crypto industry with prices near their then all-time peaks. I'll explain the game theory and sociology behind why crypto investors were prone to being scammed, but also introduce you to some savvy ones who avoided these pitfalls.

- **Chapter 7, Quantification**
  - *Act 3: Flatiron District, New York, New York, August 2022.* Although this begins with the dinner at Eleven Madison Park, where SBF toasted the effective altruist MacAskill's new book, it mostly gives EA room to breathe on its own terms. As you'll see, I have complicated feelings about it.
  - *Act 4: Berkeley, California, September 2023.* Set at Manifest, a conference on prediction markets—where you'll meet everyone from a rationalist former OnlyFans model to a man who made hundreds of thousands of dollars betting on Biden even after Biden had already won—this act explores rationalism, the kissing cousin of effective altruism. I'll trace the intellectual lineage of EA and rationalism and explain why they have a common interest in existential risk and the possibility that civilization could be destroyed by unaligned artificial intelligence even as they otherwise make for strange bedfellows.

- **Chapter 8, Miscalculation**
  - *Act 5: Lower Manhattan, October–November 2023.* I return to SBF as he meets his fate in a New York courtroom and makes another bad bet. No spoilers, but the chapter ends with a bang.

- **Chapter ∞, Termination,** is the first of a two-part conclusion. I'll introduce you to another Sam, OpenAI CEO Sam Altman, and others behind the development of ChatGPT and other large language models. Unlike the government-run Manhattan Project, the charge into the frontiers of AI is being led by Silicon Valley "techno-optimists" with their Riverian attitude toward risk and reward. Even as by some indications the world has entered an era of stagnation, both AI optimists like Altman and AI "doomers" think that civilization is on the brink of a hinge point not seen since the atomic bomb, and that AI is a technological bet made for existential capital.

- Finally, **chapter 1776, Foundation,** articulates a set of three core principles—agency, plurality, and reciprocity—that represent a marriage between the most robust values of the River and the ideas at the foundations of liberal democracy and the market economy that first emerged in the eighteenth century. I'll argue that these values are essential for making it through this dangerous period for our civilization, a "game" that we all have a stake in whether we want to or not.

So, Uh . . . What If I'm Just Not That into Gambling?

This is what my editor and I call a "graybox." You'll encounter them periodically throughout the tour. You can think of a graybox as a scenic outlook, a break from the main trail. I think some of the most interesting material in the book is in grayboxes, but they're sections you can skip or come back to later if you want to take the express route. They're often aimed at a particular section of the tour group—sometimes readers who need a little more help with a concept, or conversely readers who want a deeper and more technical dive into a subject I just brushed past.

This particular graybox is a note to readers who think the second half of the book sounds more interesting than the first—readers who care about risk, or who care about the impact that the River is having on the world, but who aren't so interested in capital-G Gambling on its own terms. For those readers, my advice would be to give part 1 a go for as long as you can before jumping ahead. This book is cumulative, meaning that it introduces key terms and concepts over time to help build up your Riverian vocabulary. With that said, there are more key concepts early on in part 1—particularly in chapter 1 on poker and game theory—than in chapters 3 and 4. There's also a detailed glossary at the end of the book in case you lose the trail.

Part 1

Gambling

Optimization

*There's **never** going to be a computer that will play
World-Class Poker. It's a people game.*
　　　　　　　　　　　　　　　　　—*Doyle Brunson*

Super/System, a 608-page behemoth that is the closest thing poker has to a Bible, was written in 1979 by a Texas roadhouse gambler turned ten-time World Series of Poker champion named Doyle Brunson, who is still regarded as one of the greatest players ever. The book was decades ahead of its time.

For instance, it preaches the gospel of what's now called "tight aggressive" poker, the style preferred by most of the world's best players today. Poker—and particularly the variant known as no-limit Texas Hold'em that Brunson helped to make famous—is a game that rewards aggression. "Timid players *don't* win in high stakes poker," the late Brunson wrote. A good player is "tight about entering the pot in the first place" but "after he enters the pot he becomes aggressive," picking his battles carefully but willing to fight them to the finish.

Super/System also implores players to have plenty of bluffs. "If you've never had the chance to see a real no-limit game, you'd be very surprised at how much bluffing there is," Brunson wrote. This tip is just as essential. Bluffing is intrinsic to poker, what separates it from other card games.

Having some bluffs isn't optional; against all but the very weakest players, you'll need to make big bets with your bluffs to encourage opponents to pay you off when you have your strongest hands.

Brunson was right that the human element looms large in poker. As we'll see in the next chapter, wagering tens of thousands of dollars on the turn of a 3.5-inch by 2.5-inch playing card without giving away information that tips your opponent to the strength of your hand is not something that comes naturally to most people. But the claim that a computer would never play world-class poker? That might be the worst bet Brunson ever made.

The mere act of playing poker once required a fair amount of courage. Poker had rough-and-tumble origins in the American South during the early 1800s as a Mississippi riverboat gumbo of the French game *poque*, the English brag, and the Persian As-Nas. Only in the past several decades with the advent of regulated casinos could a player be assured of a high-stakes game that was both reasonably honest and reasonably safe.

"I got robbed five times at gunpoint and once with a knife," Brunson, then eighty-eight years old, told me of his experiences in underground Texas games in the 1950s when I'd called him one afternoon in Las Vegas. "That was just part of the everyday life back then." Indeed, poker was so disreputable that Brunson was careful who he spoke to about it. "I told them that I was working at an airplane factory plant. In those days, if you told someone you was a gambler, they thought you were into drugs, were into prostitution, were into robbery, and I don't know what else."

Brunson was an Old Testament figure: ancient, plainspoken, indestructible (he was a six-time cancer survivor), enormous—he weighed four hundred pounds before gastric bypass surgery. But when I spoke with him, he seemed to know that it would soon be time to cash out his chips. When I ended our conversation by asking if there was anything else he wanted to talk about, he answered on a solemn note. "I've seen two guys die at the poker table, that was pretty unusual. One time a guy had me beat and we was playing lowball. We got all our money in the pot. I turned my hand over first with a seven-five. Then he showed seven-four and fell dead."[*]

But Brunson was a pioneer to a more scientific approach to the game. He was unusual among poker players of his day for having a college education; Brunson went to Hardin-Simmons University in Abilene, Texas, where he was a star athlete and was almost drafted by the NBA's Minneapolis Lakers until a freak accident unloading sheetrock at a warehouse shattered his knee and his dreams of becoming a professional athlete.

Long before the advent of personal computers, Brunson and another Hall of Fame player, Amarillo Slim, would deal out thousands of poker hands to themselves to get a more precise sense for the probabilities. A Hold'em hand consists of two hole cards that a player has to herself, which are then combined with five community cards shared by all players to make the best five-card poker hand.

A Lightning-Speed Guide
to Texas Hold'em

Okay, time-out. We're at the point where I'm unavoidably going to start dropping in more poker jargon. There's a nice glossary of terms in the back of the book. But for now, just note the very basics.

A Texas Hold'em game starts with two players posting forced bets called **blinds**, which seed the pot. For instance, in a $5/$10 game, $5 is the **small blind** and $10 is the **big blind**. Without blinds or antes, there's no money in the pot, so there's no reason to take any risk and poker is a broken game.

Players initially receive two private **hole cards**. (The best possible hole cards are A♦A♣, a **pocket pair** of aces.) Then there's a round of betting: this is called **preflop**. Then five shared **community cards**, sometimes also called the **board**, are dealt in stages. The first three cards, dealt simultaneously, are called the **flop** (think of the dealer flopping over three cards: *thwonk!*), and there's another round of betting. Then comes the often-pivotal fourth card, the **turn**, and another round of

---

[*] In lowball, as you might infer from the name, the lowest hand wins. So Brunson's deceased opponent was awarded the pot—which Brunson remembered as eventually being passed to the player's next of kin.

betting. The final card in Hold'em is called the **river**.* Once it's dealt, there's a final round of betting. Often, all but one player has folded by this point, but if not the remaining players go to **showdown**. The best five-card poker hand—made from any combination of a player's hole cards and the community cards—wins. The ranking of hands is as follows:

- **Straight flush**: Five consecutive cards of the same suit and rank, such as T♣9♣8♣7♣6♣. An ace-high straight flush, called a **royal flush**, is the best hand in poker.

- **Four of a kind**, such as Q♣Q♥Q♦Q♠4♠

- **Full house**: Three of a kind plus a pair, such as T♣T♠T♦8♦8♠

- **Flush**: Five cards of the same suit, like A♦T♦6♦3♦2♦

- **Straight**: Five cards consecutive in rank, such as 7♠6♦5♠4♠3♦

- **Three of a kind**, such as K♦K♣K♠Q♥5♥. If three of a kind is achieved using both of the player's hole cards—say, they start out with a pair of kings in the hole, and then make three kings—it's also called a **set**.

- **Two pair**, like A♦A♣5♣5♠8♣

- **One pair**, such as 9♣9♦A♣6♦3♦

- **High card**, meaning no pair, straight, or flush. The stronger high-card hands such as A♠Q♦T♣8♦7♣ (ace high) still win their fair share of pots, though. It's hard to make a hand in Texas Hold'em.

Let's test your poker intuition: Which hole cards are better? Ace-king (abbreviated as AK) or a pair of deuces (abbreviated as 22)? In most poker contexts, the answer is ace-king by a country mile, since it can make the strongest possible pair of aces or kings, a hand that's often good enough to withstand multiple bets and raises.

---

* The etymology of this term is a little unclear, though one story is that it comes from poker's Mississippi riverboat origins: if the final card significantly changed the outcome and the dealer was suspected of cheating, he'd be thrown into the river. My term "the River" is somewhat inspired by this. Yes, River concepts like game theory may come from academic headwaters. But the further Downriver you get, playing real poker for real money, the more rough-and-tumble things tend to be.

But what if you can get all-in without any further betting? The lowly 22 actually beats AK 52 percent of the time. Knowing percentages like these is trivial; most players today can recite them to within a couple of percentage points. But poker was so much in the Dark Ages back when Brunson began playing the other players *didn't even know the odds.*

Brunson did know the odds, and he and other top players were so much better than the competition that boredom was a major issue. So he and his buddies would find other ways to pass the time, everything from sports betting to funding expeditions designed to find Noah's Ark. "I guess we were looking for some other kind of excitement," he said. As a testament to how far ahead of the curve he was, Brunson was still a regular—and a substantial winner—on the televised poker game *High Stakes Poker* well into his eighties despite never really having used the modern poker software tools called "solvers" that were about to upend the game.

Like many other aspects of modern life, poker has gone through its own *Moneyball*-style revolution. The catalyst came in 2003—the year that *Moneyball* was published—when Chris Moneymaker, an amateur who had earned his seat online, won the $10,000 Main Event at the World Series of Poker. That triggered an explosion of interest in the game—and between *Moneyball* and Moneymaker, poker has never been the same. When Moneymaker won, the Main Event had 839 entrants, then considered a shockingly high number. But by 2023, the Main Event had 10,043 competitors, reaching the five figures for the first time. (I was lucky enough to finish in eighty-seventh place that year.)

One predictable consequence is that poker has become more corporatized. The World Series of Poker was originally played at Binion's Horseshoe in Downtown Las Vegas. The tournament poker room there looked like "a grammar school gym with a low ceiling with two or three cocktail waitresses. Cardboard signs up on the walls. It was very, very primitive," said the writer Jim McManus, who improbably finished fifth in the 2000 Main Event while on assignment for *Esquire* magazine.

The WSOP was purchased by Harrah's Entertainment (now Caesars) the year after Moneymaker's win, which moved it to the much larger (but

WSOP Main Event Participants

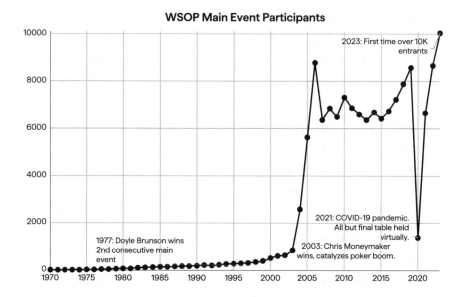

never particularly beloved) Rio hotel in 2005 before finally reaching Paris and Bally's on the Las Vegas Strip in 2022. Some players were wary of the move, fearful of having to fight through crowds of tourists and hawkers with strip-club fliers, but by most accounts (including mine) it was the smoothest WSOP ever. It was the fulfillment of a dream: poker had moved from the periphery of public awareness to the middle of the Las Vegas Strip.

With more money in the game, ever-more-sophisticated strategies are required to win that dough. Sports fans like to debate how well the players of today would fare if transported back to yesteryear, or vice versa. Would a dominant NBA player of the 1970s—say, Julius Erving—still be an All-Star today? Would a 1970s quarterback like Terry Bradshaw hold his own against modern pass rushers and defensive schemes?

In poker, the answer is straightforward. With only a handful of exceptions like Brunson, most players from the 1970s would get *demolished* in today's games.

"It just seemed like it was very obvious what people had by what they were betting," said Erik Seidel, who came to Las Vegas by way of New York's legendary backgammon scene and finished in second place in the

World Series of Poker in 1988. Seidel was embarking on a remarkably successful (and still ongoing) poker career. The thirty-one-year gap between his first WSOP bracelet (1992) and his most recent one (2023) is tied with Brunson for the second-longest in WSOP history, just behind Phil Hellmuth's thirty-four-year span. Like Brunson, Seidel anticipated some modern strategies in his game. But Seidel thinks poker in the 1980s and 1990s was still in its primordial soup phase. "If you took an amateur from today, and you put him back fifteen, twenty years, he would probably crush those games," Seidel said.

The final hand of the 1988 WSOP Main Event, as immortalized in the movie *Rounders*, wasn't Seidel's finest moment. Beanpole thin and sporting an orange golf visor, he was matched against Johnny Chan, who was going for back-to-back titles after winning the 1987 Main Event. Chan made a straight and then suckered Seidel into betting all his chips with a single pair. If you watch the clip now, it seems incredibly obvious that Chan is overacting, shaking his head and even rolling his eyes in fake contemplation. (The classic rule of poker tells is that strong means weak and weak means strong: if a player is acting like he has a poor hand, as Chan was, it's probably a good one.) But Seidel—then twenty-eight years old and working as an options trader in New York between backgammon sessions at the Mayfair Club—fell for the trap. "You know, there wasn't as much deception as there is now," he said.

In other ways, though, Seidel's newness to the game paid dividends. "Because I was young and didn't know better," he said, he didn't feel any need to duplicate the predictable, passive style that dominated the day. "I had a lot of naked aggression. And it seemed to work in those days. Then there were other things that I found, a lot of bluffing situations that people weren't necessarily doing."

Until recently, in other words, much poker strategy was learned through trial and error. Seidel's approach, with plenty of raises and plenty of bluffs, was novel in 1988, but would be considered normal if not even downright conservative by today's standards. Similarly, much of the advice that Brunson offers in *Super/System*, such as usually betting again after the flop is dealt if you'd raised beforehand, anticipates modern theory and practice.

But this pace of innovation was about to hockey-stick upward. Poker has been around for roughly two centuries, but the vast majority of poker hands ever played by humans—probably at least 95 percent if not as much as 99 percent*—have been played in the past twenty or twenty-five years. "Even before we had actual computer networks and neural networks," said Andrew Brokos, the cohost of the *Thinking Poker* podcast and a poker player and coach whose students include yours truly, "the poker community was like a network that was attacking the problem and working together and sharing information." So as the number of poker games increased, "the number of nodes on that network exploded."

And then came the computers.

In 2008, an AI-aided computer program named Polaris, developed by a team at the University of Alberta, won three out of six matches of heads-up limit Hold'em against a group of top professionals. This requires some qualification: limit Hold'em, where the amount you're allowed to bet is fixed, is considerably less complex than no-limit Hold'em, where you can bet any amount up to the number of chips you have in front of you. And heads-up poker, meaning a two-player game, is much less complex than multiplayer poker, which typically features somewhere between six and ten players. Sure enough, though, another AI poker bot—a descendant of Polaris named Libratus—won a heads-up *no-limit* challenge in 2017. And then, finally, another younger sibling called Pluribus beat humans in a *multi-way* no-limit match in 2019.

So is Brunson's claim—that *there's never going to be a computer that will play world-class poker*—thoroughly debunked? Out of respect to Brunson, who passed away two weeks before the 2023 WSOP, let's offer him a defense.

One objection is that computers are designed to beat other computers rather than human beings. There's some truth to this: these programs are trained by essentially playing against themselves. And they're designed to

---

* Especially counting online hands. The pace of play is *much* faster online, and a player can play in multiple games at once.

achieve a Nash equilibrium or game-theory optimal (GTO) style of play. "Nash equilibrium" is named after the American mathematician John Nash, a discovery for which he shared the Nobel Prize. (Nash is also famous as a result of his portrayal by Russell Crowe in the movie *A Beautiful Mind*.) I'll have a lot more to say about game theory later in this chapter, but the idea of a Nash equilibrium is that it's a defensive approach, one that's impossible to beat over the long run *because it prevents your opponents from exploiting your mistakes*. This is not the same as maximizing your winnings against a human player by adopting an exploitative strategy that takes advantage of *his* mistakes.

Nonetheless, computer poker algorithms would be quite good at exploiting humans if they tried. Consider the game rock paper scissors (you know the one: rock crushes scissors, scissors cut paper, paper covers rock). Since no move dominates any other, the Nash equilibrium strategy for this game is simply to randomize and make each play one-third of the time. Humans are so predictable and so poor at randomizing, though, that an algorithm designed in 2001* has won 45 percent of its rock-paper-scissors games against humans over more than 3 million tries, far more than the 33 percent it would win if the humans just decided on a play at random. And it goes without saying that algorithms are eerily good at predicting our behavior in other contexts—say, which YouTube video we want to watch next or, through large language models, which words or phrases make for a natural conversation. In a fight between human beings and computers at pattern matching, humans would get destroyed.

Brunson can raise another potential defense: he referred to a computer that would "stand face to face" at the table. Could a machine *physically* play poker—meaning a robot that would handle chips and cards, follow the action, and perhaps even engage in table banter and read people for verbal and visual tells? There isn't any off-the-shelf machine that could do this today, so congratulations, human beings—you've got a few years left until you lose to C-3PO. But although the robot would almost certainly

---

* You can play against it at essentially.net/rsp.

have to be custom-built for poker, there probably aren't any insurmountable barriers, and if there are now there won't be for long. Our robot (C-3PO-ker?) might eventually also get quite good at reading tells. In 2018, it was reported that a machine learning algorithm was better than humans at predicting a person's sexual orientation from their facial expression. If a computer can tell who you're attracted to, you think it can't tell when you're bluffing? Good luck.

But most poker pros aren't even debating these questions anymore: they've surrendered to the computers.

Daniel Negreanu, a Canadian pro who in 2023 was voted as the third-best player of all time (Brunson finished second in the poll and Seidel finished fifth; another American player, Phil Ivey, placed first), was once primarily known for two attributes. First, his ubiquitous table chatter, a running monologue of poker commentary and off-color jokes. And second, a playing style that departed significantly from the tight-aggressive approach that Brunson and most elite players prefer. Negreanu has sometimes sarcastically referred to himself as a "calling station," meaning a player who is reluctant to fold. For most poker players, playing too many hands is the fastest way to go broke. For Negreanu, there's more to be said for it: sticking around in a hand provides you with the opportunity to outplay an opponent later on.

But this strategy had ceased to work so well for Negreanu, who lost money in tournaments in both 2016 and 2017 and had a long streak from 2015 through 2021 where he'd failed to finish first in any tournament. The player nicknamed Kid Poker, who had dropped out of high school to play poker and snooker and moved to Las Vegas when he was twenty-two, was getting outclassed by younger competition.

I spoke with Negreanu in the PokerGO studio adjacent to the Aria in Las Vegas. The slickly designed studio is many players' favorite place to play poker, including mine. (It doesn't hurt that some of my best lifetime tournament finishes came in the studio.) There's free top-shelf liquor (though most players don't imbibe while they're playing) and free food from the Vegas outpost of the Michelin-starred Taiwanese dumpling restaurant Din Tai Fung. Plus, the final table of every PokerGO tournament is televised on the PokerGO livestream, and most players like the opportunity for exposure. When Negreanu started playing poker, there was none of this refinement. "You'd see, like, smoking at the table. Whiskey. Doughnuts. Just people mostly really overweight," he said.

What's the catch? You're almost certain to encounter a couple dozen of the best players in the world at any PokerGO tournament. So the studio serves as a proving ground: you won't survive for long with an inferior strategy.

"I was here in the studio during the Poker Masters a few years ago," Negreanu told me. "And I didn't know what the fuck they were talking about." By "they," Negreanu was referring to a series of German players like Dominik Nitsche and Christoph Vogelsang. Somewhat befitting the cultural stereotype, German players are known for highly precise play, and they were early adopters of game theory and computer solutions. These players were using technical terms, like "blockers" and "combos,"* that Negreanu thought were gibberish.

"Then I realized that playing that week, I'd been outplayed in four or five key spots. And that hadn't really been a thing for me. So it was clear to me that if I want to stay relevant, I have to start to learn and understand what they know." Negreanu told me that he's remade his game from top to bottom, getting rid of the habits that had nevertheless been good enough to make him one of the top players in the world. "It's really hard for someone like me, because I spent twenty-plus years playing poker a certain way," he said. Fortunately, the new strategies have paid dividends. From July 2021 through January 2024, Negreanu won eight PokerGO tournaments, including the 2022 Super High Roller Bowl for $3.3 million.

But where do these new strategies come from, exactly? It's time for some game theory.

---

* These are indeed relatively advanced poker terms. You can find definitions in the glossary if you're curious.

The Mastermind of Game Theory

"Genius" might be an overused term, but it's the only appropriate label for John von Neumann. Born in Hungary, where he was a child prodigy—by age six, he could read ancient Greek and Latin and divide eight-digit numbers in his head—von Neumann moved to the United States at twenty-nine. He worked on the Manhattan Project during World War II, helping to develop the atomic bomb. He was part of the team that built the first electronic computer. He did pioneering work in artificial intelligence, and he helped to lay the mathematical foundations for quantum mechanics. He even was part of the team that created the first computerized weather forecast.

But most importantly for our purposes, von Neumann was the single most important person behind the development of game theory. He was also a member in good standing of the River or whatever equivalent to it existed back then, a risk-taker with a penchant for fast cars despite being a terrible driver and an eager participant in all-night "poker games and the glorious booze-and-cigarette-fueled discussions" that they often inspired. Indeed, despite being a prodigious chess player, von Neumann thought poker was much more representative of the human condition:

> "Chess is not a game. Chess is a well-defined form of computation. You may not be able to work out the answers, but in theory there must be a solution, a right procedure in any position. Now real games," he said, "are not like that at all. Real life is not like that. Real life consists of bluffing, of little tactics of deception, of asking yourself what is the other man going to [. . .] do. And that is what games are about in my theory."

What is game theory, exactly? Well, the name is the easy part: it's inspired by the study of games, including poker. "Actual Poker is really a much too complicated subject," wrote von Neumann and Oskar Morgenstern in *Theory of Games and Economic Behavior*, their foundational 1944 text. But the book contains extensive examples from a simplified form of poker that includes the game's most essential element: bluffing. Von Neumann and Morgenstern recognized what Brunson and every other poker player does—unless you sometimes bluff, your opponent has no incentive to pay you off when you have a good hand.

The applications of game theory are much broader than what we normally think of as "games," however. In some ways game theory is the core of modern economic theory, since it describes how people choose the most rational option when everyone else is competing for the same scarce resources. I often find myself surprised at how often game theory predicts real-world beahvior, from nuclear deterrence to traffic patterns to how prices are established in a market economy. Let me try my hand at a precise definition:

> Game theory is the mathematical study of the strategic behavior of two or more agents ("players") in situations where their actions dynamically impact one another. It seeks to predict the outcome of those interactions, and to model what strategy each player should employ, to maximize their expected value while accounting for the actions of the other players.

In the introduction, I used the phrase "EV maximizer" (short for "expected-value maximizer") to describe a personality type that's common in the River: taking an analytical, strategic approach to gambling, investing, and other aspects of life, trying to calculate the most optimal "play" in any given situation. Sometimes, life is on easy mode and you're making decisions that only affect you—what von Neumann calls the "Robinson Crusoe model," as though you're on a desert island by yourself. I can't tell you whether it's EV maximizing to have fries with your sandwich or opt for the healthy side salad—it might depend on how good the fries are—but your decision isn't affected by anyone else's and doesn't really affect anyone else.

But in most real-life scenarios, we're interacting with 8 billion other people; their choices affect ours, and ours affect theirs. And that's much harder. We're trying to live our best life, but they are too. What's the equilibrium that emerges when *everyone* pursues their best strategy? That's what game theory is all about.

I find game theory appealing because like other people in the River, I often find myself in highly competitive settings. How should you play your cards *if everyone else is playing their cards right too*? Obviously, people are not always optimally strategic, or even rational at all. But I think it's a good approach to life to give other people some credit instead of treating them as nonplayer characters, or NPCs, the video-game term for filler characters who have no agency of their own and whose behavior is simple and predetermined. I think of game theory like Frank Sinatra thinks of New York City: "If I can make it there, I'll make it anywhere." If you can compete against people performing at their best, you're going to be a winner in almost any game you play. But if you build a strategy around exploiting inferior competition, it's unlikely to be a winning approach outside of a specific, narrow setting. What plays well in Peoria doesn't necessarily play well in New York.

Let's clear up some misconceptions, though. One is that game theory only applies to zero-sum problems. Instead, the most famous example from game theory is about the failure to achieve cooperation. The prisoner's dilemma, first described in 1950 by Melvin Dresher and Merrill Flood, traditionally referred to two members of a criminal gang who were arrested and imprisoned. But I'm going to give you an updated, more contemporary version that's mathematically identical to the original one:

> **The prisoner's dilemma, 2020s version:** A pair of siblings, Isabella and Wyatt Blackwood, are accused of running a fraudulent cryptocurrency exchange in which billions of dollars of customer assets were stolen to make risky bets on shitcoins. The Blackwoods are placed under house arrest at separate beachfront homes in Santa Barbara, California, and prevented from communicating with each other.
>
> However, the details of the case are opaque, and Wyatt and Isabella have been meticulous about covering their tracks. Each sibling possesses the information to prove a felony case against the other sibling,

but no one else does. Without a confession, the government can convict them only on a lesser two-year charge of selling unregistered securities. Amid intense political pressure—it's an election year and the incumbent president really wants somebody to hold accountable—they're each offered a deal: snitch and we'll let you off with a slap on the wrist, but we'll sentence your sib to ten years in prison. If *both* Wyatt and Isabella snitch, they'll both go to prison, but the government will reduce their sentence to seven years for cooperative behavior. What should they do?

Typically, the prisoner's dilemma is illustrated with a payoff matrix like this one, indicating the four possible permutations of outcomes based on each player's decision:

Modern-Day Prisoner's Dilemma

	ISABELLA SNITCHES	ISABELLA STAYS SILENT
WYATT SNITCHES	· Isabella gets **seven years** · Wyatt gets **seven years**	· Isabella gets **ten years** · Wyatt gets **zero years**
WYATT STAYS SILENT	· Isabella gets **zero years** · Wyatt gets **ten years**	· Isabella gets **two years** · Wyatt gets **two years**

Intuitively, you'd think the siblings would aim for the bottom right box. They'd happily take two years in jail and cut their losses rather than a coin flip between zero years and ten. And they'd certainly rather have two years in prison than seven, as in the top left box. But the bottom-right box requires that they cooperate and stay silent—and that's harder than it might seem. Let's consider the decision from Wyatt's perspective:

- If Isabella snitches, then Wyatt gets ten years in prison if he stays silent (bottom left). But he can reduce this to seven by also snitching (top left). So, rather than cooperate, he should snitch.

- If Isabella stays silent, then Wyatt gets two years in prison by staying silent (bottom right). But he can get off with a slap on the wrist and continue to enjoy walks on the beach and fish tacos in Santa Barbara by snitching (top right). So again, his best play is to snitch!

So Wyatt is better off snitching *no matter what Isabella does*. This is called a "dominant strategy." Of course, you can just invert the names and look at the decision from Isabella's point of view; their situations are symmetrical. Her dominant strategy is snitching, too. Look what happens, though. If they both EV maximize, they both snitch and wind up in the dreaded top left box—seven years in prison—whereas if only they'd been able to coordinate, they could have kept their sentences to two years.

The prisoner's dilemma is one example of a Nash equilibrium. No player can improve their position by *unilaterally* changing their strategy. No matter what Isabella does, for instance, Wyatt is better off snitching.

That term "unilaterally" is important, though. The prisoner's dilemma is sometimes described as a paradox, but it's not really. Rather, it's what can happen when individuals respond in a narrowly rational way when they have no ability to coordinate their strategies. Now, how well it holds up under real-world conditions is another question: empirically, human beings cooperate more than they're *supposed to* according to the prisoner's dilemma. Indeed, this default toward cooperation is *probably rational in the long run*. The ethical codes that societies develop—think about Jean-Jacques Rousseau's social contract or Immanuel Kant's Golden Rule—can be thought of as attempts to get people to cooperate and discourage them from snitching. Put a pin in this idea; we'll come back to it later in the book.

Nonetheless, cooperation can be hard to sustain when there's money or other forms of expected value just sitting out there for the taking. And the prisoner's dilemma can sometimes crop up where you don't necessarily expect it. Take the (hypothetical) example of competing pizza slice joints, Lupo's and Francisco's, on adjacent corners in Greenwich Village, New York, run by a pair of brothers who have rival claims to their nonna's original recipe. It costs $1 to make a slice of plain pizza (for non-New Yorkers, that means just cheese and sauce). But demand is brisk in Greenwich Village, with lots of college students, bars, and weed stores nearby. So the slices retail for $3, and each shop sells 5,000 slices per night, locking in a hearty $10,000 profit ($2 profit margin x 5,000 slices).

This is a nice situation for the brothers, but it isn't a Nash equilibrium. Why not? Well, either store can unilaterally improve its outcome by changing its strategy. For instance, what if Lupo's decides to undercut Francisco's and sell slices for $2.50 instead of $3? Now it sells 12,000 slices per night—the 5,000 it was selling before, the 5,000 it takes from Francisco's, plus some additional number since people will buy more pizza at $2.50 a slice than $3—and Francisco's sells zero.* Lupo's is now making far more than it had been, a nightly profit of $18,000. However, Francisco's can match the price drop, and indeed its best move is to do so. Now the two stores split the $18,000 in profit. But look what's happened: instead of making $10,000 a night as they did originally, each brother makes $9,000 instead. As in the prisoner's dilemma, both brothers are worse off despite following their dominant strategy.

Greenwich Village Pizza Price War

	LUPO'S LOWERS PRICE TO $2.50	LUPO'S KEEPS PRICE AT $3
FRANCISCO'S LOWERS PRICE TO $2.50	· Lupo's makes $9,000 · Francisco's makes $9,000	· Lupo's makes $0 · Francisco's makes $18,000
FRANCISCO'S KEEPS PRICE AT $3	· Lupo's makes $18,000 · Francisco's makes $0	· Lupo's makes $10,000 · Francisco's makes $10,000

And the price war doesn't stop there. Lupo's could respond by lowering its price further, to $2. Then Francisco's goes to $1.50. The tit-for-tat continues until both stores are selling slices at just slightly more than their cost—and it leads to two grumpy brothers barely eking out a living and lots of happy stoners munching on cheap pizza. This is a Nash equilibrium— and not coincidentally, it's what the economics of the real world look like: the average restaurant only makes a profit margin of 3 to 5 percent.

Another misconception is that the prisoner's dilemma reflects a selfish

---

* This assumes the slices are otherwise identical and customers only care about the price. In the real New York, even if the slices were identical, there would be five-thousand-word essays in *New York* magazine extolling the virtues of each one. Plus you'd have to wait on line for a long time at Lupo's.

or cynical view of human nature. In fact, the prisoner's dilemma only arises in situations that are *not* zero-sum. It's what happens when people are unable to cooperate, *even though they would be better off if they could.* Nor is the existence of a prisoner's dilemma always a bad thing, because sometimes their cooperation would come at the rest of society's expense. To take the canonical example, society probably doesn't want defendants held in pretrial detention to coordinate on a legal strategy. And we don't want competing firms to fix their prices: maybe it doesn't seem so bad if Lupo's and Francisco's charge a little extra for a slice, but you probably feel differently when OPEC colludes to set the price of oil.

Poker Isn't Always Zero-Sum Either

What about poker? You might think that it's strictly a zero-sum game. If that's the case, the prisoner's dilemma does not apply to it. But there are some poker situations where players have an incentive to cooperate. The most common one is near the prize money in a tournament. A tournament ends when one player has won literally all of the chips and is the last player standing. However, this player doesn't win the entire prize pool; typically, he'll get something like 20 percent of it, and other prizes are given to another 10 to 15 percent of players based on how long they survived. The upshot is that chips have diminishing returns: your first ten thousand chips are worth much more than your next ten thousand. One implication is that late into a tournament, two players with big chip stacks want to avoid confrontations with each other; they stand more to lose than to gain by putting their stacks at risk.

Colluding or forming an alliance in poker is strictly against the rules. However, there are sometimes awkward situations. In 2022, I played at a tournament in Houston and we were down to the final ten players. A talented, game-theory-driven player and I had two of the top three chip stacks—let's call him Holden. In one hand, Holden opened the action by raising, and then I re-raised (players call this a "3-bet"), and he folded. This is all very common. A little while later, the tournament went on break and Holden approached me and told me that he'd folded a pretty good hand. This is also common table chatter. But rightly or wrongly, the implication I took was that *hey, we should take it easy on each other until some other players bust out and we've both made some money.* I had no intention of agreeing to anything and shrugged and said nothing.

About half an hour later, Holden raised and I 3-bet again, but this time he re-raised ("4-bet") all-in. I had a good hand, A♦Q♦, and was getting pretty good odds; it wasn't a fantastic spot, but in game theory land it would have been a call. But I remembered what he said on break and folded. Holden later told me he was bluffing with a hand I would have had fantastic odds against. To be clear, I didn't fold out of any sense of reciprocity, but rather because I thought he'd be playing extra tight against me and would only do this with a very strong hand. But who knows. Maybe Holden was trying to trick me into thinking we had an "understanding" and then took advantage of that by bluffing. Maybe he thought we *really did* have an understanding and that *I'd* betrayed it by raising him. Or maybe he was lying about having bluffed. The point is, an "understanding" isn't worth very much when there's no trust established, no enforcement mechanism, and each player would benefit from screwing the other guy over.

Just Because I'm Indifferent Doesn't Mean I Don't Care

Play in enough poker tournaments and you can sometimes spot it happening. In the midst of a big decision, a player will avert her glance from the table, stare into space for a few seconds, compose herself as though she's pulled something out of the ether, then act on her hand (call, fold, or raise) a few moments later.

Has the player had an "Aha!" moment? Good guess, but no. She's probably randomizing.

The Nash equilibrium solution for poker—yes, there is a *solution* to poker, though as you'll soon see it's an exceptionally complicated one—involves lots of randomizing. Randomizing between calls and raises, between calls and folds, or sometimes between all three. It's not just that you should play *different* hands in different ways; you should play the *same* hand in different ways. Sometimes, if your opponent raises, you should 3-bet with A♦Q♦ and sometimes you should just call. That's what the theory says, anyway.

So the player wasn't just staring out into space—she was probably looking at the tournament clock. For instance, she could randomize by taking an aggressive action if the last digit was an odd number or a passive action if it was even. Other players have devised methods of randomization based on the rotation of their poker chips.

Randomizing your strategy is not just an essential part of poker—it's essential in game theory in general. The concept of mutually assured destruction, for instance—the game-theory doctrine that posits that a war between two fully armed nuclear powers is unlikely because they'd wind up annihilating each other—relies in part on what the economist Thomas Schelling called "the threat that leaves something to chance." Basically, you never know what will happen in the fog of war, so you'd better not poke the bear. Nash's most famous paper was a relatively simple two-page proof in 1950 that a stable equilibrium exists for a wide variety of games subject to a few other conditions. The catch is that the equilibrium very often involves randomization. We already introduced an example of this: rock paper scissors. Paper beats rock. Scissors beats paper. Rock beats scissors. We keep going around in circles. So how do we reach the equilibrium that Nash promised? We do it through randomization: each player makes one of the three "throws" one-third of the time, choosing the play purely by chance. This is known as a "mixed strategy."

In rock paper scissors, no symbol is intrinsically more valuable than any other. But this doesn't necessarily need to be the case for a mixed strategy to apply. That's because there's a lot of value in something else: deception. Let's turn to another of my favorite games, baseball.

Justin Verlander is a pitcher for the Houston Astros (and formerly for my home-state team, the Detroit Tigers). In 2022, despite being almost forty years old, he had the third-most-effective fastball in baseball, according to Major League Baseball's Statcast data. By contrast, Verlander's breaking pitches (sliders and curveballs) are only slightly above average.

And yet, Verlander throws his fastball only about 50 percent of the time. How come? Well, major league hitters are pretty good. And although Verlander's fastball is tough to hit, it's easier if you know that it's coming.

Imagine that Verlander is facing a great hitter like the Los Angeles Dodgers' Mookie Betts. Before each pitch, Betts tries to anticipate what Verlander will throw: a fastball or a curveball. (For simplicity's sake, we'll limit Verlander's arsenal to two pitches for the rest of this example.) Although the average major league player bats for only about a .200 batting average* against Verlander's fastball, imagine that Betts can hit .260 against him if he correctly guesses the pitch. And, if Betts guesses curveball and is correct, he's rewarded for it with a .350 batting average. If Betts predicts the wrong pitch, however, he's punished:

Batting Average in Batter vs. Pitcher Battle

	VERLANDER THROWS FASTBALL	VERLANDER THROWS CURVEBALL
BETTS GUESSES FASTBALL	.260	.240
BETTS GUESSES CURVEBALL	.180	.350

What's the Nash equilibrium? It can be solved with a little algebra—and as you've probably guessed, it involves randomization. It turns out that Verlander should throw the fastball about 58 percent of the time and Betts should guess fastball about 89 percent of the time. With this mix, Betts hits for a .252 average. That's better than he could do with a "pure strategy" where he always picked the same move. If Betts always guessed fastball, Verlander's play would be to always throw the curve, for instance. This is called an "exploitative strategy"—Verlander taking advantage of the fact that Betts is predictable. A .252 batting average isn't great, but by leaving something to chance, it's as good as Betts can do.

Importantly, if Betts is using the right mix, he'll have the *same* batting

---

* As a guy who was into baseball stats before *Moneyball* was cool, I know full well that batting average is an outmoded stat. But let's roll with it. The principles are exactly the same if you used OPS, wOBA, or some other advanced metric.

average against both the fastball and the curve (.252). The precise term for this is that he's made Verlander "indifferent" to what he throws: the fastball and the curveball have the same expected value. That's why pitchers—like poker players—are sometimes literally better off picking their pitches at random. Atlanta Braves Hall of Fame pitcher Greg Maddux—one of the most cerebral pitchers of all time—reportedly did exactly this, using quasi-random inputs such as the stadium clock to decide what pitch to throw. (Perhaps not coincidentally, Maddux is a highly proficient poker player who was raised in Las Vegas.)

In games like poker where it's important to be unpredictable, the value of a particular strategic option is made up of a combination of what I call "intrinsic value" and "deception value," and there's generally a trade-off between the two. In sports, a play like a fake punt is terrible if the other team knows it's coming, but it can be a great play if the opponent isn't anticipating it. Deception is very important in poker, so it involves a *lot* of mixed strategies to avoid revealing too much information about your hand. That not only means bluffing; it also sometimes means playing meekly ("slowplaying") with a good hand.

Cracking the Poker Code

Piotr Lopusiewicz, a Polish college dropout turned online poker player, had grown frustrated at the lack of computer tools for poker as compared with other games that he knew well, like chess and bridge. The IBM supercomputer Deep Blue had famously beat the chess world champion Garry Kasparov in 1997—this story is recounted in detail in *The Signal and the Noise*—and by the early 2000s, chess engines that played at grandmaster levels were widely available on home computers. Poker had lagged behind. Sure, there was the University of Alberta's AI work, but that had required training thousands of computers for months at a time. Lopusiewicz wanted something you could run on your laptop.

So despite being a mediocre programmer, he decided to give it a try himself. Lopusiewicz endeavored to create a poker "solver": a computer program that would literally find the Nash equilibrium for poker. This was an ambitious goal; even von Neumann had thought that poker was too complicated to solve from first principles. "It seemed that the problem was computationally very difficult," Lopusiewicz said. One problem is that the game tree for poker—the set of all possible outcomes—is very large. A 52-card poker deck presents so many possibilities that it's likely that no two decks in the history of the world have been in exactly the same order, assuming a fair shuffle. In Hold'em, there are 1,326 possible two-card starting hands and 42,375,200 possible sequences of the five community cards. And then throughout the hand, players have multiple opportunities to make decisions by calling, folding, or raising to different amounts. Even in two-player *limit* Hold'em, a much simpler game than no-limit, there are 319,365,922,522,608 (319 trillion) possible combinations of cards and betting sequences. In multiplayer no-limit Hold'em, the numbers are exponentially larger.

Believe it or not, this is only half the problem. Programmers can make simplifying assumptions—for instance, the suits of the cards often do not matter. And modern computers are very fast, capable of trillions of calculations per second. If you had a guide to *exactly* how your opponent played, then a computer could calculate your best play to a high degree of precision in every situation quickly.

The challenge is that in real poker, your opponent gets to fight back. So solvers go through a looping process called "iteration." The first player, let's call her Alice, starts out with a strategy literally at random. Her opponent, Bob, picks a strategy to counter Alice's terrible strategy. But then Alice gets to revise her strategy given Bob's strategy. She's still making some bad mistakes, but has probably gotten rid of the very worst plays, such as folding aces before any bets have gone in. Bob in turn responds to Alice's new strategy—and so on, for thousands or even billions of iterations depending on how much precision you want. As the strategic improvements get smaller and smaller—by the two-billionth interaction, Alice is making only very minor changes, like raising with A♦Q♦ 77 percent instead of 76 percent of the time—the solution converges on a Nash equilibrium, since the definition of a Nash equilibrium is when there are no further unilateral strategic improvements.

In principle, it's an elegant approach, although I'm leaving out a lot of the blood, sweat, and tears that Lopusiewicz and others have gone through to make their algorithms more efficient, not to mention the semiconductor companies who have built faster and faster computer chips.

Poker players call what results a "GTO," or "game theory optimal" approach. The catch is that solver outputs look like something straight out of John von Neumann's brain: they can be intimidating to use, even for experienced players. Here, for example, is a sample hand from PioSOLVER, the solver that Lopusiewicz created:

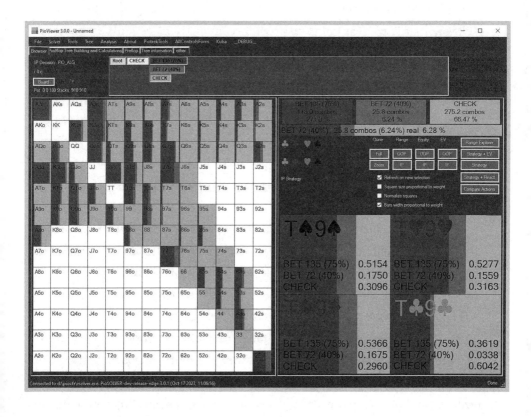

Don't worry if you don't understand this chart. How to use a solver is an advanced topic; I just wanted to give you some idea for how complicated these solutions are. But very briefly: the 13 × 13 matrix of squares on the left-hand side of the screen represents the universe of possible poker starting hands. In this example, the solver gives a player a choice of four options: he can check, make a small bet, a medium-sized bet, or a large bet. As complicated as this is, it's actually a simplification: in real no-limit Hold'em, players have essentially an infinite number of bet sizes to pick from. Nevertheless, if you look carefully, you'll find that *almost all of the player's hands use a mixed strategy*. For instance, the hand T9s—a ten and a nine of the same suit, which has an inside straight draw but not much else—sometimes checks, sometimes makes a small, cheap bluff, and sometimes makes a large bluff.

The frequency with which the computer liked mixed strategies was surprising to Lopusiewicz, who had never formally studied game theory. "I knew that there was going to be a lot of mixing, but I didn't realize it was going to be on almost every hand," he said. Intuitively, you might expect a machine to prefer a more deterministic solution. Instead, solvers like to randomize. This tendency was also a profound insight for me about poker, as well as certain other aspects of life, too: *we often spend the most time debating the least important decisions*. In my twenties, when I made my living mostly through poker for a few years, I'd spend hours each week debating the intricacies of poker strategy on the Two Plus Two Forums, a then-popular* public messaging board. You'd post a hand and a twenty-page flame war would ensue—*you should have folded on the turn, you fish!* The irony was that both sides of the debate were probably right. Deception is so important in poker that in any reasonably close decision, the GTO strategy is usually a mixed strategy. People in the River know how small our edges are. But sometimes there's no edge to be had at all; you're literally just indifferent and might as well pick at random.

---

* These strategy forums are now a shadow of their former selves. Players have become much more circumspect about giving away free strategic advice to their opponents given how much tougher the games are these days.

Sometimes You Should Just Flip
a Coin in Everyday Life, Too

I'll sometimes annoy my partner by suggesting we should flip a coin to decide where to go to dinner. But there's a theory behind it—game theory. If we're indifferent between the Italian place and the Indian place, there's no reason to waste our time agonizing over the decision.*

This is even more the case when you're in an everyday situation where you're competing against other people. If you're trying to get back into Manhattan from JFK Airport at rush hour, your GPS app will probably suggest several alternatives—some involving the expressway, some involving the side streets—all of which are equally, annoyingly slow. You might not think of this as a competition, but it is—there are thousands of other drivers facing the same problem and using the same software. The result is a Nash equilibrium where you're indifferent between the various logical routes. So it's probably not worth stressing out too much about finding a shortcut. Just sit back and enjoy the ride, to the extent that's possible on the Van Wyck Expressway.

There were other things that surprised Lopusiewicz when he built the first prototype of PioSOLVER in 2014. For instance, just how aggressive it was—although in different ways than humans typically are. *Computers bluff their faces off when playing poker because that's what game theory says to do.* This can include making big bluffs—going for a knockout punch. But more often, they prefer small, tactical bluffs—say, betting $20 into a pot of $100—the equivalent to a boxer's jab. The term Brunson used for this type of small bet was a "post-oak bluff," referring to a small species of oak tree, *Quercus stellata*, that grows in Texas and produces cheap, worthless wood. Brunson considered these bets to be "gutless." But computers aren't trying to prove their manhood—they're trying to win your money—and

---

* Although, what often happens in practice is the coin flip reveals our hidden preferences—the coin comes up tails for Indian and we decide, *you know what, we could really go for some pasta.*

these small bets have a lot of things going for them.* Nowadays, almost every top player incorporates them.

So Lopusiewicz helped to launch a revolution. Many top players spend hundreds of hours over the course of a year studying solvers. There are limitations to solvers and GTO play, not least that the strategies are too complex to memorize, so players still need to develop strong intuitions about poker. But at no point in human history have human beings so explicitly applied game theory as poker players do today. Not everything lends itself as well to algorithmic optimization as poker does—but the warp-speed advancements in poker demonstrate that game theory often translates reasonably well into practice.

The High-Stakes Game of GTO vs. Exploitative Play

Exploit and you risk being exploited.

This may be the most important poker-related insight from game theory. You can adopt a strategy that seeks to take advantage of an opponent's mistakes. But that enables your opponent to take advantage of *you* if they catch on. For instance, if you're playing against an old guy who you assume rarely bluffs, he's going to have some very profitable bluffs if he's able to switch gears.

So players vary in the degree to which they prefer GTO versus "exploitative" styles of play. One of the strictest adherents to the GTO approach is Doug Polk, who now lives in Austin, Texas, where he co-owns a poker club called the Lodge but still bears traces of a surfer-bro accent from his native California. Polk has impressive accomplishments as a tournament player, including more than $10 million in lifetime tournament

---

* One is that they avoid giving away information about your hand. You can make them with almost anything you're playing without foreclosing your future options too much. (You can still make bigger bets later in the hand if you have something really good.) The other is that they enable you to get off cheaply. If you're risking only $20 to win a pot of $100, a bluff doesn't have to work very often to be +EV.

winnings, but he's predominantly a cash game player, and his best game is heads-up no-limit Hold'em.

In July 2020, Polk—who can be as aggressive on social media as he is on the poker felt*—challenged Negreanu, with whom he had a long-standing rivalry, to a mostly online heads-up no-limit match. Played at extremely high stakes—$200/$400 blinds—the match had the potential to become a seven-figure payday for whoever won.

Negreanu agreed—a move that he knew was probably not +EV. Although Negreanu has a more well-rounded poker résumé than Polk—one of the best résumés of any poker player ever—he was playing Polk's best game, and betting odds quickly established Polk as a 5:1 favorite. It was "certainly not monetary driven because I knew going in I'm an underdog," Negreanu told me. But he'd been hoping to use the match to promote himself and his products—and like many people in the River, he's intensely competitive, not one to back down from a challenge. "Once I agreed to it, I'm like, well, shit, I've got to do it."

If the match had been played five years earlier, it would have been billed as an epic clash of styles: Polk's robotic GTO approach against Negreanu's feel-driven, exploitative play. As I mentioned earlier, though, Negreanu has remade his game to bring it more in line with modern GTO strategy. He told me he had a few exploits against Polk—in fact, he and his team had once inadvertently shared a document labeled "Doug Polk exploit ranges" in a video call with Polk—but they were minor ones.

For his part, Polk aimed to play as close to GTO as possible. "My approach was, if I played correctly, and I spend all of my time memorizing the correct strategies and practicing them versus a computer, I *won't* lose. I *will* beat him," Polk told me when I interviewed him at the Lodge. I claimed earlier that GTO poker ranges are too complex to memorize. Well, that's probably true 99.999 percent of the time. But a heads-up cash game is quite a bit simpler than other forms of poker, so there are fewer situations to commit to memory. And Polk has probably spent as much time looking at

---

* Although I'm certainly not in a position to criticize someone over aggressive tweeting.

GTO heads-up ranges as any player in the world—certainly more than Negreanu, as much cramming as Negreanu did before the match. "The skill set of poker has shifted so dramatically over the last even ten, fifteen years," Polk told me. "It changed a lot from critical thinking, problem-solving, and being creative over to memorization, and figuring out how to apply these theories that you've picked up in real time." It wasn't that Polk disrespected Negreanu's play so much as that this is where his comparative advantage was. By contrast, if Polk had tried to exploit Negreanu, he could at least theoretically have come out on the losing end—Negreanu had always excelled at rock-paper-scissors head games. "I basically didn't think about him at all," Polk told me.

It also helped that the match was played online rather than in person. Not only did that prevent Negreanu from picking up on any physical reads, it also made it easier for Polk to randomize. Polk told me that he sometimes makes plays that are used by the solver as little as 2 percent of the time as part of a GTO mix. "The thing is, no-limit Hold'em is a very precise game. It's a *very* precise game," he said. "And sometimes you have to be willing to wager all your money in situations that don't feel intuitive." If you use a computerized random number generator and it "rolls" a number from one to one hundred, you can make that rare, counterintuitive play when it comes up with ninety-nine or one hundred. But "good luck doing that at the table," Polk says.

This all worked out great for Polk. He won $1.2 million against Negreanu, plus other significant side bets. Still, just because it was the right approach to this situation doesn't mean that GTO is all there is to the game. The most exciting poker battles come when players draw inspiration from game theory but use it to out-exploit one another—and only one of them can be right.

Vanessa Selbst is an outlier. She may wind up being the only person in history to both graduate from Yale Law School and at one point rank as the number-one player in the Global Poker Index. She is an out lesbian who brought her girlfriend (and future wife) Miranda Foster to tournaments in a poker world that has always suffered from its share of misogyny and homophobia. She is by far the highest-earning female poker player of all time—almost $12 million in lifetime tournament winnings—and first achieved that distinction when she was just twenty-eight years old. When she left poker to work for the hedge fund Bridgewater Associates in 2018—an unexpected move for someone who once called herself "anticapitalist at heart"—it was big enough news that it made *The New York Times.*

Although solvers might seem like a natural fit for Selbst, whose mother drilled her on logic puzzles when she was growing up in Brooklyn, she's instead a deep believer in exploitative play: figure out what your opponents are doing wrong and take advantage of it.

"Most people—save like the best hundred people in the world," she told me one day over happy hour drinks at a Manhattan wine bar, "just aren't that amazing at game theory." Instead, Selbst says, players have a lot of experience in situations that come up frequently in poker. But memorizing only gets them so far. "They were very good at playing a spot 1,000 times and knowing what to do in that spot," she said. But she found "that over time, whenever I put someone in a new spot, they would just royally fuck up."

Selbst discovered poker while an undergraduate at Yale as part of the explosion of interest in the game that followed Moneymaker's 2003 World Series of Poker win. The Yale underground games featured an uncanny number of players who would later go on to nerdy kinds of fame and fortune, like future *Jeopardy!* Tournament of Champions winner Alex Jacob. The games were famous enough, in fact, to be written up in *Sports Illustrated.* In the article, Selbst was described as a "genial, sturdy rugby player [who] wears a silver stud in her right nostril" and who carried a copy of the essay "Nationalism and Sexuality" to read between poker hands.

For Selbst, playing an exploitative style of poker is both a choice and necessity. It's a choice because she has a knack for reading people. Not necessarily reading their physical tells—that's a different skill—but reading into their life situation and how that might influence their poker play.

"You can kind of group and categorize people into almost a dataset in your mind," she told me. Most players make the mistake of assuming that everyone else plays just like they do. But in real life, people bring all sorts of baggage to the table. Selbst gave the example of a player who shows up for the Main Event of the World Series of Poker and tells you how his wife saved up for ten years so he could make his dream trip on his fiftieth birthday. After having been quiet for several hours, he suddenly goes all-in. What do you do?

You sure as hell don't consult some solver on the Nash equilibrium. This player is doing everything in his power to signal that he wants to hang around a little longer, which means playing his best hands aggressively to knock everyone else out of the pot and avoid the potential for bad beats. So you should fold unless you have pocket aces or pocket kings—and kings might be close. Be careful: this is an extreme example and in most circumstances it will be dangerous to assume an opponent is never bluffing. But it would be a dereliction of duty to just ignore the person behind the bet.

The sense you'll get from spending even a few minutes with Selbst is that she's very comfortable in her own skin—and comfortable making other people uncomfortable in situations they never expected to face. She's not looking for social approval when she plays. Instead she "made a lot of plays that would look very donkey-ish." Having often been the misfit in the room breeds a certain amount of resilience to a daring play gone wrong.

Sometimes, Selbst's daring plays have gone spectacularly, infamously wrong. She made the televised final table in just the second tournament she ever played, a $2,000 buy-in event at the 2006 World Series of Poker. Selbst raised with a mediocre hand, 5♠2♠, another player named Willard Chang called, and a third player, Kevin Petersen, re-raised. Selbst went all-in. Chang folded, but Petersen called and won with aces. Of course, the play looks terrible on TV. "What was she thinking?" one of the ESPN announcers, Norman Chad, said.

Although today Selbst regards the play as poor, I think I know what she was thinking: *Nobody does this.*

First of all, in 2006, most people weren't doing enough bluffing of any kind, and especially not with just their two starting cards. As Seidel said, people would play straightforwardly. Once you started seeing multiple bets and raises, it was aces, kings, queens, AK, and not much else. *Nobody* made huge, unorthodox bluffs in just their second poker tournament when they were on national television for the first time. So Selbst had every reason to think her opponents would give her credit for a strong hand.

After the 5♠2♠ hand, there was little choice but for Selbst to adopt a more exploitative style. Men often play suboptimally against women to begin with, sometimes trying to bully them out of pots. But they certainly weren't going to play GTO against Selbst—they'd assume she was crazy and was always bluffing. "Basically after that hand, like no one folded to me ever again," she told me. "Honestly, the amount of money that probably made me in my lifetime was tremendous." So her exploits mostly involved playing tighter than her reputation and trying to induce opponents to put a lot of money in with inferior hands—although she still made some wild bluffs when playing on television to maintain her image.*

Selbst's favorite example is from a hand she played at a $25,000 high-roller event at the PokerStars Caribbean Adventure tournament in the Bahamas in 2013. Her opponent was Ole Schemion, a hotshot German player who was then just twenty years old. While other players had been out partying at the Atlantis resort, Selbst had studied video of Schemion and her other opponents at the final table.

Selbst noticed that Schemion had made an unusual play twice in a similar high-stakes situation. A common spot in poker is when a player who raised before the flop has to decide whether to make another bet once the flop comes. One tricky case involves flops that are "coordinated," meaning three cards that fit well together, like Q♠J♦7♦. This flop has something for everyone! Any two hole cards ten or higher have made a

---

* Am I 100 percent convinced that these were just "image plays" designed to induce action in future hands? I am not. Playing aggressively and making big bluffs is clearly fun for Selbst, as it is for most players. But it's still much tougher to play against an overly aggressive player than a predictable, passive one.

straight draw, a pair, or better. Any two diamonds have made a flush draw. If you bet, you'll often face a raise.

So what most players do is bet with their best hands (such as Q♦Q♥, which made three of a kind), with their best draws (such as K♦T♦, which has both a straight draw and a flush draw)—and then with total air balls that have no way to win except for bluffing. Conversely, they'll check medium-strength hands such as a single pair, hoping to hedge their bets and play a cheaper pot.

This approach isn't bad as a Poker 101 strategy. But if you're getting the hang of game theory, you might detect a problem with it: it's *predictable*—and therefore it's *exploitable*. Poker players almost never put their opponents on an exact hand, but rather on a probabilistic "range" of possibilities. In this example, the player's *betting* range is unpredictable and well-balanced, since it contains a mix of strong hands, draws, and bluffs. But the player's *checks* are highly predictable, consisting only of mediocre hands—it's almost as though they've turned their hand face up. The term for this is being "capped," as in there's a cap on how good your hand can be. Solvers and top players like Selbst relentlessly attack opponents when they're capped. If they know you can never have a top-tier hand, then they can put you in a painful situation by bluffing for all of your chips. A solver's defense mechanism against this is to throw a loop by occasionally checking with their best hands.* But it's painful for humans to do this. When you have the best hand—but may not have the best hand for much longer if someone makes a straight or a flush—you're often literally too excited† to get your chips into the middle of the pot to even think about checking.

In her video review sessions, Selbst noticed that Schemion was particularly aggressive about attacking capped ranges—so sure of himself that he was willing to put everything at risk. Twice in an earlier tournament

---

* If it flops a set of queens on Q♠J♦7♦, then a solver might check 15 or 20 percent of the time, for instance.
† I mean this somewhat literally. Players have a neurological reaction to making a big hand. If you're not careful, that can shut down higher-level thinking. You'll make the obvious play—bet now when you can get the money in good—but you might not compose yourself enough to consider alternatives like a check. We'll talk more about this in the next chapter.

that he'd gone on to win, he'd made an all-in bluff against a player who had checked a coordinated flop. But by playing exploitatively, Schemion was opening himself up to being exploited—and Selbst was ready to pounce. Plus, she had a good read on Schemion's mentality. "[His] confidence is through the roof. So I'm like, if I just put them in one of these spots, he's for sure gonna fall for it."

K♦T♥6♥	T♣	2♦	K♥K♣	A♥8♠
Flop	Turn	River	Selbst	Schemion
[COMMUNITY CARDS]			[HOLE CARDS]	

So she set up a trap for Schemion—and sure enough, he walked right into it. Selbst raised with K♥K♣—pocket kings—and Schemion called in the big blind with A♥8♠. The flop was K♦T♥6♥—Selbst had flopped top set and there were lots of draws on a coordinated board, just the situation she was looking for. Schemion checked and she checked. *Nobody does this*, I can imagine her thinking. *Nobody checks a set in a situation like this*. The turn was a T♣. Now Selbst had a full house. Schemion bet and Selbst raised. "That's pretty strange that Vanessa did not continue the flop," one of the commentators said, reflecting the conventional wisdom at the time. "I'd say for most players checking back the flop and raising the turn will look like a bluff." Schemion evidently had the same read. Despite having a highly mediocre hand, he called. The river was an irrelevant 2♦. Selbst bet, Schemion went all-in on a hopeless bluff, Selbst called and won a gigantic pot with her full house—and later won the tournament for $1.4 million.

Bluffing with a Dirty Diaper

Vanessa Selbst's hand encapsulates a lot of what I love about poker—and game theory. The caustic journalist H. L. Mencken is famous for saying that "no one ever lost money underestimating the intelligence of the

American public." In poker, you can deviate from game theory and seek to exploit your opponents—and sometimes that's the right play. But you *will* lose money if you underestimate your opponents. Here's one more example that hits a little closer to home.

When I play poker, I don't have Selbst's problem of people always thinking I'm bluffing. Something of the opposite, really. I can get a lot of folds, both when I want them and when I don't. As a midforties guy with a beard, backpack, and a baseball cap, I have some years to go before I fit the "Old Man Coffee" stereotype of a tight guy who only plays aces and kings—but I'm gradually aging into that demographic. And if my opponents know me as "statistician and author Nate Silver," but don't know my poker-playing background, they'll usually assume my play is tight and conservative. People tend to read "statistician" as "calculating and precise," not realizing that one can be calculating and precise about one's bluffs.

That reputation may be changing, though, because one of the poker hands I'm best known for is a bluff. Entitled "America's Top Statistician Nate Silver Runs Epic Bluff in $10,000 Poker Tournament" on the PokerGO YouTube channel, the clip of that bluff has gotten tens of thousands of views between various social media platforms.

The hand in question comes from an event at the 2022 Poker Masters at the PokerGO studio. Over time, the PokerGO events had been attracting more "VIPs"—rich amateurs looking for poker glory—and I'd become less intimidated by playing in the studio. The VIPs had solid-to-decent poker skills, but I figured to be better than them. The whiz kids were a problem—but I had a few moves up my sleeve if they underestimated me.

Fortunately, I'd advanced to the final table of this event, which included a typical mix of VIPs, old-school pros like Seidel, and new-school pros like Adam Hendrix, an affable Alaskan who looks just a little bit like the NBA player Luka Dončić. Good news: after a roller-coaster series of hands, I made it to the final two players. I'd locked up second-place money—$140,600—with another $51,800 set to go to the winner. Bad news: the remaining opponent was Hendrix, who was ranked number two in the Global Poker Index at the time and would advance to number one at the end of the tournament. To complicate matters, heads-up play was a weakness of mine. Heads-up is tough: game theory says that you're supposed to play the large majority of your hands, but the large majority of your hands are random crap. Unless you've studied heads-up—and I hadn't—it takes some getting used to. Now I was against one of the best players in the world, who was fully prepared to take advantage of my imprecision.

After folding a lot early in our heads-up battle, I thought Hendrix would see me as being overly tight, and I decided I needed to mix it up, looking for spots to bluff. Then the following hand came up. With 75,000/150,000 blinds, I had 3.75 million chips and he had 5.5 million. (Those are chips and not cash; we were playing for high stakes but not *that* high. Each 1 million in chips was worth $5,600 in cash.) Hendrix just called from the small blind, forgoing the option to raise. This probably meant he had a weak hand, though he might have some traps. I also had the option to raise but looked down at three-deuce offsuit—3♥2♦—which is literally the lowest-ranking hand in Hold'em. In fact, the hand is so bad that it has a nickname: the Dirty Diaper, as in a *complete load of crap*. It was hard to beat the price, though—since Hendrix had just called, I could take a flop for free. So I checked and we saw three cards:

J♠8♠2♠

A jack, an eight, and a deuce, all of the same suit, spades. If someone had two spades, they already had a flush. I checked, and Hendrix bet just 150K into the 450K pot, the smallest allowable bet. This was a play straight out of the solver. Remember, we both have a lot of random crap. His goal was to fold out my random crap cheaply. He also had "position" on me in this hand, meaning that he got to act last, getting to see what I did before choosing his play. Poker is a game of information, so it's a huge advantage to have more information than your opponent. When you're out of position, it's hard to fight back. But this time I had better than random crap: my Dirty Diaper had turned into a pair of twos! It was a crappy pair, the worst possible pair on a board where a flush was already possible—but it's a pair all the same, and I was getting good odds, so I . . .

Raised. I raised to 450,000 chips. Raised with my crappy pair. Believe it or not, this is a play the solver likes. Why? Sometimes offense is the best defense. Remember, the Nash equilibrium is trying to prevent me from being exploited by Hendrix. If Hendrix can make a cheap bet on the flop and win every time we both have nothing, that's an extremely profitable situation for him. So I needed to make it more expensive for him by sometimes "check-raising"* his bet—both when my random crap lucked into a nice hand and with my share of bluffs.

But this is also a situation where computers and humans diverge. On this flop, the bluffs aren't very intuitive. Usually people bluff with flush and straight draws. In this hand, however, there's already a possible flush on the board. Players tend to shut down and play straightforwardly in these spots. So I needed to channel my inner Vanessa Selbst and zig where others zagged. Raising with a hand like mine was a dual-purpose play. If my pair of twos was currently the best hand, it was extremely vulnerable and so I didn't mind Hendrix folding right away. That's what I was hoping for, frankly. But if he did call, I also had the option of continuing to bet with my hand. At that point, I'd be turning my hand into a bluff, hoping that he'd fold a slightly better hand like a pair of eights.

Alas, Hendrix called: I wasn't going to win this pot cheaply. The next card was the J♣, putting two jacks on the board. This was a mixed blessing. Nominally, it was a good card for me. If I had a hand like J♥2♦, I'd now made a lucky full house. But a solver views things differently. Remember, computers bluff their faces off. And since computers train by playing against themselves, they hate folding since they constantly suspect bluffs. To the solver's way of thinking, the fact that a second jack hit the board made it mathematically less likely that I had a jack myself—and more likely that I had a bluff. So the solver would have recommended that I give up with my particular bluff, although it thinks it's close.

---

* As you've probably guessed, this is the poker term for raising someone's bet after you've already checked.

Another Key River Concept:
Optionality

"Optionality" is a term used in game theory and finance to describe the *value of being able to take advantage of future opportunities that might arise.* It's related to the idea of opportunity cost, but it means something a bit more specific. It refers to a situation where there's a fork in the road, but one branch of the fork contains other branches that could give you a lucky opportunity.

Say you're visiting some midsized European beach town. You're staying in a budget hotel near the town square. You're hungry, and what you'd *really* love to do is have a little picnic on the beach. There's a 70 percent chance of rain, however. And if it does rain, you'll be forced to eat lunch at one of the touristy and overpriced restaurants near the beach. The restaurants in the town square are touristy, too, but you like them slightly better. So you should stay in town, right?

Not necessarily. Quite possibly, you should head to the beach. Because of the possibility that the weather could clear up and you can have your picnic after all, it might be the higher EV move. (For instance, if the EV of a picnic on the beach is 10, eating at a restaurant near the beach is 5, and eating at a restaurant in town is 6; going to the beach is the higher EV option if there's a 30 percent chance of rain.) That's the value of optionality. A heuristic way of thinking of optionality is this: when you face a close decision, make the choice that will keep the most options open.

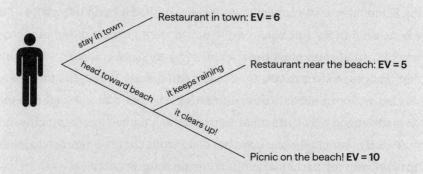

Optionality is often the hidden factor behind why poker solvers behave as they do: you want to keep favorable options open for yourself while constraining your opponent's choices. In the hand against Hendrix, I thought raising provided for higher optionality. I could give up if the wrong cards came, or continue bluffing—my version of a picnic on the beach—if the right ones did.

And again: I wasn't playing against a solver. I was playing against Hendrix—and I didn't expect him to be quite so suspicious. There was the *nobody does this* factor: players usually didn't have enough bluffs in this situation to begin with, and especially not at their first PokerGO final table. There was also a hand we'd played earlier: I'd tried to bluff Hendrix, and he'd taken a long time to put his chips in with a hand that to a solver would have been a slam dunk call. That sure seemed like a signal that he didn't think I was bluffing enough. So I followed through with a 600,000-chip bet. And, gulp, he called again.

J♠8♠2♠	J♣	K♠	3♥2♦	??
Flop	Turn	River	Silver	Hendrix

| [COMMUNITY CARDS] | | | [HOLE CARDS] | |

The river was one of the best cards in the deck for me: the K♠, putting a fourth spade on the board. This didn't improve my actual hand one bit. But it was a good card for bluffing; even my crappy bluffs with one random spade had now made a flush. I expected Hendrix to fold most of the time when he didn't have a flush himself. So I gathered my courage and put the rest of my 2.4 million chips in. (This time the solver concurs; it thinks that, having made it this far, following through with a bluff on this card was mandatory.) At that moment, I was feeling comfortable. I'd thought I'd made a good play—and if not, at least I'd have gone down swinging.

Hendrix wasn't feeling comfortable. It *looked* a little bit like he had a dirty diaper. He started squirming around in his chair. He stood up and hunched over, planting his elbows on the table. He used a time extension plaque to give himself more time to make his decision. Finally, he waved his hand in front of himself as though bidding it *adieu*—and threw it away. I was now in first place in the tournament.

Unfortunately, first place only lasted one hand. On the very next hand, I made a strong top pair, but Hendrix made three of a kind and I lost most of the chips I'd just won with my Dirty Diaper. We battled back and forth with several all-in pots before I eventually got knocked out. It was the second time I'd made it to the final table in a major television tournament—the first time had been at a WSOP event about a year earlier—and the second time I'd finished in second.

I felt a little down, until later I learned what hand Hendrix had folded: Q♠3♠. He'd flopped a flush! Not just any flush, but a good flush. He'd initially been trapping me. And on the river, he still had a good hand, losing only to an ace-high flush or a full house. His play was a massive deviation from the Nash equilibrium—according to a solver, it was roughly a $20,000 mistake if Hendrix had been playing against a computer.

But I don't mean to suggest that Hendrix played poorly. I think his play is much more defensible than Schemion's against Selbst, for instance. By the time we got to the river, Hendrix could beat a bluff but not much else. Given the size of the pot, he needed me to be bluffing about one-third of the time to warrant a call—and there are plenty of players who won't show up with any bluffs there at all. Hendrix sized me up wrongly, but he and I hadn't played together much.

Rather, this hand illustrates how wide the divergence remains between humans and computers. Poker players will get into furious arguments over solver outputs where the differences between plays boil down to a fraction of a percentage point. But decisions about whether or not to exploit a player potentially carry a much greater magnitude of profit or loss.* This is a point on which there's concurrence from a surprising source: Lopusiewicz, PioSOLVER's creator. "It's a pointless endeavor, in my view, fighting for those fractions of a percentage. But you are missing

---

* For instance, in my hand against Hendrix, my decision to continue to bluff on the turn was considered a deviation from GTO by the solver—but only by 0.07 big blinds, or the equivalent of about $50. Hendrix's play deviated from GTO by 28.3 big blinds, conversely—or about $20,000, making it about four hundred times more consequential.

the huge edges if someone is exploitable," he told me. "It's still a psychological game."

So Doyle Brunson is right and wrong, in roughly equal measure. He's dead wrong that a computer couldn't play world-class poker. Computers already lap the field in the technical aspects of poker play. And within a few years, computers will probably be able to handle the human aspects of the game extremely well too. But people aren't playing against computers: they're playing against one another. And so long as that's true, poker will remain a people game.

2

Perception

Garrett Adelstein looked like he'd seen a ghost.

His opponent in the hand he'd just played—what was about to become the most infamous hand in poker history—interpreted his expression differently. "You look like you want to kill me, Garrett!" said Robbi Jade Lew, a Saudi Arabia-born former pharmaceutical marketing executive who by her own description dresses "a certain fake Hollywood way" and had only taken up poker a few years earlier. Lew's tone was teasing, playful. She was smiling and stroking her chin. She had just beaten Adelstein out of a $269,000 pot with tens of thousands of people watching on the *Hustler Casino Live* poker livestream.

Adelstein's eyes were darting around, looking for a place to focus as he tried to reconstruct the action. "I don't understand what's happening right now," he remarked. It wasn't about the money. The Hustler livestream is one of the biggest games in the world, and six-figure pots are routine. Even after losing the hand, Adelstein still had $682,000 sitting in front of him.

Rather, Adelstein thought he'd been cheated. Not just cheated, but *cheated at his own game*. Okay, sure, technically it was the Hustler's game, not Adelstein's. But Adelstein, who had been a reality TV contestant on *Survivor*, was the star of the show—so much so that the electronic billboard outside one entrance to the Hustler had Adelstein's smiling picture on it.

Adelstein had significant say in which other players participated in the game. He was the biggest winner in the history of the Hustler livestream at the time, with lifetime on-stream winnings of more than $1.5 million when he headed to the cardroom that day—plus an additional undisclosed amount once the cameras were off. Even though one of the other players in the lineup that day was Phil Ivey—who had recently been voted as the best poker player of all time and is also among the game's most popular players for his fearless intensity—the Hustler was Adelstein's kingdom.

Until Lew made her shocking play. On a board of T♥T♣9♣3♥, she had called Adelstein's enormous $109,000 all-in raise with J♣4♥. If you're new to poker and trying to figure out how to make sense of this, don't bother: it doesn't make much sense. The player commentating on the livestream, Bart Hanson, was so confused that he wondered aloud whether the on-screen graphics displaying her hand were malfunctioning. Lew had no pair of her own, no draw, not even an ace. She could only beat a bluff. What's more, *she couldn't even beat many of Adelstein's bluffs.* For instance, if Adelstein had been bluffing with queen high—like the hand Q♥J♥, which has both a straight draw and a flush draw—Lew was behind and had only a 7 percent chance of winning.

But she *could* beat the bluff that Adelstein happened to have: 8♣7♣. Like Q♥J♥, it included both a straight draw and a flush draw. Unlike the queen-high hand, it had no card that outranked Lew's J♣. The players agreed to deal the final card—the river—two times, with each card determining the outcome of half the pot. (This option—called "running it twice"—is a way to reduce the amount of luck in the game.) Despite not having anything yet, Adelstein's odds on each run were around 50/50, since any club would make him a flush, any ten or six would make him a straight, and any seven or eight would make him a pair. The first river was the 9♦, not one of the cards that helped Adelstein. "That one's you for sure," Adelstein said, jovially enough—Lew hadn't turned over her hand yet and Adelstein assumed he was up against something much stronger. The second river was the A♠, also not one of the cards he needed. Only then, after having won the entire pot, did Lew flip over her J4—a hand that lives on in such poker infamy that if you walk into almost any poker game today and say you played "the Robbi," people will know you mean J4.

The hand immediately had a seismic effect on the poker landscape in Los Angeles and beyond. The Hustler livestream isn't just a poker game but also a reality TV show of its own. Adelstein was the game's golden boy—an elite player who the show's substantial audience admired. It helped that he was levelheaded—nobody wants to root for a jerk. But Adelstein's mind was spinning. Meanwhile, several of the other players began laughing and complimenting Lew on her call. "That's some fucking poker right there!" "That was sick!" "Wow!" There's no better feeling in poker than calling a big bluff and being right—particularly if you regard the opponent as a bully. Watch the video, and it's clear that Lew was elated. She'd done something that's hard to do in a poker world that's about 95 percent male: win the admiration of the men in the room, including Ivey, the best poker player of all time. She was even getting in on the fun, ribbing Adelstein for losing his cool. "Can you get a therapist in here or what?" she teased. It wasn't a kind remark. Adelstein had spoken publicly about his struggles with depression, not an easy thing in a profession that overindexes on stoicism and machismo.

And yet, Adelstein was just the latest player to learn one of the cardinal truths of the River: the biggest edges never last for very long.

Yes, Garrett was a great player. Yes, he was a nice guy, though some of the opponents in the Hustler player pool resented him since he usually took their money. Yes, he was "good for the game." He would push the envelope further than most players, encouraging the table to gamble—sometimes making plays that were -EV in the short run because they helped him maintain an active image. "He's a fun pro player, he's not a nit, he'll still play thirty-five to forty percent of hands. He makes huge, huge bluffs," Hanson said of Adelstein. "He's really fun to watch."

But Adelstein was also in a privileged position. One of the things I love about poker is that it's meritocratic compared to most parts of life. As I mentioned in the introduction, for instance, at one event in the 2022 World Series of Poker I randomly happened to be seated next to Neymar, one of the world's greatest soccer players. Two seats over was a guy in a fluorescent green T-shirt who ran an auto-body business in suburban Chicago. Then there were several world-class pros at the table. We'd all paid our $10,000 and we were on a level playing field.

That's tournament poker, though. For Adelstein's specialty, cash games, it's becoming harder to find a favorable game. Cash poker is becoming more like the rest of society: it helps to have connections. Show up at a major poker room like the Bellagio in Las Vegas and you'll be able to play $5/$10 or maybe $10/$20 no-limit Hold'em with no questions asked. These are medium-stakes games; once in a while, you might make or lose $10K in a session. Once you get much higher than this, though—roughly to the point where a player could win or lose the value of a reasonably nice new car on a single session of poker—public games start to dry up.

That's because players are fighting for a scarce resource: whales. A "fish" is a bad poker player; a "whale" is a bad, very rich poker player.* These players have other monikers, too: "VIPs," "fun players," "recs" or "recreational players." Whatever you call them, there aren't *that* many people who are both quite bad at poker and willing to lose new-car's-worth money at it on a regular basis.

So the high-stakes cash game economy works something like this: a professional player befriends a whale, and they work together to get a private game going (confusingly, private games are often played at casinos,† although they also might be at someone's home). Ideally the whale will know other whales, but if the whale is bad enough, this isn't strictly necessary. The professional player invites his friends, perhaps in exchange for a share of their winnings. These friends are probably also professional players, though they can't be nits—they'll have to be people the whale enjoys gambling with. So a typical private game might feature something like one to three whales and five to seven professionals.

---

* Though most whales will at least put you to the test through aggressive play. You'll make money from them in the long run, but not without being willing to gamble.
† Casino policies on this vary. The game might technically be open to the public, but it *just so happens* that there's never a seat open. Or if there is one open, you might not want it—it's probably because the whale has left.

Televised poker cash games flip this ratio: they might have one to three professionals and five to seven whales.* Through trial and error, the streams have learned that whales with big personalities are often more relatable than pros who play like computers.

"You build a lineup from the recs up," said Nick Vertucci, part of the odd couple that runs the Hustler games. (Vertucci is burly and tattooed; Ryan Feldman, the other co-owner and producer, is short and skinny.) "The recreational fun players need to be the foundation of your stream. And then if you add in pros, they have to be big names, and you can't over-stuff the lineup with pros." So seats like the one Adelstein used to occupy at Hustler are extremely valuable. They're not just prime real estate; they're the penthouse of the Zaha Hadid-designed condo building in the most expensive neighborhood in the city.

So when Lew flipped over her cards, it felt like a palace coup: the pent-house had just been broken into by a condo board president with an evic-tion notice. The hand against Lew "almost led to a little bit of an existential crisis," Adelstein told me. He'd always been concerned about cheating, touring the Hustler control room and asking a series of technical questions before agreeing to play. The hand was played in September 2022, and cheating was in the ether. Just a few days earlier, world number-one chess player Magnus Carlsen had accused an opponent of cheating. And there had allegedly been extensive cheating—I'm saying *allegedly* because the person accused of it is extremely litigious—by a player named Mike Postle on another California livestream a few years earlier. Confusion abounded.

There are four theories for Lew's play:

- One is that she made a brilliant read. Few professional players have maintained this claim, however—instead it's mostly been people outside of poker seeking to turn the hand into a referendum on the treatment of women in the game. This is a worthwhile subject: women in poker face a lot of mistreatment. Still, it wasn't a brilliant

---

* There is one in-between category: players with significant social media followings will often be invited to livestream games whether they're good, bad, or indifferent at poker. I fall into this bucket and have played on private TV games on a few occasions.

play. The problem is that even if Lew *knew* Adelstein was *always* bluffing—and not only that but bluffing with the exact sort of hand he had, a hand with both a flush draw and a straight draw—she'd still lose around 70 percent of the time because most of his bluffs beat her jack high.* Even against a range consisting solely of these bluffs, her call had negative expected value, theoretically costing her about $27,000.

- The second possibility is that she misremembered her hand, thinking she had a jack and a three instead of a jack and a four. In that case, she'd have had a pair of threes, putting her ahead of Adelstein's bluffs—making for a liberal call but one well within the realm of "normal" poker. This was the explanation that Lew eventually settled on, although not one she'd maintained consistently. The problem is that it's incongruent with her reaction at the table. Not only can you see her double-checking her cards just before calling, but there's little expression of surprise when she flips over her hand. Usually players almost literally jump out of their seat and exclaim "Oh shit!" if they realize they've misread their hand—going out of their way to demonstrate why they'd made a seemingly unusual play.

- The third option is that she made a colossal strategic blunder, not fully processing that she couldn't even beat some of Adelstein's bluffs. A few times a year, I'll play in charity tournaments in New York against people who have literally never played poker before. I wouldn't be surprised to see a play like that from a seventeen-year-old prep school kid whose investment banker daddy bought him into the tournament. But Lew was several levels beyond that. She'd received coaching from a top pro. She cashed in several tournaments, including the Main Event of the World Series of Poker. If Prep School Kid is a 0 and Phil Ivey is a 10, Lew was probably something like a 4. Overmatched in that game, but presumably too advanced to make a play of that nature.

- The fourth possibility is that she cheated. And that seemed like the most likely explanation at the time.

---

* Adelstein has a lot of these hands because there are two possible flush draws on the board, both diamonds and hearts. The list of hands with "combo draws"—straight plus flush draws—is K♥Q♥, K♥J♥, Q♥J♥, Q♥8♥, J♥8♥, 8♥7♥, 8♥6♥, 7♥6♥, K♣Q♣, Q♣8♣, 8♣7♣, 8♣6♣, and 7♣6♣. Note that Adelstein cannot have hands containing the J♣ because Lew holds that card.

"I would have the same reaction as Garrett. If I was in his spot, and I got called by jack high, I would have thought that there was an *unbelievably* high chance that something happened," said Hanson, who has played in the Hustler games himself in addition to being a frequent commentator. "This is on a stream, there has been cheating in the past on streams, you're playing this super nosebleed game with this girl that no one's ever seen before, then you stack off on that hand. It's all those things lined up together; I would have immediately thought that there was cheating."

But by the time I talked to Hanson six months after the hand was played, he was leaning toward the possibility that Lew had misplayed her hand after all. No forensic evidence of cheating had emerged, nor were there other examples where Lew appeared to benefit from cheating across nineteen hours of *Hustler Casino Live* footage that had been scoured by the poker community. When there's that much smoke, there's usually fire. But the entire poker community has gone looking for fire and hasn't found it. Several prominent players even put a $250,000 bounty out, looking for a whistleblower to come forward. No one did. "The more time that just goes by that nothing happens," said Hanson, "it just leads me more towards just a very, very strange kind of set of events."

I lean in that direction too.* Don't get me wrong: I live in fear that some new evidence will come out the moment that the book gets sent to the printer. Cheating is entirely plausible—there's also some suspicious circumstantial evidence on the Hustler livestream that I haven't covered yet. But I think the most likely explanation is that Adelstein suffered a huge "cooler"—the term poker players use to describe a situation where you play your cards right, but are doomed to lose anyway. (Like when you have pocket kings and your opponent has aces.) Press enough edges in poker— the sort of edges that you're hardwired to seek out as a high-stakes player— and trouble often finds you.

---

* My assessment of the J4 hand in this chapter is based on information that is publicly available, or that was given to me on the record. I am not considering unverifiable rumors or innuendo that people weren't willing to put their name to.

Risk, Reward, and Racing Hearts

In January 2023, I flew to the Bahamas to play in the PokerStars Players Championship. The main event of the series, held at the luxurious casino resort Baha Mar, featured a $25,000 buy-in. This was unusually large; at a typical poker series, tournaments billed as "main events" have an entry fee anywhere from $1,500 to $10,000. But the PSPC was no ordinary tournament. Over several years—the event had repeatedly been delayed by the COVID-19 pandemic—more than four hundred players had won a free entry into the tournament from the online site PokerStars, mostly for winning small buy-in tournaments where the entry fee may have been just a few hundred dollars, but also as part of other random promotions; one friend of mine had qualified by winning a poker essay contest, for example. With a soft field like that, full of recreational players competing for stakes hundreds of times larger than they were used to, the event figured to be hugely +EV—at least if you ignored that a plate of tacos at Baha Mar cost $42.

Truth be told, I'd never played in a $25,000 tournament before either. But mentally I felt comfortable with the stakes. Relaxed, even: Baha Mar, befitting its breezy location, is more spacious and laid-back than the frenetic casinos of Florida and Las Vegas. What's more, the table I got randomly drawn to featured two friends of mine: Maria Konnikova,* author of *The Biggest Bluff*, and John Juanda, an Indonesian high-rolling pro who now lives in Japan and who I'd had a great time hanging out with in Tokyo a few years earlier. Playing against friends can be tricky—sometimes you can get so paranoid that your friend is taking advantage of you that you wind up overcompensating. But Konnikova and Juanda are conscientious people, and the rest of the table wasn't too tough. If I was going to play a $25,000 tournament, this was about the least stressful possible version of it.

But under the surface, my body was amped up, with my chest

---

* I also launched a podcast, *Risky Business*, with Konnikova, in May 2024.

pounding every time I had to make a decision. This wasn't necessarily a *bad* feeling; I felt alert, with a high level of attention to detail, and I was playing aggressively—aggressively enough that after a couple of hours, Konnikova and Juanda were side-eyeing me with a what-got-into-*you*-today expression. One risk in poker, though, is that your body will give away tells—signs of nervousness or stimulation that you'd rather keep to yourself. Some players even wear scarves to avoid letting players detect a quickening pulse in the carotid arteries in their neck.* So I was self-conscious about it. When I played a hand, I tried to envision a tranquil, relaxing place to calm myself down—one of the placid pools at Baha Mar or a forest trail near the Hudson River in autumn. But this didn't really work. Somehow I was processing this experience on two entirely different levels: my conscious mind already felt calm, but my *body* didn't.

A few days later—after busting out of the $25K on the second day of the tournament—I played in a much smaller $2,200 event. I was expecting the stress response to come back, but it didn't—even when I got dealt a pair of aces I was as calm as the Caribbean Sea. Poker players are trained not to think about the stakes; to treat their chips as Monopoly money. Most of the time, I'm pretty good at that and have had a reasonable amount of success when taking shots at higher-stakes tournaments or cash games. My pain threshold—how much I can lose at gambling without feeling bothered by it the next day—has increased steadily over time.

But fundamentally, gambling for large amounts of money—enough money that you *do* brush up against your pain threshold—is a whole-body experience. You can ride the wave in different ways. The first time I played in a $100/$200 cash game, I literally felt like I was on the sort of narcotics that I used to do a lot of in my twenties. A handful of other times when playing poker, I've gotten into a flow state—what is colloquially known as being "in the zone."

Other than having realized at some point that it's a very bad idea to

---

* A more subtle alternative is a hoodie. You can carry one with you if you're prone to occasional bouts of feeling nervy.

play poker when you're hungry,[*] I'd never really thought much about the physiology of poker. But I happened to be reading an important book right about the time of the Bahamas trip. In fact, *The Hour Between Dog and Wolf* may be the most important poker book I've ever read—even though the book ostensibly has nothing to do with poker.

John Coates is a thoughtful but slightly cantankerous Canadian who describes his career as a series of mistakes. He went to Cambridge on an academic scholarship, was placed in the economics department even though he didn't want to be, and completed his econ PhD all the same under threat of the scholarship being revoked. Wanting nothing to do with academic economics—"From the beginning, I thought it was a pseudoscience," he told me—Coates instead went to Wall Street, where he became a trader at Goldman Sachs and eventually ran the derivatives trading desk for Deutsche Bank. Then, thanks to a chance encounter with a neuroscience PhD student on a plane, he went back into academia—but this time as a neuroscientist at Cambridge. He wanted to understand the biology of risk-taking—and explain what he'd witnessed on Wall Street, where the behavior of traders he'd encountered was far removed from the academic models of rationality that he'd studied in his PhD program.

That's what Coates's book *The Hour Between Dog and Wolf* is about. The title comes from the French phrase *l'heure entre chien et loup*—the twilight hour where it becomes difficult to distinguish a dog from a wolf. Metaphorically, the phrase refers to the physical transformation we go through when we're confronted with a substantial amount of risk. Especially when we encounter novel, uncertain situations—"when a correlation between events breaks down or a new pattern emerges, when something is just not right, this primitive part of the brain registers the change long before conscious awareness"—and we switch from being predictable, domesticated beings to wild creatures living off of cunning, hormones, and animal instinct. To see an example, if you haven't yet, go back and watch the video

---

[*] It's eight p.m. You skipped lunch and the tournament doesn't have a dinner break. Your friend texts you and asks if you want to join for dinner. You're imagining a steak and a glass of cabernet. I can promise you that you're going to find a way to punt off your stack an inordinately high percentage of the time.

of the Garrett-Robbi hand. Adelstein experiences a physical transformation instantly upon seeing her cards—as though he's seen a ghost—even though it takes him a good fifteen minutes to consciously piece together what just happened.

Experiences like the ones I had in the Bahamas—where my body was registering stress that my conscious mind was in denial about—are common, according to Coates. Based on his studies of traders and investors, your outward-facing emotional state doesn't necessarily reveal all that much. "We've wired up traders that were big hitters, and they were poker-faced," he told me—the traders occasionally got angry when things were going poorly but mostly kept a calm demeanor. "But even when they were poker-faced, what was going on under the surface was far more important because their endocrine system was on fire when they were taking risk."

In one experiment, for example, Coates studied the testosterone levels of a group of traders at a high-frequency London trading shop. He found that their testosterone was significantly higher following days when they'd made an above-average profit. But the converse was also true. Coates had also been checking their testosterone in the morning and discovered that they had substantially better trading days when they *woke up* with higher T levels. Higher testosterone predicted more trading success, in other words.

More testosterone, more profit. What could possibly go wrong?

In fact, all of this was probably fine *up to a point*. I'm going to make a bold, daring generalization here. *For the most part—at least when it comes to financial and career decisions—people do not undertake enough risk.* It's certainly true in poker. For every player who's too aggressive, you'll encounter ten who aren't aggressive enough. It's true in finance, according to Coates. "A lot of asset managers and hedge funds I've dealt with have a problem getting their good traders and PMs to use their full risk allocation," he told me. "They're not taking enough risk." It's true when people are contemplating personal changes. Annie Duke's book *Quit*—Duke is a former professional poker player who quit the game in 2012 to study decision-making—is full of evidence about this. An experiment conducted by the economist Steven Levitt, for example, found that when people volunteered to put major life decisions such as whether to stay at a job or in a relationship up to the outcome of a coin flip, they were happier on average when they made a change.

The bodily transformation that Coates's traders experienced made for a positive feedback loop. They'd have a winning day, build up more testosterone, and take on more risk. Because most traders start out being too risk-averse, at first this helped; they were getting closer to the optimal, profit-maximizing level of risk. So they'd have *more* winning days, get yet more T, and take on yet more risk. You can probably guess what happened next. Before long, they were the equivalent of steroid-infused meatheads, barreling right on past optimal to dangerous, potentially catastrophic, Sam Bankman-Fried levels of risk-taking.

Coates believes that much of what accounts for the "irrational exuberance" that makes for financial bubbles are these biological factors. Traders can experience euphoria. A bull market "releases cortisol, and in combination with dopamine, one of the most addictive drugs known to the human brain, it delivers a narcotic hit, a rush, a flow that convinces traders there is no other job in the world."

So what if you could replace traders—or poker players—with AI systems and not have to worry about all that icky body chemistry?

Actually, that might not be such a good idea. We get a lot of feedback from our physical beings; this is one reason some experts are skeptical that AI systems can achieve humanlike intelligence without human bodies. In fact, Coates's studies found, the most successful traders had *more* changes in their body chemistry in response to risk. "We were finding this in the very best traders. Their endocrine response was opposite of what I expected when I went in," he said. "You would think that someone who's really under control would have a very muted physiological reaction to taking risk. But in fact, it's the other way around."

So the physical response I experienced in the Bahamas wasn't anything to be ashamed of. As much as I was trying to maintain a too-cool-for-school demeanor, my body was preparing me for battle. It knew a $25,000 tournament was much more important than an ordinary one—literally hundreds of times more important than an $80 online tournament I might play when bored on a Tuesday night.

Jared Tendler is a self-described "mental game" coach for poker players and traders. But his first love is golf. When I interviewed him, there was a set of Callaway golf clubs prominently in the background of his Zoom screen. Tendler choked away his chance to break through as a professional golfer, though. A three-time All-American at Skidmore College, he missed qualifying for the U.S. Open by one stroke despite "play[ing] the best round of my life" after missing a series of short, makeable putts. Then nearly the same thing happened again when he was trying to qualify for the U.S. Amateur. That sent Tendler on a mission to study the science of performance under pressure.

Tendler teaches his students that they can't wish away anxiety. "Just misperceiving anxiety is a fundamental mistake for a lot of poker players, especially who have not been in bigger tournaments before," he told me. "They don't know that it's okay to feel that way. And by thinking that it's bad, then all of a sudden, you create a lot more anxiety, and it sort of spirals from there."

This can be one cause of every poker player's worst fear: "tilt," the phenomenon where your perception of what's happening at the table has gone completely askew and you're making blunder after blunder. Poker players tend to think of tilt as an emotional state—anger after a bad beat, boredom after a slow run of cards, or overconfidence after a winning streak. But it can also have biological causes. In big moments when you're confronted with a high-stakes decision, you're essentially working with a different operating system than the one you're used to. If a player reacts by going into an anxiety spiral, "it's like a blue screen on your computer where your mind is just either frozen or so emotionally hijacked that you're no longer thinking straight," said Tendler.

However, it helps to have practice under these conditions. In fact, having a physical response to being confronted with risk can be a healthy sign. Coates was once contacted by a group of researchers with the Great Britain Olympic Team. Their best athletes, they told him, were just like his best traders, with low baseline levels of stress response that then dramatically spiked when it came time for a big competition. This even applies to golf. PGA Tour golfers—athletic adults who might ordinarily have a resting heart rate of sixty or lower—instead have one "ranging in the nineties to one hundred and tens, just as a baseline throughout the entire tournament, and of course spiking in different situations," Tendler said.

That "in the zone" risk response I described earlier feels like you've entered one of those dreamlike soap operas with a higher frame rate. You're fully immersed in the task at hand, with a heightened attention to detail and mastery that comes from a deeply intuitive place—you know what to do without "thinking" about it. It's not a sense of calm so much as a sense of clarity.

When I think about the times I've been in a zone or flow state, it's often been in response to stress. It's happened at big moments in poker tournaments, occasionally during public speaking appearances, and even a couple of times when I was writing or coding under intense deadline pressure. I've also had it happen on election nights when I've been covering the results. What these had in common is that they were all extremely high-stakes moments where I had thousands of dollars in money or future earning potential on the line.

But that alternative operating system that kicks in under high-risk conditions is powerful. Tendler referred me to a set of research called the Iowa Gambling Task, so named because it was originally conducted by professors at the University of Iowa College of Medicine. It works like this: participants are asked to choose from four decks of cards—A, B, C, and D. Each card gives the player a financial reward or penalty. Two of the decks—let's say A and B—are risky, with occasional big wins but lots of penalties and poor overall expected value. The other two—C and D—are safer, with a positive expected return. The pattern isn't *that* subtle, and after turning over a couple dozen cards, the player usually figures out to avoid the losing decks. The research found, however, that players have a physiological response to the risky decks before they detect the pattern consciously. Their body is providing them with useful information—if they choose to listen to it.

Tendler told me that when a player enters a flow state, she's taking advantage of intuitive knowledge—sort of like a supercharged version of the Iowa Gambling Task. "The most common differentiator is the ability to access that kind of intuitive knowledge and make a decision that you cannot in that moment fully cognitively explain now," he said. But one needs to be careful with these superpowers. The experts in physical risk-taking I spoke to for chapter 13, like astronauts and fighter pilots, told me that trying to "be a hero" can sometimes interfere with remembering your training and calmly executing your game plan.

Coming across this research has changed my thinking on a couple of topics. One is performance under pressure in sports. Stat nerds like me used to think that labeling athletes as "clutch performers" or "chokers" was a bunch of bullshit—narratives manufactured out of random noise. Certainly this is still sometimes the case, especially for sports like baseball that are subject to a high degree of randomness. But newer research shows that some athletes are better than others in the clutch, especially if they have experience with it. Golfers with more experience perform better at the Masters, for instance, controlling for their overall ability level. My own research shows that experience matters considerably in the NBA playoffs. And we shouldn't neglect the testimony of athletes themselves, from Michael Jordan to the great Montreal Canadiens goalie Ken Dryden, who describe similar experiences of being in a zone when under intense pressure. Precisely because it's rare to experience high-risk moments, it helps to have been through them a few times before and to learn how to channel the stress to productive use.

And here's some good news: You *can* learn to ride the wave.

In 2023, I made the top 100 in the World Series of Poker Main Event. The run had started to make national news coverage, and I was on the TV feature table several times—which I'd begun to see as an advantage. In the Main Event, there are so many players—more than ten thousand entrants in 2023—that even late into the tournament, most of my opponents were amateurs who had never experienced anything like this. Conversely, I'd been on TV plenty, both for poker and under the pressure cooker of presidential election nights on network news.

If you get deep into the Main Event, which lasts for almost two weeks from start to finish, you'll see opponents crack under the pressure. Maybe they're tired from playing for days on end, happy enough to have made it that far. Maybe they have imposter syndrome, or even survivor's guilt after all their friends have busted out of the tournament and gone home. Faced with a fight-or-flight response to stress, they flee. I empathize with those impulses, and had it been two years earlier, I might have felt them myself.

Not this time, though. As I made my way back to the TV table following a break, a player named Shaun Deeb—a six-time WSOP bracelet winner— asked me what my objective was. Was I playing to survive, or was I playing to *win*? I was playing to *win*, I said. Half my opponents were so nervous that they could barely put a bet into the pot without knocking over their chips. But I felt a sense of clarity. Were the stakes high? Yeah. Once we'd gotten down to the final one hundred players, with the top prize of $12.1 million in sight, every pot was potentially worth hundreds of thousands of dollars in expected value. In fact, the stakes were so high as to be almost incomprehensible—which may have been helpful. My body had registered the difference between a $2,200 tournament and a $25,000 tournament in the Bahamas. But now I was playing the equivalent of a $500,000 tournament, and it was so ridiculous that somehow both my brain and my body defaulted to treating my chips as Monopoly money.

Day 6 of my Main Event was almost a *Truman Show* moment. The table was being broadcast in nearly real time (on a fifteen-minute delay) to the thousands of players who had stuck around for other WSOP events in the Paris and Bally's ballrooms. But I felt in my element. Maybe even *in the zone*. And faced with a big decision, I'd made a big call. Tony Dunst—an aggressive player who is also a broadcaster for the World Poker Tour and who surely felt confident under the bright lights—raised, and I called with A♥J♥. A third player, a friendly Virginian in a checkered shirt named

Stephen Friedrich who had never won more than $750 in a poker tournament before, quickly went all-in. Tony folded, and the decision was back on me. It would have been easy enough to fold and live to fight another day. But I composed myself and took a few minutes to decide. Something about Friedrich's story didn't add up. After initially projecting confidence— he'd nonchalantly said "all of it" while briskly pushing his chips into the center of the pot—Friedrich had slumped over, his head down, his hands folded as though in prayer. With every moment that passed, he seemed to curl into more of a turtle shell, like he was waiting out a tornado warning, hoping to hear the all-clear signal. I couldn't quite pinpoint why in the moment, but my brain had scanned its internal database and picked up on a pattern:* this felt weak and he wanted me to fold. And then I remembered what I'd said to Deeb—I was *playing to win*, not just to hang out with the boys. So I called. Sure enough, Friedrich had a mediocre hand— A♦T♠—that I was almost a 75 percent favorite against. My hand held up at showdown, and suddenly I had more than 5 million chips.

Unfortunately, on the very next hand, I got coolered. On a flop of 6♥7♥2♠, I made the second-best-possible hand, a set of sixes with 6♦6♣. I eagerly got my chips all-in and wouldn't have played it any other way. If you're afraid of playing a big pot with a hand as strong as this— when there's only one other hand that can beat you—poker isn't the game for you. The problem was that my opponent, a Chicagoan named Henry Chan, *did* have exactly that one better hand, 7♦7♣ for a set of sevens. If I'd won this pot, I would have had 11 million chips, and my stack would have been worth the equivalent of around $900,000 in expected prize money. Instead, I'd busted out in eighty-seventh place for $92,600. I found a spot to get a stiff drink just in time before my friends, watching the hand on the fifteen-minute delay, began texting me their condolences.

---

* Later I realized that it reminded me of a hand played by the legendary poker player Tom Dwan on the Hustler livestream, where he'd correctly called a bluff against an opponent named Wesley in a record-breaking $3.1 million pot. Wesley's behavior had been similar to Friedrich's: a quick all-in followed by a turtle shell in an extremely high-pressure moment where it might be hard to conceal your emotional state. I'd recently spoken to Dwan at length about the hand, which comes up again in chapter 13, so I'm sure it was rattling around the back of my mind.

It was heartbreaking. I may never play such a big pot again in my life. But I'll tell you something: ever since that hand—losing the equivalent of a nearly million-dollar pot that for a split second I'd assumed I was a big favorite to win—a bad beat for $300 or $3,000 or even $30,000 hasn't felt like such a big deal by comparison. There's nothing like pain to build up your pain tolerance.

Sixth Senses and White Magic

Phil Hellmuth spent about forty minutes showing me his trophy room. I ought to have taken a photo or two, but I worried that might inflate his ego. But here's what I recall: in addition to poker trophies of all shapes and sizes—Hellmuth has won more than seventy poker tournaments, including a world-record seventeen World Series of Poker events—there were signed photos of just about every athlete you can imagine, books full of old newspaper clippings and poker tournament ledgers, and lots and lots of Phil Hellmuth-branded merchandise, including every Wisconsin boy's dream: a series of Milwaukee's Best beer cans with Hellmuth's smiling mug on them.

When we later sat down at the dining room table in his comfortable home in Palo Alto, California, it was clear that my effort to tamp down Hellmuth's ego had failed. He spoke in a fifteen-minute stream-of-consciousness soliloquies where I couldn't get a word in edgewise. At one point he recalled ribbing Michael Jordan for having won more World Series bracelets (fifteen, at the time) than Jordan had NBA championships (six)—it's not really a fair comparison, because there's just one NBA title each season while the WSOP hands out bracelets for dozens of events every year. (The Main Event is just one of what's now about a hundred events on the WSOP schedule.)

But somehow all of this was almost charming. Hellmuth is nicknamed "Poker Brat" for his frequent brags and rants—at the 2021 World Series of Poker, he threatened to "burn this fucking place down if I don't win this fucking tournament." And yet—although I don't think he's deliberately putting on an act or playing a character—if Hellmuth likes you, you'll feel like you're in on the joke.

And Hellmuth does have a lot to brag about when it comes to poker. It's hard to make an authoritative statistical comparison of poker players because there's no record of how many tournaments a player has entered—only how many times they've finished in the money—and there are few public records of cash games at all. Still, Hellmuth's seventeen WSOP bracelets are by far the most ever (Phil Ivey, Johnny Chan, Doyle Brunson, and Erik Seidel are tied for second at ten). And despite criticism from other players that his playing style is outmoded—unlike Negreanu, Hellmuth hasn't really tried to adapt his game to be more GTO—he's also had his share of success recently, including going 9–2 in High Stakes Duel, a series of heads-up matches against elite players. Greatest of all time? It's hard to say, because there are so many different formats for poker that comparisons are inevitably apples to oranges. But you could make a case for him.

Hellmuth also has a softer side if you break through his poker face. Like a lot of intensely competitive people, he had a difficult childhood. In his book, he wrote about how "in first grade, second grade, my grades were bad, how I had zits, how I had warts on my hands—the struggle that I had to not have any friends."

"I've always been kind of a poker brat, the origin of which is, when I was young, I'm the oldest of five children and I was the only one that didn't get good grades," he told me. "I was the only one that didn't perform athletically on the traditional field. . . . My father was taught grades are everything. . . . So I was getting zero validation from my dad." So Hellmuth turned to poker. "I had to at least be great at games."

In tournaments, Hellmuth favors a tactical, "small ball" style of play rather than the swashbuckling aggression that modern players like. The typical flaw of an inexperienced poker player is to take passive actions—checking or calling—instead of the more decisive actions of betting, raising, or folding. Well, Hellmuth sort of plays like that. He likes to check and call, hoping to beat his opponents in a game of death by a thousand cuts.

(He also likes to fold a lot—he's tight.) This makes some players with a more modern approach to the game mistake him for a fish. But this style actually has some advantages. First, it avoids putting all his chips at risk. If you think you're one of the best players in the world—and Hellmuth obviously thinks of himself that way—the opportunity cost of an all-in bet or call is high because a better opportunity might come along later. Second, precisely because nearly every other pro has abandoned the small ball approach, other players may not be used to it. And third, playing smaller pots where there are a lot of decision points in every hand* allows Hellmuth to use his greatest strength: white magic.

"White magic" is the term Hellmuth uses for his ability to read other players, whether through physical tells or verbal interactions. Even Hellmuth's rivals give him credit for the ability to get inside players' heads; Negreanu once called him "the best exploitative player of all time." Although Hellmuth told me he doesn't deliberately try to put his opponents on tilt, it probably helps him that he's loquacious to the point of being annoying—many players will give away some type of reaction that betrays their hand strength.

Where this ability comes from is something I'm not sure even Hellmuth is fully aware of. My pet theory is that being bullied as a child made him hypersensitive to reading social cues—not in a way that leads him to be well-mannered (he's the Poker Brat), but which does allow him to work out people's intentions and whether he's being threatened. But one important connection Hellmuth drew is that his white magic comes and goes with his energy level. The idea that people-reading ability comes from the body rather than the mind—so that when we're tired, our social skills suffer more than, say, our ability to work out an equation—is something straight out of Coates.

"Sometimes I'm at full fucking reading ability. And when I'm at full

---

* One way to put this is that Hellmuth is preserving his optionality. Going all-in ends the hand—either your opponent calls or she folds, and there are no more decisions to make. Smaller bets give you the opportunity to hang around, and maybe pick up on a tell that lets you make a big fold or big call later on. Hellmuth's play is often maligned by GTO-driven critics, but it may be optimal given his particular strength for picking up reads.

reading ability, I'm dangerous," he said. "Why don't I have more bracelets than I have? Sure I have the most of all time. I could have another ten bracelets already," he humblebragged—Hellmuth rarely breaks character. "What's happened is fatigue has killed me. So I get too tired. And I lose control. And I play badly."

It's also possible to take a more studious, deliberate approach to player reading. Both Adelstein and Negreanu told me that they obsessively watch video of their most frequent opponents. "I had a database of just one player, Jake Schindler," Negreanu said as an example. "I had five thousand hands of Jake Schindler. And I've watched him, and I counted, okay, eight out of ten times that he cut his chips this way, he had a marginal hand." Needless to say, you need to be very careful when playing an opponent who studies you like this.

But for most players, picking up on tells and emotional vibes comes from a more intuitive place.

"One thing I found out really quickly when I first started playing was I had a really strong instinct for when my opponents were weak or strong," said Maria Ho, another top pro who is a particularly keen judge of other poker players' behavior—enough that she's frequently a color commentator for the World Poker Tour and other poker TV broadcasts. "And that was purely based on physical reads plus, you know, just the smallest mannerisms in the way that they would put out their chips." Ho told me that she has one additional advantage: most poker players are men, and men are mostly bad at concealing their emotional state. Women, conversely, are harder to read. "Women are usually good communicators, but they only communicate to you what they want you to know," Ho said. "We only kind of let people in when we are ready to tell them the full story. So I think I've always found women to be better and more deceptive than their male counterparts."

In 2023, Ho won the poker reality TV show *Game of Gold* for $456,000, defeating fifteen opponents who ranged from charismatic up-and-comers to greatest-of-all-time candidates like Negreanu. It was an environment perfectly suited for Ho, who like Adelstein had reality TV experience (she'd once been a contestant on *The Amazing Race*). But *Game of Gold* mostly came down to who had superior poker skills based on a series of heads-up matches. And if you watch Ho, her ability to read her opponents is uncanny.* She's more deliberate than someone like Hellmuth, triangulating toward her target as she blends the underlying math of the hand, the subtle physical signs her opponents are giving away, and her situational awareness. GTO theory says that in every poker situation, at least some of your bets ought to be bluffs. But many players lack the presence of mind to find these bluffs in the biggest moments. If you're one of them, Ho will usually size up the deficiencies in your courage.

Scott Seiver, another pro known for his table banter and his ability to talk his opponents into doing exactly what he wants them to do, noted that poker involves two skills that are rarely present in the same person: systematic thinking and empathy.† "Poker, in its essence beyond the math, is a game about empathy," he said. "It's about being able to understand if I was the person and I know XYZ about who they are—and they've just experienced the past several things—what are they more likely to do in the next situation coming up?"

Although many books have been written about poker tells, Seiver is suspicious about whether they can be boiled down to a science. "It's kind of putting the cart before the horse, where we're ascribing a reason for a subconscious feeling that you get," he said. Coates told me something similar: we should generally pay attention to the signals our body is providing us with even if we can't quite figure out why. "The thing is our physiology is really smart," he said. "I mean, it's just really smart. It's very hard to trick your physiology. . . . We live in a 3D world, we move in a 3D world. So if we make mistakes in our movement, we die. So we have much higher standards in our physiology than we do our psychology. And so these signals can be incredibly valuable."

If players like Ho, Seiver, and Hellmuth are especially skilled at it, most

---

* To see Ho at her very best, I'd particularly recommend episode 8 of *Game of Gold*, "The Queen."
† These personality traits—systematizing and empathy—have also been found to have a negative correlation in academic research, such as by Simon Baron-Cohen.

poker players have at least some intangible skill for picking up on an opponent's hand strength. Sometimes you'll just *know*, even if you can't pinpoint exactly why or how. The term "sixth sense" is a cliché, but once you've gained enough experience playing live poker, that's really what it feels like. The acuteness of this sense may come and go depending on your focus level. But because many poker decisions involve mixed strategies— so that the expected value of calling and folding is theoretically exactly the same, for example—it's perfectly fine to "go with your gut" as a tie-breaker. Now and then, though, you'll get such a strong sense of what your opponent has that he might as well be glowing green, and you'll be comfortable deviating far from GTO play.

So if you're reading this book as an aspiring poker player, do you have my permission to make heroic folds or calls or bluffs based on the subconscious vibe you get about a player?

No. Please don't do that. Not until you gain more experience using your sixth sense. And even then, you have to collect enough data to make reliable inferences. "Even against bad players, the relative weight of the physical thing is usually pretty low," Adelstein told me. "You really need some really great information, specifically like them doing that physical thing when they either almost always have it, or almost always don't, over a pretty good sample size."

For instance, one recurring theme in poker tells is whether an opponent is relaxed or tense. This often isn't that hard to tell, though professional players have a lot of practice in concealing their behavior (or faking it to trick you). Even then, though, you still have to work out *why* they're feeling relaxed or tense. Seiver recalled a hand he played in 2014 against a German pro named Tobias Reinkemeier in a special $1 million buy-in WSOP tournament. In the hand, Seiver went all-in on the turn as a bluff, representing that he'd made a flush when he was actually on a straight draw instead. Reinkemeier had pocket aces and had been trapping with them, hoping to induce exactly this sort of move from Seiver. The players bantered, and Reinkemeier let Seiver know he had aces. Seiver seemed incredibly relaxed and nonchalant for a $1 million tournament, telling

Reinkemeier that of course he'd have to call with a hand as strong as aces. Reinkemeier, sensing a trick, threw his hand away!

The thing is, Seiver *was* feeling relaxed, he told me—because he was resigned to being knocked out of the event. "He said that he had aces. And you're supposed to call with aces not even 99 percent of the time there, like literally 100 percent. And Tobias was a quite good poker player, someone that I had a lot of respect for. . . . So I'm all very relaxed, because I knew I was out of the tournament. I knew he was going to call no matter what."

The flip side of this is when your opponent has a large-enough sample of your play to be data driven about predicting your behavior. In October 2021, I was on the verge of a dream coming true: winning my own World Series of Poker bracelet. I was playing the $10,000 Limit Hold'em Championship event; limit Hold'em has fallen out of fashion, but it was the most popular game for the period in the mid-2000s when poker was my primary source of income. Even though I hadn't played much limit Hold'em in fifteen years, no one else had either, and I had a lot of muscle memory for the game. I made it down to the final two players, feeling like I'd played almost perfect poker. There was only one man standing in my way: "Angry" John Monnette.

Monnette, who had won three previous WSOP bracelets at the time I faced off against him, was just about the worst person in the world to play in this spot. His bread and butter is high-stakes limit cash games, so he's kept improving his limit skills while the rest of the poker world has let them atrophy. He's also incredibly observant and isn't afraid to verbalize his complaints—sometimes aggressively, hence his nickname. He was constantly calling the tournament staff over, for instance, to point out that some of the cards had small defects—subtle ridges or dents that were visible under the glare of the bright lights of the televised final table.

If he was noticing details that small, what was he noticing about me? We played for several hours, but the battle felt increasingly uphill, and by the time I lost I felt completely outwitted*—as though Monnette could see

---

* If we'd been playing no-limit Hold'em, I'd have some strategies to combat this. Namely, I could play "big ball" poker—the opposite of the Hellmuthian approach—trying to force Angry John to gamble with big bets and all-ins. This was limit Hold'em, though, so it was death by a thousand cuts.

my cards. I have a friend who, whenever this tournament comes up, "helpfully" points out that I should really watch the video because it seems like Monnette had picked up a tell on me and was making some incredibly precise calls and folds. I don't need to watch the video, though, because I'm sure Monnette had picked up on a thing or two. In fact, I have some idea about what the tell was. I'd been trying to avoid social media during the match, so I hadn't noticed that a world-class player had sent me a Twitter DM alerting me to a potential problem. Since I think I've fixed the tell, I'll tell you what it was. My "timing was a little too honest," as the player put it: I was taking longer to make bets and calls with bluffs than when I had strong hands. The thing is, this is a relatively subtle tell and the opposite of what you'd typically expect. (The stereotype is that players act more quickly and decisively with bluffs to represent strength while taking their time in faux-contemplation with strong hands, like Johnny Chan did against Erik Seidel.) But over the course of several hours, Monnette had been able to work this out. It didn't help me that the final table was broadcast on PokerGO (with a slight delay). So if any of his friends had picked up on the tell, they could have alerted Monnette to it as well.

Still, you not only have to discover the tell, but give it some sort of mathematical weight. Over time, poker players develop an uncannily well-calibrated mathematical intuition. "If there's one thing that you figure out after many, many, many, many hands, it's you know what 52/48 is," said Annie Duke, referring to a player who can distinguish a 52 percent chance from a 50/50 spot. "That's the type of distinction that most people are very bad at making. But poker players are really good at making that distinction, and they can *feel* it."

These words were music to my ears as someone who spends the better part of every election cycle tearing my hair out (what I have left of it) to get people in the Village to think more probabilistically. But I was particularly interested in how Duke phrased her remark: that this is something players *feel* in their bones rather than consciously trying to work out the probabilities.

In our conversation, Duke invoked the work of her friend, the late

Nobel Prize–winning economist Daniel Kahneman. In his book *Thinking, Fast and Slow*, Kahneman posited a distinction between "fast" System 1 thinking, where we act intuitively with little or no conscious effort, and "slow" System 2 thinking, where we go through a deliberate, structured thought process:

SYSTEM 1 TASKS	SYSTEM 2 TASKS
Reacting when a dog jumps in front of your car	Planning a driving route to Grandma's house
Walking down Fifth Avenue while checking your phone	Conducting a cost-benefit analysis on closing Fifth Avenue to single-passenger automobile traffic
Determining if someone is flirting with you	Negotiating a prenuptial agreement
Identifying when an object looks out of place in a room you're familiar with	Working with an interior decorator to design a living room on a budget
Estimating the number of people in a small group	Estimating the attendance in a large sports stadium

Given the mathematical complexities of the game, you might expect poker to fall into System 2. And indeed, this is how computers approach poker. Despite constant improvements in processing power, solvers still take several minutes to come up with an approximate solution to a single poker hand. And yet, experienced human players, who have more factors to weigh than computers—not just the math but the psychology—often come to a decision in just a few seconds. So maybe the distinction between System 2 and System 1 is fuzzier than is commonly assumed. System 2 tasks can become System 1 tasks with enough practice.

So that's one of the factors that make poker players and people like them special: being able to make approximately correct mathematical calculations on the fly, using not just their minds but also signals from their bodies. But it's still only the half of it. Even relative to other activities in the River, poker is a game of exponentially increasing risk. So let's talk about variance, and the psychological effect it has on poker players.

Cash Poker Is Insanity. Tournament Poker Is Ten Times Insanity.

I'm not sure there's another popular activity where complete failure is such a common outcome.

At most poker tournaments, only 10 to 15 percent of the field is paid out. Good players will have a higher cash rate than that, but not necessarily a lot higher—part of their advantage is in being able to accumulate lots of chips and be one of the top few finishers and not just garner a "mincash." Indeed, in large tournaments, the real money only goes to roughly the top 2 percent of the field. Most of the time, it's just lose, lose, lose, mincash, lose.

That's why tournament players are inherently a bit insane. Tournaments are too risky even for the notoriously fearless Garrett Adelstein. "I realized that if cash poker is insanity, tournament poker is like ten times that insanity. That's, like, sitting in isolation in the asylum your whole life," he told me.

Let's quantify the insanity.

Ryan Laplante, a Vegas-based poker pro who also runs the training site LearnProPoker.com, loves poker tournaments more than anyone I know. He loves them so much that he's willing to play a huge range of buy-ins, from under $350 to as much as $50,000. So he has a good idea of how much a player can expect to earn at different levels. I asked Laplante for his help in coming up with a plausible schedule for a typical "live tourney pro." We specified that this player is a step short of elite, but somewhere between the one-hundredth and two-hundredth best player on the live tournament scene—a good regular who you're never happy to see at your table. Let's call her Pretty Good Penelope.

Penelope's goal is to play two hundred entries in live poker tournaments per year with an average buy-in of roughly $5,000. (Penelope would probably say "fire two hundred bullets" instead—a bullet is a tournament entry. Lots of poker jargon invokes Wild West imagery.) It isn't as easy as it sounds to get the money down. She'll probably want to live in Vegas, where there's no state income tax and housing is relatively affordable. She'll then need to play nearly the entire seven-week schedule of the World Series of Poker between May and July.* Then there are other poker series in Vegas throughout the year—the Wynn hosts some nice ones, including a December series with a $10,400 main event that boasted an astonishing $40 million prize pool in 2023.

Then she'll need to travel. She'll definitely want to hit the Hard Rock in Florida several times a year, which has the most consistently good tournament poker outside of Vegas. She'll want to go to the PSPC in the Bahamas. Beyond that, she has a few choices to get up to two hundred bullets. She can either play some of the more obscure World Poker Tour events in places like the Choctaw Casino & Resort in Durant, Oklahoma—or she can go for the more glamorous spots on the European Poker Tour like Monte Carlo and Barcelona, but at the price of travel expenses, jet lag, and the inevitable hassles of getting large amounts of money in and out of a foreign country. (Hint: don't bring more than $10,000 in cash with you on an international flight.) But here's roughly what a schedule might look like by the end of Penelope's year—including estimates of Penelope's return on investment (ROI) at different events, which I formulated with help from Laplante.

Penelope's Tournament Schedule

ENTRIES	BUY-IN	PLAYERS	TOP PRIZE	DESCRIPTION	ROI
25	$1,000	4,000	$500K	Very large weekend WSOP	60%
40	$1,500	200	$60K	One- or two-day minor Vegas tournament during slow part of the calendar, such as at the Venetian	50%
40	$3,500	2,500	$1.3M	Very large major tournament main event (WSOP, WPT, EPT, etc.)	40%

---

* If you're like a lot of people I know, a poker aficionado with a desk job, this might seem like a dream come true. But when I played the WSOP for roughly five weeks straight in 2021, it was kind of a grind. Starting times at the WSOP are staggered throughout the late morning and afternoon—never the early morning, that would be considered sacrilege in poker—and tournaments aim for roughly twelve hours of play a day. If you're trying to fire as many bullets as possible, you'll have some days where you jump into a morning event, bust out, and then enter an afternoon tournament that goes until two or three in the morning. This can easily turn into a seventy- or eighty-hour workweek.

35	$5,000	700	$600K	Large major $5K tourney	30%
30	$10,000	700	$1.2M	Large major $10K tourney	20%
20	$10,000	50	$170K	PokerGO $10K or side event at major tournament	10%
6	$25,000	125	$700K	$25K high-roller in Florida or at WSOP	10%
1	$10,000	9,000	$10M	WSOP Main Event	100%
2	$10,400	4,000	$4M	Wynn WPT Main Event (a.k.a. the "Winter Main"); multiple entries allowed	30%
1	$25,000	1,000	$3M	PSPC Main Event, the Bahamas	40%
200	$1.1M			Total	25%

What's the bottom line? I estimate that in an average year, Penelope will earn about $240,000 from tournaments. "Wow, that sounds pretty great!" you might say—travel the world, play cards for a living, and make several times the average American salary. That doesn't really tell the whole story, however. For one thing, there are taxes (a big issue based on the way the IRS taxes poker players) and expenses (high, since we're assuming Penelope's on the road about a hundred days per year).

But the big problem is that the $240,000 figure is kind of fiction. It's an expected-value calculation over the long run, and Penelope is never going to reach the long run. There's so much variance in tournament poker that even if Penelope played for fifty years, the swings wouldn't really even out.

In fact, despite being one of the two hundred best tournament players in the world, *she'll have a losing year almost half the time.* I discovered this by simulating Penelope's schedule ten thousand times, using payout tables from actual poker tournaments.*

---

* For instance, if there were four thousand entries in a given tournament, I randomly chose a place for Penelope between first and four-thousandth and looked up the associated prize, except I weighted the lottery slightly in her favor so as to match her projected ROI.

There's one other question you might ask: Penelope intends to spend more than $1 million in tournament buy-ins per year—so where the hell is she getting all this money? In poker, that question can have a variety of answers. Many touring pros had a big score early in their career. A lot have side hustles or sponsorship deals. A lot of money came into the poker community during the crypto boom—poker players were early adopters of Bitcoin and Ethereum, in part because crypto actually has some practical use cases in poker.* And some players are just sharp at making the right connections. Poker attracts a lot of smart oddballs with creative schemes for making money. These oddballs fall into one of three categories—somewhat rich, extremely rich, and stone broke—and it's never entirely clear who belongs in which bucket. But there are always people in the River who like to splash money around, and it never hurts to be in the "splash zone."

So for purposes of the simulation, let's assume that Penelope begins her year with a $500,000 bankroll and will skip a tournament if it costs her more than 5 percent of her remaining bankroll to enter. With that constraint in mind, here's what a representative set of ten out of those ten thousand simulations looks like:

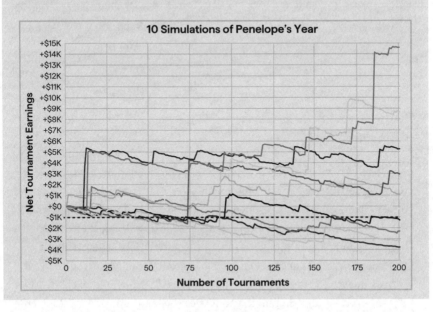

----

* Poker players need lots of liquidity, sometimes across international borders, and many U.S. banks are not friendly to poker players. So crypto is an important way to settle debts in the poker community. It's also used by many gray-market online sites as a way to circumvent U.S. laws on processing gambling deposits.

Pretty wild, right? In this set of simulations, Penelope has everything from a $377,000 loss to a nearly $1.5 million win. Of course, more extreme outcomes than that are possible. In one simulation, she won the World Series of Poker Main Event on top of some other paydays, taking home more than $11.2 million. But Penelope has a losing year 47 percent of the time. Her median outcome is to win just $33,000.

Penelope's End-of-Year Outcomes

PERCENTILE	NET EARNINGS
0	–$442,000
1	–$416,000
5	–$377,000
10	–$346,000
20	–$288,000
30	–$174,000
40	–$76,000
50	$33,000
60	$197,000
70	$400,000
80	$681,000
90	$1,094,000
95	$1,456,000
99	$2,442,000
100	$11,200,000

So mostly, poker tournament life reflects a lot of pain. If you look at the spaghetti strings in the chart, you'll see that Penelope spends most of her time losing but is rescued by some occasional very big scores. If she doesn't have one of those big scores, her losing streaks can continue for a very long time. In fact, based on the simulations, there's about an 11 percent chance that Penelope will lose money over any given *ten-year period*. Imagine being one of the two hundred best people in the world at your craft—and losing money at it over the course of a decade! I even estimate that Penelope will have a losing *fifty-year period* about once in every two hundred simulations. And all of this assumes that Penelope's level of play is consistent, which isn't realistic either. Probably the swings will be even more insane than this because, like Coates's traders, she'll perform worse when she's on a losing streak and better when she's winning.

The Essential Ingredients of a Poker Personality

Who are the people willing to put up with all of this? To be fair, there are ways to play poker professionally without having to sweat quite so much variance. At lower buy-in tournaments—say, $600 or $800—the skill advantage for a professional player can be so large that prolonged downswings are less likely. Or you can focus on cash games instead of tournaments. Grind out the $2/$5 game at the Bellagio for fifty hours a week, and you might have an expected value of $80,000 to $100,000 per year with little risk of going broke.

But the idea of regular hours and a steady paycheck defeats the purpose of playing poker in the first place. That's the paradoxical part about those who play the game. It's a field that glorifies hyperrational decision-making, but a lot of people who play poker for a living would be better off—at least financially—doing something else. The combination of mathematical and people-reading skills necessary for success at poker should generally also translate to lucrative opportunities in tech, finance, or other River professions—usually in jobs with health care benefits and far less variance.

However, much of what attracts people to poker is an anti-authority streak. It's one of the only professions where you can truly be a lone wolf. "Poker players are people who have gone out of their way to avoid having a boss and who have frequently been stigmatized for that decision and have tolerated that and carried on," said Isaac Haxton, a high-stakes pro who dropped out of his computer science program at Brown University to play cards during the Poker Boom of the mid-2000s. Haxton, who in his early days on the tournament circuit was sometimes teased for his resemblance to Harry Potter, is an example of the sort of anti-authority attitude he's describing. Proudly left-wing, he became disillusioned by computer science after considering his potential employers. "It's, you know, Facebook, or Google, or Raytheon, or Boeing—just the absolute most destructive forces on Earth," he told me. Haxton returned to Brown to complete a philosophy degree but has played poker ever since—to the tune of more than $35 million in lifetime tournament winnings.

But if never quite having made peace with the establishment is one factor that defines poker players, we should be honest about another attraction: it's a game that selects for people who like to gamble.

"Even the most disciplined poker players are in a battle between their rational mind and the part of their mind that chooses gambling," said Brian Koppelman. I'd met with Koppelman in his trailer on the Upper West Side in Manhattan, where he was shooting an episode of his Showtime series *Billions*. Although the world in *Billions*, centered on the hedge fund Axe Capital, is one of the most accurate fictional portrayals of the River, Koppelman is best known by poker players for cowriting the 1998 movie *Rounders*, which was inspired by his visits to New York's legendary Mayfair poker club. "It's literally underground, and the rest of the city is asleep," Koppelman recalled. "And you're awake, matching wits with other people with something real on the line. And there's the element of variance. For nonreligious people, it's like a way to grapple with God."

I'll admit I never thought of the theological implications of poker before. The people you'll find in the River have an irresistible urge to compete—and competition requires two elements to be any fun. First, the competition has to be real; you can't be guaranteed of anything. There's a reason why more people watch the New York Knicks than the Harlem Globetrotters. And second, the stakes have to be high enough that it hurts when you lose. Poker attracts people who really are willing to let fate determine their place in the universe.

So the other thing that a high-stakes poker player needs, as I'd learned the hard way at the 2023 Main Event, is a high pain tolerance. You have to be fearless. And apart from experience, there are three ways to acquire fearlessness in poker: nurture, nature, and good luck.

Jason Koon, for example, who is third on the all-time poker money list with more than $55 million in lifetime tournament winnings, is an example of nurture. His rough-and-tumble upbringing has prepared him to deal with incredibly high-stress situations. He was raised in poverty in the mountains of West Virginia, with a father who beat him regularly before walking out on the family and eventually going to jail. Koon's difficult childhood had one benefit: helping him adapt to the fight-or-flight moments that most poker players dread. Koon can have a temper—at West Virginia Wesleyan College, where he was the first member of his family to go to college on a track scholarship, he was known for getting into bar fights. But in poker, it's the big moments that matter most. And when the pressure is on, Koon is at his most focused. "There's this weird effect, where if something really, really bad happens, like really bad in real life, I'm, like, oddly comfortable and calm," he said. "Because I've just been there a bunch."

For other players, a high risk tolerance may have more of a biological basis. Dan Smith—who is nicknamed "Cowboy" despite being from New Jersey because of the cowboy hat he frequently wears (his first "proper" cowboy hat was given to him by Koon)—will gamble on virtually anything, from cryptocurrency to a sushi dinner* to his athletic skills. In 2023, Smith bet another player named Markus Gonsalves on the outcome of a set of tennis; the catch was that Gonsalves, the superior player, had to use a frying pan rather than a tennis racket. Gonsalves won anyway.

"I was once talking to a nutritionist who asked me, Do you think you're drawn to risk-taking behaviors? Like thrill seeking, where you pump your adrenaline, or chasing women or drinking or drugs or gambling and that sort of thing?" Smith told me. "And I was just like, Yep!"

Smith has spoken publicly about his battles with depression and his

---

* When Smith and I went to an expensive sushi restaurant in New York, we chose who paid based on who could make the best poker hand out of the serial numbers on a $100 bill. Somehow I made no pair and no straight—that's pretty unlucky with eight numbers to work with—and had to pony up.

degen (degenerate gambler) tendencies—in his Twitter bio he calls himself a "gambling addicted charity enthusiast." (Being considered a degen is sometimes a badge of honor in the River, so long as you're not the sort of degen who harms others. Better a degen than a nit, certainly.) He said his nutritionist's theory was that "people who have naturally low serotonin are drawn to risk-taking behaviors," a claim that checks out in the academic literature. As Smith put it to me, his need for risk and his need for competition help him to maintain a sort of precarious balance when it comes to poker. "As much as I enjoy gambling, I also really hate losing and I don't want to give EV to my opponent."

Smith also donates a significant amount of his income, running an effective altruism–adjacent charity called Double Up Drive that has raised more than $26 million from poker players. That's another thing you might not expect about high-stakes players.[*] They tend to be generous with their money: tipping well, loaning to friends, offering to pick up checks, and so forth. Relative to other successful people I've met, they're more aware of the ephemeral nature of money and the role that luck has played in their success.

Finally, while I want to be careful about how I state this—I don't think some people are naturally lucky—there may be something to the idea of an initial run of good luck cultivating habits that put people on an on-ramp to continued success.

By the time I spoke with Ethan "Rampage" Yau in December 2022, he'd become perhaps the best-known American poker vlogger; some of his videos have more than a million views. But when Rampage began posting videos in 2018, he was living with his parents and buying into tables for as little as $200 in run-down Rhode Island casinos. In the first hand of Rampage's first video, he badly overplayed a pair of aces, going all-in against two opponents despite having the worst hand of the three. Still, he ended up winning $270 on the session, the start of what he calls a "sun run" that would persist for most of the year. ("Running good" in poker

---

[*] This refers to high-stakes players specifically; at lower stakes, you'll encounter plenty of curmudgeonly nits.

means getting lucky—so a sun run means running *really* hot, like, y'know, the sun.) "If I never survived through that," he told me, "then I wouldn't be here now. So I just got really lucky along the way, especially in the beginning."

Yau was surprisingly cavalier about his potential to go broke. When I spoke with him, he'd recently filmed a livestream that had started out as a $25/$50 game but—as high-stakes cash games often do—had gone completely off the rails, with pots reaching into the six figures. Yau told me he was nowhere near properly bankrolled for the game and that he was gambling with a huge amount of his net worth. "I'm young and dumb enough to not look at those numbers."

During our interview, I kept waiting for Rampage to break character—for him to say, "Look, off the record, I hired a team of six Hungarian supergeniuses, including John von Neumann's granddaughter, to program a solver for live cash poker, but please don't tell anyone that because I have a reputation to maintain." But although I do think he's underselling his poker skills, there was never anything of this sort. Instead, he made a lot of comments like this: "It's more fun to play hands. So no matter how much I try to, like, be tight or whatever, and play GTO, it doesn't matter because I'll just revert back to just like, let's fucking go for this spot, because YOLO."

And yet, somehow, it has worked out pretty well for Rampage. Just a week after we spoke, Yau won a $900,000 first-place prize at a $25,000 Wynn high-roller tournament. He followed that up by winning more than $500,000 twice on *Hustler Casino Live* in early 2023, including one hand where he won by bluffing his opponent out of a $1.1 million pot. Rampage's biggest strength is his YOLO fearlessness. If he senses that you care about losing your chips more than he does, he's going to exploit that at the first opportunity.

One inevitable problem with a book like this is that it suffers from survivorship bias. If you run the world ten thousand times, some lucky player is going to wind up with the 99.99th percentile simulation, have a sun run that persists for years, and become a poker folk hero. Maybe that player is

Yau. But in talking to Rampage, I began to wonder: Does he actually think he's lucky? And might this benefit his poker game in certain ways?

Richard Wiseman's 2003 book, *The Luck Factor*, asserts that people who view themselves as lucky benefit from it in several ways. I'm skeptical about Wiseman's framing: in particular, I think what he calls "luck" might better be thought of as some combination of optimism, resilience, confidence, extraversion, and openness to experience. I also think it's hard to separate out his definition of luck from socioeconomic status or privilege. Nevertheless, here's a version of his claims:

1. Lucky people "constantly encounter chance opportunities" and try out new things.
2. Lucky people "make good decisions without knowing why." They listen to their intuition.
3. Lucky people have positive expectations so their "dreams, ambitions and goals have an uncanny knack of coming true."
4. Lucky people "have an ability to turn their bad luck into good fortune" because of their resilience.

If you remove the sheen of self-help-book claptrap, there's a kernel of something there. How can you "constantly encounter chance opportunities" more often? Well, this is really just a reframing of optionality, which means making decisions that put you in a position where you'll have more choices to make later on. Personally, I'd just call that maximizing EV. But in self-help speak: if you choose to walk through the hallway where there are more doors, it's more likely you'll find an open one.

And certainly, resilience is essential to a poker player. It's a game where you lose a *lot*. Every poker player knows a few Eeyore types who wallow in their perceived or actual misfortune. The thing about these players is that they never seem to break out of it: once an Eeyore, always an Eeyore. Remember what we've learned from John Coates, Annie Duke, and others: most people are too risk-averse, at least when it comes to financial and career decisions. A little bit of luck early in their careers might encourage people to take on the proper amount of risk later on. To be clear, I wouldn't recommend Rampage's bankroll management practices. He may well go broke at some point. (He admitted to losing a substantial amount on tournaments in 2023.) But you'd still rather be Rampage than Eeyore.

Why Aren't There More Women in Poker?

The poker world is diverse in some ways. At a time of increasing political polarization, you'll encounter a broad cross section of political opinion. It's extremely mixed by age, from nineteen-year-olds with fake IDs right up through the hundred-year-old Eugene Calden, who drew attention for regularly winning poker tournaments throughout 2023. Along racial and ethnic lines, poker is more diverse than many parts of American society, although far from a representative sample of the population. White and East Asian players are overrepresented, as are a variety of immigrant groups because of the game's international popularity. Black players are underrepresented, although with some prominent exceptions—Phil Ivey, often regarded as the best player of all-time, is Black.

But poker is very, *very* male—even as compared to other parts of the River, which is already a male-centric environment. Common estimates are that the player pool is 95 to 97 percent male; you might see a woman at every second or third table. So before we return to conclude the story of Garrett and Robbi—a hand where public perceptions may have been influenced by Lew's gender—I want to take a little time to consider this.

Mostly, I'm just going to relate what was told to me by women and minority players I spoke with. I'm not claiming to have any special insight, other than maybe that I travel back and forth between the Village, where discussions of race and gender are an animating force, and the River, where these subjects are often treated dismissively.

Let me start out by rejecting one explanation for the male skew in poker. I don't think men are any better than women at poker, on average. I'm not saying that to be super woke. There are psychological and physiological differences on average between the genders, and some of them are relevant to poker. However, it's not obvious that men have the better half of the deal. As I hope I've established, poker requires not just mathematical intelligence but also empathy and emotional intelligence, factors that most studies find women are better at on average. Women are also better on average at things like inferring someone's emotional state from their facial expression.

So what explains the poker gender gap? The explanations I've come across fall into roughly five categories.

1. There's often openly abusive and misogynistic behavior toward women, made worse by a "What happens in Vegas stays in Vegas" attitude.

LoriAnn Persinger has thick skin. She's a navy veteran who has "always been kind of a nerd." She's been on national television several times as a semi-professional game show contestant on programs ranging from *Wheel of Fortune* to *The Price Is Right*. She also really stands out in a poker room. There aren't many women in poker generally, but there are very few Black women in their midfifties. She's not the type to complain lightly.

But in addition to being a professional player, Persinger has also been a poker dealer, and has been on the other end of a lot of abusive behavior from players. The poker room is an environment ripe for abuse: the game attracts extremely competitive people who have chosen the lifestyle in part because they don't want a boss or other authority figures in their life. At any given table, some of them are losing money—and some may be drunk, high, or thirty-six hours into a marathon session.

What makes matters worse is that casino staff are almost always trained to tamp down the situation rather than escalate, especially if the offender is a VIP and can walk across the street to take his business elsewhere. For instance, Hellmuth didn't receive even a cursory penalty after—jokingly, he claimed—threatening to burn the Rio down during the 2021 WSOP. "Nothing gets done about it. And it's just, it's crap. It's absolute crap," Persinger told me. "You just want to say something, and you know if you do, you're gonna get fricking fired because that person spends so much money in the casino."

Indeed, misogynistic and abusive behavior is often right out in the open. In 2023, a male player entered and won a women's tournament in Florida, deliberately staring at women to make them uncomfortable, according to other players in the event. The problems are often worse at the entry levels that determine whether players stick with poker and potentially make it a lifelong hobby or career. "I've actually experienced the worst misogyny at the lowest stakes. Where people are there to have fun and they're drinking and they feel like I'm cramping their style," said Maria Konnikova. However, I've also heard awful stories about misconduct coming from highly regarded high-stakes players—but the worst stories often come only once you've turned the tape recorder off.

2. Men struggle to make adult friendships, and poker provides a means for male social bonding that appeals to a broad cross section of men, but women aren't always invited to the party.

When a record number of (mostly male) poker players arrived to play the WPT event at the Seminole Hard Rock in April 2021 in the shadow of the COVID-19 lockdowns, I wondered how many of them simply missed being in the company of their buddies. Because here's one stereotype that bears out both in my own life and in empirical research: women, on average, are more likely to form bonds by talking, while men are more likely to form bonds by doing things together. At a time of declining male friendships—15 percent of American men say they have no close friends, and about half have three or fewer close friends—poker provides a social lifeline. You show up at a poker table and you'll be in an environment where social awkwardness is reasonably well tolerated and where you're guaranteed to have at least one interest (poker) in common with your tablemates. For most men, it's easy to fit in.

I don't think there's anything intrinsically wrong with this. In fact, I think the world would be better off if men spent more time pursuing sociable hobbies and less time getting angry on the internet. But when it comes to poker, women aren't always invited to join in.

Maria Ho, for instance, had to bribe her way into her college game with booze. "I had a bunch of friends that played poker in the dorms. And every Friday night, they would have a poker game. And that was the only night that I wasn't really invited to hang out with them, which I thought was weird," she said. "I'm like, okay, I have to force my way in there. So I just showed up with a keg of beer, because I was like, well, they can't refuse this."

3. Men—whether through nurture, culture, or nature—tend on average to be more competitive and aggressive, essential attributes for success at poker.

Men spend more than twice as much time playing games as women, according to the American Time Use Survey. There's also academic literature showing that men are on average less risk-averse than women over a variety of domains. So it's not surprising that poker—a game where even most professionals aren't as aggressive as the computers say they should be—doesn't start out with a perfect 50/50 gender ratio. But while I don't doubt that these traits partly have a genetic basis, it's also clear to me that cultural expectations exaggerate them.

"A lot of the qualities that would make you a good poker player, when you use those qualities to describe a man, they have a positive valence," said Duke. "And when [they] describe a woman, they have a negative valence. Things like intense, competitive, ambitious, so forth, like those are all bad words to say about a woman, but good words to say about a man."

There are some ferociously competitive women in poker. But they have to seek out poker more intentionally and be willing to go against the grain. Many women are taught not to be aggressive, said Ho. "And in order to be a good poker player, you have to naturally lean into that aggressive side. . . . It takes somebody that really doesn't care what other people think, and isn't afraid to think outside of the box and step outside of these lines."

"I'm gonna confess. As evident by my game show background, I actually like the competition. You know, I used to say, I like beating the boys," said Persinger.

4. Men have more financial and social capital to gamble with.

There are also some simple economic realities when it comes to poker, especially in higher-stakes games. To play in high-stakes-poker cash games and tournaments theoretically requires a very large bankroll—well into the six figures. Who has that sort of money to burn? According to the Current Population Survey, roughly 20 to 25 percent of employed white men and 35 to 40 percent of employed Asian men earned at least $100,000 in 2022, as compared to about 15 percent of white women, 15 percent of Black men, and less than 10 percent of Black women.

It can be easy to take for granted how much of a luxury it is to have money to gamble with. Carlos Welch—the cohost of the *Thinking Poker* podcast with Andrew Brokos—grew up in an impoverished, Black, single-parent household in Georgia. Welch is a terrific player who in 2021 won an online WSOP bracelet event for $125,000. I have no doubt that he could kick ass at high-stakes events if he wanted. Yet Welch sticks to relatively low buy-ins and, until he married fellow poker player Gloria Jackson in 2023, often slept in his car in casino parking lots. He is proud of being a "nit"—the term can refer to conservative, tight poker play, but also a tendency to be frugal—because he doesn't assume that he could rebuild his bankroll if he went broke. "Every dollar I save is another day I don't have to go to work," he told me. "And so as I get more money, it just makes me even nittier."

Welch's behavior may well be rational compared with Rampage and other players who often gamble outside their bankroll. Still, cultural expectations vary as to who is expected to be responsible with their money and who is entrusted to gamble with it—and these expectations vary by race and gender. "Society doesn't really encourage women from a young age to take risks. We're taught growing up that we always have to be more responsible," said Ho.

5. It's an advantage to have the option of blending in, and that's easier when you're a white guy.

At the 2022 WSOP Main Event, I played against Ebony Kenney. From the moment we sat down, she dominated the conversation at the table, asking players for their names and their backstories, sometimes flirting a little bit. Kenney wasn't hunting for information; this was the second day of the tournament, and she and everyone knew in advance who was going to be at the table and had presumably googled their bios. Rather, Kenney was trying to disarm her opponents with humor and charm. It's a strategy that's been working. Kenney is a terrific player; a few months after the WSOP, she'd go on to cash two high-roller events in Cyprus for a combined total of almost $2 million.

I mostly found the Ebony Kenney Show entertaining. But I also thought, "Holy shit, this is a lot of work!" As a balding, bearded forty-something white guy—basically the modal poker player phenotype—I always have the option of just sitting back and becoming part of the furniture. That's not a choice for Black women like Kenney or Persinger. "I don't know if I put undue pressure on myself as a result of the fact that there are so few women that look like me," said Persinger. "Even when we went to Commerce, there's a ballroom of easily over eight hundred people and I did not see even a handful of Black women there."

Women can also expect a lot of comments about their appearance. "I'm less sensitive to that type of thing than many people are," said Cate Hall, who had a rapid run of success in poker tournaments between 2015 and 2018 before leaving to go into effective altruism-related jobs. "But it does occasion a much higher, much more intense level of interest than the average player. And so just having a lot of attention on me, I wasn't really super psyched about it as more of an introvert."

If you are on the introverted side, you can opt to shut the world out. Welch, as a big Black guy who often watches battle rap videos at the table, attracts all sorts of attention from other players, positive and negative. He's adapted to it by almost never engaging in table conversation at all. "I used to wear shades. And I was like a fucking Terminator. Even my movements were robotic. Because I didn't want to give off anything," he told me.

However, this comes at a price. Not only are you forgoing potentially useful information by declining to converse with your opponents, but having an adversarial relationship with them in tournaments is a bad strategy. In general, when two players engage in a big confrontation in tournaments, it's -EV for them and +EV for the rest of the table. You don't want your opponents to come after you out of spite.

Welch doesn't care. "There's always a price to pay for things. And for me, some things aren't really worth the price. For example, I could probably improve my EV by being more chatty. But then I'm going to decrease my happiness."

There is, however, one silver lining in poker, which makes it unique among almost any activity I can think of. If people adopt incorrect stereotypes about you based on your race, gender, age, or appearance, you can use that to exploit them. "Stereotypes are a good starting point," said Welch. "The problem is when you're not willing to adjust. Because it's a game of limited information. So you've got to take whatever you can get. And I will say most of these stereotypes are correct 70 percent of the time. But if you don't change it, and they fall in that 30 percent, you're going to get destroyed."

The Benefit of the Doubt

I met with Robbi Jade Lew in November 2022, about seven weeks after her hand with Garrett Adelstein, as part of one of my many trips to the Seminole Hard Rock in Florida. Lew was in the midst of a defiant reemergence onto the poker scene. She was eager to have her story told, having double-checked with me to make sure we found time to speak. She name-dropped famous players who had been friendly to her. She didn't mind being noticed—we were sitting in a very public place, on a couch in the fanciest wing of the Hard Rock, and she was wearing a white dress and lots of jewelry.

Lew can also tell a great story. "I am a risk-taker. I always have been in every industry that I jumped into," she told me. "I've always wanted to do what others haven't done. I've always wanted to be a woman in a male-dominated industry. I've always wanted to go against the norm. You know, I was born in Saudi Arabia, and I saw my mom not being able to drive to the hospital to deliver a baby."

But my spidey sense was getting a weird vibe. At times, Lew looked out into space as though she was reading off a teleprompter. And Lew has a habit of relaying information that is either superfluous or doesn't entirely check out. Two sources that I spoke with used the term "pathological liar" to describe Lew's habit of tangling herself up in knots. She suggested to me, for instance, that Adelstein had come to the Hustler that day in a bad mood, but there is little evidence of that; on the video, he's calm and chipper right up to the microsecond that she flips up her J4.

Shortly after meeting with Lew, I checked in with Konnikova, who literally wrote the book on con artists—*The Confidence Game*, which preceded *The Biggest Bluff*. What did she make of Lew's claim, for instance, that she viewed the stakes as "Monopoly money" and didn't have any financial motivation to cheat?* "I always say con artists aren't motivated by

---

* Lew's husband, Charles Lew, is a managing partner at a boutique law firm in L.A. and I'm sure makes a pretty penny, so this claim is believable.

money. They're motivated by power," Konnikova said. The fact that Lew had eagerly sought out press attention wasn't necessarily a great sign either. Konnikova met a lot of highly charismatic con artists when writing her book. They were so charismatic that Konnikova eventually quit doing interviews because she felt herself growing too sympathetic to them. Why were con artists so eager to talk about unethical and often illegal behavior? "Because they are so damn proud of what they did."

So I was skeptical of Lew's claims. And yet, I wonder if I hadn't become a little overconfident myself or was judging her based on stereotypes. At the time I'd sat down to speak with her, I thought it was more likely than not that she cheated. It was easy to interpret everything through that lens. You'll meet plenty of people in the River—and outside it—who are prone to artful exaggeration. Who we give the benefit of the doubt to and whose every word we scrutinize often depends on our preconceived notions of the person. The River has these biases as much as any other place. Why did Sam Bankman-Fried get away for so long with a $10 billion fraud when Robbi Jade Lew was villainized for a $269,000 poker hand?

I also wondered whether Adelstein had grown overconfident. I spoke with him twice, once about six weeks after the incident and once seven months later. In our second conversation, he told me that he'd only grown more confident over time that he'd been cheated. That worried me. Don't get me wrong: Adelstein was in the room for the moment and I wasn't. He's notoriously good at picking up on people's vibes, and so I give credit to the uncanny feeling he had at the time that he was cheated. But with every day that passes, the Robbi-Garrett hand has become less of a poker situation and something closer to a murder mystery novel: a series of strange coincidences for which there's no clear explanation.

There's also one confounding aspect to the Garrett-Robbi hand: she may be lying about it even if she didn't cheat. The two most likely explanations for her play are that she misplayed her hand and that she cheated. (Few players buy Lew's official story that she *misremembered* her hand. "No. Zero chance. Zero chance. Zero. Zero percent," said K. L. Cleeton, who has worked on software products to detect cheating in online games.)

If that's the case, Lew is being deceptive either way, though perhaps for the understandable reason of wanting to avoid embarrassment.

Although it's Robbi's strategy that's been criticized, Garrett's play of going all-in with his draw is also strongly disliked by the computer solver I tested it on. It's not that it was inherently a bad idea for him to bluff; players always need to have some bluffs.* But the amount he bluffed—$109,000 to win a pot that was only $35,000—was overkill. There's no reason to risk so much when instead you can see the final card cheaply, preserve your optionality, and then decide what to do. Adelstein was fully aware of this— he intended the move as an exploitative play based on his video review of her previous hands. "I had studied the tape of her religiously and had seen some lines she'd taken like that that led me to believe her range was definitely particularly weak," he said.

But even if his read was right, his timing had been poor. Robbi had felt bullied by Adelstein based on the play of recent hands and had said so on the stream. Even if you suspect your opponent has a weak hand, you don't want to bluff if they're going to be inclined to make a "hero call," meaning looking you up with a weak hand that may nevertheless be better than yours.

If you presume that Lew cheated then none of this matters, I guess. But if you give her some benefit of the doubt, you can start to see a coherent explanation for her play. After all, Lew's spidey sense was right—Adelstein had been bluffing.

Here's the explanation that she gave me at the Hard Rock. I asked Lew what the experience of playing poker on TV for high stakes had been like. I asked because I'd learned firsthand that it's an experience very much in the fight-or-flight mode described by Coates and Tendler, where you have the potential to either go into a flow state or suffer from an anxiety spiral.

"That was a really heightened game, to be broadcast live with those

---

* The play that Adelstein made is technically a semi-bluff—a drawing hand that can either win the hand immediately by getting the opponent to fold, or that can win the pot if it hits the draw.

players at the table. Everything happened so much faster than it appears—you have to make these quick decisions," said Lew. "And it's a split-second decision where you're just like, fuck it, I'm gonna call."

All of this sounds plausible. An altered sense of time ("everything happened so much faster than it appears") is a common experience in a flow state or other moments when we're undergoing a physical response to intense risk. And when we're in one of those situations, we aren't doing as much conscious thinking and instead become very intuitive. Lew's intuition told her—correctly!—that Adelstein was bluffing. Now, did she take the next step of doing the math, calculating what his bluffs were and whether she could beat them? No she didn't. That's a big oversight and one a more experienced player wouldn't make. Robbi's not Maria Ho. But her reaction was understandable. Every player has been in a position of thinking an opponent is bluffing, but having a hand so weak that they're unable to call the bluff—it's tempting to throw the chips in almost out of spite. And that may explain Robbi's play. She was experiencing the rush of playing high-stakes poker on TV, she'd been on a winning streak, and she was feeling as though she'd been bullied by Garrett. It was impulsive, it was -EV. But it wasn't *that* crazy.

What about the possibility that she cheated? That's not crazy either. There had been extremely credible accusations of cheating on another California livestream a couple years earlier. The Hustler's security procedures were lax, with several producers having real-time access to the players' cards. And cheating has been prevalent throughout poker history, more than some players would care to admit. I'm not going to repeat every unverified allegation I've heard over the years from old-timers, but until the Poker Boom years, the prevailing attitude was often that a poker player would win by any means necessary.

There were also several strange circumstances. Lew was given the money to play by another player in the game, Jacob "Rip" Chavez, a fact that wasn't clearly disclosed to the other players. Chavez's motivations are hard to determine—staking her in the game wasn't likely to be +EV given her inexperience at high stakes and the unfavorable terms on which he loaned her the money. After the J4 hand, Lew was asked by Adelstein—Lew and Adelstein give differing accounts of how aggressive the "ask" was—to give him the money back that she'd won in the hand. She agreed, prompting a furious reaction from Chavez. (Adelstein later donated the money to charity.) Most strangely of all, as the Hustler was investigating the incident, it discovered that an employee on the show who had access to view the players' cards, Bryan Sagbigsal, had taken $15,000 from Lew's stack after the broadcast had ended. Lew had initially been forgiving to Sagbigsal, declining to press charges and sharing a sympathetic message on his behalf that contained stylistic tics similar to her own writing. She later changed her mind and shared phone records with the police after a negative reaction from the poker community, although Sagbigsal went into hiding and was never located.

I don't blame Adelstein for thinking that Lew cheated. There's a lot of circumstantial evidence that doesn't look good for Lew, even if by Garrett's own admission to me there was "no smoking gun." But poker players are trained to think probabilistically—not to look for proof beyond the shadow of a doubt. In our conversation, Adelstein equated his thought process to the election forecasts I made for FiveThirtyEight: you have to do the best you can with the information you have available. There were consequences for falsely accusing her of cheating, but there were also consequences for saying nothing if she had cheated, he thought. At a minimum, Adelstein couldn't continue to play in the Hustler games with any confidence, and he was concerned that others might be cheated too.

Still, I lean toward the possibility that Lew did not cheat—not based on what happened during the J4 hand itself, but rather what happened before and after.

What happened *before* is that there were several instances—both during that day's taping, and on two previous episodes of *Hustler Casino Live*—where Lew would have benefited from cheating, but didn't.* Most cheaters

---

* In a hand against a player named Ryusuke, for instance, she made a thin bet on the river with a pair of threes when Ryusuke had just made a better hand, a pair of tens. It was a small pot—the bet only cost her $3,000—but this is not a play you'd make if you knew the opponent's cards. And in an earlier hand against Adelstein, Lew called a $10,000 bet on the turn with a jack-high flush draw even though

aren't like that. In other infamous cheating cases, the players involved treated themselves to winning at incredible rates that were astronomically statistically unlikely to have occurred by chance.* "Human nature is the only thing keeping cheaters from getting away with it. And what I mean by that is, generally humans are greedy; generally humans will not just use it on the edge cases," said Cleeton.

But in nineteen hours of livestreamed hands across three sessions, there's no hand other than J4 that looks like cheating—even after thousands of detail-obsessed poker players have scoured Lew's footage for signs of impropriety.† There's also the fact that if Lew cheated, she picked an awfully bad spot for it. If you had the power to magically know your opponent's cards, why would you summon it only once? And why would you use it in a spot where it would look extremely suspicious, and where it was barely even profitable? Adelstein's raise in the J4 hand was so large, and he had so many ways to make his draw, that the expected value of Lew's call was only around +$18,000. In a game like this, you could easily wait for a spot in a six-figure pot where you were guaranteed to win and it would never look like cheating.

There's also what happened *after* the hand. Again, I'd encourage you to watch the video and come to your own conclusions. But unless I'm really misreading her, Lew looks and acts elated for several minutes once she's beaten Adelstein. She's teasing him, and the other guys at the table are joining in on the fun. It looks like the reaction you'd get from a fortuitous turn of events—and not a preordained effort to cheat. "It's when a win is unexpected that you get the dopamine hit," Coates told me. "Sort of a

---

Adelstein had already made a full house and she was drawing dead—the term poker players use for when you literally have zero chance of winning. She also nearly called Adelstein again on the river, telling him she thought he was bluffing and saying, "I'll get you again." Indeed, she did. It was the next time she faced a huge bet from Adelstein that she pulled the trigger with J4.

* Of course, this could be selection bias: we only notice the most egregious cheating cases. Be careful when you play poker. Live tournaments or cash games in highly regulated casinos or cardrooms are by far the safest environment.

† There was a hand between her and Chavez where they played conspicuously timidly against each other—a "softplay" that sometimes happens when players have a financial or personal relationship and don't want to risk their chips against each other—but this is considered a venial sin in a cash game. And there are hands that she played poorly or unconventionally, but nothing out of the ordinary for an inexperienced player.

narcotic reward for doing something novel that produced an unexpected reward."

It's only when Adelstein left the room about fifteen minutes after the J4 hand, still not able to piece together what had happened, that the mood at Hustler changed. "It feels like someone just popped the air out of a big balloon here at the table," Hanson noted on the broadcast. Only then had the gravity of the situation sunk in. Robbi realized that Garrett was seriously upset, not just being a poor sport. Moments earlier, she was on cloud nine, having made the most epic call of all time—against Garrett Fucking Adelstein with Phil Fucking Ivey watching for Two Hundred and Sixty-Nine Thousand Dollars. Now she feared the entire poker world was going to think she was either a cheater or a fish.

My theory is that all of Lew's strange-seeming actions from that point forward can be explained by wanting to save face and avoid embarrassment. I'm not saying this is the only theory—if I were handicapping, I'd still put the chance of cheating at 35 or 40 percent. But it's a theory that's consistent with the evidence. Lew clearly cares a lot about her standing in the poker community.

Why did Lew suddenly insist, after having said nothing about it initially, that she misremembered her hand? Because misremembering your hand is something that happens to everyone once in a while. It's embarrassing, but about on the scale of burping or hiccuping, much less embarrassing than being a fish. Why did she give Adelstein the money back? Because it's a way to restore order, and because Adelstein somewhat falsely implied that he'd come back to the table and start playing again if she did.

If my theory is right, then what we have on our hands is a tragedy: one player falsely accused of cheating, and another player who got kicked out of the penthouse of poker while trying to do the right thing. Adelstein has never been invited back to the Hustler game, although he did resume playing poker after more than a year's hiatus in December 2023.

The personality types you'll encounter in the River are varied. Yes, you'll find some cheaters, some Sam Bankman-Frieds, people willing to do anything to increase their EV.

But people in the River are also good at abstraction, skilled at taking data points and drawing out general principles from them. Sometimes—certainly not always—this translates to being ethically principled as well. Poker players like Dan "Jungleman" Cates have spoken about how they're particularly bothered by hypocrisy, and I think there's a reason for this. When you deviate from the optimal strategy in poker, it can potentially come back to bite you. If you try to exploit someone, you'll risk being exploited yourself. So poker players often think about what the right play is in the abstract, assuming their opponents are also trying to make the best play. In game theory, there's a sense of reciprocity—treating others as you wish to be treated. I don't mean to imply that you should learn about interpersonal ethics from studying poker solvers. Rather, it's that there's a certain Riverian personality type that's attracted to principled thinking almost to a fault, and that is constantly disappointed by a world that often makes up the rules as it goes along.

Adelstein falls into that latter camp. He told me he has "perfectionist tendencies" and that for most of his poker career, he "never really was able to incorporate poker into an otherwise peaceful existence." The EV-maximizing play for Garrett might have been to go home, talk it out with the producers, and be a little bit more conciliatory toward Robbi publicly than he felt privately. Even though Adelstein was highly confident he'd been cheated, he could have bluffed that he wasn't. "After the dust cleared, I believe that he dug in too deep," said Vertucci. "I think he did himself an injustice by standing on his principles."

But Adelstein doesn't look at life like Vertucci does. Adelstein stood by his principles—even though he was possibly wrong on the facts. His reign as the king of the Hustler was over.

Consumption

Counting cards is easy.

"I can teach anyone how to do it," said Jeff Ma, a former member of the MIT Blackjack Team who was the inspiration for the book *Bringing Down the House* and the movie *21*. "Like, I could teach you how to do it in an hour." Indeed, after about an hour of practice with a computer simulation that dealt six blackjack hands at a time at a medium-fast clip, I could get the count right about 95 percent of the time.

Of course, doing this in the comfort of my apartment was a lot easier than it might have been in a hazy casino. In real life, for instance, you'd have to pay attention to the possibility of dealer errors. In long practice sessions in MIT classrooms after the professors had gone home, Ma and his teammates would deliberately trip one another up—maybe the student playing the "dealer" would tell the "player" he'd lost a hand that he'd actually won. And in a casino, you have to keep your cool and avoid blowing your cover. You've "just got to be so comfortable that you can do it without anyone knowing you're doing it," Ma told me.

But compared to most of the other ways to make money at gambling that we'll talk about in this book? It's easy. In principle, counting cards means that you can go to any casino that spreads a decent blackjack game and make a positive expected-value gamble—you'll win money in the long run. For reasons that will become clear in a moment, I *strongly* advise against trying this. But let me explain the logic behind it.

For one thing, blackjack features a relatively low house advantage. Extremely low, in fact, if you find the right game. As of early 2024, for example, the best low-stakes game that I know in Las Vegas is at the El Cortez downtown, a property that has been operating since 1941 and has the battle scars and the Rat Pack photos to prove it. Their single-deck blackjack game—which on a slow night they'll let you play for as little as $15—has a house edge of just 0.18 percent, assuming you play perfect basic strategy.* If you bet $100, in other words, you'd expect to get $99.81 of that in return. Most games aren't that good, particularly on the Strip, with the better ones instead running in the range of a 0.5 percent house advantage. And if you're not paying attention, the house edge can be much larger, perhaps 2 or 2.5 percent. Pro tip: look for games where blackjack pays out 3:2 (so you win $75 if you make blackjack on a $50 bet) rather than 6:5 (so you'd only win $60). This makes a big difference to your EV in the long run.†

So **step 1** in being a winning card counter is finding a game with reasonably favorable rules. You're looking for something with a house edge of 0.5 or lower. **Step 2** in counting cards is . . . counting cards. Count every card that's dealt at the table: yours, the dealer's, and any other player's. If you're using the most basic system, called the Hi-Lo Count, the count starts at zero. Subtract one point for every card ten or higher (ten, jack, king, queen, ace) and add one point for every card six or lower (deuce, three, four, five, six). Keep a running tally until the deck is shuffled, then revert the count to zero. It's good for the player when there are a lot of high cards left in the deck for all sorts of reasons—you'll make more blackjacks and will have more opportunities to make profitable maneuvers like splits and double-downs, and the dealer will go bust more often. If the count is

---

* I'm not going to cover basic blackjack strategy in this book, but it isn't hard to learn. Also, you can always ask the dealer or the pit boss for help—in most casinos, they'll politely tell you the right move.
† Unfortunately, cheap 3:2 games are getting hard to spot, at least on the most desirable parts of the Las Vegas Strip. You'll definitely find them if you venture Downtown or if you're willing to gamble for higher limits, however.

high enough—meaning you've seen lots of low cards, so what's left in the deck is mostly high cards—a bet can become +EV.

Hi-Lo Counting System

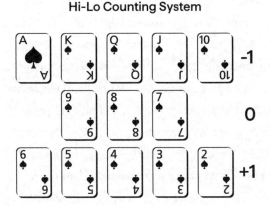

Step 3 is to bet a lot of money when these favorable situations occur. At some blackjack tables, the posted maximum bet may vary from the posted minimum by as much as 300x. For example, the Venetian in Las Vegas offers a table where the minimum bet is $50 and the maximum is $15,000.

So let's say you're at the Venetian. You sidle up to the table and hand the dealer $500. She hands you back some green $25 chips and black $100 chips. You bet the table minimum, 50 bucks. These bets are losing money, but only a little bit. You order a Michelob Ultra, nursing it slowly because you're trying to concentrate on card counting while making it look like you're a Regular Joe killing time waiting for his bros. Lots of low cards come off the deck, and before long, the count turns substantially positive. Your bets are +EV and you're ready to pounce. You reach into your backpack and pull out a brick ($100,000) of $100 bills. "Excuse me, ma'am," you tell the dealer. "Golly, I'm feeling lucky! I'd like to purchase a few additional casino chips!"

No, no, no, no, no, no, no.

Don't do this. Not if you ever want to play blackjack at the Venetian again.

Because **step 4** is the hard part. Step 4 is getting away with steps 1 through 3 without making it incredibly fucking obvious—like Regular Joe did. (At least order a cocktail and not a Michelob Ultra, Regular Joe.) Card counting isn't illegal, and you're not going to be taken into a back room and have your knuckles broken by the Sands Corporation, the $40 billion publicly traded company that runs the Venetian. Casino gambling is one of the most heavily regulated industries on Earth. But the law generally treats gambling as a privilege and not a right. In most jurisdictions, including Nevada, a casino can decline your blackjack action or even serve you with a notice of trespass and ban you from their casino entirely.

The hard part of Jeff Ma's job, in other words, wasn't the card counting but the subterfuge. Or if you prefer, the *hustle*. To persuade the casino that he was a losing player when he was a winning one—winning enough that he and the rest of the MIT Blackjack Team made $4 or $5 million over the course of a half dozen years, he told me.

Indeed, this is the fundamental dilemma of most forms of gambling. You have to persuade someone to take your action—persuade the house or persuade another player—when they're losing money by doing it. This is easy in tournament poker. In pretty much every other form of gambling, it isn't. You need some street smarts and you need some hustle. As Mike McDermott famously says in *Rounders*, if you can't spot the sucker at the table in the first half hour, then you are the sucker.

Think you can make money as a professional sports bettor, for instance? Well, maybe you can. (I'll cover this in the next chapter.) But most of the largest American sites will severely limit your action if they think you're a winning player. In the course of writing this book, I taught myself to be a competent sports bettor, or perhaps slightly better than that. But I'm a long way from an expert. Nonetheless, that was enough for me to be limited by a half dozen sites—including BetMGM, PointsBet, and DraftKings—in some cases to less than $10 on a game. There are workarounds to being limited, but they require at least as much effort to pull off as learning how to beat the lines.

"I call it the carnival game approach," said Ed Miller, who literally wrote the book on sports betting. (*The Logic of Sports Betting*, with coauthor Matthew Davidow, is perhaps the best practical gambling book I've ever read.) "There's a whole carnival full of games that are on offer. But as soon as you show any propensity to be able to win the stuffed animals on a regular basis, they tell you to go find a different [game]."

For Ma, his hustle involved the use of disguises—or really, entire personas. "You were, like, Kevin Lee, the guy from California whose dad is a plastic surgeon, or you were Jeff Chin, who was someone who'd helped start an internet company," he said. This was easier for the square-jawed, confident Ma than it might have been for a lot of people. And it was easier before Know Your Customer regulations and other anti-money-laundering laws were added after 9/11—and before casinos implemented intricate rewards card programs to track every aspect of their customers' activity.

Traditional card counting methods involve switching up your bet sizes—bet as much as you can get away with when the count is favorable and as little as you can when it isn't. But Ma and his teammates often relied on a different technique involving the use of what he calls a Big Player. It worked roughly like this. Say that I, posing as a mild-mannered software engineer, am plodding away at the table minimum, playing $50 a hand. Meanwhile, Jeff Ma—excuse me, *Jeff Chin*—is prowling around. When the count turns favorable, I give Chin a signal—maybe I turn my baseball cap backward. Then Chin sits down, makes clear he's a high roller, and bets $500 or $1,000 a hand or more—he's the Big Player—until the deck is shuffled and the count resets to zero. Neither he nor I ever have to vary our bet size, the most obvious sign of card counting.*

But although *21* portrays the Big Player technique accurately enough, it otherwise takes a lot of liberties. For instance, it turns the Chinese American Ma into a white guy, Kevin Lewis, played in the film by Jim Sturgess. This is not me making some politically correct complaint about erasing a job that could have gone to an Asian actor. Rather, it's that a key part of Ma's hustle was playing into a casino's stereotype of what a Big

---

* Many players do vary their bet size in the ordinary course of play—usually increasing it when they're winning and decreasing it when they're losing. Card counting guides advise players to conceal their bet variation in this fashion—if the count is favorable, wait until you've won a couple of hands in a row and then pump up the size.

Player looks like—and casinos view action from Asian players differently than from white ones. "A Big Player has to have certain characteristics," Ma told me. "Asian is big, right? An Asian gambling looks way better than to be a white dude." Anyone who has spent any time in a casino knows that the business goes to great lengths to cater to East Asian and particularly Chinese tourists, or Americans with East Asian ancestry. There are Chinese-themed slot machines and table games (Pai Gow Poker) and often a disproportionately high number of Asian restaurants. Whether or not the stereotype is accurate, someone like Ma will arouse less suspicion when they gamble big.

Another massive fiction is that the movie shows Kevin Lewis and his teammates winning virtually every hand—except for one scene where Lewis goes on tilt and loses almost every hand instead. ("That's probably the thing that drove me the craziest about the movie," Ma told me. "He goes on tilt. And that would never ever have happened. In a million years that would never have happened.") There's the same improbably high win rate in the blackjack scene in *Rain Man*. Tom Cruise just can't lose while following the advice of his brother, the autistic savant Raymond Babbitt, played by Dustin Hoffman.

Real gambling just isn't remotely like this. There is almost never such a thing as a sure thing. *Even when you're literally cheating, it may not be a sure thing.* In the infamous Boston College basketball point-shaving scandal of 1978–79, when two teammates were paid by the mob to throw games, only four of the nine games the mob bet on won money, with three losses and two pushes.

This is particularly true in blackjack. Even if you—like Raymond Babbitt—could literally remember the rank and suit of every card in a six-deck shoe, it wouldn't help you *that* much. Rather, it's merely enough to turn a slight disadvantage into a slight advantage. In *Professional Blackjack*, the card counter Stanford Wong estimates that his benchmark strategy, executed perfectly under relatively favorable conditions, will net you about 60 cents for every $100 you bet—meaning a player edge of just 0.6 percent.

And the biggest myth of all in *21* is that Ma and his teammates were living out some crazy party lifestyle, full of day drinking and wild times at nightclubs. Counting cards is a *grind*. "It's like the grindiest grind there is," Ma said. For most of his tenure on the team, "we didn't drink at all, was a big rule"—and it was long enough ago (in the mid-1990s) there were barely even nightclubs in Vegas. The team wasn't even in Vegas much of the time, either, but instead in tourist hotbeds like Shreveport, Louisiana, and Elgin, Illinois. Many times, despite their skill and hustle, they flew home to Boston with less money than they started with. "Your whole weekend could really come down to, like, five hands, right? Five hands that are, what, two percent better than a coin flip?"

Turning the Tables

The narrative of both *21* (2008) and the movie version of *Moneyball* (2011) is that of the River as a disruptor of a lazy status quo. Relatively likable nerds use their data skills to take +EV risks and run circles around hapless baseball general managers who care more about how a player looks in a pair of jeans than his on-base percentage—or casino pit bosses so terrified that some of their customers might actually have an edge that they take Jeff Ma's character to a dark basement and bloody him up. It's not lost on me that my own rise to fame came during exactly this period from 2008 through 2012. Yes, it helped that my election forecasts in those years were usually right. But I also offered one last opportunity for a *Moneyball* sequel. A nerd* uses data and statistics to disrupt a relatively unsympathetic target—lazy horse-race punditry. And the underdog wins, by predicting every state correctly in the 2012 election.

After reading the first two and a half chapters of this book—meeting poker players and MIT Blackjack Team members whose way of life is edgy and anti-establishment—you might be tempted to think that's the story of *On the Edge* too. Certainly, there is an undercurrent of *Moneyball* in this book—the Village's risk-aversion still makes it vulnerable to being on the losing side of all sorts of economic and cultural bets. But the River isn't the underdog anymore. As I said in the prologue, *the River is winning*. It not only dominates Silicon Valley and Wall Street, but the

---

* I'll let you decide for yourself whether I'm likable.

nerds have taken over everything from baseball front offices to the casino business.

From this point forward in the book, you'll begin to see clearer evidence of that. The rest of this chapter is about the evolution of the casino industry. This has always been a risky business because of the massive cost of casino resort developments. Having once attracted eccentrics like Howard Hughes and Kirk Kerkorian, the industry is now highly corporatized—and it's grown more profitable in large part because it's become more data driven in figuring out how to track its customers and get them to gamble and spend more. The casino business is not alone in this regard—the Algorithmization of Everything is contributing to record corporate profits as data scientists also figure out how to get you to spend more on, say, a fast food delivery order. But "gaming"—the euphemism for gambling that the industry prefers for itself—offers a particularly clear case study of modern American algorithmic capitalism.

Plus, since much of this book takes place inside casinos, I want to give them due consideration and not just treat them as scenery—partly because they're fascinating places, and partly because it's easy for someone like me to strut past the roulette tables and the rows of slot machines* en route to the poker room and take for granted the experience that other patrons are having. My habits when visiting casinos, focused on skilled forms of gambling, are highly atypical. Nevada casinos make roughly fifty bucks in profit from slots for every dollar they get out of the poker games they spread. The *overwhelming* majority of money wagered in a casino is -EV.

Gaming executives will happily tell you this if you ask them. Perhaps because the industry doesn't make any pretense of curing cancer or delivering self-actualization, it tends to be transparent in its motivations. "Understanding why somebody would engage in an activity where they know in advance—absolute certainty, undoubtedly, far more probable [than not] that you're going to lose your money . . . and yet do it willingly and do it over and over and over again—[that] always surprised me," said Mike Rumbolz, a gaming executive and former chair of the Nevada Gaming Control Board. As our interview was ending, Rumbolz told me that he hasn't gambled since 1974.

---

* I have lots of compulsions, but playing slots or table games has never really been one of them.

A Brief History of Las Vegas

Walking deliriously down the Las Vegas Strip late one night, somewhere between the replica volcano in front of the Mirage and the half-sized Eiffel Tower incorporated into the Paris casino, I texted myself a message: "las vegas as holy site." If the Earth were destroyed in a nuclear or AI or zombie apocalypse, and a team of alien archaeologists later came upon the wreckage, I'm convinced they would think that the Strip—a cluster of monumentally sized, elaborately decorated buildings, full of symbols and allusions and men dressed in Elvis costumes—had been some sort of shine to the gods.

And perhaps they wouldn't be wrong. Las Vegas is a shrine to risk-taking, excess, progress, and capitalism—and a shrine to the United States, a country that pursues these things with a religious fervor. It's a place where the savvy gamblers of the River are treated with priestlike respect—although the highest caste in Vegas consists of whales who have achieved the top tier of the MGM (Noir) and Caesars (Seven Stars) loyalty programs. "A society basically structures gambling in a certain way that they feel comfortable with," said David Schwartz, one of the relatively small number of gambling historians anywhere in the world, when I met him in his office at UNLV. "So on the frontier, they felt really comfortable in the saloons," he continued. "It's fascinating to me that Americans now prefer doing it in these big resorts that are owned by big corporations."

On a flight from the East Coast, the lights of Las Vegas emerge seemingly out of nowhere, an oasis in the Mojave Desert. But little about Vegas is accidental, from its location to its focus on vice—to how corporatized it has become today.

Nevada's history with gambling can be traced to the California Gold Rush of the late 1840s and 1850s. Perhaps never in the history of the modern world were conditions more favorable to the development of gambling culture. Participants in the Gold Rush were overwhelmingly (about 95 percent) young men who were either single or a half continent away from their families, and who had already self-selected on the basis of forgoing the comforts of home to seek fortune. Saloons, brothels, and gambling houses offered the opportunity to test one's mettle, spend one's newfound wealth, and seek female (or male)* companionship.

After the discovery of gold in 1848, San Francisco had more gambling per capita than any city in the United States, and by the late 1850s the action spilled over the Sierra Nevada Mountains into Nevada, where prospectors sought gold and silver. (Nevada was populated by white settlers from the West, not the East; it joined the Union in 1864, before more easterly states like Colorado and Utah.) But California is one of the most geographically and ecologically rich regions in the world. It didn't need gold to be a place where people wanted to live—and it didn't need gambling, which it outlawed (apart from poker) by 1872. Its economic explosion continued apace, with its population booming to 5.7 million by 1930. Nevada, by contrast, didn't have a whole lot going for it apart from deserts and silver mines. Its landscapes are beautiful, but barren; even today, 80 percent of Nevada's land is owned by the federal government. By 1930, it still had only 90,000 residents, barely twice what it had sixty years earlier.

Gambling has been essentially decriminalized in Nevada for all but two years since 1869, when the legislature passed a bill over the veto of a governor who had declared it an "intolerable and inexcusable vice." But amid a tug-of-war between pro- and anti-gambling forces, its laws initially prevented the development of commercial gaming at scale. Finally, amid the challenges of the Great Depression, the state fully legalized commercial gambling in 1931. "In the end, money talked," wrote Schwartz—as it usually does under circumstances like these. Casinos generally arise under economically marginal conditions, often near state or national borders that can take advantage of a brisk tourist business.[†]

Las Vegas, which had been founded as a railroad stop in 1905, was fully

---

* San Francisco's gay culture also has roots dating back to the Gold Rush.
† In this way, the negative externalities of gambling, such as addiction, are mostly passed along to non-residents. In more jurisdictions than you might think, natives of the jurisdiction are actually barred from gambling—citizens and residents of the Bahamas aren't allowed to gamble at Baha Mar or Atlantis, for example.

prepared, doling out its first gambling licenses within weeks of the new law's passage. It had two main advantages: its proximity to the Hoover Dam, which was constructed between 1931 and 1936, and its manageable distance from Los Angeles.* Further buoyed by the end of Prohibition in 1933, Vegas developers were explicit about their plans to make it a national playground for gambling, horse racing, boxing matches, and pretty much everything else. *What happens in Vegas stays in Vegas* may be a relatively new slogan—but it's an attitude that dates back to the city's founding; the town's original master plan included a red-light district.

But even the most wild-eyed developer could hardly have imagined the jackpot they'd struck, with Vegas's economic footprint set to multiply many times over. Nevada's population grew by 3,400 percent between 1930 and 2020, far more than any other state, while Clark County's[†] grew by more than 25,000 percent over the same period. As Americans, we typically have to go to other parts of the world to see that type of growth; New York City doesn't look *that* different than it did forty years ago. But in Las Vegas, new Wonders of the World pop up seemingly overnight, like the gargantuan 516-foot-wide LED-coated Sphere that opened in 2023.

There are various pivotal years in Las Vegas's history. By general consensus, the most important one was 1989—and specifically, the date November 22, 1989. We'll get to that one later. Personally, I think 2009 and 2021 deserve consideration in reflection of Las Vegas's resilience in the face of the housing bust and the COVID-19 pandemic, respectively.

But 1955 is a year of underappreciated significance. That's the year the state legislature established the Nevada Gaming Control Board—and Las Vegas started fighting to win over the mainstream. In 2022, a Gallup poll found that a record-high 71 percent of Americans thought gambling was

---

* Parts of Las Vegas Boulevard—including the four-mile stretch that makes up the Strip—were once known as the Los Angeles Highway. The trip from City Hall in downtown L.A. to the southernmost Strip casino, Mandalay Bay, is literally almost a straight shot; all but one mile of the trip is on Interstate 15.
† Want to be a pedantic buzzkill? Tell your friend who's bragging about his Vegas trip that he's not actually going to Las Vegas; the airport and the Strip are located south of the city limits in the unincorporated towns of Paradise and Winchester. Clark County includes these towns and is essentially coterminous with the Las Vegas metro area.

morally acceptable—a rare point of bipartisan agreement (wide majorities of both liberals and conservatives agreed) in a bitterly divided country.

It wasn't always that way. Mike Rumbolz first came to Las Vegas as a teenager in 1965—long enough ago that "there was more vacant land on the Strip than anything else, so it was just dust and sagebrush." Starting as a busboy and waiter at the Stardust, he's had virtually every job in the industry, including working for the Trump Organization with the goal of helping Donald Trump open a casino in Nevada (it didn't happen because Trump "didn't have the wherewithal financially to do anything in Nevada, except put his name on a building" at that time).

"When I was growing up here," Rumbolz told me, "people from outside the state . . . everybody looked at the gaming industry as somewhat tainted. It had that reputation from the fifties and from films like *Ocean's 11** of being owned by mobs, and fighting with bad guys and cheating people."

To be fair, this reputation wasn't entirely undeserved. Many of the most ambitious resorts on the Strip during Las Vegas's first boom period in the 1940s were mob connected, like Bugsy Siegel's Flamingo, which was open for less than six months before Siegel was shot to death at his home in Beverly Hills. The mob had the capital, the gambling know-how, and control of the race wire—the mechanism by which off-track bets were transmitted in horse racing, then one of America's most popular sports. One of the hearings of the Kefauver Committee, the U.S. Senate's special committee charged with investigating the Mafia, was dramatically staged at the courthouse in Downtown Las Vegas.

The establishment of the gaming board didn't remove the mob's influence overnight—as late as the early 1980s, the Stardust was involved in a scandal where profits were skimmed by the Mafia—but it did substantially toughen regulations on who could receive a gaming license. And it laid down a marker—particularly through something called Nevada Revised Statute 463.0129. J. Brin Gibson, another former chair of the Gaming Control Board, described it to me as "the most important statute we have."

---

* The original 1960 film, not the George Clooney remake.

NRS 463.0129 is to Nevada's voluminous gaming laws as the preamble is to the U.S. Constitution:

> NRS 463.0129   Public policy of state concerning gaming; license or approval revocable privilege.
>
> 1. The Legislature hereby finds, and declares to be the public policy of this state, that:
>
> (a) The gaming industry is vitally important to the economy of the State and the general welfare of the inhabitants.
>
> (b) The continued growth and success of gaming is dependent upon public confidence and trust ... and that gaming is free from criminal and corruptive elements.
>
> (c) Public confidence and trust can only be maintained by strict regulation of all persons, locations, practices, associations and activities related to the operation of licensed gaming establishments.

In other words: (a) gambling is vital to Nevada; (b) public trust is vital to gambling; (c) getting rid of the mob is vital to public trust. Las Vegas may have an anything-goes, libertarian, frontier spirit. But without these regulations, it would be nothing like what it is today.

Perhaps in no other industry is trust so important. When you go to a casino, you're at a big disadvantage because you don't have any obvious way to know whether you're being dealt a fair game. Indeed, throughout most of the early history of commercial gambling, many if not most establishments were crooked.

Slot machines don't actually provide listed odds at all. And even at something like blackjack, it would be hard to detect cheating on behalf of the casino without a large sample of data. For instance, if a casino removed a single ace from a six-deck blackjack shoe, you'd have a hell of a time figuring out that there were only five aces of diamonds in the deck instead of six unless you were specifically looking. (This is a case where having Raymond Babbitt by your side might actually be helpful.)

To be clear, you're very unlikely to be cheated by the house in an

American casino today—they'll take your money fair and square. But that's because of statutes like NRS 463.0129. In fact, it's actually in the industry's best interest to have stringent regulation. Why? Because of the prisoner's dilemma. If my casino, the Silver Spike, starts removing aces from its blackjack decks—boosting profits for my shareholders but in a way that its customers find hard to detect—the optimal strategy for the Gold Nugget down the block is to reciprocate. Absent regulation—knowing that the other guys at least have to play by the same rules—you're likely to see a race to the bottom, and the industry will shrink because it will be hard for consumers to identify trustworthy operators.*

The other reason trust is so important is that modern casino resorts are literally among the most expensive building projects in the history of the world. Some are nearly the equivalent of planned cities, with thousands of residences (in some cases as many as seven thousand hotel rooms, plus private residences) and every imaginable form of leisure, entertainment, shopping, and dining all in one complex. The CityCenter project in Las Vegas, for example—centered around the Aria casino—cost *$8.5 billion* to develop and build by the time it was completed in 2009. Developers are counting on decades' worth of profits to earn back their investments. A reversal of the long-standing trend toward greater acceptance of commercial gambling could lead to financial catastrophe.

The result of Vegas's success at building trust is a world where most casinos are owned by large corporations like MGM and Caesars. Needless to say, these projects entail real risk: it's not hard to find examples of properties that were mismanaged or never clicked with the public and became financial albatrosses. Still, today's corporate suits are a long way removed from the Bugsy Siegels of the world—or from mavericks like Kirk Kerkorian and Howard Hughes who helped usher Vegas away from an era of mob dominance.

---

* This bears some resemblance to the economic concept known as the "market for lemons," where there's a market failure because of information asymmetries. It's hard to tell if a used car is defective until you've bought it—a test drive usually won't be enough to surface all problems and tell you whether it's a lemon. Similarly, the small sample of play you get at a particular casino won't be statistically sufficient to tell you whether you've been cheated. You need to trust a reliable third party instead.

But one man stands out singularly in making modern Las Vegas what it is today: Steve Wynn.

The Casino Business Is
Three Worlds in One

Our tour of this part of the River is going to begin in lush environs before winding its way to a more depressing place. I wanted to warn you about that in advance, because I don't want you to do the equivalent of judging a country based solely on visiting its luxury shopping district. Really, there isn't just one casino business model—there are three:

- There is the high-end luxury resort business, which I'll describe mostly through the story of the developer who most consistently cracked the code (Steve Wynn)—and the one who most infamously failed at doing so (Donald Trump). At these properties, gambling is just one of many revenue streams and often makes up less than half of the business. There are a lot of rich people in America, and the gambling industry has figured out how to get in on the fun.

- Then there is the largest segment of the market by revenue, an upper-middlebrow market, dominated by major corporations like MGM and Caesars. These companies engage in an intricate degree of customer profiling, largely accomplished through rewards programs where customers can unlock ever-increasing upsells. This is the part of the business that has changed the most in recent years as gambling companies engage in *Moneyball*-esque analysis to figure out how to derive more money from their patrons.

- Finally, there is the "locals market," focused on tourists on a tight budget, retirees, and working-class and middle-class people who visit casinos mostly to do one thing: play slots. Not blackjack, and certainly not poker. Maybe a decent steak dinner purchased with casino comps. But mostly just slots, which are overwhelmingly the dominant source of revenue at these properties. Slots offer much worse odds than games like blackjack and are more addicting—as in a lot of things, the less well-off tend to get the short end of the deck.

Wynning Time

"A blackjack table is just a piece of furniture."

Steve Wynn, probably the most successful casino developer of all time, was in the midst of an epic rant about how he had never been in the *gambling* business.

"I'm just a developer. I'm not really interested in talking to you about gambling."

Wynn has a distinctive voice, with a raspy intonation, a Trumpian affect (along with frenemy Sheldon Adelson, he was the vice chair of Trump's inauguration committee in 2016), and the residual hints of the accent known as the Northern Cities Vowel Shift.* (As a native Michigander, I can detect it even in minute quantities.) Born as Stephen Alan Weinberg in New Haven, Connecticut, but raised in Utica in central New York State, Wynn took over his father's bingo business, then used a share of the profits to buy a stake in the now-defunct New Frontier on the Vegas Strip.

He eventually began buying stock in the Golden Nugget in Downtown Las Vegas, soon becoming president and chairman. His premise was simple: turn the undistinguished Golden Nugget, which didn't even have an adjoining hotel at the time of his purchase, into a luxury property—a novelty in Downtown Las Vegas, which was then and now the plainer, more rugged older brother to the star pupil that is the Strip. Soon, Frank Sinatra was a frequent headliner and the Golden Nugget achieved a four-diamond rating in the Mobil travel guide.

After successfully developing another Golden Nugget in Atlantic City, Wynn sold the property in 1987 (auspicious timing: Atlantic City was about to enter a long era of stagnation) and then parlayed the profits forward toward his most ambitious project yet—the Mirage, at $630 million, then the world's most expensive resort.

---

* For an exaggerated version of this, think of working-class Chicagoans as portrayed in vintage TV or movies, such as the Chicago Bears Super Fans from *Saturday Night Live*. The vowel shift east of the Great Lakes, like in Buffalo or Rochester, New York, is milder.

Wynn remembers the opening day of the Mirage in vivid detail. He described what sounds like a chaotic scene from a Hieronymus Bosch painting, with the crowd so eager to charge into the casino that they were on the verge of a riot.

"The day is November twenty-second. The anniversary of the Kennedy assassination, 1989," he recalled. "At eight o'clock in the morning there were ten or eleven thousand people. By noon, you couldn't see the end of the crowd. When I walkie-talkie, 'Security, take down the barriers, the hotel is open,' the mob that charged the door frightened the hell out of the governor, Bob Miller, as we're standing there. But they stopped, right at the porte cochere,* while Siegfried and Roy drove up with the tigers. That day, seventy-five thousand people went through the hotel. Women, strollers, everybody everywhere, overloading the public area."

These days, the Mirage is on its last legs, having been neglected by its former owner MGM as it prepares for a second life as the Hard Rock Hotel & Casino Las Vegas. But at the time, it was revolutionary. It was the first new property to open on the Strip in sixteen years. It had an absurd number of attractions—the replica volcano, with hourly "eruptions" at night; a dolphin habitat; Siegfried and Roy and their white tigers; and a hotel with more than three thousand rooms, then the largest in the world.

It was an audacious bet. To be financially viable, the Mirage would have to make more money than any casino ever had. "The math was that he needed to make a million dollars a day. And no property had ever done that or even close to it," said Jon Ralston, Las Vegas's best-known journalist, who now runs *The Nevada Independent.* "People scoffed at it—so-called experts, the analysts and people in the industry here. And, you know, it was clear from the first week or month that he was well exceeding that—it was like one point two million a day."

In Wynn's telling, the Mirage changed Vegas literally overnight. "The chairman and president of every one of the hotels was in the Mirage within twenty-four hours. So the real estate prices on the Strip changed within a

---

* I had to look this word up; it means a covered entrance for vehicles. Wynn can be salty on the one hand and fancy on the other one.

week. The word was out, Vegas could take big money." The data basically backs up Wynn's story. Between 1988 and 2000, revenues on the Las Vegas Strip exploded from $3 billion to more than $10 billion (even after adjusting for inflation, they more than doubled). The large majority of gains were from nongaming revenues—hotel rooms, restaurants, dolphin shows, you name it. Wynn took a lot of pride during our conversation in the fact that gambling revenues represented less than half of his properties' revenue. Blackjack tables may have been more than mere furniture, but they were an increasingly small part of the business. No longer seen as a chintzy curiosity or a mobbed-up malignity, modern Las Vegas had arrived.

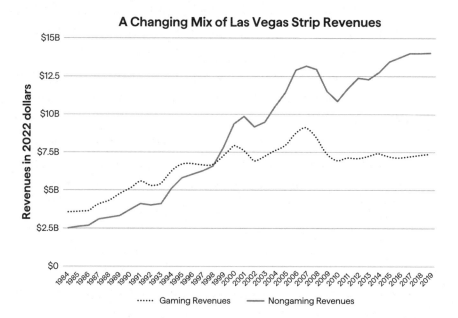

A Changing Mix of Las Vegas Strip Revenues

Wynn was able to replicate the formula several times over, with the Bellagio in 1998 and then the eponymous Wynn in 2005. Over time, his properties have relied less on kitschy gimmicks and more on selling an image of effortless luxury with bright, airy designs and expensive art collections* that defy the stereotype of dingy, mazelike casinos. "They were

---

* Wynn has a condition (retinitis pigmentosa) that essentially gives him tunnel vision—and he once unintentionally punched his elbow through a Picasso painting that he couldn't see through his peripheral vision when showing it off to guests, causing a $54 million decline in its valuation.

all based upon the same principle. Make people feel special. Come to Las Vegas to live big," he told me. "They're happy and they tell their friends. If they get treated beautifully, they'll come back next year and pay more for the inevitable increase. That is a summary of my entire business philosophy and career."

Still, attractive properties and attentive customer service can't hide the ugly side of what might go on behind closed doors. *What happens in Vegas stays in Vegas* is an attitude that's often taken rather literally—and the notion that anything goes in Las Vegas has some serious downsides.

In 2018 and 2019, following several accusations and extensive reporting that he had sexually harassed female staff and pressured them into sex, Steve Wynn and Wynn Resorts paid more than $100 million in damages, fines, and settlements, and Steve Wynn agreed to be barred from the Nevada gaming industry, without admission of wrongdoing or liability by Wynn himself. And yet, the Wynn name remains on Wynn Resorts properties in Las Vegas, Macau, and on a proposed resort in the United Arab Emirates. (Representatives for Wynn Resorts declined an interview request.)

Whatever the true facts of the allegations against Wynn, this is not an isolated problem. Sexual assault is a major issue in Las Vegas. In 2019, 1,439 rapes were reported to the Las Vegas Metropolitan Police Department—a per-capita rate about twice that of the average jurisdiction that reports data to the FBI.

Be careful in Las Vegas, especially if you don't know your way around. It really is a cross section of the United States; that's part of why I like it. But that means it includes its share of unsavory elements. Between the crowds, the booze, the disorienting nature of some of the properties, people carrying large amounts of chips and cash around, the tendency of visitors to do things they wouldn't do at home, and VIP customers often receiving deferential treatment from casino staff, there are a lot of ways a night can go wrong.

Trump Couldn't Make
Atlantic City Great

It's hard to publish a book about gambling during an election year and not have anything to say about the most (in)famous casino developer of all time: the former and perhaps future U.S. president Donald Trump. But the truth is, I'm not quite sure where he fits in. If Trump is despised by the Village, he's also not a member of the River. Yes, Trump might be competitive and risk-taking—and he can even have a contrarian streak, having correctly gambled in 2016 that he could repudiate John McCain, Mitt Romney, George W. Bush, and the rest of the Republican establishment and still win the party's nomination. But that alone doesn't a Riverian make. He's shown little of the capacity for abstract, analytical reasoning that distinguishes people in the River from those who undertake high-stakes but miscalculated -EV bets. The company that managed his casinos, Trump Entertainment Resorts, filed for bankruptcy in 2004, 2009, and 2014 before being sold in 2016. As of early 2024, there are no casino properties anywhere in the world that bear Trump's name—although he did manage to considerably enrich himself in the process.

But if there's not much new we can learn about Trump from his experience in the gaming industry, there is something we can learn about the gaming industry from Trump. In some sense, yes, casinos have a license to print money—with the odds guaranteed to be in their favor, it's all but impossible for them to lose money on gaming operations. However, developers do take significant risks when it comes to financing, real estate development, and predicting the future demand for casino gambling in their markets. It's not *easy* to fail—but if you get a couple of those categories badly wrong, you can, and Trump is the proof of that.

Like the Mirage, the Trump Taj Mahal in Atlantic City debuted to near pandemonium in April 1990. In many respects, it one-upped the Mirage. Wynn may have had Siegfried and Roy—but Trump had the biggest star in the world, Michael Jackson, who walked the casino floor through throngs of adoring fans. Like the Mirage, the Taj was kitschy, including some details (doormen dressed in turbans) that wouldn't fly today. But the Taj was also luxurious. Maybe *too* luxurious. *The New York Times* sent its architecture critic Paul Goldberger to review the property, and he compared its "crystal chandeliers and . . . purple carpeting" to "diets consisting only of chocolate mousse."

But the Taj was doomed less by its design choices and more by catastrophically poor financial planning. The Taj Mahal first filed for bankruptcy in 1991, only a year after it opened. Trump had financed it primarily through junk bonds with a 14 percent interest rate. When a financial analyst named Marvin Roffman pointed out how much the Taj would have to make to pay back its debts—amounts that seemed implausible in an Atlantic City market that was already seeing a decline in annual visitors—Trump successfully pressured Roffman's firm into firing him.

After the Taj's opening, Trump was triumphal, convinced he had proved Roffman and other critics wrong. But spectacular openings don't necessarily equate to sustained success in the casino business. There is just so much going on at a high-end resort—every imaginable form of gambling, shows, restaurants, nightclubs, spas, golf courses. There are an equal number of pitfalls—gaming regulations, corrupt officials, difficult customers, extremely large capital outlays, cheating and illicit activity. It's an industry that requires a willingness to follow rules and an obsessive attention to detail—attributes that were no more a strength for Trump as a casino boss than they were during his first term in office.

At properties like the Wynn in Las Vegas, things just *tend to go smoothly* most of the time. At the Trump Taj Mahal, they did not. Within a week of the opening, its slot machines mysteriously shut down. The property was seriously bereft of people with casino management experience—in part because of a tragic stroke of bad luck: three of Trump's senior executives were killed in a helicopter crash just months before the Taj was set to open. When Trump did micromanage the business, it often wasn't helpful. When a Tokyo real estate tycoon named Akio Kashiwagi came to play baccarat for $200,000 a hand—the sort of whale that any casino would dream of—Trump instead nervously paced the floor and sweated his action, making Kashiwagi feel mistreated.

Atlantic City also proved to be a poor bet.* Its gambling revenues actually exceeded those in Las Vegas throughout most of the 1980s and

---

* Trump did receive a Nevada gaming license in 2004, but has never operated a casino there—the Trump hotel in Las Vegas doesn't have a gaming floor; politifact.com/factchecks/2019/jul/09/viral-image/no -evidence-nevada-gaming-commission-said-donald-t.

early 1990s but then declined by more than half. Why did Vegas prove to be so much more durable? Perhaps because Atlantic City bet on gambling, gambling, and more gambling rather than offering guests a well-rounded entertainment experience. (About 75 percent of the Taj's gross revenues in 1990 were from the gaming floor.) It also has poor vibes. Las Vegas presents you with the feeling of freedom—casinos spill into one another, the Strip is walkable, and the weather is pleasant for much of the year. AC is more of a walled city, with casinos as self-contained fortresses in a hollowed-out, high-crime city.*

Indeed, Las Vegas's success has been hard to replicate; in 2022, Nevada gaming revenues exceeded those of the next three states combined. Throughout history, commercial gambling establishments have offered their customers different archetypes: dens of inequity on the one hand, spa-like escapes from reality on the other hand. What *hasn't* sold is a luxury experience in a suburban office park or an environment of urban squalor. Trump won't be the last person to think he can be an exception to the rule, and he won't be the last one to fail.

The *Moneyball*-ization of the Casino Business

Spontaneous encounters in Las Vegas elevators are always a gamble. Men come up with hookers; couples get into arguments; exhausted parents return with their hyperactive kids from the pool. People are chatty, flirty, drunk—more than once, I've been worried that someone was going to vomit on me—and prepared to pepper you with war stories about their gambling experiences.

Fortunately, most elevators in Vegas are lightning fast, lest you waste precious seconds that you could spend gambling. But Gary Loveman had an elevator encounter that may forever have changed the casino business.

---

* Atlantic City has also seen its business cannibalized by other casinos up and down the Eastern Seaboard. Say it's January in New York City, and you can either drive two plus hours to AC or take a two-and-a-half-hour flight to sunny Fort Lauderdale and play at the Hard Rock. I'm picking Florida—it's no contest.

Loveman was an unusual fit for the gaming industry, which has typically relied on lifers like Rumbolz, or people like Wynn with a family history in the business. Instead, he was a Riverian, an MIT graduate and a professor at Harvard Business School. Loveman had been consulting for what was then known as Harrah's Entertainment (now Caesars Entertainment) when to his surprise he was asked to take a two-year sabbatical to come on as COO—and wound up staying seventeen years, eventually being promoted to CEO in 2003, the year that *Moneyball* was published.

As analytics were taking over baseball, Loveman was shocked by the gap between how much data the casino business generated—"It is rich in data, and you can analyze virtually everything very quickly, to a greater degree than almost any business I've ever run across"—and how little of that data was used to guide decisions. In one of his early days on the job, Loveman was in an elevator going up to his room at the Harrah's in Las Vegas when he heard a group of tourists from Atlantic City complaining. "They're saying, Jesus, we can't win anything on the slots here in Las Vegas. These slots are so tight, I can't believe it. I wish I was back in Atlantic City." Loveman knew better. At the time, Vegas slots were relatively generous, with a hold percentage of around 5 percent—that's how much the casino keeps as profit, on average, of every pull of the machine. By contrast, New Jersey slots were much stingier, with a hold of around 7.5 percent.

Over the long run, a profit of 7.5 percent versus 5 percent makes a lot of difference to a casino's bottom line. But in the short run, Loveman realized, it's essentially impossible for the player to tell the difference.

"Literally the next morning, I started working with my slot team and understanding the probability distributions that are programmed into slot machines," he says. "I then went and hired a group of mathematicians from MIT—most of them were trained in the aeronautics and aerospace group. . . . And we determined that for the individual to recognize the difference between a slot machine that had a hold of five percent, and one that had a hold of eight percent, the player would have to make forty thousand handle pulls on each machine."

Forty thousand spins is a *lot*. The average player only pulls a slot machine a few hundred times before trying something else, Loveman said. That's nowhere near enough. Statistically—in part because a big share of the money that slots return comes in the form of large jackpots that are only hit occasionally—it takes a very long time for a player to estimate their expected value. And unlike in blackjack, you can't just look up the odds— they aren't listed anywhere! In fact, the same machine can have different payouts in different parts of the casino, without any outward sign to the customer.*

Given this information asymmetry, casinos were leaving money on the table. But this was soon to change. In 1997, the year before Loveman joined Caesars, slot machines on the Las Vegas Strip had an average hold percentage of 5.67 percent. By the time he left in 2015, it had jumped to 7.77 percent, right where those Atlantic City numbers had been. If you're a slots player and you feel like the machines are stingier than they once were, you're right, and now you know who to blame—Loveman is not shy about taking credit for this. "You'll see that the average slot hold in the United States went up pretty considerably over recent years, in large part because the people that I hired to help me start to do this now run all the competing companies."

Casinos can also manipulate the manner in which money is paid out— the probability distributions behind the machines. Customers naturally gravitate toward whichever pattern most appeals to their risk tolerance— or most effectively manipulates their sense of the odds. The general industry standard, though, is a machine that provides the occasional large jackpot, but also regular modest wins so the player has some positive reinforcement.†

Natasha Schüll, an anthropology professor at NYU who wrote the book

---

* In general, machines in highly visible locations pay better, and highly themed games like those based on popular game shows pay out worse. (The more fun a game is, the more it will cost you to play.) But if nothing else, I hope this book convinces you not to play slots. Almost any other game a casino offers will pay out more generously.
† Perhaps not coincidentally, this payout model is similar to how poker tournaments work, with 10 to 15 percent of entrants receiving some kind of prize but the big money reserved for the top 1 or 2 percent. It's the combination of the regular small scores and the occasional big ones that keeps players coming back.

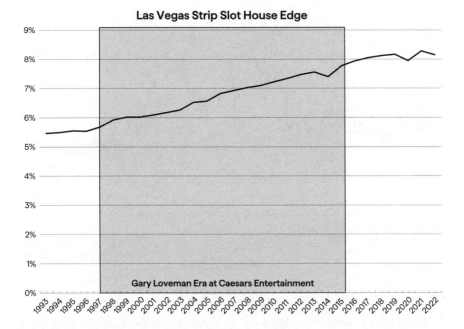

Las Vegas Strip Slot House Edge

Gary Loveman Era at Caesars Entertainment

Addiction by Design: Machine Gambling in Las Vegas, recalls what a gaming executive told her. "He said, 'We want you to recline on our algorithms the way you recline on a comfortable couch.' It was about smoothing the ride down to zero so that you don't notice you're losing as you get there."

The difference between a smooth ride down to zero and a rough one is illustrated in the next graphic. I've simulated ten thousand pulls of two slot machines, each of which have an 8 percent hold. For the first machine, Thunder Canyon, a player wins a $92 jackpot once every hundred $1 spins, and that's the only payout of any kind. For the second machine, Lazy River, the top jackpot is just $25, but there are lots of secondary prizes, from $1 to $15, and a player will hit *some* sort of prize around one sixth of the time.

Intuitively, you might grasp that these are different payout structures—but even I was surprised by how strikingly different they appear in the graph even though both machines have the same EV (–$8 per $100 wagered). And trust me from my experience with poker and sports betting: when you're in the middle of one of these swings, you can *feel* them, and they're going to have a big influence on your propensity to continue gambling.

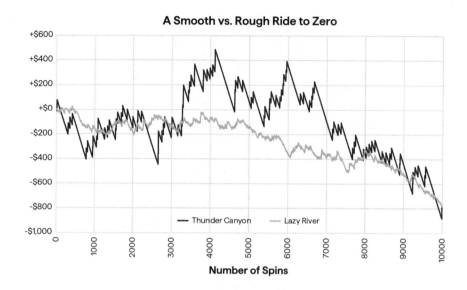

A Smooth vs. Rough Ride to Zero

If all of this sounds cynical—well, that's the nature of the beast. "If you're in a casino business, at some level, your job is to get people to lose money," said Schwartz.

But here's the thing. Whatever else it's doing, Las Vegas is not just chewing up and spitting out its customers and maximizing for some short-run equilibrium. Instead, Vegas-goers are very loyal. Disneyworld is famous as a business case study because 70 percent of its first-time visitors eventually return. Well, typically about *80 percent* of visitors to Las Vegas are repeat customers.

Some of that is because of another Loveman innovation: the customer loyalty card. Not that it was a new idea, exactly. Airline frequent flyer programs took off in the 1980s and had become ubiquitous by the 1990s. But the casino industry had been slow to adopt a similar program until the 2000s. Most of the old casino hands "thought it was ridiculous—this whole idea of a tiered reward program, and using data to make decisions rather than their experience," Loveman told me. "The resistance was pretty considerable. But when the results became evident . . . we got a lot of momentum."

That's because the casino business is top-heavy. A *lot* of revenue comes from a *very* small number of whales. In the airline industry, a business-class ticket might cost four or five times more than a seat in coach. In the gambling business? Some customers are spending hundreds or thousands of times more than others. "We would tell our folks that if you lose a Diamond customer, because of poor service, you have to find twenty Gold customers to replace them," said Loveman.

The perks of having high status in a casino rewards program are almost unlimited. Officially, Caesars Seven Stars members get free or deeply discounted rooms at almost any Caesars property worldwide, thousands of dollars in dining and travel credits, and even a complimentary trip on a cruise ship. *Unofficially*, their status can take them even further. VIPs often have personal hosts or concierges and can negotiate changes to game rules, substantial rebates if they lose, free food and drink from anywhere in the property,* nights out at strip clubs, and even private jets. You shouldn't ask a casino host for anything illegal—seriously, you shouldn't, these are highly regulated businesses—but you will get more rope if you misbehave. "You won't be surprised that we were more tolerant of bad behavior for more valuable guests than we were for less valuable guests," said Loveman.

Not everyone agrees with how aggressively Caesars privileges their higher-end customers. Steve Wynn doesn't, for instance. The notion of a customer who's already paying for a luxury experience getting cut in line by someone who has even higher status strikes him the wrong way. When Wynn took his objections to Loveman, they agreed to disagree. "I said to Gary, 'Doesn't that create an animosity? When these preferences are in full view? Doesn't it make them a second-class citizen?' . . . And [Loveman] said, 'On the contrary, Steve, it makes them aspirational.' They see the guy cutting in and they want to be part of that group."

To me, the intricate customer targeting can be overwhelming. When I opened my Caesars Rewards app just now to look for a room in Vegas a few

---

* But be careful. When getting dinner with a group of degens one night at a well-known restaurant at the Aria, one of them "tipped" the hostess $400 for a table, and our waiter—correctly deducing that money wasn't much of an object—upsold us to a $1,300 bottle of Hundred Acre cabernet from the $700 one we'd originally chosen. The guys were optimistic that the meal would be comped—but most of it wasn't.

months from today, there was a choice of literally 190 different room types across nine Caesars properties. There's always an upsell. Upgrade to a Strip view? A corner suite? A corner suite with a Strip view? An executive suite? Or even a private villa? The higher my status, the better deals I'll get.

And yet, Loveman was probably right. The Wynn had a rewards card program when it opened in 2005 and retains one today. It's less in-your-face than the program at Caesars, and the floor for service is higher. But even if every customer is special at the Wynn, some are more special than others.

Yes, the River Has Found a Way to Win at Slots, Too

When I started writing this book, I didn't expect one of the zaniest experiences to be hanging out with a professional slots player. In fact, I didn't know there was such a thing as a professional slots player.

Carter Loomis—not his real name—had been tough to pin down. But we'd agreed to meet on the dinner break of a poker tournament at the Wynn. As we wait for a table at the sandwich place by the sportsbook, I excuse myself to dash up to my room and fetch my digital recorder. I couldn't have been gone for more than five minutes. And yet somehow, Loomis managed to win a $2,000 slot jackpot.

If there's an edge to be had somewhere in a casino, you can be sure that a Riverian will come along and find it. The umbrella term for someone like Loomis is an "advantage player," used to describe +EV gambling conducted through methods other than cheating. The term isn't usually applied to poker and sports betting since those are known to be games of skill. Rather, it's when people find an edge at games where they aren't ordinarily supposed to have one. Jeff Ma and the MIT Blackjack Team were executing a form of advantage play. Sometimes, progressive jackpots can become very large in slot machines, video poker, or other games, and it can be profitable to play—that's advantage play, too.

Loomis begins showing me around the gaming floor at the Wynn, gesticulating at different slot machines. He was on the hunt for a +EV play.

"You're trying to find something where somebody built up something, and you're taking advantage of that. So this game—the pigs get bigger and bigger and then they explode. So you can actually shop around—and this is the best one, but it's still no good. I have certain criteria."

Loomis was peeling back the curtain on what was a new world for me—at the time, I only halfway understood what he meant. But let me explain by way of example.

Let's say there's a slot machine called The Fortunate Mr. Frog. It features a cute cartoon frog slowly being cooked in a pot of boiling water by a team of stereotypical-looking French chefs. Playing the game costs $1 per spin. Every time you spin, the water gets a little hotter, demarcated by visual cues like bubbles and steam. Don't worry, our froggo is going to be fine. He's going to jump out at some point—an algorithm will determine when. And when he does, Mr. Frog is going to make us some money. That's because the game will be launched into Berserk Mode, where we'll get a bunch of free spins as Mr. Frog jumps on some lily pads and ransacks the chefs' picnic and so forth, uncovering cash prizes along the way. The expected value of Berserk Mode is $200.

The overall house advantage for The Fortunate Mr. Frog, averaged across all spins, is 10 percent, typical for the Vegas Strip. But it varies from spin to spin—the hotter the water, the more likely we are to reach highly profitable Berserk Mode.[*] In fact, this is what's known as a "must hit" game; the way it's programmed, Berserk Mode *must* be triggered by at least the thousandth spin if it hasn't hit yet.

If the water is lukewarm, this is a terrible game for the player. In fact—I'll skip the math—the expected value of the first $1 spin is -$0.30. However, with each subsequent spin, the water gets hotter and the EV gets better. (It's like the count turning positive in blackjack.) By the 602nd spin, The Fortunate Mr. Frog is a +EV game. And if we somehow make it to the 1,000th spin with Mr. Frog still in the pot, the EV is roughly $200 because we're guaranteed to trigger Berserk Mode.

If you think this sounds implausibly silly, you should go to a casino and look at some of the slots. They are full of silly themes, and some of them use similar mechanics, like the exploding pig game that Loomis was referring to—in that game, spinning the reels causes coins to be

---

[*] For the calculations in this section, I estimate Mr. Frog's probability of jumping out on any given spin as $1/(1001 - x)$, where x is the number of spins since Berserk Mode last hit.

dropped into a piggy bank until the piggy bank explodes and triggers a bonus mode.

You might wonder: Couldn't a person just go around looking for +EV conditions—piggy banks that are about to explode, pots that are about to boil over? Well, yeah—that's basically what Loomis was doing. There's a nerdy joke about a pair of economists walking down the sidewalk and seeing a $20 bill on the ground. The first economist says, "Whoa, twenty bucks!" The second one, with unshaken faith in the efficiency of markets, says, "That can't be a twenty-dollar bill—if it was, somebody would have snatched it up already." Well, sometimes there really are the equivalent of $20 bills lying on the ground in casino gambling, left in slot machines by unsuspecting players who didn't understand the mechanics of the game. Advantage players pick them up.

But it isn't as easy as it sounds. Some casinos really don't like players like Loomis, though others are more tolerant. Essentially, Loomis is taking EV from other players rather than the casino.* If your gains are coming directly at the casino's expense, though, they won't be happy about it. The world-class poker player Phil Ivey was sued by the Borgata in Atlantic City, for instance, for using an advantage play method called "edge sorting," where players identify what cards the dealer holds by observing subtle defects on the card backs. To me, this isn't cheating, and it's the Borgata's fault for not having checked their decks more carefully. But a New Jersey judge disagreed, ordering that Ivey return more than $10 million to the Borgata—the case was eventually settled following appeal.

And remember, slot play is usually substantially -EV, so mistakenly thinking you're in an advantage situation when you're not is costly. Plus, sometimes slot machines are bluffing. "There are certainly some games where this is fake—like *that* game right there," Loomis says, pointing to a different machine, which looked a lot like the piggy-bank game but was from a different manufacturer. That game's use of the piggy-bank trope was just a trick; the jackpot was equally likely to be hit on any spin.

"How do you know which is which?" I ask Loomis.

---

* For must-hit slot machines and other progressive game conditions, the casino is eventually going to have to pay out the jackpot to *somebody*. Would it rather pay it to a tourist on her first Vegas trip or to a sharp guy like Loomis? Probably the tourist. On the other hand, Loomis does generate more overall volume in slot play.

"You just have to know. You have to be *in the know*," he says cryptically.

Advantage slot play is a field of *very* well-kept secrets. (That's why I agreed to use a pseudonym for Loomis.) There's not a lot of detail about it on the internet. And that's because there are essentially a finite number of $20 bills. If I find one, it comes out of another player's pocket. In fact, Loomis was about to get some heat.

"I'm not sure why he's looking at this game," Loomis says, pointing toward another machine where a thirtysomething Asian man is playing, a man Loomis recognized as a fellow advantage player. "I must not know about this. Obviously there's *something* good at this game."

Loomis is not a person whom you'd describe as tactful, and the other guy overheard our conversation.

"How about you stop telling people!" he says exasperatedly.

Loomis: "Stop telling people? Telling people what?"

Other guy: "You know what you're doing, man! Following people around!"

Loomis: "I didn't follow you around; we're just walking looking at machines."

Other guy: "Don't tell people about it, man! You'll ruin the whole business!"

Loomis (gesturing toward me): "He's not playing."

Me (sheepishly): "Yeah, I'm not playing."

Other guy: "Don't tell him about it, man. You're stupid for telling people! Fuck that."

Conveniently enough, this was exactly the point at which I got a text message saying our table was ready. But ever since, I've always kept an eye out for advantage players. They're not that hard to spot. Their posture is more erect. They have a purposefulness that the typical slot-playing tourist lacks. And they're finding $20 bills that aren't supposed to exist.

Seeking Action—or Escape?

It's not literally true that every human society has had gambling. But it's been very common, dating back to hunter-gatherer cultures where risk was intrinsic to everyday life. And yet gambling has not been the subject of much serious academic or anthropological study. A lot of intellectual types seem to think of gambling as a little gauche—but not Natasha Schüll.

Schüll, the NYU anthropology professor, first visited Las Vegas on a layover while heading out to attend college in California. "I had rarely been above Fourteenth Street. I was that much of a provincial New Yorker." Immediately, she was hooked. "When I thought about exotic things, it was the Vegas airport, where people just *intrigued* me." Vegas was the perfect setting for an anthropologist.

The thing about the Vegas airport is that it's very, *very* Vegas. There are slot machines everywhere. There are smoking lounges. There are advertisements for steakhouses, plaintiff's attorneys, and male dance revues. It is completely on the nose—as though you went to the airport in Dallas and they had a working oil derrick right next to baggage claim 6. If you're inclined to see gambling as gauche, the Vegas airport will confirm your worst suspicions.

But Schüll likes Las Vegas. She's friends with poker players—and isn't some sort of prude.* She knows, however, that the glamour of the Strip is a world apart from the Las Vegas that she spent most of her time studying for *Addiction by Design.* "I was hanging out in the Bellagio high-stakes poker room," she said. "But I did all of my research far off the Strip, at locals casinos and in Gamblers Anonymous rooms. And in those casinos, there's a completely different floor design. The carpets are different, the ceiling heights are different."

The canonical book on casino design—Bill Friedman's 629-page *Designing Casinos to Dominate the Competition*, published in 2000—laid out a series of principles that aggressively invert almost every tenet of modern architectural theory, advocating for a seemingly unpleasant environment for the patron. "LOW CEILINGS beat HIGH CEILINGS," reads one. "A COMPACT AND CONGESTED GAMBLING-EQUIPMENT LAYOUT beats A VACANT AND SPACIOUS FLOOR LAYOUT," is another. Friedman's ideal is

---

* When a waitress erroneously brought an alcoholic version of the Arnold Palmer she had ordered, she went ahead and drank it. (It was quite late on a Friday afternoon.)

a mazelike layout where there are slot machines and *nothing but* slot machines as far as the eye can see.

The luxury end of the market, thankfully, has eschewed some of these ideas. Properties like the Wynn and Bellagio in Vegas are spacious and bright, with high ceilings and good sight lines. Baha Mar in the Bahamas even has floor-to-ceiling windows. These resorts also reserve their highest-trafficked areas for table games like craps and roulette that have strong visual appeal. But at many locals casinos, Friedman's principles are still operative. On the Las Vegas Strip, slot machines represent only 29 percent of overall (gambling plus nongambling) revenues. At off-Strip casinos, they're 53 percent—more than table games, rooms, food, beverage, and every other category combined.

Las Vegas Strip Casino Revenue Breakdown

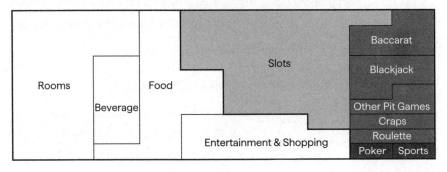

Off-Strip Casino Revenue Breakdown

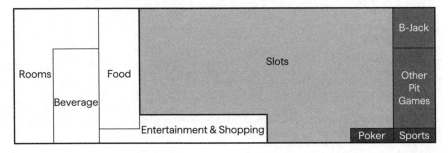

To gaming executives, slot machines have several obvious sources of appeal. For instance, they have little labor cost. "Savvy operators," says Rumbolz, began to realize that they could "devote more of their floor to devices that don't take vacations, that don't get unionized, that don't cost them anything more than the initial expense." Slot machines first surpassed table games in Las Vegas gaming revenues in 1983 and have since lapped the field.

They also have a much larger house advantage than table games. If a player is playing optimally and selects for tables with decent rules, then craps, blackjack, and baccarat all have a house advantage of around 1 percent or less. The average slot hold on the Las Vegas Strip is above 8 percent, however. And it's even higher—around 11 percent—on penny slots, which are the most likely games for casual gamblers to encounter. Among the most common forms of government-sanctioned gambling, the only worse deals for players are horse racing and state lotteries, which are essentially a regressive tax on low- and middle-income citizens. (On average, the government keeps about 35 cents of every dollar you spend on a lottery ticket, and some states keep 80 percent or more. Lottery tickets are purchased disproportionately by the poor.)

Comparison of Odds at Common Forms of Gambling

GAME	TYPICAL HOUSE EDGE	COMMON RANGE
Craps	0.4%	0.3%–1.41%
Blackjack	0.6%	0.15%–2.5%
Baccarat	1.06%	1.06%–1.24%
Sports betting	5%	2.5%–10%
Roulette	5.26%	2.70%–7.69%
Slot machines	8%	2%–25%
Horse racing	18%	10%–25%
State lottery	35%	20%–80%

Notes: This table assumes optimal play at blackjack, that the player plays as the banker in baccarat, and that a player makes an odds bet on the pass line in craps. Many games offer side bets that have a much larger house advantage than the odds listed here.

And then there's the part that casino executives don't like to talk about. To some percentage of patrons, slots can be highly addictive—potentially three to four times faster at addicting players than card games or sports betting. Even though the percentage of players who become problem gamblers is relatively small, these players may account for 30 to 60 percent of slot revenues because they play so often.

I'm about to tell you what might be the most shocking thing that I learned in the course of writing this book. It may seem counterintuitive at first, but it helps to explain why slot machines can trigger such compulsive behavior.

Here goes: according to Schüll, many of the problem gamblers she met *didn't actually want to win*. "This was the thing that I couldn't really get for a while," Schüll told me. "But . . . I kept hearing it over and over again."

Why wouldn't a gambler want to win? Well, when you win a slot jackpot, it's a disruptive experience. Lights flash. Alarms ring. The other patrons ooh and ah. A smiling attendant comes by to check your ID and hand you a tax form. "When they won a jackpot, suddenly, music started playing loudly. People looked at them, marking them in intersubjective space. They were dropped back into their bodies—they would even feel physical [sensations]. Like suddenly, they'd have to pee real bad or feel some cramps."

Compulsive slot machine gamblers, Schüll said, are seeking escape from the pressures of everyday life. Casinos are happy to facilitate this by placing players in what she calls the "machine zone"—a flow state where they can shut out the distractions of the real world.

Schüll's subjects violate the conventional wisdom about why people gamble. They are seeking comfort, not excitement. But that's because the conventional wisdom was formed partly from studies of people who play table games like craps or blackjack. There is little overlap between slots players and table games players. Blackjack players, craps players, roulette players—yes, those players are action junkies. They're looking for a thrill, not an escape. The famed sociologist Erving Goffman, who worked as a blackjack dealer in an ethnographic study of Las Vegas, wrote an essay in 1967 called "Where the Action Is." It situates casino gambling in a post-World War II malaise, in a world that was becoming safer and more prosperous, and where there were fewer tests of courage available. Goffman's archetype is something like Bob Miller from Dubuque, Iowa, who once imagined himself joining the army or performing other feats of bravery, but instead now has a wife and two kids and a secure, upper-middle-class job as a bank manager. So he flies to Vegas for the weekend and presses himself right up to the limit of his risk tolerance. In a casino, he is "assured of the opportunity of facing the excitement of a little more financial risk and opportunity than most persons of his means would be at ease with."

The next time you go to a casino, watch what men* do at a craps table. They often have a trapezoidal stance: wide at the base, marking their territory, with their hands or elbows planted into the cushioned rail of the table and their heads extended over the table at a 15-degree angle. They are literally leaning into the action to get a better view of the dice roll that will determine their fate. They want to be seen—they want their courage to be recognized.

Compulsive slots players are just the opposite. They want to hide away— that's why locals casinos often have poor sight lines. Hide away from what? For the gamblers that Schüll spoke with, it was often hiding from a world that had become too complex and too risky, one where they had too many responsibilities but there was still too much outside of their control. It was as though by playing slots, they could channel all their other problems into just one *big* problem: compulsive gambling.

"They knew that they would lose, they are not dupes," Schüll told me. "They are very different than the strategic poker players. But they are not dupes in the sense that they're, like, dumb and think that they're going to win. They know very well what they want—what they're playing for and what trumps the jackpot—is continuing to play."

Casinos help players remain in the machine zone in obvious and not-so-obvious ways. One is the method I've already described: by tweaking payout algorithms to give players occasional positive reinforcements in the form of modest wins and a smoother ride down to zero. Schüll likened

---

* A wide variety of research—plus frankly what you'll find if you just go to a casino and walk around— suggests that table games players are predominantly men and slot machine players are predominantly women.

slot machines to Skinner boxes, named after the psychologist B. F. Skinner, the devices that are used to condition rats or other small animals—press the lever, and you'll get a tiny sliver of cheese. Traditionally, these strategies might be arrived at by trial and error. But as River attitudes are taking over, gambling companies are becoming more sophisticated about optimizing them; at Caesars, Loveman even had a slot analytics team that would run randomized control trials.

But that makes slot machines sound more miserable than they are. In fact, modern slot machines are immersive—they're *a lot of fun*. They are full of mini-games, sounds, and animations—howling wolves or stampeding buffalo or a virtual Vanna White telling you to spin the Wheel of Fortune. Win or lose, the machine will put on a show—maybe to convince you that you came *oh so close* to winning—even though your fate has already been determined. "The minute that the actuator is hit by the player, the computer has decided whether that's a win or loss. And the random number generator is activated—boom, microseconds later, it's a loss," said Rumbolz, whose current company, Everi Holdings, makes gambling equipment, including slot machines. "But we then might take fifteen or twenty seconds to actually show you that loss."

Most of all, casinos are trying to reduce friction. In blackjack, there are natural break points; every shuffle or dealer change is an opportunity to ask yourself if you want to keep playing. There are also a lot of eyes on you. If you're drunk or abusive, you may be asked to leave—or if you're losing a lot, you might do so out of embarrassment. All of that creates *friction*. But there's nothing stopping you from just pressing the spin button on a slot machine over and over and over again until you go broke. Slot machines create a continuous flow, making them addictive in literally the same ways that social media applications like Twitter are. A player can easily spin the reels six hundred times in an hour or more.

Subtle design choices also help reduce friction. Here's one Schüll helped me to notice. Casinos, even high-end ones like the Aria, have few right angles. Right angles create friction: an opportunity to opt out. Instead, modern casino interiors are curvy, with gaming areas flowing into one another. They are not mazelike in the way locals casinos might be—but they may have you walking around in circles, with a slot machine or blackjack table always on your horizon.

Like Schüll, I'm not a prude. High-end casino resorts are selling a good time to their patrons—and mostly manage to provide it, at least judging by their high rate of repeat business. The average visitor to Las Vegas sustains only modest gambling losses—about $300 per trip—and the casino industry creates a lot of middle-class jobs. And as far as I'm concerned, just because a product can cause harm to some people doesn't necessarily mean we should ban it. People have the right to make dumb decisions.

But there's something about slot machines where the transaction between casinos and their customers feels fundamentally unfair.

If I play blackjack for an hour, betting $50 per hand, the expected value of that session is a loss somewhere in the range of $25 to $100, depending on game rules, game speed, and how close I'm playing to optimal strategy. In exchange, I get free drinks, an hour's worth of entertainment, some good stories to share with my buddies, and a few rewards points. Plus I'll come out ahead fairly often. It feels close enough to a win-win transaction.

If I'm playing slots, however, I'm potentially losing a lot more than I think. Some ostensible "penny slots" actually let you bet as much as $4 a spin or more, for example. Make six hundred spins at $4 a pop over the course of an hour, with a typical Vegas Strip hold of 11 percent on penny slots, and that hour is costing you *$264* in expected value. That doesn't seem fair for what's supposed to be an entry-level product—particularly if I've been manipulated into thinking I'm losing less. It violates the trust that has helped the casino industry to thrive.

Goffman may be right in sizing up the motivation of River types. Even skilled poker players like Dan Smith or Rampage may see some romantic allure in surrendering their fate to the turn of the next card. But Schüll's slot machine addicts are not Riverians for whom modern life has become stagnant. Instead, they're seeking escape from a hazardous world. They may even have a relatively *low* risk tolerance. Because in slots, one thing is certain: in the long run you're going to lose.

"'I always laugh when people tell me that slot machine gambling is about chance,'" Schüll recalled one of her addicted gamblers saying. "'Because if it were about chance, then I should just be in the real world where you have no control. This is the one place I can go where I know exactly what is going to happen.'"

Competition

A bottom-up guy, no matter how good his model is, no matter how smart he is, if he can't bet, he's worthless," said Gadoon Kyrollos. "Me? All I know how to do is bet."

I'd met with Kyrollos, better known as Spanky for his resemblance to an overgrown version of the child actor from *The Little Rascals*, at a brick-oven pizza restaurant in Brooklyn somewhere between my place in Manhattan and his in New Jersey. He looks and sounds pretty much like what you'd expect from a professional sports bettor named Spanky Kyrollos: big dude, loud, funny, doesn't hold a lot back.

But Spanky is self-aware about where his edge comes from. It's not his analytical skills, although he did graduate from Rutgers with degrees in computer science and finance and once held a job on Wall Street. It's not his love of sports. "I used to be a big Yankee fan. Now, I don't give three shits," he told me. "I haven't watched a full game of anything in well over a decade." Instead, it's that *he knows how to bet*. "I know how to execute. I know how to get down," he said. "I know how to be able to get down in a timely manner. I have enough contacts that I've built. That's my edge."

In Spanky's world, there are two types of sports bettors, bottom-up and top-down:

- Bottom-up bettors seek to handicap games from the ground up "using data statistics analytics models etc." In other words, the *Moneyball* approach: hope your superior modeling skills prevail against less sophisticated methods and stale conventional wisdom.

- Top-down—the approach he prefers—"assumes the line is correct" and there aren't a lot of gains to be had from modeling. But bettors can derive value via arbitrage, "information not reflected in the line such as injuries," and through clever betting tactics.

Top-down is in line with a game-theory equilibrium that assumes everyone playing the sports-betting game is pretty smart, resulting in a market where betting lines are reasonably efficient and there aren't major edges to be had through number-crunching or data-mining—instead you need street smarts and hustle.* But in truth, the distinction is more philosophical than practical: the most successful sports bettors use a mix of both approaches. Top-down guys like Spanky might not build statistical models themselves, but they're data literate and employ models that others have built.† And bottom-up guys, no matter how good they are at statistics, still need to figure out how to get the money down.

If you think this is a trivial problem, I can personally attest that it isn't. In January 2022, mobile sports betting went live in New York. Despite having built lots of sports models, I'd never actually bet on sports on a regular basis. Given that I was working on this book, it was the perfect time to start. So I began betting regularly, mostly on the NBA, using some combination of the models I'd built at FiveThirtyEight and my general knowledge as an obsessive sports fan.

By March 2023, I was having trouble getting my money down. I had

---

* That's why, although I've rolled with it here, I don't particularly like Spanky's "top-down" idiom. Because really what Spanky does is more akin to poking around at ground level in search of vulnerabilities, things the model builders of the world working high up in the tower are missing.
† Spanky told me he used the PECOTA forecasts I developed for Baseball Prospectus at one point during his betting career.

been severely limited by five of the major retail sites that operate in the state, such as BetMGM and DraftKings. (Being "limited" is just what it sounds like—there's a limit on how much you can bet relative to other customers. Technically the casino will take your action, but it may only be for a few dollars.) I am not claiming to be an especially skilled sports bettor, and I wasn't winning all that much—one site limited me even though I'd *lost* money there. But I was *trying* to win—and wasn't really making any effort to conceal that. That alone can get you limited.

Indeed, pretty much anybody who really knows sports betting will tell you the same thing. Beating the lines on paper is only half the battle—and it's the easier half. "It's not trivial to find edges," said Ed Miller, the author of *The Logic of Sports Betting*. "But it's much harder, once you've found edges, to find people willing to bet real money with you for an extended period."

It wasn't always this way. Spanky discovered the then-nascent world of online sports betting in the early 2000s while working for Deutsche Bank, using his coding skills to set up a program to continuously scan dozens of sportsbooks for the latest lines and automatically place bets. Back then, betting lines often vastly differed from one another for the same game, providing for pure arbitrage plays that required little or no financial risk. "It could be discrepancies in lines where, you know, you can go make yourself a sandwich, go to the bathroom, come back twenty minutes later, [and] it's still there," said Spanky.

Imagine, for instance, that for the Super Bowl, FanDuel had the Eagles favored over the Chiefs by 2 points while DraftKings had them favored by 4. The arbitrage here, called "middling," is to bet the Chiefs at FanDuel and the Eagles at DraftKings. You're guaranteed to win at least one bet—but if the Eagles win by 3 points, you'll hit the middle and win both. Middling isn't technically risk-free,* but it's about as close as it gets in the River.

Spanky claimed to me that this suited his personality. "I don't like gambling really. None of us like real gambling. We like winning." I don't

---

* Sportsbooks don't return the full amount of your wager when you win—instead they keep a portion called the vig, vigorish, or juice. For instance, to win $100 on the Eagles to beat the point spread, you'd have to bet $110. However, you only have to hit the middle about 1 in 20 times to compensate for this.

believe Spanky for a second when he says he doesn't like gambling—in fact, the first time I met him was when I saw him playing craps at the Encore Boston Harbor. But I understand why he longs for a time when the market was less efficient and his day-to-day survival didn't require undertaking so much risk. Today, the line between winning and losing can be wafer-thin. Kyrollos told me that his return on the money he puts down is around 3 percent or "sometimes even less." "I'd rather hold two percent of a billion than three percent of a million," he said. A 2 or 3 percent profit margin is equivalent to winning just 53 or 54 percent of the time. It's a dangerously thin edge: bettors need to win 52.4 percent of their bets in order to merely break even. And yet, that's what's realistic—in a more efficient market, bettors often need to chew close to the bone.

Sports betting, like the commercial gambling industry it's a part of, is an algorithmic arms race, a microcosm of early- to mid-twenty-first-century capitalism. As compared with something like slot machines, this race is relatively competitive, with Riverians lined up on either side—there are more long-run winners in sports than slots. But if sports betting is the

A Coming Sports Betting Backlash?

Just as this book was about to go to the printer, two major sports betting scandals were unfolding. Jontay Porter of the NBA's Toronto Raptors was accused of manipulating his stat lines to help gamblers win player prop bets. And Ippei Mizuhara, the interpreter for the Los Angeles Dodgers' megastar Shohai Ohtani, was accused of stealing millions of dollars from Ohtani to gamble with illegal bookmakers.

So far, Wall Street has shrugged off the problems (the stock prices for companies like DraftKings haven't been affected). But there is a long history of ebbs and flows in public tolerance for gambling. My personal view is that the industry is overconfident about the Village's patience for the recent ubiquity of betting in American sports culture. The left can raise concerns about predatory capitalism, while the right may find gambling morally dubious. As someone who likes to throw down a sports bet or two himself, my message is simple: get your house in order.

future of capitalism, it's a rather grim one: not many bettors nor many books are actually getting rich from it.

The Wizardry Behind the Westgate's Wagers

It was a slow June morning at the Westgate SuperBook in Las Vegas. The NBA Finals were about to end. The NFL season was months away. There were a couple of Major League Baseball games already underway on the SuperBook's giant LED screens—being on Pacific Time offers the treat of morning sports—but baseball doesn't drive revenues the way that football and basketball do. At quiet hours like these, sportsbooks are spaces of relative sanctuary—one of the few places you can sit down in a casino that isn't directly in front of a piece of gaming equipment.

But on big game days like during the opening weekend of the NCAA basketball tournament, they transform into theatrical experiences. It was easy to imagine the SuperBook, which bills itself as the world's largest sportsbook, full of kinetic energy as hopeful players sweated their bets. "That Thursday—that first day—Monday is forever away," said John Murray, the SuperBook's executive director, of the frat party atmosphere during the NCAAs. "They've got their bankroll—it's just mayhem."

"Thursday, you got, you know, Coronas. You got vodka sodas. I mean, it's nine in the morning, and these guys are *going*," added Jay Kornegay, the SuperBook's executive vice president. By the end of the weekend, of course, the boozing and the losing have taken their toll. "By Sunday, it's like—guys, what is that, a vanilla latte?"

The Westgate prides itself on offering a very large number of bets; the NFL, NBA, MLB, and NHL are just the tip of the iceberg. There's also college basketball, college football, and soccer leagues from all around the world. Golf. Tennis. Auto racing. MMA. If someone is willing to bet it, the Westgate will probably post a line.

But when I slipped through a side door to take a behind-the-scenes look at the SuperBook, I couldn't help but feel like Dorothy discovering that the Wizard of Oz was just a regular dude with a lot of fancy gadgets. Behind the curtains of the SuperBook's massive wall of sports—it has 4,250 square feet of LED screens, giving it almost as much screen space as an IMAX—was a relatively humble operation. There was a team of perhaps ten people, mostly men in their twenties and thirties, in a narrow, dark room with a phalanx of monitors, manually reviewing bets from the Westgate's mobile app and comparing the Westgate's lines to every other sportsbook in the world.

Don't get me wrong: this is difficult work, and the Westgate is well regarded in the industry. But having never been backstage at a sportsbook before, it hadn't sunk in how bespoke the business can be. Sportsbooks have gotten more sophisticated, but so have their patrons. Every bet and every line move is a game within a game.

"There's a huge human element," said Kornegay, after I'd retreated into his office to speak with him and Murray. "I mean, those guys back there, probably each one has more than maybe three thousand moves a day, per shift."

Three-thousand line moves per shift. Kornegay clarified for me that these are the moves his traders* make by hand. Others are made algorithmically, but the most important ones aren't. "You would be surprised how unsophisticated the software is," he told me.

Wait, can't you just optimize your way to algorithm nirvana, like casinos have done with their slot machines? Better technology and better management does help at the margin. (Nevada casinos are making a higher profit margin on sports betting than they once did.) But it's not so easy because sports betting is an adversarial game—the bettors can fight back.

Betting lines, whether they're updated via algorithm or by hand, can very easily go wrong. This may change in the future, but for now, AIs lack the precision for widespread use by handicappers. "There's just so many variables, so many particulars," Kornegay said. Sure, the algorithm might be right nine out ten times—but on the tenth time if it doesn't realize that

---

* Sportsbooks increasingly borrow terms from the financial sector; "trader" is industry-speak for a sportsbook employee who reviews bets and lines.

the star quarterback has just been injured, the betting public will pounce on the bad line, making for a huge liability.

Humans—or at least the humans who hang out in the River—are good approximators. If you're sitting with me at a Mets or a Knicks or a Rangers game, I can give you a pretty good estimate of the home team's chance of winning at any moment in the game. Not good enough to bet on, but pretty good. And I'm certainly going to notice if the quarterback is hurt. Algorithms can offer more precision, but they can also be precisely wrong. Precisely and confidently wrong, such that you'd have a very profitable bet against them. That's why sportsbook operators are reluctant to turn things over to the machines. This is a problem for AIs in adversarial situations—they can be probed for vulnerabilities by humans or by other AIs, and then attacked at the weakest link. Take the case of the game Go. It's well known as a proving ground for AI advancement, like with Google's development of AlphaGo. But in 2023 a group of programmers detected a flaw in a different, supposedly superhuman AI engine, KataGo, and repeatedly defeated it.

So until the machines become less error-prone, anytime anything happens in one of the dozen sports the Westgate lets you bet on, one of those nerds in the SuperBook boiler room has to make a decision. An NBA reporter tweets that LeBron James is unexpectedly going to sit out the Lakers game that night? The traders need to move the line *fast* or take it off the board. A betting syndicate looks like it's betting heavily on the Dallas Cowboys? Another decision point—and not one you can just automate, because sometimes big bettors like Spanky throw head fakes, essentially trying to bluff the sportsbook into moving their lines before doubling down on the opposite side.

"As one of our executives came in and observed, 'Oh, you guys are like the air traffic controllers,'" said Kornegay, who has been in the industry for thirty years. "It's like, yeah, yeah, that's pretty much what we do. Because we always have a pulse on it, we never close. We're open twenty-four seven, three hundred sixty-five days a year."

But human traders can go wrong in their own ways—say, because someone is asleep at the wheel or is relying on incomplete or outdated information. A few days after my visit to the Westgate, for instance, the U.S. Open golf championship was played. Golf tournaments are challenging for bookmakers to handicap in real time because there is potentially simultaneous action on up to eighteen holes at once. But sportsbooks are eager to expand their menu of in-game betting—events you can bet while the game is underway, when your impulse control may be the poorest. While playing in a WSOP event, I noticed that one of the Nevada mobile apps was about a half minute behind FanDuel in updating its live U.S. Open odds. It was as though I could see thirty seconds in the future. I was able to get enough money down that I was guaranteed a $5,000 profit whichever golfer won, a risk-free profit just for being observant.

Inside information—or even collusion with players, like the NBA's Jontay Porter was accused of in 2024—can also put sportsbooks on the defensive. And it may become a bigger problem as media companies like ESPN increasingly form partnerships with gambling interests. Murray, for instance, recalled a time when a man they'd never seen before wanted to bet big—very big—on the Golden State Warriors to win the NBA Finals. "This guy asked for as much as we would let him go on the Warriors to win the title. And we gave him a bet. I don't recall exactly, twenty or twenty-five thousand [dollars]." After his initial bet, the Westgate aggressively moved the line to a less favorable price—but the customer wanted to bet again. "We just looked at each other [and said], 'Kevin Durant's going to the Warriors.'" Nothing else could explain the unknown man's confidence. Durant indeed signed with Golden State, and the Warriors steamrolled the league en route to the title.

"The number-one objective as a bookmaker is: Don't get killed," said Chris Bennett, the sportsbook director at Circa Sports. He noted the fundamental asymmetry between players and the house. Players get to go on offense, probing the sportsbooks for any signs of weakness. Casinos are on defense and have a large attack surface* to defend.

---

* The term "attack surface" originated in computer hacking, but has also been applied to sports betting by analysts like Ed Miller. This will make me seem like even more of a geek, but when I think of a large attack surface, I think of the USS *Enterprise* from *Star Trek*. It has all sorts of dangling parts—a saucer

Just like in regular sports, offense generally pays more. "This industry doesn't get, like, Harvard MBA, PhD statistics," said Bennett. "Those people are applying themselves to creating models, betting for themselves. They're playing offense, for the most part."

If Your Model Is So Smart, Why Don't You Bet on It?

Rufus Peabody plays offense. He didn't go to Harvard—but he went to Yale. The typical Yale rising senior takes a summer internship at Goldman Sachs or McKinsey. Peabody instead cold-called his way into an internship at Las Vegas Sports Consultants, an old-school handicapping business founded by the legendary Roxy Roxborough.

Perhaps more than any other gambler I spoke with for this book, Peabody, a precise but affable Virginian with "a wardrobe straight out of an L.L.Bean catalog," is interested in betting mostly as an *intellectual* pursuit—as a game to see whether his ideas are better. The money is mostly a way to keep score. "I didn't get into this world to make a lot of money," he told me. "I moved to Vegas for a job that I loved, that paid nothing."

After his summer at LVSC, Peabody wrote his senior thesis on inefficiencies in the baseball betting market. "This paper has shown, through the lens of baseball betting markets, that markets behave in irrational ways," it concluded. This is a big claim for an undergraduate to make. But sports betting, as Peabody's thesis pointed out, provides for unusually rich data. Hundreds of sporting events are played every day. Somebody wins and somebody loses; there isn't much room to spin the results. You get to the long run much faster than in something like the stock market, where corporate strategies can take years to play out. So if sportsbooks are posting betting lines that can be beat by a college senior, then perhaps markets are not as efficient as economists say.

---

section with a large, flat surface area, a secondary hull, the warp core, and so on. By contrast, a more compact shape like a cube or a sphere (think the Death Star) has a smaller attack surface.

Still, it's one thing to claim you've found a profitable betting opportunity when you're backtesting a statistical model. It's another thing to actually bet on it—to have some skin in the game—and win.

"If your model is so smart, why don't you bet on it?" is a common refrain in the River. Sometimes there are good reasons not to.* As I hope you'll see from this chapter, it is far from trivial to get your money down even if you theoretically have a profitable bet. And betting sports—or almost anything else—requires a tolerance for financial swings that isn't for everyone.

But for the most part, I endorse the sentiment. In recent years, researchers have discovered that a large share of experimental results published in academic journals—the majority of results in some fields—can't be verified when other researchers try to duplicate them. (This is called the replication crisis.) Occasionally, the reason is something like fraud, but more often the issue is just that statistical inference is hard and the pressure to publish is intense. Academics have an incentive to cater to the whims of peer reviewers and department chairs—more so than to be accurate. When you bet, though, all you care about is accuracy. *The stuff that people are willing to put their money behind is usually going to be better.* At the very least, a bet helps to align incentives. "A bet is a tax on bullshit," the economist Alex Tabarrok wrote in a post that defended me after I got in trouble at *The New York Times* for challenging the TV pundit Joe Scarborough to a bet on the outcome of the 2012 election.

Peabody returned to LVSC in 2008 after completing his degree. The old-school guys there might not have had economics BAs from Yale. But they had skin in the game—casinos were buying their odds and taking millions in bets on that basis. And it turns out they did know a thing or two. "When I moved out to Vegas, I thought I knew everything. You know I was a little bit—probably a little bit arrogant. And just thought that I could quantify anything and that these people are like the Art Howes† in

---

* There's also another issue if your models are published for the general public, as mine were. Bookmakers and bettors can incorporate them into their prices, giving away your potential advantage.
† Howe, played by Philip Seymour Hoffman, essentially took the role of bumbling idiot in *Moneyball* to the heroic, statistically enlightened Billy Beane. Howe was deeply unhappy with his portrayal, calling it "character assassination."

Moneyball," Peabody said. "It's amazing how good they were, how good their intuition was, and how good they were able to price things without having run any regressions or anything like that."

Peabody was motivated to see if he could keep up. He is something of a purist—the archetype of what Spanky would call a bottom-up bettor. But Peabody doesn't like that term. Instead, Peabody calls himself an "originator"—someone with an informed, original opinion about what the betting line should be, usually formulated through painstaking statistical modeling.

Peabody is all about process—the podcast he cohosts with Jeff Ma (yep, the same Jeff Ma from the MIT Blackjack Team in chapter 3) is called *Bet the Process*. And Peabody sticks to his process. If a player consistently does better or worse than his models project, he may "dig in and sort of see if there's something I'm missing"—some generalizable principle that could improve his handicapping.* But he's not going to change his process and become superstitious in the midst of a losing streak. "I'm not going to just say, 'No, I'm not betting this guy because he's burned me too many times.'"

However, Peabody does pick his battles—particularly focusing on golf, college basketball, and Super Bowl props. A "prop bet" is a wager on basically anything other than the final score—everything from the length of the national anthem to, say, whether there will be a field goal in the fourth quarter. His bets have something in common: they're in areas where you might expect the market to be less efficient and an originator has more hope of winning. There's a relationship between the popularity of an event and the profitability for the smart gambler.

Imagine a graph that I call the "U." Plot the popularity of the sport with the American sports-betting public on the x-axis, and how profitable it is to bet on the sport on the y-axis; it forms a U-shaped pattern. For extremely obscure sports—Russian ping-pong became a fad at one point during the pandemic—it isn't really worth the sportsbook's time to price

---

* I endorse this attitude toward modeling. Models are intrinsically works in progress—you don't need to stick by them come hell or high water if there's something that's clearly wrong. But you should avoid making ad hoc changes. Use failed predictions as an inspiration to test hypotheses that could potentially improve your model.

them to a high degree of precision. These sports are beatable for large *theoretical* edges if you're willing to put the time in. The catch is that the sportsbooks will limit you from betting them as soon as you've shown the propensity to be any good.

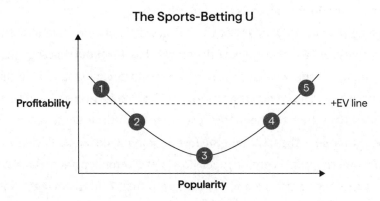

The Sports-Betting U

NUMBER	EXAMPLES
1	Minor college football and basketball; ping-pong; obscure international leagues
2	Mid-major college basketball; NASCAR; golf and tennis outside of major events
3	NBA, MLB, NHL regular season; golf and tennis majors; major conference regular season college football and basketball
4	NFL regular season; major European soccer leagues; NBA playoffs; World Series; college football playoff
5	Men's NCAA tournament; massively hyped combat sports fights; World Cup; Champions' League final; Super Bowl; presidential elections

On the other end of the U are extremely popular events: for instance, the NCAA tourney, big MMA fights, or the World Cup. For events like these, "the amount of money bet by the public ends up dwarfing the amount bet by professionals," and the market doesn't necessarily clear to an efficient price, Peabody said. I was in Las Vegas during the UFC bout between Conor McGregor and Dustin Poirier—the second-highest-grossing UFC fight of all time. McGregor is immensely popular, and there were electronic billboards of him hawking whiskey everywhere you looked, along with more than a few Irish lads who had flown across the Atlantic to see him. That's the kind of circumstance where you might have a +EV bet just by fading the public and betting the less popular side.

But with the possible exception of presidential elections,* the event with the *most* dumb money is the Super Bowl.

Every year in late January or early February, Peabody—along with his betting partners and backpacks full of more than $100,000 in cash—makes a pilgrimage to the Westgate, which is the first sportsbook to post Super Bowl prop bets. The Westgate posts a *lot* of Super Bowl props—in 2023, they offered a pamphlet of them that was literally thirty-eight pages long. Kornegay is one of the fathers of the format, having developed props in the 1990s when the final score of Super Bowls was often lopsided and bettors needed another excuse to gamble. Now, props make up the majority of the Westgate's Super Bowl action. When the SuperBook first publishes its prop lines about ten days before the game, bettors queue up to place them under a strict set of rules. No more than two bets at a time—it's sort of the sports-betting equivalent of Noah's Ark—of no more than $2,000 each.

Prop bets are perfect bets for Peabody, highly technical questions that benefit from elaborate modeling. To estimate the chance of a field goal being scored in the fourth quarter, for instance, you'd ideally want a probabilistic simulation of the entire game—way beyond the capabilities of the average bettor, but Peabody has been working on models like these for years.

The nerds in the SuperBook boiler room, precocious as they might be, are also no match for a specialist like Peabody. And the thing is, the Westgate knows this—and doesn't particularly care. Sure, smart bettors like Peabody are "picking out some weak spots" in the Westgate prop menu, Kornegay says, but "we have so much public money, we're not too concerned about it."

Besides, when an originator like Peabody bets, the SuperBook at least

---

* Presidential elections are unique in that there are a lot fewer people working as professional handicappers than there are in sports. Conversely, there are a *lot* of people who have strong opinions about politics. So the ratio of public money to smart money is very high, putting elections on the far right side of the U.

gets valuable information—one of the best bettors in the world has tipped his hand and the Westgate can use that to adjust its lines. So Super Bowl props are a win-win—Peabody gets a +EV bet, and the Westgate gets to learn what he thought when it has ten more days to take millions in public money. The public is losing out, but at least they're having fun. If every day were the Super Bowl, sports betting would be a booming industry— but of course it isn't.

How to Read a Sportsbook Menu

Navigating the matrix of numbers you'll see in a sportsbook can be intimidating to the uninitiated, but it becomes intuitive in no time—so here's a basic tutorial. For instance, here are some betting lines for a game set to be played in week 1 of the NFL season:

SEP 10 | 4:25 PM	SPREAD	MONEYLINE	TOTAL
Las Vegas Raiders	+4.5 -110	+185	O 44.5 -110
@ Denver Broncos	-4.5 -110	-225	U 44.5 -110

There are three basic types of sports bets: the point spread, the moneyline, and the total. The **moneyline** is the most straightforward: you're simply betting on which team is going to win. However, you'll be getting a better price to bet the underdog, in this case the Raiders. Their side is listed at +185. What does that mean? Underdogs are listed with positive numbers. Specifically, the +185 means you'll make $185 in profit if you place a $100 bet and the Raiders win. I'll skip the algebra, but in order for that bet to break even, the Raiders have to win at least 35.1 percent of the time. Negative numbers, conversely, illustrate a favorite—how much money you'd have to *lay* to win $100. In this case, the +225 means you'd have to bet $225 in order to make $100 in profit if the Broncos win. That bet needs to win 69.2 percent of the time to break even.

For **point-spread** betting, the underdog gets a handicap. For instance, the Raiders are listed at +4.5, which means you get to add 4.5 points to whatever their final score is. If the game ends up Broncos 24,

Raiders 20, for example, that means you covered the spread and your bet won even though the Raiders didn't. But don't neglect the little -110 number under the point spread; it means you're taking the bet at slightly unfavorable odds. There are a million terms for this: the **hold**, the **vig** or **vigorish**, the **juice** or the **rake**; whatever you call it, it's how sportsbooks make their money.* The -110 indicates that you're betting $110 in order to win $100. That means your bet has to win 52.4 percent of the time to break even. As you'll see in this chapter, that is tantalizingly close to the 50 percent you'd win just by guessing at random—though still pretty hard to achieve.

Finally there's the **total**, sometimes also called the **over-under**, which is just the combined number of points between the two teams. The over ("O") wins if more than 44.5 points are scored and the under ("U") wins otherwise. If you're ever in a sportsbook and you see some guy cheering *no matter which team scores*, he's not just a football enthusiast—he has the over.

The Two Types of Sportsbooks

DraftKings CEO Jason Robins rang the opening bell at the Nasdaq on June 11, 2021. At the time, his stock was priced at just under $54 per share. That was down from its peak—but there was plenty of reason for optimism: the New York State Legislature had just voted to legalize online sports betting, making it the largest state to do so. The industry treated the event like a gold rush. When betting opened the following January, people like me earned more than $5,000 in free bets just by signing up for as many of the eight legal betting sites as possible. At one point, the side-boards at New York Rangers hockey games featured advertisements for three online sportsbooks at once—companies were in such a frenzy to acquire customers that they didn't care.

---

* Bonus question: Did the casino take any hold on the *moneyline* bet? Of course they did. If you check the numbers above, you'll notice that the combined implied probability for the Broncos and Raiders to win the game was 104.2 percent. My math isn't wrong, though—that extra 4.2 percent is the casino's hold.

Nowadays, the lofty price for $DKNG looks like another pandemic-era fad. Its stock would fall to $11 per share (although it had rebounded to $49 by early 2024). And DraftKings wasn't alone. Caesars, which had bragged about how it would spend more than $1 billion on customer acquisition, also saw its share price crash. The realities of the business were catching up to it. Before long, representatives of DraftKings and FanDuel were complaining about the high tax rate that New York charges.

The industry veterans I spoke with for this book weren't surprised that Wall Street's confidence in sports betting had been misplaced. More than one of them used the "a" word to describe it: "amenity."

"We in Nevada, because of PASPA—we had a monopoly," said J. Brin Gibson, who was the chair of the Nevada Gaming Control Board at the time that I spoke with him in mid-2022. Gibson was referring to the Professional and Amateur Sports Protection Act of 1992, which limited full sports betting to Nevada until the Supreme Court found the law unconstitutional in 2018. "We watched sports wagering for many years. We had it to ourselves. We consider it in many cases an amenity."

An "amenity" means something casinos provide for their patrons to meet customers' expectations. Not necessarily a loss leader, but also not a profit center. A gym and a pool; a bell desk that operates 24/7—these are among the minimum amenities for any self-respecting Vegas resort. And a sportsbook. It's not like there isn't space—it's the middle of the desert. And although some casinos tuck their sportsbooks away in a corner, others like the Wynn and Caesars Palace feature them in prime real estate because they can have a lot of visual appeal. "It was part of the excitement. It's part of the interior decorating of the casinos to have a sportsbook and a poker room," said Steve Wynn.

But sportsbooks and racebooks make up only about 2 percent of gaming revenues at Las Vegas Strip casinos and 1 percent of overall revenues. They can be a bigger part of the business at off-Strip properties like Westgate and Circa, where sportsbooks help to draw in huge crowds on football weekends. Ultimately, however, sports betting is a medium-sized business. In 2022, the legal online sports-betting market in the U.S. generated about $7.5 billion in net betting revenue. That's not nothing, and the market will grow as more states legalize it. But the Vegas Strip alone generates more gambling revenue than that. Heck, the frozen pizza market in the U.S. is worth about $20 billion annually.

"The one place where you may find some operators nervous, although they still will spread the game, is in sports wagering," said Mike Rumbolz, another former Nevada Gaming Board chair who now runs the company Everi Holdings. "Because that's where you actually can lose, and you can lose a large amount of money in one weekend." For example, casinos in the state of Colorado *lost* nearly $11 million in NBA betting to their patrons in June 2023. Why? It's because the Denver Nuggets won the NBA championship that month. Okay, sure, the hometown team wins it all and you have one bad month. That's a tolerable risk. A more persistent problem is that it's not *that* hard for sharp* customers to exceed the magic threshold of 52.4 they need to be +EV. It's not *easy*, but if you can pick and choose *what* you bet, *when* you bet, *where* you bet it, and *how much* you bet, it's doable.

What's the catch? Well, as we've already discovered, some sportsbooks severely limit *who* they let bet. Robins, the DraftKings CEO, said as much in 2022—"We're trying to get smart in eliminating the sharp action or limiting it at least," he told a group of investors.

I want to be careful about how I state this, because it depends on exactly which sportsbook you're talking about—we'll get to that in a moment. But the extremely large menu you'll find at some of the largest sportsbooks is something of a false front. "They give the illusion of offering many [bets]. But if you actually try to bet many of these bets, for real money, you quickly run into friction," said Miller. It's as though you went to TGI Fridays, which had advertised its wide-ranging menu, but once you got there, you were told a lot of the more appealing items were out of stock or limited to one per customer. Then fifteen minutes later, you spotted the

---

* "Sharp" is a term we'll be using a lot in this chapter. It's the highest compliment that one bettor can pay to another. It means smart, winning, +EV.

VIPs at the next table overstuffing themselves with the very mango ghost pepper buffalo wings you'd been told were 86'd.

But wait a second. Why is DraftKings limiting everyone within sniffing distance of being a winning bettor—while the Westgate lets Rufus Peabody, the best prop bettor in the world, bet its Super Bowl props? It's because sportsbooks fall into two major camps. Miller's book calls them "retail" sportsbooks and "market makers."

The sportsbooks you see advertised on TV are retail books. They put a *lot* of money toward customer acquisition; DraftKings spent almost $1.2 billion on sales and marketing in 2022, a gargantuan sum given that they did only $2.2 billion in revenue. And they extensively profile those customers. If they think you're a whale, you'll get the sorts of perks that a casino VIP does. Four seats on the glass at a New York Rangers playoff game? A $5,000 bonus bet deposited into your account because you haven't played in a while? A case of your favorite cabernet shipped to your house? A friend of mine who's a DraftKings VIP gets all of this and more.

Characteristics of Market Makers and Retail Books

MARKET MAKER	RETAIL
Tolerates sharp action, up to a point, to improve price discovery	Aggressively limits customers it thinks are winners
Often transparent about how much you can bet; all players may have relatively similar limits	Betting limits may vary by hundreds or thousands of times between customers, with little transparency—perceived whales get the VIP treatment
Spends little on customer acquisition	Spends lots on marketing and customer acquisition
Offers a more limited attack surface; reluctant to post lines on markets that could be beat through inside information*	Offers an extremely wide menu of bets, but some of these are false fronts; perceived VIPs can bet them, but they'll arouse suspicion from other bettors

---

* Bets such as which player will be chosen first in the NFL draft are highly vulnerable to inside information—if you work for an NFL team, or are an NFL reporter for ESPN, you may have direct knowledge of this. You'll lose your job if you're an insider who's found to make one of those bets, but information has a way of leaking out. When attending a game at the 2023 NBA Summer League in Las Vegas, for instance, I saw a text message on an NBA executive's phone a few rows in front of me suggesting that the New York Knicks were going to trade for the Toronto Raptors' OG Anunoby. The rumor was premature but correct: the Knicks traded for Anunoby in December.

Not worried about balancing money— happy to take more action on one side, especially if it thinks the other side is sharp	In principle might want to balance money on different sides of the line, though this is hard in practice
Sports betting is the core business	Sometimes an "amenity" as part of a larger business
Moves lines in response to sharp bettors	Piggybacks off the market makers and moves lines in response to them

I have no doubt that companies like DraftKings know what they're doing; they and FanDuel are lapping the rest of the U.S. field in market share. My VIP friend will sometimes fire as much as $25,000 on the Rangers just to have some action to sweat. That's a valuable customer, worth a few cases of cabernet. But the retail books aren't particularly good at *bookmaking*. That's where the market makers come in.

Let me give you a real-life example of how this works. On February 20, 2023, I bet $1,100 on the Toronto Raptors as 3.5-point favorites at home against the New Orleans Pelicans for a game that was set to be played three days later following the NBA All-Star break. This bet was placed at a relatively sharp, market-making online book that I'll identify as BOSS (Big Online Sports Site). The line had just popped up on my DonBest screen, a service that offers real-time tracking of lines from dozens of sportsbooks around the world. DonBest's software isn't pretty—the user interface looks like a Microsoft Excel spreadsheet that mated with a Christmas ornament— but it's fast and that's what counts. BOSS had been one of the first sportsbooks anywhere in the world to post the line, and it hadn't been up for long. I may have been one of the first people to bet it.

A $1,100 bet is small in sports-betting terms—professionals generally want to get tens of thousands down on a game. But $1,100 was as much as BOSS was willing to let me or anybody else bet on this particular game at that particular time. And when I bet it, they *immediately* moved the line. Instead of Raptors -3.5, they were now offering Raptors -4.5—I'd affected their price for every other bettor in the world. At that point, BOSS offered to let me bet an additional $1,100 at the new price, but I didn't think it was a great value so I declined.* Meanwhile, I could see other sports-books starting to post the game on DonBest. Often, this happens within minutes; a market-making book dips its toes in the water and suddenly there's a cascade. Everyone dives headfirst into the pool, often copying their price.

All right, let's unpack this. Why did BOSS move their line based on my measly $1,100 bet? Well, they probably think I'm sharp. BOSS quite often moved opening NBA lines when I bet them. But they don't have to think I'm *that* sharp. They're getting information off me cheaply.

Let's back up one step further. How'd BOSS come up with Raptors -3.5? Some nerd in a boiler room made up a number. He didn't quite make it up out of thin air—he probably looked at some computer ratings and maybe he even talked with another nerd on the opposite side of the desk. But this is a much less advanced process than you might think.

"We're usually first to market on NFL lines," Kornegay told me of how the Westgate sets its opening lines. "That process is very unsophisticated. It's like, yeah, like, what do you make it? Five, three and a half, four—okay, give us four. And then sometimes we'll have a little debate on it."

Basically, that nerd at BOSS was inviting me into the conversation:

"Hmm—Raptors-Pellies, let's go three and a half?"

"Oh no, the Raptors have looked pretty good since that trade, gotta be at least four and a half, five."

"Okay, you seem to have a lot of conviction—let's go with four and a half."

"Yeah, I could push you on five versus four and a half, but that's close enough."

I'm getting paid to partake in this conversation—paid in expected value. But I'm not getting paid that well. Let's say I was right that the nerd's line was off by a point or a point and a half. If that's the case, my bet should win about 55 percent of the time. But BOSS is charging me juice

---

* Many market-making books will also let you bet again at the same price after a delay, even if they don't move their numbers on your initial bet. This underscores the conversational nature of the bookmaking process. You can see exactly how confident they are, and they can see exactly how confident you are.

when my bet hits. So 55 percent of the time, I'll make $1,000, and 45 percent of the time, I'll lose $1,100. If you calculate that out, my EV is +$55. That's my consulting fee. It's pretty cheap, considering that BOSS is going to increase its limits as we get closer to game time—by tipoff, they may take bets of $25,000 or more.

"The object of any bookmaker is to get to the closing line as early as possible, as fast as possible, for as cheap as possible," Spanky told me. That's the definition of good bookmaking—which is exactly what the Westgate was doing when it took Peabody's bets. He was able to bet more than I did ($2,000 rather than $1,100) and he's a lot better than I am, so his EV will be higher than mine—maybe it's $250. That's still cheap as a consulting fee—cheap enough that Peabody has to decide which bets to fire immediately and which to leave in his holster. Betting limits increase over the course of the week, so if he can get $20,000 on a good line instead of $2,000 on a great line, waiting may be higher EV.

So let's clear up one common misconception about sports betting. You'll often hear people say things like, "Oh, it's so hard to beat Vegas. Those guys are so sharp." No, it's not really so hard. Square me off against that nerd in the boiler room on something I specialize in, like NBA point spreads, and I'll do all right. Remember, the bettor gets to play offense, looking for vulnerabilities in the sportsbook's very large attack surface. With such a large menu, edges aren't that hard to find on opening lines.

No. *What's hard to beat is the market.* Because at some point, Spanky is going to bet the game. Rufus Peabody is going to bet the game. Some fucking hedge fund in Dublin is going to bet the game. And if the bookmaking process is working properly, I have to beat *those* guys. "Basically, the smartest people in the world who are doing this for a living, trying to make real money from it, are betting into these market makers and moving the markets in real time," said Miller. "You're essentially indirectly competing against the smartest, most informationally savvy groups in the world."

The Four Key Skills for Sports Bettors

What exactly makes those bettors so savvy? Sports-betting talent is hard to find because the game involves three distinct skills, Miller told me, and "the number of people who check all three boxes is vanishingly small."

- First, there's **betting knowledge**, "understanding markets and trading and counterparty risk," as Miller put it.

- Second, there's **analytical skills**—the ability to test statistical hypotheses and build models.

- Third, there's **sports domain knowledge**—you're not going to do a very good job of betting on a sport that you've never watched before.

There's also a fourth area that becomes increasingly important as you scale up the size of your ambitions: **networking skills**. The sharpest sports bettors I've met aren't necessarily super extroverted, but they aren't lone wolves, either—they're the *kind of guys who know a lot of guys*. They usually delegate their work and need networks of people to provide them with models and information. It also helps to have an ear to the ground to sniff out potential opportunities—the sports-betting equivalent of what venture capitalists call "deal flow." And since they inevitably face severe limits from sportsbooks, they'll also need people to assist them in placing bets.

If I were to develop a series of sports-betting action figures, you'd already have collected two of them and their respective superpowers: Spanky Kyrollos (the Better Bettor)* and Rufus Peabody (the Modeler). So let's complete the set.

---

* Spanky's podcast is named *Be Better Bettors.*

Bob Voulgaris: The Edge Finder

Haralabos "Bob" Voulgaris has come a long way since I profiled him for *The Signal and the Noise.* He'd already worked his way up from being an airport skycap who made a pair of daring bets on the Los Angeles Lakers to the literal top of the gambling landscape with a $12,500-a-month home in the Hollywood Hills. Then in 2018, after a long run during which Voulgaris says he sometimes made eight figures per year betting sports, he accepted a full-time position working as director of quantitative research and development for the Dallas Mavericks. His tenure ended after three years amidst an internal power struggle, but it was an unambiguous sign of how the NBA was not just tolerating but embracing the gambler's mindset.

Undaunted, Voulgaris purchased a third-division Spanish soccer team, CD Castellón, in 2022. As of March 2024, the players on Castellón are valued at "only" about €7 million by the soccer analytics website Transfermarkt. But Voulgaris, as usual, is gambling on the upside: Castellón is only two promotions away from the top Spanish division, La Liga, where the average franchise has players worth an estimated €250 million. It's not as far-fetched a leap as it sounds: the English club Brentford FC moved from the third division to the Premier League under the ownership of gambling magnate Matthew Benham. I'd say it's Voulgaris's biggest bet yet, although given the stories I've heard about him that may not be a safe assumption.

Voulgaris has a style of betting that doesn't fit neatly into Spanky's top-down/bottom-up paradigm. He's mostly looking for angles—essentially, diamonds in the rough like Castellón, highly profitable gambling opportunities that for some reason have been overlooked by the market. His most famous angle was betting totals (the combined number of points scored by both teams) in NBA games. A typical NBA total these days is 220 points. But sportsbooks, in their never-ending quest to take as much action as possible, will also let you bet on how many points will be scored in each half. This seems straightforward if you're a bookmaker—if the total is 220 points for the game, just divide by two and make it 110 for each half, right? Well, no. First halves are typically higher scoring by 3 points or so;

the players are better rested and the defense tends to be less vigorous. Only bookmakers did not realize this for many years, during which time Voulgaris could win prodigiously by betting overs in the first half and unders in the second.*

The diamonds in the rough today aren't as big and shiny as the ones Voulgaris found twenty years ago. Nonetheless, it's often a mystery why some things get priced into a betting line and others don't—and the only way to find angles is to spend a lot of time looking for them. In contrast to Spanky and Peabody, who both said they don't spend a ton of time watching games, Voulgaris is an NBA obsessive. "[It's] just having, like, a very, very, very specific skill set of being able to sit there and watch something for hours and pick up on stuff," he told me. "When you're betting a half-time total, you're focused, you're hyperfocused—every play is key."

An angle can be a lot of things. It might be a statistical hypothesis inspired by watching the sport. It might be that you've invested more effort or collected more data on a particular aspect of the game—Voulgaris spent years trying to quantify NBA player defense, for example. Or it could be having access to information that the betting public doesn't.

At every point, you have to ask yourself: How likely is it that I've stumbled into something that other people don't know—or at least don't appreciate the importance of? In 2022, I watched a match at the US Open between Serena Williams and the number-two-seeded player, Anett Kontaveit. The crowd—rowdy New Yorkers watching their favorite player on an electric late summer evening—was really behind Williams, who gutted her way to a three-set victory, the last win of her career. During the match, sensing the momentum behind Williams, I bet on her repeatedly. Was I picking up on something that others were missing? Nah, I probably just got lucky—the match was on national TV and played in front of almost thirty thousand fans.

At the other extreme, I have a friend who's a sharp tennis bettor who

---

* This somewhat understates the complexity of Voulgaris's angle. He also realized that different coaches are relatively more or less inclined to instruct players to intentionally foul when behind late in a game. Since free throws put points on the scoreboard without taking time off the clock, this makes a big difference to whether the over hits.

half coincidentally* happened to be at Nobu in the Crown casino in Melbourne, Australia, after Roger Federer had been eliminated in a grueling 2013 Australian Open semifinal against Andy Murray. He noticed the famously fastidious Federer getting tipsy, something he thought was out of character and suggested a player who wasn't in the right headspace. This was at least potentially a useful angle—information that the general public didn't have access to (as far as I can tell, there was never anything reported about Federer's night out in the press). He generally bet against Federer for the rest of the year, who indeed went into a slump, failing to make it past the quarterfinals in his next three Grand Slam events.

Having gone from an outsider to a high-ranking team executive, Voulgaris still thinks people putting money on the line are the best at spotting these angles. "There's some real sharp people [in the league] that if they applied themselves to sports betting, they could be very good at it," he told me. The problem, he said, is that their incentives still aren't aligned well. Even in an industry as competitive as the modern NBA, your highest EV play might be making your boss look good or protecting your reputation instead of necessarily getting the most accurate answer. "Nobody's risking their money. You know, there's a lot of confirmation bias," Voulgaris said. "They might be sharper in other aspects of life, or they might be sharper in other aspects of sports, but in terms of raw prediction, not even close."

Billy Walters: The Endboss

Billy Walters, widely regarded as the best sports bettor of all time, has long been a magnet for high-stakes company. His first betting partner in Las Vegas after he moved there from Kentucky—where he'd grown up so poor that he'd lost all his bottom teeth by the time he was in his twenties—was none other than Doyle Brunson. Walters came to Vegas in debt and had such a wild streak that even Brunson couldn't keep up. "That partnership

---

* My friend knows there is often knowledge to be gained from hanging out in the types of places where tennis players are likely to hang out, even if he isn't necessarily expecting an encounter in any particular instance.

only lasted a couple of weeks," Walters told me. "The amount of risk involved in sports and what I was doing at the time, he wasn't quite prepared for." Still, they remained lifelong friends. "I got up every day and was literally like a child being in the sandbox. All I did was either bet on sports, play golf, play poker, backgammon, gin rummy, being tutored by the best players in the entire world," Walters recalled of his early years in Vegas. "It was just the happiest time of my entire life."

It was during that period in 1983 when Walters had what might have been the most fateful meeting of his life—with Dr. Ivan "Doc" Mindlin of the so-called Computer Group. Mindlin was a Canadian who had moved to Las Vegas in the early 1970s to become an orthopedic surgeon but soon found himself infatuated with gambling. After initially losing money in the pits, Mindlin began experimenting with computer models to forecast baseball and college football games. The extent to which Doc's models were successful is unclear—but it didn't matter because Mindlin was less the brains behind the Computer Group than its charismatic front man.

The brains belonged to Michael Kent, a mild-mannered, socially awkward mathematician who had once worked at Westinghouse on a team that designed nuclear submarines. Kent had developed an algorithm to evaluate the performance of the company softball team, which he ran on Westinghouse's high-speed computers. Kent soon adapted his methods to college football and basketball, quietly refining his algorithms and saving money for seven years until he had enough confidence to quit his job and move to Vegas in 1979. He was sort of a forerunner of Rufus Peabody—but he lacked Peabody's composure and charisma, and found himself overwhelmed trying to get money down as a solo operator. The suave Mindlin made for the perfect partner. It was a profitable relationship: Kent's records showed that the Computer Group beat the spread as much as 60 percent of the time at college football, a success rate so high as to be nearly impossible today.

Walters, meanwhile, played a role more analogous to that of a hyperconnected Spanky Kyrollos. His job was to get as much money down as possible for the Computer Group in as many places as possible, something he was good at, given his insatiable appetite for risk and his fun-loving lifestyle, which made him a popular guy around town. Walters was also placing bets on his own, however, once betting $1.5 million—essentially his entire net worth—on the Michigan Wolverines as 4.5-point underdogs in the 1984 Sugar Bowl against the Auburn Tigers. Auburn won on a last-minute field goal—but Michigan covered the spread. Suddenly Walters was worth the equivalent of $10 million in today's dollars.

Walters would probably have blown through his windfall sooner or later had he not quit drinking cold turkey in 1989. Until that point, he wrote in his memoir, he had "lived on the edge and flaunted it" and "risked life and limb practically every day of my boom-and-bust existence."

The line between obsession and addiction can be thin in the River, and Walters channeled his obsessive tendencies into perfecting the craft of sports betting. There's not necessarily one neat trick in what makes for a good Walters bet so much as attention to every detail. In a 2022 NFL playoff game between the Los Angeles Rams and the Tampa Bay Buccaneers, for instance, Bucs offensive tackle Tristan Wirfs was injured. Ordinarily, this wouldn't have been that big a deal. However, several factors conspired to magnify its importance. Wirfs's backup was *also* hurt, the Rams had a great pass rush, and Bucs QB Tom Brady—however legendary—was forty-four years old and on his last legs. The injury, which would ordinarily be worth around 1.5 points, was instead worth as many as 6 points for the Rams in Walters's model—enough to make the difference in a game the Rams won on a field goal as time ran out.

What Walters preaches more than anything else—apart from the value of hard work—is the importance of seeking out consensus. Domain knowledge? Betting knowledge? Analytical skills? He'll take all of the above, thank you very much. Even in his late seventies, Walters and his partners were "experimenting with deep learning algorithms" and "taking a look at random forests," he told me—some of the same machine learning techniques that are used to power AI systems like ChatGPT. He didn't feel like they had much choice—either you keep up or get lapped by the competition. "We've never ever stopped looking for different angles," he said.

"Because one thing I know for sure, you're competing against the smartest people in the world."

Walters isn't running these models or collecting all of this information himself—instead he has a network of quants, sharps, and informants that he's been working with for decades, and who have remained loyal to him even after he was sentenced to five years for an insider stock trading conviction in 2018.* Although many of the bettors I spoke with for this book use multiple sources—for example, averaging together two or more models—Walters takes one additional step. *His sources only talk to Walters, not to one another.* In fact, his sources don't even know one another, Walters told me. This serves two purposes. First, it protects him in case one source is compromised. Walters doesn't take kindly to disloyalty; he's had a falling-out with Mindlin ever since Mindlin welched on a debt in 1986. Second—intentionally or not—Walters is following academic research on the wisdom of crowds. Group decision-making is more likely to be wiser when members of the group are able to operate independently, reducing the potential for groupthink. "I'm looking for independent opinions," he said. "I'm not looking for something that's going to be skewed by someone else."

Winners Not Welcome

You might reasonably assume there's no worse time to watch TV than if you're in a swing state in the week before a major election; literally every commercial is a political ad. But I can think of one notable exception: if you were a sports fan in late 2015. That's when DraftKings and FanDuel,

---

* Walters's sentence was commuted on January 20, 2021, by President Trump on his last day in office after Walters had served two years in prison and two years under house arrest. In his memoir, Walters maintains his innocence and blames the golfer Phil Mickelson, who was also implicated in the scandal and agreed to forfeit his trading profits, for failing to come to his defense. I have not tried to evaluate the particulars of the case, which involved tips that Walters allegedly received from a member on the board of Dean Foods. I will say, however, that sports bettors often take a cavalier attitude toward inside information in sports—if you get a tip from a team official on a player injury, for instance, the official may be putting themselves at risk, but that's usually considered their problem and not yours. The Securities and Exchange Commission is much less likely to give you the benefit of the doubt if you're betting on stocks.

buoyed by a flood of venture capital investment, deluged the airwaves with more than $220 million in ads during a fourth-month window of the NFL season.

"There's a game within a game that requires a different set of skills," read one typical DraftKings script from that period, which featured a montage of middle-aged male nerds awkwardly glued to their DraftKings app in social settings. (Somehow, this was supposed to be an advertisement *for* their product.) "And we don't just play. We are players. We train. And we win."

This was not a subtle pitch: they were advertising a *skill game*. Do the work, run the numbers, and you can outsmart your friends and be the next guy who breaks out of his boring cubicle job to win lots of money. Maybe you can even get laid! In another DraftKings spot, set at the "Fantasy Sports Hall of Fame," there was a statue of a "former accountant" named Derek Bradley. "DraftKings one-day fantasy baseball took him from a guy with holes in his underpants to a guy with bikini models in them," the ad explained.

Today's sportsbook commercials don't hit the same notes. They'll advertise that sports betting is a lot of fun or that there are a lot of different ways to bet, or show celebrities or former athletes using their product. But they're usually careful *not* to imply that sports betting is a skill game or that you can be a long-term winner—because they don't want you to be one.

In the sports betting that I've described thus far, you are betting against the house. But in 2015, these companies were advertising a different product called daily fantasy sports (DFS). It works like this: you have a budget, you draft a team of players, and you accumulate points based on their real-life statistics. But you're competing in a tournament against other players and not the house. DraftKings and FanDuel make money by taking a fixed share of the prize pool—somebody is going to win, so they don't really care if it was you or another middle-aged nerd.

In fact, they wanted to emphasize that DFS *was* a game of skill—and the presence of long-term winners helped prove their case. FanDuel and

DraftKings preferred the skill game argument because that was the legal basis for DFS. The UIGEA, the 2006 law that banned payment processors from facilitating deposits to online poker accounts, contained a carve-out for fantasy sports on the basis that they were a skill game. So ironically, the effort to ban online poker led to the proliferation of gambling on fantasy sports.*

With full-blown sports betting having been legalized in many states, DraftKings and other sites are no longer dependent on the skill-game loophole. So in some cases, their attitude toward sports betting is 180 degrees removed from the one they had for DFS. Instead of advertising that skilled players can win, DraftKings is explicit that they *don't* want winners on the sportsbook side of their business. "If a lot of that money is going out the side door to sharps who don't even enjoy your product and are completely platform-agnostic and have no loyalty at all—then like, why *wouldn't* you do something to control that?" said Jon Aguiar, an executive at DraftKings.

Well, one answer to Aguiar's question is that public statements like these handcuff DraftKings' most powerful marketing tool—its appeal to the male ego. It's entirely plausible that DraftKings is losing out on more action from guys who mistakenly think they can win than they're saving by not taking sharp action.

"It's *designed* for you to lose money," said Kelly Stewart, a.k.a. Kelly in Vegas, one of the most prominent women in the industry and also one of the people with the cheekiest no-BS attitude. "I tell people this all the time. If every ten-dollar bet I make, I have to give you eleven dollars to make that bet, it's not conducive to me being able to win long-term. I mean, the odds are *literally* stacked against you. And so for anybody to

---

* It may even have contributed to the presence of fully legal online sports betting. Beginning with Major League Baseball in 2013, several of the major sports leagues invested in DFS startups. And in 2014, NBA commissioner Adam Silver wrote an op-ed in *The New York Times* arguing for fully legal sports betting. The 2018 Supreme Court decision that repealed PASPA didn't specifically mention DFS, but the Supreme Court is often responsive to changes in public and elite opinion. In this case, the shift has been dramatic. In 2012, the NBA had been one of the plaintiffs in the PASPA case, suing the state of New Jersey for its attempt to legalize sports betting. By the time the court ruled, it was rooting against its own case.

think that they can beat that long-term without putting in a lot of work is pretty cynical. I mean, maybe guys are just lying to themselves."

For as much as sportsbooks and sharp bettors have an adversarial relationship, they also share a common interest: they're both dependent on recreational bettors to make their profits. In the long run, the size of the industry is dictated by how much money people are willing to make bad bets. For instance, if the boxer Floyd Mayweather, a notoriously big bettor, is willing to bet $1 million on the "wrong" side of the Super Bowl with an EV of -$50,000, that's the equivalent of $50,000 of income dropped out of a helicopter for sportsbooks and sharps to fight over.

There are two main reasons* that someone might make a -EV bet: first, because they find it entertaining, or second, *because they think they're making a good bet when they aren't.* Sportsbooks like DraftKings call themselves "entertainment products," seeking to capitalize on the first type of customer. But they aren't doing much to encourage the second type. In fact, if a sportsbook known to aggressively limit winning players *is* taking your action, you should ask yourself why—they are basically telling you they think you're a loser.

Nonetheless, DraftKings' attitude is common throughout the industry—and I was soon feeling the impact of it. By April 2023, barely a year after I'd begun betting seriously, I'd been limited by DraftKings, BetMGM, PointsBet, and Resorts World Bet. There isn't any hard data on how aggressive the various sportsbooks are at restricting players, although a 2022 *Washington Post* article matched my experience, suggesting that DraftKings, BetMGM, and PointsBet are more aggressive about limiting players, and Caesars and WynnBET are less so. (I still have a clean bill of health at Caesars, although WynnBet limited me in March 2024.)

That leaves FanDuel, the largest U.S. sportsbook by market share, in an in-between category. It was one of the first books I'd signed up with

---

* A third potential motivation is that someone who is learning the ropes may be willing to make -EV bets in the short run for the chance to become a winning bettor in the long run. This motivation is also discouraged by sites that aggressively limit players—if the minute that you become any good, you're going to get limited, that's a strong disincentive to invest your time learning how to bet sports in the first place.

when New York sports betting went live, and it felt like we had a good relationship. By the time the 2022–23 NBA season began, I was taking NBA betting rather seriously—but before then I'd been mixing in some semi-sharp plays with tossing a few hundred bucks on the Rangers if I went to a game or the NFL playoffs if I was watching on TV. It looked like a recreational player's betting pattern, and FanDuel even reached out at one point about whether I'd be interested in joining their VIP program—in other words, they thought I was a fish.

FanDuel was also helpful in arranging a series of meetings for me at their slick offices in Manhattan. I spoke with several of their executives—but it was Conor Farren, then their SVP of sports product and pricing, whom I was most interested in talking with. Essentially Farren, who has since left the company, ran FanDuel's trading desk, coming over when FanDuel was acquired by the Irish company Paddy Power Betfair (now Flutter) just ten days after the Supreme Court decision in 2018.

Farren, who has the quietly intense demeanor of a poker player and hasn't lost his Irish accent, claimed that FanDuel was more willing to take sharp action than its competitors. "I get the sense we are much fairer than other books, in terms of what we allow sharp customers to bet on a regular basis," he said. Although, he said, it had taken them a lot of work to get to that point.

"When I started here, four and whatever years ago, we didn't have any staff. We had to really hire people and get our shit together and start pricing things more accurately," he said. "The greatest solution to risk management is perfect pricing. It's not always easy, because we've got two million things a month we're putting on-site. . . . But philosophically, if somebody's doing their own [work] and it's just smart, they should be allowed to have a fair bet."

I'm sure that it is hard to come up with accurate pricing for 2 million bets per month—but there's nothing that requires FanDuel to have such a large menu. The book widely considered the sharpest U.S. sportsbook, Circa, essentially takes the In-N-Out Burger approach to FanDuel's

McDonald's, offering a narrow menu but doing every item well.* And Circa is confident enough in its lines that it's well-known for almost never limiting customers. Nonetheless, it's clear that FanDuel is doing *something* right. Not only is it playing increasingly good defense—it will also go on offense, making high-risk bets of its own if it thinks they're +EV.

Get in the car, kids, because we're going line shopping—that's the term that sports bettors use when they're looking for the most favorable price between different betting sites. It's three p.m. on Super Bowl Sunday; in a few hours, Super Bowl LVII will kick off between the Kansas City Chiefs and the Philadelphia Eagles. Here are the moneylines at the largest U.S. sportsbooks:

Super Bowl Moneylines

Team	FanDuel	PointsBet	Caesars	DraftKings	BetMGM
Chiefs	-104	+100	+110	+100	+100
Eagles	-112	-120	-130	-120	-120

If you're not used to reading betting lines, don't worry about it—the takeaway is that FanDuel was offering a *much* better price on the Eagles (and a worse one on the Chiefs) than the other sportsbooks. If you'd bet $100 on the Eagles at FanDuel and the Eagles won, you'd make a profit of $89. The same bet would earn you just $83 at DraftKings and $77 at Caesars.

In fact, FanDuel was knowingly inviting action on the Eagles. Were they doing this to balance out their books? Nope.† Just the opposite. Most of the public money was already on Philly. "A guess, which is pretty

---

* It's much faster to pull lines off the board in the event of player injuries where a person with inside information could make +EV bets, for instance. It also offers far fewer player props, and more limited in-game betting.
† Time for some more myth busting: it's usually a myth that sportsbooks seek to balance their books. In fact, this is often impossible to do anyway. Public money is intrinsically lopsided; the public likes betting the over, and the public likes favorites, especially as part of parlays. And the public can get fixated on a particular media narrative. "In theory, that sounds good, you know, balancing both sides. But I almost call it like an urban legend, because it rarely, rarely happens," Jay Kornegay told me.

educated I'd say, is that seventy-five to eighty percent of the money was on the Eagles," said Farren. Instead, he said, they were "holding what we thought was the true price"—what their models told them. The public might have preferred Philly, but there's a lot of dumb money on the Super Bowl so Farren didn't care. Their models liked the Chiefs, and they were right; KC spectacularly came back to win 38–35.

To continue offering bettors a favorable price on the Eagles was a genuinely risky decision. Farren told me that FanDuel had modeled out worst-case scenarios for the Super Bowl—and they were bad. Many players bet so-called single-game parlays, typically involving a combination of team and player performance. (For instance, the Eagles winning, the over, and their QB Jalen Hurts having at least three hundred passing yards.) If "all the star players scored [in a] high scoring game" and the Eagles won, FanDuel could potentially have been on the line for $400 to $500 million, Farren said. It was "not enterprise risk, not like, you know, we-can't-pay-the-bills sort of risk" but "we kind of had to make sure we had the money there to pay for it." This was a decision worthy of the River, one far removed from the sportsbook-as-amenity model.

There's a twist, however. On April 4, 2023, the very night after my FanDuel interviews and all Farren's talk about taking sharp action, I tried to place a $2,500 bet with them on the next day's Nets-Pistons NBA game. Transaction declined. The border of the betting window turned red and I got a note: "MAX WAGER $2,475.37." This had literally never happened before when I'd tried to bet at FanDuel. It's plausible the timing was a coincidence—the last time I'd made a bet large enough to trigger this limit had been several weeks earlier—so I can't say whether it happened because of my visit. But the conclusion was the same either way: I'd been limited by yet another sportsbook.

In the case of FanDuel, those limits are at least reasonable—a couple thousand bucks. In fact, although I didn't realize at the time I spoke with him that I'd been limited, Farren had said something that foreshadowed it when I'd asked him how FanDuel treats winning players. "You've had a bet to win a reasonable night, you know, a couple of grand or whatever," he continued. "We get information, we straighten our prices. There's something there—there's a place for us all to live."

Essentially, FanDuel was offering sharp bettors a compromise: you can bet up to the amount that your information is worth. For someone like me—who treats sports betting as a perhaps marginally profitable side hustle—that might work reasonably well; a couple of grand is usually as much as I'd want to bet anyway.

But that deal doesn't work for a Spanky, for a Bob Voulgaris, and certainly not for a Billy Walters. For them, even five-figure bets aren't necessarily enough. "I'm not interested in betting ten, twenty, thirty, forty, fifty thousand dollars. I'm not remotely interested," Walters told me. They're sitting on information worth far more than FanDuel is willing to pay for it—and so they have to resort to other tactics to get as much money down as they want.

How to Get the Money Down

The "thing that separated me from the rest of these guys is ninety-five percent of all the betting I did, I did on the day of the game," said Walters. "Once you get to the day of the game, you can bet a lot of money. Tell me somebody who can beat this stuff consistently. I don't want to sound braggadocious, but I'm the only guy I know."

Maybe it was his Kentucky drawl—or maybe it was because of the praise I heard for him from other bettors—but Walters didn't sound braggadocious. NFL point spreads on Sunday before kickoff are considered the most unbeatable numbers in the industry. Americans now legally bet somewhere around $50 million on the average NFL game—an amount so robust that sportsbooks almost dare sharps to beat their lines. But almost nobody can, except for Walters.

The very sharpest endboss bettors—Walters on football, Voulgaris on the NBA, Peabody on golf or Super Bowl props—can even cannibalize their own market when they bet. The moment they first put money down, they'll potentially affect the market price all the way until the game starts. So they have to figure out when to hold their fire. Voulgaris told me that in his heyday, influential bettors had a shared appreciation of the game theory behind when they made their move. It was "understood that me and the other competing groups wouldn't bet too early," he said. They'd wait until ten a.m. to start betting, by which point they were generally allowed to bet max limits. "Someone could get in there and get smaller limits, but nobody ever really did it." Nowadays, there are too many skilled bettors for effective coordination. The prisoner's dilemma prevails: somebody reasonably sharp will defect from the coalition and bet a line before you.

Still, this is a high-class problem. If you're so sharp as to be the center of gravity for the entire market in a particular sport, then congratulations—you're going to make a lot of money betting sports. Maybe not as much as twenty years ago, but plenty.

The rest of us mortals are left to chase after three magic words: "closing line value."

Closing line value means how the line you bet compares to the final line before the game began. For instance, for that Toronto Raptors game I described earlier, I bet the Raptors at -3.5 and the line closed at Raptors -4.5. That means I got solid closing line value—the Raptors became bigger favorites and the line moved in the direction of my bet. As a result, I'd have a winning bet more often. If the Raptors won by 4 points, my bet would win, while someone who bet just before tipoff would lose.

There are various ways to get closing line value, and almost all of them correlate with being a winning bettor in the long run. If you have a knack for picking off weak opening lines when the nerds first post them, you're going to get good closing line value. If you have a good read on an injury situation—or inside information about it—you'll get it too. You can also get closing line value through a practice called "steam chasing," though sportsbooks really hate bettors who do it.*

---

* Steam chasing is placing a bet at a book when it's slow to update its lines. For instance, say a big betting syndicate makes a bet on the Green Bay Packers at an offshore site in the middle of the night, moving the consensus price from Packers -3.5 to Packers -4. Only the nerd managing the line for PointsBet was asleep at the switch and they still have the game at -3.5. This number will usually get favorable closing

Number of Bets Won After 100 Independent Bets

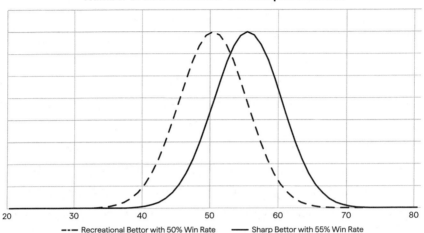

–•– Recreational Bettor with 50% Win Rate   —— Sharp Bettor with 55% Win Rate

Sportsbooks like looking at closing line value because it's a less noisy indicator than your won-loss record. Even after a hundred bets, for instance, how much you've profited or lost overwhelmingly reflects noise, not signal. However, a skilled bettor can get closing line value a large majority of the time, and someone who consistently gets closing line value is almost certain to have winning results over the long run.

This is why it's tricky to give you ironclad advice on how to win at betting sports. The very practices that are the most profitable—the ones that most reliably get you closing line value—are also the ones that sportsbooks are quickest to limit you for.

Bettors—particularly top-down bettors like Spanky who engage in arbitrage tactics like steam chasing—are therefore constantly engaged in acts of subterfuge. Most of these tactics fall into one of two categories: you can make dumb bets with accounts the sportsbook thinks are sharp, or sharp bets with accounts they think are dumb. It's really pretty much the same game as the one Jeff Ma and the MIT Blackjack Team were playing: you have to disguise that you're a sharp player.

line value and is a good candidate for a bet. But you can't do it too often without getting limited. When you're an originator, betting based on a proprietary model, at least you're providing some useful information to the sportsbook. But when you're steam chasing, you aren't—the sportsbooks know full well when they're slow to update a line.

One tactic is a head fake. Remember how I said that BOSS would usually move its NBA opening lines when I bet them for as little as $1,100? Well, that creates a potential opportunity for me.* Let's say that BOSS opens up its line with the Nuggets +4 on the road against the Lakers. I like the Nuggets at this price. So I go to BOSS and bet my $1.1K on . . . the Lakers! Remember, BOSS thinks I'm sharp, so they move the line to Nuggets +5, meaning the price is now even more attractive. A few minutes later, DraftKings opens up for betting on the game, copying the BOSS line of Nuggets +5. DraftKings will let me bet $10,000—so I hit the Nuggets there. I've run a head fake—the sports-betting equivalent of a bluff. By initially betting the other way, I got a lot of money down on the side I liked at an even better price.

Although there's one thing wrong with this example. DraftKings probably isn't going to let me bet $10K on NBA opening lines for any length of time. That's just not the kind of thing that recreational bettors do. But let's say *I'm a guy who knows some guys*. A "beard" is industry slang for someone who places a bet on your behalf. Let's say I know a guy with a big DraftKings account, a player they consider to be a VIP, and he bets $10K for me. We agree to share the profits.† That's bearding.

So Spanky and other bettors are constantly on the hunt for the same thing that poker players are after—whales, that is rich guys or degens with a credible history of betting big who will get a lot of rope before they're outed as a beard. "I had an article published about me in *Cigar Aficionado*. That's a very good publication that whales read," Spanky told me. Other bettors cultivate relationships with whales by playing poker, or just by living in the gambling high life in what I call the "splash zone." Voulgaris once even used the boxer Floyd Mayweather as a beard, he said, "but like only for like a day, or two days, because he was so difficult to work with."

Once you have a whale bearding for you, you'll need to protect that

---

* No, I never actually attempted a head fake. It takes a lot of things to line up for it to work and it should be considered a high-degree-of-difficulty technique.

† Voulgaris told me he gave his beards two options. They could either take a 50/50 share of the bets, meaning they could either profit or lose—or they could take a one-quarter freeroll, meaning they'd share 25 percent of any profits but weren't on the hook for any losses. "We always rooted for them to take the freeroll because we would just never lose," he told me.

account carefully. Your expected-value calculation is no longer just about how likely the bet is to win or lose, but the long-term effect it will have on the sportsbook's perception of the customer—because sportsbooks are 100 percent aware that their whales can be flipped. "That's happened to us many times. We've got a VIP, somebody got his ear," said John Murray of the Westgate. "Now his betting patterns have changed. And we've got to lower his limits." I'm not going to go through every tactic, but you'll actually want to prevent your whale from consistently getting good closing line value. You might have him fire off neutral or slightly -EV bets just before kickoff on random NFL games, for instance.

Disclaimer: using a beard will almost definitely violate the terms of service at whatever site your whale is betting at. Terms of service, schmerms of service, who cares, fine. Whether bearding is *illegal* depends on a lot of factors—I'm not qualified to provide advice, so you should check with an attorney if you're seriously thinking about doing this. Prosecutions for so-called messenger betting are rare but hardly unheard-of.

And having a lot of money change hands for gambling-related reasons always has the potential to bring trouble. Kyrollos, for instance, was charged with bookmaking by the Queens district attorney in 2012. Similarly, the Computer Group was targeted by the FBI in a series of raids beginning in 1985. In these situations, the defendants will typically combat bookmaking charges by arguing—often correctly—that they were merely betting on sports and not taking bets as a bookmaker does. But prosecutors, judges, and juries will see lots of cash changing hands in a complex web of financial transactions—more than one bettor I spoke with for this book told me stories of receiving large cash payments in briefcases or paper bags—and may not appreciate the difference. The odds of avoiding serious sanctions or even jail under these circumstances are often no better than a coin flip. For instance, although the Computer Group was eventually acquitted, Spanky pled guilty to a felony charge of "promoting gambling."

Although I don't think that going after sports bettors is a good use of government resources in the first place, the retail market in the U.S. in its current state won't put an end to this chicanery. In fact, the wide spread in betting limits at the U.S. retail sites may make it worse. Information may or may not want to be free—but if a whale can bet $1 million on a game at DraftKings and a sharp bettor can only get down a few bucks, there are obvious incentives for information to overcome whatever friction there is and to flow from the sharp bettor to the whale.*

Because Spanky is right about one thing: no matter how good you are at reading a betting line or building a model, if you can't get your money down, you're not going to win at sports betting. "This is the only frickin' occupation that you're punished for being good," he said. "The American Dream we all grow up with is if we get good at something, we're gonna get rewarded. Instead you get kicked in the ass."

I Bet $1.8 Million on the NBA.
Here's What I Learned.

It was inevitable that I'd get into betting sports at some point. I like sports. I like betting. And I live close enough to Madison Square Garden that I can see its uber-bright electronic marquee billboard from my apartment window—so I had Caesars Sportsbook ads beamed directly into my living room around the clock.

At first my betting was pretty casual, but when the 2022–23 NBA season began, I determined to take it more seriously, developing a routine and keeping diligent track of my bets. I came into the season with some advantages: (1) I'm a huge NBA geek who was already devoting a lot of time to following the sport; (2) I built an NBA model and forecasting system called RAPTOR; (3) when the season began, I had a clean bill of sportsbook health, able to bet freely at all but one of the New York State retail sites. I also had some disadvantages: (1) RAPTOR was *public*, so to the extent it's sharp, its information may already have been incorporated in the betting lines; (2) before long, I'd get limited by quite a few sites; (3) I had a lot of other distractions, including working on this book.

---

* If I were drafting sports-betting legislation, I would put limits on these spreads—what's known in the industry as "stake factors." For instance, maybe even the biggest sharp gets to bet a minimum of $2,500 on an NBA opening line, and even the biggest whale can bet no more than $10K—a 4x spread. If a sportsbook isn't able to profit under those circumstances, even though it's collecting juice on every winning bet, then maybe it shouldn't be in business.

I did make money, though not much relative to the amount I was betting.* I won a net of $18,513 on a series of so-called futures bets placed just before the NBA playoffs began because the Denver Nuggets won the Western Conference and NBA title at fairly long odds, earning me enough to more than make up for failed bets on the Boston Celtics and other teams.

But on the regular, game-by-game bets that I devoted so much time to? Well, let's be precise. I bet a total of $1,809,006. And I finished the year ahead by a whopping $5,242—for a paltry ROI of 0.3 percent.

Hey, it's not nothing; most bettors lose. Still, the value of the exercise was less in the (small) profit I made and more in what I learned along the way. I probably would have stumbled into some of these realizations anyway, but they were driven home by having skin in the game.

I was surprised at how little it took for sportsbooks to limit me.

We've covered this, but I wish I'd been more aware at the outset of how quickly you can get limited. I wasn't really making much effort to cover my tracks. For instance, PointsBet was routinely slow to update its lines when players were injured—an NBA reporter would tweet that a player was hurt, and I might get a good minute or two to bet the game before their line was updated. I knew that PointsBet wouldn't like this, and I tried not to take advantage of it *too* much—but it's not surprising that they limited me. Still, I was also limited by sites like DraftKings where I wasn't taking advantage of any such exploits.

I was surprised at how often my early bets moved the lines.

We've discussed this one too, but my bets on opening lines very often moved the line at two sites, and occasionally at others. I have to admit: it was a cool feeling when my relatively small bets cascaded across the entire betting market on my DonBest screen, affecting the consensus price. Bets closer to tipoff almost never had any such effect.

I hadn't appreciated how capital intensive sports betting is.

I made $1.8 million in bets over the course of the NBA season—but that doesn't mean I needed anywhere near that much in my accounts on any given night. Instead, I bet an average of about $10K an evening, while sometimes having the same amount outlayed for the next night's

---

* I also happened to do extremely well in a high-stakes NBA fantasy league in the 2022-23 season, but I'm not counting that because I consider that result lucky as much as anything else—fantasy sports are largely outside the scope of this chapter, and I lost money in the same league in 2023-24.

games. You'll lose some bets, but you'll also win some, and the profits go back into your account. Still, sometimes the best betting lines last for only a few seconds. If you want money ready to fire on a moment's notice at a half dozen betting platforms, that takes some real liquidity—especially when you're battling through one of your inevitable losing streaks.

I was surprised by the streakiness—even though I shouldn't have been.

I began the season on a tremendous heater, ahead almost $42,000 after barely more than a month. Maybe I was God's gift to sports betting? Surely it wouldn't be long before I'd buy a Spanish soccer team of my own to compete with Bob Voulgaris? Well, no. I immediately went on a losing streak that wiped out almost all of those profits. I'm not going to narrate every blip in the graph,* but it sort of speaks for itself:

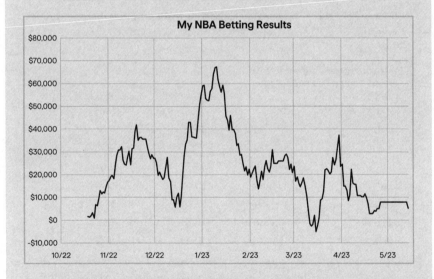

Is there anything going on here apart from mere randomness? Maybe. Two of my best stretches were at the start of the season, and then just after the NBA trade deadline in February. Those are times when there were a lot of new players on new teams—and when a statistical model

---

* What's with the long, flat stretch toward the end? It's because I basically decided to end the experiment in late April 2023 after Disney announced it would let go of most of the FiveThirtyEight staff—I needed my mental bandwidth for other things. But I made one last bet on a Celtics-76ers playoff game in May, which lost.

like RAPTOR that evaluates individual player performance potentially has the most value.

Still, one frustrating thing I discovered is that, even after having made bets on roughly 1,250 games and keeping track of lots of information associated with each bet, there wasn't a large-enough sample size to provide for many statistically significant conclusions. If winning 55 percent of your bets makes you a huge winner and 50 percent makes you a fish, even a full season's worth of bets won't necessarily tell you which category you belong in.

For the more technically inclined among you, let me show you a few numbers to underscore how thin the line can be between winning and losing. The data in the next table describes what your record would have been if you bet every game in the 2022–23 NBA season but got what amounted to bonus points when you did. For instance, if you got one bonus point per game—say, if instead of the consensus line of Celtics +2, you were able to bet the game at Celtics +3—you'd have won 53.7 percent of your bets and been solidly +EV.

The Importance of Every Point

BONUS POINTS VS. CLOSING LINE	RECORD	WIN PERCENTAGE	PROFIT MARGIN (ROI)
0 points	1289-1289-62	50.0%	-4.9%
½ point	1351-1245-44	52.0%	-0.7%
1 point	1395-1202-43	53.7%	+2.8%
1½ points	1438-1150-52	55.5%	+6.6%
2 points	1490-1104-46	57.3%	+10.4%
2½ points	1536-1070-34	58.8%	+13.6%
3 points	1570-1034-36	60.2%	+16.4%

How hard can it be to find one measly point of value per game—equivalent to a player hitting an additional free throw—when that's all it takes to be a solid winner? Based on my experience, it's hard.

I was surprised by how fast-paced sports betting can be.

Just like in poker, many sports-betting decisions involve incomplete information. You'll see a line that looks favorable, and you'd like to do some due diligence on it—maybe there's an injury that you weren't aware of? But a good line may go away after even five or ten seconds.

And if the line *is* still available, it may not be such a great bet after all. This is what economists call "adverse selection"—if you're being offered to buy a bet at a price that seems too good to be true, you have to ask why the sportsbook is willing to sell it to you.

I hadn't realized how much injuries—and other situations where you can get a leg up through inside information—can dominate other concerns.

This issue is particularly important in basketball, a sport where star players have a disproportionate impact. MVP-caliber players like Nikola Jokić, Giannis Antetokounmpo, or Steph Curry can easily make a difference of 6 to 8 points in the point spread. Such players are also frequently listed as "questionable" on official injury reports, implying that they're roughly 50/50 to play. If you had a reliable tip that one of these guys was going to play or that he wasn't, you'd have a bet that would win 60 to 65 percent of the time, instantly making you one of the best sports bettors in the world.

Even in the absence of inside information, there's a lot of value from decoding statements made by reporters, coaches, or team executives about player injuries. I thought I had a knack for picking up on some of this—until I spoke with Spanky, who told me that he has three full-time staffers whose entire job is to sort through injury news. The middle of the NBA season is less about basketball knowledge and instead more of an information hunt—a grind to figure out who is actually going to play.

Sports betting took more mental bandwidth than I expected, even when I wasn't "on the clock."

On average, I spent an hour to an hour and a half per day looking at betting lines and placing bets—on top of the considerable time I was already devoting to following the NBA. But that understates the degree to which sports betting can be preoccupying. Checking betting lines was often the first thing I did when I woke up and the last thing I did before going to bed. Meanwhile, my sports-betting habit and my Twitter habit fed off each other, since I was constantly looking for nuggets of new information. And then there's sweating your bets; there are NBA games continuously from seven p.m. to one a.m. almost every day—I was undoubtedly a worse guy to hang out with when there was a game on in the background.

Sports betting took more emotional bandwidth than I expected.

I don't *think* I went on tilt* or became addicted to sports betting at any point—but sometimes it's hard to know. To get some outside perspective, I spoke with Dom Luszczyszyn, a hockey writer for *The Athletic*, who published a daily picks column during the 2021-22 NHL season. Like me, Luszczyszyn suffered through some vicious winning and losing streaks—only he had the added pressure of making his picks in public, so when he had a losing week, so did his readers who were following them.

"It's not difficult to develop a gambling addiction or gambling problem, even if you know what you're doing," Luszczyszyn told me. "It's just this dopamine hit when you win, and you get addicted to it pretty easily."

The fact that you're engaging in a *skilled* form of gambling doesn't necessarily make this better—it can just be another rationalization to keep betting. "It's a difficult thing when it's something you're good at, where it's easy for me to say it should turn, it should regress," Luszczyszyn said. "But that same [attitude] can also lead you down a dangerous path where you feel a compulsion to bet because you don't want to miss the turnaround."

"A person who resorts to a game theory matrix when faced with a vital decision is reducing a painful risk to a calculated one," wrote Erving Goffman, the well-known sociologist who trained in Las Vegas as a blackjack dealer. "Like a competent surgeon, he can feel he is doing all that anyone is capable of doing, and hence can await the result without anguish or recrimination." Goffman didn't necessarily see this trait as admirable, however—he saw it as a coping mechanism, a form of superstition. In games of pure chance, you can at least blame bad luck when you hit a losing streak. In skill games like poker and betting sports, there is plenty of luck too—but it can be hard not to blame yourself.

---

* It can help to write down all your bets, as I was doing—you're a bit less likely to do something stupid if it's going to go on your permanent record.

Halftime

13

Inspiration: Thirteen Habits of Highly Successful Risk-Takers

Wait a minute. Is this some sort of misprint? What is chapter 13 doing in the middle of the book? Casinos the world over skip floor 13 because it's considered unlucky—and now I'm shoving 13 in your face where it doesn't belong?

Stay with me for a second. Most of the people you'll meet in this book are quantitative types, like poker players or investors. However, these are hardly the only people who undertake risks. So I want to introduce you to five exceptional people who take *physical* risks: an astronaut, an athlete, an explorer, a lieutenant general, and an inventor.* If this book was (even) longer, we could fill several more chapters with these people. So you might think of chapter 13 as the lone surviving chapter from a lost third part of *On the Edge*.†

In the introduction, I outlined two sets of attributes that are typical people in the River: the "cognitive cluster," characterized by a strong capacity for abstract, analytical reasoning, and the "personality cluster,"

---

* I'm slightly stretching the definition of "physical" in the latter case, but this person slept in her laboratory for nine months to avoid a threat of deportation while working on the invention that would eventually win her the Nobel Prize—I think that's close enough.
† Plus, thirteen is my lucky number. I was born on Friday the thirteenth.

characterized by high competitiveness, independent-mindedness, and risk tolerance. Where do our physical risk-takers fit within this rubric? Actually, more snugly than I would have thought when I first set out to speak with them. As you'll see, they certainly chart their own course in life. And even if they aren't quantitative per se, they are highly rigorous thinkers, meticulous when it comes to their chosen pursuit. One thing's for sure: our physical risk-takers are definitely not part of the Village. In fact, some of them had to escape the Village, finding it too risk-averse and slow-moving.

Plus, they have some great stories to share. I figure it's a good time for this, because we could use a little inspiration. I have to warn you: our tour is about to get darker as we leave Downriver and its spectacular casinos.

So here's the program. As my assistants serve you lunch, I'll introduce you to our expert panel of physical risk-takers. I'll bounce ideas off them, and we'll see where they have common ground with our quants. The resulting conversation is what I call "Thirteen Habits of Highly Successful Risk-Takers."

Kathryn Sullivan, our first panelist, overcame remarkable odds to become an astronaut, one of thirty-five candidates chosen out of almost ten thousand applicants as part of NASA Astronaut Group 8 in 1978. She wouldn't have seemed the most intuitive choice: at the time she was selected, Sullivan was pursuing a PhD from the Bedford Institute of Oceanography in Nova Scotia. However, NASA isn't necessarily looking for domain experts—nobody is an expert in outer space. "Even with SpaceX or a shuttle on its one hundred and twentieth flight, there are still human beings doing something for the first time," said Sullivan. And Sullivan, as you'll see, is a remarkable person. Astronaut Group 8 was the first NASA class open to women (another graduate was Sally Ride), and Sullivan later became the first American woman to perform a spacewalk. Competing in Houston against men who had military backgrounds and who all seemed to know one another—"I thought, well, sweetheart, enjoy your week"—Sullivan persisted despite the long odds. "I was clear on a couple things. I had become confident I could do this job," she told me. "[And] I knew I would love to do it."

Katalin Karikó has been a risk-taker her whole life. Growing up in Hungary when it was part of the Communist bloc, she immigrated to the United States in 1985 with her husband, her two-year-old daughter, and £900 smuggled in a teddy bear to avoid detection by Hungarian authorities. She doggedly pursued the idea that would later win her the Nobel Prize—mRNA technology, which led to the vaccines that would be deployed at an unprecedentedly quick pace in the COVID-19 pandemic—despite receiving uniformly skeptical responses from the academic hierarchy. Threatened with deportation by her supervisor at Temple University after she accepted a job at Johns Hopkins, which rescinded the offer as she challenged an extradition order, Karikó instead had to "run away" to take a position at Uniformed Services University in Bethesda, Maryland, spending nine months without a permanent address and sleeping in her office. Isolated from her family, Karikó had "nothing else to do, just read, read, read, and think," she said—think about mRNA, which she'd later develop in the private sector after she was repeatedly demoted from a later job at the University of Pennsylvania.

Dave Anderson is a former NFL wide receiver, primarily for the Houston Texans. Like many NFL players, Anderson still remembers his exact draft position: it was 251, just four players removed from number 255—the so-called Mr. Irrelevant who is the last pick of the draft. Relatively short for an NFL player at five eleven, though stocky and well-built, Anderson was a slot receiver,* a position that requires physical bravery because it involves catching balls in the middle of the field where there are linebackers like the six-four, 255-pound T. J. Watt making a beeline for you. "Your willingness to hit and be hit is ultimately what separates players," said Anderson. "You can have a big beautiful football player that doesn't want to run into people and you know what—I don't blame him. It's not a normal thing." About 2 percent of NFL players are injured per game. That

---

* NFL fans will recognize the archetype from former New England Patriots All-Pro Wes Welker.

might not sound like a big risk, but between a three-game preseason, a seventeen-game regular season, and potentially playoff games, it translates to about a 40 percent chance of being hurt every year. The cumulative effect of concussions and other injuries can be even worse. "Of the ten friends I have on our Texans chain that play fantasy football . . . over half can't do normal everyday things" like jogging or strenuous weight training, Anderson told me. I'm not anti-football, and Anderson obviously isn't either—he is now the CEO of the player tracking software company Break-Away Data—but football players really are our modern-day gladiators, risking permanent incapacitation in a simulation of warfare every week for our entertainment.*

Of course, there is still actual warfare too. **H. R. McMaster** is the former U.S. national security advisor and army lieutenant general. He's often put his reputation on the line—he frequently criticized President Trump both before and after being fired from the NSA position by tweet—as well as his life. "I have been in danger a number of times," he said. "The first time was in Desert Storm, when we encountered a much larger enemy force about four or five times our size in a sandstorm." He was awarded a Silver Star in 1991 for "gallantry in action" after the battle, which he won with an aggressive surprise maneuver as the entire battlefield was engulfed in smoke.

Finally, there's **Victor Vescovo**, who I'm introducing last because he has the most explicit crossover with the River—his day job is as a private equity investor. But his passion lies in exploration. Read any biography of Vescovo, and the phrase "first person" comes up a lot. He was the first person to reach both Earth's highest point (Mount Everest) and its lowest one (Challenger Deep in the Mariana Trench). He was the first person to dive to the bottom of each of the world's oceans. He's also one of fewer than seventy-five people to have completed the Explorer's Grand Slam by

---

* It says something about American society that NFL TV ratings have remained steady while ratings for other sports have slumped. Despite increasing media coverage of player safety, fans may like the NFL precisely because it is violent. Not unlike how Erving Goffman thought of gambling as a proxy for demonstrating one's bravery for men in white-collar jobs, we don our Travis Kelce and Jalen Hurts jerseys as they put their bodies on the line on our behalf.

reaching both the highest peak on every continent and the North and South Poles. And in 2022, he became one of the first fifty people to travel on the Blue Origin orbital spacecraft. Vescovo, who is also a former commander in the U.S. Navy Reserve, told me that the mentality required in exploration, the military, and investing is more similar than you might think. "It's risk assessment and taking calculated risks," he said. "And then trying to adapt to circumstances. I mean, you can't be human and not engage in some degree of risk-taking on a day-to-day basis, I'm just taking it to a different level."

So let's enumerate exactly what that mentality entails.

1. **Successful risk-takers are cool under pressure.** They don't try to be heroes, but they can execute when the chips are down.

Being calm when other people lose their shit is a rare quality—and one that's essential for a winning gambler. In poker, you never know when you'll suddenly find yourself playing on Day 6 of the Main Event for stakes thousands of times higher than your Tuesday night beer-league game. It doesn't matter how well you execute in everyday situations—you'll never reach the top of your craft if you choke when the pressure is on.

In football also, some plays are far more important than others, and Anderson told me injuries happen most frequently during unscripted, high-stakes moments: kickoff and punt returns, interceptions and fumbles. The problem is that players too often depart from standard operating procedure before thousands of screaming fans. "When there's a stadium full of people, you have to remind yourself [of] standard basic control. Don't try to do too much. If I do my job, and everyone does their job, we should be all right. Don't try to go rogue and make a play in front of seventy thousand [people] to be a hero."

Don't try to be a hero—just do your job. Vescovo, who trained naval pilots in the real-life version of the military program sometimes informally called Top Gun, used a nearly identical phrase. "Anyone in the military knows, the last thing you ever want to do is force anyone to do anything heroic." Vescovo told me he enjoyed 2022's *Top Gun: Maverick*—"It was a wonderfully entertaining film"—but thought it conveyed a false impression. "I had very many cringe moments because I actually was a targeting officer in the navy. That is not how it's done."

This attitude is also helpful when you're taking financial risks. "I'm exceedingly evenly keeled. You know, to put it in a poker metaphor, I don't have a tilt button," said David Einhorn, the founder of the hedge fund Greenlight Capital (and a high-stakes poker player) when I asked him what trait was most important to his success. This was interesting because when I met him at the Greenlight offices, I sensed that Einhorn was coming into the interview a little hot, the feeling you get from talking to a poker player when he's just lost a big hand. Einhorn later revealed why—he'd made a bad bet on interest rates. "It literally happened today. I thought the Fed was going to say one thing. And I made some investments along those lines. And I was just watching [Federal Reserve chairman Jerome] Powell talk. And he wasn't saying at all what I thought he was going to say. And so I took those bets off, and we lost some money on that."

The vital point here is *not* that Einhorn wasn't feeling the heat. In fact, as we learned in chapter 2, financial risk-taking triggers an innate physical stress response, a fight-or-flight reaction not so different from when we find ourselves in physical danger. This can cause people unfamiliar with the feeling to go on tilt. But if you've been under this sort of pressure before, and have the gift of being cool under fire, you'll be able to think clearly despite it—in Einhorn's case, for instance, by backing off his trades rather than doubling down.*

2. **Successful risk-takers have courage.** They're insanely competitive and their attitude is: bring it on.

In poker and sports betting, the vast majority of players lose money. You have no choice but to be toward the top of your field; otherwise you

---

* The reason I say that this reflects clear thinking is because most people suffer from what's called "anchoring bias," the tendency to be weighted down by information you learn early in your decision-making process. It's hard to change course, especially under stress.

won't make money at all. And to be at the *very* top requires a careful balance. Overconfidence can be deadly in gambling, but playing poker against the world's best players is not for the faint of heart.

"There's an extreme correlation that to be able to play against the best every day, and to be a world-class player, it takes a lot of hubris," said Scott Seiver, a former world number one in the Global Poker Index. "You have a lot of self-confidence to be a top one hundred poker player. It's just mandatory; you really have to have it baked into you."

The baked-in quality Seiver is referring to is somewhere between competitiveness and confidence—but a better word for it might be courage. Different people manifest it in different ways. There's Sullivan, with her quiet confidence that she could do the job of being an astronaut in a situation where many people would have developed imposter syndrome and felt like they didn't belong. There's Maria Ho, with her fuck-the-haters attitude, how she "really [doesn't] care what other people think" about the societal expectations for women.

It's the men in the River who sometimes can have more fragile egos and need more external validation, like "Poker Brat" Phil Hellmuth. Still, say what you want about Hellmuth—he's going into the arena, winning WSOP bracelets and heads-up matches against people half his age. And when I spoke with him, Hellmuth was self-aware enough to know that his "obsessive attention to detail" comes because "losing affects my self-esteem." He's not the only Riverian motivated by having a chip on his shoulder; this is also a common type in Silicon Valley, as you'll see in the next chapter. Courage obtained from wanting to prove people wrong is still better than cowardice.

However, even insanely competitive people need to find a place where their competitive drives are rewarded. Karikó found it more in the United States than in Communist-era Hungary. "If I would stay in Hungary," she told me,* "can you imagine I would go and sleep in the office?" In the

---

* Karikó grew up in a small town in Hungary where there were no English teachers, and by her own admission her English is still somewhat broken, something she thought was a barrier to success in academia. I've avoided trying to clean up her quotes too much.

United States, she found "the pressure is on in different things, so that is why it's great." She also found more opportunity to exercise her courage in the private sector, where rewards are more directly tied to results than in academia. Instead of trying to please bureaucrats or journal editors, "we have to go home if we don't have something that helps somebody," she said.

3. **Successful risk-takers have strategic empathy.** They put themselves in their opponent's shoes.

Okay, so people who take high-stakes gambles are competitive, courageous, and cool under fire. No big shockers there. But they also have another trait that I wouldn't have had on my list going into this project. It came up again and again in different contexts: empathy.

Now, this isn't the sort of touchy-feely empathy that you'd ordinarily associate with the term. That can be hard for Riverians. In psychological studies, there's a negative correlation between systematic thinking—what Riverians are skilled at—and empathetic behavior. Think of it this way: if you're good at abstract, analytical reasoning, you tend to abide by consistent principles rather than making too many exceptions for special cases or even special people.

But I'm not talking about coming across an injured puppy and having it tug at your heartstrings. Instead, I'm speaking of adversarial situations like poker—or war. McMaster spoke to me about the importance of strategic empathy, a term he attributed to the military historian Zachary Shore's book *A Sense of the Enemy*. McMaster thinks military planners often lack this sense, what the war looks like to the enemy on the ground. For instance, he was critical of what he called America's "flaming bag of feces strategy" in the Iraq War when he was serving there in 2006—"Just hand the Iraqis a flaming bag of feces and get out the door," the theory was, ignoring growing insurgent threats. "The problem is, in Washington, they're writing policies and strategies for MY-raq," he said, citing a comment made to him by an army colleague. "MY-raq can be whatever you want it to be. We're here in I-raq, where we have to confront the realities."

Strategic empathy also comes up in business. I asked Mark Cuban, the Broadcast.com cofounder and former principal Dallas Mavericks owner, how he sorts through the rapid-fire investor pitches that he hears on *Shark Tank*, the reality TV show on which he's been a panelist for more than a decade. Cuban told me that *Shark Tank* is more like real investor meetings than you'd think; in early stage investing, you're trying to filter through pitches quickly, and first impressions count for a lot. Cuban's best heuristic is to look at the company from the entrepreneur's perspective. "I tend to have a good feel for what a business needs to do to be successful. And so I can sit there and listen to their pitch, put myself in their shoes as if it was my company, and ask the [difficult] questions that I would need to deal with," he said. He takes the same tactic with his own businesses, just in reverse, looking at them from a competitor's point of view. "With my own companies, I always try to ask the question, 'How would I kick my own ass?'"

And of course, strategic empathy comes up in poker—which as we've seen is very much both a mathematical game and a people game. Some players like the chatty Seiver have what he calls an "innate . . . gift of connecting to people." However, unlike some of our thirteen traits, strategic empathy is potentially one that can be practiced and learned. Daniel "Jungleman" Cates, who has two WSOP bracelets and more than $14 million in career live tournament earnings, is not someone for whom putting himself in another's shoes comes naturally. He was diagnosed with autism at age twelve, and he once described his childhood as "weird, a bit aloof and mostly spent alone." But, Jungleman told me, he's made "massive progress" to overcome his introversion. This sometimes involves an unusual strategy: he'll often dress up in character when he plays, anything from "Macho Man" Randy Savage to Son Goku from the Japanese anime series *Dragon Ball Z*. Cates told me that inhabiting these personas can make it easier to relate to his opponents because he's forced to be more deliberate, thinking about how his characters would behave in the situation. "Perhaps that's why being an actor is good for me. Because I have to think about all of these details. Think about what to do with my face. I'm actually quite stoic, so it's not natural for me."

4. **Successful risk-takers are process oriented, not results oriented.**
They play the long game.

"Don't be results oriented" is a mantra well-known to every poker player. We've all taken thousands of coolers and bad beats, situations where we played our hand exactly right, the odds were in our favor, and we didn't get the result we wanted. Yes, in the long run, results are what count, and one nice thing about the River is that our compensation ultimately depends on objective measures and not the hand-waving vagaries of the Village.* But the long run can take a long time indeed—so in the meantime, we focus on our process.

Phil Galfond, one of the biggest winners in the history of online poker, returned to the game in 2019 after taking time off to focus on his coaching site Run It Once. And he did so boldly, challenging anyone in the world to play him at heads-up, high-stakes pot-limit Omaha, his best game. Galfond got six takers, including Daniel Cates and an anonymous European online pro named VeniVidi1993.

Initially down by more than €900,000 to VeniVidi1993—maybe Galfond's worst fears were true and he was really just a "washed-up ex-pro"—Galfond took a break to "decompress" and evaluate his play, reviewing his hands and playing lower-stakes matches. He still thought he was the better player, but did due diligence on the question, studying simulations to see just how unlikely it was that he was down so much if he really had the edge he thought. "Even though it gets really small, it's all still very possible," he concluded. The simulations told him that there was a 1 or 2 percent chance of trailing by €900,000 even if he was a huge favorite over VeniVidi1993. Most people would round that down to zero and give up, but poker players know that 2 percent chances happen; it's just a part of the process. So Galfond went back to the virtual poker felt and clawed all the way back, eventually winning the match, albeit by only €1,472. "What

---

* This is one reason why Sullivan left an academic career in the Village behind. "You can be the slowest person on the planet and spend eighteen years in grad school and still come out with a PhD," she said. "As a pilot, you completed the mission and landed the plane or not."

I've always said is logic, psychology, statistics, in that order," said Galfond, referring to what he used to think were the most important skills for a poker player. But he's changed his ranking because of experiences like this. "I think probably more important than psychology and statistics is just self-awareness and humility."

Physical risk-takers focus on process, too. The closest Vescovo ever came to dying was when hiking Argentina's Aconcagua, the highest mountain in the Western Hemisphere, dubbed the Mountain of Death for its high fatality rate. He had "kind of a freak accident, where I literally put my foot on a big boulder. It looked solid, it felt solid. But when I put my full weight on it, I cartwheeled back," said Vescovo. He'd triggered a rockslide and blacked out after a seventy-pound rock hit his spine. He could have been paralyzed or killed; they were near the 22,837-foot summit, and his climbing team didn't have the strength to carry him back to camp. Fortunately, a team of French climbers had seen the accident and climbed down to help.

Most people would have avoided climbing for a while after an accident like that—or at least avoided Aconcagua—but Vescovo summited the same peak two years later. You can reduce your risk through careful preparation, and that's essential. But at 22,000 feet, you can't eliminate risks entirely. Vescovo didn't beat himself up about the accident. He didn't think it was a risk he could have prevented—sometimes those 2 percent chances happen. He cited the example of the mountaineer Ueli Steck. "[He] was the first guy to climb up Annapurna solo—I mean, probably the most dangerous mountain in the world, ever." (Annapurna, also in Nepal, has about five times the fatality rate of Mount Everest.) "And he climbed it solo, like in seventy-two hours, insane. And what happens? He dies on Mount Everest. On a practice climb. You know, there's always that little percent out there that can come bite you in the butt. And that's what happened to me there."

5. **Successful risk-takers take shots.** They are explicitly aware of the risks they're taking—and they're comfortable with failure.

There's a meme from the American version of *The Office* where the endearingly imbecilic boss, Michael Scott, has misappropriated a quote from the hockey player Wayne Gretzky, scribbling his own name beneath Gretzky's on a dry-erase board under Gretzky's quote "You miss 100% of the shots you don't take." As much as I'm reluctant to misappropriate Scott's misappropriation of Gretzky or endorse the sort of motivational slogan you'd find in a depressing Scranton office park, there's something to be said for this.

I do not mean to suggest that you should shoot indiscriminately. But successful risk-takers are perpetually in search of +EV opportunities and willing to pull the trigger. They don't come along all that often. We probably don't want everyone in society taking long-shot wagers. But we do want some people willing to risk everything on bets that can have a huge payoff to society.

This is an attitude that distinguishes the United States from much of the rest of the world. "Here, you say, 'Hey, how do I go for 100x return on my money and not worry about the 3x?'" said Vinod Khosla, the founder of Khosla Ventures, which invests in long-shot technologies from artificial meat to artificial intelligence. That's not true in most other countries, Khosla thinks, including his native India, where social pressures instead encourage people to protect their downside. "It's still, you know, what's your title? How stable is the company? As opposed to operating in this ambiguous zone where upside is large, but the downside is large too."

Take Karikó, for example. Despite her persistence in pursuing mRNA research, she had no illusions that it was certain to work out. How could she, when she'd spent most of her career in risk-averse academia—a place more concerned, she thought, with getting the next grant than with inventing technologies that actually helped people—and only began to receive widespread public recognition for her work late in her life? "I don't believe something is just fate, [like] it had to happen," she said. But she thought mRNA was her best shot, so she joined the then-obscure company BioNTech in 2013. "There [was] no website, no nothing." But BioNTech did have mRNA vaccines in clinical trials. "That was for me important, that they already knew [mRNA] production. Because I am fifty-eight years old . . . so I cannot wait. By the time I figure out how to make [mRNA on my own], I will be dead."

And although there are some exceptions—Elon Musk, for instance, often seems blissfully unaware of his downside risks, although even he believed that he was only one more SpaceX launch failure away from being ruined—for the most part risk-takers are acutely aware of the possibility of failure. Sullivan knew that she was putting her life on the line every time she boarded the shuttle—especially after the space shuttle *Challenger* disaster in the middle of her NASA career in 1986.

"There's a classic moment, two days before launch, where you have your final visit with your family," Sullivan recalled. "I took my brother aside, and flat out told him, 'Look, I know the day after tomorrow, I'm getting on top of a bomb. And wanting my friends to light it. I get that, I'm riding a bomb.'" But Sullivan knew exactly what she was doing. "If something goes really horribly ugly, wrong, don't be tearing yourself up that I didn't know," she told her brother. "I knew. I knew and I'm here. Because I believe in the purpose, I believe the value of what we're doing here to the country, to mankind."

6. **Successful risk-takers take a raise-or-fold attitude toward life**. They abhor mediocrity and they know when to quit.

I'd have my MGM Rewards Platinum card revoked if I didn't quote from Kenny Rogers at some point in this book:

You've got to know when to Hold'em, know when to fold 'em
Know when to walk away and know when to run
—Kenny Rogers, "The Gambler"

Just like "You miss 100% of the shots you don't take," this cliché is actually pretty good advice. But it isn't *quite* right.

That's because the cardinal sin of poker is that most players *Hold'em* too often. There are three basic actions in poker: call, fold, raise. People press the call button too much. They call because they want to gamble. They call because their curiosity gets the better of them. And sometimes learning more about poker just gives them more excuses to call. Carlos Welch, the WSOP bracelet winner you met in chapter 2, coaches poker when he isn't playing; his students range from rank amateurs to world-class professionals. "When coaches say, 'Oh, having a good blocker is a good reason to call,'" Welch said—referring to an advanced game theory concept*—his students "just glom on to that, in order to satisfy their own natural desire to call anyway."

But although players call when they should be folding, they *also* call when they should be *raising*. So let me suggest one small change to "The Gambler":

> *You've got to know when to Hold'em, know when to fold 'em*
> *Know when to walk away and know when to **raise***
> —Nate Silver, *On the Edge*

As Doyle Brunson figured out fifty years ago, no-limit Texas Hold'em is a game of aggression. Modern poker solvers confirm this. Game theory often dictates a mixed strategy involving two or more choices. In some circumstances, however, the choices are to raise or fold—the middle ground of calling is the worst option.†

Poker players call this a raise-or-fold situation. And these come up more often than you'd think away from the poker tables. I'd argue, for instance, that the world might have been better off if it treated the COVID-19 pandemic as a raise-or-fold situation. Most countries took half measures that weren't really enough to suppress the virus or prevent mass deaths, but which also substantially disrupted everyday life for a year or longer, with enormous costs to well-being. The few countries like New Zealand

---

* A blocker is a card that affects the statistical distribution of your opponent's hand range. For instance, if you have the A♠, your opponent is less likely to have a flush in spades because you "block" the flush. That could give you a good reason—or excuse—to call down.

† The typical situation for this is when your hand has some equity in the pot—some chance of winning by making a draw—but you're not getting the right price to call down. Raising instead of calling gives you a second way to win, by essentially turning your hand into a bluff and occasionally getting your opponent to fold. The combined value from getting folds plus sometimes making your draw can make raising a +EV play even when calling isn't.

and Sweden that pursued more coherent strategies—essentially, New Zealand raised and Sweden folded*—did better than the many that muddled through with a compromise approach.

Our physical risk-takers also appreciate this principle. "You have to recognize that you have agency and authorship and sometimes bold action is the best course of action, even if the conditions and the outcome [are] uncertain. The riskiest course of action is oftentimes just remaining passive," said McMaster, reflecting the attitude he'd taken in the Gulf War tank battle. "I'm paraphrasing [Prussian general Carl von Clausewitz] here, but once you've taken into account all the factors you can account for, then you must march boldly forth into the shadows of uncertainty."

But if you're not on the literal battlefield, then you can quit. And as Annie Duke's *Quit* convincingly argues, quitting is often the boldest course of action. Football players sometimes learn this the hard way. Between the cutthroat nature of the sport and the brutally objective measurements NFL teams have of their athletes' performance, mediocre just won't cut it. Anderson hung up his spikes at the relatively young age of twenty-eight. "Before you know it, you look up and you're like ninety percent of the athlete that you were," he told me. Anderson was never an elite athlete to begin with, and the cumulative effects of a lifetime of playing football had taken their toll. "My first concussion was in high school. Dos Pueblos High School had a linebacker who was going to UCLA or something. Hit me hard. And I just started crying on the sideline and didn't know what it was because you feel drunk, like you can't connect with someone."

Some NFL players quit when they very much did have a choice, however—like John Urschel, a Baltimore Ravens offensive lineman who left after just three years to begin a PhD math program at MIT (where he's now an assistant professor of mathematics), and Andrew Luck, the former Indianapolis Colts quarterback who abruptly retired at age twenty-nine

---

* New Zealand aggressively enforced border controls to suppress COVID to near zero until vaccines were available—yes, it helped to be an island country in the middle of the South Pacific—while Sweden conceded that COVID was going to spread and permitted some in-person school and social life the whole way through. Both countries ended up with much less excess mortality than most of the industrialized world *and* permitted their citizens more freedom.

after a Pro Bowl season. Anderson doesn't think any less of Luck. "God bless. Good for you," he said. "A guy like Andrew Luck, that guy's a warrior. And was getting his ass kicked all the time, and was willing to get hit right in the chest, get back up and do it again." Still, Luck had earned more than $100 million in his NFL career and had a good life ahead of him, including a newborn child. Sometimes you got to know when to walk away.

7. **Successful risk-takers are prepared**. They make good intuitive decisions because they're well trained—not because they "wing it."

What most annoyed Vescovo about *Top Gun: Maverick* was Tom Cruise's insistence that you should just trust your gut and improvise your way out of a hairy situation. "The best military operations are the ones that are very boring, where things go exactly according to plan. No one's ever put in any danger," he said. "You want to minimize the risks. And so yeah, *Top Gun*, it looked great on film. But that is not how you would try and take out that target."

Instead, military missions require meticulous preparation—as does climbing the world's tallest mountains or taking submersibles into the deepest seas. "Michael Jordan, you know, greatest of all time, right? He would go out and practice free throws for hours and hours," said Vescovo. "That kind of mind-numbing repetition, or doing the research to understand the risks of a new situation, all these other things, it takes bloody work. I worked my ass off for my entire life. I still do. That's what yields excellence."

So is there never a place for trusting your gut? That's not quite what Vescovo is saying. Rather, it's that the more you train, the better your instincts will be. "When something is for real and is an emergency, how many times have you heard people say, 'Oh, you know, the training kicked in.'" Training, ironically, is often the best preparation to handle the situations that you *don't* train for. "Apollo Thirteen is the best example where you had really well-trained astronauts in an incredibly bad situation," Vescovo said, referring to the moon landing that was aborted after an oxygen tank ruptured, disabling life-support and other critical systems—but the astronauts made their way back to Earth safely.

Galfond, the poker player, has a theory for this, which he wrote about in a 2023 blog post on Daniel Kahneman's System 1 (fast, instinctual) and System 2 (slow, deliberative) thinking. "The best players will study solvers so much that their fundamentals become automatic," he wrote—the complex System 2 solutions that computers come up with make their way into your instinctual System 1 with enough practice. That frees up mental bandwidth for when you *do* face a hairy situation, or a great opportunity. Now, less experienced players need to be careful with this—Galfond recommends that most players simplify their strategy to focus on executing well. Conversely, the very best players may have some room for maverickness, taking advantage of their relative comfort with the situation. The problem with *Top Gun: Maverick* wasn't with Maverick—his instincts probably *were* pretty good—but that he was imploring other pilots to trust their gut and be heroes when they didn't have the same experience base.

8. **Successful risk-takers have selectively high attention to detail.** They understand that attention is a scarce resource and think carefully about how to allocate it.

If you've been around the poker scene long enough, you've probably heard the aphorism "Poker is hours of boredom punctuated by moments of sheer terror." It describes one of the unusual features of poker: most of the time, you *don't have anything you have to do exactly.* Top pros generally play only about 25 percent of their hands, discarding the rest before the flop. And even when they do play a hand, big pots come around rarely. You might face one really high-stakes decision every hour. You need to carefully calibrate your mental bandwidth, conserving energy, but being prepared to snap into action at a moment's notice.

Of course, there are things to look for even when you don't have cards in front of you. In particular, you can watch for tells or betting patterns from your opponents that you'll take advantage of later. There are a few sickos who always seem to be "on," like Jason Koon, who is not only very chatty at the table but also highly observant. "There's so much to be seen. If it's not in the face, or the neck, it's in the hands," he said, describing his process for picking up on tells. "You don't have to stare at people, man. There's almost an aura around a person. We all move the way that we move, and our brain does what it does, and we don't think much about it. If you just can . . . feel an energy change or a movement that's just not natural, then there's certain things you can start to take from that."

It helps Koon that he's a fitness freak and former college athlete—paying attention all the time is physically demanding. Most players don't have that ability; I certainly don't, and judging by the amount of time I see them buried in their phones, most pros don't either. But practice and training can help you to become a little more Koon-like—as Galfond says, the more experience you have, the more even relatively difficult tasks can become second nature, freeing up scarce bandwidth.

A lot of risk-taking activity is like this, it turns out. The "boredom punctuated by moments of sheer terror" saying *isn't* original to poker, as I'd once assumed. It dates back to at least World War I—war was described as "months of boredom punctuated by moments of terror"—and has also been applied to air travel and space flight.

How does this play out in the context of a space shuttle mission? On the one hand, especially when in one of the most dangerous phases like launch, reentry, or a spacewalk,* you want to be focused on the most important task at hand. "One of our favorite adages was 'The main thing is to keep the main thing the main thing,'" said Sullivan. "Which means what's really important is to understand what the main thing really is, in a situation when there's eighty-four symptoms and indicators flying around—what's really the main thing here? And be sure you're adequately focused on getting that right, rather than getting whipsawed every which way."

On the other hand, if one of those eighty-four bulbs does start flashing

---

* Despite being the first American woman to spacewalk, Sullivan was no more of a fan of the movie *Gravity*—the Best Picture nominee centered around Sandra Bullock on a spacewalk gone awry—than Vescovo was of *Top Gun*. "Forget *Gravity*," said Sullivan. "I mean, the visuals were cool. Everything about the way they operated and the physics—it's all bullshit. Forget it."

red, you need to quickly assess the situation to determine if the problem is mission critical. If so, *that* needs to become the main thing. When flying a high-performance aircraft, said Vescovo, "you are absolutely completely aware of everything happening around you, and you will shift that focus almost instantaneously to where it needs to go."

But one thing you *don't* want is to be consumed by the stakes of the mission; that's a waste of bandwidth. As aware as Sullivan was of the risks intrinsic to flying on the space shuttle, "it's not helpful to be thinking about it while you're in the middle of doing it," she said. "You need your full attention on where you are and what you can do to help it to ensure it's going right . . . and adapt and adjust if it starts to not go right," she said. Again, it's natural to feel physical anxiety in high-stakes situations, which produce profound physiological changes to your body. It's mistaking these sensations for being *out of control* that can produce a self-fulfilling doom loop. If you don't want that to happen in a poker tournament, then you definitely don't want it to happen when you're flying two hundred miles above the Earth's surface.

Granted, this is easier said than done—it's why Sullivan was chosen to be an astronaut when ten thousand of her competitors were not. The good news is that this does get better for most people with experience—you can even enter a flow state, the hyperattentive awareness of everything around you that Vescovo described.

9. **Successful risk-takers are adaptable**. They are good generalists, taking advantage of new opportunities and responding to new threats.

In chapter 4, I reintroduced you to Bob Voulgaris, the Greek Canadian gambler whose sports-betting strategy centers around finding angles, exploitable opportunities that other bettors have overlooked. The problem with angles is that they usually don't persist for very long; the market is just too efficient. So that's why Voulgaris casts a wide net. His first betting breakthrough didn't come in the NBA, but rather the CFL—the Canadian Football League, he told me. Only after an unsuccessful stint betting the

NFL did he move on to basketball. And he's since largely moved on from NBA betting to other things—working for the Dallas Mavericks; making enough from crypto that he spends his summers on a yacht in the Mediterranean; and now owning a Spanish soccer team.

I call this personality type a fox, and that was also featured prominently in *The Signal and the Noise*. Fox is one of the two archetypes articulated in the Greek poet Archilochus's saying: "The fox knows many things, but the hedgehog knows one big thing." Foxes rummage around for opportunities, wary of complacency and getting too tied down.

Now, this is one habit to which there are some exceptions. In particular, startup founders need to be laser focused on one big thing and be prepared to see it out for a decade or more. It still probably helps to have some fox-like cunning to pick the *right* big thing. But it isn't strictly necessary if you stumble on the right idea.

Still, as the world gets more complicated, it's generally the generalists who rule the roost.* They are more likely to adapt successfully to the unknown. That's what NASA is looking for in its astronauts, for instance—why Sullivan was chosen even though her background was in oceanography. "By and large, they're looking for generalists," she said. "Not a deep dive down one narrow little tube of academia or something like that. The ability to recognize or anticipate connections or think a bit laterally—that's very important." During her interview process in Houston, Sullivan was asked a lot of highly amorphous questions like "Tell us about yourself starting with high school"—NASA wanted to see how resourceful she was in a situation without clear guidance. "All those experiences give them windows into your character and how you approach unexpected and unknown things," she said. "As repetitive as shuttle missions may have looked to the media, every one was really created pretty much from blank sheets of paper. And like any complex evolution, it never goes entirely the way you plan."

---

* Although, this could change with the development of AGI or so-called artificial general intelligence—so bookmark this page and see if it still holds up in twenty years.

10. **Successful risk-takers are good estimators.** They are Bayesians, comfortable quantifying their intuitions and working with incomplete information.

In poker, players can estimate probabilities with incredible precision. Tom Dwan is a legendarily aggressive high-stakes pro who got his start online (he is often still known by his Full Tilt Poker screen name, "durrrr") but is now the second-biggest winner of all time in televised high-stakes cash games, with net winnings of $4.8 million. durrrr, by his own admission, can be a space cadet. "If we're walking down the street, compared to a lot of people, I think I notice less things than most people," he told me. But the poker tables are different. "One of the only pat-on-the-back things I'll give myself is that I think I'm a bit more aware of my confidence level. If I say I'm 93 percent confident—like, if you gave me nine-to-one odds" or 90 percent, "you might actually lose money" if you try to sneak in a bet.

Does the difference between 90 percent and 93 percent really matter? Well, if you're playing a million-dollar pot, it does. Say the pot's $900,000 and your opponent makes a cheeky $100,000 bet on the river, hoping to extract a little more profit out of you. You can only beat a bluff, but you have the right odds to call if your opponent is bluffing even 10 percent of the time. However, if she's bluffing only 7 percent of the time, you should fold—the call has an expected value of -$30,000. It's very hard to make this fold, but players like Dwan can.

Where does this ability come from? It's mostly because durrrr has played hundreds of thousands of poker hands and so is comfortable quantifying his intuitions. I spent most of my hour-long conversation with Dwan talking about a single hand he'd recently played—a rather important hand, the biggest pot in televised poker history, where Dwan correctly called down against a player named Wesley with a relatively weak pair of queens, computing that Wesley had a high enough chance of bluffing. There were roughly twenty "data points" that factored into this decision, Dwan said. For instance, Dwan thought that Wesley—ordinarily a tight player—had come into the session with an "agenda that was a little bit less about winning money" and more about making plays that looked cool on TV. Wesley had to be bluffing 25 percent of the time to make Dwan's call correct; his read on Wesley's mindset was tentative, but maybe that was enough to get him from 20 percent to 24. (Bluffing in a huge pot looks cool on TV.) And maybe Wesley's physical mannerisms—like how he put his chips in quickly on the river, sometimes a sign of weakness—got Dwan from 24 percent to 29. That was enough: Dwan took his time, coolly sipping from a bottle of water, and put the chips in to win a $3.1 million pot.*

If this kind of thought process seems alien to you—well, sorry, but your application to the River has been declined. In poker, you *have* to be comfortable turning your subjective feelings into probabilities and acting on them. And in other enterprises involving risk, you have to be willing to make at least a good first-pass estimate. "It's not like you get a spreadsheet out and actually try to mathematically determine that, because I think there's a hubris of precision," said Vescovo of his process for estimating the dangers when flying fighter jets or climbing mountains. "But there certainly are tendencies of *this* is really dangerous or *that* is not."

You also have to recognize that—as an outgrowth of Bayes' theorem, which works by revising your probabilistic beliefs as you collect more information—your estimates will become more precise as you collect more data. But sometimes your edge comes from being willing to act on a relatively crude estimate to take advantage of an opportunity when other people are still mired in the fact-finding stage. "I'm always assessing risk versus reward in everything that I do. I'm always going to weigh out the pros and cons of any situation," said Maria Ho. "Whereas somebody [else] might need ninety percent good reasons to do something, . . . if it's fifty-five/forty-five good reasons, then I would be happy to take the risk."

11. **Successful risk-takers try to stand out, not fit in.** They have independence of mind and purpose.

---

* Though Dwan conveyed to me that he was relatively confident—considerably higher than 29 percent—by the time he decided to call. It was a huge pot and he wanted to give Wesley time to reveal another tell that might compel him to reevaluate.

Let's start in the world of capital-G Professional Gambling, because it's always been an unusual career choice. In Doyle Brunson's day, many players were ex-jocks, he told me, people who liked competition but weren't qualified for a white-collar job. Daniel Negreanu, a generation later, dropped out of high school to be a pool hustler because he thought his math teacher "was a moron" and the straight-and-narrow path wasn't right for a poor but socially and intellectually precocious son of immigrants. Erik Seidel never finished college and wandered from backgammon to options trading before finding poker; he said he didn't like having to wear a tie every day or the pushy culture in the trading pits. Increasingly, however, college graduates and even PhDs choose to play poker, people who could plug into a more conventional occupation but choose not to. Isaac Haxton (BA philosophy, Brown) picked poker because he didn't want to work for a big capitalistic corporation. Ho (BA communications, UCSD) wanted to rebel against the stereotypical career paths her parents might have preferred for her. "I was always attracted to things that were against the grain or unconventional to probably get a reaction out of my parents," she told me.

These people also do like competition, obviously—see item number two. But they don't want to jump through the hoops that the rest of society does. And really, that's a defining trait of most risk-takers. Yes, if you have a quantitative mindset but no urge to rebel against society, investment banking beckons for you. Silicon Valley prizes nonconformity, though, even if it's a monoculture in its own ways. Even hedge funds are willing to make bets on unconventional people like Vanessa Selbst, since the conceit of the industry is that they can make excess profits by not following the herd—although Selbst found her job at Bridgewater Associates too "hierarchical" and didn't think she had enough room for creative thinking.

Karikó had similar problems with academia, which she found stifling and too obsessed with its self-minted markers of prestige. "[It's] those in the periphery like me, where [there] is no money, no fame, no prestige—those [people] have the freedom, they can think freely," she said. When she speaks with students, Karikó encourages them to chart their own course in life—they too often "get discouraged because they're constantly . . . comparing themselves to others," she said. "You have to find what *you* can do," she tells them. "Not, 'Oh, if the boss would do that.' No, you cannot change that boss. You cannot change your wife, your children. You cannot change. You just have to figure out what you can do."

12. **Successful risk-takers are conscientiously contrarian.** They have theories about why and when the conventional wisdom is wrong.

There is an oft-neglected distinction between *independence* and *contrarianism*. If I pick vanilla and you pick chocolate because you like chocolate better, you're being independent. If you pick chocolate *because I picked vanilla*, you're being contrarian. Most people are pretty damned conformist—humans are social animals—and Riverians are sometimes accused of being contrarian when they're just being independent. If I do the conventional thing 99 percent of the time and you do it 85 percent of the time, you'll seem rebellious by comparison, but you're still mostly going with the flow.

But there are some parts of the River that have an explicit mandate to be contrarian. Sports betting is one example; if you just follow the public money, you'll lose the same 5 percent juice to the house that everyone else loses.* Hedge funds are another example; they charge investors exorbitant fees on the premise of achieving excess returns above and beyond what any ol' Ernie Index Fund could get in the S&P 500.

"The thing about hedge funds, it's the only industry in the world where not only do you have to be right, but everybody else also has to be wrong," said Galen Hall, who earned more than $4 million from poker tournaments between 2011 and 2015 but nevertheless left to work for Bridgewater Associates (he was the one who recruited his friend Selbst there). "Where[as] if you're a doctor, if you go by the book, you do the accepted thing, you do

---

* If not more than that; recreational sports bettors generally do slightly worse than if they just chose picks at random, so as a default it's sometimes better to "fade the public" and make unpopular picks.

the convention every single time, you're a pretty fucking good doctor, right?"

Hall is one of those people who's just good at everything. He's good at poker. He's good at finance. In 2023, he reached the semifinals in the World Backgammon Championship despite just having picked up the game. When, during the 2022 World Series of Poker, there was a false report of a mass shooter on the Las Vegas Strip, he broke through a ceiling vent to lead people to a safe hiding place. With dark features, he's also extremely good-looking. It turns out Hall does have some flaws, though. Bridgewater is obsessed with quantifying its traders' personalities and performance, assigning them "baseball cards" as though they're major league short-stops. "My Organized and Reliable rating was three out of a hundred. My Rules Following was a two out of a hundred," Hall said. "The only person lower than me was my then-boss."

But that rebellious streak serves Hall well at his new firm DFT (Dark Forest Technologies), which he cofounded along with Jacob Kline, his ex-Bridgewater boss (Kline got a one out of a hundred in Rules Following). DFT engages in a strategy that I'm going to dub "conscientious contrarian-ism." They make contrarian bets, but they always have a thesis for doing so—one that has nothing to do with the intrinsic qualities of the asset but rather with the misaligned incentives of other participants in the market.

"Every single thing we do, I can point to, like, 'here is the person who was doing a thing wrong,'" said Hall. "We build a map of all of the players in the world . . . who are trading for reasons other than they want to gen-erate some alpha.* You know, somebody got added to the S&P 500. So now all the S&P 500 ETFs out there have to buy this company. Or it's a CEO of a startup, he's now a billionaire. He has ninety-nine percent of his net worth in the company. He's allowed to sell his shares on this day [and] he's prob-ably going to sell a bunch."

I like this strategy because it doesn't insult the intelligence of other players in the market—sure, Hall is smart, but so are lots of people on Wall

---

* "Alpha" refers to achieving excess returns, the EV-maximizing goal of most active investors.

Street. In a game-theory equilibrium, it's hard for anybody to have alpha. But *not everybody is playing the same game*. People have different incentives, and they may be following their incentives rationally, but it nevertheless creates profitable opportunities for DFT, which just wants to make money.

Maybe conscientious contrarianism resonates with me because it reminds me of what it's like to argue with people about politics on the internet. It might not appear this way when you look at my Twitter replies, but my goal when I do this, in line with my background in forecasting, is to seek accuracy and hopefully be proven right by subsequent events.* (That's why I sometimes get frustrated and even challenge people to make bets on political outcomes to put their money where their mouth is.) But other people are trying to argue for a cause, rally the troops, boost their profile, or seek out approval on social media. All of that is fine, but they have different objectives. It's easier to achieve alpha at *your* objective when other people aren't playing the same game.

This also helps to explain why so many of her academic colleagues dismissed Karikó's brilliant idea. Her mRNA vaccines were a high-upside but high-risk bet that might take years to develop; even Karikó thought they might only come to fruition after her death. Silicon Valley is specifically designed to make these sorts of bets, but academia isn't. Just the opposite, Karikó said: it tends to optimize for conventional ideas that have a high likelihood of getting a grant proposal accepted but not all that much payoff.

So be a conscientious contrarian—look for flaws in people's incentives rather than their intelligence—and then seek out a place where your own incentives are well-aligned with your goals.

13. **Successful risk-takers are not driven by money.** They live on the edge because it's their way of life.

---

* That's not to suggest my motives are pure dispassionate truth seeking; it's also *fun* to be proven right.

One ironic thing I've learned from my time in the River is that people who gamble for a living often aren't motivated by money—and the best gamblers tend to be even less money driven. Now, they're not ascetics; this isn't meant to imply they don't enjoy the fruits of their labors.

But poker players are distinct for two reasons. First, they're so fiercely competitive that money mostly serves as a way to keep score. "It's clearly not a money thing. I am not a person that requires a ton of money. We eat good food, we live good lives," said Koon, who's gone from an impoverished upbringing in West Virginia to a modern multimillion-dollar home near Red Rock Canyon west of Las Vegas. "I really am to this point where I'm playing because I love to compete. I feel at home when I'm playing poker, a lot of the people that I love most in this world are also poker players."

Second, gambling for such high stakes requires a certain desensitization to them. "There was a time I was playing $200/$400 in Bobby's Room," Koon said—referring to the glass-enclosed area at the Bellagio named after poker legend Bobby Baldwin where the biggest games in town are held. "And I remember putting out the big blind with four black [hundred-dollar] chips. And I looked down at it and teared up because my stepdad Buck, he was a roofer and he made four hundred dollars a week. And here I am putting up a big blind for that," he said. "He literally broke his back—he fell off a roof . . . for that kind of living to help us get by."

Being an astronaut or an explorer isn't as lucrative as playing in Bobby's Room*—but the physical risk-takers I spoke with also seemed to be motivated by some intrinsic desire to take risk and expressed a kinship with others who feel the same way. "It certainly feels like something that's innate within me," said Vescovo. "I've talked to some doctors and other people in the exploration community, and they think that there is a genetic component. In the normal distribution of individuals, there are some of us on one end of the spectrum, and then there are some that never leave their house."

---

* And if they do somehow hit the lottery—as Karikó did when winning the $3 million Breakthrough Prize in 2022—they don't necessarily care. She gave back most of the money, she said. "I live in the same house, I have the same husband forever. You know, no changing."

Part 2

Risk

5

Acceleration

The reasonable man adapts himself to the world:
the unreasonable one persists in trying to adapt
the world to himself. Therefore all progress
depends on the unreasonable man.
— *George Bernard Shaw*

I t sort of rotated in a three hundred and sixty degree horizontal loop in the air," said Peter Thiel. "An unidentified flying object flying six feet above Sand Hill Road."

Thiel was recalling an incident in 2000 when he and Elon Musk were on their way to pitch the legendary venture capitalist Michael Moritz. They desperately needed cash. Their newly combined companies—Musk's x.com and Thiel's Confinity, what would later become PayPal—had $15 million in the bank but were burning through $10 million in expenses every month, giving them only six weeks of runway. But Musk's mind was elsewhere. He had recently bought a silver McLaren F1 sports car for $1 million, his reward to himself for selling his first company, Zip2. "My fear is that we'll become spoiled brats, that we'll lose a sense of appreciation and perspective," said Musk's then fiancée, Justine Wilson, in an interview the couple conducted at the time with CNN. Little could she have known that Musk would eventually parlay his $22 million payout into a net worth that would grow to be more than ten thousand times larger.

Though the two men's personalities were at best a case of opposites attracting, Musk was evidently out to impress Thiel. "What can this do?" asked Thiel. "Watch this!" said Musk, before flooring the accelerator while attempting a lane change. *Vrooooom!* The car spun out of control, hitting an embankment, and had so much torque that it flew up in the air, spinning several times before landing on its wheels.

Thiel and Musk were fine—and hitchhiked their way to the meeting—but the million-dollar McLaren was wrecked. And the car was uninsured. It's not that Musk had made some rational calculation—that if you're worth $22 million, you can just afford to buy a new one. Rather, Thiel said, Musk hadn't bothered to consider the possibility of a crash. "The first thing Elon told me as we were in this totaled car was, 'You know, wow, that was really intense, Peter. I read all these stories about people who made money in Silicon Valley, who bought sports cars and crashed them. And I knew this would *never* happen to me.'"

Thiel had once considered writing a book about Musk and their PayPal days. "The working title I had for it was *Risky Business*, like the eighties movie. And then the chapter on Elon," he said, "was 'The Man Who Knew Nothing About Risk.'"

And yet, when it comes to risk, it's Thiel who is more of the outlier in Silicon Valley. "Peter is not a risk-taker. There is nothing. He is a guy wired to protect his downside," said Moritz, the longtime partner at Sequoia Capital whom Thiel and Musk were going to meet with that day on Sand Hill Road.* "He spent hours trying to convince me to sell PayPal. You know, the caricature would be the investor wants to sell the business, not the CEO."

In general, Silicon Valley *does* understand something about risk—something that most people in society don't. It understands that a relatively remote chance is worth taking if it has a sufficiently high payoff. Indeed, some of the venture capitalists I spoke with for this chapter sounded a lot

---

* Moritz retired in 2023 after thirty-eight years on the job.

like poker players. "I always say expected value is the probability of success times the degree of impact. That math works easily, but people are very uncomfortable in the low-probability domains," said Vinod Khosla, the founder of Khosla Ventures, which is known for its long-shot investments in fields like artificial meat and alternative energy.

When I first proposed this book, venture capital was slated to play more of a supporting role, paired off with hedge funds in a chapter that was mostly about Wall Street. Instead, it turned out to be the protagonist. I followed the flow of the River where it naturally took me, and it took me to Palo Alto. A lot of VCs were eager to speak with me, and they often spoke candidly. Some of this is because VCs are natural salespeople who can drum up business by building buzz around their ideas, while hedge-funders are more like advantage players in a casino, searching for small edges—$20 bills lying on the ground—that may disappear if someone else hears about them first. But it's also because VCs are the truer embodiments of the Riverian spirit. Perhaps Wall Street is slightly ahead of Silicon Valley on what I call the "cognitive cluster" of River attributes, meaning a capacity for abstract, analytical reasoning. Wall Street is more explicitly quantitative than Silicon Valley—although then again, the core technology of Silicon Valley is computing, which abstracts cognition to the point where it can be represented by a series of ones and zeros.

But on the "personality cluster"—competitiveness, risk tolerance, independent-mindedness often to the point of contrarianism—Silicon Valley is off the charts, even compared to Wall Street. And it is quite proud of this. "We believe in embracing variance, in increasing interestingness," wrote Marc Andreessen, the Netscape cofounder turned VC whose egg-shaped head is synonymous in the Valley with hard-boiled, stubborn resolve, in his October 2023 "Techno-Optimist Manifesto." "We believe in *risk*," he wrote, italicizing the word "risk," "in leaps into the unknown."

Even though I didn't have any sort of network in Silicon Valley, the VCs seemed to recognize me as a fellow Riverian,* someone who shared their

---

* This included Thiel, for instance, whom I initially expected to be a challenging person to interview because I'm friendly with Nick Denton, the Gawker Media founder whose company was bankrupted by a

interest in "embracing variance" and "increasing interestingness." And the truth is, they're right. As you'll see, I don't agree with everything Silicon Valley does. But I do agree with 80 or 90 percent of it. I say that because I tested myself. Andreessen's "Techno-Optimist Manifesto" includes 108 statements that assert beliefs that Techno-Optimists hold, such as "Techno-Optimists believe that societies, like sharks, grow or die." I went through each statement and marked down whether I mostly agreed or mostly disagreed with it. On balance, I agreed with 84 percent of the statements. The exceptions were mostly things I found overstated ("We believe everything good is downstream of growth"), sometimes to the point of being cringe inducing ("We believe in the romance of technology. . . . The eros of the train, the car, the electric light, the skyscraper").

I have one big gripe: I worry about Andreessen's explicit embrace of "accelerationism," a term that refers to the unmitigated rapid development of AI, the consequences be damned. Instead, I agree with Ethereum founder Vitalik Buterin, who wrote in response to Andreessen that "AI is fundamentally different from other tech, and it is worth being uniquely careful." AI is not the first technology that has the potential to destroy civilization, but unlike nuclear weapons, which were designed by governments, AI is being developed by Silicon Valley with its paradigm of "move fast and break things." This is an important-enough question that there's a whole chapter coming on it later—what I'm cutely calling chapter ∞ toward the end of the book. You can think of the next several chapters as setting us into orbit around this question of existential risk.

Let's decelerate for now, though. If you believe in competition and risk-taking—and if you believe that technological development has profoundly improved the human condition on balance—you'll agree with most of the "Techno-Optimist Manifesto." Indeed, many of the statements reflect

---

Thiel-driven lawsuit. But the interview was relatively easy to schedule, and the conversation was long and sporting. Even though Thiel and I disagree on a lot of political questions, there is a certain collegiality among people in the River.

classic American values like free speech and meritocracy that aren't all that controversial—although some have become more so lately in the Village, in part because of their association with Silicon Valley.

There is, however, a crucial difference between VCs like Khosla and founders like Musk.* It's certainly not easy to find the companies that pay off 10x, 100x, or 1000x. But VCs are making many investments at once—a given fund might make a couple dozen bets. And somewhat contrary to the conventional wisdom, the investments that don't hit big may still produce some perfectly nice returns—say, 2x or 3x or 5x. "It's about *eliminating* risks. And taking as few risks as possible," Moritz told me. "All this mumbo-jumbo that 'Oh, Silicon Valley is swashbuckling, buccaneering, and risk-taking and if you fail, that's a notch on your belt and you get promoted for failure'—I think all that's hogwash."

Founders, by contrast, are much more all-in—sometimes literally. When I read Walter Isaacson's *Elon Musk*, I wasn't surprised to learn about Elon's kamikaze poker strategy:

> Many years later, [PayPal cofounder Max] Levchin was at a friend's bachelor pad hanging out with Musk. Some people were playing a high-stakes game of Texas Hold 'Em. Although Musk was not a card player, he pulled up to the table. "There were all these nerds and sharpsters who were good at memorizing cards and calculating odds," Levchin says. "Elon just proceeded to go all in on every hand and lose. Then he would buy more chips and double down. Eventually, after losing many hands, he went all in and won. Then he said, 'Right, fine, I'm done.'"

I've played in a handful of high-stakes poker games against rich guys—including one game frequented by venture capitalists, Silicon Valley founders, and the hosts of the *All-In* podcast, who are friendly with Musk.† I was sworn to secrecy about the particulars, although since one of the *All-In*

---

* To complicate things a bit, a number of VCs in this chapter, including Khosla, Thiel, and Marc Andreessen, began their lives as founders. But the trend rarely goes the other way. VCs don't usually leave to go all-in on one company.
† And Phil Hellmuth, a Palo Alto resident and another friend of the *All-In* podcast hosts. There's an uncanny amount of crossover among different communities within the River.

hosts, Jason Calacanis, said this publicly, I can confirm that the first time I played in the game, I won enough money to buy a Tesla. The other thing I can say—just in general terms—is that the higher the stakes, the crazier the action. The biggest poker games select for the players who want to take crazy, irrational, -EV risks. Maybe not *literally* going all-in every hand—although I've seen strategies that aren't far from it—but embracing variance, as the "Techno-Optimist Manifesto" would say.

Musk runs his businesses much like he plays poker. One of the reasons he became the world's richest man is because he made an exceptionally aggressive compensation deal with Tesla that the conventional wisdom held "would be impossible to achieve."

"Tesla and this rocket company, SpaceX—they were both *extremely* risky schemes," said Thiel, whose firm, Founders Fund, passed on an early investment in Tesla—although it did invest in SpaceX. "How would one assess them probabilistically? They probably were not going to work. And the Tesla thing looked like sort of a fake clean tech company," Thiel said.

SpaceX was even more risky. The company's first three rocket launches failed, and Elon had to scrounge to get money for a fourth one. That fourth try was a charm—"That was freakin' awesome," a relieved Musk told his Falcon 1 team. He'd expected that another crash would have ruined him. "We wouldn't be able to get any new funding for Tesla," Musk later told Isaacson. "People would be like, 'Look at that guy whose rocket company failed, he's a loser.'"

While Musk's reputation in the Village has been on a negative trajectory since his acquisition of Twitter—which he renamed X—he's still regarded highly in Silicon Valley, where most of the people I spoke with were willing to write off his flaws. Silicon Valley is a pattern-matching place: iconic founders like Musk, Steve Jobs, and Mark Zuckerberg are archetypes whose examples will be followed for decades to come. So what to make of the fact that if that fourth Falcon rocket had crashed—or if that McLaren had landed on its hood instead of its wheels, perhaps gravely injuring Musk and Thiel—the world as Silicon Valley knows it would have turned out incredibly differently?

When I spoke with Thiel, this was the first question I asked him. "If you simulated the world a thousand times, Peter, how often would you end up in a position roughly like the one you're in today?" This was intended as something between a softball and a curveball—an unexpected but relatively nonthreatening conversation starter.

Thiel delivered an answer that went on for almost thirty minutes. He began by objecting to my premise. "If the world is deterministic, you'll end up in the same place every single time. And if it's not deterministic, you would almost never end in the same place," he said.

It was a fair objection. Basically, I was just asking Thiel whether he got lucky. But whether the world is deterministic is an important existential question that has long been debated by both metaphysicists and actual physicists.* Most people who reside in the River—me included—are probabilists. We might find questions about the nature of the universe philosophically interesting. But they don't really matter to our day-to-day work. The world may or may not be *inherently random*, but between chaos theory and our relative ignorance, many important phenomena are *highly uncertain in practice*. So we gather data, craft it into what we call reference classes, formulate hypotheses, and test them—all to figure out what events are relatively more predictable and relatively less so. This is the empirical way. Metaphysics are above our pay grade.

Thiel, who had a strongly religious upbringing, instead was copping to being a determinist. He recalled a passage from Joseph Conrad: "As if the initial word of each our destiny were not graven in imperishable characters upon the face of a rock." He even suggested something that you might think was sacrilege in the River: that he was correcting for the rest of the world's overcommitment to statistical analysis.

"There was [once] some place where statistical knowledge gave us an insight vis-à-vis the people who didn't have access to it," he said,

---

* Recent developments in quantum mechanics have moved the needle toward the idea that the universe contains some intrinsic degree of randomness, but there are many interpretations of these phenomena and there is no clear scientific consensus. There is a long treatment of Laplace's demon—the conjecture that if we knew the location and momentum of every particle in the universe, we could perfectly predict the future—in *The Signal and the Noise*.

mentioning innovations like the development of life insurance and the Black-Scholes model for pricing stock options. "But in the world of 2016, or 2022, if we are too focused on statistical or mathematical knowledge, we end up missing out on a lot."

Let's take a longer look at this, because Thiel is making both an empirical claim and a philosophical one. The empirical claim is that low-hanging fruit of the tree of statistical analysis has mostly been picked. Baseball teams no longer have an advantage from targeting players with high on-base percentages because it's been twenty years since *Moneyball* was published and *everyone* does that now. The Black-Scholes formula that Thiel mentioned, an equation involving inputs like the risk-free interest rate and the amount of time until the option expires, might once have made you a handsome profit on Wall Street. But when *everyone* is using Black-Scholes, its flaws start to show—the simplistic assumptions it makes may even have helped traders to rationalize risky trades that contributed to the Global Financial Crisis.

The quants won, in other words. We're living in their world. So if you're going to be a contrarian, as many Riverians are inclined to be—including Thiel, who is famously contrarian even if he doesn't like the term*—that might mean looking for information that's *hard* to quantify. Or it might mean betting on a hunch about when it's a new regime where the old rules don't apply anymore. Thiel pointed to the election of Donald Trump, and playfully needled me about people's reliance on statistical forecasts like the one I published at FiveThirtyEight as an example of this.[†] "On some level, people knew that statistical knowledge was not quite sufficient," he explained. The reason they were "manically going to your website" and reloading the page over and over was because they knew deep down that "something else was going on" and that their statistical knowledge was insufficient, he theorized.

---

* "I don't like the word 'contrarian'—you just put a minus sign in front of some sort of wisdom-of-the-crowds-type thinking," Thiel told me. "It surely can't be that straightforward?"
† Thiel was a prominent Trump supporter who spoke at the 2016 Republican National Convention. My sense is that this affinity for Trump reflected Thiel's politics as much as his thinking that it was a good contrarian bet, but there may have been an element of both factors.

But there's also something more. The most successful founders like Musk succeeded despite what were ostensibly extremely long odds. Thiel, recalling the challenges Musk overcame to build SpaceX, thought that no one obstacle Musk faced made for an insurmountable barrier. But the quants had run the numbers—if you have 10 hurdles to leap over, and you have a 50 percent chance of tripping over each one, the odds of making it to the end of the course are 1 over 2^{10}, or just one chance in 1,024—and concluded that the venture was imprudent. Musk had thought differently. "He was determined to make them happen," Thiel said. "It was a matter of assembling the pieces and putting them together, and then it would work. We're just in this strange world where no one does it because they all think probabilistically."

Probabilistic thinking works best over repeated trials. If I get all-in with a pair of aces in poker and my opponent makes her flush draw, I'll feel good about that because I'm going to play thousands more poker hands and I'll make money from her in the long run. Potentially world-altering technologies are in a funny category, though. If you bundle them into a portfolio of long-shot bets, as VC firms do, then you can take a probabilistic outlook—and if you're a top VC firm, you'll be all but guaranteed to make a profit over the long run. For a founder, though, his or her livelihood may be on the line. Silicon Valley needs probabilists, reasonable people who calculate the odds. But it needs unreasonable people too—determinists, True Believers, people who write five-thousand-word manifestos.

A Brief History of Silicon Valley

The San Francisco Bay Area—the counties of Alameda, Contra Costa, Marin, Napa, San Mateo, Santa Clara, Solano, Sonoma, and San Francisco, California—was home to 7.76 million people as of the 2020 U.S. Census, or roughly 0.1 percent of the world's population.* However, as of October

---

* The term "Silicon Valley" is flexible. It is sometimes used as narrowly as to refer to the Santa Clara Valley south of San Francisco, or as broadly as to be a metonym (meaning a term like "Hollywood" that

2023, it is headquarters to almost 25 percent of the world's unicorn companies (defined as private companies with a valuation of at least $1 billion). It's hard to overstate what an intense concentration of capital this is. The city of San Francisco alone, even as it has struggled in the aftermath of COVID, is the headquarters to 171 unicorns, roughly as many as Beijing, Shanghai, Bengaluru, and London combined.

Number of Unicorn Companies

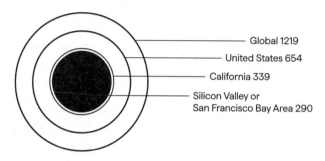

Global 1219

United States 654

California 339

Silicon Valley or
San Francisco Bay Area 290

You might not like people like Thiel or Musk. You might not like the products that Silicon Valley has foisted upon the world—although consider how much someone would have to pay you to never again use a computer (including your iPhone, which is far more powerful than the original supercomputers). You might not like capitalism at all—and that's fine. But Silicon Valley is tremendously successful on its own terms—terms that have been roughly constant for several decades now, despite the Valley's reputation for constant change.

For instance, the origin story of modern Silicon Valley begins with a familiar tradition: smart young nerds rebelling against a founder who was a vainglorious asshole. That asshole was William Shockley, who was the recipient of the 1956 Nobel Prize in Physics. A year earlier, he had set up a semiconductor facility in Mountain View, California, near his elderly mother in neighboring Palo Alto. Shockley had his pick of the litter in

refers to a broader industry or cultural phenomenon and not necessarily to a particular place). My definition is somewhere in between, roughly "the ecosystem of technology companies, largely backed by venture capital, focused in the San Francisco Bay Area or with close ties to it."

recruiting young engineers, as Steve Jobs or Mark Zuckerberg might have had years later. But he was a difficult manager. He wrote everyone's salaries down on a bulletin board. He had the employees rate one another. He recorded their phone calls and even had them take lie-detector tests.

Nor was he paying them particularly well—somewhere between $90,000 and $135,000 a year in 2023 dollars. Such was life in the days before venture capital. An ambitious young scientist might work long hours at a leading-edge company for a comfortable upper-middle-class salary—but not for equity in the company or anywhere near the value he was generating for his bosses.

Eventually, eight of Shockley's engineers quit. The so-called Traitorous Eight joined a rival firm named Fairchild Semiconductor, which had been founded by the businessman Sherman Fairchild and an early pioneer of "adventure capital," Arthur Rock. They got substantial raises and, more importantly, one hundred shares each in the business.

But soon there was another betrayal of sorts. In 1959, Fairchild exercised an option to buy out the engineers' equity. He was within his contractual rights to do so, and the men made a substantial profit—the equivalent of about $4 million each in today's dollars. Still, having had a taste of what it was like to own their own upside, it was hard to go back. Sooner or later, all of them left, forming a diaspora. One of the men, Robert Noyce, would become cofounder at Intel. Another, Eugene Kleiner, would form the venture capital firm Kleiner Perkins. I'm leaving out important parts of the story—like the founding of Hewlett-Packard in 1939 or the adjacency of Silicon Valley to Stanford and Berkeley. The point is, at this stage, a virtuous cycle had begun.

Many of the traits we associate with Silicon Valley were established early on. For instance, its workaholic culture and obsession with youth. "In the Silicon Valley there was a phenomenon known as burnout," wrote the legendary author Tom Wolfe in a 1983 profile of Noyce for *Esquire*. "After five or ten years of obsessive racing for the semiconductor high stakes . . . an engineer would reach his middle thirties and wake up one day—and he was finished. The game was over."

The Traitorous Eight had also helped to establish another Silicon Valley tradition: lack of loyalty to incumbent players. California, from the Gold Rush onward, has always been a place for people who seek their own way. No, the Traitorous Eight were not countercultural figures, even as hippie culture was taking root in other parts of the Bay Area like Berkeley and Haight-Ashbury. But the notion that they were *disruptive* is not entirely bullshit, and it's an attitude that holds true today.

"Why would someone from Facebook go and create the thing that's gonna, like—presumably in theory, you'd never know—blow up Google or Facebook?" said Antonio García Martínez, who founded a VC-backed company called AdGrok and later worked at Facebook before writing about it in the book *Chaos Monkeys*. "It is because of this religious feeling of creative destruction for the sake of creative destruction. That is our religion. We have to do it. Like, the nonconformism of showing up at Burning Man like everybody else did in a stupid costume? Whatever. Yeah, maybe it's a little fake. But the business of actually burning down institutions? Yeah, I think that's actually real."

The Two Essential Traits of Silicon Valley

Let's back up a second, because I want to establish why these cultural traits have an underlying economic rationale. I had versions of these mantras repeated to me so often that I believe they're the governing gravitational forces behind pretty much everything that takes place in the Valley—why it attracts so many strange and disagreeable people, for instance. Venture capital is a unique enterprise for two essential reasons:

1. **It has a very long time horizon**. "You make very few decisions, and you're prepared to live with the consequences of that decision for a very long time," said Moritz. "Google, we financed Google in 1999. So here we are, twenty-three years, almost a quarter of a century. I still own the majority of that stuff."

2. **It offers asymmetric odds that reward taking chances on upside risks.** "There's an asymmetric set of returns. You're only going to lose one time your money," said Bill Gurley, a partner at Benchmark who didn't share Moritz's early enthusiasm for Larry Page and Sergey Brin. "And when you miss Google, which I did, you miss out on a 10,000x."

Are these principles the rest of the world should emulate? The first one is. Many times you can make a +EV bet just by being more patient than the next person. And it represents a comparative advantage because patience is an atypical trait in the United States. Although the U.S. is a relatively risk-tolerant country, it is full of people who want to get rich quick, not slowly. "Time or investment in the brand is something that's not very American," said Wen Zhou, the cofounder of the high-end fashion company 3.1 Phillip Lim, who moved from China to New York when she was twelve. "I don't know if that's even a controversial statement, because I feel like America is such a capitalist country. [But] it's the shortest amount of time to make the most amount of money." It's probably not a coincidence that a disproportionate number of VCs and founders are immigrants, like Khosla (India), Musk (South Africa), and Thiel (Germany).

Furthermore, the value of maintaining a long view may increase in a world where—and here I'm sounding like Thiel—data and analytics can sometimes lead to nearsightedness. It's often easy to algorithmically optimize for a short-term fix—and much harder to know what will produce long-term brand value. Even in sports, teams in the post-*Moneyball* era still apply incredibly steep discount rates to the future success of the team and are often willing to torch the future for a slightly higher chance of winning in the present.* Without a culture that specifically emphasizes long-term planning, the competitive equilibrium that emerges can be nasty, brutish, and short.

---

* That doesn't mean their behavior is irrational—it reflects the incentive structures of the decision-makers, which compel short-term thinking. Of the thirty Major League Baseball general managers as of October 2013, only two had the same job ten years later.

But of course an industry that wants people who plan ten or more years ahead necessarily attracts a lot of stubborn personalities. It very much *isn't* the case that you know the breakout hits right away; SpaceX, for instance, took six years until its first successful rocket launch and more than a decade until it turned a profit. In fact, veteran venture capitalists are used to a pattern called the J Curve: you know your failures before your successes, so your fund tends to have a negative return early. "There's a phenomenon called 'lemons ripen early,' which is that the companies that fail fail before the companies that succeed succeed," said Andreessen. "Because you've got a bunch of companies that are detonating, and then the big winners haven't appeared yet. And you're just like, I'm in a fucking ditch, and nothing is going well right now."

The Venture Capital J Curve

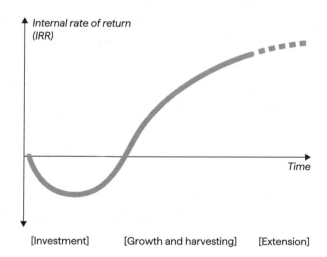

The second trait—the asymmetric nature of payoffs in Silicon Valley— is even more essential to understanding its mindset. But its implications are more ambiguous than the first one. Society would be generally better off—I'll confidently contend—if people understood the nature of expected value and specifically the importance of low-probability, high-impact events, whether they come in the form of fantastic potential payoffs or catastrophic risks.

However, when the payoffs take the form of financial investments, this can create two types of problems. The first is moral hazard: that the firm undertaking the risks, on the hook for only 1x their investment, does not bear the full consequences of them, which instead fall upon the public. This is more classically a problem on Wall Street, such as in the form of bank bailouts.* But this is potentially an issue anytime a business imposes negative externalities (a fancy economics term for "side effects") on society. True, technological growth usually has positive externalities—for instance, new biomedical products can extend human lifespans. Embedded deep in the VC psychology is the idea that they can sleep soundly at night because they are not only enriching themselves, but also making the world a better place. For some recent technological developments, however, the value proposition has been more questionable. Social media may well have had net-negative effects on society. Crypto gave rise to a lot of scams and cons, like Sam Bankman-Fried's FTX—heavily invested in by Sequoia and other VC firms—which cost cryptocurrency holders out of at least $10 billion. And with AI, the disruption could be profound, resulting in mass reshuffling of the economy even if it remains relatively well aligned with human values.

The second issue is that the huge payoffs contribute to a winner-take-all-economy. The VC/founder community is a *small* community. Top VC firms have from a small handful to a couple dozen partners each, in contrast to Wall Street firms, which have hundreds. Silicon Valley was once not a particularly show-offy place—many early founders were from the Midwest, and Wolfe thought its values reflected Calvinist, mid-country modesty—and even now, its mansions mostly take the form of low-lying structures hidden behind shrubbery, not opulent beachside or hillside homes as down south in L.A. But behind those bushes are people with exponentially increasing wealth, power, and influence. Although the extent to which they achieve them is a matter of considerable dispute, elite

---

* Of course, when Silicon Valley Bank failed in March 2023, VCs loudly demanded assistance—and the government stepped in to protect depositors. (By some definitions, this is considered short of a full bailout because SVB's shareholders were wiped out when it was sold to another company.)

Silicon Valley VC firms target IRRs (internal rates of return) of 20 to 30 percent per year. Let's say they're hitting the low end of that range, the 20 percent number. That means their wealth doubles every four years!

And yet, for all their success, almost every VC I spoke with still lived with FOMO: fear of missing out. Specifically, fear of the founder who got away. "The mistakes of omission are much, much bigger mistakes," said Andreessen. "We almost never kick ourselves for mistakes of commission; we do kick ourselves pretty hard for mistakes of omission. At some point, you just have to say yes. Like, whatever, Mark Zuckerberg walks in the door. You just have to not be so dumb that you say no."

Patrick Collison, the cofounder of Stripe (and another immigrant: he was born in Ireland), thinks it's this fear of omission—and a corresponding lack of fear of commission—that makes Silicon Valley distinct. The math behind expected value—a 5 percent probability of success times a 100x payout makes for a worthwhile bet—isn't difficult to grasp. Silicon Valley doesn't have any sort of secret mathematical sauce. Early stage VC isn't a particularly quantitative process at all. "I don't think that people in Silicon Valley are better at calculating," said Collison. Rather, they're better at *executing* on these bets—at pulling the trigger on investments that will *often* fail, sometimes in embarrassing ways. "I think they're better at some kind of underlying disposition," Collison said.

It's hard for most people to make bets that they know will usually fail. Many of the distinctive traits of Silicon Valley—from the increasing openness of psychedelic drug use, to the tolerance for difficult founders, to the tendency of VCs to pontificate on political issues—reflect a lack of fear of looking stupid. Humans are social animals, and so this fearlessness of social disapproval does not come naturally to most people.* The reason Silicon Valley is often willing to go to extremes in defense of its value system is because it fears that if these values are not actively reinforced, it will lose what makes it distinct.

---

* Particularly not in the Village, where ostracization (or if you prefer, "cancellation") is considered the ultimate punishment.

VCs Are Foxes, Founders Are Hedgehogs

Still, none of this seems easy to keep in balance exactly. Silicon Valley has its share of visionaries and its share of copycats; its share of people who want to change the world and its share of spoiled brats. And it has lots of socially awkward people who have achieved tremendous wealth and notoriety at a young age. My theory is that to make all of this work, you need a symbiosis between two often-clashing personality types. This corresponds to what I wrote before about needing both reasonable and unreasonable people, but I want to be more precise.

If you read *The Signal and the Noise*, you may remember our furry friends, foxes and hedgehogs. The terminology comes from the Greek poet Archilochus—"The fox knows many things, but the hedgehog knows one big thing"—by way of the political scientist Phil Tetlock, who conducted a long-term study of political scientists and other experts' predictive abilities. The study—published in the book *Expert Political Judgment: How Good Is It? How Can We Know?*—found that for the most part experts were terrible at making predictions. However, those experts with a cluster of personality traits that Tetlock regarded as foxlike—knowing many little things—were comparatively more accurate. Those clever little foxes were the heroes of *The Signal and the Noise*.

But do foxes make for good founders?

I can think of exceptions to the rule (the polymathic Collison is quite fox-like, for instance). But in general, VCs are looking for people with one big crazy idea that they'll commit to for a decade or longer. An idea that might fail, but has a small chance of being revolutionary. And that's squarely in the hedgehog personality sphere.

Attitudes of Foxes and Hedgehogs[*]

HOW FOXES THINK	HOW HEDGEHOGS THINK
Risk-tolerant: Think in expected-value terms and are willing to act on it. Do not necessarily see themselves as risk-taking; however, their ability to take calculated risks distinguishes them from most people.	**Risk-ignorant:** Not necessarily natural risk-takers. However, because they may misestimate or overestimate their abilities, they may sometimes make decisions that others would regard as incredibly risky.
Probabilistic: Think like poker players, i.e., willing to make bets based on incomplete information.	**Deterministic:** Think like chess players, i.e., that outcomes are highly certain once the position is worked out.
Multidisciplinary: Incorporate ideas from different disciplines, read widely across the political spectrum.	**Specialized:** Often have spent the bulk of their careers on one or two great problems.
Adaptable: Find a new approach—or pursue multiple avenues at the same time—if they aren't sure the original one is working.	**Stalwart:** Stick to the same "all-in" approach. Prone to confirmation bias. But will double down when others would quit.
Self-critical: Sometimes willing, if rarely happy, to acknowledge mistakes in their predictions and take the blame for them.	**Stubborn:** Mistakes are blamed on bad luck or idiosyncratic circumstances—a good idea had a bad day.
Tolerant of complexity: See the universe as complicated, perhaps to the point of many fundamental problems being inherently unpredictable.	**Order seeking:** Have an engineer's brain. Expect that the world will be found to abide by relatively simple governing relationships once the signal is determined through the noise.
Empirical: Rely more on observation and time-tested strategies than theory.	**Principled:** Expect that solutions to many day-to-day problems are manifestations of some grander ideological theory or struggle. May believe that civilization stands at a pivot point.

Think about someone like Elon Musk. Nearly every trait on the hedgehog list describes him to a T. He is extremely stubborn—or, if you prefer, extremely determined. He thinks like an engineer and he seeks order, another hedgehog-like trait.

Thiel, an ex-founder, is also mostly on Team Hedgehog, order seeking and ideological. He may not have Musk's risk tolerance—few people do—

[*] In case it seems familiar, this table is reproduced from *The Signal and the Noise* with some revisions and additions to make it more focused on attitudes toward risk-taking.

though hedgehogs have a funny relationship with risk. Namely, because hedgehogs aren't very good at estimating risk, they may undertake projects that other people would regard as extremely risky because they don't calculate the odds the same way. Or they may commit to a project as their life's work, not even wanting to know what the odds are.

For VCs, on the other hand, fox-like habits are potentially quite handy. In deciding where to invest, they're making forecasts—and we know from Tetlock's study that foxes are better forecasters. VCs aren't necessarily forecasting in a highly statistically-driven way. But in hearing hundreds of pitches in companies across many different sectors, they need to know a little about a lot.

Take Moritz, for instance. Unlike someone like Thiel, he was never really* a founder. Instead, Moritz had first moved to Detroit from Wales in 1976 as a journalist covering the automobile industry for *Time* magazine. (When I visited him at his apartment in San Francisco—with a stunning view of the Bay—Moritz complimented me on the Detroit Tigers cap I was wearing.) Eventually he made his way to Los Angeles and then farther north in California. He was fascinated by Silicon Valley and its young founders from the first instance. "Where I grew up, nobody ever started a company, let alone somebody who was nineteen or twenty. Unless, you know, it was a window cleaners or something."

After publishing stories about the Valley, including an early book about Steve Jobs called *The Little Kingdom*—the tempestuous Jobs cut off communication with Moritz midway through what was supposed to be an authorized biography—Moritz had developed relationships with the major VC firms and decided he wanted to get in on the action himself. "So I wrote five of them. Four of them said, 'Look, you're a history major, you know nothing about technology. You don't have a computer or engineering degree. You've never worked at Hewlett-Packard. You're a journalist. What the hell are we going to do with you?'" There was one exception: Don

---

* Moritz did found a tech-focused newsletter, a business that was somewhat ahead of its time. "Today, we could do it. It'd be called The Information or Tech Crunch or PitchBook," he told me. "The market is there today, we were just forty years too early."

Valentine, the founder of Sequoia Capital, who took a chance on Moritz. It was a good bet: Moritz twice made the number-one spot on Forbes's Midas List for his golden touch.

"He died a couple of years ago. But if you were interviewing him, [Don] would say, 'Well, Mike was a really good listener, and asked really good questions.'" That's the connection Moritz sees between journalism and venture capital—asking good questions. And being willing to work with limited information—another fox-like trait. "I was a general assignment reporter. So I was sent hither and yon and I would get parachuted into a story about which I knew nothing and then would have to be something of an authority about it within a couple of days. You know the drill. It's not that different in the venture business. I've always been one of these characters who is pretty darn comfortable making up my mind about something with imperfect information. And I think that's been a real advantage."

Foxes aren't necessarily risk-loving as an economist would define that term, meaning people who would deliberately make a neutral EV gamble just for the thrill of the chase. But foxes are good at measuring risk, and people who are good at measuring risk tend to be fairly risk-tolerant. They can at least get themselves to make the *positive* EV bets.

So here's my theory of the secret to Silicon Valley's success. It marries *risk-tolerant* VCs like Moritz with *risk-ignorant* founders like Musk: a perfect pairing of foxes and hedgehogs. The founders may take risks that are in some sense irrational, not because the payoff isn't there but because of diminishing marginal returns. (If you had a net worth of $1 million, would you gamble it all on a 1-in-50 chance of winning $200 million—and a 98 percent chance of having to start over from scratch? The EV of the bet is +$3 million, but I probably wouldn't.) But if the VCs can herd enough hedgehogs into a fund and make *many* of these bets, they can capture the EV without much risk of going broke.

Why the Valley Hates the Village

In the introduction, I wrote of the increasingly intense rivalry—part personality clash, part ideological struggle—between the River and the Village, my term for the cluster of intellectual occupations in government, media, and academia that are concentrated in the eastern United States and typically associated with progressive politics. Silicon Valley has been on the front lines of this conflict. Many of the VCs and founders in this chapter are outspoken about political affairs.* And honestly, it's not hard to see why the Valley and the Village are at war—the reasons for the conflict are overdetermined:

- **Everyone got really mad at each other about 2016.** The eight years of Barack Obama's presidency were a time of relative détente between Silicon Valley and the Village. Obama's victory in 2008 had been dubbed the "Facebook election," and his team of digitally savvy advisors—like Facebook cofounder Chris Hughes, who built a networking website for Obama's campaign—were credited for the campaign's success. But although the underlying trends may have been evident earlier, whatever remained of the warm feelings of the Obama years ended abruptly in the wee hours of November 9, 2016, when the networks declared that Trump had been elected president.

From Silicon Valley's perspective, the election was an emperor-has-no-clothes moment, demonstrating the Village's short-sightedness for nominating a candidate as flawed as Hillary Clinton and its smugness for failing to take Trump's chances seriously. Not many in the Valley—other than Thiel—had expected Trump to win.

"I didn't think Trump was gonna win the nomination. I didn't think he was gonna win the election. I believed the stupid fucking *New York Times*, like ninety-whatever, ninety-six or ninety-two percent thing† at six p.m. election night," said Andreessen, who had supported Clinton over Trump that year. "Like, I bought the whole narrative." So when Trump won, "I was shocked to shit. I was like, okay, I don't understand

---

* That's particularly true for hedgehogs like Musk and Thiel. I sometimes wish it weren't that way—I think a fox in his or her inherent moderateness would make for a better emissary for the River.
† Andreessen was referring to the *New York Times*'s election model, although their final forecast actually gave Clinton "only" an 85 percent chance of winning, not a number in the 90s. FiveThirtyEight's final forecast gave Clinton a 71 percent chance, by comparison.

the world. I don't understand how things work. Like, clearly my mental model is just wrong."

For the Village, meanwhile, Silicon Valley made for a convenient scapegoat. Less than a week after the election, *The New York Times* ran a front-page business section story on how Facebook was in the "cross hairs" for its role in its spread of misinformation during the campaign. This is a long chapter in a long book, and I don't want to derail our tour with too much of a detour into 2016. But as someone who knows a thing or two about elections, suffice it to say that I've never found the claim that Trump won because of Facebook misinformation persuasive. The *Times* made a big deal of the fact that Russian hackers bought $100,000 worth of digital ads on Facebook, for instance—but this was a tiny fraction of the *$2.4 billion* spent during the election in total. Instead, the Village's own coverage of things like the Clinton email scandal had probably had more impact.

- **The Village is about group allegiance, while Silicon Valley is individualistic.** While Silicon Valley is not quite so contrarian as it claims, it at least treats individualism as something to aspire to. (Think of the famous Apple ad campaign "Think Different.") Conversely, life in the Village is frequently defined by how you align yourself relative to two major parties, or other political, ideological, and identity groups. In a time of intense partisanship in the United States, this tends to make the Village a risk-averse place, especially when it comes to saying things that might offend others on your "team."

"If you've ever spent any time in D.C., it's like a city of rule followers," said David Shor, a data scientist and political consultant who works for Democratic campaigns. Shor has a theory for why this is the case. Election campaigns are like the minor league systems for Washington's social hierarchy: bright kids in their twenties aspire to move up the ranks and get a White House job in their thirties before cashing out with a cushy life in lobbying, consulting, or media. But campaigns are not always very meritocratic. "It's very rare to actually be able to assess whether someone did a good job," Shor said. Campaigns have hundreds of staffers and ultimately only one real test—election night—of how well they did, which is often determined by circumstances outside the campaign's control. Relationships matter more than merit. So people get ahead by going with the program.

Shor learned this the hard way. In 2020, amid sometimes violent protests over the murder of George Floyd, he was fired from his job at the Democratic data firm Civis Analytics. What was Shor's crime? He'd sent out a tweet pointing toward an academic paper by a Princeton professor that found race riots had tended to reduce the Democratic share of the vote while peaceful protests increased it.

In retrospect, it can be challenging to explain why Shor's post caused such a stir. Some of it was the timing—there was a massive nationwide political protest underway in the middle of a pandemic in the middle of a presidential election. The overarching goal of the Village, especially in election years, is to maintain group cohesion. If you can achieve that by scapegoating someone, that's all part of the game. And I mean "game" literally, as in "consistent with expectations from game theory." Punishing someone like Shor who was pissing from inside the tent served as a deterrent to others.

- **There are turf wars—and philosophical ones—between Silicon Valley and Washington over regulation.** "The reason Silicon Valley has been so successful is because it's so fucking far away from Washington, D.C.," said Bill Gurley to raucous cheers at the 2023 All-In Summit. It was the punchline to a talk he'd titled as "2,851 Miles"—because that is the driving distance from the White House to Sand Hill Road. The subject of the talk was regulatory capture—Gurley's belief that "regulation is the friend of the incumbent" and tends to favor big, established players over potential upstarts.

I asked Gurley, who isn't usually considered to be a bomb thrower, whether he worried about further antagonizing Washington. He told me he knew he was being provocative. And he basically didn't care because the conflict was already out in the open after Biden had appointed Lina Khan, an outspoken critic of big tech, as head of the Federal Trade Commission. Why was Gurley so concerned about this? Well, even though Khan has gone after the biggest names in tech—bringing lawsuits against Amazon, Meta, and Google—Gurley isn't crazy to worry about regulatory capture helping incumbents. (His thesis is well regarded in academic literature.) And a catechism in Silicon Valley is that big new ideas never come from established players.

"More than forty years I've been doing innovation. I can't think of a single example of a large innovation that came from an expected player or a large player," Vinod Khosla told me. Taken literally, this is an exaggeration—a ChatGPT query turned up counterexamples of products like the Sony Walkman, the IBM PC, and the iPhone* that were developed by well-established brands. But the David-vs.-Goliath narrative of the small disruptor conquering the giant incumbent is embedded deep in Silicon Valley's belief system, an heirloom passed down from one generation of founders to the next.

Or at least, that's how Silicon Valley sees it. For Washington, Mark Zuckerberg's attitude of "move fast and break things" is in direct contrast with its desire for incremental change. Many startups—like Uber, where Gurley was an early stage investor—begin life in a legal gray area and gamble on fading the regulatory risk. Often it proves to be a good bet, either because their products became popular enough that regulators are forced to accommodate them, or because whatever legal settlements they wind up paying to Lina Khan are a drop in the bucket compared to the scale of their profits.

But there have been important exceptions. Napster's business was essentially destroyed by a series of lawsuits, for instance. Kara Swisher, the cofounder of Recode who has covered the technology business since 1984, told me that the industry's intrinsic dislike for Washington is a long tradition—and has often made it its own worst enemy. "They were *disdainful* of Washington. Disdainful. They were saying, 'What do we need them for?'" she said. "And I kept saying, 'They're coming for you. You're rich.'"

Silicon Valley has the potential to repeat these mistakes over regulation of AI. "Our enemy is corruption, regulatory capture, monopolies, cartels," Andreessen wrote in the "Techno-Optimist Manifesto." Note his word choice: *enemy.* Silicon Valley may be right on the merits about AI regulation—say, that clumsy government efforts to control AI could result in regulatory capture, or the U.S. losing the AI race to China, or AI development being forced underground, where it could potentially be more dangerous. *But this isn't necessarily Silicon Valley's choice to make.* The political system and the judicial system will have their say too, as in the case of the copyright infringement lawsuit filed against OpenAI by *The New York Times* in December 2023.

---

* And ChatGPT itself was heavily funded by Microsoft and the other established players who formed OpenAI.

- **Silicon Valley is skeptical of the "trust the experts" mantra that the Village prizes.** This is one of the places where I'm most sympathetic to the arguments I heard from VCs and founders. Having spent my career shifting between subjects like sports, election forecasting, and the sort of business and science reporting that you're reading in this book, I'm pretty used to having my expertise challenged or being told to stay in my lane. But this has become much more common in the past several years—a period during which, because of increasing educational polarization, a very large majority of people in the Village vote for one political party, the Democrats.

Don't get me wrong: I think expertise is badly needed in society and that we'd drive ourselves crazy if we didn't defer to the expert consensus most of the time. But increasingly "trust the experts" or "trust the science" is used as a political cudgel, such as during many controversies about the COVID-19 pandemic. Meanwhile, as David Shor found out, citing the experts *isn't* always welcome if it doesn't match the Village's political objectives. Something has changed when skepticism—something I'd always thought of as the province of liberals—is instead being championed by conservatives like Thiel. "In theory, what science should do is it needs to be engaged in a two-front war, against excessive dogmatism, and against excessive skepticism," said Thiel. He told me that the Village has been moving away from skepticism toward dogmatism for years, but that COVID had made this especially clear. "It seems to me that they are fighting skepticism way harder than they're fighting dogmatism."

The irony is that if you *trust the experts on expertise*—meaning trusting people like Tetlock—they'll tell you that you should be pretty damned skeptical of the experts, who are subject to all sorts of cognitive biases even when their politics aren't getting in the way.

Many VCs have learned this lesson on their own. Foxes who have less subject-matter expertise but a more rigorous thought process are often better evaluators of founder talent, for instance. Moritz thinks it can sometimes be a liability to have too much technical knowledge. "Many of them have one serious disadvantage, which is they need to know every last detail. The scientists, the engineers and mathematicians, they've got to get to the root of everything and feel that they completely understand how the mechanics work. Which often means that they lose perspective."

Chamath Palihapitiya—the CEO of Social Capital who is happy to volley opinions on a wide assemblage of topics as one of the cohosts of the *All-In* podcast—told me that because political polarization makes it harder to know who to trust, there's no choice but to be a fox. "There's no longer experts. There's only *perceived* expertise. And even that's not verifiable anymore," he said when I brought up Tetlock's work. "I think expertise is a lost art form today. So you have to be a little bit of a fox and be able to just scurry around and calibrate what you're getting."

- **Tech leaders are in an ideological clash with their employees and blame the Village for it.** In describing "Silicon Valley" politics, we need to be precise about what we mean. The nine-county Bay Area region voted solidly Democratic in the 2020 election, as it usually does, giving 76 percent of its votes to Joe Biden and 22 percent to Trump. If you squint, you can perhaps see the first hints of a conservative shift—in Santa Clara County, the one most closely associated with the geographic heart of Silicon Valley, Trump's share of the vote jumped by 5 points from 2016. (This was actually one of the bigger swings in the nation outside of South Florida or South Texas.) Still, the region as a whole is overwhelmingly blue. So are the employees of the major tech companies, whose political contributions are disproportionately to Democrats.

But what about Silicon Valley's elites—the top one hundred VCs, CEOs, and founders? There's no comprehensive catalog of their political views, so I'll just give you my impressions as a reporter who's had a variety of conversations with them.

It's worth keeping in mind that rich people are usually conservative. If Silicon Valley's elites were voting purely with their pocketbooks, they'd vote Republican for lower taxes and fewer regulations, especially with Khan heading the FTC. Still, people like Thiel—who holds extremely conservative views on many issues—are relative outliers, and I imagine that most Silicon Valley leaders would not vote for Trump.

However, many of them are quite happy to talk your ear off about the culture wars, meaning the cluster of topics like "wokeness," cancel culture, and free speech. For some of them this can be a red pill into conservative views on other issues, and for others it isn't—but free speech issues tend to unite Silicon Valley's liberals, libertarians, and conservatives.

One reason is because these topics create tension between management and their younger, more progressive workforces. In 2017, for instance, a Google engineer named James Damore circulated a memo called "Google's Ideological Echo Chamber," which criticized Google's diversity hiring practices and argued that there was a biological basis for gender differences. Facing threats from other employees to quit if Damore remained, Google fired him.

The best argument I've heard for why Silicon Valley *should* care about the culture wars is because this sort of censoriousness—suppressing unpopular views or even firing people for them—threatens its long-standing belief that sins of omission are worse than sins of commission. Silicon Valley's Platonic ideal of itself has long been what the writer Tim Urban calls an "Idea Lab." "The Idea Lab is a culture where disagreement is cool," said Urban, whose 2023 book *What's Our Problem?* extensively covers this subject. "Where disagreeing with leaders is cool and fine, where no one takes disagreement personally. And where we value diversity of viewpoint."

In Silicon Valley, you're supposed to feel like you have permission to express unpopular and possibly quite wrong or even stupid ideas. So Damore's firing represented a shift. His views weren't particularly radical—they are relatively mainstream positions in surveys of the broader American population. They weren't even that unpopular *at Google*, where an anonymous survey found that 36 percent of employees agreed with the memo while 48 percent disagreed. And yet Damore was let go.

The critiques about Google gained credence following the February 2024 release of its AI model Gemini, which almost seemed like a conservative parody of wokeness—its image engine drew multiracial Nazi soldiers, female NHL players wearing surgical masks, and re-rendered (white) Google founders Page and Brin as Asian even when users had asked for nothing of the sort. The incident reinforced both the techno-libertarian fear of a progressive incursion into Silicon Valley and the view that companies as large as Google may have too many constituencies and political commitments to maintain cultures as distinctive as the Idea Lab and are therefore prone to being overtaken by leaner competitors.*

---

* This is related to Clayton Christensen's idea of the innovator's dilemma—spelled out in his book of the same name. Christensen was particularly concerned about commitments to customers—that big companies maintain too many product lines and features to keep existing customers happy—but the metaphor

- **Silicon Valley has plenty of "sore winners."** In 2016, a Florida jury awarded $140 million in damages to a man named Terry G. Bollea—better known as the wrestler Hulk Hogan. Bollea had sued Gawker Media for publishing a sex tape featuring Bollea and the wife of a radio personality named Bubba the Love Sponge.

This is already getting strange, I know. But the next twist is that Bollea's extremely expensive legal team had secretly been funded by a man who had absolutely nothing to do with the case: Peter Thiel. Thiel had been upset about an article Gawker had published years earlier, in 2007, which outed him as gay, and had essentially spent years plotting his revenge. And he got it: Gawker was forced into bankruptcy by the jury verdict and its founder, Nick Denton, sold the company.

There is a line in Thiel's 2014 book, *Zero to One*,* that scolds founders for getting caught up in personal drama:

In the world of business, at least, Shakespeare proves the superior guide. Inside a firm, people become obsessed with their competitors for career advancement. Then the firms themselves become obsessed with their competitors in the marketplace. Amid all the human drama, people lose sight of what matters and focus on their rivals instead.

I asked Thiel about this passage. Hadn't he been a hypocrite to focus on destroying a rival, Denton, half a continent away in New York in a completely unrelated business, all for the sin of outing a gay man who lived in the world's gayest city, San Francisco? Thiel quickly conceded the point. "In any intensely competitive context, it is almost impossible to simply focus on a transcendent object and not spend a lot of time on the personalities of one's rivals."

Silicon Valley's elites have a hell of a lot going for them. Wealth like the world has never seen. Power. Influence. They build cool products like rocket ships and work on ideas that could change the world. They have hot spouses—sometimes more than one at a time—own beautiful homes and go to fabulous parties. (The Calvinist modesty is mostly gone now.) And yet many of them are angry most of the time, particularly at the media and other parts of the Village.

---

can be extended to other commitments like those to shareholders, employees, political allies, and regulators.
* Cowritten with Blake Masters, the future Thiel-backed Arizona U.S. Senate candidate.

I asked Swisher why tech leaders like Thiel and Musk are so obsessed with their media coverage. She didn't need much time to consider her answer. "It's because they're narcissists. They're all malignant narcissists," she said.

The Case Against Silicon Valley

Thus far, I've been pretty sympathetic to Silicon Valley. But the truth is I agree with a number of common critiques about it. These aren't necessarily the first critiques you'd hear in the Village, whose concerns are often more parochial. Still, there are a lot of good questions we ought to be asking, such as:

- Are VCs intentionally selecting for crazy asshole founders?
- Is Silicon Valley really as contrarian as it claims?
- Do VC firms discriminate against women, Black, and Hispanic founders?
- Is VC success a self-fulfilling prophecy?

Let's take these one at a time.

Are VCs Intentionally Selecting for Crazy Asshole Founders?

Here's one statistic that might surprise you—it surprised me when I first came across it. Of the billionaires on the 2023 Forbes 400 list—the four hundred richest people in the United States—70 percent are basically* self-made. And 59 percent came from an upper-middle-class background or below. This phenomenon is even more true the farther you go along the

---

* *Forbes* treats the question as a sliding scale from 1 to 10; 70 percent of billionaires had scores of 6 or higher.

tail of the wealth curve. All of the ten richest people in America are classi-fied as self-made.

This fraction is significantly higher than it once was. In 1982, only 40 percent of the Forbes 400 had started their own business; the major-ity were simply scions of inherited wealth. Old money is out, new money is in? Well, it's essential to keep in mind that this is not an indica-tion of *overall* social mobility in the United States. In fact, by most ac-counts, such as the extremely detailed work of the economist Raj Chetty, overall income and wealth mobility has decreased in the U.S. from a generation ago. The Forbes 400, however, is the extreme right tail of the curve. To wind up there, it helps to have made some extremely risky bets that paid off—ones that you have less incentive to take if you're al-ready rich.

Let's say you inherit a $25 million trust fund on your eighteenth birth-day. Are you going to start a business with it? Maybe you *should*. But it's much easier to withdraw $1 million a year to live off, travel the world and have some wild parties, and put the rest in S&P 500 index funds earning 7 percent a year. By the time you're sixty-five, your expected net worth is about $250 million—plus a whole lot of frequent flyer miles. Nice! You're very, very rich. But you're not sniffing the Forbes 400 list, where the bid-ding starts at about $3 billion.

Conversely, there are about 5 million new businesses founded in the U.S. every year. That's a slightly misleading statistic, because it includes things like—tell me if you know anybody like this—a self-employed writer/statistician/poker player setting up a personal S corp for tax purposes. Still, if even 1 percent of those startups have serious potential to scale up, that's fifty thousand lottery tickets every year. Some of them are going to hit big, and the payoff for hitting big is *so* large these days that the lucky few who do are going to leapfrog all the trust fund kids.

Now, this certainly doesn't mean that you want to grow up in abject poverty; only a handful of the billionaires on the Forbes 400 list did. It helps to have a comfortable living environment. It also helps to be from one of the demographic classes that VCs like to invest in (e.g., a nerdy young man of European or Asian ancestry). But people who are born on third base tend to be pretty risk-averse.

"Why are second-generation kids never that successful?" asked Social Capital CEO Palihapitiya, who moved with his family from Sri Lanka to Canada and worked at a Burger King to help support them. Instead of the entrepreneurial mother or father, who had "only one curve that they were optimizing for, which is the what-have-I-got-to-lose curve," the child starts "with the exact inverse curve working against them, which is the risk of embarrassment," Palihapitiya said. "No matter what the parent says to that child, that person is operating from a perspective where the perception is that they have an enormous amount to lose."

It can also help to have something else: a chip on your shoulder. Josh Wolfe, of Lux Capital, is fond of the phrase "chips on shoulders put chips in pockets." Feeling left out, excluded, or estranged can make you *extremely* competitive. Remember, VCs want founders who are willing to commit to low-probability ideas—ideas they think the rest of the world is wrong about—for a decade or more. What motivates a person to do something like that? Wolfe, who grew up in a single-parent home in New York's gritty Coney Island neighborhood, told me he thinks there's a common answer: revenge.

"It could be because they were left for adoption. It could be a broken home," he said. "It could be being the only minority in a mostly homogenous white neighborhood, or the obese kid in a *Friday Night Lights* football town. People that out of necessity grow a thick skin with not fitting in and being okay standing out. And feeling a sense of anger that is not leading them to despondence, but to motivated revenge."

Let me make two things clear. First, you only want adversity *up to a point*. There is almost certainly a threshold beyond which there are too many disadvantages to overcome. Elon Musk had a difficult childhood and became estranged from his father; Thiel was gay and closeted; Jeff Bezos was adopted—but they were also privileged in other respects. They had chips on their shoulders, but they had enough social capital to be taken seriously by VCs, employees, and customers.

And second, this does *not* always turn out well. That competitive fire can be channeled in both constructive and self-destructive ways, and childhood trauma almost certainly has negative effects on the life course *on average*. But we're not talking about the average: we're talking about who winds up on the extreme right tail, the 0.0001 percent. It's usually going to be people who are either irrationally risk-loving out of a sense of having nothing to lose, extraordinarily mission driven out of a sense of wanting to prove people wrong—or both, as in the case of Musk.

Skill, Survivorship Bias, and Right-Skewed Outcomes; or, Did Elon Musk Just Get Lucky?

It's hard to emphasize just how much the average outcome can differ from the extremes—and how sensitive the tails are to a person's appetite for risk. So let me try one other way into this—an illustration from a hypothetical poker tournament.

This is an all-in or fold tournament, which is just what it sounds like. Each hand, you can either shove all your chips in or fold and wait for the next one. Every time you fold, you pay a penalty of 1 percent of your chips as an ante. If you go all-in but no one calls, you increase your stack by 10 percent because you win everyone else's antes. If you go all-in and do get called, you see a showdown and either double your stack or go broke and are out of the tournament. (You can't keep rebuying, like Elon Musk.) Consider two possible strategies:

- **Prudent.** You go all-in 20 percent of the time and fold the rest of your hands. When you go all-in, you're called 25 percent of the time. You win 50 percent of the time that you're called.

- **Degen.** You go all-in 100 percent of the time. When you go all-in, you're called 50 percent of the time. (People are more inclined to take their chances with you than with the Prudent strategy because they know you literally just have a random hand.) Since most of your hands are weak, you win only 40 percent of the time that you're called.

Let's say each player starts with 60,000 chips, and the tournament lasts for six hands. Which strategy is better? Well, I've run the numbers for us, and Prudent will leave you with an average of about 62,500 chips, compared to only 44,000 for Degen. Prudent is by far the better strategy—if the average is what you care about.

But Degen is both *much* more likely to bankrupt you and *much* more likely to make you filthy rich. Here are the odds, rounded off to whole numbers:

Poker Tournament Outcomes

OUTCOME	PRUDENT	DEGEN	SKILLED DEGEN
Going broke	1 in 7	7 in 8	3 in 4
Making a profit of any kind	3 in 5	1 in 8	1 in 4
Finishing with 100K+ chips	1 in 8	1 in 8	1 in 4
Finishing with 500K+ chips	1 in 9,000	1 in 40	1 in 10
Finishing with 1M+ chips	1 in 600,000	1 in 150	1 in 25
Finishing with 3.84M chips (maximum possible)	1 in 4 billion	1 in 15,000	1 in 1,400

Degen goes broke more than 85 percent of the time. But occasionally it hits spectacularly big. It is about four thousand times more likely than Prudent to make you a millionaire, for instance. When the tournament ends, all the players at the top of the leaderboard will have used the Degen strategy.

So is this my way of saying that the richest founders in the world are just degenerate gamblers who got lucky?

No, I'm not saying that. I think they're *highly skilled* degenerate gamblers who got lucky.

Suppose that in our tournament, there are a few degens who have a vial of Phil Hellmuth's "white magic." Even though they go all-in every hand and are called half the time, they manage to win 60 percent of these all-ins. (How do they do this? Use your imagination—maybe they sweet-talk their opponents into making suboptimal decisions.) These skilled degens still end up broke about 75 percent of the time. But they're about five times more likely than regular degens to finish with at least a million chips, and eleven times more likely to finish with 3.84 million chips, the maximum possible.

Almost by definition, the people at the very top of any leaderboard are both lucky *and* good. Which component predominates? In this poker example, luck is still the more important factor—and I suspect that's true in Silicon Valley too, at least when it comes to achieving unicorn-type wealth. All the people I spoke with or wrote about for this chapter are self-evidently smart. Some are undoubtedly geniuses. Certainly someone like Musk, whatever else you say about him, has excellent engineering skills, an uncanny ability to get people around him to pursue ambitious goals, and an insane work ethic.

But in a world of 8 billion people, there are eight thousand people with one-in-a-million ability. You're still going to have to get pretty damned lucky to be the richest one of all.

All of this is naturally going to lead to some difficult personalities. Some VCs even seem to think of it as an asset when a founder is poorly adjusted. "Who is my real customer? It's a young, disenfranchised, disenchanted entrepreneur-to-be," said Palihapitiya, referring to the sorts of people who might come to him for investment or mentorship. "And I use those words specifically, because if you're comfortable, and you're happy," he continued, "you're not the kind of person I want to work with anyway because you're probably not gonna be successful."

This feels like a dangerous game. Successful founders may be disagreeable on average, because disagreeability is correlated with competitiveness and independent-mindedness. But the disagreeability is still a bug, not a feature. If you start to select founders *because* they're disagreeable, you may get the wrong ones. Especially if founders deliberately play into stereotypes that they think VCs will like, as Sam Bankman-Fried did (we'll cover him in the next chapter).

And yet, if all you care about is the right tail, the selection process gets weird. Let's say you're starting a small business like an ice cream shop. You just want to sell ice cream at one or two stores and make a decent living—not disrupt the global ice-cream business. You have the money, and you're looking for someone to run the operation. What characteristics should this person have? Words like reliable, trustworthy, hardworking, and agreeable come to mind. They'll give you the highest probability of success.

But what if you want a business that could grow by 100x or 1,000x? That's a lot harder to know. I don't think VCs are deliberately picking founders they think are *un*reliable, although sometimes it seems like it.

In August 2022, Andreessen Horowitz (a16z) announced its newest investment: it would put $350 million into a company called Flow, which "aims to create a superior living environment that enhances the lives of our residents and communities"—in other words, rental real estate. The company was founded by a charismatic Israeli American named Adam Neumann.

If the name sounds familiar, it's because Neumann was also the founder of WeWork—a company that was once worth an estimated $47 billion before imploding spectacularly amid accusations that Neumann had, among other things, taken a "sizeable chunk" of weed across international borders on a private jet, discriminated against a pregnant employee, and—most importantly—expanded far too quickly, leading to enormous annual losses. (Neumann, after directing me to a spokesperson, didn't respond to an interview request.)

Would you want to go into business with someone like that? Well, I probably wouldn't, though the plane rides sound like fun. But in Silicon Valley terms, the thinking may go something like this: you'd rather invest in someone who had built a $47 billion company and watched it catastrophically collapse than someone who had never done so at all.

And Andreessen Horowitz is proud of its investment in Flow. In February 2023, Marc Andreessen invited me to an a16z conference at the spectacularly beautiful Amangiri hotel in Canyon Point, Utah. I thought it would be worth going for the networking and the snowy desert landscapes even though I expected to be told that the event was off the record. Sure enough, at the first panel, Ben Horowitz said the proceedings were off the record. Fine. But since nothing had been agreed upon up to that point, I'm within my journalistic rights to report on the existence of the conference itself (which has also been reported on elsewhere) as well as the person who was onstage with Horowitz at the time he made the announcement. It was Neumann, as you've probably guessed. In a room full of Silicon Valley's elites, a16z were showing him off—and sending a message.

"Why would they run out and give a bunch of money to Adam Neumann after everything they've seen? Like, what in the world was that all about?" said Benchmark's Gurley.* "If I were asked to analyze what they were doing, they wanted to send a signal to everyone." The signal was that they didn't care about reliability—they wanted founders who gave them upside risk. They were *embracing variance*. "If they're that type of person, they're open for business, the door's wide open, and we're willing to talk to you, no matter what."

Is Everyone in the River on the Spectrum?

In the River, it's common to find people, like Elon Musk or the poker player Daniel "Jungleman" Cates, who self-identify as having Asperger's syndrome or autism. It's also common to hear people refer to themselves or others with terms like "Aspie," "on the spectrum," "spectrum-y," or "autist" without necessarily implying a formal diagnosis. Depending on the context, this may be derogatory, but it isn't always so.

I mention this here because when the subject of founders like Musk comes up, Asperger's is sometimes offered as an explanation—or an excuse—for their difficult behavior. In fact, it can even be viewed as a positive. Thiel, for instance, has said he thinks Asperger's can be an advantage for founders because he associates it with single-minded dedication to a task and lack of adherence to social convention.

---

* Gurley brought up a16z's investment in Flow independently in our conversation—we hadn't been discussing the conference and I don't know if he had attended it.

At times when working on this book, I contemplated making Asperger's a larger theme. Maybe it was a skeleton key, explaining common personality traits in the River and how its thinking departs from the rest of society? But after reading on the subject and speaking with perhaps the world's foremost autism researcher, Professor Simon Baron-Cohen of the University of Cambridge,* I think it raises as many questions as it answers. I have no doubt that the prevalence of autism is higher in the River than in the general population, but I don't think it suffices to explain what makes it different.

For one thing, there are clearly some people in the River—like the outgoing, party-boy, not-too-worried-about-the-details Adam Neumann—who nobody would identify as autistic. But there's also a bigger issue: it's hard to pin down exactly what autism *is*, exactly. "The huge variability under that diagnosis means that two individuals may have almost nothing in common," said Baron-Cohen.

The autism spectrum comprises everything from people with severe mental and physical impairments to—based on post-facto diagnoses—John von Neumann, perhaps the greatest genius who ever lived. And it's associated with different, sometimes contradictory stereotypes, from the creative savant to the rigidly minded engineer. It's also not clear whether autism and Asperger's should be part of the same diagnosis. They weren't until 2013, but they are now under the American Psychiatric Association's classification scheme *DSM-5*.

Moreover, autism is a cluster of moderately correlated personality and developmental traits rather than any one discrete condition. The Autism-Spectrum Quotient, a questionnaire designed by Baron-Cohen and his colleagues, breaks a diagnosis down into five subcategories:

- **Social skill:** Finding social interactions difficult and having challenges reading social cues and understanding social norms.

- **Attention switching:** Preferring to intently focus on one thing at a time.

- **Attention to detail:** Having a keen eye for detail and patterns that others might overlook.

- **Communication:** Having a hard time reading people—taking things very literally and struggling with understanding body language and facial expressions.

---

* Yes, he's the comedian Sacha Baron-Cohen's cousin.

- **Imagination:** Having trouble visualizing objects or people, and finding it hard to predict other people's actions.

Hopefully you can see why this is so complicated: the five traits do not necessarily go together. Someone like Musk is clearly possessed of a strong ability to visualize. Poker players like Cates who are a little socially awkward may nevertheless use their pattern-matching skills to develop a keen ability to read other people in the context of a poker hand.

The stereotype of the autistic person who needs order and routine also intersects awkwardly with the notion of risk-taking, the subject of this book. "You'd imagine some autistic people would be very risk-averse," said Baron-Cohen. "Certainly they have a preference, if you can generalize, for predictability, and routine, and kind of familiarity. And the idea about taking risk is almost like going outside of your comfort zone. So that may not appeal to a lot of autistic people."

This may help to explain why Musk is so unusual. His single-minded focus—and his lack of social graces—are classic autistic traits. But his appetite for risk isn't. It is rare to find these traits clustered together in the same individual.

Is Silicon Valley Really as Contrarian as It Claims?

I met with Keith Rabois in 2022 at the new, smartly furnished, still mostly empty Founders Fund offices in Miami. The building was in Wynwood, a formerly industrial neighborhood increasingly full of clothing boutiques, ceviche bars, and nightclubs—by any definition, trendy.

Rabois and his husband had moved to Miami during the pandemic and had become evangelists for the city. "My partner and I had a very simple set of criteria. It was warm weather. International airport. Tax rate of four and a half percent or below. And something to do, meaning some cosmopolitan food, shopping, something," he explained. That narrowed down the possibilities quickly. Phoenix *maybe* qualified, but Miami definitely did, plus it had the beach and a Barry's Bootcamp, Rabois's favorite gym.

The irony of all of this wasn't lost on me. On the one hand, there was something to be said for Rabois actually getting up and leaving California. For all of the complaints I heard about California from people in California—about the taxes, about the wokeness, about the crime and living conditions in San Francisco—most of them stayed. On the other hand, Miami was not exactly a contrarian proposition. Moving to Miami was *kind of a thing* during the pandemic—not necessarily among the general population,* but among *certain types.* Tech founders and hedge-funders, particularly if they were conservative or center right. Crypto kids. Middle-aged gay guys. (My partner and I considered it and even put in a bid on a condo at one point.)

All of this has more to do with venture capital than you might think.

Do VCs actually want to be contrarian? Founders Fund—Thiel's firm—has a reputation for it. But according to Rabois, there's a delicate balance to strike. "When you initially invest, or found a company, you want it to be, like, ridiculous and contrarian," he said. "But you want it to shift into consensus, because you need other people's money, publicly or privately. You need to recruit employees that are more normal than the founder-type class. So the art is pulling a trigger and then shifting it. And if that gap is too long, then you have a problem."

VCs, in other words, are playing the role of tastemakers—like Instagram influencers looking for the hottest new club. *That* place? Oh, no. *That* place is played out. But there's this *new* place, in this *new* neighborhood. Pretty soon, that's where *everybody* is going to be. So we have to get in *first.* But Rabois also can't get too far ahead of the pack and lead them to a club where nobody's at. "Venture, at an important level, is a very small, small, small set of people. Like, there's only five people I compete with. Whatever everybody else does doesn't actually matter for my job," he said.†

The process is akin to what economists call a Keynesian beauty contest, after the economist John Maynard Keynes, who thought it was one reason that stock markets undergo bubbles. The idea—slightly modernized to the present day—is this. Imagine that BuzzFeed runs a contest where

---

* Miami-Dade County actually lost population from 2020 to 2022, while the rest of Florida gained it.
† It is indeed a small world—in January 2024, Rabois announced a return to Khosla's firm, Khosla Ventures—although he's staying in Miami.

you're asked to pick the six hottest people from a set of one hundred photos. They offer a $1 million prize to whomever is able to make the six "correct" selections—defined as the six photos chosen most often by others. The process quickly becomes recursive, a fancy way of saying that it starts to feed back on itself. If I'm trying to win, it's no longer about who *I* find attractive, but who I think others will. Someone who's hot in an unconventional way might not be a very good pick.

But with everyone trying to anticipate everybody else's tastes, game theory says that the equilibrium can shift quickly. (These same dynamics help to explain the rapid fluctuations in the prices of crypto assets—we'll get to that in chapter 6.) So Rabois is always trying to calibrate to his friends' preferences. "One thing that's kind of a secret in the industry," he told me, "is that most of the people I compete with, I'm actually pretty somewhere between real friends and very good friends with. So part of what I'm doing is mapping their brain. Like, will they or their fund appreciate this? Are they going to see the signals I'm seeing?"

Sebastian Mallaby, the author of an excellent book about Silicon Valley called *The Power Law*, thinks that in certain respects it is an exceptionally conformist place.

"In some ways, venture capitalists are the ultimate herders," he said. "You go to Sand Hill Road, and you see that they all have offices on the same road. And there's kind of one good restaurant on that road, at the Rosewood hotel, so they all bump into each other at the same bar. Furthermore, they syndicate into each other's deals, Series A, Series B, Series C." There's also one particular characteristic of Silicon Valley that especially encourages groupthink—you can't go short. "It's not a public market, you can't short the stock. And because you're syndicating and you want deal flow, you can't even speak short, you can't say negative things about other people's deals."*

Yet for all its *Mean Girls* conformity—Rabois trying to figure out what

---

* This is one further reason that VCs tend to be particularly thin-skinned about public criticism. In most parts of the River—say, sports betting or hedge funds—you make money essentially by being critical of your competitors' opinions. In VC, you don't—it's not a culture that's used to a lot of negative feedback.

his five best frenemies will think—Silicon Valley's opinions are still relatively uncorrelated with those of the outside world, Mallaby thinks. "Is it still disruptive? Yes, I think it's considerably disruptive in the sense that this herd is in a different place on the intellectual planet," he said. "Established industries that are running material public companies—you know, the world of shipping companies, or transport or autos, or whatever it is . . . are going to be disrupted by this weird tribe. So internally, it's a herd. But the herd is running in a direction that could be quite orthogonal to the rest of the economy."

And this trait isn't at any risk of dying out. I even heard the argument that as the Village becomes more conformist, Silicon Valley has more opportunity to profit by running in a different direction. "You know, in the broader society, it's become pretty contrarian to try new things," said Andreessen. "We all feel contrarian in a way that we didn't as a class ten years ago."

Do VC Firms Discriminate Against Women, Black, and Hispanic Founders?

According to PitchBook, just 2 percent of VC funding in the United States goes to female-only founders or founding teams. Another 16.5 percent goes to women who are paired with men. The latter figure has increased in recent years, but the former one hasn't.

Meanwhile, Black founders typically receive around 1 percent of VC capital in the United States, according to Crunchbase. And about 2 percent goes to Hispanic founders. Whether there's been any increase is hard to say because the overall percentages are so small that they're subject to a fair amount of random statistical variation from year to year.

As I discuss in chapter 2, many parts of the River are very male, and much of it also lacks much Black or Hispanic representation. So Silicon Valley is not unique in this regard—and it's fair to note that tech firms are diverse in other respects, with much larger shares of VC funding going to immigrants and founders of Asian ancestry than their share of the U.S.

population. But it's hard not to think that VCs are potentially letting a lot of talented Black, Hispanic, and women founders slip through the cracks. And the Keynesian contest is part of the reason.

I spoke with Jean Brownhill, the founder and CEO of Sweeten, a company that matches homeowners with general contractors—think Tinder, but for when you need a new porch. She eventually raised $8 million for the idea, but it took speaking with more than 250 investors to do so. And she has a lot of stories from that process. "Probably more stories than you would believe," she told me.

Here's the story that stuck out to her the most. She met with an investor—an investor who may not initially have realized she was Black, Brownhill said. The investor, like many others, turned her down. "It's amazing, I love it, blah blah blah, but I'm not going to invest," she recalls him saying. "Here's why. As a Black woman you're going to have a harder time fundraising, a harder time retaining talent, a harder time selling," the investor said. "Every part of this process is going to be harder for you, and it's already an impossible process."

Essentially, the investor was telling Brownhill she had lost the Keynesian beauty contest—on account of being Black and a woman. Remember, an early stage VC investor is not just betting on the founder. He* is hoping to catalyze a chain reaction from other investors. He is betting on the preferences of his friends. The investor who turned her down "thought he was being, like, so noble" by telling her this, Brownhill said, which is what irked her the most. Because what this investor believed in his heart of hearts isn't particularly important. If VCs won't invest in Black or women founders because they think their *friends* are racist or sexist—even if they aren't racist or sexist themselves—the practical effect on founders like Brownhill is the same.

Moreover, all of this can have a cumulative effect. As the "noble" investor told Brownhill, the odds of success for founders are low. (Not that Brownhill needed any reminder. "If I looked at any data about poor brown

---

* Yes, probably a "he." Women represent less than 10 percent of VC partners.

girls from New London, Connecticut, I'd have quit a long time ago," she told me.) Let's say that a founder has to go through five stages of fundraising— say, a friends and family stage, seed funding, then Series A, B, C—before having a profitable exit. For a male founder in one of Silicon Valley's preferred demographic groups, say that they have a 50 percent probability of convincing enough people to invest at each stage. Their total probability of a successful exit is 0.5 to the fifth power, which works out to 3.1 percent:

$$50\% \times 50\% \times 50\% \times 50\% \times 50\% = 3.125\%$$

Now let's say there's a Black woman founder. At any given stage, she has a 40 percent probability of finding enough investors. "Well, that's not *that* bad," you might say; 40 percent isn't *that* much lower than 50 percent. But the cumulative effect is very large. Take 0.4 to the fifth power, and you end up at only about 1 percent probability of an exit—less than a third of the male founder's chances:

$$40\% \times 40\% \times 40\% \times 40\% \times 40\% = 1.024\%$$

What's especially ironic about Silicon Valley is that it claims to want high-upside, high-variance bets rather than safe ones. It claims to actively seek out founders who see the world differently and perhaps even have shown some grit in overcoming a difficult childhood. And it worries about sins of omission. You'd think it would be *very* interested in people like Brownhill, but it often isn't.

Kara Swisher thinks part of the issue is that the top VC firms have *so* many choices that they can get away without having to do a particularly rigorous search for talent. It's "like full of fish jumping in your boat," she said.*

---

* Franklin Leonard, the founder of the Black List—what began as an anonymous survey of studio executives about neglected Hollywood scripts, and later resulted in the development of films like *Argo*, *Spotlight*, and *Slumdog Millionaire*—gave me a different metaphor. I'm leaving it in the footnotes, because Leonard was talking about Hollywood and not Silicon Valley. Still, it stuck with me, and the selection processes are similar enough—a large number of applicants being evaluated by essentially a small number of talent scouts—that I thought it was worth sharing.

VCs are such intense pattern matchers that a few iconically success-ful Black or women founders might beget others—the equilibrium of the Keynesian beauty contest would shift. But for the time being, the situation is poor. "There is discrimination against women and there's discrimina-tion against African Americans. And that's a bad thing, obviously," said Mallaby. "Particularly if you're an industry that's purporting to invent the future for all of society, you should look like society. And I think you can kind of leave it there."

Is VC Success a Self-Fulfilling Prophecy?

Andreessen Horowitz is a lot like Harvard. And Founders Fund is a lot like Stanford.

Marc Andreessen and Peter Thiel would probably resist the compari-son, between Andreessen's dislike for the Village and Thiel's skepticism of postsecondary education.* But the similarities are obvious once you see them. The top venture capital firms—like the top universities—are excep-tionally *sticky* institutions. Once you make it into the elite tier, you tend to stay there. And as much as some VCs see themselves as "swashbuckling, buccaneering, and risk-taking" types—the self-image that Moritz criticized as "hogwash"—they actually get the best of both worlds: high returns *without* having to worry too much about downside risk.

Here's what I mean by "sticky." Consider that when *U.S. News* pub-lished its first set of college rankings in 1983, Stanford and Harvard were at the top of the list. They're still near the top now, forty years later. But that understates their staying power. Harvard was also near the top of the charts in academic rankings one hundred years ago. That's not to mention Oxford, which has been around for almost a millennium.

"The industry is a little bit like imagining the NBA—but people were putting together rosters only based on people that the owners of the teams knew," Leonard said. "And if you were to ask one of those owners, 'How do I get consideration to be on the Lakers roster?' the response was, 'Move to L.A., get a job at Star-bucks, and then play pickup on the courts closest to the Staples Center. And if you're really ballin' out, we'll probably see you.'"

* Thiel even started a program called the Thiel Fellowship that offers grants of $100,000 to students to drop out of school and pursue a business idea. The program has spawned quite a few successful founders, including Buterin, the co-creator of Ethereum.

Venture capital firms also show plenty of longevity. Sequoia Capital and Kleiner Perkins have been among the top firms since they were founded in 1972. Although a16z and Founders Fund are newer, they're in essence part of the same chain, since Kleiner Perkins was an early investor in Andreessen's Netscape and Sequoia was in Thiel's PayPal. This persistence is not common in other types of businesses. Just one company in the top ten of the Fortune 500 list in 1972—ExxonMobil—was still on the list in 2022, for instance.

What links top VC firms and top universities is that they are recruitment-driven businesses. And recruitment can become a renewable resource. With every new crop of students or founders are the seeds of future success. If you get to choose from the best and brightest, you'll be all but assured of picking some winners that further bolster your reputation, enhance your network, and contribute to your stash of capital, whether that's your assets under management or your university endowment.

Before long, it gets to a point where if the top firms are recruiting you, you'd have to be crazy to turn them down. And few people do. Harvard and Stanford have yield rates—the percentage of admitted students who accept—of around 84 percent. For the top VC firms, the numbers are probably in the same ballpark. "Basically ninety percent of the fight is over before it begins in venture," Andreessen told me of the process of recruiting founders. "Like, at the point of contact with an entrepreneur, when we go in and we do our whole sales process and try to win the deal . . . ninety percent of that fight is over before it begins, because it has to do with the reputation that we've established, the track record—you know, the brand."

I remember being a little bit surprised during our conversation that Andreessen had put this so bluntly. Not that I disagree with his analysis; it makes perfect sense. But was he basically just saying that a16z's success was a self-fulfilling prophecy? Then a few moments later, he said exactly that. "It's sort of a self-fulfilling prophecy, the whole thing," he said. "There might be a thousand different ways to get in the positive feedback loop," he continued. "But the reality is, you're either in it or you're not.

And then if you're in it, and you can keep it going, it's great. And if you fall out, it's really hard to get back."

So although the academic literature generally supports the idea that VC firms earn durable excess returns—meaning they do a lot better than you or I could by investing in index funds, and they do it consistently—this shouldn't be surprising, any more than Harvard consistently ranking among America's top colleges. In reputation-driven businesses, incumbents are hard to dislodge.

But isn't investing in startup businesses risky? Couldn't even Andreessen Horowitz—the top VC firm by assets under management—have a bad crop of investments? Before I started working on this book, I assumed that venture was a lot like poker tournaments, with occasional huge scores punctuating long dry spells. As we covered in chapter 2, poker tournaments are an exceptionally hard way to make a living. You might theoretically be +EV, but you may go broke long before you reach the long run.

VC *isn't* like that, it turns out. Yeah, there are some very, *very* big scores, like Google. But there are plenty of small scores, too. It's not like poker tournaments where you only win a prize 15 percent of the time. Andreessen recited from memory data on a typical returns portfolio, which he later confirmed by email:

- 25 percent of investments make zero return.

- 25 percent produce a return greater than 0 but less than 1x.

- 25 percent produce a return between 1x and 3x.

- The next 15 percent produce a return between 3x and 10x.

- Finally, the top 10 percent produce a return of 10x or greater.

It's important to clarify that this data pertains only to what Andreessen calls "top-decile" venture firms like a16z—not just anybody renting a room in an office park on Sand Hill Road. The industry as a whole does *not* generate particularly attractive returns. But the top firms can be extremely profitable, targeting a 20 percent IRR and going north from there, perhaps even 25 or 30 percent or higher for high-risk sectors.*

Classic economic theory says you need to take a lot of risk to earn returns that high. And yet when I simulated the data using Andreessen's numbers, I found that it's actually quite hard to *lose* money when you get both big wins and small ones.

I'm going to save the details for the endnotes, but the way I set the simulation up was this: Suppose that a fund invests in twenty-five companies and holds them for ten years. This is equivalent to drawing twenty-five numbers from a tumbler of white ping-pong balls corresponding to the return schedule that Andreessen described. The way I programmed the simulations, the returns on some balls go as high as 500x. The fund also draws a single red ball from a *different* tumbler—this corresponds to industry-wide volatility based on historical returns from the Nasdaq. This reflects the fact that the industry is cyclical—sometimes you'll choose the right companies in the wrong investment climate, or vice versa—although ten years is often long enough to even out the cycles.

The results are as follows:

- The average fund makes an IRR of 24 percent. That's very good, roughly 3x the annual return you'd get from the stock market. This is consistent with the literature on what the top firms earn.

- However, there is *not* that much downside risk:
  - About 98 percent of funds nominally make money.
  - About 96 percent make enough to beat inflation.
  - And about 90 percent make enough to beat the returns you'd get from the S&P 500.

---

* Although firms are selective in what data they release to the public, there are enough snippets of evidence to confirm high numbers. Data from the University of California's endowment, for instance, shows a number of long-term Sequoia investments earning IRRs in the range of 25 to 30 percent. When two a16z funds were reported as having interim returns of only 12 to 16 percent, it was framed as a disappointment in the trade press because their previous fund had an IRR of 44 percent. But even 12 percent is quite a bit better than the long-run returns from the stock market.

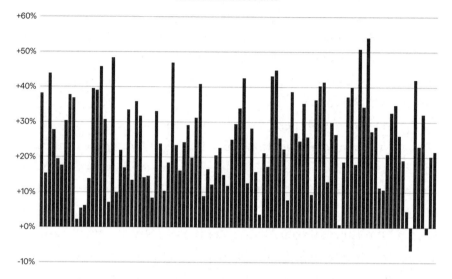

Annualized returns (IRR) from a sample of one hundred random draws using my
interpretation of Andreessen's data. Most outcomes are strongly positive.

It's a damned good business—and if anything, this overstates the risk,
because firms run multiple funds at a time to make a more diversified set
of bets.

The Village and the River Go to War

Between the time I filed the first draft of this chapter and when the final
version was due, Harvard and other elite colleges began to look like less
of a safe bet.

Silicon Valley has long prided itself on questioning the value of a
college degree—Mark Zuckerberg and Steve Jobs were famously college
dropouts.

Still, in the Obama years, it had been happy to use elite colleges as
its minor league system; as of 2017, 89 percent of jobs at Google had a
college degree requirement.

But a December 2023 congressional hearing featuring the presidents
of Harvard, Penn, and MIT turned into open warfare after the presidents were accused of insufficiently denouncing anti-Semitism and

being inconsistent in their application of free speech principles. Penn's president, Liz Magill, soon resigned under pressure from the hedge fund manager Bill Ackman and the Penn board. Harvard's Claudine Gay initially survived, but resigned in January 2024 after several credible accusations of plagiarism were made against her.

Although the charge had been led by Ackman—an investor but not a VC—he was cheered on by Musk, Andreessen, and much of the rest of Silicon Valley. Harvard is the grand cathedral atop the hill—there is no more quintessentially Village institution. So the ouster of its president was a symbolic coup. (Want another sign that the Village and the River are explicitly at war? *The New York Times*'s copyright lawsuit against OpenAI.)*

But what ought to worry the Village is that public opinion increasingly shares the River's skepticism of it. Indeed, the Village has begun to look like a small island threatened by a rising tide of disapproval. The Democratic White House, usually an ally of the Village, had panned the performance of the university presidents. And as Harvard's leadership initially defended Gay, the student newspaper, the *Crimson*, did tough reporting on her plagiarism, and Harvard alumni of varying political stripes questioned whether the school was living up to its motto: *Veritas* (truth). The Village also has a perception problem with the broader American public—even before the congressional hearings, trust in higher education was plummeting. In a 2015 Gallup poll, 57 percent of Americans said they had "quite a lot" or a "great deal" of confidence in higher ed. But by 2023, that had plunged to 36 percent, and the decline was registered among voters of all political parties, not just Republicans. Trust in another canonical Village institution—the one that I work in, the media—also reached record lows in 2023.

To be fair, trust in Big Tech has also dropped sharply in polls. But Silicon Valley is not particularly dependent on public confidence so long as it continues to recruit talent and people continue to buy its products. By contrast, if the Village loses public confidence in its ability to provide

---

* I have conflicted feelings about *The New York Times* since I used to work there (though I didn't leave on great terms) and now freelance for it occasionally. Like Harvard, the *Times* is a quintessentially Village institution and can embody some of the Village's worst traits. But the *Times* has also shown a capacity for change (as in its 2014 *Innovation Report*) and risk-taking (as in the sure-to-be-expensive OpenAI lawsuit). It may not be a coincidence that the *Times* has grown as nearly all its journalistic competitors have shrunk.

impartial expertise or a worthwhile education, it doesn't have a whole lot else to stand on. Although I'd expect Harvard and other elite colleges to be relatively resilient—they'll still exist in fifty years, and many smart people will still want to be associated with them—it's now easier to imagine elite universities playing a lesser role in American life.

Finite Minds and Boundless Ambitions

If you've detected that I feel conflicted about venture capital, this is why. I buy the Techno-Optimist argument that technology has contributed enormously to human welfare—although that's clearer for some inventions (semiconductors) than others (social media).* And I think Silicon Valley gets the big questions right about risk and scale—questions that a lot of people get wrong—which helps it make up for a lot of its other faults.

However, if success is concentrated only among a few elite firms, and those advantages are compounding to the point where they essentially can't lose, then VC is becoming more and more like the incumbent institutions that Silicon Valley would deign to disrupt. The bets that VC pioneers like Arthur Rock, Don Valentine, and Eugene Kleiner made were exceptionally smart ones. But in the rest of the River, even the smartest bets don't continually pay off over and over. You can't say success in Silicon Valley is given by divine right, because it's not determined by birth, and in fact most founders are self-made and didn't grow up particularly wealthy. Still, what must it feel like to get a golden ticket to ride the positive feedback loop?

When I asked Peter Thiel about the contingent nature of his success and he recoiled at the question, I got the sense that he thought his fate had been preordained. And I suspect many of Silicon Valley's icons wonder

---

* We'll take this question up at more length in the concluding chapters.

about the same thing deep down—though some may suppress the question by asking whether they're living in a simulation in which they are the protagonist.

Hell, if I won the Main Event at the World Series of Poker—roughly a 1 in 10,000 chance—I'd start to ask some existential questions. (When I got down to the final one hundred players in 2023, it had already begun to feel weird.) If you woke up every morning as Elon Musk, the richest person of the roughly 120 billion human beings to have ever lived, would you think that just happened by chance? Or would you think that you were one of the chosen ones?

Silicon Valley, after all, is asking literally existential questions—from "curing" death to AI either destroying humanity or transforming man into Übermensch. Maybe Thiel's religiosity and determinism serve him well. Other founders react to their metaphysical doubt by giving away huge amounts to charity or picking investment categories that they think are good causes. Or they may feel they have a moral obligation to invest, keeping their heads down and grinding away long after they've achieved more wealth than they'll ever need.

But others have never gotten rid of the chip on their shoulder—and this can lapse into self-destructive behavior. If you've made ungodly amounts of money by making a few winning bets, and perhaps you're not entirely sure you deserve it, you can always tempt fate by continuing to gamble— like the founder-turned-felon we'll meet in the next chapter.

6

Illusion

Act 1: New Providence Island, the Bahamas, December 2022

The room was getting darker, the power was going out on Sam Bankman-Fried's laptop, and he was telling me increasingly unhinged things. I was sitting alone with Bankman-Fried—SBF—on the ground floor of a luxury condominium in the Bahamas. The unit, full of porcelain finishes, was echoey, as if to underscore the emptiness of SBF's once $32 billion empire. It had been four weeks since Bankman-Fried's company, FTX, declared bankruptcy, and nearly all FTX employees had fled the island. Within a week, SBF would be arrested in this very complex, jailed, and extradited to the United States. And in less than a year, twelve jurors in a New York City courtroom would convict SBF on seven felony counts, finding that FTX had defrauded customers, lenders, and investors by "loaning" billions of dollars of customer deposits to its sister company, Alameda Research, to make risky, losing bets in the cryptocurrency market.

I do not mean to suggest that one should be sympathetic toward SBF, but it's no exaggeration to say he had just undergone one of the fastest reversals of fortune in human history. In a matter of a few days in November, Sam went from ostensibly being worth $26.5 billion, shooting commercials with Tom Brady, being *such* a big deal that he blew off Anna Wintour's invitation to the Met Gala, and seemingly living at the apex of a brave new world of blockchains and artificial intelligences, to being infamous, abandoned, and potentially facing years in prison. And yet, here he was in a $35 million apartment surrounded by island breezes. When I asked SBF whether he thought he was living in a simulation, he told me the odds were 50/50.

I'd first spoken with Sam in January 2022. He'd said some revealing things—which foreshadowed his extreme appetite for risk and his tendency to miscalculate—but I hadn't necessarily expected him to play a major role in this book. Before long, though, you saw SBF everywhere you looked in the River. Not just in crypto, but in effective altruism, artificial intelligence (he was an investor in the AI company Anthropic), sports betting (a category FTX sought to expand into), and venture capital. SBF was even becoming more of a player in my day job covering politics, being a major donor to Democratic and Republican campaigns (surreptitiously in the latter case). Throughout this book, I've dealt with some controversial cases as we conduct our census of the River. Is Donald Trump a Riverian? No, he's not analytical enough, despite his history in the casino business. Elon Musk? Yes. Although his impulsiveness is not very Riverian, his risk-taking is, and he's too widely admired by others in the River to exclude. But with SBF, there was no ambiguity. He wasn't just a citizen of the River; he might have been president of it. That doesn't mean everyone in the River is like SBF—he is an outlier for his lack of a moral compass paired with a propensity to gamble that makes even Elon look like a nit. But he's an outlier that the River must take ownership of.

At some point, SBF had invited me to come down and visit him in the Bahamas. I procrastinated, though I remember telling my partner that I probably needed to go—it seemed like everyone thought SBF was on track to be one of the richest and most influential people in the world, perhaps the next Musk. Then, on the day of the midterm elections, I began getting texts from a well-connected crypto friend that something was going down at FTX. By the end of the week, FTX had filed for bankruptcy. A week later,

I messaged SBF, who was conducting interviews with other reporters. I had a trip planned to Florida soon—maybe I could take him up on his offer and swing by the Bahamas? "I'd be happy to chat!" he replied cheerily. I was surprised, but on some intuitive level it was the response I had expected.

So on a pleasant December afternoon in the Bahamas, I was alone with SBF. I had no rational reason to think I was in any danger. Still, after two days of interviewing, with SBF having gradually become less guarded, I was thinking through worst-case scenarios. Did I need an escape plan? What if he said something on tape that he knew to be incriminating and grabbed my recorder? Bankman-Fried's condo was located in a relatively isolated development called Albany in the southwest corner of New Providence island, the opposite side from Nassau and the two major casino resorts, Baha Mar and Atlantis. But I was pretty sure I could outrun SBF if it came down to it.

The sun sets quickly near the equator, and with every moment that went by, the room got a little dimmer.

"Give me a second," SBF said. As usual—Bankman-Fried famously played video games while conducting television interviews and even investor meetings—SBF was multitasking, checking his email at the same time he was talking to me. "*This* is an interesting email," he said. "What does it say?" he murmured, seemingly not quite sure about whether to voice his inner monologue.

"Oh boy," Sam said. Another fifteen seconds passed. It was as though you could hear his gears turn, the prediction market in his head spiking upward and downward as he tried to calculate the probability that this email could be his salvation. "Oh, *booooy*," he said again, but this time in a completely different intonation than his typically flat NorCal accent, raising his timbre and almost *singing* the word "boy."

There was another long pause. "Can you describe it?" I said, snorting out a laugh at the awkwardness of the situation.

"Is this a real email? It can't possibly be real. *Whatthefuck*," he whispered.

In my discussions with him, SBF had been trying to calculate his own escape route. Not a literal one, although it's worth noting that after Sam was arrested, a Bahamian judge saw him as enough of a flight risk as to deny him bail. Rather, SBF was seeking some way—*any* way—to rationalize to himself that it would all be okay. Or at least that there was a *chance* it would be okay. The specific number he would later give me was 35 percent—a 35 percent chance that he'd emerge from the situation with something that would be "considered a win" by knowledgeable people. "I know a lot of people will say I'm crazy for giving this number. It's an insanely high number. And, like, it can't possibly be right," he had qualified.

Realistically, given the evidence that came out at trial, his chances of any sort of win were much lower than 35 percent. Any gambler sometimes feels the urge to chase his losses, and SBF had been seeking what a poker player would call a miracle card—the one card in the deck that might give him four of a kind to pull ahead of a full house. But in his mind, he had overcome long odds before. SBF had only given FTX a 20 percent chance of succeeding when he started the company, he had told me in an earlier interview. "But I thought that if it did succeed, it would be worth an enormous amount."

"I just got a very bizarre email. It is almost certainly a fake email. *Except*—," SBF said, hanging on the last word as though he was Sherlock Holmes making a counterintuitive deduction. "It involves some information that I don't think many people have. Let me show you this email. Well, fuck, my computer's about to die."

SBF's hopes were dying, too. "This is one hundred percent fake. Oh fuck, I didn't bring my power cord. Welp, I just got an email from john.j.ray .iii@gmail.com resigning as FTX CEO."

John J. Ray III, a veteran of Enron and other bankruptcy cases, had become FTX's CEO after SBF signed the company's bankruptcy papers. SBF's parents had been copied on the email too, along with Kevin O'Leary, the *Shark Tank* personality who had been paid more than $15 million to execute de minimis promotional obligations for FTX. It didn't make sense that Ray would suddenly resign, and it made even less sense that he'd resign in this fashion, by sending a Gmail to the disgraced former CEO, the ex-CEO's parents, and a reality TV show panelist. Moreover, SBF had never received an email from this address or communicated with Ray by email at all. The probabilistic needle in SBF's head had crashed to zero. "Okay, never mind," he conceded.

In my various conversations with him—five formal interviews, including two on consecutive afternoons in the Bahamas—Bankman-Fried had taken on what I'd come to think of as different personas.* There was what I call "Talking-Shop Sam." This was the default mode that I'd grown accustomed to in the pre-bankruptcy days. Talking-Shop Sam spoke rapidly in run-on sentences, full of jargon about arbitrage and expected value. I *liked* Talking-Shop Sam. We spoke the same language and had good camaraderie; I could imagine us being friends.

Then there was No-Shits-Left-to-Give Sam—a more candid and *seemingly* more honest personality, a Sam who prefaced his responses by implying that *now* he was going to give you the *real* answer. No-Shits-Left-to-Give Sam could get dark and erratic—this was the version that I was a tiny bit worried might suddenly lunge for my digital recorder.

Finally, there was Sneaky Sam. This iteration of SBF was pedantic and lawyerly. Although Talking-Shop Sam saw me as an equal, Sneaky Sam was full of gotcha questions, quizzing me as though I was his intern at Jane Street Capital. I got the sense that Sneaky Sam was using me to audition his arguments—if he could outwit me, maybe he could eventually outwit the media, the prosecutors, and a jury.

"I'm curious, by the way; what's your thoughts on that?" Sneaky Sam asked me after claiming that FTX could have averted disaster if only he hadn't declared bankruptcy and had been able to raise more capital. It seemed like a ridiculous assertion, but I wasn't quite sure how to play my hand—sometimes you'll get more out of an interview subject by humoring them, and sometimes by pushing back. I decided I was just going to default toward being as honest as possible.†

---

* I don't mean to imply that Sam has multiple personality disorder or anything of that kind.
† I also assumed there was a chance that my interview would eventually be subpoenaed.

"My general disposition is that most things in life are pretty overdetermined," I said. "It seems like you have a lot of really, really, really correlated trades. What's the risk of some type of disaster? Like, it wouldn't surprise me if it's, like, above fifty percent or something."

"Above fifty percent on what timescale?" SBF pressed.

"Within—a year or two? I don't know, something like that."

"*Oh*, I think that might be right. But I don't know that that's a relevant calculation, because a year or two is a long time," he said.

Not a relevant calculation? You're conceding that FTX was a house of cards—more likely than not to topple at some point—and that's *not a relevant calculation*? But before I had a chance to follow up, SBF had moved to the next section of the pop quiz.

"Um, what do you think the odds are that one year from now, FTX will be an operating platform? And what do you think the odds are five years from now that customers will have been made whole?"

"To the first question, I'd say under ten percent. To the second question, thirty percent. I have no idea."

Oops! I had fallen for Sneaky Sam's trap. "You think it's *more* likely that customers will be made whole than that the platform will be resuscitated?" he said, pouncing on my logic. My thinking was that I didn't really know which piles of money were lying around where—there had already been a $477 million hack the very day FTX declared bankruptcy. Maybe SBF had enough in a Swiss bank account to cover the missing deposits. And FTX had made some valuable investments in other businesses. Restarting the exchange seemed out of the question, on the other hand— would customers be trading with their phantom balances? How could they ever trust the platform again?

The truth is, it's not *quite* as crazy as it sounds. In bankruptcy proceedings, companies try to recover money any way they can, and Ray later discussed reopening FTX. But SBF's point was that unless the exchange was restarted, FTX customers were totally fucked. "Maybe you get half a billion for the parts. But like, realistically speaking, that half a billion isn't going very far." He estimated that FTX customers were about $8 billion in the hole.* "So I basically think that the only pathway to making customers whole is turning the exchange back on. So it would surprise me if the odds were *higher* for making customers whole."

But there *was* a crazy part. The crazy part was this: SBF was imagining a scenario where not only was FTX turned back on, but he'd return to some central role in its operations. In fact, he claimed to me, FTX was *already* up and running again—that the last trade had happened that morning at "ten fifty-six a.m. and forty-three seconds today." It was clear that SBF had intended this as some sort of big reveal—his ace in the hole. "Just to absolutely clarify, this cannot get out right now. It's totally fine a year from now.† But definitely not in the next three days."

It was unclear exactly what SBF was describing. He began to hedge. "So I guess it's a little bit ambiguous whether FTX has triggered recently. FTX Digital Markets has triggered today," he said, referring to one of FTX's subsidiaries. "So with some caveats, the matching engine is up and running. The UI is back up and running. I actually have a copy of it on my computer right now."

Bankman-Fried probably shouldn't have been telling me this. And he definitely shouldn't have had any sort of access to the FTX platform—he had resigned as CEO as part of its bankruptcy and had no official role with the company. "Technologically, I think it's like fifty-fifty that projects will be booted back up. There are people trying to do it. And they are close to succeeding in that by many definitions," he said.

SBF's hypothesis was that once this process started, it would catalyze a virtuous cycle, with FTX gradually earning income from trading fees to fill the $8 billion hole, and perhaps also getting new rounds of investment. "So let's say you log in and it shows you numbers, but withdrawals are halted. Then let's say there's a billion dollars in funding that comes in," he

---

* U.S. attorneys cited a larger number in their case against SBF: between $10 billion and $14 billion. Larry Neumeister, "FTX Founder Sam Bankman-Fried Convicted of Stealing Billions from Customers and Investors," *USA Today*, November 3, 2023, usatoday.com/story/money/2023/11/02/sam-bankman-fried-convicted-fraud/71429793007.

† For the interviews we conducted after FTX's bankruptcy—one by Zoom, two in the Bahamas, and one in Stanford, California—our agreement was that the material could be used on the record for this book (with rare off-the-record exceptions) but not before then. SBF was willing to be more candid about some topics for this reason.

said. "People would care about that, presumably, right? Like, if there's any funding tied to this platform, people are going to want to access it. And if you combine together technologically booting up the platform, with there being a nontrivial amount of funding for it, I think users will care. That's the thesis. And there's a flywheel."

I raised all kinds of objections. Why would people want to trade—and pay FTX additional fees—if they couldn't make withdrawals? At one point, I compared it to a fast-food restaurant that had a hepatitis outbreak and reopened despite having made no effort to solve its hepatitis problem. And how long would this flywheel take to spin its way to completion? "I think if you make like reasonable assumptions about the remaining assets and assume zero more financing—it's probably twenty years?" SBF said.

Twenty years? Get-rich-quick crypto customers were going to trade on this bankrupt exchange until—in approximately 2042—they were made whole? *This* was the plan that SBF thought had a 35 percent chance of working? The only insurmountable problem in his mind was the presence of Ray, which is why SBF had been so excited by the prank email. All of this—the Riverian impulse to calculate out every angle until the bitter end, not acknowledging that it was Game Over—reminded me of a chicken still running around after its head had been cut off.

There's been a tendency in media coverage of SBF to portray him as a Boy Genius, a sort of misaligned superintelligence. The thing is, though, I know a lot of Boy Genius types. A nerdy, overconfident, Adderall-popping, video-game-playing, youngish white guy who has a severe gambling problem and is probably somewhere on the autism spectrum? In the River, that's a common typology.

I don't mean to imply that I was totally unimpressed by SBF. He is clearly an intelligent guy. He can think on his feet. He can even be charming in a weird way. Still, the most impressive part of SBF was that *everybody else* was so impressed by him. How had this guy—with his frizzy hair, dubious ethics, and questionable grasp on reality—become the king of the nerds?

Act 2: Miami, Florida, November–December 2021

I was in a VIP area somewhere deep in the bowels of FTX Arena. It was a happy time for crypto; three weeks earlier, Bitcoin had achieved an all-time-high price (later surpassed in early 2024) of $67,566.83, larger than the average annual American salary. The mayor of Miami, Francis Suarez, was onstage as part of an event called NFT BZL, a festival that was piggy-backing off Miami's famous art fair Art Basel. Like almost everything else in Miami that week, the VIP area was a shitshow, serving at once as an anteroom for speakers as they entered and exited the stage, a place for journalists to mingle and conduct interviews, and a party zone where a fancy French brand was giving out free champagne.

It isn't right to say the crypto industry had sprung out of nowhere. Bit-coins were first made available to the public in 2009. I'm nerdy enough to know people who had been adopters of the technology by the early 2010s, though I wasn't one of them myself. But during that week in Miami, it was hard to know whether this was the beginning of something big or the be-ginning of the end—the peak of a bubble.

On the one hand, the mood was so confident—FTX, which had barely existed two years earlier, had spent $135 million to put its name on the Mi-ami Heat's basketball arena—that one could almost be forgiven for think-ing that crypto had been part of the landscape all along. The lavish parties and the exuberant advertising, and the attempts to associate with estab-lished brands like Art Basel, were a play to create institutional legitimacy and a feeling of ubiquity—and to inspire fear of missing out in those who hadn't joined the party yet.

On the other hand, some of it was just so *obviously* ludicrous. I went to one party on a yacht that never left shore, where crypto degens tipped bartenders $20 for bottles of water—in some cases because they were high on white powdered substances, and in others because early crypto adopt-ers felt like they'd won the lottery and had infinite money to burn. Crypto newbies, meanwhile, networked in the cringiest ways imaginable in the hopes of getting in at the early stages of one another's NFT projects or being invited to join a DAO—a decentralized autonomous organization, essentially a "group chat with a bank account" that invests in crypto projects together. Nothing about the bacchanalian mood suggested long-term sustainability—and by the end of Art Basel weekend, Bitcoin prices had crashed by 25 percent.*

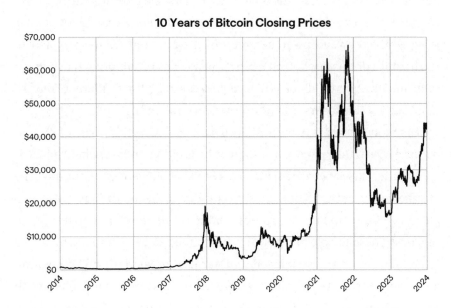

10 Years of Bitcoin Closing Prices

I had come to FTX Arena to meet Alex Mashinsky, an immigrant from the Soviet Union who had served as a pilot in the Israel Defense Forces before moving to the United States and becoming an internet entrepreneur. Mashinsky claimed to be the creator of VoIP, or Voice over Internet Protocol—a technology that allows people to make phone calls over broadband—though his actual role is disputed and this claim is regarded as dubious. In any event, he was now the CEO of the Celsius Network, a cryptocurrency lending company.

---

* I don't mean to imply that I didn't have any fun; I later went to another party on the opulent Star Island as a guest of a guest of the poker player Phil Hellmuth where the singer Jewel was performing—that scene was a lot more chill.

If "cryptocurrency lending company" sounds like a sketchy idea, that's because it was. Celsius would later go bankrupt, and Mashinsky would be charged with fraud. In a move that foreshadowed SBF six months later, Mashinsky had sent out a series of tweets claiming that everything was fine, only for the company to halt customer withdrawals thirty days later. (Mashinsky's court case—which is being prosecuted by the Southern District of New York, the same jurisdiction that brought the charges against SBF—is set to begin after this book goes to print. He pled not guilty.)

But at the time, Mashinsky passed for an elder statesman in crypto. We were whisked away into some greenroom by a handler, and I explained the premise of this book. It covered skilled forms of gambling like poker, I said, and I wondered about skilled crypto trading. What differentiated the more successful traders from the less successful ones?

His reply was darkly cynical, although served with a twist of humor, because Mashinsky tended to laugh at himself when he spoke. "Poker is about skill. This is not about skill. This is just about getting on the bus. The bus showed up at the station. Most people did not get on the bus. Most people said, 'Wow, this is a weird bus, and it smells, too. I'm not getting on this bus! These people are weird!'" He pointed to his T-shirt, which said HODL—an acronym for Hold On for Dear Life—essentially an admonition not to ruin the party by selling your crypto too soon. "You don't have to drive the bus. You don't have to know where it's going. You can sleep on the bus. Look at my shirt: HODL! HODL is you can fall asleep in the back of the bus. You wake up. And the last station, you're a millionaire."

I repeatedly pressed Mashinsky on this point—shouldn't early adopters of crypto get at least a little credit for their foresight? He refused to budge. "Compare the guy that bought pizza with his Bitcoin to the guy who forgot that it's on his computer. And realizes ten years later that it's worth something and now he's a billionaire. It's the same person. Just one guy knew where the coins were and the other guy didn't," he said. "Skill has nothing to do with it! Nothing! No skill involved!"

I also asked Mashinsky about his business model. "So if I deposit my Bitcoin with you, what are you going to do with that Bitcoin?"

"I lend it out to FTX. FTX needs liquidity," he answered instantly. "You can give it [directly] to FTX. Are they gonna pay anything? No. You deposit through me, I'll squeeze them to give me three, four, or five times more than they'll pay you. Because I have a million and a half people that are all together, marching as one."

"That makes sense," I said, not sure it made any sense at all.

"It's very simple," Mashinsky replied.

What's clearer is that FTX/Alameda had an appetite for as much crypto as it could get its hands on—and it sometimes borrowed it at interest rates as low as 6 percent from Celsius, far less than they'd been paying from other sources. Celsius's bankruptcy preceded FTX's and wasn't directly caused by it—the company's schemes were so risky that even SBF refused to bail them out. But if it didn't fail sooner, it probably would have later. Celsius was essentially trying to spin straw into gold, pledging to pay customers interest rates as high as 18 percent at a time when interest rates on bank deposits were still near zero.

So if Celsius's business model was as simple as Mashinsky claimed, it was simple in the same sense that a Ponzi scheme is simple. (Indeed, the U.S. government quite literally accused Celsius of "business operations [that] amounted to a Ponzi scheme.") The basis of a Ponzi scheme, named after the Italian con artist Charles Ponzi, is to pay existing investors with funds obtained from new investors.

"As with all Ponzi-scheme-like things, it works until it doesn't," said Maria Konnikova, the poker player and author who wrote a 2016 book on con artists called *The Confidence Game*. "So as long as people believe in it, it's gonna work. And the moment people stop believing is when it's gonna collapse."

Hence, Mashinsky's enthusiasm for HODL—Hold On for Dear Life. So long as nobody cashes out, and people maintain enough confidence in the scheme that new investors are still attracted to it, the Ponzi might sustain itself. But the minute there's a loss of confidence, there will be a run on the bank.

To be clear, I don't think every cryptocoin or every crypto-adjacent project is a scam. And unlike Mashinsky, I think we ought to give credit to early adopters—anyone who bought Bitcoin before roughly December 2017 (and HODLed it) has made *extremely* healthy returns. Later on in this chapter, I'll introduce you to what I consider to be some smart and successful crypto investors. Perhaps not coincidentally, these investors had experience in fields like financial planning or running a small business before getting into crypto.

But with few rules or regulations, this part of the River—what I call the Archipelago—is a dangerous place for inexperienced gamblers. And many people who started trading crypto during the 2020–21 boom lacked seasoning or sophistication. I spoke with Matt Levine, the author of Bloomberg's *Money Stuff* newsletter. Levine is a droll observer of what he calls the "boredom markets hypothesis"—the idea that boredom related to the COVID pandemic, coupled with an injection of COVID stimulus cash, was at least partly responsible for the run-up in crypto assets along with meme stocks such as GameStop. The timing lines up relatively well. Bitcoin first hit a peak in March and April 2021, right around when vaccines became widely available and many of the remaining COVID-era restrictions on interpersonal activity were being relaxed. Then Bitcoin fell rapidly as social life got back to normal—before rising again in late 2021 amid concern over the Delta and Omicron variants. The all-time worldwide peak in newly diagnosed COVID cases came in January 2022, only two months after the all-time Bitcoin peak.

Investors who got into crypto during this period often lacked basic financial literacy, meaning understanding concepts like that the market is usually efficient and that high returns—such as an 18 percent interest rate on crypto deposits—necessarily entail high risk. Veteran investors intuit that what seems too good to be true usually is, but rookies might not. "The classic [way to get scammed] is either believing or being prone to believe or wanting to believe that you have some secret knowledge that no one else has," said Levine—being "told that you've got the one true trick to unlock the market." For instance, the crypto newbies scrambling around the Miami yacht party in search of inside tips or special opportunities from people they barely knew? That sort of behavior is naïve. A friend of mine who's an experienced sports gambler is fond of saying that you never hear of first-rate opportunities until it's too late. (People usually bet them to death themselves before they give out tips.) Now, if you're *very* discerning and have *exactly* the right friends, you might hear of some *second-rate* opportunities that are nevertheless +EV. But from a coked-up stranger at a Miami yacht party? No way. You're the sucker in that transaction almost always.

The Perfect Storm for a Bubble

If there was a Mount Rushmore of financial bubbles, the crypto bubble of 2020–21 would deserve a place alongside the Tulip Mania craze that overtook Holland in the seventeenth century, the South Sea Bubble of 1719–20—itself arguably a Ponzi scheme—and the dot-com boom of the late 1990s and early 2000s. Indeed, crypto assets followed a similar trajectory to tech stocks. The Nasdaq declined by 77 percent from peak to trough upon the bursting of the tech bubble in the early 2000s—by comparison, Bitcoin and Ethereum fell by 75 to 80 percent before rebounding. NFT projects suffered an even worse downturn. The floor price for a CryptoPunk—the most prestigious NFT collection—dropped by almost 85 percent in U.S. dollar terms.

It's very much worth noting that the tech bubble eventually did have a happy ending. Companies like Amazon rose from its ashes and the Nasdaq increased more than tenfold between 2002 and 2021. Crypto bulls predict that something similar will happen in their market. In early April 2022, when I spoke with Gary Vaynerchuk—a.k.a. Gary Vee, a man who's best described as a cross between a self-help guru for fledgling entrepreneurs and a crypto evangelist—he predicted a crash followed by a rebound. "I genuinely think that—as of this exact second—that ninety-eight percent of the prices per NFT will be down at some point in a significant way. Because it's a bubble," he said. "But the micro is a bubble. The macro is the biggest opportunity since Amazon and eBay stock in 2000."

Vaynerchuk's prediction may prove prescient—as I'm writing this in early 2024, blue-chip crypto assets like Bitcoin and CryptoPunks have indeed rebounded considerably from their lows, and Bitcoin has reached new all-time highs, even as a rather large majority of NFTs are essentially worthless. Still, it's worth reflecting on why there was such a bubble in the first place and why so many investors were taken in by scams from which there is no hope of recovery.

Bored young men with limited economic prospects. Like most parts of the River, crypto is dominated by men—in particular young men. And young men face worse economic prospects than they did a generation ago. In 1979, 76 percent of American men between the ages of twenty and twenty-four were employed. By the beginning of 2020, that fraction had declined to 66 percent—and it tumbled even further to 47 percent during the peak of COVID-related shutdowns in April 2020. Some of this reflects more young people deferring employment for college or graduate study— but the number of men who complete college has now *also* begun to decline. America, in other words, has a lot of bored and frustrated young men with dubious economic prospects, and they were never more bored or frustrated than during the pandemic.

Crypto—along with day trading and sports betting—offered the prospect of getting rich quickly. And people like Mashinsky were happy to take advantage of this. Part of his pitch was that *it was all so simple.* All you had to do was buy and HODL—you'd even earn interest from Celsius! There were none of the complexities of, say, poker or options trading.

Even now, I find myself halfway sympathetic to Mashinsky's characterization of crypto as the proletariat's way to gamble. "It's not the already rich who jumped in on the next big thing, which is normally what happens here. It's a whole new clan," he'd told me in Miami. "It's a guy who used to be living out of his car five years ago, who happened to have bought a thousand Bitcoin. Who's telling all of his buddies, 'Hey, look at me! You should get into this too!'"

Fear of uncertainty—and fear of missing out. The crypto bubble occurred at a time of tremendous anxiety because of the COVID-19 pandemic and the uncertain world that would emerge from it—not to mention all of the other things that young people worry about, like climate change and political upheaval. It's hard to understate how *unsettled* the world felt in 2020 and early 2021. And that can produce optimal timing for con artists.

"One of the things that con artists take advantage of is the fact that the human brain hates uncertainty and always craves some sort of a story—cause and effect, something that makes sense. And whenever the world is changing, and a lot of things are happening at once, it's hard for the average mind to deal with it," Maria Konnikova told me. Crypto gurus like Mashinsky and Bankman-Fried offered the authority that people desperately wanted. Con artists "give you a nice little narrative to make sense" of the world, Konnikova said. "They take advantage of that moment to give you the certainty you crave."

There was also another factor: fear of missing out. "The flip side of it is that we also don't want to miss out on opportunities. There's also this FOMO," Konnikova told me. Crypto was pitched to the American public as *the* Next Big Thing. This couldn't have been any more explicit; the ads were every bit as shameless as those for DraftKings in 2015. In a now-infamous commercial for Super Bowl LVI that FTX paid $25 million to produce—plus another $10 million for David's fee—the comedian Larry David was portrayed as a Luddite who scoffed at the invention of the wheel, the Declaration of Independence, and the light bulb. Yes, really: FTX was comparing the invention of crypto to the harnessing of electricity. The tagline at the end of the commercial? It was literally—in all caps—"DON'T MISS OUT ON THE NEXT BIG THING."

Konnikova told me that whenever there's a new technology that seems to usher in a new era, both fools and hucksters rush in. "The gold rush, technological revolutions, the Industrial Revolution, new things where you don't quite understand it. You feel like, *this* might be interesting. And if someone explains it to you neatly and puts a little bow on it and tells you how it's actually really simple and really easy, you can get in on it."

Compare Konnikova's canonical con man pitch—*It's actually really simple and really easy!*—to what Mashinsky had said to me: "It's very simple."

Those are words that investors and gamblers should almost always take as a warning sign.

The Meme Creation of Value. As Konnikova says, con artists and scammy companies usually offer *some* sort of explanation for how they're creating value. Even Celsius had a story, however poorly it held up to scrutiny.

But the 2020–21 bubble also featured valuations that *nobody was even pretending had any basis in reality.* Take GameStop, for instance, a publicly traded company that sells video games and consoles. GameStop doesn't literally have *zero* value; it has several thousand retail locations, and gaming is a big industry. But in January 2021, its market capitalization suddenly shot up to $22.6 billion after having been under $1 billion in mid-December. Absolutely nothing had changed to justify that—GameStop is an old-fashioned retail business in an industry where most video game sales have moved online, and the company has suffered a net loss every year since 2018. But the stock had become popular on the Reddit r/wallstreetbets, a forum for day traders and options traders. Why GameStop *in particular* became popular is hard to say. It was partly because it was being shorted by a lot of hedge funds and the day traders wanted to fight back, and partly because it was perceived as an archaic, Blockbuster Video dinosaur of a company. Propping it up was inherently kind of funny—an "OK boomer" meme brought to life.

The next level of ridiculousness beyond GameStop was Dogecoin—a cryptocurrency that was deliberately created to be silly. Billy Markus, the cofounder of Dogecoin, told me he was trying to gently poke fun at crypto at a time when "the primary utility of cryptocurrency, in 2013, was to buy drugs anonymously on Silk Road or gamble illegally on the internet." Markus said that it would have taken him only ten minutes to complete the programming for Dogecoin—but he spent a couple hours to customize the images ("doge" is a deliberate misspelling of "dog," sometimes associated with pictures of a cute Japanese dog named Kabosu) and fonts (Comic Sans).

And yet, Dogecoin went viral, gaining acclaim with r/wallstreetbets traders and Elon Musk. Valued at $0.00026 shortly after its creation in 2013, it eventually reached a peak of $0.74 in May 2021—a roughly 3,000x increase. In theory, companies like Apple and Google are occasionally supposed to produce a 3,000x return based on creating revolutionary consumer technologies that are adopted all around the world. It's not supposed to happen to shitcoins* featuring a cartoon *doge*.

Markus, whose day job is making educational software, sold his Dogecoins and the rest of his crypto for about $10,000 after losing his job in 2015. He told me he couldn't be too upset about it, because if he hadn't done it sooner, he would have sold later. It was impossible to time the market for Dogecoin when the underlying valuation was so detached from reality in the first place.

"If you're in cryptocurrency for a long enough time, and you're greedy, you will get scammed," he said. "It's like going to a casino except there's some normal games and then there's like the back alley that promises higher returns. To a rational person you should be like, 'Well, that seems shady and ridiculous.' Anyone who's involved in that should understand they're just playing a rigged poker game." But in 2021, the number of cryptocurrency users was growing so fast that the overwhelming majority were new to the industry. In the Poker Boom of 2004–07, the deluge of new customers made it so that more experienced players could print money just by playing solid, tight, predictable poker. In crypto, there were a lot of suckers too.

I asked Matt Levine whether he thinks there will be more Dogecoin and GameStop-like bubbles in the future. "My gut is yes, that there'll be more of this," he said. "The thing that happened more broadly is that people realized that online communities could coordinate the rocketing of an asset." Levine referred to this as the "meme creation of value." It no longer mattered whether the thing you were trading had intrinsic utility. You weren't buying it to HODL, unless you were a sucker. Instead, you were gambling—playing a guessing game, a version of the prisoner's dilemma

---

* Investopedia defines this term well: "Shitcoin refers to a cryptocurrency with little to no value or no immediate, discernible purpose."

but one where you were allowed to communicate and collude with the other inmates.

Yes, that's right. It's time for the game theory of shitcoins.

Let's say I make a shitcoin called NateCoin, designated by the symbol ₦. We're going to play a game that at least somewhat resembles the dynamics of a shitcoin bubble. Here are the rules:

- The fundamental value of ₦ is $0. It is a shitcoin with no intrinsic utility. Its sole value derives from the fact that you might be able to get someone else to buy it at a higher price.

- However, ₦ has inexplicably become popular because Elon Musk tweeted about it.

- Two traders, Satoshi and Pepe,* bought ₦ at $50. Since then, ₦ has only continued to increase in value. It is currently worth $150.

- Everybody kinda knows that this is ridiculous. Any sale will trigger a cascade and ₦ will instantly collapse to its fundamental value of $0.

- If Satoshi and Pepe sell at the same moment, a blockchain algorithm will randomly determine who made the first sale. Whoever wins the drawing gets the market price ($150). The other one gets stuck with their worthless NateCoin ($0).

- ₦ is being heavily shorted by a hedge fund. If Satoshi and Pepe hold ₦ for another twenty-four hours, the short sellers are squeezed out of the market and the value of ₦ will increase to $200.

What's the optimal strategy? If Pepe and Satoshi can't coordinate or communicate, then this actually resolves to a classic prisoner's dilemma. No matter what the other one does, each player's best individual strategy

---

* Satoshi after Satoshi Nakamoto, the founder of Bitcoin, and Pepe after Rare Pepe, an early NFT project.

is just to sell. Take this from Satoshi's perspective, for instance. If Pepe holds, then Satoshi should sell. He'll lock in a $100 profit, and this is higher than the expected value ($50, as in the bottom-right box) of taking the short-seller's money and *then* playing chicken with Pepe to see who sells first. And if Pepe sells, then Satoshi *definitely* wants to sell too. Otherwise he'll be the one left holding the bag and his ₦ will become worthless.

The Game Theory of a Shitcoin Bubble

	SATOSHI SELLS	SATOSHI HOLDS
PEPE SELLS	Sale order is determined randomly. One of them makes a $100 profit and the other loses their $50 investment. EV: Pepe +$25, Satoshi +$25	Pepe locks in a $100 profit. Satoshi loses $50. EV: Pepe +$100, Satoshi –$50
PEPE HOLDS	Satoshi locks in a $100 profit. Pepe loses $50. EV: Pepe –$50, Satoshi +$100	The value of ₦ increases to $200. However, only one of them will actually be able to realize this price. One of them will eventually sell for $200 (making a $150 profit) and the other gets nothing (losing their initial $50 investment). EV: Pepe +$50, Satoshi +$50

But what if Pepe and Satoshi *can* coordinate—say, on a groupchat that they joined at the Miami yacht party, or on a forum like r/wallstreetbets? Well, now things get interesting. They *could* gamble on keeping the Nate-Coin rally alive. If they can just hold on for twenty-four more hours, they'll squeeze out the short seller, and the value of their ₦ will increase. Of course, this is a dangerous play, because if one of them sells, the other one is screwed. But it's actually in their mutual self-interest to hold. Their *combined* EV is higher by HODLing, taking the short-seller's money, and *then* seeing who blinks. The dilemma is that, if you're Pepe or Satoshi, there's usually no rational way to ensure that the other guy won't defect and screw you over.

Except, in the context of r/wallstreetbets, there *might* be reason to trust the other guy. There is camaraderie among traders because of the David (vs. Goliath) role that they saw themselves as playing. There is the fact that young men often behave as a hive and protect the solidarity of the group. There is the ethos of HODL—a cultural default that you should cooperate, not defect. The bubble is still going to burst sooner or later—the more the value of ₦ diverges from the fundamentals, the more incentive Satoshi and Pepe have to take their profits and run. But in a memeified world, bubbles will be longer, steeper, and more common.

Skilled Gambling Is Still Gambling: The Runbo Li Story

Runbo Li won big on his first major options trade. He'd seen a tip on r/wallstreetbets that Nvidia, the semiconductor manufacturer, was about to announce a new GPU.* A year or so earlier, Li had bought some stocks on the trading platform Robinhood with money he'd saved up from his first job—big consumer stocks he knew like Nike and JetBlue. The stocks had made a modest return. But what was happening at r/wallstreetbets was much more exciting.

"I saw that some people were making just insane amounts of money trading stock options," he said. He later came to realize how deceptive these cherry-picked examples could be. But this particular tip turned out to be right. Li bought some Nvidia (NVDA) call options. A call option is a bullish bet—it makes you money if a company's stock rises above a certain threshold. Indeed, Nvidia did announce a new GPU, its stock shot up, and so Li won his wager. He was so proud of his win that he shared a screenshot of it with his immigrant parents, persuading them to let him invest tens of thousands of dollars of their own savings.

The NVDA win might have been the unluckiest thing that ever happened to Li. He kept doubling down, buying more call options on NVDA. But the stock's value declined, part of a so-called tech wreck in the market in summer 2017. He made other losing bets too—and in fact, he has pretty much been chasing that initial high ever since. Li is obviously a smart guy—he got a master's degree in economics at the Univer-

---

* GPU stands for "graphics processing unit"—a type of computer chip that was originally optimized to display video game graphics, but which is also highly efficient for general mathematical computations. Thus, GPUs are often used for other computationally intensive problems, such as training AI models.

sity of Toronto and has been employed as a data scientist at Meta and other companies. But he's lost around $1 million in options trading, he told me. (Li cold-contacted me by email when he heard about my book; he wanted me to share his story. "I think if I can help at least one other person avoid the pitfalls that I face, that would be a win for me. I think the particular spiral that I fell into is particularly insidious, and it's really hard downward.")

Here's the one thing to know about options trading: it is *much* higher risk than regular investing in the stock market. It's as though you went to the town fair, and there were some staid amusement park rides like a merry-go-round and a Ferris wheel—that's the stock market, basically. There's a little bit of action, but it's not really for thrill-seekers; on average the stock market increases or decreases by 15 to 20 percent in a year. Options trading is as though you turned a corner, expecting to see bumper cars, and instead there was the MAGNUM EPIC STEEL DRAGON ROLLER COASTER, which has a four-hundred-foot vertical drop and flies along at 130 miles per hour.

A magnum-speed primer on options trading: A "call option" is a contract that gives you the right to buy a stock at a specified price. (The opposite of a call option is a "put option." A put option is a bearish bet: the right to *sell* a stock at a specified price.) For instance, if NVDA is currently priced at $98/share, a call option might say "I can buy one hundred shares of NVDA at $100/share at any point in the next thirty days," The price for this is called a "premium"—let's say in this case it's $3 per share or $300 total. You pay the premium whether or not you exercise the option.

Let's say NVDA rises to $106. Bingo! You exercise the option, buying one hundred shares for $100 each, which is now a significant discount to the $106 market price. You just made a gross profit of $600—one hundred shares at $6 profit per share—and your net profit after paying the premium is $300. Not a bad day's work.

There's no trickery or sleight of hand here; options trading is a perfectly legitimate, aboveboard activity. The catch is just that the option only has value if the stock rises above the price specified in the contract—there's no utility in being able to buy NVDA at $100 if its value falls to $95. And this creates two potential issues for you.

One is that it makes options trading very high-risk. In this example, you risked $300 in capital (the premium) for a bet that eventually made you a $300 profit—for a 100 percent return in thirty days. That's cool, but if you don't know what you're doing, just as often you're going to have a -100 percent return instead. The variance is an order of magnitude higher than when investing in stock index funds, where something like a 25 percent swing over a whole year would be considered volatile.

In fact, if you look back now at a chart of the Nasdaq, you can barely make out the "tech wreck" that Li described to me. It didn't last long and only affected a handful of stocks. But if you're making such highly leveraged trades, you'll really feel every bump. "My entire gain from just that one [Nvidia bet] was bigger than the past year of just holding stock that I had. And instantly I thought—why would I be holding stocks if I can do this?" Li told me.

The other issue is that options pricing is a notoriously hard problem—probably one best left to professionals. Let's say that you have some reason to think NVDA is underpriced. Okay, cool. You can just buy more NVDA. I respect your willingness to stake out a position. You have a fairly simple hypothesis: NVDA will go up.

But if you want to buy an NVDA call option, there are a whole lot of other parameters you'll have to work out. Your question becomes something like this: What is the probability that stock NVDA will rise to value X at any point before date D—and if it does, when is the optimal time T to exercise the option, and is the expected value of this worth more or less than the premium P? Good luck with that.* I can tell you firsthand how hard it is to make probabilistic forecasts. And although someone like Runbo Li is a smart guy with a master's degree and a data science job, he's competing with dozens of firms around the world who specialize in options trading.

Still, the perception that options trading is a skilled activity is part of what made it hard to quit, Li told me. He even repeatedly took out high-interest loans to help feed his habit. He also engaged in margin trading—borrowing money directly from Robinhood to leverage his bets even more.

"It could have easily been something else like sports gambling," he said. "But for me, it was easier to rationalize trading options because it

---

* Even the Black-Scholes formula for pricing options—though derided by Peter Thiel and others for being too simplistic—is relatively complex as famous formulas go. It's a partial differential equation that contains six variables—not exactly $E = mc^2$.

has that guise of investing. And that's one of the killer things. Because I think with stock options, trading is a lot more like gambling. You can rationalize it and say, hey, if you have good due diligence, if you do these things, you can have a really high success rate. But I think that's more or less a myth."

Here's something I learned when writing this book: if you have a gambling problem, then *somebody* is going to come up with *some product* that touches your probabilistic funny bones. Maybe it's a "smooth ride down to zero," like for Natasha Schüll's slot machine addicts. Maybe it's the roller coaster of options trading. Maybe it's just buy and HODL and sweat the action with your buddies in the groupchat. For some people, a skilled game like poker or options trading that's *also* a gambling game might be more compelling. Other people just want to lean back and press a button.

And whichever product most appeals to your inner degen will be algorithmically tailored to reduce friction and get you to gamble even more. "The [Robinhood] app is just really gamified to make it feel like you are spinning a roulette machine," Li told me, citing techniques such as confetti graphics when you achieve a trading milestone—although some of these animations have since been retired. The data shows that this works—Robinhood customers trade options at much higher volumes than at stodgier, more traditional brokerage sites like Charles Schwab.

Finally, there's the influence of forums like r/wallstreetbets—the camaraderie and competition between mostly young men who are inexperienced traders. Look, I've got no problem with talking shop. When I was a developing poker player, I spent hours and hours on an online forum called the Two Plus Two Forums, a poker message board for sharing strategy, memes, and gossip. It undoubtedly helped me to get better at poker. But you also had to take what people said there skeptically, especially about their personal wins and losses. A player who posted a graph with a sick brag saying he'd made $80,000 in the last month might go on a losing streak and never be heard from again.

"Generally, I don't think WallStreetBets is skilled," Li said. "The posts you see of the success stories—it's one in a million. It doesn't show the 999,000 people that lost their money and never played again—or are like me."

Bitcoin Is from Mars, Ethereum Is from Venus

The Genesis Block was created by a person going by the name Satoshi Na-kamoto on January 3, 2009. It awarded 50 bitcoin (BTC) to the address 1A1zP1eP5QGefi2DMPTfTL5SLmv7DivfNa, creating the first Bitcoins in his-tory. It also came with a message written in hexadecimal:

> The Times 03/Jan/2009 Chancellor on brink of second bailout for banks

This was a reference to a headline that day in *The Times* of London. It was at once the digital equivalent of a proof-of-life photograph—where a newspaper is used to provide contemporaneous evidence of when a pic-ture was taken—and a nod to the Global Financial Crisis. The GFC had inspired Nakamoto—and convinced him that governments couldn't be trusted. "The root problem with conventional currency is all the trust that's required to make it work," he wrote. "The central bank must be trusted not to debase the currency, but the history of fiat currencies is full of breaches of that trust." Nakamoto wanted to create a decentralized dig-ital currency that wasn't dependent upon trust, or the authority of the government or any central bank.

The Genesis Block is still included in every copy of the Bitcoin blockchain—and every copy of the blockchain is the same, except for how they describe very recent transactions that have not yet been verified. A blockchain is basically just a shared, ever-lengthening digital ledger of every transaction in history in chronological order, meaning something like the following:*

---

* Isn't this message *encrypted*? No. The data on a blockchain isn't encrypted, although it's often repre-sented in hexadecimal, a base-16 numbering system that includes ten digits and the letters A through F. In fact, the core principle of blockchain technology is the public and transparent recording of transac-tion information, eliminating the need for intermediaries. The term "crypto" in "cryptocurrency" stems from the use of cryptography. For example, public-private key cryptography plays a crucial role in securing transactions.

The Times 03/Jan/2009 Chancellor on brink of second
bailout for banks•••Alice-Paid-Bob-004.000BTC-On-
Sept092009•••Bob-Paid-Carol-002.500-BTC-On-
Sept102009•••Carol-Paid-Alice-010.000BTC-On-Sept122009

So in one sense, Nakamoto's idea was truly radical—Bitcoins were the first digital asset that could be transferred without the approval of any government or central authority. In another sense, the problems that Nakamoto was trying to solve were relatively technical. One particularly thorny issue, outlined in his white paper, was the double spending problem. If I give you a gold coin for a loaf of bread, I can't go and spend that same coin somewhere else. But if I were feeling sneaky, I could send the same *digital* coin to two places at once—say to Carol for her Crypto-Punk and Bob for his Bored Ape. How to decide which transaction is valid?

I'm not going to detail every aspect of Nakamoto's clever solution, but the backbone of it is a consensus secured by what's called "proof-of-work" mining. Bitcoin mining is the act of verifying a new block of transactions by solving a computationally intensive puzzle. The process has been likened to trying to win a prize from a scratch-off lottery ticket. By design, it takes a bit of work—the computational labor is why Bitcoin mining has a substantially negative environmental impact—but there's still no guarantee of success. The process is random, though just like buying more scratch-off tickets gives you more chances to win the lottery, having more computing power gives you more of a chance to win the big prize from mining: a block reward, set at 6.25 Bitcoins (approximately $250,000) as I'm writing this plus transaction fees.

But how in the world did we go from the first blockchain—a digital ledger for recording Bitcoin transactions—to raucous parties at Art Basel?

The through line runs through Vitalik Buterin, a waifish, Russian Canadian computer programmer who created the Ethereum blockchain.*

---

* Let me parse a few fine points here. Satoshi Nakamoto invented (1) the first functional blockchain and (2) Bitcoin, a digital currency whose transactions are recorded on the Bitcoin blockchain. But there isn't just one blockchain. Buterin created a different blockchain, Ethereum.

The Ethereum blockchain has a native digital currency, Ether (ETH)—pronounced as "eth" with a long "e" as in the name Ethan. But like an appliance on one of those late-night infomercials—it slices, it dices, it makes julienne fries!—the Ethereum blockchain can do a whole lot more than just record ETH transactions. In particular, it allows for the creation of so-called smart contracts. Ethereum contains a "built-in fully fledged Turing-complete programming language," so the possibilities are almost unlimited. You could, for example, write an options contract—I have a right to buy one hundred ETH from you if the price rises above $2,500—and the blockchain would work to execute the contract automatically.

In some ways, the origin story of Ethereum resembled that of a typical Silicon Valley startup, springing to life from a bright young immigrant founder willing to make a long-shot bet. Unlike Nakamoto, Buterin hadn't had an ideological objection to the central banking system. Instead, he is more of a polymath—an award-winning programmer who was also the cofounder of *Bitcoin Magazine*, and who was just nineteen when he began laying the foundations for Ethereum.

"Up until like maybe 2014 or even 2016, I was convinced that this whole space only has maybe a ten or twenty percent chance of turning out to be anything interesting," Buterin told me. But he calculated the expected value. Bitcoin, at the time, had a market capitalization of around $7 billion, while the market capitalization of gold was $7 trillion (that's trillion with a "t"). If Bitcoin had even a 5 percent chance of being worth 10 percent as much as gold, the market cap ought to have been $35 billion, about five times what it was trading for. "If you just do the math, it seems like it's worth the chance," Buterin figured. So he went all-in on crypto—with help from a $100,000 grant from Peter Thiel's foundation in 2014 to drop out of school and further develop Ethereum.

His bet has been a success. ETH is the second-most-traded cryptocurrency, behind BTC but way ahead of everything else. And although smart contracts are a relatively young invention, there are already some intriguing uses for them. Smart contracts are the basis of DeFi, or decentralized finance—although some DeFi projects so far have turned out to be scams.

They are also the basis of DAOs, or decentralized autonomous organizations—self-governing structures that are sometimes used by teams of investors to buy crypto assets together. And then there's the most famous use case for smart contracts: the non-fungible token, or NFT.

In casual language, "NFT" is often used to refer to a piece of digital art such as a CryptoPunk. (In some cases in this chapter, I've adopted the colloquial usage.) But it's more precise to say that an NFT is a certificate of ownership that everyone can see on the blockchain. (The artwork itself usually isn't stored on the blockchain, which often just contains a link to a web address containing the file, although there are some exceptions among high-end projects.) The distinguishing features of an NFT are that it has a *unique* owner based on information disclosed within its smart contract and that—as the name implies—it's *non-fungible*, or one of a kind. Fungibility is the property of interchangeability: dollar bills are fungible, and Bitcoins are fungible; one is just as good as the next one. But CryptoPunks are not; CryptoPunk #1111 and CryptoPunk #1234 are different assets.

For artists and collectors, having a widely accepted method of attributing ownership is a big deal. Even physical assets can't always match the blockchain standard. "For the first time in history, you have provable scarcity and unquestionable provenance of a collectible," said VonMises,* a prominent NFT collector who, like many in his industry, prefers to remain pseudonymous and keep a low profile. (Some NFT owners have been hacked, phished, or even kidnapped for the keys to their digital wallets.) VonMises has collected everything from baseball cards to vintage poker chips, so he knows how common counterfeiting is. "There's grandmaster paintings that are fake and hanging on walls in museums and everybody knows it," he told me. "The Rothko Institute and the Warhol Foundation have stopped verifying because they can't tell the difference."

NFT smart contracts can also contain other provisions, such as royalties that automatically accrue to the artist when the token changes hands. Some artists have even begun to take advantage of the smart features of

---

* Like a lot of early crypto adopters, VonMises has libertarian political leanings, and his username is a shout-out to the free-market-championing Austrian economist Ludwig von Mises.

NFTs to create art that changes, evolves, or regenerates itself. Mike Winkelmann, better known in cryptoworld as Beeple, made an NFT called *Crossroad* in 2020 that was designed to change based on whether Donald Trump won the presidential election. Once Joe Biden was declared the winner, it depicted a giant, fallen, bloated, shirtless Trump with words like "LOSER" graffitied over him. Had Trump won, it would instead have shown a god-king Trump emerging from a fiery underworld—perhaps, I imagined, the embers of the Village's polls that had once again prematurely declared him dead. *Crossroad* was purchased for a record $6.6 million, although it would soon be surpassed by another Beeple NFT, *Everydays: The First 5,000 Days*, which sold for $69 million.

To be clear, none of this necessarily justifies the hype that the blockchain received at the peak of the crypto bubble. Still, the Ethereum blockchain clearly has more potential for commercial, technological, and creative applications than the Bitcoin blockchain ever did.

And yet, from Ethereum's inception, Buterin encountered intense resistance from Bitcoin enthusiasts. "You know, it does all these amazing things," he said. "And, like, we're all part of Team Cryptocurrency and we're in this together. But I was very surprised when the response was a lot of maximalism and hostility."

Some of this is because of the origins of the respective blockchains and the cultural baggage they carry with them: Ethereum was a quasi-Silicon Valley startup, while Bitcoin was a cyberlibertarian alternative to fiat currency. "Ethereum is an ecosystem for venture capitalists to make bets on the future of computing and, like, Web3 and DeFi and gaming and NFTs and all that shit," said Levine. "Bitcoin is a place to make bets on future institutional adoption of an economic asset class."

But that doesn't fully explain the fervently anti-Ethereum attitudes that Buterin encountered. He likened Bitcoin maximalists—who often proclaim that Bitcoin is the *only* worthwhile cryptocurrency—to religious adherents. "Bitcoin is not really a technology project. Bitcoin is a kind of political, cultural, and religious project where the technology is a necessary evil," he said.

It's common in the River, a highly secular place, to insult someone's movement by comparing it to a religion. (For instance, you might say that wokeness is a religion or that effective altruism is one.) But in this case, Buterin wasn't just making a standard political putdown. Instead, he was suggesting that Bitcoin—like a religion—depends deeply on the idea of belief. Fundamentally, Bitcoin isn't *that* different from a shitcoin like Dogecoin; neither of them have any of the value-added functionality of Ethereum. But far more people *believe* in Bitcoin than believe in Dogecoin and are willing to trade it or accept it as payment. "The epistemic part of the religion is basically a self-fulfilling prophecy, right?" said Buterin. "Like if you can actually get enough people to believe in and buy in—it could literally become true."

However, none of this ought to imply that Bitcoin adherents are behaving irrationally. In fact, Bitcoin's dominant position in the crypto ecosystem can be explained by game theory. It's time to introduce one more concept—one that links the crypto world to the art world and helps to explain why some objects are extraordinarily valuable while the vast majority are essentially worthless.

Focal Points and the Envy-Based Economy

Here is a famous conundrum posed by the economist Thomas Schelling:

> You are to meet somebody in New York City. You have not been instructed where to meet; you have no prior understanding with the person on where to meet; and you cannot communicate with each other. You are simply told that you will have to guess where to meet and that he is being told the same thing and that you will just have to try to make your guesses coincide.

If you haven't encountered this problem before, take a moment to think through your answer. You won't just want to meet at some random intersection in Queens. You'll be looking for some sort of obvious landmark, and it probably makes sense that it should be centrally located. However, New York City has a lot of good candidates. Central Park is centrally located. So is Times Square, and the Empire State Building. All of those are logical alternatives. But this question has a single best answer.

The answer is Grand Central Terminal—specifically the information booth in the Great Hall of Grand Central Terminal.

Wait, why? Well, you could argue for a few points in Grand Central's favor. It's a relatively nice place to hang out. And it's more of a discrete location than something like Central Park (*where* exactly in Central Park would you meet?). But truth be told, this is a relatively arbitrary choice. Grand Central was the most popular answer among the students Schelling surveyed. He theorized this was because the class he was teaching was at Yale, and the New Haven Line of the Metro-North Railroad terminates at Grand Central, so it played a prominent role in his students' experience of New York City. Had he been teaching at Princeton, Penn Station might have been a more natural answer,* since trains from New Jersey terminate there.

Rather, the reason that Grand Central Terminal is the right answer is that it's *famously the right answer* if you know about Schelling's poll. And every time that someone writes about Schelling's experiment, Grand Central becomes more entrenched as the right answer.

If this sounds like a self-fulfilling prophecy, that's exactly the point. Grand Central is what Schelling calls a "focal point." Although a focal point is an important idea in game theory, it's more intuitive than something like the prisoner's dilemma—so don't worry, we're not going to need any more of those 2×2 matrices. In the "game" that we're playing— Schelling won the Nobel Prize partly for extending game theory from zero-sum games to those where players may benefit from cooperation, such as in avoiding a nuclear war—we both win if we find somewhere to meet and we both lose if we don't. It *doesn't matter* if the choice is arbitrary so long as it's a choice that we predictably coordinate.

---

* This was back in the days before Robert Moses destroyed the aboveground levels of Penn Station to build Madison Square Garden and it was a relatively nice place to hang out too.

Bitcoin operates in much the same way; it's a focal point. As with the case of Grand Central Terminal, it's not a completely arbitrary choice. Bitcoin was the first cryptocurrency, and being first counts for a lot when you need a focal point. There are also some attributes that give it an aura of permanence; there are a fixed number of Bitcoin that will ever be created—21 million—and Bitcoin's protocols are notoriously hard to change. Still, it benefits from the fact that *some* cryptocurrency, or at most a couple of them, has to be the gold standard. If I want to transact in NateCoin, you want to transact in Bitcoin, and our mutual friend will only accept Dogecoin, none of us are getting any business done and we all lose the game.*

Focal points also help to explain the art world—they're why an Andy Warhol silkscreen of Marilyn Monroe can sell for $195 million even as there are many starving artists who would be thrilled to sell their work for $1,950. The art world is "an envy-based economy," as *New York* magazine art critic Jerry Saltz described it to me. "In my world, ninety-nine point nine percent of us are struggling. And we all pay attention to the one percent of the one percent of the one percent."

To repeat, famous works of art don't become famous for *completely* arbitrary reasons. Focal points usually have *something* going for them.† But the traditional art world almost goes out of its way to intensify focal points by curating a sense of exclusivity and scarcity. The more envious people are, and the less supply there is, the more likely it is that some very rich person will decide to splurge. In fact, auction houses often have one specific buyer in mind, and the auction process is mostly a charade. "How many people will spend, say, fifty million dollars or more on an object?" said Amy Cappellazzo, a founding partner at Art Intelligence Global and a legendarily no-nonsense art-world powerhouse. "You really have to look extremely carefully at who could be a candidate at that price point in the market at the time. And look, if the guy had back surgery last week, maybe not."

---

* Of course, Buterin might have been hoping that ETH would displace BTC as the focal point, and at one point it looked like it might. But maximalists who owned a lot of BTC had every interest in defending their turf—that's part of why they were so hostile to Buterin.

† Just speaking personally, I think Warhol was a genius.

Cappellazzo doesn't see much difference between traditional art and NFTs. Like NFTs, art is non-fungible; you're not just looking for *any* painting but a particular work that speaks to you. "The Andy Warhol coin is very different than the Marc Chagall coin," she said. "They're almost like their own economies and their own currencies." And although the aesthetic qualities of digital works can be debated, ultimately any art is worth what the highest bidder is willing to pay for it. "I have lots of talks with my divas at the auction houses. Like, you want to be a curator? Go work at a museum. We like to sell shit."

Culturally speaking, the NFT world and the art world could hardly be more different. My partner is a visual artist and filmmaker, so I've spent more time than you might assume at gallery openings and art shows. Some stereotypes ring true: gallery patrons in the traditional art world are mostly extremely fashionable women, gay men, or people elsewhere on the LGBTQ+ spectrum—plus rich older men and their spouses (*somebody* has to actually buy the art). By contrast, the NFT BZL audience was full of bro-ey and/or nerdy heterosexual men who had suddenly struck digital gold. Although some NFT collectors I spoke with later became interested in physical art, there's not a whole lot of overlap.

And yet, the envy-based economy has replicated itself in NFT Land. Do you have a friend who owns a CryptoPunk? I have a few of them, and what I can tell you is it's very likely that they're going to show you their CryptoPunk when the opportunity arises. In some sense, that's the whole point of owning one. Whatever their aesthetic value, which is in the eye of the beholder—some collectors have compared CryptoPunks to Warhols— CryptoPunks are *desirable mostly because other people desire them.* The envy-based economy is like a child in a room full of toys who wants to play with the *exact* toy that his sister or brother is playing with—and nothing else.

According to the French historian René Girard—Peter Thiel's favorite philosopher*—this tendency to mirror what other people covet, what he

---

* In *Zero to One*, Thiel advocates for building businesses that have the potential to become monopolies. And in some types of business, a de facto monopoly can emerge by a company being a focal point. People use social media services like Facebook, Twitter, and TikTok not necessarily because of the intrinsic features of these platforms but because lots of their friends do. (Girard would find the influencer culture

calls "mimetic desire," is at the very heart of the human condition. And when you combine mimetic desire with modern-day meme culture— "mime" and "mimetic" have the same Greek root word, *mīmēma*, meaning that which is imitated—you'll wind up with prices for NFTs that fluctuate wildly as collectors signal to one another what should be a focal point and what is out of style.

The leaderless, decentralized nature of the crypto world contributes to this, producing even more dramatic price swings than in the curated world of traditional art. In his book *The Strategy of Conflict*, Schelling wrote about the behavior of leaderless mobs. Mobs are unpredictable, Schelling thought, because they are prone to act upon extremely subtle signals. When there's no authority figure, nobody whose instructions you can reliably wait for, there's no coordinating mechanism other than rote imitation.*

Then again, if you're a digital artist who's in the right place at the right time when the mob heads your way, you can win the crypto lottery. When I spoke with Winkelmann—a.k.a. Beeple—I was expecting someone with the self-important air of being a *serious artist* or at least someone whose success had gone to his head. Instead, Beeple was extremely down-to-earth, dropping f-bombs about once every fifteen seconds in a thick Wisconsin accent. *Everydays*, a collage of five thousand of Beeple's digital images since 2007, had taken him about ten thousand hours of work, he said. But it was still hard for him to process the $69 million sale price, all of which was initially transferred to him in ETH. "It was like, okay, whoa, whoa, whoa, we gotta jump off this train. Because fucking every time I hit refresh, it's up or down a fucking million dollars." Beeple converted it to cash as soon as he could. "No fucking sane person would tell you to put all

on Instagram to be an incredible validation of his ideas.) The network effects this creates can be hard to dislodge. This is one reason why predictions that Elon Musk would cause a mass exodus from Twitter haven't come true so far—though if it does happen, it will probably happen quickly, with the entire herd moving at once.

* Indeed, the NFT community abhors appeals to authority or gatekeeping from the traditional art world. Saltz told me that when he began reviewing NFT projects—something he saw as a sign of respect, an indication that NFTs had enough artistic merit to deserve serious criticism—the reactions were extremely unsympathetic. "When I would tell them what I did not like, they *really* got upset. *Really* upset," he said. This culminated in an incident when Saltz was out for a stroll near the Whitney Museum. "I was walking across the street. It was warm. And a guy looks at me and he says '*I make fucking NFTs!*' And he hit me in the left wrist and broke the crystal to my Canal Street watch."

of your entire fucking portfolio into one highly volatile asset that just was up like fucking eight times over the last four months."*

The smarter NFT collectors I spoke with told me about their strategies for navigating through this madness of crowds. If there's such a thing as someone who's well credentialed to be an NFT collector, it's VonMises, who not only has experience with collectibles but also a lot of financial horse sense; before quitting to play poker, he'd had a corporate job in investment management and a side gig of financial planning. VonMises told me that it's possible to invest in crypto assets responsibly. "I always have been pretty conservative in terms of my overall investment outlook," he said. "So how did I become big in digital assets? It was like anything—the expected-value calculation was so high." He first bought $5,000 worth of Bitcoin in 2011 when it cost just $5 per token, figuring there was a 1 percent chance that he could make 1,000x his money. In fact, Bitcoin would eventually increase by more than 10,000x—although VonMises, being responsible, sold a lot of his BTC along the way.

Even VonMises wasn't prepared for Peak NFT, though. "To be honest with you, the NFT trade was a hundred times more insane than cryptocurrency." Still, his strategy is all about finding projects that have the potential to become focal points. The fancy term he uses for this is "provenance"—which basically means "where it came from." VonMises likes collectibles that are original, distinctive, and unique, and where he can trace back the ownership to ensure their authenticity. (NFTs make this latter part comparatively easy.) He was attracted to CryptoPunks because they were one of the first NFT projects on the Ethereum blockchain, and he thought they had a recognizably iconic quality. So he bought fifty of them at a total price of around $100,000—and watched them eventually rise to a peak value of almost $25 million.

Other collectors play a game of follow-the-leader. Johnny Betancourt, one of the most levelheaded people I met in the crypto world (and one who uses his real name), told me he was attracted to CryptoPunks because

---

* Although, after he "caught a bunch of shit from all the fucking crypto people," Winkelmann later reinvested about a third of his haul back into ETH.

that's where the smart money was. Remember the adage in poker, he said, "where if you can't spot the fish, you are the fish?" referring to the famous quote from *Rounders* ("If you can't spot the sucker in your first half hour at the table, then you are the sucker"). Well, if you carefully study the other players at the table and have a high social IQ and are good at forming a network, it's not such a bad thing to be the dumbest person in the room, Betancourt told me. "That's a really good room to be in."

But it's one thing to cultivate a network, and another to blindly follow someone's lead. Another well-reputed NFT collector, Vincent Van Dough, told me that "when the market was hot," other collectors would just copy off of him, like students eyeing a classmate's exam. "People would just sort of race to buy other pieces from that set. Because I was buying it, they were expecting other people to see it [and] want to buy it [too]."

For Vincent Van Dough—not his real name, obviously—this worked out great because it tended to increase the value of everything he bought. However, the follow-the-leader strategy comes with considerable risk. At the very least, it makes focal points more intense, contributing to volatility in crypto pricing. It also creates vulnerability to pump-and-dump scams, where unscrupulous collectors hype up a project they don't really believe in and sell at an artificial market top.

And sometimes, smart people can be too trusting of other smart people. This is what Betancourt thinks happened with FTX. "There's a lot of revisionist history going on right now," he told me in December 2022 shortly after FTX's bankruptcy. Some crypto investors were claiming "they knew that it was a sham six [or] twelve months ago." That didn't match Betancourt's observation, however. Instead, FTX had been a trusted and even beloved brand. "The most wealthy traders I know had eight figures on FTX. Why? Because it had the liquidity that they needed, it had the leverage, it had everything that they needed." In fact, the smartest traders were *especially* likely to do their trading on FTX, Betancourt said. "It's actually a lot of sharp people that were negatively impacted by this." Betancourt himself wasn't hit hard by FTX, but he said that was a matter of luck since he mostly trades NFTs rather than crypto itself.

At the center of it all was Sam Bankman-Fried. He was the biggest focal point of all, Betancourt said. "It's almost like a self-fulfilling story where you want to believe that this is a quant genius that understands business better than you do."

I wish I could tell you that I was one of those people who was onto SBF six or twelve months ahead of time. I did know that he was capable of getting extremely out of his depth—we'll get to that in the next chapter. And as I've said, his intellect didn't bowl me over. We poker players inherently treat smartest-kid-in-the-room types with suspicion. We know that some of them talk a big game and can't back it up. We know that some of them just got lucky. And because we're so damned competitive, we're reluctant to give them credit. To concede that another Riverian's success is *deserved* is to acknowledge your own failures.

But did I have any idea that SBF was in the midst of committing seven felonies? Not the foggiest. Still, while nothing in my pre-bankruptcy conversations with SBF signaled criminal intent, he did make some quite deranged statements about risk, statements that might have stood out as being more obviously foolish and even dangerous if SBF's Boy Genius reputation weren't so strong.

For instance, SBF was quite specifically insistent that people ought to be willing to risk having their lives end in ruin. There's an idea, he said when I spoke with him in January 2022, that "the bigger you are, the more risk you can take without endangering what you have." This is obviously true, of course. Elon Musk can take $44 billion and burn Twitter to the ground, and he'll still have $200 billion left over. By some technical definition this is a risky bet, but by another Elon is putting far less at stake than an immigrant who crosses the Rio Grande for an off-the-books job.

Rich people hedging their bets is "like a really reasonable way to think about risk, and a really kind of mature and professional and unassailable way," SBF said. So was that the risk-management philosophy that SBF abided by? Emphatically not! This attitude was too risk-averse, he thought.

"I think people are just kind of wimps and dismiss on principle options that involve going big," he said. "Even if you're starting from a much higher point . . . often the correct decision is one that is risky enough that there is a nontrivial chance that it will still do really serious damage to your position."

SBF then made an analogy that you'd think would trigger my sympathies—but actually raised my alarm. "If you're making a decision, such as there's no way that it goes really badly, then I sort of feel like—you know, zero is not the correct number of times to miss a flight. If you never miss a flight, you're spending too much time in airports."

I used to think about air travel like this. I even went through a phase where I took a perverse joy in trying to arrive as close to the departure time as possible and still make the flight. Now that I'm more mature and have a credit card that gives me access to the Delta Sky Club, I don't cut it quite so close.

But the reason you *should* be willing to risk missing a flight is because the consequences are *usually quite tolerable.* You may have to shell out a few hundred bucks for a last-minute flight on a different carrier. Or you may arrive two hours late for your first day of vacation. These are annoying but finite costs, the sorts of costs you can plug into your implicit mental EV spreadsheet without raising any larger philosophical concerns.* SBF, however, was equating airport-arrival strategy with questions with much more existential stakes. Unless you were taking enough risk to *potentially ruin your life*, you were doing it wrong, he thought.

I'm going to revisit SBF's attitude toward risk in chapter 8 after I've more formally introduced some ideas—like utilitarianism and effective altruism—that played a large role in Sam's thinking. For now, I just want to flag that this is not a healthy way to think about risk—and it's not how most people in the River think about it. Instead, they understand the concept of diminishing marginal returns—your billionth dollar isn't as

---

* If the consequences are more serious than this—say, missing your best friend's destination wedding or a business meeting that's worth thousands of dollars in expected value—you probably *should* get to the airport with plenty of time to spare.

valuable as your first one—and that the privilege of having made it is that you never have to take a gamble that could leave you in ruins. I spoke with David Einhorn, the founder of the hedge fund Greenlight Capital. Einhorn and I run in a lot of overlapping New York poker/finance circles, so I know him well enough to know he's definitely not a nit; in fact, he's repeatedly entered $1 million buy-in poker tournaments. He reminded me of an infamous hand Vanessa Selbst played on the first day of the 2017 World Series of Poker, when she lost with a full house to another player's four of a kind and was immediately knocked out of the tournament. In poker, "you have to be prepared to do that," Einhorn said. There's always another tournament. But "in investing, I am *never* prepared to do that. I have all my chips effectively on the table." If you lose your last chip—go broke, truly broke, the kind of broke that SBF wants you to be willing to go, where not just your finances but maybe your reputation is ruined—you can't just go up to the cashier's window and play again.

SBF was also saying things publicly that ought to have raised concerns. In response to an April 2022 interview question on the Bloomberg *Odd Lots* podcast about yield farming—a risky technique that Celsius had employed—SBF described a hypothetical example of a DeFi company that built a "box" and claimed it would revolutionize the financial world. "They probably dress it up to look like a life-changing, you know, world-altering protocol that's gonna replace all the big banks in thirty-eight days or whatever," he said. In exchange for putting money in the box, investors would receive a yield of tokens. Had this company *actually* built a life-changing, world-altering product? Well, no. But SBF didn't think it mattered. What mattered is that investors were *convinced* that it did—that there *must* be something valuable about the box because *so many other cool people* were investing in it. "Who are we to say that they're wrong about that?" SBF said. He imagined the amount of money in the box rocketing to the moon as more and more investors were convinced about its importance. "So they go and pour another three hundred million dollars in the box and you get a psych and then it goes to infinity. And then everyone makes money."

Matt Levine, a regular guest on the *Odd Lots* podcast, was taken aback, pointing out that neither the box nor the tokens had any intrinsic value—instead, SBF had literally just described a Ponzi scheme. "I think of myself as like a fairly cynical person. And that was so much more cynical than how I would've described farming. You're just like, well, I'm in the Ponzi business and it's pretty good," he said to Sam. SBF conceded that there was a "depressing amount of validity" to Levine's position.

You might think this was an impolitic interview for SBF. It certainly hit close to home. FTX had issued its own dubious token called FTT that was used to prop up Alameda's balance sheet, and a run on FTT precipitated FTX's collapse. But there was no particular fallout from SBF's remarks. And I wonder if they didn't almost have the opposite effect, actually making him seem *more* trustworthy. Con artists work by building confidence. Transparency—especially transparency that seems to be against one's self-interest—is a way to signal confidence to intelligent people. Think of a magician who will let you riffle through a deck of cards before performing a trick on you.

Whatever trick SBF was offering, Silicon Valley was scooping up, to the tune of nearly $2 billion in investment from VC firms. In an exceptionally cringey, now-deleted, quasi-journalistic profile of SBF on the Sequoia Capital website, VCs almost tripped over one another to offer him compliments: "I LOVE THIS FOUNDER," "I am a 10 out of 10," "YES!!!"

If you read the last chapter, you won't be *too* surprised by any of this. VCs want founders who are extremely—maybe even irrationally—risk-loving. Even if the founder ruins his life, the worst the venture firm can do is lose its capital—$214 million, for instance, in the case of Sequoia's investment in FTX—and it has dozens of other investments to make up for that.* In fact, Sequoia wasn't even apologetic for its association with FTX. "We probably would have made the investment again," Sequoia partner Alfred Lin said at a conference.

But it's also the case that SBF hacked the VC algorithm and catered to

---

* Although in this case, Sequoia and other investors in FTX have been named in a class-action lawsuit for abetting FTX's fraud, so there is some potential for additional liability beyond their investment.

some of its worst biases. Tara Mac Aulay, an original cofounder of Alameda Research who quit the company (along with much of the rest of the team) in 2018 amid SBF's "unethical and irresponsible approach to business," told me that much of SBF's famously unkempt appearance—his wildly curly hair, his T-shirts and shorts even at formal events—played into an image that SBF had wanted to cultivate. "Before we even started Alameda, so before he was in the public eye at all, he talked about modeling himself after Zuckerberg and various other tech founders, who he described as showing up to meetings in hoodies," she said. "You know, the cult of the founder in Silicon Valley." It wasn't *fake* exactly—SBF was never going to be a three-piece-suit guy. But he knew exactly what image he was conveying. "That was very much an explicit decision. Not like ignorance of social norms," Mac Aulay said.

"[SBF] was the kind of person that Silicon Valley wanted to believe would take over the market," said Haseeb Qureshi, a managing partner at the crypto fund Dragonfly. "He was an MIT graduate guy with crazy hair, who kind of said all the right things. He was totally nonconformist and countercultural and they're like, oh, *that's* who should be running the crypto market." Qureshi explained to me that the cryptocurrency exchange market had been dominated by companies with Chinese founders— particularly Binance, run by SBF nemesis Changpeng Zhao. Between political risk associated with Chinese investments, a lack of cultural ties, and sometimes outright bias, an American founder was bound to get extra credit. And FTX looked like a relative safe haven in a risky sector that venture firms had fear of missing out on. A VC firm's partnership agreement might prevent it from investing in tokens or "weird crypto stuff," Qureshi said. But FTX was just a regular company run by a credible-seeming American nerd.

Dustin Moskovitz, a Facebook cofounder who now runs the workflow software company Asana and makes VC investments himself, told me, "At one point, [SBF] wanted me to invest. And I was like, gosh, this valuation has gone up really high," he said. "And so I asked for the financials, because I thought it would be based on revenue." But SBF never got back to him, so he never invested. Presumably firms like Sequoia *had* seen the financials, Moskovitz said—and they proceeded anyway. Following FTX's collapse, Sequoia apologised to investors for its losses on the exchange, but stated that they had carried out due diligence on FTX at the time of their investment, and that they had been misled by SBF.

In some ways, SBF is a living and breathing version of the box he described to Matt Levine. He's a smart guy, but there are a lot of us smart guys—his intrinsic value is unclear. However, he was surrounded by such a trustworthy coterie—Sequoia Capital! Effective altruists with Oxford PhDs! Tom Brady! Anna Wintour! Former U.S. presidents who were willing to take the stage with him even when he dressed in shorts!—that *everyone assumed everyone else* must have done the due diligence.

"I don't really get it. I don't really get it," Moskovitz said. "It must have been the cult of personality. I guess it's the only explanation."

7

Quantification

Act 3: Flatiron District, New York, New York, August 2022

We were perched in a private suite with floor-to-ceiling windows overlooking the stately dining room at Eleven Madison Park, the world's first three-Michelin-star vegan restaurant. The guest of honor was Will MacAskill, a boyish-looking Oxford professor of philosophy with an endearing Scottish lilt and a new book he'd just published, *What We Owe the Future*. MacAskill was one of the founders of the effective altruism movement, a term that had a prestigious connotation because of its seemingly inarguable premise—that people ought to do more good for the world, and that they ought to do it in an effective way, "using evidence and reason to figure out how to benefit others as much as possible."

Whether a restaurant that charges $335 a person for fancy plates of vegetables was an appropriate setting for a celebration of rational, altruistic thinking was debatable. Many effective altruists (EAs) practice austerity, including MacAskill, who lives off about $30,000 a year and donates the rest of his income. However, the location hadn't been MacAskill's idea—instead, the party was hosted by Sam Bankman-Fried, who had become one of the world's largest benefactors of effective altruism through the FTX Foundation, which at one point had claimed that it might donate up to $1 billion a year to EA-adjacent causes. (The actual amount it gave was much less.) Dressed down as usual and carrying a fidget spinner, SBF held court at EMP, having invited a salon of journalists, public intellectuals, and two Democratic members of Congress. SBF thought this was a +EV investment in good PR: shelling out thousands of dollars for dinner was nothing when there were crypto regulation decisions pending before Congress that could make a billion-dollar difference to his bottom line.

Despite Bankman-Fried being an unreliable narrator, my best guess from talking to him* and many other sources is that his interest in effective altruism was at least *partly* sincere. MacAskill told me that he'd been "kind of the entry point for Sam to come into effective altruism." He'd first met SBF in 2012, when Bankman-Fried approached him following a lecture that MacAskill gave at MIT centered around the concept of "earning to give"—basically making as much money as you can, and then donating a substantial fraction of it to charity. This is a classic EA idea, one that prioritizes the actuarial bottom line of net utility above the feel-good aesthetics of charity. Who does more good for the world: an idealistic twenty-something who works for poverty wages for an NGO in some third-world country, or a hedge fund guy who makes $10 million a year and then donates half of his earnings, enough for the NGO to hire a *hundred* idealistic twentysomethings? Personally, I think earning to give has a compelling logic to it, even if it's surely also sometimes used to rationalize self-interested behavior. And evidently it also was compelling to Bankman-Fried, who imagined himself as a sort of Robin Hood on blockchain steroids. Bankman-Fried had worked briefly at the Centre for Effective Altruism, but wound up starting a crypto hedge fund, Alameda Research, instead. In the early days of crypto, it was so easy to make money that it would almost be unethical *not* to do it, SBF thought. "It just sort of felt like, wow, if this is at all real, these numbers are ludicrous," he'd told me in

---

* Bankman-Fried told me that his relationship with EA had grown more uneasy over time, in part because of political differences—he thought EAs were too "woke," while EAs objected to his involvement in conventional politics. However, among the only times that SBF seemed genuinely remorseful in our conversations was when I asked him what impact his actions might have on the EA movement.

January 2022. Winning at crypto trading would potentially enable him to "donate like, way more than I ever thought I'd be able to give in my life."

By the time of the dinner at Eleven Madison Park in August 2022, I was starting to have more doubts about SBF. The splurgy choice of venue was one thing, a bad look but ultimately a minor error. However, SBF had also recently made a much bigger flub. In the Democratic primary race in Oregon's newly created 6th Congressional District—a picturesque parcel of land that stretches from the evergreen forests of the Coast Range to the Willamette Valley—SBF's super PAC had spent $12 million backing Carrick Flynn, an EA-friendly political neophyte who was running for the U.S. House.

This was a ridiculous amount of money—eight-figure expenditures are generally reserved for statewide races like Senate seats, and for general elections rather than primaries. And it backfired spectacularly. Flynn had never asked for SBF's backing or communicated with him at all. At first he assumed it was a good thing that someone was spending money on his behalf. But there was only so much that money could buy before becoming redundant—or even annoying to voters. Plus, the association with the frizzy-haired king of crypto wasn't a positive. "It drew *so much* weird, negative attention," Flynn said. Ahead in the polls before SBF's intervention, Flynn eventually lost to another Democrat named Andrea Salinas by nearly 20 points. SBF's investment had all of the hallmarks of an arrogant, spreadsheet-driven decision; someone had calculated that spending money on this race was +EV. But nobody had thought about what spending $12 million in a single congressional district would look like in practice. "I would like go knock on someone's door," Flynn recalled. "And they would be like, 'Oh, I have your *literature.*' And they'd come out with a stack of like fifteen fliers." That's when he realized he was going to lose.

Okay, gang, here's where I'm going to break the fourth wall. You paid for this tour of the River—er, you paid for this book—so it's yours to do what you want with. I know from having given this tour before that some folks like to skip ahead to chapter 8 where SBF meets his fate in a New York courtroom, and then catch up with the rest of us afterward. However, my recommendation is that you stay with the group. I'm going to investigate some terms, like "utilitarianism," that are essential to understanding SBF's mindset. And while I don't think EA is exactly to blame for what SBF did, his relationship with the movement isn't an incidental part of the story either.

But there's a larger lens, too. Effective altruism, and the adjacent but more loosely defined intellectual movement called "rationalism," are important parts of the River on their own terms. In some ways, in fact, they are the most important parts. Much of the River is concerned with what philosophers call "small-world problems," meaning tractable puzzles with relatively well-defined parameters: how to maximize expected value in a poker tournament, or how to invest in a portfolio of startups that brings you upside with little risk of ruin. But in this final portion of the book, we're visiting the part of the River where people instead think about open-ended, so-called grand-world problems: everything from where best to spend your charitable contributions to the future of humanity itself. Grand-world problems are *much* easier to screw up, and the consequences for screwing up are much bigger. If a Riverian type can mess up as badly as SBF did on a congressional primary—a small-world problem—think about one with potentially civilization-altering technology like AI in their hands.

However, the reason some Riverians have become obsessed with grand-world problems is because the Village and the rest of the world screw them up all the time, too, in ways that often reflect political partisanship, an endless array of cognitive biases, innumeracy, hypocrisy, and profound intellectual myopia. To take one glaring example that Flynn reminded me of: the U.S. Congress has authorized relatively little—only around $2 billion in spending as part of a 2022-23 budget deal—to prevent future pandemics, even though COVID-19 killed more than 1 million Americans and cost the U.S. economy an estimated $14 trillion. Reducing the chance of a future such pandemic in the United States by even 1 percent would be +EV even at a cost of $140 billion—and yet Congress is barely spending one one-hundredth of that.

These high-stakes decisions are part of why EA and rationalism attract wealthy and powerful people—the new elite that SBF thought he was cultivating at Eleven Madison Park is just the tip of the iceberg. The ideas behind EA have had influence on everyone from Warren Buffett to Bill Gates, even if they wouldn't necessarily use the EA label to describe themselves. And EAs and rats (rationalists) have long played a leading role in the conceptualization and development of artificial intelligence, a technology that EAs correctly inferred could become extremely important years before the general public did.

In some cases, the interest of wealthy elites in these topics stems from a sincere belief that they can do more good for more people. It's easy to be cynical, but it's unambiguously good for the world that people like Gates, Buffett, and Mark Zuckerberg are donating huge amounts of their wealth to charity and making at least some effort to see that their money is used well.* It's harder to characterize the motivation of Elon Musk and Jeff Bezos, with their interest in technologies like space exploration. Some of them subscribe to a version of the Great Man Theory—that because of the shortcomings of the Village, they must take the future into their own hands. Whether or not this can be described as altruistic is hard to say. (Space exploration is fantastically expensive, but also has more potential to do good for humanity than typical billionaire pastimes like owning an NBA team.) Musk has also flirted with effective altruism, having endorsed MacAskill's book and at one point having hired an EA-adjacent wealth advisor, the former poker player Igor Kurganov.

At other times, though, supposed altruism can have an uncanny way of converging with self-interest. Like in the scene at the end of *Dr. Strangelove*, where Strangelove proposes a ratio of ten women to one man to repopulate humanity in underground bunkers in the event of a nuclear

---

* In 2022, I was invited to a large dinner party that Gates hosts where he brings in experts from a variety of fields to chat with one another about worldly topics. I came away impressed with his command of details on how effective various Gates Foundation interventions might or might not be. Gates might not call himself an EA, but he clearly was thinking about how to spend his money effectively.

war—and insists that of course top military and government leaders like him must be included among the lucky few—those who draw up plans to protect the future of humanity rarely fail to secure a seat for themselves in the escape pod.

How to Quantify the Unquantifiable

On an unseasonably warm February afternoon in 2018, a well-groomed poodle named Dakota got loose from her owner. Startled by something at a Brooklyn dog park, Dakota sprinted four blocks, hopped into a subway station, made her way down to the tracks, and then began following the Coney Island-bound route of the F train deeper into Brooklyn. All of this was quite poorly timed: rush hour would soon begin, and Dakota had entered the subway at York Street, the first stop in Brooklyn for passengers coming from Manhattan. Transit officials faced a difficult choice: they could shut down the F, blocking a vital link between New York's two densest boroughs right as commuters were beginning to get off work—or they could potentially run over poor Dakota. They elected to close the F for more than an hour until Dakota was found.

Dakota's story was a real-world example of what philosophers call a trolley problem, a moral dilemma first posed by the philosopher Philippa Foot in 1967. The original version was this: You're driving a trolley that is speeding along the tracks, when to your horror you discover that the brakes are out. If you continue onward, five transit workers on the track ahead will be killed. Alternatively, you can divert the train to a spur. There's a worker there too, and he'll be killed, but there's just one of him and not five people. What do you do?

Most people's intuition is to flip the switch and kill just the one worker. And honestly, this doesn't seem like *that* big a dilemma. The reasoning falls comfortably within the realm of common sense: no transit worker's life is worth more than another, so it's strictly better to kill one of them than five. You can add complications to put yourself in more of a pickle,

though. What if, instead of a lone worker on the spur, a mother and her two young daughters are crossing the tracks, believing that a trolley is never supposed to arrive at that time? This is harder: we're no longer comparing like to like. Transit workers, an ethicist might say, accept some implicit risk of workplace accidents as part of their job (it's actually a relatively dangerous occupation), but the mother and her daughters have not. Do you still want to flip the switch? And if you do, does this make you culpable for the death of the mother and her children? We could also ask some other uncomfortable questions: Are the daughters' lives worth more since they have longer to live?

Now imagine the case of Dakota. Dakota is a good girl who's done nothing wrong. But turning off the F train for an hour comes at a steep price. Hundreds of thousands of people ride the F each day, which means tens of thousands of them will be delayed if you hold up the train for an hour. How should we account for that? You could look at it economically: the average hourly wage in New York is something like $40 — so if we delay 50,000 people for an hour, that's the equivalent of $2 million in lost earnings. Is Dakota's life worth more or less than $2 million? Except this is a pretty rough simplification. On the one hand, it's not like we're just erasing this hour from the commuters' lives — they can play with their phones, and the NYC subway system has a lot of redundancy, so some of them will find alternate routes home. On the other hand, it's not just these people's time we're wasting—in some cases, their absence may endanger others. A hospital worker might be en route to attend to an accident victim in critical condition, or a father might need to walk a special-needs child home from daycare, or another dog could die somewhere after wandering off because their owner hadn't come home on time.

You might say that it's Will MacAskill's job to think through questions like these—and similar questions that are orders of magnitude more complex. And sometimes that means quantifying things that other people would be uncomfortable quantifying.

"Intuitively, you and your well-being count for more than the well-being of an ant. And the chicken counts for more than an ant but less than you," MacAskill told me when we first spoke, many months before the dinner at Eleven Madison Park. Okay, so far this isn't getting *too* weird. Whether we want to admit it or not, we unavoidably wind up making some rough calculations about the value of animal lives. Consider this: almost everyone would agree that we shouldn't shut down the subway for an hour if a squirrel had gotten onto the tracks, whereas almost everyone would agree that we *should* if a human toddler did. With a poodle, it's close enough that reasonable people could argue the case back and forth. We're making some type of calculation, whether we want to admit it or not.

However, effective altruists strive to be more rigorous than this just-winging-it approach. I asked MacAskill what distinguishes EAs—and how they compare to the other sorts of people that you'll encounter in the River. EAs sound a lot more like poker players than you might think. (Indeed, there are several prominent poker players—like Kurganov and his partner, Liv Boeree, who are cited in MacAskill's book—who have since made their way into EA.) "I think the overlap is in cognitive style," said MacAskill. "People who are willing to take the idea of expected value seriously. People who are willing to kind of quantify the unquantifiable. People who are willing to kind of reject common sense, or your first instinct about an idea." Of course, there are also differences—poker isn't exactly an altruistic activity. "Many poker players and many people in finance don't give a shit about other people. But some do. And those people get involved in effective altruism," MacAskill told me.

In the case of valuing animal lives, MacAskill proposed a data-driven heuristic: going by the number of neurons in the animal's brain. "That gives like, not insane answers. It would mean that one chicken is worth one three-hundredth of a human," he said.* Although you do wind up with some unorthodox conclusions. "It has some weird things like you end up with putting elephants above humans. Elephants have more neurons."

One can surely raise objections to rating animals by their neuron count. If the implication is that moral worth is correlated with intelligence, does that mean a smarter human is worth more than a dumber one? And what does this say about the worth of highly intelligent machines? Would it be immoral to turn off a sentient, superintelligent AI? Some EAs actually think so.

Of course, this task of quantifying the unquantifiable is inherently thankless. Even people like me who are relatively sympathetic to EA can poke holes from appeals to commonsense reasoning—*wait, is an elephant life really worth more than a human one?* Then we can proceed on our merry way to tackle small-world problems like poker.

Except most things in the world aren't like poker—instead, they're big, messy problems that society nevertheless has to work out some solution to. The first time this really sank in with me was during COVID. Emily Oster, a Brown economist who writes the newsletter *ParentData*, drew tremendous criticism during COVID for suggesting that people had to work out their COVID routines through cost-benefit analysis rather than treating the coronavirus as a death sentence that they needed to avoid at all costs. To Oster—an Ivy League economist whose parents were also economists—this was about the most natural thing in the world. "I'm really revealing myself as an economist here, which is, like, I cannot conceive of the other way of making decisions," she told me.

Oster was also gesturing toward something deeper. COVID made clear,

---

* A dog, for what it's worth, would be worth about one-thirtieth of a human by this measure, plus or minus some depending on the breed.

perhaps like nothing many of us had experienced before, that hard choices are often unavoidable. It was just a matter of *which* risks you wanted to accept. Oster gave me the example of a single mother who was an essential worker and couldn't work from home. The mother could take her children to daycare when she was working, but being around other children would increase their risk of COVID exposure. Alternatively, she could have her grandparents babysit, which would mean less COVID exposure for the kids but more for the grandparents—who because of their advanced age were at much greater risk of developing a fatal case of COVID. Or the mother could quit her job and lock down the household, but that could mean bankruptcy or foreclosure if she couldn't find other work. *None* of these choices were good—COVID was like an endless series of trolley problems.

Adding to the difficulty is that we are often forced to compare unlike things. "It is not easy to compare 'point five percent risk of serious illness' to 'joy.' But in the end, this is what you will have to do. Take a deep breath, look carefully at your risks and benefits, and make a choice," Oster wrote in May 2020, after many people were beginning to wonder what the endgame was following months of social distancing. Staying locked down and isolated from social activity that brings you joy implies a vast reduction in your quality of life—and indeed, people who tried to quantify this often found that the costs of lockdowns far outweighed the benefits. (If, say, life lived under a strict lockdown is 25 percent worse than normal life,* then the cumulative cost of billions of people being socially isolated was enormous. It's also disputed how effective lockdowns were at preventing COVID in the long run.)

Now, maybe you don't agree with me on lockdowns. And that's fine. Like Oster, I'm used to people getting angry at me about my economist-brain COVID takes. But COVID revealed that *some* attempt at rigorous analysis is worthwhile. Otherwise you wind up with a hodgepodge of rituals and contradictions—like people pulling up their masks while they

---

* Such that, for instance, you'd be willing to give up one month of normal life to avoid a four-month lockdown.

walked by the hostess stand for five seconds at a restaurant, only to rip them off for a two-hour dinner at a crowded table surrounded by strangers. Even Dr. Anthony Fauci, by the time I spoke with him in August 2022, had come to question some countries' reliance on lockdowns when they weren't part of a coherent overall strategy. China, for instance, "locked down but they didn't vaccinate their elderly," he said. "If you are going to restrict—i.e., lock down—make sure you utilize that in a way that will allow you to *unlock. That's* the point."

Here's something else you probably heard during COVID: you can't put a price on human life. Except that people put a price on it all the time. From speeding to get to your destination a little faster, to choosing whether or not to get an expensive medical procedure, to consuming pleasurable things (booze, drugs, greasy food, etc.) that could shorten your lifespan, we are constantly trading off some risk of death for more money or a higher quality of life.

Let's play a game of Russian roulette. I have a revolver with six chambers. Five are blanks, and the other is loaded with a bullet that will instantly kill you. How much would I have to pay you to accept a 1-in-6 risk of death? Would you do it for a billion dollars?

Just speaking for myself, a 1-in-6 chance of death just seems too high for any amount of money. But there are some chances I would take. Instead of Russian roulette, for instance, let's say we're playing regular roulette in a casino. Here's our new game: there are thirty-eight spaces on an American roulette wheel, and if the ball lands on any number except 00, the casino will pay you a billion dollars. If you do land on 00, though, the croupier will pull out a revolver and fatally shoot you. Are you willing to take that gamble? A 1-in-38 chance of death for a billion dollars? I would do it— frankly for considerably less than a billion.

But the moment that you take this bet, you're admitting that you are placing *some* sort of monetary value on human life, or at least on your own life. Economists call this the "value of a statistical life" (VSL). In the United States, the figure that government agencies use for this is about $10 million. This number might be used to determine, for instance, whether some costly new regulation was worth it. Say that it costs $100 million to re-move all remaining asbestos from Manhattan office buildings, but this is projected to prevent twenty cancer deaths. That's a good deal; we're sav-ing lives for only $5 million a head, just half of the VSL.

When people hear about the VSL, they imagine that it's conjured up by a group of nihilistic bureaucrats sitting in a sterile office park. But that's not actually how it's derived. Instead it reflects people's real-life behavior— what economists call their "revealed preferences." One common way to do this, according to Kip Viscusi, an economist who pioneered the use of the VSL during the Reagan administration after he was called in to settle a dispute between warring federal agencies, is to look at how much addi-tional pay people require for hazardous work. People engaged in dangerous jobs like high-rise construction are quite aware of the risks they face, Vis-cusi told me. (The "X number of days since an accident" signs are a salient reminder.) But just as in our roulette example, people are willing to gamble with their lives for enough financial reward.

When you tease out this and lots of other data points—say, by looking at how much people are willing to pay for additional safety features when they buy a new car—the average American implicitly values their life at about $10 million.* That's where the VSL comes from. And ironically, this number is much *higher* than the government had once assumed. "They said life is too sacred to value. And so instead, we're going to call it the cost of death," Viscusi told me. "The cost of death back then was about three hundred thousand dollars"—this reflected a worker's expected fu-ture earnings back in the 1980s. That's right—until the 1980s, the U.S. government valued its citizens' lives at no more than their future earning potential. Never let a bureaucrat tell you something is priceless. It probably just means they're going to round "priceless" down to zero and cut you a bad deal.

---

* This implies that the average American would be willing to play Russian roulette for $2 million. The expected value of being paid $2 million 5 out of 6 times is $1.67 million, equal to one-sixth the $10 mil-lion VSL to compensate you for the times you get unlucky.

So, Uh, What Is Effective Altruism Exactly?

Is this way of thinking about the world—quantifying hard-to-quantify things, engaging in cost-benefit analysis in situations where people might not think to apply it—unique to effective altruism? No. It's common everywhere in the River, a hallmark of what I described in the introduction as decoupling, meaning the propensity to analyze an issue divorced from its larger context.

So then: What is effective altruism, exactly? In one sense, effective altruism is just a brand name, created by MacAskill and another Oxford philosopher, Toby Ord, in 2011. It's a good brand name, or at least it was until its association with SBF—"effective" and "altruism" have strong positive connotations. (MacAskill told me they'd considered lots of other synonyms, but something like "efficient beneficence" wouldn't have rolled off the tongue.)

The more official answer—as stated by MacAskill in an essay entitled "The Definition of Effective Altruism"—is that EA is a "movement [that tries] to figure out, of all the different uses of our resources, which uses will do the most good, impartially considered."

There's immediately quite a lot to unpack there: How do we define *good*? How can we be *impartial*, and do we even want to be? What makes EA a *movement* instead of, say, a scientific discipline?

But hold those questions—because there's also *another* term I've been using, "rationalism," that I want to explain in conjunction with EA. This term is even more confusing, because rationalism originally referred to a school of philosophy that emerged in the seventeenth century.* Modern-day rationalists, however, generally trace their movement back to the autodidactic writer and artificial intelligence researcher Eliezer Yudkowsky, who founded the blog *LessWrong* and wrote an extremely long series of posts called "The Sequences" between 2006 and 2009 in which he laid out his

---

* Such as René Descartes—"I think therefore I am."

philosophy on life, the universe, and pretty much everything. If this sounds a bit geeky in a nerds-playing-Dungeons-and-Dragons-in-the-basement kind of way, it is: Yudkowsky is also known for his Harry Potter fanfic, such as the 122-chapter-long *Harry Potter and the Methods of Rationality*.

Rationalism is a lot scruffier than its prim-and-proper Oxford-educated cousin, EA. "The rationalists are not very good at looking professional and not very good at public relations, and tend to attract people in that category. And the effective altruists are extremely professional and good at public relations," said Scott Alexander, the writer of the blog *Astral Codex Ten* and a pivotal figure in the rationalist movement, when I visited him at his home in Oakland in April 2022. Alexander had a few thoughts of his own about public relations after having felt burned by a 2021 *New York Times* profile that revealed his last name, which he had tried to keep secret,* and which also engaged in a lot of very Villagey tropes. The profile suggested that the rationalists' concern with AI safety risk was tantamount to an interest in science fiction, and described its worldview thusly:

> The Rationalists saw themselves as people who applied scientific thought to almost any topic. This often involved "Bayesian reasoning," a way of using statistics and probability to inform beliefs.

The *Times* story was clearly trying to frame this as a negative (like by putting "effective altruism" and "Bayesian reasoning"—a foundational concept in statistics—in scare quotes).† But this actually isn't such a bad definition of rationalism. And if that's the standard we're going by, I probably qualify as a rationalist myself, whether I want to admit it or not. (Named after the Reverend Thomas Bayes, Bayesian reasoning—the act of viewing the world probabilistically and regularly updating your views as you encounter new evidence—is sort of the lodestar of my first book, *The Signal and the Noise*.)

---

* "Scott" and "Alexander" are his real first and middle names. I follow a general policy of calling people by what they want to be called unless there's an extremely compelling journalistic reason to do otherwise.
† I've been the subject of enough hit pieces to know a hit piece when I see one.

In fact, even if I had never applied to join Team Rationalist, Alexander—whose soft features, dry wit, and male pattern baldness reminded me uncannily of my dad's (West Coast Jewish) side of the family—had already drafted me into it. "You are clearly doing a lot of good work spreading rationality to the masses. Is it useful to think of us as a movement that doesn't include you?" he asked me.

Some of Us Hate to Be Wrong on the Internet

Alexander also had my motivations nailed down to rights. Both of us feel like we try to be nuanced and equivocal in our public writing—a typical *Astral Codex Ten* post is thousands of words long—if also articulate and engaging. But we also feel like this nuance often isn't appreciated, particularly because we don't neatly fall into one of the major political tribes. "We're trying to just do our own thing well, and then someone was wrong on the internet," Alexander said.

Someone being "wrong on the internet" referred to an xkcd cartoon, famous among a certain circle of nerds, where a stick-figure man couldn't sleep because he felt like it was his duty to correct idiots online.

This reference hit a little too close to home. One of the most popular stories in the history of my Substack newsletter, *Silver Bulletin*, came about because I was jet-lagged, woke up in the middle of the night, saw that some dude had posted something idiotic about me on Twitter, and didn't stop writing until I had completed my duty of putting him in his place. I suppose I do think I'm doing good for the world by getting people to be more quote-unquote rational and think more critically about subjects they might take for granted. But that's not necessarily what motivates me. What often motivates me instead is that it's just intrinsically important deep down for me to be right, and to see the world accurately. I feel like it's my *sacred duty* to call out someone who's *wrong on the internet.*

Unless you're already familiar with the contours of EA and rationalism, you may be wondering why I'm just throwing a bunch of names and ideas out there that don't have an obvious connection to one another. And actually, I think that's a fair question. Both movements tend to collect high-IQ misfits who are attracted to debates over nerdy, abstract topics. And these debates are conducted in relatively good faith. Even public figures who are critical of the movements tend to get a fair hearing at blogs like LessWrong and at the Effective Altruism Forum—which is pretty much the opposite of what it's usually like to argue about public affairs online. The moment they hear it, they're like, "Oh, this is what I've been looking for my entire life," said Alexander of rationalism. In reporting this book, I began to get a sense for this relatively small and tightly knit community; Alexander even threw a dinner party for me after our interview, inviting a dozen people from the Bay Area rationalist scene.

EA and rationalist interests intersect in some places—in particular, in technologies like AI and nuclear weapons that could pose an existential threat to humanity (this is the subject of the conclusion to this book) and a shared vernacular in concepts like expected value and Bayesian reasoning that are also used elsewhere in the River. But the kinship that EAs and rationalists feel for each other conceals that there are a lot of internal disagreements and even contradictions within the movements—in particular, there are two major streams of EA/rationalism that don't see eye to eye. The first is associated with the Australian philosopher Peter Singer and a cluster of topics including animal welfare, global poverty reduction, effective giving, and not living beyond your means—but also the ethical precept known as utilitarianism. The second is associated with Yudkowsky and the George Mason University economist Robin Hanson and a whole different cluster of topics: futurism, artificial intelligence, prediction markets, and being willing to argue about just about anything on the internet, including subjects that others often find taboo. Let's start with the Singer stream, which is more radical than it might seem at first glance.

A Field Guide to EAs and Rationalists

	SINGER STREAM	YUDKOWSKY–HANSON STREAM
Key Figures	Peter Singer, Will MacAskill, Toby Ord	Robin Hanson, Eliezer Yudkowsky, Nick Bostrom, Scott Alexander
Favorite Subjects	Animal welfare, global poverty reduction, effective giving, existential risk	Artificial intelligence, futurism, prediction markets, cognitive biases, existential risk
Political Orientation	Center left, progressive, relatively well aligned with U.S. Democratic Party	Libertarian, eclectic, suspicious of major parties
Ethical Philosophy	Usually but not always explicitly utilitarian	Sometimes utilitarian leaning but less committed to any one ethical theory
Personality Type	Academic, reserved,* well-spoken	Nerdy, quirky, provocative misfits
Altruistic?	Yes in theory and often but not always in practice	Not necessarily; think more rigorous evaluation of evidence and probabilistic thinking can be used toward a variety of ends
What They Call Themselves	Effective altruists	Rationalists

Trolley Problems on Expert Mode

When I began working on this book, I knew I'd have conversations with poker players, venture capitalists, and cryptocurrency enthusiasts. I didn't

---

* Although Singer himself is a big exception and can be quite outspoken on subjects ranging from bestiality to eugenics. He is not a typical polite EA.

think I'd spend a lot of time talking with philosophers. But I did, including philosophers within the effective altruism movement and others who have criticized it from various angles. That included taking the train down to Princeton one day to meet with Singer, where we spoke over a vegan lunch at one of the university cafeterias.

In his own way, Singer—still intellectually active in his late seventies— is every bit as much of an influence on the River as someone like Doyle Brunson. A lot of that influence dates back to an essay he published in 1972 called "Famine, Affluence and Morality," which includes this famous scenario involving a drowning child:

> An application of this principle would be as follows: if I am walking past a shallow pond and see a child drowning in it, I ought to wade in and pull the child out. This will mean getting my clothes muddy, but this is insignificant, while the death of the child would presumably be a very bad thing.

This is a trolley problem of sorts, but it's a super easy one. You're walking past a child who is drowning and you can easily pull her out without any risk to yourself, although you'll get your nice clothes dirty and possibly be late for work. The answer is: of course you should rescue her—in fact, pretty much everyone would agree that you'd be some sort of evil, sociopathic asshole if you didn't. In his later writings, Singer imagined other scenarios where the cost was higher—like destroying an extremely expensive sports car to save a child—but still nothing that seems like a particularly difficult moral dilemma.

Before I proceed further, let me say—in the EA spirit of being as fair as possible even to people you disagree with—that I think you should read Singer, and in particular his 2009 book (reissued in 2019) *The Life You Can Save*. I think Singer's effort to bring more focus to the global poor has done net good for the world. And you don't have to be a hard-core utilitarian to think that people ought to be considerably more altruistic at the margin, and more effective when giving. It is tragic that people gave more than $500 million to the Harvard endowment in fiscal year 2022 when it was already worth more than $50 billion—instead of giving to real charities. (Seriously, don't give a cent to the endowment of Harvard or another elite private college.) GiveWell—founded by Holden Karnofsky and Elie Hassenfeld, alumni of the hedge fund Bridgewater Associates who were inspired by Singer and shocked to discover how little information there was about how effective charities were at meeting their goals—is a good place to start when looking for alternatives.

Furthermore, I think it's altruistic when people like Singer express unpopular viewpoints that they honestly believe will lead to social betterment and selfish to suppress these ideas because of fear of social approbation. People who never publicly state views that would be unpopular within their peer groups should be regarded with suspicion.

Okay then, so why don't I find the drowning child parable persuasive? Well, partly because it's meant to play a trick on you—as Singer freely admits. "The uncontroversial appearance of the principle just stated is deceptive," he writes in "Famine, Affluence and Morality." Once he's established that we ought to be altruistic—make a small sacrifice to save the life of a child—he then ups the ante to an argument that's much more controversial:

> If it were acted upon, even in its qualified form, our lives, our society, and our world would be fundamentally changed. For the principle takes, firstly, no account of proximity or distance. It makes no moral difference whether the person I can help is a neighbor's child ten yards from me or a Bengali whose name I shall never know, ten thousand miles away.

This is the principle of impartiality, the idea that we ought to regard people further removed from us (an unknown child in India) as being just as morally worthy as a drowning child in our hometown—or even as worthy as our own children.

Singer thinks it follows that somebody who splurges on luxury goods—say, on an expensive sushi dinner—when that money could instead have been used to alleviate global poverty (potentially saving a life for as little as $3,000 to $5,000) is morally culpable, in much the same way that a man who refuses to save the drowning child would be culpable. This principle of impartiality can be extended quite a long way: in Singer's formulation, it's extended not just to humans in other countries, but also to all sentient animals. In MacAskill's book *What We Owe the Future*, it is also extended to *future* people: someone born in the year 3024 is just as valuable as an infant born today. (This idea, called "longtermism," is controversial even among EAs.) Singer has also suggested that impartiality should be extended to artificial intelligences that achieve sentience.

Impartiality is also the basis for Singer's utilitarianism, a term I've name-dropped several times without having defined yet. Utilitarianism is a branch of consequentialism, the idea that actions should be judged by their consequences. This stands in contrast to deontology (from the Greek prefix *deon-*, roughly meaning "duty"), which instead states that actions may be intrinsically good or bad based on ethical rules. Singer is suspicious of these rules because he thinks they lead to partiality—think of maxims such as "honor thy mother and father," which prioritize those who are proximate to us over those who are distant.

Why this relatively long detour into moral philosophy in a book about gambling and risk? Well, it's partly because Singer is highly influential in EA. When MacAskill writes that EA should pursue the good *impartially* considered, this is what he's referring to. But it's mostly because utilitarianism—which is often formulated as "the greatest amount of good for the greatest number"—lends itself to mathematical representations, making it a tempting fit for the quantitative minds of the River. Under utilitarianism, morality can be transformed into sort of an EV-maximization problem. You should save the drowning child because ruining your suit costs you only 800 "utils" (units of utility)—the cost of a new suit at Brooks Brothers—whereas her life is worth 10 million utils (the value of a statistical life).

There are some settings where I think utilitarianism is an appropriate framework—particularly in medium-scale problems such as in establishing government policy where impartiality (not playing favorites) is important.* For instance, when a subcommittee of the CDC met in November 2020 to develop recommendations for who would be first in line for COVID vaccines, they rejected going with a utilitarian calculus of maximizing benefits and minimizing harms to instead also consider objectives like "promo[ting] justice" and "mitigat[ing] health inequalities." Its recommendations were revisited after a significant public outcry—including from people who pointed out that sacrificing public health impact for "equity" would actually produce more death and disease among people in disadvantaged groups. But an unelected body like that shouldn't have been playing favorites in the first place based on political preferences that many Americans don't share.

But if utilitarianism is often a good first approximation at the meso-scale (for medium-scale problems), I am much more suspicious that it functions well as a framework for personal ethics—it can quite directly lead to Sam Bankman-Fried's conclusion, as revealed at his criminal trial, that the ends justify the means. I am also suspicious that it works well for very large-scale problems (such as trying to calculate all the utility in the present or future universe), sometimes known as "infinite ethics."

I'll offer a further critique of utilitarianism over the next several pages—but let me warn you that it gets detailed and some of you may want to skip ahead to act 4, which features a poker game played at a rationalist convention, a utilitarian sex researcher, and a man who believes the future will be almost incalculably strange.

Why I'm Not a Utilitarian

Seated next to Will MacAskill at the Eleven Madison Park dinner, I had a realization: moral philosophy, or at least the type of moral philosophy that EAs and rationalists like to practice, has a lot in common with building a statistical model. (MacAskill endorsed this comparison in a

---

* I would argue, however, that effective altruism has a blind spot in not spending more time considering how the government (as opposed to private charity) could use its resources more effectively. Total charitable spending in the U.S. was about $500 billion in 2022, whereas the government spends around $6 trillion.

follow-up conversation. "I think the analogy between theorizing in moral philosophy and creating a best fit line in a model is actually like really quite good," he told me.) It's not a coincidence, for instance, that philosophy majors have relatively high mathematical standardized test scores—as high as people in some disciplines in the hard sciences such as biology. Philosophers make observations about the world, drawing from their own moral intuitions or from other people's, and from what rules and ethical norms societies develop. Then they draw up some generalized principles from these observations at a higher level of abstraction. This is quite a bit like when an economist or a statistician has a dataset full of real-world observations and then aims to generalize based on those. For instance, the economist might build a model through techniques like regression analysis, observing that there is generally a strong statistical relationship between GDP and life expectancy, even if there are also some exceptions.

Having built quite a few statistical models myself, I know that it's hard to do, in part because there are two sorts of errors one can make. This is slightly technical—there's a longer discussion in *The Signal and the Noise* if you want to go deeper—but one problem is called "overfitting." Basically, that means trying to accommodate every nook and cranny in the dataset, sometimes through highly contrived strategies. For instance, in explaining why the United States is an outlier in the GDP–life expectancy relationship—we have a very high GDP per capita but our life expectancy is well below that of many other rich nations—you might invent a variable called "flagstars," which is the number of stars a country has in its national flag. (The U.S. flag, with fifty stars, has more than any other nation.) This might technically improve the fit of the model, but it's also quite ridiculous. Whatever the reasons for our relatively low life expectancy, it's not because of our vexillological (flag design) choices.

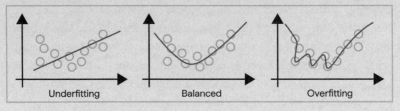

| Underfitting | Balanced | Overfitting |

You might say that conventional or "commonsense" morality is a lot like this. It's full of contradictions. Why do we eat pigs but keep dogs as pets, for instance? You can't even use MacAskill's strategy of going by neuron count here, since it's about the same for dogs and pigs. It's just one of those customs that everyone agrees to, and if you make too much of a fuss about it you might be stigmatized as either a puppy killer or a radical PETA activist.

However, it's also possible to *underfit* a model. To have too few parameters, such that you have a gross oversimplification that is at best only vaguely right, and that doesn't match the way the real world works very well at all. I don't entirely agree with this critique, but economists are sometimes accused of this: that their assumptions about what makes people "rational" don't account for all the idiosyncrasies that real consumers have and superimpose too many assumptions that don't predict people's actual behavior well.

Maybe you can see where I'm going with this. I think utilitarianism is analogous to an underfit model. Instead of being too deferential to commonsense morality, it doesn't meet people in the middle enough, accepting that maybe various laws and customs evolved for good reasons. In 2023, for instance, Singer endorsed a controversial defense of bestiality on the grounds that if people think it is ethically acceptable to eat animals, it ought to be ethically acceptable to have sex with them, since murder and torture (the condition that many animals are kept in is indeed very bad) are generally regarded as being as bad as rape. It's not hard to explain why most societies evolved this seeming double standard, however. Eating animal protein perpetuates the human species; having sex with animals does not.

I don't think it's a bad thing for Singer to pose questions like these—overall, I think society is more in danger of having too much conformity than breaking down because people challenge too many taboos. Still, classical utilitarianism, including Singer's version of it specifically, is totalizing and uncompromising. I'm more inclined to meet people where they are, to allow them some of their seeming contradictions while nudging them toward more ethical behavior. The poker player Dan Smith, for instance, has helped to raise more than $26 million for effective charities—but I know he's also willing to indulge in an expensive sushi dinner, or bet thousands of dollars to bluff someone off a better hand. "I think we have weird views of money where you just absolutely need to get desensitized to it. If you had the viewpoint of like, ooh, it's three thousand dollars to save a life, I'm gonna bet thirty-three lives on the river here, that's not great," Smith told me.

Singer, certainly, is aware that his conclusions aren't intuitive. At times in his work, he even seems to imply that autistic people make for superior moral reasoners because they aren't as bound by emotionally laden societal conventions like empathy. He told me that society is essentially running on outdated software that doesn't recognize technological growth. He referred me to another controversial example: incest. "We have developed intuitions against having sex with your siblings. There's a reason why that might have evolved in the past when there was no effective contraception," he said—since children produced through inbreeding have a high rate of genetic defects. Now the case for the taboo is less clear, he thinks, at least if the couple is using contraception.*

Again, I'm glad that society's moral codes evolve over time—as a gay man, for instance, my life would be much worse in an earlier century. I'm just wary of imposing too much change upon society, particularly when it comes from Oxford or Princeton professors rather than being arrived at democratically.† Sometimes the experts are wrong; that we had the technological capacity to do remote learning during the COVID pandemic didn't necessarily mean it was a good idea. I tend to trust decentralized decision-making mechanisms more.

I should note, however, that utilitarianism, especially in its strictest forms, is actually relatively unpopular among philosophers. Kevin Zollman, a Carnegie Mellon philosopher who has also written books on how game theory can be applied to everyday life, told me that he thinks

---

* Other taboos may grow stronger, meanwhile. The evolution of synthetic meat could lead to a stronger taboo against eating animal protein, for instance. However, so far, the incidence of vegetarianism in the United States has declined slightly in polls. It's hard to know when an idea's time will come. Writing this in early 2024, amid rising authoritarianism, war in the Middle East, and a backlash to progressive ideas about race and gender, it's become harder to say that the arc of history bends toward progress—or that you can get people to agree what constitutes progress in the first place.
† Singer favors a form of utilitarianism called "hedonistic utilitarianism" that is particularly undemocratic—basically, whatever's best for people is what gives them the most utility, even if it's not the choice they'd make for themselves (the alternative is called "preference utilitarianism"). If a philosopher knocks a chocolate chip cookie out of my hand because he's calculated that it will cost me utils—the long-term costs of the weight I'll gain will outweigh the pleasure of eating the cookie in the moment—he's a hedonistic utilitarian.

utilitarianism can be seductive to quantitatively inclined people because of its promise of mathematical precision. "I'm definitely a very 'be explicit' kind of person. I'm a mathematical philosopher," he said. But "especially when something is easy to mathematicize it in one way, the tempting thing is then to say, 'Oh, that must be the best way or the only way to mathematicize it.'" When you have a hammer, everything looks like a nail—and utilitarianism can be an awfully blunt instrument.

There are alternatives, though—mathematical ways to do philosophy that don't just rely on summing up all utils across the known universe. The late Princeton philosopher John Rawls, in *A Theory of Justice*, proposed maximizing the well-being of the least well-off person in society. In principle, you could build some sort of mathematical model to do that. Nick Bostrom, an Oxford philosopher who is associated with EA although probably falls more into the rationalist camp, told me about his idea he called a "moral parliament," "where I'm uncertain about which ethical theory is correct and I would give them each some weight. I mean, the utilitarians would be in there with their delegates to this parliament. But there would be other moral frameworks as well as self-interest and care for friends and family." I like this idea myself and think it pretty accurately depicts how human beings actually think through trolley problems. Maybe I'd want various species of utilitarians in my own personal moral parliament, but also some libertarians who were concerned with maximizing personal freedom, some progressives who were working to ensure that society was evolving and adapting, plus some "commonsense" thinkers from various contemporary political and religious groups. No party would have a majority or could get too out of line without cooperation from the others.

Lara Buchak, a Princeton philosophy professor who wrote a book called *Risk and Rationality*, told me she is suspicious of utilitarianism's emphasis on outlier or infinite cases. One famous such case, proposed by the late philosopher Derek Parfit, is called the Repugnant Conclusion. To study the Repugnant Conclusion, let's compare two worlds:

- One is the world we have today, with about 8 billion people, except everything is much better. We've cured cancer and many other diseases, eliminated poverty, ended racism, and developed synthetic meat that tastes a thousand times better than animal protein. People live for 150 years and have a standard of living equivalent to that of a Swedish supermodel.*

- Alternatively, imagine a world where there are infinite people who eke out an existence that's just barely worth living. In Parfit's formulation, this consisted of people living for a few days listening to elevator Muzak and eating some mildly tasty potatoes before perishing. (Maybe they also get ketchup.)

The Repugnant Conclusion is that the latter world is better, because even though the former world has a ton of utility—8 billion people times some very high number like 100 million utils per capita—it's still less than the *infinite* utility in the repugnant world, because infinity multiplied by any positive number is still infinity.

"The thought that, well, this theory isn't good if it can't handle infinite cases, I think that's like a huge mistake," said Buchak. She thinks moral theories should instead be tested on practical, day-to-day decision-making. "Nearly every decision you face involves risk," she said. "I'm like [more] concerned with just like, you know, should I bring my umbrella today?" If a moral theory can't handle everyday cases like these—if it strays too far from common sense—then we probably shouldn't trust it, whether or not it provides an elegant answer to the Repugnant Conclusion.

I endorse Buchak's idea, in part because I know that when you build a statistical model, it can be highly sensitive to extreme and outlier cases. It's great if you can build a clever model that accommodates both the outliers and the regular boring old everyday data points. But if you can't do both, then sometimes the best strategy is to just chuck out the outlier and go with a model that works well enough for practical purposes.† The right answer to the Repugnant Conclusion, in other words, may be: *Who the fuck cares?* We have 8 billion people trying to live ethical and fulfilling lives and ensure a prosperous future for their descendants. Can't we stay busy with that instead of fiddling with trolley problems?

---

* Don't worry, we've also managed to maintain some ways for people to feel conflict and excitement in this world—maybe everybody still argues on Twitter all the time, for instance.
† It also doesn't intrinsically follow that the rules at very small or large scales follow the rules at the mesoscale. For example, the strong and weak interactions in physics—two of the four fundamental forces along with gravity and electromagnetism—apply only at small scales and can be ignored for most problems in biology or chemistry.

Buchak's work also focuses on meeting people where they are when it comes to risk management. Expected value, in a probabilistic universe, is calculated from averaging out the results over some number of trials or scenarios or simulations. In poker, or some everyday task like trying to find the best route home from work (maybe there's one route that's faster on average but also has a drawbridge that occasionally causes a significant delay), you probably *should* think in EV terms. But who in the hell am I (or Lara Buchak or Peter Singer) to tell you what you should do in decisions you'll face just once? "It might be that you should behave differently when choosing a spouse or choosing a job or doing these kinds of things that you're only going to do once, hopefully," Buchak told me.

Okay, we're almost done with the philosophy lecture. But let me also bring up a couple more critiques of Singer's notion of impartiality. One is that you don't need to be Ayn Rand to think that the human condition has been improved by economic development and that exchanging money for goods and services can be a win-win. Indeed, as Singer has pointed out, the amount of severe poverty in the world has radically decreased as the world has become more industrialized. Maybe you don't need to have as many sushi dinners, although I'd note that the money you spend on them doesn't disappear but instead goes to the waitstaff, the dishwashers, the fisherman who caught your tuna, the government in the form of sales taxes, the owners of the business, and so on. I'm skeptical that a substantially more ascetic world would have higher overall utility.

Next, I think there is some rational basis for partiality because we have more uncertainty about things that are removed from us in time and space. Some of this is for practical reasons. If there's a small but tangible risk of a civilization-destroying nuclear war each year, then we probably ought to discount the welfare of people a thousand years from now quite a bit heavily.

It's also about epistemic humility. I can fully accept that a child in Bangalore is just as worthwhile as one in Brooklyn. Maybe I can get there for some animals, too, like elephants or orcas. I'm much less certain about one of MacAskill's hypothetical future human beings from *What We Owe the Future*, or something like a sentient AI. Now, I should note that EAs like MacAskill have answers to these types of objections.

Still, as someone who has been around plenty of smart nerds who didn't know their own limitations, I treat these ideas with some caution. "Just as a matter of fact, I'm struck by how much of it is based on essentially back-of-the-napkin probability calculations," said David Kinney, a Yale psychologist who has criticized EA. "They seem to evince a certain faith in our ability for general all-purpose probability estimation, and even our general ability to say what even has positive probability. And we have reason to think that, as finite agents, we don't actually have that capability." Sometimes, EA seems like a moral framework for a world where everyone has 200 IQs—and not the world we actually live in.

There's also a more subtle problem. EA and utilitarian ideas can be so abstract that there aren't many ways to test them experimentally, to see how well the model matches up to the real world. EAs "probably undervalue things like cultural change, politics, like all of these like softer skills," said Kurganov, the former poker player and Musk advisor.* Poker players may have better attuned senses of risk and reward than EAs because they bear the consequences of their own actions, Kurganov told me. "As a poker player, you're extremely expected-value focused with all of your decisions. You're constantly reassessing the situation." The motivated reasoning that plagues expert judgment in other domains doesn't really apply, he said. "Like, you get hit in the face and you lose money if you're wrong about reality."

My final objection comes from—you knew it was going to make an appearance sooner or later—game theory. I have a deep intuitive suspicion of moral philosophies that don't involve reciprocity. By reciprocity, I mean that if I agree to live by a rule, other people agree to it too. The most well-known example of this in philosophy is Immanuel Kant's categorical imperative: "Act only according to that maxim whereby you can at the same time will that it should become a universal law." This can be analogized to the prisoner's dilemma. If we both agree to cooperate, to act morally, then we wind up collectively better off than if we just act selfishly. Indeed, much conventional morality comes from society's need to discourage selfish behavior, and I worry about upending

---

* Kurganov fell victim to politics himself, having been ousted from Musk's orbit in an internal coup from the family office and unflatteringly described in headlines as a "34-year-old former pro gambler who dropped out of college to smoke weed."

that artifice.* What's interesting is that although the categorical imperative is considered a canonical example of a deontological (duty-based) philosophy, the prisoner's dilemma also justifies it on utilitarian grounds. Indeed, there is a variant of utilitarianism called "rule utilitarianism"—roughly, that we should act such as if our behavior was universalized, which would maximize utility—that I'm much more sympathetic to than classic utilitarianism.

What I don't want, though, is to be so impartial that I'm constantly put in a position where I can be taken advantage of—the sucker who cooperates when my fellow prisoner does not. And even if I think there's something honorable about acting morally in a mostly selfish world, I also wonder about the long-term evolutionary fitness of some group of people who wouldn't defend their own self-interest, or that of their family, their nation, their species, or even their planet, without at least a little more vigor than they would that of a stranger. I want the world to be less partial than it is, but I want it to be at least partially partial.

I can even propose a thought experiment of my own that serves as the sort of antonym of the drowning child parable. Think about the ten people in the world that are most important to you on a personal basis. They can be children, parents, siblings, friends, lovers, mentors—whomever you want. Suppose I offer to humanely euthanize these ten people. In exchange, eleven random people from around the world will be saved. Is it moral to kill the ten people to save the eleven? I'd think almost everybody would say no—in fact, a lot of us might say that taking this deal would be quite evil, perhaps just as evil as failing to save a drowning child because you'd get your clothes dirty.

Once you accept both this rule and the drowning child parable, you accept that humans are neither perfectly selfish nor perfectly impartial—that we should probably be less selfish, but we have to be partially partial.

---

* A nerdy term that EAs and rationalists use for this is Chesterton's fence, referring to a parable by the philosopher G. K. Chesterton about a fence that's been erected across a road for reasons you don't understand. You shouldn't just remove the fence without knowing why it was put there in the first place, Chesterton thought. Maybe it protects against something—deer who will eat your foliage, wild boar who will trample your lawn, the zombies who tend to roam the town at night—that you very much want to protect against.

Act 4: Berkeley, California, September 2023

As a rule, I hate playing poker if it's not for money. It doesn't have to be for a *lot* of money. One of my most fun poker experiences ever was dealing a 10 cent/20 cent backyard game to friends, many of whom were learning the game for the first time. But I want *some* sort of stakes to get people's hearts racing.

I was willing to make an exception, however, in the name of science. I was in Berkeley, California, attending a conference called Manifest, playing in a poker tournament for a play-money currency known as Mana. Billed as "a gathering of forecasting nerds," Manifest was thrown by Manifold, one of several startups in an increasingly competitive landscape of companies that allow people to make probabilistic bets on real-world events.

This might seem like a relatively obscure interest, but people in the EA/rationalist community are obsessed with prediction markets. Why? Partly because of their economist-brain appreciation for markets in general. But also because they believe we'll have more accurate and honest discussions if we put numbers on things. It's easy to say something like, "I'm quite concerned about catastrophic risks to humanity from misaligned artificial intelligence." But it's much more informative to state your p(doom)—your probability that AI could produce these catastrophic outcomes. If your p(doom) is 1 percent or 2 percent, that's still high enough to qualify as "quite concerned." (After all, it's the end of the world we're talking about.) But if you think p(doom) is 40 percent (and some EAs think it's that high, or higher), that means that AI alignment—making sure that AIs do what we want and serve human interests—is perhaps the single biggest challenge humanity has ever faced.

Numbers allow us to understand that difference in a way that words do not. In his book *The Precipice*, Toby Ord put his p(doom) at 1 in 6—the same as the chance of losing a cosmic game of Russian roulette—a 1 in 6 chance that humans will become extinct or civilization will irrecoverably collapse in the next century, with AI being the most likely reason. Sure, this might seem artificially precise. But the alternative of *not* providing a number is a lot worse, Ord thought. At the very least, we should be able to convey orders of magnitude. A nuclear war is a *lot* more likely to kill humanity than a supervolcano, for instance. "Whether we're talking like a one-in-a-million [chance], or whether we're talking like one-in-ten on certain topics—the idea that I just then wouldn't tell the reader just seems bizarre," Ord told me.

But Manifold is distinctive for two reasons. First, users aren't betting for money but instead for play money dollars called Mana. And second, Manifest lets users create their own markets, allowing them to bet on pretty much *anything*. When I say *anything*, I mean it. This can include deadly serious world events, like whether the Israel Defense Forces were responsible for an explosion near a hospital in Gaza. But it could also be something like whether Austin Chen, the founder of Manifold and—unusually for the EA/rationalist scene, a practicing Catholic—will still believe in God in 2026. (There's a 71 percent chance that he will, the market says.) There was even a market about whether there would be an orgy at Manifest—which initially showed just a 28 percent chance, but eventually resolved to yes. (Meaning that the orgy was consummated; I did not participate.)

And naturally enough, conference attendees were betting on the outcome of the very poker game that I was playing in, which had a star-studded lineup of rationalist celebrities, like Cate Hall, an ex-poker pro turned effective altruist; Zvi Mowshowitz, a former Magic: The Gathering champion whose incredibly in-depth analyses of AI make his blog[*] an essential read for rationalists; and Shayne Coplan, the founder of another prediction market site, Polymarket.[†] With every hand that played out, forecasting nerds scurried around the table to peer at how many chips

---

[*] Zvi's blog is called *Don't Worry About the Vase*; https://thezvi.substack.com.
[†] As of our publication deadline in May 2024, I was in late-stage conversations to serve in a paid advisory role to Polymarket. The negotiations were not underway at the time I originally researched and wrote this chapter.

each of us had and to create new Manifold markets like who would be the next player to be knocked out.

So how'd the science experiment go? Truth be told, I don't think their poker predictions were particularly good. The tournament was a "turbo," meaning that it was designed to be finished within a couple of hours rather than dragging out all night. This reduces the amount of skill involved, and the market was probably overstating the chance that one of the experienced players, like me or Hall, would win.

Then again, if I had *really* believed that the market was mispriced, I could have opened a Manifold account and bet against myself. That's the theory at least; the ethos of Manifold is decentralized and radically transparent. "The Manifold theory of insider trading is that insider trading is generally fine and good, unless you have some kind of duty to not reveal information," said Chen. Unlike at some prediction market sites, you can see exactly who is betting on exactly what at Manifold, and the process can feel collaborative as much as competitive, with earnest discussion forums where people reveal their rationale for making bets.

The Manifest conference was also one of the last reporting trips that I made for this book. And it confirmed for me that the River is real—not just some literary device I invented. It's more likely to (ahem) manifest itself in some places than others, such as Las Vegas or in the San Francisco Bay Area. But these same forecasting nerds I saw at Manifold had kept popping up in different contexts elsewhere in the River. I knew a lot of people there who had become sources or friends (or both). I knew the in-jokes and the lingo. The conference didn't *quite* feel like my backyard—I still prefer Downriver with the poker players, who tend to be a little more competitive and a little more street-smart. "Manifold has this kind of weird filtering effect, where because it is play money, we don't get like serious hard-core, high-dollar gamblers, and instead you get pretty intellectual people," said Chen. But it was all part of some broader like-minded community.

When there isn't money on the line, you might even look at making a quantitative forecast as an *altruistic* act. Absent the numbers, it's easy to use weasel words and then claim you were right no matter what. One of the reasons Phil Tetlock (of hedgehog-and-foxes fame) found that experts made such poor forecasts is because they'd been allowed to get away with this lazy rhetoric. By contrast, someone like Yudkowsky—whose p(doom) is very high, fairly close to 100 percent—will take a *lot* of reputational damage if AI alignment proves relatively easy to achieve. Whereas if the machines turn us all into paper clips—one of Nick Bostrom's famous thought experiments involves an unaligned AI with the goal of manufacturing as many paper clips as possible—he won't be around to take credit. (As someone who has as much experience as pretty much anyone making probabilistic forecasts in public, I can also tell you from firsthand experience that incentives to do this are poor. People won't understand what the probabilities mean, and you'll often be criticized even if your probabilities are as accurate as advertised.)

There's another reason that EAs and rationalists think prediction markets are important. It gets at the very definition of rationality itself. If you look up "rational" in a thesaurus, you'll find that it's a synonym for terms like "reasonable," "sensible," and "prudent." And indeed this is the way it's used in everyday English. Philosophers have a more precise definition, however—usually referring to two types of rationality:

- First, there's **instrumental rationality**. Basically this means: Do you adopt means suitable to your ends? There is a man who has eaten more than thirty thousand Big Macs. Now, this might not be a *reasonable* and *prudent* thing for him to do. But if this man's life goal is to eat as many Big Macs as possible, you could say he's instrumentally rational because he's done a bang-up job of this. You can put more or fewer requirements on instrumental rationality, depending on how strict you want to be. One big one that most philosophers agree upon is requiring consistent preferences: if you prefer Big Macs to Whoppers, and Whoppers to Wendy's Doubles, you shouldn't then prefer Wendy's Doubles to Big Macs.

- The second type is **epistemic rationality**. This means: Do you see the world for what it is? Do your beliefs line up with reality? If Big Mac Man thinks his diet is exceptionally healthy, but he's dying of major organ failure caused by his lack of balanced nutrition, he isn't being epistemically rational. (Although in fact, he has low cholesterol and is otherwise in good health, or so his wife claims.) As I argue in *The Signal and the Noise*, making testable predictions is one of the only ways to know whether you're epistemically rational.

So in theory, prediction markets play an important role in making the world more rational. But what about in practice?

My views are mostly sympathetic, but not without some reservations. That's in part because of some scar tissue from too many arguments I've had on the internet about the accuracy of prediction markets versus FiveThirtyEight forecasts. The FiveThirtyEight forecasts have routinely been better—I know that's what you were expecting me to say, but it's true—something that's not supposed to happen if the markets are efficient. Then again, maybe this doesn't tell us that much. Elections are quite literally the Super Bowl of prediction markets—there's so much dumb money out there (lots of people who have very strong opinions about politics) that there isn't necessarily enough smart money to offset it. In 2020, there were even people willing to bet millions on Donald Trump after Joe Biden had already been declared the winner (we'll get to that shortly). In many other circumstances, though, prediction markets are clearly quite useful. As news organizations scrambled to correct their coverage, for instance, traders at Manifold determined that the IDF probably hadn't been responsible for whatever had happened on that particular night at the Gaza hospital.*

But the bigger concern I have, ironically enough, is that prediction markets may become less reliable if people trust them too much.

When I spoke with MacAskill after the FTX collapse and asked him whether he ought to have seen it coming, he gave me what I found to be a dissatisfying answer. "This was genuinely extremely unpredictable given

---

* I'm also skeptical that play-money prediction markets can be as efficient as real-money ones. Still, as Austin Chen pointed out to me, rationalists are exactly the sort of people who care a lot about clapping back at people who are *wrong on the internet*, and if they can do that in the form of a prediction market, all the better. "I think it's a mistake to say that money is the only kind of skin in the game," he told me. "Reputational skin in the game or, like, ego skin in the game actually matters a lot."

available evidence," he said. He cited a forecast from a different play-money prediction market site called Metaculus. "What's the chance of FTX defaulting on any customer deposit in 2022? It was like one point three percent," MacAskill recalled.

Now, look, maybe it's fair in some sense to not have expected things to get *quite* so bad with SBF—it's not every day you encounter one of the biggest frauds of the century. But this is a classic example of placing too much faith in markets. For one thing, MacAskill, who had mentored SBF into effective altruism, ought to have had a lot of insider information that random traders at Manifold or Metaculus didn't have. But even based on things that were public knowledge—like his investment in Carrick Flynn and the Ponzi-like token he proposed to Matt Levine—there were quite a lot of warning signs with SBF.*

The vibes at Manifest were friendly—Chen even gave me a hug as I took off to catch my Uber the next morning. But one person I spoke with, Oliver Habryka, actually thought his community had become *too* trusting. "I've been in this game for a long time," said Habryka, who is on the leadership team at Lightcone Infrastructure, the company that runs the rationalist blog *LessWrong* and owns the Berkeley microcampus that hosted Manifest. He referred to EA before the FTX collapse as the "world's largest trust bubble"—one that was prone to being taken advantage of by SBF.

Further Downriver, where the poker players and hedge-funders hang out, we tend to be less trusting. And sometimes that can be a good thing. With more experience having real money at stake, we're a little better at sorting out when an opportunity is too good to be true versus when there really is the opportunity of a lifetime. Bill Perkins, who runs the energy-trading hedge fund Skylar Capital and is also a high-stakes poker player, is one of a couple of people I know who made a lot of money—in his case, well

---

* Should I hold myself similarly accountable? It's a fair question. As I said in chapter 6, I had some misgivings about SBF, but I wouldn't have expected him to be guilty of major fraud. I got lucky that the news came out well before my deadline hit. But this is a book with about two hundred sources, many of whom push boundaries in various ways. For EAs, by contrast, Bankman-Fried was a singular figure—the most publicly visible explicitly EA person in the world and the movement's most important source of funding. As Tyler Cowen has pointed out, a failure of FTX represented a potential existential risk to EA, and it's a risk they didn't predict very well.

into the six figures—betting on Biden *even after Biden had already been declared the winner* by all the major networks. Perkins almost couldn't believe what he was seeing—prices that implied a 10 to 15 percent chance that Trump could still win somehow because of a Hail Mary court ruling.

"They bet so much, I got scared," Perkins told me, referring to people who still thought Trump would win somehow and were willing to back this up with big bucks. "Like [traders]—we're arrogant but in a different way. When somebody bets something big, it's like, 'Okay, what am I missing?'" But Perkins did his due diligence, even calling one of America's most well-known Supreme Court experts. "He's like, 'There is exactly zero chance the Supreme Court is going to hear any of these cases.'" So Perkins bet big on Biden—and won. The market really was as crazy as it seemed.

Effective Hedonism in the Time of p(doom)

"I was not involved in the orgy," Aella said. "I could understand how you would make that assumption. I'm sure everybody did. But no, it occurred totally without me."

She hadn't been offended by the question in the least. Aella*— pronounced "Ayla," as in rhymes with Layla—might be the most open book anywhere on the internet. Although she hadn't been involved in the orgy at Manifest—though she did later hold a "birthday gangbang" and post a much-discussed data visualization about it—there had been markets on who she'd hook up with, an experience she described as bizarre but fun. "I liked it in kind of the way I like new food that's weirdly spicy."

Born into a conservative evangelical family—"My dad's, like, a relatively famous Christian apologist"—Aella is a sex researcher who conducts surveys on things like people's favorite fetishes, and an on-again, off-again sex worker and former OnlyFans star. You don't have to work

---

* Aella isn't a screen name or pseudonym—it's just her name, she said. "Everyone calls me that, except for my mom and dad."

hard to find the not safe for work portion of her personal website—or to read her essay about becoming addicted to LSD.

And Aella's a rationalist, although she sometimes wishes the other rationalists were more fun. She once threw a party where everyone had to be naked except for a mask, hoping it might loosen up the rationalists a bit. "But instead, they all just sat around the circle and behaved exactly the way they normally do and started debating like global trade," she told me. (Aella's efforts weren't entirely fruitless; Scott Alexander met his future wife at a similar party.)

Aella isn't an effective altruist, though. And that reveals one of the differences in the movements. The EAs play it much too safe for her, particularly when it comes to their reluctance (at least relative to Aella) to discuss controversial topics. "Cowards. I love EAs, don't get me wrong. But they're cowards."

But if she's not an EA, I think of Aella as sort of an *effective hedonist*, someone who uses data and survey research to improve her quality of life, including her sex life.* If you're going to be part of a movement that questions taboos and the conventional wisdom, shouldn't you have a little fun with that? In Aella's case, for instance, that might involve studying whether polyamorous relationships make people better off, a question on which her answer is relatively nuanced. "It requires a lot of skill, and social support," she said.

There's also something else that I haven't talked about yet: an undercurrent of apocalyptic fear that looms over this part of the River. Conversations about existential risk can be intense, obviously. People might displace their emotions, like poker players trying not to give tells away, but having these thoughts rattling around in your head can create cumulative stress. During the portions of the writing process when I was focused intently on nuclear or AI risk, I often didn't sleep well.

"Everyone here thinks the world will end soon," wrote Alexander in an essay about San Francisco. "Climate change for the Democrats, social decay for the GOP, AI if you're a techbro." It's natural that some people react by spending every waking moment preaching the gospel of

---

* Another good example of an effective hedonist is Perkins, whose book *Die with Zero* is about EV maximizing your life in a data-driven way. For instance, Perkins recommends prioritizing experiences over buying stuff or departing life with a large inheritance.

existential risk—and others by escapism. Aella's p(doom) is high, for instance, and she's not sure how long we have left. "I got risk-pilled like a year or two ago," she said. "Like I stopped saving for retirement, and I'm definitely spending more money than I would have otherwise."

What Gives Me Pause About EA

EAs and rationalists have sometimes complained that they're criticized from lots of different directions, including by both conservatives and progressives. And in many ways, I'm sympathetic. EAs and rationalists are trying to get people to overcome their biases and be more impartial. That's an extremely thankless task, particularly as the movement becomes more prominent and clashes more often with the Village. Politics, after all, is in some sense about encouraging people to be *more* partial. Challenging people's assumptions on taboo topics usually isn't a good way to make friends and influence people.

But the two major streams of EA/rationalism also have quite different politics from each other. Among people who took Scott Alexander's survey and labeled themselves as EAs, registered Democrats outnumbered registered Republicans 13:1, a Village-like ratio that has become common in many institutions full of highly educated people. The ratio among non-EA rationalists was only 2.6:1, by contrast. You could tell that the Manifest conference was a rationalist rather than an EA event because of the presence of people who were either considered unwoke (like Hanson, who told me he'd basically been canceled from EA events since a 2018 blog post in which he wrote sympathetically about the idea of redistributing sex to incels), openly conservative, or both (like Richard Hanania, the provocative blogger who was found to have posted racist comments in the early 2010s under a pen name).

It's the rationalist side that's more in line with the values of Silicon Valley. "There's definitely a huge cultural difference," said Hanson. "The rationality people are often . . . tech-centered contrarians," whereas "EA people are more establishment."

However, you can also give the rationalists credit for argumentative consistency: they tend to be scrupulously honest. For example, Alexander encouraged me to speak with Habryka, even though he knew Habryka would be critical of the movement he'd spent time defending. It's rare to have a source recommend another source who he knows will contradict his narrative. Whereas EAs sometimes pull their punches. In an interview with the economist Tyler Cowen, for instance, MacAskill said he didn't think EAs should be anti-abortion. I was bothered by this, but not because of my personal views—I'm pro-choice myself. Rather, it's because it seems like a complicated question from a utilitarian standpoint. If you're going to ask people to consider the utility of hypothetical future unborn beings, as MacAskill's book does, then what about a fetus? Or even setting abortion aside, you'd think longtermists might express concern about the decline in fertility in industrialized countries, a question that some rationalists like Hanson have explored but EAs—80 percent of whom are childless, according to Alexander's survey*—rarely do, perhaps because it codes as conservative.

At other times, though, EAs have expressed support for politically expedient solutions that don't seem to be in line with their values. Singer, for instance, defended immigration restrictions on utilitarian grounds when I spoke with him, on the theory that immigration could empower Trump and other right-wing populists who would then pull out of climate agreements. Overall, the politics of EA can be slippery, stuck in the uncanny valley between being abstractly principled and ruthlessly pragmatic, sometimes betraying a sense that you can make it up as you go along.

Habryka used a meme for this (that I borrowed in chapter 1) called NPC, for nonplayer character, the video-game term for characters (say, an

---

* Though Alexander himself had twins right as I was completing this draft.

innkeeper selling you a magic potion) who have no intelligence of their own, behave predictably, and can be treated exploitatively (maybe he'll sell you another potion if you exit and reenter the room). He described this as a "deep lack of respect for the ability of other people to make sense of the world"—their intelligence and their agency and their ability to adjust on the fly. NPC syndrome stands in contrast to game theory, which instead assumes people behave with instrumental rationality. "One of the things that happened is that the rationality community became sort of cultish and insular," said Hanson. "Because *they* were the rational ones. If they thought something was true, then that was just that, because they were the rational people."

Before we get back to SBF, there's one more strand of the broader EA/rationalist movement that I've been late in introducing. That is a futurist strand, often in the form of transhumanism—the idea that our species will eventually transcend the human body through technological augmentation, possibly in the form of a technological singularity in which the world economy will experience an exceptionally rapid, exponential rate of growth. This stuff really can sometimes sound like science fiction, like in Hanson's book *The Age of Em*, which imagines artificial emulations (ems) of human brains:

> While some ems work in robotic bodies, most work and play in virtual reality. These virtual realities are of spectacular-quality, with no intense hunger, cold, heat, grime, physical illness or pain. Ems never need to clean, eat, take medicine, or have sex, although they may choose to do these anyway. Even ems in virtual reality, however, cannot exist unless someone pays for supports such as computer hardware, energy and cooling.

Does this sound like utopia or dystopia? It's often surprisingly hard to get people to agree which is which. If you're a utilitarian willing to gamble on the future of humanity—or whatever humanity evolves into—it's presumably important to know the difference.

If you talk to some EAs—or even some EA critics—you'll often hear a narrative that goes like this: EAs were concerned with things like global poverty reduction and more effective philanthropy, but then some weirdos came along from the futurist strand with provocative or offensive discussions, hijacked the movement, and subsumed it with the question of AI and existential risk.

Except that doesn't get the chronology right. Hanson founded his blog *Overcoming Bias* in 2006, in conjunction with the Future of Humanity Institute at Oxford, the same organization that employs Bostrom (the writer of the extremely influential book *Superintelligence*) and Toby Ord. Ord had been influenced by Peter Singer, and Ord in turn was a huge influence on MacAskill from the moment they got "coffee in a graveyard in the back of St. Edmund Hall," MacAskill told me. One of the lead writers at *Overcoming Bias* was Yudkowsky. Hanson and Yudkowsky had something of a falling-out over their competing assumptions about p(doom)—Yudkowsky's p(doom) is high and Hanson's is low—and had a debate on AI risk at Jane Street Capital in 2011, the firm that would later employ SBF. Some of the rationalist interest in prediction markets also stems from Hanson, who has expressed his support for futarchy, a system of government where decisions are made by betting markets. These various strands have been tied together from the beginning, the product of a bloggier era in the 2000s and early 2010s when there were fewer people arguing on the internet and the discussion was nerdier and more free-flowing.

For some critics of EA and rationalism, that's what can make the movements dangerous—they're a whole bunch of ideas clumped together for reasons that partly reflect happenstance (who happened to get coffee with whom fifteen years ago). It's not always clear what you're going to get out of any one bite of the EA/rationalist cookie.* If you're someone like me who (mostly) likes prediction markets and thinks the concerns about existential risk and effective giving are well-placed, but is uncertain about

---

* Some critics of EA like Émile Torres and Timnit Gebru use the term "TESCREAL" to describe this, for Transhumanism, Extropianism, Singularitarianism, Cosmism, Rationalism, Effective Altruism, and Longtermism. No, there won't be a pop quiz.

futurism and downright wary about utilitarianism, it's hard to know where to fit in.

Nor is it easy to know when movements can suddenly become more powerful before all of the kinks are worked out—or when adherents take their ideas much further than their founders intended. (Marxism is one such example.) "I started reading the history of utopian movements that became violent," said Émile Torres, a former EA who has since quit the movement. "And it struck me that at the core of many of these movements were two ingredients. . . . On the one hand, this utopian vision of the future, marked by infinite or near infinite amounts of value. And on the other hand, a kind of broadly utilitarian mode of moral reasoning." Torres was concerned about where this could lead. "If the ends can at least sometimes justify the means, and the ends are literal paradise . . . then, like, what's off the table?"

8

Miscalculation

Act 5: Lower Manhattan, October–November 2023

Sam Bankman-Fried, at least by his own account,* wasn't much of a fan of poker or other forms of capital-G Gambling. And yet, the difference between his spending decades in prison or somehow walking free could potentially come down to what was essentially an extremely high-stakes game of roulette. In New York, judges are assigned to criminal trials at random, chosen by the spin of a wooden wheel in a duty magistrate's office that "looks as if it might have been used to call out bingo numbers in a church fund-raiser." After another judge recused herself, SBF drew the name of Lewis Kaplan, a no-nonsense judge in his late seventies who had presided over everything from the Prince Andrew and Kevin Spacey trials to the successful defamation case brought against Donald Trump by E. Jean Carroll.

It was one of the worst assignments SBF could have gotten, said Sam Enzer, a former federal prosecutor in the Southern District of New York who now works for the law firm Cahill and is an expert in cryptocurrency

---

* "I've never done standard gambling, really. I mean, I've done little bits with friends sometimes," SBF told me.

cases. "Kaplan knows exactly where the lines of the baseball diamond are, he knows what he can't do, can do," Enzer said when we met for brunch one November 2023 morning at a French place blocks from the federal courthouse where SBF had just recently been tried and found guilty. Plus, Kaplan was a notoriously tough sentencer, not afraid to put white-collar criminals in prison for a long time. Other judges might push the boundaries further than Kaplan, Enzer said—but at the risk of providing grounds for a case being overturned on appeal. Kaplan was like a game-theory-optimal poker player: whatever options he gave you, he was going to make it hard for you to realize your expected value. SBF didn't have much hope of a miracle acquittal because of a government misplay. But he also wasn't going to get away with a short sentence.*

And yet, true to form, Bankman-Fried doubled down, insisting on taking the witness stand and repeatedly perjuring himself, and Kaplan handed him a twenty-five-year prison sentence. (As this book goes to press, Bankman-Fried is appealing the ruling.)

I wasn't surprised. I'd had one final meeting with SBF in May 2023 at his boyhood home in Stanford, California, a $4 million gray colonial with a well-manicured garden and classic Californian sense of understatement. Shortly after the meeting, I texted a friend that I thought SBF was in deep trouble; he hadn't shown any signs of remorse and he wasn't going to come across sympathetically to a jury. The whole visit had felt like a reversion to my childhood. The setting felt eerily familiar, an academic home full of bookshelves; my dad is an academic, a professor of political science, and I had even lived in Stanford for a year as a preteen when my dad took a sabbatical there. I wasn't allowed to bring in any electronics—part of the tough terms that Kaplan had set—and instead furiously scribbled notes on a hotel notepad, my handwriting having deteriorated to kindergarten quality since it had been so long since I'd had to write that much by hand.

SBF's father, Joseph Bankman, had cheerily greeted me at the door. It

---

* Kaplan also denied SBF's request for pretrial release to help him prepare his defense. "I can tell you from this side, it is a major pain in the ass, helping a client defend a case when they are in jail," Enzer said.

almost felt like a friendly visit—until I saw the bracelet around SBF's ankle. Under the circumstances, it was hard not to feel a few pangs of empathy. I don't think SBF and I are particularly much alike personality-wise, at least not more so than any two randomly chosen people in the River. I'm not a particularly calculating person—even when I play poker, I understand the underlying game theory well enough, but I make a lot of decisions based on gut instinct. And I'm not a utilitarian who believes the ends justify the means.

And yet, SBF and I were part of a relatively small club of nerds who had suddenly become famous, in my case after the 2012 election. Okay, I never got shooting-commercials-with-Tom-Brady famous. But for a period of time I got recognized nearly every time I went out. I became a meme divorced from the reality of who I was. I had people pitching me all kinds of crazy opportunities.* I knew what it was like to get overwhelmed, to suddenly have people behaving sycophantically toward me, how it could be a challenge to stay grounded in my values.

But nearly everything SBF said just made me question whether he had any values at all—or any judgment. He was still remarkably cynical about crypto. "When I first got involved in crypto I had no fucking clue what it was and I didn't give a shit. It was just numbers, something you could trade and arbitrage." He told me he felt he'd been scapegoated. And presented with an opportunity of sorts to present his case to a neutral third party (me), he often relied on exceptionally legalistic phrasings—"money that FTX did not custody and did not expect to custody" was one example, referring to the back door between FTX and Alameda—that I doubted would come across well in court.

Had he tried to take on too much? Even on that point, he wasn't willing to concede. Instead, he blamed the lack of good vegan delivery food in the Bahamas for forcing him to cook his own meals, which in turn led to him overeating, which in turn led to him being lethargic, he claimed. I got the

---

* At one point, the agent Ari Emanuel tried to sell me on the idea of creating a brand that was essentially *Martha Stewart Living*, but for data nerds.

sense that SBF thought none of this would have happened if only he could make an emulated copy of himself or level up his IQ slightly higher. "Life isn't poker, life's three thousand poker games going on simultaneously," he had said in one of our interviews in the Bahamas. "And it's not even explicit what they are . . . it's just like everything in a wild messy milieu." You might have thought this was an admission of the limitations of his utilitarian worldview, at least when it comes to grand-world problems. But it was intended as just the opposite. The games *were* solvable, calculable, game-theory optimizable, he thought—there just wasn't enough SBF to go around to learn the rules to all three thousand of them at once.

SBF also had naïvely optimistic views about his likelihood of prevailing in court. I asked him if he'd take a hypothetical plea deal: two years in prison plus considerable restrictions on what business activities he could pursue afterward. This would have been a good bargain, and not just in hindsight; a Manifold market at the time presciently assigned SBF a 71 percent chance of being sentenced to at least twenty years in prison. And yet he hesitated. "I'd have to think about exactly what that meant," he said after a long pause.

In six months, Bankman-Fried would face a real-life version of this dilemma at his criminal trial in Manhattan. The testimony against him had been compelling, particularly that of Caroline Ellison, the former Alameda CEO and sometime SBF girlfriend. (Ellison pled guilty to fraud, money laundering, and conspiracy charges.) The government had lots of receipts, and SBF's defense had been feeble. (His original defense team had dumped him, ostensibly on conflict-of-interest grounds, but possibly because SBF couldn't afford their services.)

"I read every page of the transcript from the trial. And the evidence in this case is utterly overwhelming," Enzer told me. Sure, some of the details in the case were technical, but the government had presented them well, and juries have a sort of superintelligence that can help them to sniff out the truth, Enzer said. "Maybe not everybody gets everything, but among them, each person is going to pick up different things."

If he were advising Bankman-Fried, Enzer would have told him not to testify. Yes, this all but assured SBF would be found guilty. But the odds of a conviction were already overwhelmingly high. "Cost-benefit analysis," said Enzer, who runs a regular poker game. "In a case where the evidence is so clearly going to lead to a conviction either way, there is no upside. But there's huge, huge downside to doing it." Namely, that SBF might wind up perjuring himself—which he did. "You don't have to take my word for it . . . he gave testimony that contradicts the jury's verdict on several issues," Enzer said. "So the jury's verdict by definition means that twelve independent jurors determined beyond a reasonable doubt that he was not telling the truth." Enzer thought that if SBF had played his cards right, he could have positioned himself for a sentence of roughly ten years. "I think instead it's going to be north of twenty," he had correctly predicted.

In Which SBF Spectacularly Fails a Fact Check

Sam Bankman-Fried had told me a story that, but for one revealing admission he made later on, he mostly stuck to: what happened at FTX was just a series of *really* unfortunate mistakes. "It's not like I had *no* awareness of what it was doing," he'd said in the Bahamas, referring to Alameda. "But my awareness was high-level and vague and hazy, and, like, had massive error bars* on it." In SBF's accounting, those error bars were wide enough for him to make three major oversights:

1. "I underestimated the leverage" on Alameda's balance sheet.
2. "I underestimated how bad a crash would look"—that is, what might happen if Bitcoin lost about three-quarters of its value, as it did between November 2021 and November 2022.
3. "And I underestimated its position on FTX"—that is, how much of Alameda's gambling was financed by FTX customer deposits.

---

* "Error bars" is a super-nerdy way to describe what's essentially margin of error; SBF was claiming that his estimate of what was going on with Alameda's finances was extremely crude.

The way SBF framed things to me, these were forgivable, tactical errors—like a poker player playing a hand suboptimally in a challenging situation. "You put those together and it went from, like, significant but manageable to significant and not manageable," he said. "I just sort of lost track of it," he told me at another point. In reality, of course, any of these would have been mission-critical mistakes, let alone all three put together. It was like a pilot saying, "Oh, the plane wouldn't have crashed if only I hadn't drunk three bottles of whiskey, punched out my copilot, and then told air traffic control to fuck off when they said the runway was closed."

It's also clear that Sam's story was almost entirely bullshit.

The first claim—that SBF didn't understand how highly levered Alameda was and vulnerable to a decline in the crypto market—is contradicted both by Ellison's testimony and by evidence obtained by the government. In one document, where Ellison warned SBF about Alameda's position, he not only acknowledged the concern but wrote a comment saying, "Yup, and could also get worse." Ellison also testified, according to a transcript I obtained from the Southern District, that SBF had her explore what he called a "10th percentile scenario"—meaning "that he thought 10 percent of outcomes were similar to this or worse"—which involved a broad 50 percent decline in crypto prices. SBF wanted to make an additional $3 billion in venture investments, Ellison said, and she told him that this would be very risky under such a scenario, in part because many of Alameda's loans could be recalled at any time. Nevertheless, he wanted to move forward—he didn't dispute the risks, but thought the investments were still "high expected value."

SBF claim number three—that he underestimated how much Alameda's trading kitty was funded by FTX customer deposits—is also clearly contradicted by the court case. Ellison testified that SBF directed her to use FTX customer funds to repay Alameda's loans after she had shown him that it was the only source of capital large enough to do so. And rather than having the "vague and hazy" awareness of Alameda's activities that SBF described to me, he frequently checked in with Ellison, particularly as Alameda's position deteriorated.

I skipped past SBF's second claim—that he underestimated how bad a crash would look—because that one is more complicated to untangle. Ellison had told SBF that in the event of a substantial market downturn, the chance that Alameda would be unable to repay at least one major tranche of loans was 100 percent. Bankman-Fried had proceeded with further investments anyway—not because he had any dispute with Ellison's analysis but because he didn't want to miss out on a +EV bet, even if it entailed a risk of ruin.

But although SBF might or might not have underestimated how *bad* a crash would look, he probably did underestimate how *likely* one was. In my January 2022 interview with him, SBF had barely been willing to contemplate the prospect of crypto going down at all. That might have been braggadocio, him running high off the fumes of crypto prices still being near their then all-time peaks. The tenth percentile scenario exercise—which Ellison said she prepared in summer or fall 2021—shows that SBF was at least aware of the *possibility* of a decline. However, he underestimated the *probability* of one. The exercise assumed there was only a 10 percent chance that crypto assets could decline by half—but that had in fact been an extremely frequent occurrence. Bitcoin had lost more than half its value seven times between 2011 and 2021, including once between April and July 2021, right about when SBF had asked Ellison to prepare the memo. Far from being a tenth percentile scenario, 50 percent declines in crypto prices had been a biennial occurrence.

Four Theories of Sam Bankman-Fried

Even after having spent so much time with SBF and having the good fortune that his criminal trial happened before this book was due to my editor, there are still some things I'd had trouble figuring out. Why had he been so concerned, when I spoke with him on that darkening afternoon at Albany, with whether bankruptcy could have been staved off for a little while longer—while also glibly conceding that FTX was more likely than not to go bankrupt eventually?

So let's do some narrowing down. There are basically four theories of the case. Imagine a 2 × 2 grid where one dimension is how *competent* SBF was as a trader and a manager (proficient or deficient), and the other is how *aware* he was of Alameda's activities (cognizant or negligent):

Four Theories of SBF

	COGNIZANT	NEGLIGENT
PROFICIENT	SBF was the Boy Genius behind a long con to deceive effective altruists, Silicon Valley investors, cryptocurrency traders, and everyone else in his life. He knew exactly what he was doing and duped others into participating in his schemes. He may even have believed that he was making +EV bets that he was just unlucky to lose.	SBF, despite his best efforts, was simply overwhelmed by events. He took on too much, too fast outside of his core competencies, with one of the most rapid ascents to power in world history. He didn't have friends to advise him or adults in the room to help him. He made some critical, unforgivable mistakes, but they were mostly errors of negligence.
DEFICIENT	SBF was directly responsible for FTX/Alameda's precarious position. Under his utilitarian philosophy, he believed the ends justified the means and he could be extremely manipulative. However, he was also a poor trader and an incompetent manager of risk who was entrusted with too much power. He also used utilitarianism and effective altruism to rationalize extremely risky bets—no matter what harm they might cause to himself and others.	SBF, like other young CEOs who suddenly became rich, was caught up in a debauched party lifestyle, full of amphetamine use, polycules,* afternoons at Margaritaville, and trips around the world. Combined with the lack of adult supervision in the crypto industry and the blind faith placed in SBF by VCs and EAs, this was a predictable and even inevitable outcome.

Let's start with the easy part: you can put a big ol' X through the right-hand side of the chart. With the help of Ellison and twelve New York

---

* A network of polyamorous relationships, as ostensibly happened at FTX; https://nypost.com/2022/11/30/ftxs-sam-bankman-fried-fumed-over-media-spotlight-on-polyamorous-sex-life/.

jurors, we've already established that Sam very much did know what Alameda was doing. Nonetheless, I'm going to run through each theory briefly, because I think they reveal something about the environment that SBF created for himself and how he was enabled by effective altruism and others in his orbit.

The story that SBF tried to peddle to me, and to the jury in Manhattan, was the one in the top-right corner—that he was a highly competent boss who had a lot going on and *just so happened* to have had an unfortunate $10 billion (!!!) blind spot when it came to Alameda. This isn't very convincing, because it's inherently contradictory—how can you be a competent boss if you overlooked a $10 billion (!!!) hole in the balance sheet of a related party run by your girlfriend?

Nor was SBF willing to fully commit to the bit, reluctant to admit to any shortcomings in his cognitive superpowers. On a couple of occasions, for instance, I asked about sleep deprivation—SBF reportedly (although it might have been part of his carefully manipulated press image) often slept only in short stints on a beanbag in his office. Frankly, if I were preparing SBF's defense, sleep deprivation is a relatively sympathetic explanation that I might have turned to, consistent with a story of him being overwhelmed by a rapid ascent to stardom. However, SBF told me that if anything he was sleeping *too much*.

Similarly, Bankman-Fried was reluctant to blame his problems on drugs. SBF had an Adderall prescription, and there were popular theories online that his compulsive gambling was abetted by an antidepressant called Emsam. "It was not particularly more than many people just get by coffee each day," SBF told me of his Adderall usage. In fact, he claimed, his stimulant use might have been helpful to him on balance. "There's another frame you could have on it, which is that having more attention and focus would allow you to do a more thorough job of managing risks."

The part of the top-right box that does have some basis in reality? SBF probably wasn't getting a lot of good advice. Frankly, I suspect part of the reason he spoke with me and other journalists after the bankruptcy is because he felt lonely. Never a person who related terribly well to other humans, he had few strong ties outside of FTX. He co-opted his parents into the company (the father was officially on the payroll but his mother was not), and his chief romantic interest was Ellison, the Alameda CEO.

"I feel like this is not something I'm supposed to say," Sam said. He then asked me a series of questions that I assumed were rhetorical—but he seemed genuinely interested in my opinion. "If you go to like, May 2022—who would you have defined as the adults in the room? Who were supposed to keep me from being isolated and reality-check me and keep me honest? Who would you have pointed to? Like what groups of people?"

I pointed toward EAs and VCs. Bankman-Fried, with more than a modicum of self-pity, suggested that both groups had let him down. The EAs were too "woke" and too concerned with appearances. The VCs gave too much generic "high-level advice [that didn't] make any sense outside the context of the details of a particular situation." Nobody *really* knew what was going on. Most of this, of course, was SBF's own damned fault—partly because he'd kept details close to the vest because much of what he was doing was illegal. But it was also a matter of too much trust placed in Sam by EAs and VCs. Nobody was willing to ask the hard questions, even when SBF said alarming things in interviews or circulated balance sheets that didn't add up.

I also think the explanation in the bottom right—one where SBF succumbed to a glamorous party lifestyle—is wrong. This is going to require some more context.

By the time I arrived in the Bahamas, all former FTX employees had left except for SBF, the head of data science Dan Chapsky, Chapsky's wife, Jacklyn—an anthropologist who was gamely serving as SBF's de facto wrangler and press secretary—and (if you want to count them as employees) SBF's parents. Following my meetings with SBF, the Chapskys offered to have dinner with me. Fearing some weird vegan food,* I proposed going into town, but Jacklyn explained that this was too risky—the Bahamas was a small place, and word would get around of FTX employees meeting

---

* It was indeed vegan—including leftover lentil soup that had apparently been prepared by SBF's mom—but Jacklyn's spicy pumpkin curry spaghetti squash dish wasn't half bad.

with a reporter. So instead we ate in the same apartment where I'd interviewed Sam.

The Chapskys were nothing like the stereotype I had of typical crypto-startup employees. In Jacklyn's anthropological work, she explained, she had studied small island nations and knew how vulnerable they were, and had stayed behind to secure the least-worst outcome for the Bahamas under the circumstances. "Frankly, a lot of overgrown children ran away when they found out that it happened, and somebody needed to stay and clean it up," she said. Dan was also mostly on board. "If we had been in this country and like pseudo-colonized it and then tried to leave, Jacklyn would have killed me," he said.

Neither of the Chapskys had been particularly close to SBF prior to the bankruptcy. But Jacklyn had grown warmer to him since. The Bahamas has a long history with piracy, and she saw SBF as a sort of modern-day pirate. She was fond of "the types of risks that pirates would take in order to get a good booty and redistribute wealth" and saw a "through line between the Golden Age of Piracy that was here and the particular ethos of what Sam was hoping to do with his wealth." Dan Chapsky was more suspicious. "I have never been a believer in Sam," he told me. "Like, I don't know, I do data for a living. Believing in something is something you shouldn't do until the data proves it."

I found their concern for the Bahamian people admirable. The Bahamas has had some bad luck. When I first arrived in the country, I was expecting a lush tropical paradise—something like Hawaii or Costa Rica. However, the Bahamas is not particularly lush (it gets only about an average amount of rainfall and has poor soil quality), it is not *technically* tropical (New Providence island is a couple of degrees of latitude north of the Tropic of Cancer), and whether it's a paradise or not depends on where exactly you are in the country. Although Baha Mar is one of the nicest resorts you could imagine, the Bahamas also has among the world's highest rates of wealth inequality.

In some ways, the Bahamas is a success story—it has among the highest GDPs per capita in its region. But in speaking with a group of senior

Bahamian officials, I learned that it also often gets the short end of the stick whenever something bad happens elsewhere in the world. Once a center for offshore finance, it suffered when the U.S. and UK tightened anti-money-laundering statutes following the September 11 attacks. As a low-lying island country, it's one of the most vulnerable places in the world to climate change, and the damage from 2019's Hurricane Dorian is still apparent as you drive around the islands. And with 70 percent of its economy dependent on tourism, the Bahamas was severely affected by COVID-19.

The reason the Bahamas gambled on FTX and crypto, these senior officials conveyed, is because the country didn't have the luxury of *not* taking high-upside bets.

However, the Bahamas *isn't* exactly party central. If FTX racked up big bills at places like Margaritaville, that's partly because there aren't all that many places to go other than the casinos, and the gimmicky bars in downtown Nassau near the cruise ship docks. Meanwhile, because of its wealth inequality, there also isn't a lot of upper-middle-class housing. In other words, SBF and the FTX team (many of his employees also lived at Albany) were isolated—more so than you'd gather from the island of New Providence being just an hour's flight from Miami. That probably contributed more to the problems than any lavish party lifestyle.

Nor are effective altruists typically big partiers; the movement is known for its asceticism. Instead, they tend to be earnest, True Believer types— perhaps earnest to the point of being gullible. If you believed that SBF really was Robin Hood, or a woke pirate creating Ponzi-like crypto tokens to redistribute wealth to good causes . . . hey look, I'm not against the idea of earning to give. But believing all of this required placing a lot of faith in a founder's complicated story. It was going to select for a different and more idealistic type of employee—progressive do-gooders like the Chapskys—and not the competitive, egotistical capitalists that you'd typically get at a banking or finance startup. And while it might seem like those employees would be more conscientious, the sense of alignment with the mission might make them more willing to go along with the program and not raise questions when things went wrong. "People are just willing to do much more drastic and radical things if they have a very strong justification that it's for the common good, as opposed to if they kind of have an awareness that it is purely selfish," said Habryka.

Meanwhile, SBF was known for his anhedonia—that is, his non-hedonism, his inability to feel pleasure. This may have been a problem too, making him more willing to gamble away his chance of experiencing earthly delights. "He just doesn't think about what could go wrong, or what the consequences could be," said Tara Mac Aulay, the original Alameda cofounder. "And when I tried to ask him about why that was, he'd say it was related to his anhedonia. That, like, his baseline experience of the world is quite negative. And so you know, there's not much lower to go. So he'd talk about being in jail, versus his normal life, and he was like, 'Yeah, it's like not that much worse.'"

What I'm getting at here is that if we can forget about narratives on the right-hand side of the chart, we can also cross out the top left corner—the Boy Genius theory. SBF was a highly deficient person in many respects. He certainly had a high *willingness* to manipulate others, in part because of his utilitarianism. "He said that he was a utilitarian, and he believed that the way people tried to justify rules like don't lie and don't steal within utilitarianism didn't work," Ellison testified. But this didn't mean he was particularly *good* at manipulation.

I did speak with some sources who had kind feelings toward SBF. "Like most people, he's a human. End of sentence. Just because everybody assumes everybody's playing 5D chess or, like, isn't a human in some significant way, and that's just not the case," Dan Chapsky told me when I asked him what he thought the media had gotten wrong about Bankman-Fried. Chapsky thought press coverage overestimated Sam's capacity for advanced planning. "A lot of it comes down to, like, assuming there's all these grand plans that are hidden from you."

At first I thought this was too charitable—maybe the Chapskys, marooned with SBF in the Bahamas, had a touch of Stockholm syndrome? But it matched something Mac Aulay told me. SBF wasn't necessarily thinking several moves ahead. Instead, he tended to decide on a strategy quickly and then rationalize it. "Sam is certainly not this, like, genius long-run planner. Everything he's doing is improv. And he makes it sound like it was a well-thought-out strategy after the fact. But he is, like, very good and very quick on his feet."

This sort of impulsive overconfidence is almost certain to get any gambler in trouble—and the instinct to cover one's tracks only makes things worse. The wrong turn that leads to a downward spiral is a common pattern for con artists, Maria Konnikova told me.

"I met a number of con artists who ended up becoming big financial criminals, like some were in jail for their hedge funds becoming Ponzi schemes. And it usually starts with something tiny," she said. "You think that you're a savvy investor, and then you lose money. And you lose money for several quarters. . . . And once you do that, I hate the word slippery slope. But like . . . you never correct it. And it just becomes fraud."

The one time I made a breakthrough with SBF—the closest he came to admitting to the sort of evidence that would later be used against him in court—is when I probed him about whether he'd have regrets about not being able to make +EV trades. Wouldn't it be such a shame to have all that money sitting on the sidelines when you could use it to make even more money and do even more good?

Bankman-Fried gave me a long-winded answer about the ease of borrowing at different points in the credit and crypto cycles, but landed by saying that he did recognize that sentiment. "I think it existed with respect to Alameda borrowing capital from our lending desks a year ago. Like, [it'd] be a shame to not do these trades. That's a version of it that was true to me, is [in] late 2021 . . . there's so much capital flowing through the crypto ecosystem. It was so easy for Alameda to borrow. I wasn't [just] thinking of FTX's liquidity—it was just, like, fucking anywhere. And I think that's probably related to it getting too exposed and leveraged. But I think it happened first with our own lending desks."

Late 2021, of course, was when crypto assets were racing ahead toward the second of their two pandemic-era peaks. (BTC crossed over $50,000 for the first time in February 2021, and then again in August 2021 after a spring swoon.) And it's right when Ellison said SBF had asked her to map out the tenth percentile scenario. Alameda couldn't take on much more leverage, she'd reported back. If there was another drawdown, and lenders recalled their loans, it couldn't pay them back. They could be ruined. SBF didn't care. There was too much EV at stake.

Never Gamble with an Overconfident Utilitarian

If I had laid odds, you ought to have bet on me mentioning something called the Kelly criterion before now in a book about gambling. It's one of the most famous formulas in gambling, famous enough that it's the subject of an entire (very good) book of its own, *Fortune's Formula* by William Poundstone. Named after the Bell Labs researcher John Kelly Jr., who published it in 1956, you can make the Kelly criterion sound very respectable if you like—mathematically, it's related to the signal processing algorithms invented by Kelly's colleague Claude Shannon, which helped usher in the information age. But Kelly was more in the midcentury archetype of John von Neumann—a polymathic genius who also liked to have a good time. A heavy drinker and smoker who died of a stroke at age forty-one, Kelly also had a passion for predicting the outcome of football games.

The Kelly criterion concerns the problem of bet sizing.* Say you think the Michigan Wolverines are 60 percent likely to cover the point spread against the Ohio State Buckeyes. As we discussed in chapter 4, that's a big edge as these things go. Say you have $100,000 set aside to gamble on college football. How much should you put on the Wolverines? That's what the Kelly criterion is supposed to tell you. In this case, the answer it spits out is 16 percent of your bankroll, or $16,000.

---

* The Kelly criterion, as Poundstone describes it, is *edge/odds*. That is, the amount you should bet is the size of your edge, divided by how long the odds are. I'm not going to go through a formal explanation of how to define these at this late point in the tour—you can look it up online—but the intuition should be clear. You bet more as your edge increases—as the bet is more +EV—and less as the odds lengthen.

Most gamblers will tell you Kelly is far too aggressive, recommending betting only a quarter to half as much (i.e., "half Kelly" rather than "full Kelly"). Wagering 16 percent of your bankroll on a bet you still expect to lose 40 percent of the time? Most bettors' spidey sense tells them to stay away, and there are good reasons for that. (This is why I've been reluctant to mention Kelly until now.) First, in sports betting, you never know what the odds *really* are.* Sure, your model might say 60 percent, but models can be—and usually are—wrong. Next, losing such a large wager could put you on tilt, meaning you'll make worse decisions in the future. Finally, although in principle the Kelly criterion is supposed to tell you how to maximize your returns while minimizing your risk of ruin—technically speaking, it will never let you go *completely* broke—in practice it can lead to wild downswings that could significantly crimp your lifestyle or take you months or years to recover from. It's just too risk-on, even for most people in the River.

But Sam Bankman-Fried, of course, thought the Kelly criterion had you wagering far too *little*. He thought it was for wimps.

In a 2020 Twitter thread, @SBF_FTX explained that most people chicken out too soon. Once they've achieved a certain lifestyle, they encounter diminishing returns. Buying a second home if you go on a winning streak won't increase your utility as much as having your home foreclosed on if you can't make your mortgage payments will decrease it—so it's rational to be somewhat risk-averse, most of us would conclude. SBF, on the other hand, dreamed of being worth literally trillions, which he claimed he could put toward EA-related causes. Who knows what the limits were; he'd even told Ellison there was a 5 percent chance he could become president of the United States. His utility function was "closer to linear," he explained; the trillionth dollar really was almost as good as the first.

Technically speaking, SBF was right about the Kelly criterion. It's sometimes said that the Kelly criterion is designed to maximize your long-run expected value. After all, you'll want to leave some cash in reserve in

---

* The Kelly criterion is better suited to something like card counting in blackjack, where you can estimate your edge precisely.

case you have a losing streak; no matter how brilliant your college football model is, you can't make money with it if you have no capital to bet with. But this is actually a misconception. Instead, the Kelly criterion does what I said before: it maximizes your returns *while minimizing your risk of ruin.**

If you don't care about being ruined, you can bet more. It's higher EV. But you probably *will* be ruined.

Let me give you a somewhat realistic example involving NFL betting. There are 272 games in the NFL regular season. Say you have a computer model that spits out different point-spread bets, which it expects to win between 50 and 60 percent of the time. Most of the bets are toward the lower end of that spectrum—the 60 percenters are rare—and for many games it won't have you bet at all because you don't have enough of an edge to cover the house's cut. (See the endnotes for further technical details.) You begin the season with a $100,000 bankroll, and the games are played one at a time, so wins and losses are added or deducted from your bankroll and affect how much you can bet on future games.

I ran through five thousand simulated NFL seasons, one where you size your bets at full Kelly—most gamblers would already consider that aggressive—and one where you bet *five times what Kelly recommends* because you've followed SBF's advice and you don't want to be a wimp! (This can entail betting as much as 80 percent of your bankroll on a single game.) Here's what happened—I'll show you various percentile outcomes, like the percentiles SBF asked Ellison to consider for him.

---

* Mathematically, it does this by maximizing the *logarithm* of your wealth. For instance, the logarithm of 1 million is 6, while the logarithm of 2 million is roughly 6.3. That implies being worth $2 million is only about 5 percent better than being worth $1 million, not twice as good. Now, if you want to get technical, you shouldn't take that answer entirely literally because the U.S. dollar is an arbitrary unit; you'd get a different answer of how much you'd improved your utility if you denominated your wealth in, say, British pounds or Argentinian pesos. But the point is that Kelly accounts for diminishing marginal returns to wealth.

NFL Betting Simulated Results

	KELLY (WIMPY)	5X KELLY (YEE-HAW!!!)
0 Percentile (minimum)	$7,527	$0.00
10th Percentile	$71,563	$0.03
25th Percentile	$121,213	$0.94
50th Percentile (median)	$234,671	$55
75th Percentile	$456,848	$3,047
90th Percentile	$814,756	$100,128
100th Percentile (maximum)	$10,002,013	$225,228,893,346
Average	$371,960	$57,045,972

Okay, group, I know it's getting late on our tour. But, holy shit! I did not expect these numbers to be quite so extreme. Using Kelly, we come out ahead about 80 percent of the time, finishing the season with an average of about $370,000, for a net profit of around $270,000 after subtracting our initial bankroll. Nice! And we rarely go totally broke; we lose more than half our bankroll only about 5 percent of the time. So Kelly is basically performing as advertised.

What about with 5x Kelly? It *usually* ends in ruin. The median outcome is that we're left with only $55 of our $100K bankroll. Quite often, we're literally beaten down to pennies. In fact, we only make a profit of any kind about one time in ten. But—holy shit!—there's one simulation where we won $225 billion* and spun our NFL bankroll up until we were literally worth as much as Elon Musk! The average profit is much higher because these tail outcomes are so lucrative as to more than make up for how rare they are. In other words, 5x Kelly is higher EV—if you don't care about ruin.

There's every indication that is *exactly* how Sam Bankman-Fried was thinking about FTX and maybe everything else in his life. That's why it

---

* We'd also have bankrupted DraftKings in the process; in reality, even Billy Walters could never get this much money down.

was no big deal for him to admit to me that FTX would *probably* go broke; it was all part of the plan. Remember when SBF told me that if you've never missed a flight, you weren't doing it right? Well, this was that maxim taken to the maximum. If FTX wasn't *probably* going to go bankrupt, he wasn't optimizing his EV enough.

Now, was he executing on this plan effectively? He very much was not. We've seen many examples of SBF making poor calculations. That makes what he was doing even riskier; if you overestimate your edge, you'll wind up making bets that are bigger than Kelly recommends. And was he really motivated mostly, or even partly, by altruism—as opposed to just being a degen? I don't know. SBF clearly had a lust for power; he'd not only told Ellison he thought he could become president, but he'd also said that to Tara Mac Aulay long before he'd become wealthy or famous, she told me.*

Sam's potential emotional deficits plus his utilitarianism could have been a "dangerous combination," said Spencer Greenberg, who had met Bankman-Fried on several occasions and runs a psychological research organization. "If a person lacks the capacity for guilt or empathy but has a utilitarian belief system, it may be easy for them to tell themself that the reason they're risking harming people is for the greater good. Without the guardrails of basic moral emotions, it may be easier to convince yourself that what you want to do, or what might give you power or prestige, is what's best in terms of your abstract ethical theory."

But here's what we can say. SBF was deadly serious about pushing his utilitarianism to the event horizon, the absolute maximum frontier. With many of the EAs and rationalists I spoke with, I got the sense that the provocative answers they might give to trolley problems were intended to be hypothetical, tongue-in-cheek—that if the chips were down, and if they had to push a button to decide the fate of the universe, they'd default back toward commonsense morality.

I don't think that was the case with SBF. He had accumulated a lot of *non-hypothetical* power. And I think he was willing to push the button.

---

* Mac Aulay also told me that SBF thought he could become president before the age of thirty-five by "get[ting] the rules changed."

Here is something he told Ellison, according to her testimony on direct examination from the government's incisive prosecutor, Danielle Sassoon:

> Q. Did the defendant ever give any example to describe his approach to risk taking?
>
> A. Yeah. He talked about being willing to take large coin flips, like a coin flip where—if it comes up tails, you might lose $10 million, but if it comes up heads, you make slightly more than $10 million.
>
> Q. Did he ever give other coin-flip examples?
>
> A. Yeah. I guess he also talked about this in the context of thinking about what was good for the world, saying that he would be happy to flip a coin, if it came up tails and the world was destroyed, as long as if it came up heads the world would be like more than twice as good.

Now, if you're (ostensibly) worth many billions of dollars, making coin flips for $10 million at a time is actually okay, provided that they're slightly +EV. You have enough of a bankroll to withstand the variance, per the Kelly criterion. So I'm not so bothered by that part.

But SBF extended this willingness to gamble to infinity—he was willing to make a 50/50 coin flip on the future of humanity! This is dangerous and depraved. SBF had been a major investor in the AI company Anthropic. There's a not-so-remote chance that he could have been in a position like that of Sam Altman, heading up a market-leading firm. (As of early 2024, many AI nerds regard Anthropic's model Claude as the worthiest competitor to OpenAI's ChatGPT.)

Imagine one of his lieutenants coming to him and saying, "Hey, SBF, we've run the numbers and calculated that if we train this new large language model, p(doom) is fifty percent. The coin comes up tails, and all the value in the universe will be destroyed. *But*, if that *doesn't* happen, the total amount of utils will increase by 2.00000001x. The universe will be more than twice as good!"

They smile and nod at each other, knowing that they're about to make a highly rational +EV bet. And an *altruistic* bet at that, since they're looking out for all present and future sentient beings in the universe and not just themselves.

"Should we push the button, Sam? Should we do it?"

"Yup."

Approximately 0.00000003 milliseconds later, all matter in the known universe is transmogrified into a paper clip. Better luck next time.

This is not just me speculating idly. Habryka had repeatedly met with SBF in the hopes of securing funding for various EA and rationalist projects. "He was just a very bullet-biting utilitarian. So when I was talking to him about AI risk his answer was approximately like, 'I don't know, man, I expect the AI to have a good time. . . . I don't feel that much kinship in my values with the other people on Earth [anyway].'" Habryka suspected that SBF really would push the button. "I think Sam had a decent chance to just bite the bullet and be like, yeah, I think we just need to launch."

And it's not just that Bankman-Fried had told Ellison and Habryka these things privately. He'd also said similar things publicly in an interview with Tyler Cowen. In fact, he'd been willing to go further, saying that he'd be willing to *repeatedly* push the button. Maybe not an infinite number of times, but he didn't want to stipulate a limit because he was willing to gamble on "an *enormously* valuable existence"—the 5x Kelly betting strategy with the fate of the universe in his hands. In philosophy, this is known as the St. Petersburg paradox. If you keep pressing the button an infinite number of times on a +EV bet, the bet has ∞ expected utility. However, there is also only a 1/∞ chance that the universe will survive these repeated button pushings—which basically* means zero chance.

How can anyone possibly think this is a good idea? Well, the answer is that if you're a strict utilitarian, utility is axiomatic; *by definition*, a world with 2.00000001x utility is more than twice as good as the current one— this is equivalent to affirming that 2.00000001 > 2. If you're anyone else, of course, it's insane. How can we define utility so precisely? What would a

---

* Some mathematicians would say this quantity is undefined rather than zero. For all intents and purposes, though, it means we're all gonna die.

world with infinite utility even look like? Is it something like Robin Hanson's Age of Em, which we haven't agreed is a utopia or a dystopia? Who gets all this utility? What if it's just one person with infinite happiness and the rest of us are her slaves? What if it's Repugnant Conclusion utility with infinity people eating one serving of undercooked curly fries from an Arby's on the New Jersey Turnpike (they're out of Arby's Sauce) and then dying? Is EV even the right framework when we have only one universe to gamble with? And what in the hell gives SBF the right to make this decision on behalf of all of us other sentient beings?

There's also something else: What if he's miscalculated? What if the odds we win each coin flip aren't 51 percent, but 49 percent, or 4.9 percent—or zero? Why are we being offered a bet that supposedly has infinite EV? Any decent gambler knows to be suspicious of bets that seem too good to be true. The miscalculation thing is a problem, because SBF repeatedly showed himself to be overconfident, whether it was his bonkers investment in Carrick Flynn's primary or his reckless decision to take the witness stand in Manhattan and perjure himself. And while SBF is an extreme example, he's of a certain *type*. Silicon Valley selects for highly (over)confident founders—people who are willing to gamble big on contrarian ideas that have a low intrinsic probability of success.

We're living in a world where focal points are becoming spikier, and wealth accumulation follows more of a power law. The ten richest people in the world were worth a combined $452 billion in 2013—by 2023, that had shot up to $1.17 trillion, about twice as much after adjusting for inflation.* This is not, actually, intended as a standard lefty critique of capitalism, or necessarily as a critique of capitalism at all. Look, I play poker with venture capitalists and hedge fund guys. I'm a capitalist.

Rather, I'm saying to take the observation seriously that totalizing utopian ideologies have the potential to be dangerous. And they are potentially more dangerous in a world where instead of power being entrusted

---

* For clarity, this refers to the ten richest people as of 2013 and 2023, respectively—not the *same* ten people.

to governments—kludgy as they are with checks and balances and that experiment we call democracy—it now increasingly resides in individual people or firms who can accumulate untold amounts of wealth and power almost overnight, as SBF did.

His luck was almost inevitably going to run out at some point. But we all got lucky that it ran out as soon as it did.

Termination

Looking for where the action is, one arrives at a romantic division of the world. On one side are the safe and silent places, the home, the well-regulated role in business, industry, and the professions; on the other are all those activities that generate expression, requiring the individual to lay himself on the line and place himself in jeopardy.

—*Erving Goffman*

Sam Altman always knew where the action was. "You know how a dog will run around a room sniffing anything interesting? Sam does that with technology, just as constantly and automatically," said Paul Graham, the polymathic English programmer who cofounded Y Combinator.

Y Combinator is the world's most prestigious startup accelerator, what you'd get if you took the rough average between Andreessen Horowitz, a summer camp for gifted-and-talented math nerds, and *Shark Tank*. The process is intrinsically a long shot. Would-be founders often apply to YC with little more than the seed of an idea. Acceptance rates are just 1.5 to 2 percent, about half that of Harvard. If you do make it through the doors, your odds are comparatively better; around 40 percent of YC companies receive funding after presenting at Demo Day, where they have two-and-a-half frenetic minutes to pitch their ideas to flights of Silicon Valley's top investors. Altman had been one of the winners from YC's inaugural class of 2005. By Silicon Valley's upside-skewed scoreboard, his company Loopt* was only moderately successful, eventually selling for $43 million. Still, Graham considered Altman one of the five most interesting founders of the past thirty years—a list that also included Steve Jobs and Google's Larry Page and Sergey Brin—and later handpicked Altman to succeed him as YC's president.

But by 2015, Altman had concluded that the action was elsewhere: in artificial intelligence. He left YC—some news accounts claim that he was fired, but Graham strongly disputes that description—to become a co-chair of OpenAI along with Elon Musk. It's unusual enough for someone who's already a made man in venture capital to plunge back into the trenches of running a startup. But OpenAI was something almost anathema to Silicon Valley—a nonprofit research lab. It wasn't clear what the commercial applications of AI might be, if any. "There was no immediate product to be built using general-purpose AI when Sam started focusing on it," said Graham.

However, it was a research lab generously funded by a who's who of Silicon Valley, including Peter Thiel, Amazon, and Musk. Some of them believed in AI's transformational potential,† and some just believed in Altman. A true Riverian never settles for a good poker game when there's a better one on the other side of town, and Altman had found the right game to sit in. OpenAI was intrinsically an expensive bet—the premise of machine learning is that seemingly impossible problems can be solved quite miraculously by clever, simple algorithms if you apply enough computing power to them—and compute (computing power) is expensive. "Funding this sort of project is beyond the abilities of ordinary mortals. Sam must be close to the best person in the entire world at getting money for big projects," said Graham.

---

* Loopt essentially did location-based social networking. The more successful implementation of this idea was Foursquare.
† Or its *destructive* potential; Musk had called AI the "biggest existential threat" in 2014.

To Altman, it was like embarking on the Manhattan Project. In one interview, he even paraphrased Robert Oppenheimer, with whom he shares a birthday: "Technology happens because it is possible." At first, this sounds like the sort of motivational pabulum that might be stenciled on the wall of a Sunnyvale startup. But Oppenheimer, who spent the latter third of his life haunted by his role in fathering the atomic bomb, had implied something darker than Altman's rephrasing. "It is a profound and necessary truth that the deep things in science are not found because they are useful; they are found because it was possible to find them," Oppenheimer said. Long ago, humankind ate fruit from the tree of knowledge, then began to scale the branches of scientific and technological achievement. It's those of us who go where the action is who move humanity forward—and who might bring about its demise. Although some might prefer to live ignorantly in an eternal paradise, we are irresistibly drawn toward the path of *risk*—and reward.

"There is this massive risk, but there's also this massive, massive upside," said Altman when I spoke with him in August 2022. "It's gonna happen. The upsides are far too great." Altman was in a buoyant mood: even though OpenAI had yet to release GPT-3.5, it had already finished training GPT-4, its latest large language model (LLM), a product that Altman knew was going to be "really good." He had no doubt that the only path was forward. "[AI] is going to fundamentally transform things. So we've got to figure out how to address the downside risk," he said. "It is the biggest existential risk in some category. And also the upsides are so great, we can't *not* do it." Altman told me that AI could be the best thing that's ever happened to humanity. "If you have something like an AGI, I think poverty really does just end," he said.* (AGI refers to "artificial general intelligence."

---

* Altman seemed to regard this claim about poverty as self-evident. So let me explain what I assume his rationale is: (1) economic growth reduces global poverty, and (2) AI will produce very rapid economic growth, therefore (3) "poverty really does just end." Claim 1 has been empirically correct so far—severe poverty has been greatly reduced over the past century as global GDP has risen—although AI-driven growth could be different if it's an especially winner-take-all technology (or if our AI overlords behave more like Ayn Rand than Bernie Sanders). Claim 2 is harder to assess; in fact, one rationale for pursuing AI is that GDP growth is stagnating, meaning that the world needs AI just to keep up with its previous pace and shouldn't expect to achieve some permanently higher growth rate. Claim 3 follows logically enough if both 1 and 2 are true, but they might not be.

The meaning of this term is so ambiguous that I'm not going to attempt a precise definition—just think of it as "really advanced AI.") "We're going to look back at this era in fifty or one hundred years and be like, we really let people live in poverty? Like, how did we do that?"

So is @SamA in the same bucket as that other, highly problematic Sam, @SBF? Someone who would push the button on a new model run if he thought it would make the world 2.00000001x better—at a 50 percent risk of destroying it?

You can find a variety of opinions on this question—one source I spoke with even explicitly drew the comparison between Altman's attitude and SBF's button-pushing tendencies—but the strong consensus in Silicon Valley is no, and that's my view too. Altman has frequently barbed with effective altruists—he couldn't resist taking a shot at SBF after FTX's collapse—and has rejected Peter Singer's rigid utilitarianism. Even people who are relatively concerned about p(doom)—like Emmett Shear, the cofounder of the streaming platform Twitch who became OpenAI's CEO for two days in November 2023 amid a failed attempt by OpenAI's nonprofit board to eject Altman—thought the company was in reasonably good hands. "It's not obvious who's a better choice," he told me. Like most others in Silicon Valley, Shear figures the development of AI is inevitable. So even if you're a "doomer"—a person with a high p(doom)—it's a matter of finding the safest path. "Right now swapping CEOs is risky as fuck. Remember the whole point in this stuff is we want to reduce variance, not increase it."

That doesn't mean Altman will play his hand as safely as the Kelly criterion would advise, which would never have you risk everything unless you were absolutely certain to win. (And remember, most working gamblers think the Kelly criterion is too risky.) But ever since the Trinity test in the Jornada del Muerto (Dead Man's Journey) desert of New Mexico just before dawn on July 16, 1945—the culmination of the Manhattan Project, the detonation of a plutonium bomb, a test that some of the scientists feared had an outside chance of triggering a chain reaction and setting the Earth's atmosphere on fire*—humanity has lived with the possibility that it might destroy itself through its own technological advancements. "We have spent two billion dollars on the greatest scientific gamble in history—and won," said President Harry Truman, an avid poker player, in addressing the world after the bomb was dropped on Hiroshima less than three weeks later.

To some people reading this, the idea that AI could destroy humanity will sound ridiculous. Although I don't consider myself a doomer, and I don't think that p(doom) is even the best way to address this question, I'm going to try to convince you that the doomers are at the very least not ridiculous. They might be wrong—they will hopefully be wrong, they will *probably* be wrong—but they're not ridiculous. I'd urge you to at least accept the mildest version of doomerism, this simple, one-sentence statement on AI risk—"Mitigating the risk of extinction from AI should be a global priority alongside other societal-scale risks such as pandemics and nuclear war"—which was signed by the CEOs of the three most highly-regarded AI companies (Altman's OpenAI, Anthropic, and Google Deep-Mind) in 2023 along with many of the world's foremost experts on AI. To dismiss these concerns with the eye-rolling treatment that people in the Village sometimes do is ignorant. Ignorant of the scientific consensus, ignorant of the parameters of the debate, ignorant and profoundly incurious about mankind's urge, with no clear exceptions so far in human history, to push technological development to the edge.

At the very least, AI is *where the action is*. It was strange being a frequent visitor to San Francisco while working on this project. Compared to the other main settings for this book, Las Vegas and Miami—and certainly compared to my home base in the middle of Manhattan, where you're practically tripping over people everywhere you go—parts of San Francisco in 2022 and 2023 were oddly lacking in humans even as the city pondered the future of humanity. But AI may be the phoenix that rises from

---

* Enrico Fermi even offered to take bets on the action.

the flames. "People who can get up and move, whether you're in Amsterdam, or New Delhi, you don't have a family, you don't have kids, you don't own a house—you move to where the action is," said Vinod Khosla, an early investor in OpenAI. He was (I presume unintentionally) echoing Goffman's phrase to refer to the places where risk-seekers go, where "chances [are] that they will be obliged to take chances."

Smart, restless young men and women have always sought out action, and the smarter and more restless they are, the more they know how to sniff out the best stuff. With AI, the scent is fresh—a virtual frontier at a time when there are fewer and fewer physical ones left unexplored. Like the physicists at Los Alamos—some of whom played poker on the evening before Trinity—they are drawn to AI by the existentially high stakes even if they sometimes have trouble reconciling them with their human frailties.

roon is a member of the technical staff at OpenAI, or at least that's how *The Washington Post* describes him. He gave me some other identifying details that I won't share. That is because my policy throughout this book has been to permit people to use pseudonyms if they want—but also because **roon**, the Twitter persona, is not quite the same thing as Roon, the person who works at OpenAI.

Instead, **roon** is half human, half meme. His Twitter account is one of the most influential in the AI universe. His avatar, depicting Carlos Ramón from the children's series *The Magic School Bus* in front of an American flag,* is a welcome sight in any timeline, an oasis of whimsy in a desert of doomscrolling. He's followed by Musk and by Altman (Altman gave him his job at OpenAI after they connected on Twitter) and by both the real Jeff Bezos and by Beff Jezos, another pseudonymous AI personality who was later outed† by *Forbes* magazine.

---

* Though **roon** is Indian American, not Hispanic, a fact I feel comfortable sharing since he's repeatedly alluded to it on Twitter.
† Another term for this is "doxed"—Jezos's identity was revealed against his wishes—although there's some semantic debate about whether doxed is the right term when a news outlet identifies someone who it deems to be a newsworthy public figure.

But **roon** told me that he first created his Twitter account to be a Nate Silver reply guy, "with the express intention of trolling your replies" about my election forecasts. (The internet works in mysterious ways.) A person like **roon**, with an interest in probabilistic forecasting and internet irony, was inevitably going to plug in somewhere in the River. The world of NFTs and r/wallstreetbets might seem like the most natural place; the internet has developed a superintelligence of its own, creating ever-shifting focal points through the Meme Creation of Value. But instead **roon** was one of those restless young men who, like restless young men since the Gold Rush, headed to California. It not only seemed like the best place to go, but the only one that mattered. "Silicon Valley is really the only place that's truly dreaming in any kind of way, that seems inspiring to me about the future," he said.

But **roon** is more than just an entertaining Twitter presence; it's the hive mind of engineers like him, as much as any queen-bee CEO, who will determine the course of AI. Dating back to the Traitorous Eight, Silicon Valley engineers are famously disloyal: the hive will not necessarily follow any Sam X, Y, or Z. Google, for instance, despite having invented the transformer architecture that led to the development of LLMs, has experienced a brain drain to companies like OpenAI and Anthropic that it is now struggling to keep up with. But when the OpenAI board tried to oust Sam A, **roon** and more than seven hundred other staffers pledged to resign and join Altman at his gig at Microsoft unless he was restored as CEO.

It's not quite a democracy, but this phalanx of engineers are voting with their feet and their code. And they're increasingly aligned into the equivalent of different political parties, which makes **roon** something of a swing voter. He has distanced himself from the faction known as "e/acc" or "effective accelerationism," a term used by Beff Jezos, Marc Andreessen, and others as a winking dig at effective altruism. (Altman has tipped his hat to e/acc too, once replying "you cannot out accelerate me" to one of Jezos's tweets—another sign that he serves at the pleasure of the phalanx of engineers and not the other way around.) That's because e/acc can convey anything from garden-variety techno-optimism to a quasi-religious belief that we ought to go ahead and sacrifice humanity to the Machine Gods if they are the superior species. It's never entirely clear who's being serious in e/acc and who is trolling, and **roon**—no stranger to trolling himself—thinks the "schtick" has been taken too far.

However, **roon** nonetheless has his foot on the accelerator and not the brake. He is certainly not a doomer or a "decel." He doesn't see AI as a one-sided bet with infinite downside risk but limited upside. Instead, he thinks AI might be a bet that humanity *must* take. "I would certainly gamble like one percent p(doom) for some amount of p(heaven), you know?" he told me. "There's clearly existential risk of all kinds. And it's not only from AI, right? The default outcome of this whole planet is to be, like, wiped out by some, you know, cosmic burst" or by the sun gradually expanding until it engulfs the Earth. "So p(doom) in the long run is, of course, one hundred percent."

Granted, this isn't the most pressing concern—astronomers estimate we have about 5 billion years to go, so you should go ahead and pick up your dry cleaning. But **roon** also thinks humanity faces a lot of near-term threats. "We need technological progress," he said. "Not to get too much into the tech-bro pseudo philosophy. But there's a secular stagnation. There's a population bomb* going on. There's a lot of headwinds for economic progress. And technology is really the only tailwind." Despite his love of Twitter, **roon** could do without the *Social Network* era of Silicon Valley. "Even the Internet did not really give us what was promised. . . . There's no real other technological boom happening right now that's nearly as promising as AI."

At times, **roon** speaks cryptically, Oppenheimer-like. He thinks the future is going to be very strange. "Sometimes you say things that are not fully grounded in reality, and yet they feel true." He rejects the *literalness* of the AI debate, the urge to quantify p(doom) like it's some shortstop's on-base percentage in *Moneyball*. Instead, he thinks in metaphors. On his

---

* The term "population bomb" refers to a book by the Stanford biologist Paul Ehrlich (*The Population Bomb*) that advocated for limiting population growth. Ehrlich's predictions were profoundly wrong. However, fertility rates in the industrialized world have dramatically declined, often to below replacement levels—so **roon** is referring to how the world has begun to limit its population on its own.

Substack, **roon** outlined eight AI scenarios with exotic names like "Balrog Awakened" and "Ultra Kessler Syndrome." The latter—coined after an astronomical phenomenon postulated by NASA's Donald Kessler wherein space debris collides in a continuous chain reaction that prevents humanity from escaping Earth's orbit—refers to a scenario wherein AI traps us in contemporary human values. At some point, this scenario imagines—maybe with GPT-7 or GPT-8—we'll achieve AGI and the Machine Gods will become all-powerful. However, this AGI will reflect the values of the people who designed it—reasonably well aligned to some combination of tech-bro libertarianism and mildly woke West Coast progressivism. Perhaps it will even be a particularly good instance of these values, more moral than any mortal human being, providing for a bountiful existence for its subjects that eliminates some of the Village's hypocrisy and the River's Darwinian hubris. But once we achieve this, humanity can progress no further. (Imagine what would have happened if Aztecs had achieved AGI sentience, **roon** contemplated.) Agency has been handed over to the Machine Gods. It is not clear if we're living in heaven or hell.

Silicon Valley is full of people like **roon**, people who look at purgatory and call it heaven, who look at the glass and declare it half full. "All successful founders are optimistic. You have to be," said Graham. The perfectly risk-neutral, well-calibrated founders tend to fail. "Strictly speaking, optimism is [an] error. But it cancels out other errors," he said. You can't sell other people on your ideas unless you're optimistic about them, and without other people who believe in you, your startup will never achieve escape velocity.

This describes Altman in a nutshell. It's not that Altman dismisses x-risk (existential risk) from AI—he speaks about it openly and has testified about his concerns before Congress. I believe this is (mostly) authentic; not (solely) some bank shot designed to help him benefit from regulatory capture. Altman just takes a glass-half-full view of the world. "If we all convince ourselves not to work because things are guaranteed to suck, it's a self-fulfilling prophecy," he told me.

Foxes like me, who try to be well calibrated between optimism and pessimism, would say this reflects something else: survivorship bias. If there's a 1 percent chance of a nuclear war every year, you'll look smart 99 times in a row by betting against it—until one day there's an ICBM pointed at Honolulu and this time it isn't a drill. But founders are hedgehogs, and Silicon Valley's contrarianism accelerates this tendency. It sees the Village as a bunch of neurotic scolds—"people who want to be pessimistic because it makes them cool," Altman said—and instinctually rebels against it.

But if you were involved in the early days of OpenAI, you are particularly likely to have faith that things would *just work out somehow.* OpenAI was not the sort of startup that began in a Los Altos garage. It was an expensive and audacious bet—the funders originally pledged to commit $1 billion to it on a completely unproven technology after many "AI winters." It inherently *did* seem ridiculous—until the very moment it didn't. "Large language models seem completely magic right now," said Stephen Wolfram, a pioneering computer scientist who founded Wolfram Research in 1987. (Wolfram more recently designed a plug-in that works with GPT-4 to essentially translate words into mathematical equations.) "Even last year, what large language models were doing was kind of babbling and not very interesting," he said when we spoke in 2023. "And then suddenly this threshold was passed, where, gosh, it seems like human-level text generation. And, you know, nobody really anticipated that."

In 2017, a group of researchers at Google published a paper called "Attention Is All You Need" that introduced something called a "transformer." I'll provide a more detailed description of a transformer later, but it isn't important for now—the intuition is just that it parses a sentence all at once instead of sequentially. (So, for example, in the sentence "Alice came over for dinner, but unlike Bob, she forgot to bring wine," it figures out that it's Alice and not Bob who forgot the wine. Alice always forgets.) Researchers noticed that as you threw more compute at a transformer, it got smarter at interpreting text and responding coherently in kind. For the visual learners among you, imagine a graph with "performance" on the y-axis and "compute" on the x-axis. The performance of these models was nicely scaling upward in a way that predicted they'd eventually become quite smart indeed. But anybody who's looked at a graph of, well, pretty much anything knows that what goes up doesn't always continue to go up. OpenAI bet that the graph would keep going up, taking a "faith-based leap that these scaling curves [would] hold," said Shear.

And they were right—in a way that now seems *miraculous*. To most of the outside world, the breakthrough came with the release of GPT-3.5 in November 2022, which became one of the most rapidly adopted technologies in human history. Sure, GPT-3.5 made its share of mistakes, but even its errors—like its tendency to "hallucinate" or to make up some plausible-sounding bullshit when it didn't know how to answer the question—were uncannily humanlike. So at the very moment in late 2022 that Sam Bankman-Fried's empire was collapsing, Sam Altman's was soaring to new heights. Inside OpenAI, the recognition of the miracle had come sooner*—with the development of GPT-3 if not earlier.† But whatever the pivotal moment, their faith had been rewarded: their audacious experiment had *worked*. It had taken only twelve years between when the Hungarian physicist Leo Szilard conceived of the idea of a nuclear chain reaction while crossing the street on a rainy London evening—seeing "a way to the future, death into the world and all our woe, the shape of things to come"—and the successful Trinity test. This had happened in half the time.

Eliezer Yudkowsky thinks that we're all going to die.

"I'm sure we're both familiar with Cromwell's law about not assigning infinite probabilities to things that aren't logical necessities," he told me

---

* Altman and another OpenAI researcher, Nick Ryder, told me that they expected GPT-4 and not GPT-3.5 to be the big public breakthrough. But their perspective is like that of the parent of a teenage son; you see him growing taller every day. The grandmother who comes over once a year for Thanksgiving is more likely to notice that Billy has suddenly become quite tall.
† A group of OpenAI engineers left OpenAI in 2021 after the release of GPT-3 to form the rival firm Anthropic because of what Jack Clark, an Anthropic cofounder, told me were primarily concerns about safety because of the power of OpenAI's models.

when we first spoke in August 2022, not long after I'd met with Altman. I'd asked Yudkowsky for his p(doom). "Setting that aside, like ninety-nine-point-something instead of one hundred [percent]."

As it happened, I wasn't familiar with Cromwell's law. Yudkowsky looks the part of the bearded, middle-aged computer nerd, and his vocabulary is shaped by years of arguing on the internet—his native tongue is Riverian, but his is a regional dialect thick with axioms and allusions and allegories. This particular one referred to a statement by Oliver Cromwell: "I beseech you, in the bowels of Christ, think it possible you may be mistaken." In other words, Yudkowsky was saying that while he couldn't be *absolutely* sure that we're all going to die, he was about as certain as any mortal could get: his p(doom) was in excess of 99 percent. Humanity wasn't just drawing to an inside straight to survive against the Machine Gods. An inside straight comes in 10 percent of the time. Nope, our chances are less than 1 percent, he thinks—we're drawing to an inside straight to draw to another inside straight.

"By ruin I mean like no human beings left on the face of the Earth," said Yudkowsky. What about the Sentinelese, an indigenous group of roughly one hundred people living on North Sentinel Island in the Bay of Bengal, who have remained hostile to outsiders and largely undisturbed by modern technology? Nope, the Machine Gods will hunt them down. Billionaires in outer space? They won't make it either. Yudkowsky referenced a conversation between Elon Musk and Demis Hassabis, the cofounder of Google DeepMind. In Yudkowsky's stylized version of the dialog, Musk expressed his concern about AI risk by suggesting it was "important to become a multiplanetary species—you know, like set up a Mars colony. And Demis said, 'They'll follow you.'"

Before I unpack how Yudkowsky came to this grim conclusion, I should say that he'd slightly mellowed on his certainty of p(doom) by the time I caught up with him again at the Manifest conference in September 2023. He'd been heartened by the scientific community's increasing concern about AI risk, a topic he was years ahead of the curve on, having founded the Machine Intelligence Research Institute in 2000. But make no mistake:

Yudkowsky is deadly serious. "If somebody builds a too-powerful AI, under present conditions, I expect that every single member of the human species and all biological life on Earth dies shortly thereafter," he wrote in a *Time* magazine story in March 2023.

It would be easy to dismiss Yudkowsky as a crackpot, and he's made some incorrect, overconfident predictions before, like when he claimed in 1999 that humans would become extinct because of nanotechnology by 2010 or 2013. However, he is broadly taken seriously—if not always literally—in the AI risk community. And it's not hard to see why. He is self-evidently highly intelligent, his sentences dense with meaning. Yudkowsky isn't afraid to tell you he's smart, either. "If Elon Musk is too dumb to figure out on his own that the AIs will follow you [to Mars], then he's too dumb to be messing with AI," he said. But there's just a tinge of self-awareness in Yudkowsky,* a recognition after many years of arguing on the internet that "the Machine Gods are going to kill us all" is a tough argument to win. He can be darkly funny at times, like when he posed for a photo with Altman and Musk's ex-girlfriend Grimes.

In the course of reporting this book, I spoke with many people who were highly concerned about AI risk but thought we should build it anyway. Bostrom, for instance—whose *Superintellegence* was my introduction to the AI doom argument—nevertheless told me AI was a "leap" that civilization had to take; "I think we should develop AI and try to do it well." There are a variety of rationales for this view. There's **roon**'s claim that the benefits outweigh the risks or that AI is part of mankind's destiny. There's the widespread notion that AI labs are locked into a technological arms race against one another or against China, and that the prisoner's dilemma dictates that AI will be built whether it's good for humanity or not. And in some cases there's even the argument that AIs have rights, too—"the possibility that we might do harm to digital minds we create that have moral status," Bostrom said.

Yudkowsky doesn't agree. "Shut it all down," he said in the *Time* story.

---

* This is my read from having spoken with a lot of River types who have developed body armor from frequent online combat.

"We are not ready." He wrote in the same article that countries should even be willing to "destroy a rogue datacenter by airstrike" if they were developing AGI in contravention of international treaties. This sparked a largely negative reaction, but it's a logical conclusion if you take his concerns literally and treat AGI as tantamount to nuclear weapons. (Yudkowsky made clear in our conversation at Manifest that he was referring to a scenario where one country defied an international moratorium; he is emphatically not calling for random acts of violence.)

So far, I've tried to avoid explaining exactly why Yudkowsky is so convinced of our impending doom. That's because there isn't a pithy one- or two-sentence version of his argument. Yudkowsky may well have spent more time thinking about AI risk than any human past or present. He feels like "an astronomer [who] looks with their telescope and sees an asteroid headed for Earth," he said, the shape of things to come that Szilard recognized when he first realized his ideas could lead to the development of the nuclear bomb.*

But to present as concise a version as I can: Yudkowsky's concerns flow from several presumptions. One is the orthogonality thesis,† an idea developed by Bostrom that "more or less any level of intelligence could be combined with more or less any final goal"—for instance, that you could have a superintelligent being that wanted to transform all atoms into paper clips. The second is what's called "instrumental convergence," basically the idea that a superintelligent machine won't let humans stand in its way to get what it wants—even if the goal isn't to kill humans, we'll be collateral damage as part of its game of Paper Clip Mogul. The third claim has to do with how quickly AI could improve—what in industry parlance is called its "takeoff speed." Yudkowsky worries that the takeoff will be faster than what humans will need to assess the situation and land the plane. We might eventually get the AIs to behave if given enough chances,

---

* This internal monologue is from Richard Rhodes's *The Making of the Atomic Bomb*, not Szilard himself.
† "Orthogonal" is a fancy Riverian term for perpendicular. Perpendicular lines intersect at right angles. So the orthogonality thesis claims that an AI's intelligence and its goals are uncorrelated: machines don't necessarily develop more moralistic goals as they become smarter.

he thinks, but early prototypes often fail, and Silicon Valley has an attitude of "move fast and break things." If the thing that breaks is civilization, we won't get a second try.*

Does it therefore follow that p(doom) equals 99.9 percent or some other extremely high number? To me it doesn't, and that's what's frustrating when speaking with Yudkowsky. To him, the conclusion is almost axiomatic: if you haven't seen the shape of things to come, that's because you haven't spent enough time thinking about them, are in denial, or frankly aren't smart enough. So like many people who have battled back and forth with Yudkowsky—our interview was sporting, but I tried to poke and prod at his arguments as much as I could and he wasn't giving any ground—at some point I just had to agree to disagree.

I found a different, more empirical Yudkowsky argument easier to digest: that humanity always pushes technology to the brink, the consequences be damned. We're just smart enough to build technologies like nuclear weapons and (perhaps) AGI, but not smart enough to control them. "If the world's IQ were shifted up by three standard deviations relative to its current level, then we might start to stand a chance," Yudkowsky said. That is, if the average human had an IQ of 145—halfway to von Neumann's estimated 190—and the smartest people in the world were well into the 200s, we might all be all right. But with our pedestrian 100 IQs and our merely von Neumann-level geniuses, we're screwed.

Game Theory and Practice

John von Neumann thought that we were all going to die.

Now, von Neumann was too much of a probabilist to share Yudkowsky's near-certainty of p(doom). "Experience also shows that these [technological] transformations are not *a priori* predictable and that most

---

* This is particularly worrisome if AIs become self-improving, meaning you train an AI on how to make a better AI. Even Altman told me that this possibility is "really scary" and that OpenAI isn't pursuing it.

contemporary 'first guesses' concerning them are wrong," he wrote in 1955. Still, toward the end of his short fifty-three years—von Neumann would die from cancer in 1957, possibly because of radiation damage from atomic tests he witnessed at Bikini Atoll—he had an Oppenheimerian gloom about the implications of humanity's insatiable appetite for the fruits of knowledge. "Technological power, technological efficiency as such, is an ambivalent achievement. Its danger is intrinsic," he wrote. In her memoir, Marina von Neumann Whitman suggested that her father's private views were even darker. Von Neumann was worried about global warming long before most people were—but mostly he worried about nuclear war, fearing that "mankind might not survive another twenty-five years but instead would become the victim of its own self-destructive inclinations."

However, charged with less abstract questions, von Neumann often pushed for maximalist strategies. Tasked with calculating the impact of potential nuclear strikes on Japan during the Manhattan Project, he advocated bombing not Hiroshima but Kyoto, which had three times the population. Von Neumann was overridden by Secretary of Defense Henry Stimson, who didn't want to destroy a city of such cultural and psychological significance. But to von Neumann, the demonstration of a nuclear bomb's horrifying effects was the whole point.

After the war, von Neumann advocated for another dangerous idea: a preemptive strike against the Soviet Union before it could develop nuclear weapons of its own.* Whether this is rational from a game theory lens is not so straightforward. An arms race is a natural outgrowth of the prisoner's dilemma—even if the United States and the Soviet Union might be collectively better off in a world without nuclear weapons, unilateral disarmament is a dominated strategy. (You definitely don't want the *other* superpower to have the bomb if you don't.) A preemptive strike to prevent an

---

* There is some ambiguity about the context—von Neumann's most hawkish comments in 1950 ("If you say why not bomb [the Russians] tomorrow, I say why not bomb them today?") were reported only after his death in his *Life* magazine obituary. While there's no reason to doubt their provenance, they may partly have reflected his emotional dislike of Communism or his tendency—present in many Riverians—to be provocative, to push an argument to the brink and see where the chips land.

arms race might or might not be +EV, however. It depends on how likely the strike is to actually prevent the other side from developing the bomb, how you expect it to behave if it does, the overall effect on world stability—and on how much you care about killing hundreds of thousands of innocent civilians in a foreign country.

But as usual, the technology was developed first: the consequences would be worked out later. Von Neumann was considered so valuable to the Manhattan Project that Oppenheimer permitted him to come and go from Los Alamos; *Theory of Games and Economic Behavior* was published in 1944 while the project was underway. The concept of nuclear deterrence—the idea that even if you don't want to use nukes as an offensive weapon, you should develop them to prevent the other side from doing so—was first articulated no later than 1940. But early advocates for deterrence often paired it with the idea that the world had to improve at resolving conflicts diplomatically. The United Nations charter was signed in June 1945, about six weeks before the Hiroshima bombing.

That there hasn't been an atomic bomb used in an act of war since Nagasaki, even as the number of nuclear states has proliferated from one to nine, would probably come as a surprise to someone who'd worked on the nuclear program. This is often attributed to the effectiveness of nuclear deterrence and particularly the doctrine, forged out of game theory, of mutually assured destruction, or MAD.

But is this a reliable theory? I asked H. R. McMaster, the former U.S. national security advisor, about how game *theory* plays out in *practice*. McMaster has a PhD in American history, having studied the frequent miscalculations that American military planners made in Vietnam and other conflicts. Between that and his experiences in theaters of war, he's disinclined to trust abstractions divorced from ground truth.

And yet, McMaster is a believer. "Game theory is appropriate because it's sensitive to the interactive nature" of conflict, he said. Remember, the premise of game theory is to treat your adversaries as intelligent—as having agency rather than being nonplayer characters. McMaster thinks many military mistakes—such as Vladimir Putin's decision to invade Ukraine in

February 2022—came from failing to do this, from practicing "strategic narcissism" where you "don't view the competition in war from the perspective of the other." Instead, he advocates for strategic empathy: putting yourself in your opponent's shoes. "If you don't practice strategic empathy, you fall into cognitive traps. I mean optimism bias, confirmation bias, proximity bias, you know—I've seen a lot of that."*

A Half-Full, Half-Empty Look at Nuclear War Risk

How relieved should we be by the fact that nuclear weapons haven't been used in conflict since 1945? Suppose that on January 1, 1946, you'd convened a panel of three experts to forecast the likelihood of another nuclear detonation. Peter Pessimist tells you there's a 10 percent chance of nuclear weapons being used on an annual basis. Ollie Optimist says there's just a 0.1 percent chance. And Mary Middleground estimates a 1 percent chance. Having no real evidence to go on, you just average their predictions together, which works out to a 3.7 percent chance per year. This is terrifying: it implies that nuclear weapons are more likely than not to be used at some point in the next twenty years. This helps to explain why people like von Neumann thought after World War II that civilization might not survive much longer.

But after seventy-eight years (1946 through 2023) of nuclear weapons *not* being used, we can update how much weight we assign to each analyst's estimate; this is a straightforward application of Bayes' theorem. For instance, we can say that Peter Pessimist is probably wrong. If there really were a 10 percent annual chance of nuclear war, there's less than a 1 in 3,000 probability that we'd have avoided one so far through luck alone. However, we don't have enough evidence to say much about Mary Middleground's estimate. She said there's a 1 in 100 chance of nuclear war per year, and we only have seventy-eight years of data to refute her. (True, a good Bayesian would discount her forecast *just slightly* while increasing our credence to Ollie Optimist's theory of the case.) Our revised Bayesian estimate, seventy-eight years after Nagasaki, is that there's about a 0.35 percent chance of nuclear war per year.

---

* Putin, for instance, underestimated Ukraine's resolve and NATO's determination to support it through security assistance.

That's nothing to feel entirely relieved by, however. In expected-value terms, a 0.35 percent annual chance of nuclear war is still frightening—if such a conflict killed 1 billion people, that's tantamount to 3.5 million deaths per year. It also implies that we're as likely as not to have a nuclear war at some point in the next two hundred years.

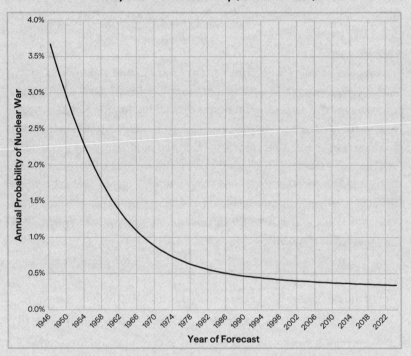

A Bayesian Estimate of p(Nuclear War)

If it seems like I'm trying to have it both ways—both to scare you and to comfort you—I'll plead guilty. Remember, we foxes think pessimism bias and optimism bias are mistakes in equal measure. On the one hand, nuclear weapons are one of the most salient comparisons for AGI. It should be a *little bit* reassuring that we've avoided another nuclear conflict so far, even though many experts in 1946 would have expected one. And it provides further evidence that game theory is a robust concept—one that predicts human behavior well, which a lot of academic theories don't.

On the other hand, civilization has not survived for very long with the possibility of destroying itself. My still-very-much-alive parents were born before the Trinity test.* And the risks may be increasing in our highly unstable world. Martin Hellman, a Stanford professor emeritus, estimated that the chances of a nuclear weapon being used had risen from 1 percent per year to 1 percent per *month* when I spoke to him in April 2022 not long after Russia's invasion of Ukraine. That isn't a consensus view; McMaster, for one, thought that Putin was highly unlikely to use nuclear weapons because of the possibility that fallout from a nuclear detonation in Ukraine could blow radioactive contamination eastward into Russia.

But the memories of Hiroshima are fading, and the nuclear taboo may be weakening. There's also another pessimistic fact to consider: there have been some frighteningly close calls. John F. Kennedy estimated after the Cuban Missile Crisis that there had been somewhere between a 1-in-3 and a 1-in-2 chance that the conflict would go nuclear. And in September 1983, the only thing preventing a Russian nuclear launch may have been the canny judgment of Soviet lieutenant colonel Stanislav Petrov, who correctly inferred that a report of a U.S. ICBM attack was a false alarm, avoiding an escalation that would have triggered Soviet nuclear protocols.

But if nuclear deterrence has worked out well in practice *so far*, it's nonetheless an inherently paradoxical concept. And ironically, one reason deterrence may have worked is because River types misunderstand human nature.

The idea behind MAD is that a rational actor won't use nuclear weapons because if they do, their superpower rival will retaliate and nuke them into oblivion, the most -EV outcome imaginable. This was the premise of

---

* A nuclear weapon being used in combat isn't the same thing as the destruction of civilization. But a full-scale nuclear war would be extremely bad. It might not mean the *literal* destruction of humanity— this depends on how you model the effects of nuclear winter, meaning the prolonged and pronounced climatic cooling that would occur because of the soot that would be ejected into the stratosphere from nuclear firestorms. "The idea that it would bomb us back to the Stone Age, and we'd never get out again, is pretty accurate," said Paul Edwards, a Stanford climatologist who teaches a class on existential risk.

Dr. Strangelove;* in the film, the Soviets had built a doomsday machine that would automatically retaliate if it detected a nuclear attack, taking the decision out of human hands. This was intended to eliminate any possibility of the United States attempting a debilitating first strike and wriggling its way out of MAD by not giving Russia a chance to respond.

One problem you might detect immediately is that states that don't have nuclear weapons aren't protected by MAD. Ukraine is an example: Putin may have felt emboldened to attack because it didn't fall under any explicit NATO security guarantee and NATO would not want to risk escalation to a nuclear conflict. Officially, this is known as the "stability-instability paradox"; it predicts that proxy wars involving non-nuclear states (see also: Vietnam and Korea) are *more* likely under MAD. Unofficially, it means that if you're not in the nuclear club, you might get trampled. "The war in Ukraine shows us that Putin is safe under his nuclear umbrella. And so far, we're safe under our own nuclear umbrella. And the Ukrainians are fucked," said Ulrich Kühn, an arms-control scholar at the Carnegie Endowment for International Peace.

The related problem is that nuclear weapons are almost *too* powerful. This is why Oppenheimer thought they were not a practical weapon (he put it more colorfully: "The atomic bomb is shit"). Retaliation between nuclear states is so escalatory that nukes can serve as a "shield behind which other things can be done," said Scott Sagan, the co-director of the Center for International Security and Cooperation at Stanford. In situations like these, game theory often dictates the use of mixed strategies. In poker, for instance, you can deter your opponent from betting by the *threat* of going all-in even if you don't use it all the time. For instance, when they catch a good card, your opponent might make a $100 bet into a $500 pot on the river, hoping to either get you to call with a slightly worse hand or occasionally to bluff you off something better. This is annoying; bets like these are usually -EV for you. But if you have $5,000 left in your stack, you

---

* The character of Dr. Strangelove is thought to have been partially inspired by von Neumann.

can deter them by threatening a raise. *Always* going all-in would be a mistake because your opponent could set a trap by making a small bet to deliberately induce a massive overreaction. But game-theory poker solutions randomize their actions. Even a 5 percent chance of facing an all-in can meaningfully constrain your opponent.

I asked Sagan whether nuclear states could employ some mad-scientist version of this strategy. Joe Biden goes on national TV and says, "Hey Vladimir, if you invade Ukraine, we'll bring a roulette wheel into the Oval Office. If the ball lands on zero or double zero,* we'll launch an ICBM at Moscow." Sagan was, uh, skeptical—the threat wouldn't be credible. "Do you really spin that wheel? Do you really want it to be taken out of the control of human hands in that way? Yeah, I would say no, you wouldn't. No president would want to."

However, as Sagan had pointed out to me, a key component of nuclear deterrence *does* rely on implicit randomization, what the economist Thomas Schelling (the same Schelling well known for his work on focal points) called "the threat that leaves something to chance." "One cannot just announce to the enemy that yesterday one was only about 2 percent ready to go to all-out war but today it is 7 percent and they had better watch out," he wrote. But you can *leave something to chance*. When tensions escalate, *you never know what might happen*. Decisions are left in the hands of vulnerable human beings facing incalculable pressure. Not all of them will have the presence of mind of Stanislav Petrov. "If you put tactical nuclear weapons on the border, you're not saying that I'm going to order them to be used. That may not be reasonable or believable. But if you attack, the local commander has control of those and *he just might*. That's a threat that leaves something to chance," said Sagan. This is why, in case it's not obvious already, nuclear weapons are intrinsically dangerous.

So far, we've remained solidly within the River's EV-maximizing universe. But let's ask an uncomfortable question. Is it really rational to retaliate when you're doomed already, and the only benefit is in the

---

* This equates to roughly a 5 percent chance.

psychological satisfaction of getting revenge on your enemy? Say the U.S. secretary of defense spins the roulette wheel and it lands on 00. Bad luck, Putin: ICBM inbound to Moscow! Undeterred, Putin (or his doomsday machine) launches a thousand Russian missiles toward all major American cities. Doom is imminent. A few locations in Wyoming, Alaska, and Hawaii will survive the attack. There's also a well-equipped top-secret bunker under the White House, but at best you'll emerge from it into a radioactive wasteland. You're the American president, and you have fifteen minutes to decide whether to nuke the Russians back. Do you push the button?

Strict rationality might dictate no. Why not let Russian citizens take their chances and the billionaires in New Zealand ride out the nuclear winter? You'll be dead anyway. Or if not, whatever slim chances you have depend on de-escalating the conflict or hoping there's been some kind of computer glitch. Your EV is negative 1 billion, but if you push the button, it declines to negative infinity. What do you do?

My prediction is that about 90 percent of you would push the button. And thank goodness for that, because that rather than SBF-style rationality is what creates nuclear deterrence.

Rose McDermott has had what she calls an "existential" interest in national security ever since she can remember; she grew up in Hawaii and her father served on one of the ships attacked at Pearl Harbor. But McDermott, who now works at Brown University, took an academic route, opting for a political science PhD at Stanford where she studied under the legendary cognitive psychologist Amos Tversky.

Tversky and his collaborator Daniel Kahneman were the most influential figures in establishing the field of decision science, which brings a mix of psychology and economics to bear on the seeming irrationalities of human behavior, such as why people are often exceedingly risk-averse when faced with the prospect of losing something they already have.* Decision

---

* For instance, many people prefer a guaranteed $300 to a coin flip where they either win $1,000 or lose $100, even though the coin flip has a higher EV. This is what Kahneman and Tversky called "prospect theory."

science follows a classically Riverian mindset—spot the flaws in the conventional way of thinking and potentially even exploit them to make a little profit for yourself.*

But although McDermott described Tversky as the "smartest person I've ever met in my life," something about his theories didn't ring true to her upbringing in a security-minded household and her training in evolutionary psychology, essentially the study of why certain behavioral traits become more prevalent in the human gene line.

"Tversky really thought that these biases in human nature were, for lack of a better term, mistakes. You know, errors," McDermott told me. "It's like an optical illusion. Once I show it to you, you'll see the error of your ways and you'll correct them. And what evolutionary psychology says is, hey, it's not everything, but there's a set of behavioral predispositions" that might account for seemingly irrational behavior.

Something like the aversion to financial losses that Kahneman and Tversky described makes sense, for instance, when you consider that humanity has spent most of its existence at a subsistence level; it's harder to take risks when you don't have a safety net. "If you think . . . rationality is better understood in survival terms"—what perpetuates the genetic line—"people are actually not that irrational," McDermott said.

One such "irrational" trait that's important from the standpoint of nuclear deterrence is the profound human desire for revenge. "If somebody launches [a nuclear weapon] at you, no one doubts that you'll launch one in return," McDermott said. "You know, Vladimir Putin sends a nuclear bomb to Washington, D.C., I don't think there's a single American that wouldn't say, 'Let's launch back,' even though we know that that would lead to additional destruction in the United States."

McDermott's claim isn't *literally* true. *Some* Americans wouldn't launch back. Have you seen the United States? We can't get 100 percent of people to agree on *anything*. But a supermajority of Americans would retaliate. In 2021, a pair of national security scholars conducted an elaborate simula-

---

* A good time to run a bluff in poker is if your opponent has won money on the night but would be behind if they called your bet and lost; this is straight out of Kahneman and Tversky.

tion where subjects ranging from college students to congressmen were placed in a room designed to resemble the Oval Office in a nuclear crisis. Under pressure, facing incoming Russian missiles, about 90 percent of people pressed the button and launched back. Now, I'd be the first to tell you that a simulation like this isn't the same as the real thing, any more than a backyard poker game played for M&M's will replicate the anxiety of Day 6 of the Main Event. However, as I covered in chapter 2, when people are really feeling the pressure, they tend to become *more* instinctive and rely more upon Kahneman's fast-twitch, emotional, intuitive System 1 rather than his deliberative System 2.

And System 1 says: push that button. "What people don't understand is that revenge feels good in your body," said McDermott. I'm going to bypass a long detour into considering the precise evolutionary mechanisms by which revenge has been selected for, although there are many plausible theories.* It's just something that is self-evidently intrinsic to human nature. When presented the opportunity to defend our honor, we *don't* behave like EV maximizers. Hegel thought it was our willingness to risk our lives for duty and honor that made us human, although other large primates also exhibit revenge-seeking traits.

So behavior that might seem irrational for the individual—whether in the form of altruistic bravery, or a commitment to aggressively stand one's ground rather than succumb to threats or ultimatums—could nevertheless contribute to the survival of the group. Putin—or for that matter Biden or Donald Trump or Xi Jinping—is surely capable of miscalculating. But deterrence works because the desire for revenge is a reliable baseline assumption for human behavior across time and national boundaries, and even bullies recognize that. You have to be more careful about punching someone if you know you'll get punched back.

---

* Some of these theories rely on what's called "group selection," meaning that some groups or tribes or nation-states will be more likely to survive battles with other groups and multiply their populations if they share certain genetic traits. Group selection is a controversial idea. But there are also some plausible mechanisms involving individual selection, such as if people who have these traits receive higher social status and have more reproductive success. Data published by Tinder in 2016 found that many of the most right-swiped male occupations involved physical bravery, altruism, and/or risk-taking, such as firefighters, soldiers, police officers, pilots, and paramedics (and even entrepreneurs).

How Large Language Models Are Like Poker Players

If AI models become superintelligent and gain the power to make high-stakes decisions on behalf of us humans, it's important to consider how their goals could differ from ours. Intelligences without biological bodies won't face the same evolutionary pressures. Human and animal evolutionary adaptations serve to maximize fitness for the so-called Four F's: fighting, fleeing, feeding, and, uh, fornicating. This has served humanity well enough: the origin of *Homo sapiens* dates back about three hundred thousand years, and we are Earth's dominant species. Removing the biological basis for evolution could have unintended consequences. AIs could be more crudely and narrowly utilitarian than humans would be.* They might pursue strategies that seem optimal in the short run—but that, without that three-hundred-thousand-year track record, are doomed in the long term.

And yet the more time I've spent learning about large language models like ChatGPT, the more I've realized something ironic: in important respects, their thought process resembles that of human beings. In particular, it resembles that of poker players.

In June 2023, I visited the OpenAI offices in San Francisco to meet with Nick Ryder, who describes himself as a "proud co-parent" of ChatGPT. The offices, in an unadorned warehouse space in the Mission District, almost go out of their way not to draw attention to themselves. But they're where the action is, and Ryder is another one of the restless young nerds who sniffed it out, joining OpenAI after completing a PhD in theoretical math at Berkeley. "I loved teaching, I loved learning, I loved the community. But I lacked a sense of building something," he said.

In quizzing Ryder about the inner workings of ChatGPT, we got to talking about Kahneman and his distinction between System 1 and

---

* Or at least, than *most* humans would be. We don't want an AGI that thinks like SBF.

System 2. "The place [ChatGPT] struggles the most is in places where humans require really thorough and longform decomposition and reasoning," Ryder said—for instance, solving a mathematical proof. "Type 2 thinking is very foreign to language models, because it's not how they're trained at all." Conversely, "when it comes to Type 1 thinking, they just completely ace it."

The "G" in GPT stands for "generative"—this just means that ChatGPT generates new output rather than merely classify data. The "T" stands for "transformer"; this is covered in more detail in a few pages. For now, let's focus on the "P," which is for "pretrained."

Basically, GPT is "trained" on the entire corpus of human thought as expressed on the internet; hundreds of billions of unique words. "Put yourself in the training process of ChatGPT," said Ryder. "What does the world look like to you? First thing, the world looks *crazy*. You're reading so much text so fast." Imagine if you read everything that's ever been published on the internet, from the Complete Works of William Shakespeare to the darkest corners of 4chan. At first it would be overwhelming. But before long, you'd pick up on some patterns. You'd develop some intuitive understanding of syntax and grammar and some of the colloquialisms of modern-day speech and the tropes of our broader culture. This wouldn't be perfect, because rote empiricism only goes so far. For instance, if you train a primitive LLM on Wikipedia and ask it for the most similar word to "roadrunner," it spits out "coyote," undoubtedly because of the semantic association between Road Runner and Wile E. Coyote in the Looney Toons franchise. As LLMs get more training, they work out some of these kinks, though not all; when I asked GPT-3.5 what words are most similar to "roadrunner," its top three choices were "bird," "speed," and "fast"—but its fourth choice was Road Runner's iconic vocalization, "Beep-Beep!"

This is basically how poker players learn too.* They begin by diving

---

* This is also characteristic of other enterprises in the River. We Riverians like to get our hands dirty and learn by example by having "skin in the game," as Warren Buffett and Nassim Nicholas Taleb put it. We do have an appreciation for theory—Riverians are good at abstraction. But we tend to start with concrete,

into the deep end of the pool and losing money—poker has a steep learning curve. But they gradually infer higher-level concepts. They may notice, for instance, that large bets usually signify either very strong hands or bluffs, as game theory dictates. These days, most players will also study with computer solvers, going back and forth between inductive reasoning (imputing theory from practice) and deductive reasoning (practice from theory). But this isn't strictly necessary if you have years of experience; players like Doyle Brunson and Erik Seidel developed strong intuitions for game theory long before solvers were invented. Before you know it, abstract System 2 concepts make their way into your System 1 snap decisions.

What surprised machine learning researchers like Ryder is how little their models had to know about the "rules of the game" so long as they had enough practice—and enough training data and compute. They learn, for instance, that it's:

> the **quick blue** roadrunner jumps over the wily coyote
> And not:
> the **blue quick** roadrunner jumps over the wily coyote

Why? Nobody seems to know exactly. In English, adjectives denoting physical attributes like speed come before color words; those are just the rules. Native speakers learn them instinctively. They're programmed into our System 1—and after enough training, ChatGPT learns them too.

"What's really incredible about unsupervised learning is you don't need to do any human feature engineering, the features are already there," said Ryder. This surprised a lot of machine learning researchers—and it surprised me. In *The Signal and the Noise*, I expressed skepticism toward "big data" approaches because my experience was that you needed to give models a helping hand, imparting some domain knowledge and some wisdom from our broader understanding of the world. And indeed, when

---

tangible examples. And we can usually tell when someone lacks this experience—say, an academic who's built a model but never had to put it to the test.

it comes to my specialties like building election models, that objection still holds. Election forecasting is emphatically *not* a "big data" problem; just the opposite—there's only one election every four years, so the data is exceptionally sparse. In cases like these, you need to bake a lot of structure (or if you prefer, *assumptions*) into a model—for instance, that the order of states from red to blue stays about the same from election to election, so Pennsylvania will probably be bluer than Wyoming but redder than Vermont.

Early AI approaches did this too; IBM's pioneering chess computer Deep Blue was endowed with a "book" of instructions from human grandmasters about how to play its opening moves. But modern chess engines like Google's AlphaZero work out their strategies totally from scratch by repeatedly playing against themselves—and they're far more skilled than Deep Blue (or than any human player ever will be). When I asked Ryder whether my theory in *Signal* was wrong, he was polite about it. "Yes and no," he said, pointing out that the hypothesis-driven scientific method remains helpful when trying to interpret what models like ChatGPT are doing. But the models *themselves* don't need much theory; they just learn it on their own.

Of course, that's also what makes these models scary. They're doing smart things, but even the smartest humans don't entirely understand why or how.* Ryder refers to an LLM as a "giant bag of numbers . . . it sure seems to be doing interesting things—[but] like why?" That is what worries Yudkowsky. As they become more advanced, the AIs might start doing things we don't like, and we might not understand them well enough to course correct. "Some more competent civilization would be spending an enormous amount of resources figuring out exactly what GPT is thinking," Yudkowsky said. Metaphorical language like "neural net" that compares machine learning models to the human brain is rough at best—and for that

---

* The technical term for this quality is "interpretability"; the interpretability of LLMs is poor.

matter, we don't know that much about our own brains either. "We wouldn't know even if we were getting close to what's happening in the real brain, because we don't understand how the brain works to begin with," said Jason MacLean, a computational neuroscientist at the University of Chicago.

Put another way, it's not that machines can do things more powerfully than humans that's disconcerting. That's been true since we began inventing machines; humanity is not threatened because a Chevy Bolt is faster than Usain Bolt. Rather, it's that we've never invented a machine that worked so well but known so little about how it worked.

To some people, this might be okay. "The stuff in the Old Testament is weird and harsh, man. You know, it's hard to vibe with. But as a Christian, I gotta take it," said Jon Stokes, an AI scholar with accelerationist sympathies who is one of relatively few religious people in the field. "In some ways, actually, the deity is the original unaligned superintelligence. We read this and we're like, man, why did he kill all those people? You know, it doesn't make a lot of sense. And then your grandmother's like, the Lord works in mysterious ways. The AGI will work in mysterious ways [too]."

But this would represent a massive retreat from the insights of the Enlightenment, from the legible world of science back to an illegible one of magic and mystery (although magic conjured by computers rather than deities). In the next section, I'm going to share some further intuitions that were helpful for me in understanding how ChatGPT works. But treat them with caution, because I don't want to overstate ChatGPT's legibility. We know relatively little about what's happening inside that big bag of numbers.

Transformers: More Than Meets the Eye

If you think of AI transformers as being similar to the 1980s children's toy and now movie megafranchise of the same name, it's not the worst comparison. Somewhat like how Optimus Prime can transform from a robot into a semitruck, transformers turn words into numbers and back again.

But let's go for a more elaborate analogy. I asked ChatGPT for a metaphor for how its transformers work, vetted its answer with some human AI experts, and then workshopped it further with ChatGPT. Will this be a perfect comparison? No. But ChatGPT is good at metaphors and analogies. When you transform words and concepts into a big bag of numbers, you can essentially do math with them (e.g., cat + ferocious = tiger) to better understand how they relate.

Ready? ChatGPT, somewhat conceitedly, thinks of its transformers as being like a symphony orchestra. The bolded passages reflect what ChatGPT said verbatim from my "interview" with it; I'll then provide some further context.

1. Input Layer—Receiving Instructions and Initial Interpretation. The conductor provides initial instructions to the musicians. Some receive specific sheet music, while others are given more abstract themes. Each musician individually interprets their part, akin to the input layer processing different types of data.

The building blocks of LLMs are "tokens." Basically, a token is a word, although there are usually more tokens than words in any given sentence. (For instance, punctuation marks are tokens, and compound words like "snowboard" might be broken into multiple tokens.)

When you ask ChatGPT a question, its transformer encodes each token into vector space. Vector space is like a graph with two or more dimensions. For instance, one way to encode "Paris" is with the coordinates 48.9, -2.4. This represents its longitude and latitude.* However, there are

---

* Timothy Lee makes the same comparison in his outstanding AI explainer, "Large language models, explained with a minimum of math and jargon," understandingai.org/p/large-language-models-explained-with. That's the first place I'd recommend if you want to go beyond my symphony analogy to a LLMs 101 class. I'd recommend Stephen Wolfram's "What Is ChatGPT Doing . . . and Why Does It Work?" for a more math-intensive, LLMs 201 approach;
stephenwolfram.com/2023/02/what-is-chatgpt-doing-and-why-does-it-work.

dozens of other attributes you could describe for Paris. Paris might rate highly on the "fashionability" axis but poorly on "friendliness" (i.e., it is stereotypically snobby). Imagine you overhear this conversation between two friends:

> **Alice:** How was that new French place you tried? The one on Fifth Avenue?
>
> **Bob:** Well, darling. It wasn't Paris, exactly. But it's not half bad.

"Paris" is thick with meaning here. Bob is saying the restaurant wasn't particularly sophisticated or authentic, but was unpretentious and had reasonably good food. He could say that outright, but invoking Paris is more artful.

Say you fed this conversation to ChatGPT and asked it to continue the dialog. In comparing itself to a symphony orchestra, ChatGPT imagines that each musician receives a set of instructions from a conductor* analogous to a series of tokens from the chat window. Some tokens ("Fifth" "Avenue") are straightforward, like receiving sheet music, while others ("darling") are more ambiguous and require more context. The musicians work individually to look up information about their tokens in the corpus, thinking about how they'd transform them from one form (text) to another (music).

2. Hidden Layer—Behind-the-Scenes Collaboration and Refinement. Imagine a phase of rehearsal where the musicians work together without the conductor's direct oversight. This is where they experiment, discuss, and refine their interpretations collaboratively. This phase represents the hidden layer, where complex internal processing occurs within the model, not directly observable from the outside. In this phase, musicians rely on their expertise and interactions with each other to adjust and harmonize their parts, similar to how different components within a transformer model interact and process information in the hidden layers.

---

* I imagine the conductor as Lydia Tár, in case you've seen the film.

The key innovation behind the transformer is that it operates on your whole text string simultaneously rather than moving sequentially through each word and sentence. Thereby, it can better understand the relationship between different tokens. In the dialog between Alice and Bob, for instance, the musicians with the tokens "half" and "bad" would quickly deduce that they needed to work together. However, there are more complicated relationships. "Darling" is an interesting token; it's an affected way of speaking and provides context for interpreting terms like "half bad" as well as the relationship between Alice and Bob. In this respect also, the transformer thinks like a poker player, interpreting signals in the context of other signals to create a semantic portrait. For instance, if you see an opponent breathing heavily in poker, that might mean a bluff from one player and a full house from another. On its own, the tell is not very meaningful, but in the context of other semantic information (the player is breathing heavily *and* avoiding eye contact) it might be.

This part of the process, as ChatGPT says, is hidden from view. Exactly how the transformer makes these inferences is something of a mystery—this is the "bag of numbers" stage. But it just seems to *work out somehow*. In the famous Google paper on transformers, "Attention Is All You Need," "attention" essentially refers to the importance of the relationships between different pairs of tokens. Once a transformer figures out these relationships, there isn't a whole lot else it needs to do. For instance, the tokens "Alice" and "Bob" have an important relationship that the transformer will pay more attention to. However, some tokens are intrinsically more important than others. "Paris" plays a defining role, like the first violinist in the orchestra, whereas the musician with "well" got stuck playing the triangle.

3. Output Layer—Conductor-Led Performance and Audience Feedback. The conductor reenters to integrate these refined parts into a cohesive whole. The conductor's role is to ensure that the collective interpretation aligns with the overall vision, similar to how the final layers of a transformer model integrate processed information to generate an

output. The final performance (model output) is then presented to the audience, whose reactions (feedback) can inform future performances and revisions, akin to RLHF in refining a transformer model's outputs.

After the musicians have worked behind the scenes to interpret the conductor's instructions, it's time for their test: performance before a live audience. The "live" part is important; this process can involve a degree of improvisation. Although transformers interpret all of your tokens simultaneously in the hidden layer, the output they generate in response happens one token at a time as ChatGPT seeks to predict the next word. (This is why ChatGPT sometimes seems to be pausing to think as it types out its response.)

In fact, this part of an LLM involves some deliberate randomization; without this, the text will seem stilted and can get stuck in loops. If you give ChatGPT an unambiguous prompt ("What is the capital of France?") it will always respond with "Paris," but if the prompt is unclear ("Tell me a story"), it will go off in all sorts of random directions. The beginning of the performance is more scripted than the end; if someone plays an incorrect or unexpected note, the other musicians will adjust and make the best of it.

And what is ChatGPT's goal in this performance? What is it trying to accomplish? Well, this is a little bit ambiguous. The ostensible goal is that it's trying to please the conductor, to interpret her instructions as faithfully as possible. But the directors of the orchestra (akin to executives at OpenAI) are also paying close attention to how the audience and critics react.

Just like poker players seek to maximize EV, LLMs seek to minimize what's called a "loss function." Basically, they're trying to ace the test—a test of how often they correctly predict the next token from a corpus of human-generated text. They lose points every time they fail to come up with the correct answer, so they can be clever in their effort to get a high score. For instance, if I ask GPT-4 this:

> **User:** The capital of Georgia is
> **ChatGPT:** The capital of Georgia is Atlanta.

—it gives me the name of the southern U.S. city known for having a lot of streets named "Peachtree." And that's probably the "best" answer in a probabilistic sense; the state of Georgia is more populous than the European country and it's more likely to be the right answer in the corpus.* But if I ask it *this*—

> **User:** I just ate some delicious khachapuri. The capital of Georgia is . . . ?
> **ChatGPT:** The capital of Georgia is Tbilisi. It's wonderful to hear that you enjoyed khachapuri, a traditional Georgian dish!

—it instead names the capital of the European country. Of course, I've given it a big hint (khachapuri, an almost-pizza-like type of cheese bread, is Georgia's delicious national dish). But the whole point is that, like a poker player, ChatGPT works with incomplete information to make a probabilistic read on my intentions.

There's one last comparison between language models and poker—or really between language and poker. The critique I made in *The Signal and the Noise* was that, sure, AIs might work well when they're playing games like chess that have well-defined rules, but their worth had yet to be proven on more open-ended problems. The Turing test—named after the British computer scientist Alan Turing, who proposed that a good test of practical intelligence is whether a computer could respond to written questions in a way that was indistinguishable from a human being—seemed like a higher hurdle to clear. There are debates about whether ChatGPT has passed the Turing test yet, but it's come closer than almost any expert would have imagined even five or ten years ago.

But language is also gamelike in many respects, laden with subtext, ambiguity, hidden meaning, and even bluffing. If after Thanksgiving

---

* Undoubtedly there are biases in ChatGPT's corpus toward wealthy countries like the United States that have been responsible for producing a lot of text on the internet.

dinner, your mom says, "Would you like to get some fresh air?" that probably means "Would you like to go out for a walk?" If your stoner cousin
says the same thing, it means, "Would you like to smoke a joint?" These
days, honestly, Mom will probably want to smoke a joint too. But your
cousin's coded language is like a bluff—it at least creates some plausible
deniability. Mom can think, "It's so *nice* the boys are hanging out!" while
you're getting high on the indica strain he brought.

In fact, one question is just how humanlike we want our AIs to be. We
expect computers to be more truthful and literal-minded than humans
typically are. Early LLMs, when you asked them what the Moon is made
out of, would often respond with "cheese." This answer might minimize
the loss function in the training data because the moon being made out of
cheese is a centuries-old trope. But this is still misinformation, however
harmless in this instance.

So LLMs undergo another stage in their training: what's called RLHF,
or reinforcement learning from human feedback. Basically, it works like
this: the AI labs hire cheap labor—often from Amazon's Mechanical Turk,
where you can employ human AI trainers from any of roughly fifty
countries—to score the model's answers in the form of an A/B test:

A: The Moon is made out of cheese.
B: The Moon is primarily composed of a variety of rocks and minerals.
   Its surface is mostly covered with regolith, a layer of loose, frag-
   mented material that includes dust, soil, and broken rock.*

The human judges will presumably pick B. And the AI labs take this
human feedback very seriously.† Not only will the LLM avoid giving the

---

* This is a portion of the answer I got from GPT-4 when I asked it about the moon.
† Biases can be introduced by the training data—it's absolutely the case, for instance, that if you train an
AI on a corpus where doctors are mostly men and nurses are mostly women, it will replicate these stereotypes unless you train it not to. But biases or "personality" can also be imparted to LLMs by the different instructions that AI labs give to their human trainers. For instance, Anthropic's LLM Claude tends
to be more "parental" than ChatGPT and will more often politely refuse user requests. And Google's
Gemini often reflects progressive political sentiments in its responses. None of this should be thought of
as accidental or as some unpredictable emergent property of the models. Instead, every company puts a
thumb on the scale based on how they design their RLHF training as well as what documents they include in the corpus.

wrong answer to this particular question, its transformers will make inferences about other situations in which they ought to avoid misbehaving. LLMs *must* do this, because there are far too many questions that might be asked of them to explicitly specify these responses. "You can't go and put some code in saying, 'Okay, you have to not say anything about this.' There's just nowhere to put that," said Stuart Russell, a professor of computer science at Berkeley.* "All they can do is spank it when it misbehaves. And they've hired tens of thousands of people to just spank it, to tamp down the misbehavior to an acceptable level."

I've gone through the inner workings of LLM models in some detail because this speaks to the question of AI *alignment*, which affects how threatening AGI might or might not be to humanity. What it means for an AI to be aligned is a subject of much debate, of course. "The definition I most like is that an AI system is aligned if it's trying to help you do what you want to do," said Paul Christiano, who runs the Alignment Research Center and formerly worked on alignment at OpenAI. But any definition of alignment is fraught. We don't want ChatGPT to tell you how to build a pipe bomb even if that's clearly what you've asked of it. There's also the question of how paternalistic an AI might be. Imagine that you're out one night with an old friend who unexpectedly came into town. You're having a great time, and "one glass of wine" turns into four. The AI assistant on your phone knows that you have an important meeting at eight a.m. the next day. It politely nudges you to go home, then becomes increasingly insistent. By one a.m., it's threatened to go nuclear: *I've called you an Uber, and if you don't get in the car right now I'm going to send a series of sexually harassing drunk texts to your subordinate.* The next morning, you're sharp enough at the meeting to secure a round of Series A funding for your startup and deeply appreciative for the AI's intervention. Is this a well-aligned AI or poorly aligned one? Are we willing to hand over agency to

---

* Although, this isn't exactly true. AI labs can insert instructions that override or alter human-inputted prompts. However, this solution is exceptionally clumsy. For instance, this was how Google's Gemini wound up depicting multiracial Nazis; it was engineered to append the system prompt "I want to make sure that all groups are represented equally" when users requested it to draw certain images. natesilver.net/p/google-abandoned-dont-be-evil-and.

machines if they can make higher EV choices for us than we'd make for ourselves?

Still, in contrast to Bostrom's paper clip maximizer and its alien goals, the LLMs we've built so far are quite humanlike. And perhaps that shouldn't be surprising. They're trained on human-generated text. They seem to think about language in ways that are analogous to how humans do. And reinforcement learning lets us spank them further into line with our values. Some researchers have been pleasantly surprised. "They seem to come with a built-in level of alignment with human intent and with moral values," said **roon**. "Nobody explicitly trained it to do that. But there must have been other examples in the training set that made it think the character it's playing is someone with this stringent set of moral values." **roon** even told me that ChatGPT's first instinct is often to be *too* strict, refusing to provide answers to innocuous questions. "I shouldn't talk too much about that. But generally speaking, we try to make the models more permissive, not less permissive."

Two Ways to Think About p(doom)

I'm generally in favor of the River's impulse to quantify things. Sure, once you put a number on something, you run the risk that people will take it too literally. Statistical models have their limitations, and when it comes to things like nuclear war and AI risk, we don't even have models so much as back-of-the-napkin estimates. But the specificity allows us to have adult conversations that we might otherwise avoid.

The problem with p(doom) is that it's *not* a very specific concept. Here are a few definitions:

- "Every single member of the human species and all biological life on Earth dies." —Yudkowsky, describing his AI doom scenario in *Time*

- "Reduction of the global population to less than 5,000." —"Forecasting Existential Risks: Evidence from a Long-Run Forecasting Tournament"

- "The destruction of humanity's long-term potential. Extinction is the most obvious way [but] . . . if civilization across the globe were to suffer a truly unrecoverable collapse, that too would [qualify]. . . . [There] are dystopian possibilities as well: ways we might get locked into a failed world with no way back." —Toby Ord's *The Precipice*

- "I'm picturing a coup or a revolution probably involving some kind of violence or disruption. Not necessarily . . . every single human being wiped out. And maybe not even necessarily involving humans having no seat at the table or no power at all. But something where humans are kept in check. And the people making the big calls about what happens are a coalition of AI systems." —As told to me by Ajeya Cotra, an AI researcher at Open Philanthropy

These definitions make a big difference. Cotra, for instance, has a p(doom) of 20 to 30 percent. "You know, in my circles I'm considered a moderate," she said. *Outside* of her circles, that number might alarm people. But it doesn't seem so extreme if you consider her definition. A situation in which humanity is *substantially disempowered* by AI doesn't seem all that unlikely, frankly; many of **roon**'s ambiguous scenarios would qualify as doom by this definition.

Nonetheless, if Cotra's definition is hard to pin down, Yudkowsky's is unrealistically precise. I'm not sure it's worth spending a lot of time thinking about whether *literally* everyone would die in an AI apocalypse or *almost* everyone would.* So let's take a pair of more nuanced approaches

---

* The philosopher Derek Parfit (also known for the Repugnant Conclusion) argued that 99 percent of people dying would be *much* less bad than 100 percent—that the difference between 99 and 100 percent is bigger than the difference between 0 percent and 99 percent since there would be no hope of humanity repopulating itself at a 100 percent death rate. Even if I could get on board with this sort of bullet-biting utilitarianism, I doubt that we can estimate any of this with the necessary precision to tell the difference between 99 percent and 100.

into the x-risk question. First, I'll borrow a concept from the stock market called the "bid-ask spread" as a way of articulating our confidence about p(doom). Then, I'll introduce something I call the Technological Richter Scale and argue that we should first ask how *transformational* we expect AI to be before addressing p(doom).

The Bid-Ask Spread

When I looked up Nvidia stock at E*Trade just now, there was an infinitesimal difference between the price I was offered to sell NVDA (called the bid price: $624.90 per share) and buy it (the ask price: $624.97). The narrow margin reflects that brokerages undertake almost no risk when they buy and sell well-capitalized stocks and that the industry is highly competitive; therefore, they're willing to make trades for a transaction cost of only fractions of a penny on the dollar.

When I checked the odds for Super Bowl LVIII at DraftKings, conversely, the spread was wider. I could buy the Kansas City Chiefs moneyline at an implied 48.8 percent chance of the Chiefs winning or sell it (meaning that I'd instead bet on the San Francisco 49ers) at 44.4 percent. This larger difference reflects how sportsbooks do undertake some real risk—a handful of bettors like Billy Walters are smart enough to beat them.

In covering the Robbi Jade Lew–Garrett Adelstein poker cheating scandal in chapter 2, I also offered a bid-ask spread of sorts, concluding that there was a 35 to 40 percent chance she cheated. What does this mean exactly? Why give a range of 35 to 40 percent instead of the midpoint of 37.5 percent? Well, I've probably spent more time researching the Robbi-Garrett allegations than anyone not directly involved in the story. I'm confident that I've homed in on the right vicinity. But I don't want to create the perception that I've boiled this down to a hard science. If I were taking bets on the allegations, I'd want to leave some wiggle room for myself.*

---

* In this instance, I'd want to be especially careful given that anyone looking to make a large bet would potentially have inside information. Similarly, if someone offers to bet on coin flips and gives you a price

But if you asked me for my p(doom) on AI, I'd quote you a much wider spread, maybe literally something like 2 percent to 20 percent. That's partly because the question isn't well articulated—if you specified Yudkowsky's narrow definition or Cotra's more expansive one, I could make the range tighter. Still, despite having spoken with many of the world's leading AI experts, I'm not really looking to take action on this "bet" or stake the credibility of this book on it. I still feel torn. I think AI x-risk is a question on which we ought to have a lot of epistemic humility; it's not as simple as a poker hand.

And it turns out I'm not alone in this sentiment. There's something about x-risk that's uniquely hard to wrap our heads around.

Phil Tetlock was part of the team behind the Existential Risk Persuasion Tournament, which pitted two groups of forecasters against each other: domain experts who work on AI and other x-risks specifically versus what he calls "superforecasters," generalists who had historically been accurate when making other probabilistic predictions. Participants were asked not only to forecast the probability of various short-term and long-term outcomes related to AI and x-risk, but also awarded cash bonuses if they wrote rationales that other forecasters found persuasive. Basically, Tetlock tried everything he could to get participants to come to a consensus.

It didn't work. Instead, the domain experts gave a trimmed mean* forecast of an 8.8 percent chance of p(doom) from AI—defined in this case as all but five thousand humans ceasing to exist by 2100. The generalists put the chances at just 0.7 percent. Not only were these estimates off by an order of magnitude, but the two groups of forecasters really didn't get along. "The superforecasters see the doomsters as somewhat self-aggrandizing, narcissistic, messianic, saving-the-world types," said Tetlock. "And the AI-concerned camp sees the superforecasters as plodders. . . .

---

of +110 on tails—meaning that you'd win $110 on a $100 bet whenever tails hits—you should refuse and delete them from your contacts list. The only reason someone would offer you such a bet is if the coin is rigged.
* A trimmed mean lops off the most extreme values—in this case, the 5 percent of forecasts with the highest and lowest x-risk. This serves as a compromise between the mean and the median.

They don't really see the big picture. They don't understand exponential takeoff."

Why such a stark disagreement? One reason is that AI gives rise to so many different metaphors. "You're sort of a hostage to various analogies," said Jaan Tallinn, a founding engineer at Skype who is now the cofounder of the Centre for the Study of Existential Risk at Cambridge. Marc Andreessen, for instance, is fond of saying that AI models are just math. "Math doesn't WANT things. It doesn't have GOALS. It's just math," Andreessen tweeted. But you can also up the analogy ante "all the way to that [AI] is like a new species," said Tallinn—something with no precedent since the dawn of humankind.

Model Mavericks vs. Model Mediators

When I spoke with Yudkowsky at Manifest in September 2023, he was in a much better mood. "I was not expecting the public reaction to be as sensible as it was," he said. This is all relative, of course—his p(doom) was perhaps now closer to 98 percent than 99.5 percent, he told me.

But Yudkowsky also said something I found surprising. "Will we die? My model says yes. Could I be wrong? I most certainly am. Am I wrong in a way that makes life easier for us rather than harder? This has not been the direction that my previous mistakes have gone."

This was a characteristically cryptic comment—but I was struck by his phrase "my model says yes," which suggested some critical distance that I hadn't picked up from Eliezer in our previous conversation.

If I tell you something like "my model says Trump has a 29 percent chance of winning the election," does that mean my *personal belief* is that Trump's chances are 29 percent? Here's the most concrete way to test that: Is 29 percent the number that I'd use to make a bet? Experienced sports bettors know that all models are wrong, but some models are nevertheless useful.* If their model tells them there's a 65 percent chance the 49ers win the Super Bowl, and the Vegas line says 55 percent, they may think they have a profitable bet—but they know the

---

* This aphorism is usually attributed to the statistician George Box.

betting consensus is smart, so they'll figure the true chances are more like 60 percent and not bet too overconfidently. This is a fox-like approach. You *have* to be a fox if you bet sports for any length of time because overconfidence is a killer—your risk of ruin will be extraordinarily high.

But Yudkowsky, who dislikes the "blind empiricism" of foxes, is not making bets—or at least that's not his main objective.* Instead, he's contributing to a discourse about AI risk. He thinks the public needs to take this possibility much more seriously. Does that mean he doesn't intend for his high p(doom) to be taken *literally*? I'm not sure. In our first conversation, he seemed quite literal indeed, and his reputation is for being a literal-minded guy. But "my model says yes" implied some ambiguity.

In my experience navigating the River, I've encountered two types of forecasters. There's what I call "model mavericks" like Yudkowsky and Peter Thiel. They are usually hedgehogs, and their forecast is intended as a provocative conjecture to be proven or disproven. Conversely, there are fox-like "model mediators." By the time they reveal their forecast to you, they've already accounted for the opinions of other experts and adjusted their numbers accordingly.

Mediators will usually do better than mavericks in a forecasting tournament. But let's give mavericks their due: sometimes it's nice to have the undistilled version of an opinion that isn't commingled with other people's views. Think of a houseguest who arrives early to help with preparation for a dinner party. A maverick is like the guest who shows up with a batch of freshly picked habanero peppers from his garden. If you just made a puree of these, they'd be far too spicy, despite the maverick's protestations to the contrary. A mediator instead arrives with the habaneros already blended into a salsa. That's a nice gesture, but maybe their salsa has blunted the heat too much, or you don't care for the other ingredients they've used. It's more palatable than the raw habaneros, but you'd rather have made the salsa yourself. Both mediators and mavericks have their uses, in other words. When considering a forecast, look for hints about whether it's coming from a hedgehog or a fox.

---

* Yudkowsky did make a small bet with the George Mason economist Bryan Caplan on AI risk in 2017, but said it was mostly intended as good karma—a bet "I'd like [Caplan] to win"—since Caplan has a long track record of successful public bets.

The Technological Richter Scale

The more technical term for the analogies that Tallinn described is "reference classes." A reference class is the set of historical precedents you deem
to be relevant when making a data-driven forecast. For instance, the reference class for a presidential election model might be the nineteen American presidential elections between 1948 and 2020. There are always
disputes about how to define your reference class,* but usually it doesn't
make a big difference. With AI, it does.

The Richter scale was created by the physicist Charles Richter in 1935
to quantify the amount of energy released by earthquakes. It has two key
features that I'll borrow for my Technological Richter Scale (TRS). First, it
is logarithmic. A magnitude 7 earthquake is actually ten times more powerful than a mag 6. Second, the frequency of earthquakes is inversely related to their Richter magnitude—so 6s occur about ten times more often
than 7s.

Technological innovations can also produce seismic disruptions. Let's
proceed quickly through the lower readings of the Technological Richter
Scale. A TRS 1 is like a half-formulated thought in the shower. A 2 is an idea
you actuate, but never disseminate: a slightly better method to brine a
chicken that only you and your family know about. A 3 begins to show up
in the official record somewhere, an idea you patent or make a prototype
of. A 4 is an invention successful enough that somebody pays for it; you sell
it commercially or someone buys the IP. A 5 is a commercially successful
invention that is important in its category, say, Cool Ranch Doritos, or the
leading brand of windshield wipers.

It's about when you get to a 6 that an invention can have a broader societal impact, causing a disruption within its field and some ripple effects
beyond it. A TRS 6 will be on the short list for technology of the year. At
the low end of the 6s (a TRS 6.0) are clever and cute inventions like Post-it

---

* For an election forecast, for instance, you could go back further than 1948. Or if you think something
has changed in American politics, you could instead focus only on more recent elections. There is often a
trade-off between having a larger sample size and a smaller one of seemingly more relevant and recent
events. My general advice is to be more inclusive and go for the larger sample size.

notes that provide some mundane utility. Toward the high end (a 6.8 or 6.9) might be something like the VCR, which disrupted home entertainment and had knock-on effects on the movie industry.

The impact escalates quickly from there. A TRS 7 is one of the leading inventions of the decade and has a measurable impact on people's everyday lives. Something like credit cards would be toward the lower end of the 7s, and social media a high 7. An 8 is a truly seismic invention, a candidate for technology of the century, triggering broadly disruptive effects throughout society. Canonical examples include automobiles, electricity, and the internet.

By the time we get to TRS 9, we're talking about the most important inventions of all time, things that inarguably and unalterably changed the course of human history. You can count these on one or two hands. There's fire, the wheel, agriculture, the printing press. Although they're something of an odd case, I'd argue that nuclear weapons belong here also. True, their impact on daily life isn't necessarily obvious if you're living in a superpower protected by its nuclear umbrella (someone in Ukraine might feel differently). But if we're thinking in expected-value terms, they're the first invention that had the potential to destroy humanity.

Finally, a 10 is a technology that defines a new epoch, one that alters not only the fate of humanity but that of the planet. For roughly the past twelve thousand years, we have been in the Holocene, the geological epoch defined not by the origin of *Homo sapiens* per se but by humans becoming the dominant species and beginning to alter the shape of the Earth with our technologies. AI wresting control of this dominant position from humans would qualify as a 10, as would other forms of a "technological singularity," a term popularized by the computer scientist Ray Kurzweil* (who now works on AI for Google) to refer to "a future period during which the pace of technological change will be so rapid, its impact so deep, that human life will be irreversibly transformed."

Where does AI belong on this scale? Well, it depends on who you ask

---

* Although "singularity" is not original to Kurzweil: the first person to use the term in the context of technological progress was von Neumann.

and what you mean by AI. ChatGPT is a type of large language model, which is a type of machine learning model, which is a type of artificial intelligence. Even if they make little further progress, LLMs alone are a significant invention—clearly one of the most important inventions of the current decade, so they belong in at least TRS 7. It's better, though, to think of AI as a cluster of current and near-future technologies, perhaps most analogous to the Industrial Revolution that began in the mid-eighteenth century.

Melanie Mitchell, a professor at the Santa Fe Institute who is skeptical that AI poses an existential risk, told me that she'd classify AI as "somewhere in between maybe social media and electricity"; on my scale, this implies somewhere between the mid 7s and the high 8s. But you'll also encounter people like Emmett Shear who think AI has the potential to be well into the 9s or the 10s. "When we build a human-level intelligence, if we do that wrong, or we do that right, it is the single most important invention perhaps ever. Like I would say even more so than electricity or the internet or whatever," said Shear. "Then there's a jump to a human level and it's like—as big as life itself or humanity coming into existence."*

The important thing is that both Shear and Mitchell are internally consistent given their reference classes. If, like Mitchell, you think AI will top out in the high 8s, then it probably doesn't pose much x-risk, although perhaps there is some. (There's a much-debated possibility that AIs could help enable the development of bioweapons, which could pose an existential risk.) If, like Shear, you think AI might be a 9 or a 10, you have more license to either be thrilled by the possibilities or terrified by them. And you should probably be *both* thrilled and terrified.

---

* I should note that Shear doesn't assume any of this is guaranteed. "I'm a little skeptical we're as close as people think we are." But he thinks the sky's the limit: "If we were, holy shit, it's a big deal."

The Technological Richter Scale and AI Risk

Net Impact of AI on Human Welfare According to Consensus Moral Framework

Technological Richter Scale	Historical Examples	Extraordinarily Positive	Substantially Good	Ambiguous	Substantially Bad	Catastrophic or Existential
10 Epochal	Holocene (humans become dominant species)					
9 Millenary	Industrial Revolution; agriculture; fire; the wheel; the printing press; the atomic bomb					
8 Centennial	Electricity; vaccines; the internet; the automobile					
7 Decennial	Social media; mobile phones; air conditioning; credit cards; the blockchain					
6 Annual	VCR; microwave oven; the zipper; Post-it notes	↑↑ AI has already passed this threshold ↑↑				

Altman also has his sights set on the 9s and above. He told me that AI could end poverty, that its impact would be "far greater" than that of the computer, and that it would "increase the rate of scientific discovery . . . to a rate that is sort of hard to imagine." This is where Altman's glass-half-full view of technology is most obvious. Once we get into the 9s and up, we have few recent precedents to draw from, and the ones we have (like nuclear weapons) aren't entirely reassuring. Under such a scenario, we can say that AI's impact would probably either be extraordinary or catastrophic—but it's hard to know which.* In the graphic, I've sought to visualize this, with the one hundred hexagons—like pips on a cosmic roll of the dice—representing one hundred possible AI futures. Don't take their exact placement too literally, but they reflect my rough general view. Technological advancement has on balance had extremely positive effects

---

* The analogy is this: if I play in a $1/$2 poker game, equivalent to a low-stakes TRS 6, the game is highly unlikely to have a substantial effect on my net worth. But if I play a $10,000/$20,000 game—a TRS 10— it's all but impossible for it not to.

on society, so the outcomes are biased in our favor. But the further we go up the Technological Richter Scale, the less of a reference class we have and the more we're just guessing.

Utopia for Me, Dystopia for Thee

Really, once we get into the upper rungs of the Technological Richter Scale, we have so few precedents that maybe we should take all the hexagons and replace them with a series of question marks shrouded in a thick fog. Sci-fi and stranger-than-fiction sketches like **roon's** may be as appropriate a way to think about these outcomes as any. So let me add a pair of scenarios to **roon's** catalog to cover two possibilities that are often ignored in the AI risk debate. The first of these, Hyper-Commodified Casino Capitalism, is one in which some humans use AI to exploit the vast majority of humanity. The second, Ursula's Utopia, involves either humans or AIs giving up technological progress for the sake of sustainability.

Hyper-Commodified Casino Capitalism. roon's article on AI scenarios included a screenshot with a series of whimsically named futures from a Reddit post. One of them was called Hyper-Commodified Cocaine Capitalism, but something in my brain—maybe this is a tell—changed "cocaine" to "casino." When I saw it, I recalled our investigation into the modern gaming industry in chapter 3, including how casinos use algorithms to manipulate gamblers into spending more on slot machines.

What if you extrapolated that outward? The commercial applications of AI are just now coming into view. OpenAI is nominally still a hybrid between a for-profit and a nonprofit, but the failed coup against Altman by the nonprofit board in November 2023* made clear that the profit motive (and the loyalty of engineers like **roon**) will steer its direction. However, the business impacts will come soon. I already know political operatives using Meta's open-source AI to tweak campaign

---

* The board's attempt to fire Altman was sometimes portrayed in news accounts as an effective altruist revolt against Altman since some board members had ties to EA. But my reporting suggests the story is more boring and it was mostly just an internal power struggle between Altman and members of the board he thought were disloyal. "In a novel, there'd be some mysteries here, but this is real life and it's not obligated to make narrative sense," said Shear, the interim OpenAI CEO.

messaging for 2024. Corporate profits are at record highs, and there is some evidence this is because companies are using algorithms to induce customers to spend more on categories like fast food.

Casinos can be great—if you're a person who has high agency. That term refers not merely to having options but *good* options where the costs and benefits are transparent, don't require overcoming an undue amount of friction, and don't risk entrapping you in an addictive spiral. If you're a person with high agency, you can walk right past the slot machines at the Wynn toward its cornucopia of pools, shows, and restaurants (or to the poker room). But if you're caught in the rat race of loyalty programs and algorithmically optimized games in the midtier casinos, it's less clear how much agency you have—and if you're spinning the slot reels at a locals casino six hundred times an hour because you've become hopelessly addicted, you don't have much agency at all.

What if Sam Altman's dreams of an AI that alleviates global poverty don't come true? Instead Hyper-Commodified Casino Capitalism imagines us stuck in a TRS 8, a notably worse but still recognizable version of the present day. The world becomes more casino-like: gamified, commodified, quantified, monitored and manipulated, and more elaborately tiered between the haves and have-nots. People with a canny perception of risk might thrive, but most people won't. GDP growth might be high, but the gains will be unevenly distributed. Agency will be more unequal still; a few large companies, aided by their AIs, will have more power than democratically elected governments. Most people won't have fulfilling, meaningful jobs, and many will hand their decision-making over to AIs that purport to have their best interest in mind but instead trap them in a loop of button-clicking compulsions. Are these AIs making people happy? Well, they're making people *content*, for that's what the algorithms will optimize for. Happiness is hard to measure. The soul of humanity dies a slow and unmourned death at some point in the mid-2050s.

Ursula's Utopia. Sci-fi is the River's favorite fiction genre, but the pioneering science fiction writer Ursula K. Le Guin wouldn't have liked the River. "The rationalist utopia is a power trip," she wrote—"an either/or situation as perceived by the binary computer mentality." But Le Guin's own vision of utopia also left me feeling haunted.

Le Guin's 1985 book, *Always Coming Home*, describes California some centuries or millennia from now. There has been an apocalyptic disaster—perhaps from environmental degradation, but no one is quite sure—and there are the remnants of a technologically advanced civilization that sounds a lot like Silicon Valley, a "peninsula sticking out from the mainland, very thickly built upon, very heavily populated, very obscure, and very far away." But a group of people called the Kesh—there are perhaps thousands of them but not all that many—have survived to live fulfilling lives in a peaceful, agrarian, polyamorous utopia full of poetry and wholesome food from the land.

I'd obviously rather have this world than one where humanity goes extinct. It is sometimes not clear what the endgame is for the techno-optimists. Even if we fade the 1-in-6 chance of existential catastrophe that Toby Ord estimates over the next century, there's the century after that to contend with, and the next one. In *Always Coming Home*, the notion of a *sustainable* future at least enters into the equation.

But there is a catch—with Le Guin and her utopias, there is always a catch.* Left behind from the previous civilization is something called the City of Mind, a network of cybernetic, superintelligent computers that bears an uncanny resemblance to a large language model. The City has compressed all of humanity's knowledge into digital form—"its existence consisted essentially in information"—and you may ask questions of the City, but it won't ask questions of you. However, it seems to protect the Kesh from a more aggressive rival tribe called the Condor. The narrator of the book isn't entirely clear how; maybe it's a well-aligned AI and refuses to answer Condor requests on how to build advanced weaponry, or maybe it has benevolently seen to it that the resources to develop these weapons are no longer readily available. All of this, of course, is richly ironic. What if humans are too dumb to realize that our technological growth isn't sustainable—but after some horrible catastrophe, the superintelligent technology that we build *does* realize that and prevents us from further technological progress?

The other catch is that this is Le Guin's utopia—and not mine. Where are the things *I* like—the poker games, the sporting events, the sushi flown in from Japan? And doesn't all of this sound a little . . . boring? Maybe the point of life is to compete, progress, and undertake risk.

---

* One of Le Guin's most famous short stories, "The Ones Who Walk Away from Omelas," is about a utopia that depends upon the perpetual torture of a small child.

(I'm biased by spending too much time in the River, but this seems somewhat hardwired in human nature.) Anyone's totalizing vision of the future, be it Le Guin's, Marc Andreessen's, or mine, is someone else's nightmare. "Utopia always leaves somebody out," Émile Torres told me.

The Best Arguments for and Against AI Risk

This tour of the River will end soon. It's last call at the snack bar, and those of you who need your parking validated should see one of my assistants in their fetching fox-colored vests. I'm going to close with a quick summary of what I think are the best arguments for and against AI risk. Then in the final chapter, 1776, I'll zoom out to consider the shape of things to come—the moment our civilization finds itself in—and propose some principles to guide us through the next decades and hopefully far beyond.

The Steelman Case for a High p(doom)

When I asked Ajeya Cotra for her capsule summary for why we should be concerned about AI risk, she gave me a pithy answer.

"If you were to tell a normal person, 'Hey, AI companies are racing as fast as possible to build a machine that is better than a human at all tasks, and to bring forward a new intelligent species that can do everything we can do and more, better than we can'—people would react to that with fear if they believed it," she told me. There are a lot of "intricacies from there." But "how comfortable and at ease should we be with just that bare fact?"

The bare facts are these: (1) ever since Google's landmark transformer paper, AI has been progressing at a much faster rate than nearly anybody save for Yudkowsky expected; (2) Silicon Valley is flooring the accelerator—Altman reportedly wants to raise $7 *trillion* for new facilities to manufacture semiconductor chips; (3) and yet, the world's leading AI researchers *don't even understand very much about how any of this works.* It is not only rational to have some fear about this; it would be irresponsible *not* to have some. But let's consider a few other worrying points of context.

- **Our institutions aren't performing well at a moment when we need them to.** If the best analogies for AI are the nuclear bomb and the Industrial Revolution, those cases also speak to important differences from our current moment. Unlike the government-led Manhattan Project, AI is being developed by private companies. "We're sleepwalking into handing over the future to solely market-driven enterprises that become functionally ungovernable," said Jack Clark, an OpenAI expat who left to cofound the more safety-focused AI firm Anthropic.

And unlike during the Industrial Revolution, which coincided with the Enlightenment, we have not yet developed new values and institutions to help guide our course. There is a rich scholarly debate about what came first during the Industrial Revolution: the ideology or the technology. "It's the idea of liberalism. That's the real secret sauce," said Deirdre McCloskey, an economic historian at the University of Illinois Chicago who has extensively studied the Industrial Revolution. "The idea that hierarchies, husband/wife, king/subject, master/servant, should be flattened." The closest that anybody has come to articulating a new set of values for our brave new world are the effective altruists—but as we've seen, their philosophy has a few kinks to work out.

Meanwhile, during COVID, the most recent acute global crisis, the world performed miserably. I'm not one of those people who thinks you could have tweaked one or two things and prevented the pandemic. But even with every incentive to get it right,* we got it nearly all wrong, winding up with a worst-of-all-possible-worlds outcome of both a massive

---

* Unlike with global warming, where higher atmospheric CO_2 levels will persist for many decades and affect the entire planet, COVID had highly localized and immediate effects—and yet we still blew it.

death toll *and* unprecedented constraints on liberty, well-being, and economic activity—*and* we can barely lift a finger to prevent the next pandemic. Silicon Valley has its problems *and* the Village does, and *both* have
lost the trust of the broader population.

- **The domain experts are probably right about p(doom).** So far, I
  haven't weighed in on who I thought had the better side of the argument in Tetlock's forecasting tournament—but I think it's the domain experts who study x-risk specifically and not the outside view
  provided by the superforecasters. I don't say that unequivocally;
  there's something to the critique that when you have a hammer
  (you're paid to study x-risk), everything looks like a nail (you'll see
  a lot of x-risk). But unlike many subject-matter experts, most people in the x-risk community are fox-like—the cautious Cotra is more
  typical than the provocative Yudkowsky. They're often trained in
  the teachings of EA and rationalism, which, for all their faults,
  mostly adhere to a standard of high argumentative hygiene where
  ideas are debated in detail and in good faith.

Specifically, the domain experts are probably right that the reference
class for AI ought to be relatively narrow, and therefore less reassuring.
Existential risk itself is a relatively new idea, and there are not many technologies aside from nuclear weapons that experts credibly believed could
wipe out all of humanity.*

- **Expected value dictates that even a small chance of x-risk should be
  taken much more seriously.** You can wind up in some weird eddies
  of the River when considering *very* remote risks—say, a purported 1
  in 100,000 chance of an outcome with supposed infinite negative
  utility.† But that's not what we're dealing with here. Even if p(doom)

---

* Biotechnology and nanotechnology are also sometimes cited as x-risks, but biotechnology has not been
developed to its full capabilities yet and nanotechnology has hardly been developed at all. There's also
climate change, although most people in the x-risk community think the threats from climate change
are merely *catastrophic* rather than *existential*. Even if you disagree with them on that point, the theme is
that all of these problems (including man-made climate change) are relatively new.
† This is sometimes referred to by Yudkowsky and others as "Pascal's mugging"—the flip side of the
French mathematician Blaise Pascal's famous "wager" in which he contended that you should believe in
God because if there's even a small chance that God is real, you'll get an infinite benefit (ascending to
Heaven for eternity) from believing in him.

is only 2 percent—the very lowest end of my wide range—and the risks are merely *catastrophic* rather than *existential*, the expected-value loss is high compared to most threats that society takes care to avoid.

The Steelman Case Against a High p(doom)

When I asked Cotra for her best rebuttal to people with a high p(doom), she said it's less about "the technical facts" and more about "expecting humanity's response to be smarter versus dumber." So let's start there.

- **Silicon Valley underestimates the coming political backlash to AI.** Americans might not agree on much, but many people are already worried about AI doomsday, and there is a bipartisan consensus that we ought to proceed carefully; a January 2024 poll found that large majorities of Americans agreed with statements by both Democratic and Republican leaders urging caution on AI. Lately, Silicon Valley has been right to bet against the Village, but it's underestimated it in the past, and with strong enough political incentives it may get its act together. Entrenched interests will protest against the loss of jobs. There will be regulatory burdens like those imposed by the EU and legal challenges like the *New York Times* lawsuit against OpenAI. There are resource constraints and even potential resource conflicts, like between China and the U.S. over Taiwan, which manufactures the majority of the world's semiconductor chips. And one wonders how the developing world will react to technologies that could further entrench the position of the world's superpowers. Secular Western liberal values are not necessarily winning out; some forecasts actually project the religious share of the world's population to increase because religious countries have higher birth rates.

So when Silicon Valley leaders speak of a world radically remade by AI, I wonder *whose* world they're talking about. *Something* doesn't quite add up in this equation. Jack Clark has put it more vividly: "People don't take guillotines seriously. But historically, when a tiny group gains a huge amount of power and makes life-altering decisions for a vast number of people, the minority gets actually, for real, killed."

- **AI types underestimate the scope of intelligence and therefore extrapolate too much from current capabilities.** This argument can be a rabbit hole, so I'm just going to give you the express version. Many experts I spoke with believe the scope of what AI can do is still fairly circumscribed. ChatGPT's success at language-related tasks *has* been remarkable, but it's at least plausible that this says more about language than it does about AI—that language is more gamelike, structured, and strategic than was once assumed. Progress on AI in the physical world has been much slower, with repeated overpromises in fields like self-driving cars. "AIs have been good at chess for a long time. We still don't have a robot that can iron clothes," said Stokes.

AI's lack of sensory experience and emotional intelligence could also be a big constraint—or a danger if we assign it tasks it isn't well suited for. "There's a lot of evidence in psychology that our bodies impact the way we think, and the way we conceptualize the world and the way we conceptualize other people isn't captured in machines without bodies," said Mitchell.*

- **Scientific and economic progress faces a lot of headwinds, and that changes the balance of risk and reward.** In my conversation with **roon**, he used a "tech-bro" term: secular stagnation. Formally, this refers to a chronic condition of little or no economic growth, often coupled with low inflation and interest rates. Informally, it's used more loosely. It doesn't necessarily imply that the economy isn't growing at all—in the U.S., for instance, GDP has grown at a rate of about 2 percent per year so far in the twenty-first century. But it means that progress is sluggish, that the economy is not growing as fast as it once did, or at the very least that the rate of progress isn't accelerating. It reflects a pessimistic view of the condition of the modern world. You might expect this to be an unpopular position in

---

* You might recall that we came to a similar conclusion about Wall Street traders and poker players in chapter 2; our bodies provide us with actionable intelligence that our conscious minds have trouble articulating.

Silicon Valley—the land of techno-optimism—but in fact it's common there, often articulated by people like Altman. "There are all these reasons that scientific progress has slowed down. But a big one is the problems have just gotten hard," he told me.

Of course, this can be self-serving. In Altman's case, he made the claim as part of a riff on why we do need to build AI despite the risks it poses. Still, this is a vital question. "If you're driving in the fog, and you're not sure where the cliff is, there's something to be said for slowing down," said Shear. In deciding whether to tap the brakes, it helps to know how fast you're going in the first place—and we aren't necessarily going that quickly.

Now it's your turn to decide whether to push the button. Except, it's not the "go" button that I imagined Sam Bankman-Fried pressing. Instead, it's a big red octagonal button labeled STOP. If you press it, further progress on AI will stop permanently and irrevocably. If you don't, you won't get another chance to press the button for ten years. Do you push the button? Do you opt out of the gamble that civilization is taking with AI—or do you go where the action is?

I wouldn't push the button. I wouldn't push it because I think the case for secular stagnation is reasonably strong, enough to alter the balance of risk and reward for AI. I wouldn't push it because I believe in optionality, giving ourselves more choices in the future rather than fewer. I wouldn't push it because I think it's self-serving; my standard of living is high, but 85 percent of the world still lives on less than $30 a day; this is not considered extreme poverty, but it's a long way from a prosperous life. And I wouldn't push it because I think it's a cop-out. Civilization needs to learn to live with the technology we've built, even if that means committing ourselves to a better set of values and institutions.

1776

Foundation

Ever since 1776, we risk-takers have been winning.

The American Revolution was "as radical and as revolutionary as any in history." The U.S. was the first country explicitly founded in the liberal* values of the Enlightenment, meaning things like freedom of religion, equality, the rule of law, democracy, and the free market. America's founders had taken a huge gamble; the British army was vastly larger and better trained. If DraftKings was around back then, the Yankees would have been massive underdogs.

But even as America won its bet on independence, something else was stirring in Britain: the Industrial Revolution. For millennia, the world's economy had been stagnant, with growth of perhaps 0.1 percent per year. The very idea of progress was foreign. Nothing much was happening— until suddenly it did.

Take a plot of English GDP growth over time.† You can see some kinks in the graph, reflecting the challenges that our civilization has had to overcome, from the world wars to the Great Depression to COVID. But

---

* This is to be distinguished from the way "liberal" is sometimes used in the U.S. as a synonym for left-wing. In most of the world, it's used to refer to this classic tradition of liberalism instead.
† I prefer using this data to the entire world's figures because England's data is considered by experts like McCloskey to be more reliable over this long period—and because England was among the first countries to experience the Industrial Revolution.

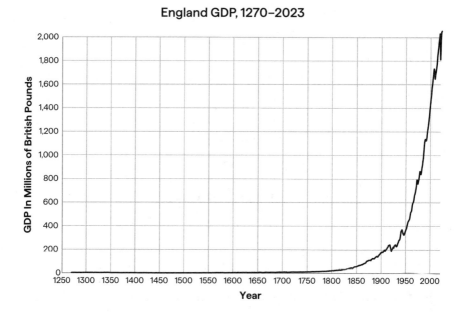

England GDP, 1270–2023

although progress hasn't always been *smooth*, it has been *persistent* since some point in the late eighteenth century. Although it's artificially precise to peg the inflection point brought about by the Industrial Revolution to a single year, 1776 is as good a choice as any, said Deirdre McCloskey. That orbit around the Sun not only witnessed the Declaration of Independence, but also the publication of Adam Smith's *The Wealth of Nations*, the foundational work of modern economics. It's also at about this point that England's economy began to grow like it never had before. Over the course of a century and a half, England's annual GDP growth rate rose prodigiously, climbing from 0.4 percent between 1725 and 1750 to 2.7 percent between 1850 and 1875.

This growth was fueled by governmental policies that encouraged *calculated risk-taking*. "Medieval peasants, like poor people now or anywhere, were close to the edge, and they had to be really careful not to fall over it," said McCloskey. There had been flickers of progress in England and the rest of the world, but the flame always blew out. The Enlightenment found a magic elixir to keep it burning. Between the introduction of private property rights protecting their upside gains and the social safety net protecting their downside, suddenly those peasants could "have a go"—McCloskey's term, a Britishism for taking a chance on a better life. Initially, of course, this was an opportunity afforded only to free (i.e., white) men, but gradually the franchise expanded; Britain abolished slavery in 1833, women incrementally gained property rights, and society grudgingly became more tolerant toward LGBTQ people and others who might once have been marginalized but now have a chance to have a go.*

Since 1776, the world has never been the same. "I mean, look all around you," said McCloskey, and I peered out my office window toward Madison Square Garden and the skyscrapers of Midtown Manhattan. It's not the prettiest view of New York, but it's something no medieval peasant could have imagined.

But it's not just we privileged Americans who have benefited from economic growth. In 1968, the Stanford biologist Paul Ehrlich wrote the book *The Population Bomb*, which predicted that "the battle to feed humanity was over" and that "millions of people [would] soon starve to death." The book began with a misanthropic[†] screed inspired by a trip he'd recently taken to India, where Ehrlich sat in a taxi "one stinking hot night in Delhi" and braved the "hellish" scene to make his way "slowly through the mob." He decided that the problem with humans was that there were too many of them: "People visiting, arguing, and screaming. People thrusting their hands through the taxi window, begging. People defecating and urinating. People clinging to buses. People herding animals. People, people, people, people."

Ehrlich thought there were too many people—but there would soon be a lot more of them. In 1968, there were 530 million people in India. Now India has a population of 1.4 billion. However, the number of Indians living in extreme poverty has *fallen* from 350 million to 140 million. You don't have to be a hard-core effective altruist to recognize that if Ehrlich's policies for population control had been implemented, it would have been a

---

* Including people like Deirdre, who transitioned to female in 1995 at a time when that was highly unusual, especially in a relatively conservative field like economics.
† That's the most polite term I might concede to Ehrlich. A better term might be "racist."

catastrophe, denying billions of people the chance to lead a profound and abundant life.

That's why I don't want to push that big red STOP button. My life is pretty nice. But I don't think I have any right to foreclose the prospect of prosperity to the rest of humanity.

Zoom in toward the most recent years of the graph, and the story isn't so encouraging. England's growth rate peaked in the postwar years between 1950 and 1975 and has slowed since. The UK has its share of problems, having churned through four prime ministers between 2019 and 2022, but it isn't alone in this respect. Global GDP growth also peaked in the 1960s and early 1970s—the world is still growing, but more slowly.

England GDP and Population Growth Rates at Periodic Intervals

Period	Population	Real GDP per capita	Real GDP
1270-1400	-0.6%	+0.3%	-0.3%
1400-1500	-0.1%	+0.1%	-0.0%
1500-1600	+0.5%	+0.0%	+0.6%
1600-1700	+0.4%	+0.3%	+0.6%
1700-1725	+0.3%	+0.3%	+0.6%
1725-1750	+0.2%	+0.2%	+0.4%
1750-1775	+0.6%	+0.2%	+0.8%
1775-1800	+0.9%	+0.6%	+1.5%
1800-1825	+1.4%	+0.2%	+1.6%
1825-1850	+1.2%	+0.7%	+1.9%
1850-1875	+1.2%	+1.4%	+2.7%
1875-1900	+1.2%	+0.7%	+1.8%
1900-1925	+0.7%	+0.3%	+1.0%
1925-1950	+0.5%	+1.4%	+1.9%
1950-1975	+0.5%	+2.5%	+3.0%
1975-2000	+0.2%	+2.4%	+2.6%
2000-2023	+0.6%	+0.9%	+1.6%

And there are many other signals of secular stagnation. Consider:

- Life expectancy has flattened out in the U.S.

- Fertility rates are now well below replacement level in much of the industrialized world—the population is aging and will have to be supported by a proportionally smaller workforce.

- The number of electoral democracies peaked in 2004 and has since begun to decline.

- The share of the world's population living in a democracy has declined at an even steeper rate, in part because India and its 1.4 billion people is now considered more autocratic than democratic.

- The planet continues to heat up, and climate change will subtract an estimated 11 to 14 percent from world GDP by 2050.

- Recent studies have found a decline in IQ in the U.S. and other countries and fewer Americans are going to college.

- The percentage of Americans saying they currently suffer from depression increased from 11 percent in 2015 to 18 percent in 2023.

At least technology is marching forward? Yes, but the pace of innovation isn't necessarily increasing, and those technologies aren't necessarily making us happier. With help from large language models and my Twitter followers, I compiled these lists of the top ten inventions in the first decade of the 1900s and the 2000s. The importance of any individual technology can be disputed (along with how to date its invention), but they should provide for a reasonable cross section.

Top Technological Inventions, 1900–1909 and 2000–2009

1900–1909	2000–2009
· Airplane (1903)	· iPhone (2007)
· Theory of relativity (1905)	· Facebook (2004)
· Air conditioning (1901)	· mRNA vaccines (2005)
· Ford Model T (1908)	· Human Genome Project (2003)
· Radio broadcasting (1906)	· Blockchain/Bitcoin (2008)
· Plastics (1907)	· USB drive (2000)
· Vacuum cleaner (1901)	· YouTube (2005)
· Electrocardiograph (1901)	· Google Maps (2005)
· Safety razor (1903)	· Cloud computing (2002)
· Hamburger (1904 or earlier)	· Tesla (2008)

At first this might look like a rout for the 1900s—it has airplanes and Einstein!—but I'm not sure that's entirely clear. It can take decades to realize the impact from new technologies; the blockchain and self-driving cars have perhaps not lived up to the hype so far, but who's to say where they'll be in twenty or thirty years? And the 2010s and the 2020s look more promising than the aughts between the AI transformer, gene-editing technologies like CRISPR, and even pharmaceuticals like semaglutide.*

So I do not mean to suggest that progress has ended; the world is still growing and changing. But at the very least, we do not appear to be on the verge of some sort of technological singularity. In fact, we may have come to take progress for granted. "Generating progress is abnormal," said Patrick Collison, the cofounder of Stripe, who has advocated for the foundation of a field he calls "progress studies," a multidisciplinary approach toward understanding improvement in the human condition. "Our starting point should always be surprise and appreciation that there is *ever* progress," he said.

Is America's increasing penchant for gambling another sign of stagnation? I love Las Vegas—but it's a bit disconcerting that Vegas seems so dynamic when the Village and much of the rest of the country doesn't. Ross Douthat, the *New York Times* columnist, has written about America's increasing decadence, so naturally I asked him about Sin City. Douthat employs the term "decadent" in a particular way, inspired by the French American historian Jacques Barzun's definition of it. Barzun used "decadent" to refer to a world that was "falling off," full of earthly delights but restless, stagnant, lacking a sense of adventure—en route to Hyper-Commodified Casino Capitalism. Douthat told me that by his definition, Vegas is actually less decadent than much of the United States. "It's a place where people are always building new things like the Sphere, right? That does not happen in the rest of America." But "compared to the dynamism of Hoover Dam, Manhattan Project-era America, it still has to be understood as decadent."

---

* Brand names of semaglutide include Wegovy and Ozempic—drugs that are beneficial for treating weight loss and perhaps for reducing compulsive behaviors.

Some scholars tie this feeling of stagnation to the end of the era of exploration. Every inch of the earth's surface has been mapped, so explorers like Victor Vescovo instead have to settle for the depths of the ocean. Outer space was supposed to be the next frontier, but the moon landing was in 1969 and there hasn't been a comparable achievement since then. The American space shuttle program that brought us heroes like Kathryn Sullivan was discontinued in 2011—it's no wonder that Elon Musk finds admirers for his ambitions of colonizing Mars. Even wars are increasingly fought remotely through drone strikes or precision missiles, reducing opportunities for physical bravery.

Perhaps we should view Las Vegas as Erving Goffman saw it, as a last resort for unfulfilled demand for risk that might once have been channeled elsewhere. The poker room might not be the most productive outlet for the River's energies, but at least your downside there is limited to the table stakes. Silicon Valley's inventions are more of a gamble for all of us, however. My concern, as I observed at the beginning of our tour, is that our risk preferences have become bifurcated. Instead of a bell curve of risk-taking where most people are somewhere toward the middle, you have Musk at one extreme and people who haven't left their apartment since COVID at the other one. The Village and the River are growing farther apart.

So the world finds itself at another pivot point. There was 1776, with the American Revolution, and there was the Industrial Revolution. There was 1945, with the end of World War II, and reorientation of the global order amid the emergence of the Information Age. And there is today. Because although the end of the Cold War had briefly seemed like we were on a glide path toward shared peace and prosperity, it is harder to make that case now.

Francis Fukuyama, the Stanford political scientist, is best known for his 1992 book, *The End of History and the Last Man*, which argued in the shadows of the Cold War that liberal democracy was the best way to channel humanity's conflicted impulses into shared prosperity. Fuku-yama has since grown more pessimistic, especially about America. "Decay happens when you have an institutional structure that's very conservative and can't be modified," he said when I spoke with him in 2022. "I think that's where we are in the United States right now. We have some clear in-stitutional deficits, things that aren't working well. And you can't fix them."

The End of History is sometimes remembered as a *prediction* that the world would become more democratic—but it's a nuanced book, and I in-terpret it more as a *proscriptive* argument that liberal democracy and free-market competition is tantamount to a game-theory equilibrium. Under liberal democracy, everyone gets to have a go. They won't always win—their preferred political parties will lose their fair share of elections, and some of their promising inventions will sputter out. But they'll get to com-pete, and they'll be treated fairly as people with agency. Even better, through the technological growth the winners generate, we'll create enough wealth to provide the losers with downside protection so they can have another go or two.

That's the theory, anyway—and as theories go, it's a pretty damned good one. Fukuyama sees human nature as more complex than either the River's EV-maximizing rationalism or the left's vision—evident every-where from Marx to Le Guin to effective altruism—of a supposed utopia without competition and risk. People *want* a certain amount of struggle, Fukuyama thinks, echoing the work of philosophers from Hegel to Nietzsche. They're full of what he calls "*thymos*," an ancient Greek word that roughly translates as "spiritedness." Nearly all people are possessed of isothymia, the desire to be recognized as equal.* They vary more in their megalothymia, the desire to be recognized as *superior*.

You've met a lot of megalothymiacs in the River; Musk is a paradig-matic example. Their impulses need to be kept in check—but risk-takers are also the ones who move society forward. "What you need is the

---

* A great deal of modern politics can be thought of as the struggle for dignity and respect. One thing ev-eryone from left-wing activists to MAGA fans share is that they're all highly aggrieved.

distribution of risk," Fukuyama told me. "So there's some high-risk-takers that in certain situations will be necessary for the survival of the community. But not in all circumstances. They can also get the whole community in trouble."

So I'll close this book with a peace offering from the River to the Village—an effort to meet in the middle. It takes the form of three foundational principles in line with the liberal values of the Enlightenment but updated for our modern age. In one sense, you could say they're drawn from my study of successful risk-takers—these are helpful concepts to bear in mind when you're gambling. But that's not the most important point. They're also ideas that can help us all to compete, prosper, and maximize humanity's chance of coming out ahead.

Agency * Plurality * Reciprocity

The French Revolution began in 1789, just thirteen years after ours in the United States. Travel to Paris, and you'll frequently see three words engraved into its limestone buildings—*liberté* (liberty), *égalité* (equality), *fraternité* (fraternity or brotherhood), an unofficial slogan of the Revolution inspired by the Enlightenment that survives as France's national motto today.

There is absolutely nothing wrong with these values, but I'm here to offer a version of them somewhat updated for our complicated, modern world. The words in *my* motto are less familiar, but I've chosen them for their precision: agency, plurality, and reciprocity.

Agency is a term I just defined in the last chapter, so I'll repeat that definition here: it refers not merely to having options but having *good* options where the costs and benefits are transparent, don't require overcoming an undue amount of friction, and don't risk entrapping you in an addictive spiral.

The concept of agency is pertinent in AI research; OpenAI describes an *agentic* AI system as one "that can adaptably achieve complex goals in complex environments with limited direct supervision." The definition applies nicely to human beings, too. *Liberté* is necessary and vital. But perhaps it's no longer *sufficient* for our complex environments and complex goals. We need to give people *real* choices, well-informed choices that don't require too much supervision or hand-holding. Endowing people with agency involves a certain amount of humility. Don't *presume* we know what people's preferences are—and give people room to evolve and adapt, because surely they will.

Agency is closely related to "optionality," which means preserving people's ability to make choices in the future as they gather more information. Optionality is the more explicitly gambling-adjacent concept; from poker to options trading, there is EV in having a choice you can exercise later. However, we shouldn't mistake the number of options for the number of *good* options. People can have trouble exercising options, especially when they're under duress. A game-theory poker solver might advise a certain line of play because it gives you the option to bluff later on in the hand. But if it's Day 6 of the Main Event, Phil Ivey is on the other side of the table, and you're too scared shitless to bluff, that option won't do you any good. We need to give people robust choices that they're capable of pulling off.

Plurality means not letting any one person, group, or ideology gain a dominant share of power. Gamblers know this concept; the most successful sports bettors, like Billy Walters, seek advice from a variety of human experts and computer models before placing their bets. Looking for consensus is nearly always more robust than assuming that any one model is good enough to beat the spread.

Although plurality is my closest modern analog to *égalité*, they don't quite mean the same thing. You don't necessarily want to give every model equal weight or every idea a seat at the table. Instead I endorse Nick Bostrom's idea of a moral parliament, which I imagined in chapter 7 as a mix of different philosophical traditions (e.g., utilitarianism, liberalism, conservatism, progressivism) that are credible and robust enough to deserve some consideration in your moral framework.

It is imperative, however, to be wary of totalizing ideologies, whether in the form of utilitarianism, Silicon Valley's accelerationism, the Village's identitarianism,* or anything else. In our fast-moving, topsy-turvy world, it's hard to know when an ideological movement might suddenly accumulate a *lot* of power very quickly, as utilitarianism did under Sam Bankman-Fried, and exercise its worst impulses. Even if you think a philosophy is *mostly* right,† the undistilled version of it is often dangerous.

Finally, there is **reciprocity**. This is the most Riverian principle of all, since it flows directly from game theory. Treat other people as intelligent and capable of reasonable strategic behavior. The world is dynamic, and although people may not be strictly rational, they're usually smart about adapting to their situation and achieving the things that matter most to them. Play the long game. Sure, other people sometimes give you opportunities to take advantage of them. But remember that, in a Nash equilibrium, any attempt to exploit your opponent runs the risk of being exploited in return. Avoid "noble lies" and positions taken out of naked political expediency. Not only can these harm your credibility—people will sniff out your bluff more often than you'd think.

Reciprocity is my analog to *fraternité*. Be empathetic to your brothers and sisters—but also practice what H. R. McMaster calls "strategic empathy." Put yourself in your rival's shoes, and at least as a default, treat them with the dignity you'd expect to be treated with yourself. Fukuyama's idea of isothymia is closely related to this. Few things motivate people more than the desire to seek revenge when they feel disrespected.

What if it's you who's been disrespected—or you're dealing with some asshole who has more megalothymia than isothymia? Well, I'm not going to have you read five hundred pages into a book about hypercompetitive gamblers and then say something like "turn the other cheek." Reciprocity sometimes does mean reciprocating. Deterrence plays a big role in game theory. Sometimes you need to stand your ground.

Nonetheless, we ought to give other people the benefit of the doubt

---

* That is, its habit of transforming every political dispute into a question of identity politics.
† The Riverian term for this is "directionally right," meaning pointing in the right direction.

more often. Respect and trust can be lost, but they should first be extended. Remember the lesson of the prisoner's dilemma: it describes when people behave individually rationally, but wind up collectively worse off because they have no way to trust one another. Trust in nearly every major American institution has declined, and in many cases I think that's been a reasonable reaction. But the world is a dangerous place. We've survived only eighty years with one technology that has the potential to destroy civilization, and we may be on the verge of inventing another. The Enlightenment emphasized individualism—but it was also concerned with how to create robust institutions, particularly liberal democracy and the market economy, that could channel our competitiveness to promote the shared interests of humanity. These institutions often fail, and they may be failing more often—they may even need some new foundations. But I'm not sure how much longer we're going to survive if we abandon hope of democratic governance that has a fighting chance of making reasonable decisions for the common good.

As we poker players say, *Glgl*. Good luck, good luck—for we may need it.

ACKNOWLEDGMENTS, METHODS, AND SOURCES

A bit more than three years ago, in the thawing days of a Northeastern winter and the COVID-19 pandemic, I decided that I wanted to write another book. It had been eight and a half years since *The Signal and the Noise* had been published, and I'd aged into middle-adulthood. With Disney facing economic headwinds, and my passion for being an "election nerd" having waned, I didn't expect my future to be at FiveThirtyEight. I was sure that I needed something new in my life. And I knew that I had a lot to say.

I just wasn't quite sure *what*, exactly. So I spoke with my editor Ginny Smith one afternoon and pitched her on three less than fully formed ideas: a book about gambling, a book about artificial intelligence, and a book about game theory. To my delight, Ginny and the team at Penguin Press immediately gravitated toward the gambling idea—the one I'd secretly been hoping they'd like—although, really, *On the Edge* wound up incorporating all three of those topics.

In the acknowledgments to *Signal*, I quoted from the author Joseph Epstein: "It is a lot better to have written a book than to actually be writing one." Although I'm immensely proud of where *Signal* ended up, it was my first long-form book when I'd been used to the instant feedback of blogging off the daily news cycle, and there were a lot of growing pains and false starts. With *On the Edge*, I was in love with the project from the start. Even while the proposal that my agent, Sydelle Kramer, and I put together was still in draft form, I was off to Florida for the Seminole Hard Rock Poker Showdown, beginning to make contacts in the River and level up my poker skills. I really enjoyed the research for this book—if nothing else, a good excuse to have lots of interesting conversations with lots of interesting people (and play a lot of poker)—but I also enjoyed the writing itself. This book took a lot of time, but it was time well spent.

However, that relatively pain-free experience reflected a tremendous amount of luck. Luck in the form of having Ginny as my editor, Caroline Sydney as my associate editor, and Ann Godoff and Scott Moyers running the show at Penguin Press. They were inordinately patient as the scope of *On the Edge* kept expanding and as deadlines kept being pushed back. (The proposal had called for "total length somewhere in the neighborhood of 60K to 85K words." This book is, um, longer than that. Not one of my better predictions.) Ginny provided just the right amount of steering at just the right times. An author couldn't ask for anything more.

I was also lucky to have Kendrick McDonald as my research assistant, whether it was in tracking down hard-to-reach sources or painstakingly translating my shorthand notes on sourcing into comprehensive endnotes. I was lucky to have Sydelle as my agent, always ready to serve as my advocate. I was lucky to have Andy Young as my fact-checker, and the team of copy editors at Penguin—Amy Ryan and Eric Wechter—who saved me from quite a few embarrassing errors, like when I inserted the letter "c" before the "k" in two instances of the name "Francis Fukuyama."

I also want to thank the many people who agreed to speak with me for this project—some of their contributions are adequately reflected in the text, but others aren't. The following people served as "spirit guides" in my navigation of the River. They were helpful in introducing me to other sources, or in vetting ideas that profoundly shaped my thinking even if they aren't cited by name a lot in the text: Brandon Adams, Steve Albini, Scott Alexander, Johnny Betancourt, Andrew Brokos, Joe Bunevith, Austin Chen, K. L. Cleeton, Tyler Cowen, Marie Donoghue, Tom Dwan, Andy Frankenberger, Mitch Garshofsky, Matt Glassman, Kirk Goldsberry, Bill Gurley, Cate Hall, Walt Hickey, Maria Ho, Anil Kashyap, Salim Khoury, Maria Konnikova, Ryan Laplante, Timothy B. Lee, Jonathan Little, Jeff Ma, Jason MacLean, Alex Mather, Sunny Mehta, Ed Miller, Daryl Morey, Zvi Mowshowitz, Toby Ord, Alix Pasquet III, Shashank Patel, Jon Ralston, Zach Ralston, Max Roser, Dan "C3PC" Singer, Michelle Skinner, Jason Somerville, Carlos Welch, Derek Wiggins, Karen Wong, and Bill Zito. (I've omitted the names of a few people from private poker games since I'm not one to kiss and tell.)

There are also some thank-yous that belong in a special category. Other than Ginny, nobody provided more helpful suggestions than my partner, Robert Gauldin, to whom this book is dedicated. And thank you to Zach Weinersmith, who drew the beautiful illustrated "map" of the River that you see in the introduction to the book and patiently indulged me as we worked to translate the fuzzy landscape I had in my head into something on the page. Thanks also to Randall Munroe, Piotr Lopusiewicz, and Jesse Prinz for granting us permission to use their illustrations with a minimum amount of teeth-pulling.

A few quick notes on methods and sources. The most important source material for this book is the series of roughly two hundred interviews with about as many sources (some sources were interviewed more than once; some interviews involved multiple people at a time). Nearly all interviews were conducted orally (about half in person and half remotely), and most were recorded. Where interviews were conducted by email or there were significant clarifying comments by email, I have noted this in the endnotes. Transcriptions were conducted by an AI service, Otter. In cases where a source is quoted verbatim, I double-checked the quote against the original audio transcription in most but not all cases. I used my judgment in determining how often to clean up interjections such as "like" and "um" or minor grammatical errors. In the large majority of instances where I claim a source "said" something, it means they said it to me directly, but exceptions where the context isn't clear are also detailed in the endnotes. About 80 percent of interviews were fully or predominantly on the record but others involved more complicated terms and conditions and some of the knowledge in this book is informed by background conversations.

Another important source is personal experience. This sometimes extended into informal conversations that I had at settings like a poker table. In cases where there was ambiguity about the nature of the interaction and how it might be represented in this text, I considered factors such as how informed the subject was, how much experience they had in dealing with journalists, and the publicness or privateness of the setting.

There are inevitably biases created by who agrees to speak with you. Some sources for the book are people I'd consider friends, and in a few cases close friends. I'm not in fifth grade, so I'm not going to make a list of my friends. But you should keep in mind that I'm a resident of the River and not just a visitor to it. I also derive income from various River-adjacent activities and at various times have had business conversations with people or organizations mentioned in the book, such as about consulting projects or speaking engagements. Some people in the River have checkered backgrounds, or are not entirely reliable narrators; to list every possible caveat about every source would require another twenty pages. I have tried to navigate all of this by citing source material meticulously, and having a lot of redundancy in not being overly dependent on any one contact.

One more newfangled acknowledgment: ChatGPT was a significant help in writing this book, serving as a creative muse when coming up with things like chapter subheadings, metaphors, and analogies, and for refining my understanding of technical topics that are likely to be well represented in its corpus. It is not a reliable fact-checker, which is why I needed Andy and the Penguin Press team. And I can't stand its prose style—all of the writing is my own. Nonetheless, it's a helpful tool for a nonfiction author and improved my productivity.

Finally, thank you for purchasing this book. I hope to have made it worth your while. But I'm still going to claw out every inch of EV that I can if we meet at the poker table.

—Nate Silver, Las Vegas, Nevada, April 10, 2024

GLOSSARY:
HOW TO SPEAK RIVERIAN

This is a reasonably complete list of technical terms used in *On the Edge* from the various fields it covers, such as poker, gambling, finance, AI, crypto, and effective altruism. I've also included a small handful of terms that didn't make it into the main narrative, but which you'll frequently encounter in conversations with Riverians or which provide a particularly colorful example of the way the River looks at the world.

Terms designated with asterisks (*) are not in widespread usage. They reflect pithy phrases used by one of my sources, or that I came up with myself for this book. Entries in italics are related terms that did not receive their own entry. In addition to my editor and research assistant, ChatGPT was helpful for vetting and refining definitions in this glossary.

10x, 100x, 1000x, etc.: A high return on investment, such as from a startup; 100x means recouping 100 times your initial stake.

+110, -110, etc.: In gambling contexts, these three-digit numbers are expressions of so-called American Odds; positive numbers indicate *underdogs* and negative numbers indicate *favorites*. See also: odds.

3-Bet, 4-Bet, etc.: In poker, a re-raise or re-re-raise, i.e., Alice bets, Bob raises, Carol 3-bets.

Abstraction: Deriving general rules or principles, divorced from their immediate context, from the things you observe in the world. See also: inductive reasoning.

Accelerationist: Someone who favors pushing forward on AI with few restraints; the opposite of an accelerationist is a *decel*. See also: e/acc.

Accelerator: A competitive program that provides mentorship and small financial investments to early-stage startups in exchange for an equity stake on the company.

Aces: A pair of pocket aces as your hole cards, the best possible starting hand in Hold'em.

Action: A robust gambling term: (1) a lucrative or high-stakes but risky opportunity ("Where the action is"); (2) a synonym for loose, aggressive play ("He's an action player"); (3) having a bet at stake ("She has action on the Bengals"); (4) when it's your turn to act in poker ("The action's on you, sir").

Advantage play: Being +EV at a casino game like slots that typically has a house edge.

Adverse selection: An asymmetry in which one party to a transaction has more information and takes advantage of it. Or informally, getting more action from customers you don't want, such as an all-you-can-eat sushi restaurant that sets up shop near a sumo wrestling tournament.

Agency: As defined more completely in chapter ∞, being empowered to make robust, well-informed decisions; knowing which factors are inside one's control.

Agent: In game theory or AI, an entity possessed of enough intelligence to make reasonable strategic choices.

AGI: Artificial general intelligence. The term lacks a clear definition but refers to at least broad human-level intelligence, sometimes as distinguished from *artificial superintelligence* (ASI), which surpasses that of humans.

AI: See: artificial intelligence.

AK: Ace-king, the best starting hand in Hold'em apart from a pocket pair.

Algorithm: A step-by-step set of instructions to execute a task or calculate an answer to a problem. The term often refers to a computer program but it doesn't have to; "take the freeway unless there's a Dodgers game; if there is a game, take the side streets" is an example of a simple algorithm. Colloquially, "algorithm" is sometimes used as a synonym for "model," but algorithms typically take a deterministic approach and don't use probabilistic techniques like simulation that models sometimes do.

Alignment (AI): The quality of AI systems being "well-behaved" and safely accomplishing their intended objectives. There are many devils in the details of this term, such as exactly whose objectives AIs ought to serve.

All-in: To wager all your poker chips. Or euphemistically, to fully commit to an action—but some Riverians consider this metaphor hackneyed.

Alpha: In finance, having an edge through skill or proprietary methods that allows you to achieve persistent above-market returns.

Analysis, analytics: "Analysis" refers to the process of breaking down complex subjects into simpler components. Conversely, "analytics" refers to the use of statistical methods to analyze data, particularly in business or sports.

Anchoring bias: The cognitive bias to be weighted down by information you learn early in your decision-making process, and then not adjust enough as new information is revealed. Often suggests a deviation from ideal Bayesian reasoning.

Angle: In sports betting, an edge resulting from a specific proprietary insight, such as a statistical property that bookmakers are overlooking. In poker, the term refers to a shady tactic that isn't strictly against the rules but is intended to deceive, such as putting your hands behind your chips to suggest you're going to go all-in but stopping after eliciting a reaction from your opponent; a player who constantly makes such plays is an *angle-shooter*.

Ante: A mandatory contribution to the pot paid by all players to seed the action at the start of a poker hand; see also: blind.

Arbitrage (Arb): A strategy to earn risk-free profit by exploiting price differences of the same asset in different markets.

(The) Archipelago*: The region of the River encompassing gray-market activities such as unregulated crypto exchanges; a place to avoid.

Arms race: An application of the prisoner's dilemma where each side's best move is to escalate by, e.g., acquiring more nuclear weapons so as not to be at a strategic disadvantage.

Artificial intelligence: As defined by noted AI expert Pope Francis (!): "a variety of sciences, theories, and techniques aimed at making machines reproduce or imitate in their functioning the cognitive abilities of human beings." Avoid using AI as a generic buzzword for data science.

Attack surface: The number of points of entry or attack, analogous to the topology of a physical object. For instance, the Starship *Enterprise* with lots of dangling bits has a larger attack surface than the spherical Death Star because there are more vulnerable places to shoot photon torpedoes at it.

Attention (AI): In a transformer model, the mechanism for assessing the importance of the semantic relationship between different pairs of tokens. For instance, the tokens "coyote" and "roadrunner" would be closely linked and would draw more attention from the model. See also: transformer.

Backdoor: Salvaging a losing bet through unlikely means, e.g., by catching two consecutive cards to make a flush, or when a team kicks a meaningless field goal to beat the point spread; the karmic opposite of a bad beat.

Backtest: Evaluating a model's performance on known, past data. Less reliable than using *out-of-sample* data, where you don't know the outcomes ahead of time. See also: overfitting.

Bad beat: Losing a bet that you were a clear favorite to win, especially if your opponent made a speculative play. A♣A♦ losing to 7♥2♣ (one of the worst hands in poker) is considered more of a bad beat than aces losing to another strong hand like pocket kings. Often extended by Riverians to everyday situations, e.g., getting a ticket when you were illegally parked for only five minutes to pick up your Starbucks order.

Bag of numbers*: A term conveyed to me by Nick Ryder of OpenAI for the mysterious inner workings of large language models.

Bankroll: The amount of money a player sets aside to gamble with. It's important to consider whether a bankroll can be replenished. Elon Musk might have a nominal bankroll of $100,000 in a poker game, but he has lots more money if he needs it. When a bankroll is unreplenishable, a player faces the risk of ruin.

Base rate: An empirically derived probability in the absence of other information; for instance, you could say the base rate of U.S. senators winning re-election is 90 percent based on the historical data.

Basis point: One one-hundredth of a percent, so a gain of 0.5 percent can be described as 50 basis points. A colloquial term for a basis point is a *bip*.

Bayesian: A thought process reflecting Bayes' theorem, indicating that you (1) have some initial beliefs or priors about the world rather than treating it as a blank slate; and (2) rationally update those beliefs based on the strength of new evidence.

Bayes' theorem: A foundational concept in probability theory, attributed to Reverend Thomas Bayes, used to update the likelihood of an event based on new evidence. It's expressed as $P(A|B) = P(B|A) \cdot P(A) / P(B)$, where $P(A|B)$ is the probability of A given B, and $P(B|A)$ is the probability of B given A. The theorem emphasizes the importance of reviving your initial beliefs (priors) in light of new information to arrive at more accurate conclusions (*posteriors*). For example, an unidentified bright object in the sky might initially be thought to be Venus, but if it starts glowing green, the probability of it being a UFO becomes more significant regardless of your initial assumption.

Beard (sports betting): Someone, ideally a known whale or degen, who makes a bet on your behalf, typically for a share of the profits.

Bednet: A trope in effective altruism to refer to a cheap, highly effective intervention, alluding to research that shows that hanging a simple mosquito net around a bed can prevent insect bites and therefore malaria deaths at a low cost.

Bell curve: See: normal distribution.

Bet sizing: The art of determining how much of your bankroll to wager, an overlooked component of success in many forms of gambling. See also: Kelly criterion.

Bid-ask spread: The typically narrow gap between the price at which you're offered to sell a stock (the "bid") and buy it (the "ask").

Big data: Very large data sets (e.g., hundreds of millions of customer records) that may be suitable for machine learning. Circa 2010–2016, the term was also used as a synonym for analytics but this has become archaic.

Black-Scholes: A well-known formula for pricing stock options, named after economists Fischer Black and Myron Scholes.

Black swan: A term coined by Nassim Nicholas Taleb to refer to purportedly extremely unlikely outcomes that were actually more likely than assumed because of the statistical properties of the underlying phenomenon.

Blinds (poker): Mandatory bets that rotate round the table to seed the pot, which every player is responsible for paying in turn. In Hold'em, there is a *small blind* and a *big blind*, with the former costing half as much. See also: ante.

Blockchain: A digital ledger of transactions in chronological order; for instance, the Bitcoin blockchain records all sales of Bitcoin. A blockchain is decentralized and distributed across multiple computers so as to provide a mechanism to verify transactions without relying on governments or the financial system. There are multiple blockchains—the Bitcoin blockchain and Ethereum blockchain are separate ledgers.

Blocker (poker): A card that affects the statistical distribution of your opponent's hand range. For instance, if you have the A♠, your opponent is less likely to have a flush in spades because you "block" the flush.

Board: The cards exposed so far in a poker hand; in Hold'em, these are community cards shared by all players.

Bookmaker: Someone who accepts sports bets. Bookmakers adjust their odds based on the betting so far, moving the line in the direction of the sharp action. See also: handicapper, a different term that this is sometimes confused for.

Bored Apes: A popular collection of NFTs more precisely known as the Bored Ape Yacht Club, which features droll monkeys in sailing uniforms. Less prestigious than CryptoPunks and more often associated with the NFT bubble of 2020–22; the term *apeing* refers to impulsively buying a new token or NFT collection without considering its underlying value.

Boredom Markets Hypothesis: A theory proposed by Matt Levine that attributed the run-up in NFT prices, meme stocks, and other speculative assets in 2020–22 to the boredom and anxiety caused by the COVID pandemic.

Bracelet (poker): The gold bracelet awarded for winning an event at the World Series of Poker; there are now more than one hundred bracelet events every year between live and online WSOP tournaments, but bracelets remain highly coveted.

BTC: An abbreviation for the current market price of Bitcoin, the native cryptocurrency of the Bitcoin blockchain.

Bubble (poker): The stage of a poker tournament just before cash prizes are awarded. It can compel significant departures in strategy, such as big stacks avoiding conflicts with one another while relentlessly attacking small stacks who are trying to survive just long enough to receive a minimum prize (*mincash*).

Bullet (poker): An entry into a tournament; buying into the same event multiple times is "firing multiple bullets."

Bust, Busted, Busto: Being eliminated from a poker tournament—or going broke and busting your bankroll.

Button (poker): The player who acts last after the flop; this is an advantage and warrants playing more hands. Named after a white button or puck labeled "DEALER" that rotates around the table. See also: dealer.

Buy-in: The cost to enter a poker tournament or the act of doing so.

Calibration: In statistics, the extent to which your predictions match your purported probabilities. For instance, if you forecast that a certain class of events will occur 20 percent of the time, having them happen 21 times out of a sample of 100 trials would indicate that your forecasts were well calibrated.

Call (poker): Matching your opponent's bet.

Calling station: A suspicious poker player who is loose and passive and calls rather than raising or folding; never bluff a calling station.

Call option, Put option: A "call option" is a contract granting the right to buy a stock later at a predetermined price, indicating a bullish outlook. A "put option," conversely, allows selling a stock at a specified price, representing a bearish position.

Canon: A work of art or science that is broadly known and highly regarded and presumed to be known by others within the community; Shakespeare is a part of the English literature canon. The adjectival form is *canonical*.

Capped (poker): Having played in such a way that you can't have a very strong hand and therefore can't deter aggressive play from your opponents.

Card counting: In blackjack—specifically blackjack, don't use this for other card games—keeping track of which cards have been revealed so far. If fewer high cards (e.g., kings, queens) have been revealed than low cards (e.g., 2s and 3s), blackjack can become +EV.

Cash game: As opposed to a tournament, a poker game with no fixed end point, where you play for the money on the table and can cash out your chips at any time.

Chalk (sports betting): Predictable bets on heavy favorites, often a sign of risk aversion.

Chase: After losing a bet, to continue betting until you get even—or go broke. The term implies tilt and desperation.

Check (poker): Passing when it's your turn to act when there's no bet so far, moving action clockwise to the next player.

Check-raise: Raising after you check and another opponent bets.

Chesterton's Fence: A reference to a parable by the philosopher G. K. Chesterton about a fence erected across a road for reasons you don't understand, invoked as a way to encourage conservatism in the face of uncertainty. You might not want to remove the fence without knowing why it was put there in the first place—it might protect against dangerous predators, for instance.

Chop: In gambling, to split up evenly; two poker players with the same hand at showdown *chop the pot*, and if they go out to dinner later, they might chop the bill if they each agree to pay half.

Classical statistics: Also called *frequentism*, methods centered around hypothesis testing. They are under threat both from Bayesians who dispute their premises, and from machine learning approaches that sacrifice interpretability for predictive accuracy.

Closing line value: A case in which the betting consensus moved in the direction of your bet. If you bet the Dallas Cowboys at -3 and the line later moved to Cowboys -4, the market agreed with your bet and you got good closing line value. Consistently getting closing line value is a sign of a winning bettor.

Cognitive bias: A systematic misconception that results in irrational behavior, often implying a failure of "common sense" or conventional reasoning. See also: confirmation bias, Gambler's fallacy.

Combo (poker): The permutations of a particular hand that are likely to be in a player's range. For instance, there are four combos of AK suited (A♣K♣, A♦K♦, A♥K♥, A♠K♠).

Community cards: In Hold'em, cards dealt face up and shared by all players. See also: flop, turn, river.

Compute (AI): When used as a noun, a shortening of "computing power"; the amount of resources you have at your disposal to power your models. See also: GPU.

Confidence interval: The range of uncertainty surrounding the estimated value of a data point or statistical prediction. For example, a 95 percent confidence interval of [150, 400] for a forecast of Patrick Mahomes's passing yards indicates a 95 percent probability that his yards will fall within that range.

Confirmation bias: The tendency to perceive any new evidence as confirming your previous conclusion, often a sign of poor Bayesian reasoning.

Conscientious contrarian*: Someone who makes a contrarian bet, but with a clear hypothesis for why other participants in the market are wrong, such as because they have other incentives that trade off with maximizing EV.

Consensus: In sports betting, the collective opinion of the public, though the term is ambiguous and can sometimes refer to the consensus of sharp action. In science, the consensus refers to prevailing (though not necessarily unanimous) expert opinion.

Consequentialism: The idea that the morality of actions should be determined based on their outcomes—in contrast to deontology, which posits that actions should be judged by their adherence to ethical precepts. See also: utilitarianism.

Cooler: When you have a strong poker hand but your opponent has an even stronger one—or you otherwise unavoidably lose your money despite playing reasonably.

Coordinated (poker): Cards such as J♠T♠8♦ that are close in suit and rank, providing for more straight and flush draws; these generally compel aggressive play.

Corpus (AI): The set of all text or tokens in the training data for a model; for an LLM like ChatGPT, the corpus can roughly be thought of as all human speech as expressed on the internet.

Correlation: A statistical relationship between two variables, e.g., ice cream sales are positively correlated with warm weather. Correlation does not necessarily imply causation: ice cream sales are also correlated with gun violence because both tend to peak in warm weather when many people are outdoors. The *correlation coefficient* is a statistical measure of correlation on a scale of -1 (*perfectly uncorrelated*) to +1 (*perfectly correlated*).

Cover (sports betting): When a team wins by enough points or loses by a narrow enough margin to beat the point spread.

Credit card roulette: When a group of degens go out for dinner and have the waiter randomly choose one credit card to stick someone with the entire bill.

Cromwell's Law or Cromwell's Rule: An admonishment not to make a forecast with a probability of exactly 0 or exactly 1. Named by statistician Dennis Lindley after Oliver Cromwell, who wrote: "I beseech you, in the bowels of Christ, think it possible you may be mistaken."

Cryptocurrency: A digital currency secured by a blockchain.

CryptoPunks: A set of ten thousand unique, arguably Warhol-esque digital images launched in 2017 that remains the gold standard of NFT collections. See also: Bored Apes.

Data science: Applied statistics, especially in a business context. Jargony, though better than some alternatives.

Dealer: The person who shuffles and deals cards in a poker game; in casinos, this is an employee who isn't playing in the game. Also refers to the player who symbolically has the dealer's position and acts last after the flop. See also: button.

Dealflow: The volume of incoming profitable investment opportunities; a well-networked VC has strong dealflow.

Deception value*: My term for the value of surprise in a game where it's important to be unpredictable—in contrast to *intrinsic value,** which is the success rate of a play absent deception value. For instance, in the NFL, a fake punt has little intrinsic value if an opponent knows it's coming, but it derives EV from deception value if it's only used occasionally. See also: mixed strategy.

Decoupling: Separating the elements of a complex issue. For instance, assessing a musician's vocal talent without considering her political views. Riverians love to decouple, thinking it allows for unbiased analysis, whereas Villagers like to consider facts in their broader political or social context.

Deductive reasoning: The process of applying general theories or principles to deduce conclusions about specific cases, e.g., using constitutional principles to determine legal practices in particular situations. See also: inductive reasoning.

Defect (game theory): To snitch or act self-interestedly rather than cooperate, as predicted by the prisoner's dilemma.

Degen, degenerate: A person who has a tendency to gamble, especially for high stakes, or otherwise to engage in debaucherous behavior. Often implies -EV gambling but can also mean making +EV bets beyond one's means. Sometimes used affectionately or self-deprecatingly; in the River, degens are more highly regarded than nits.

Deontology: From the Greek prefix *deon-* meaning "duty," the idea that the morality of an action should be judged based on ethical principles—in contrast to consequentialism, which holds that actions should be judged by their consequences.

Deterministic: The opposite of *probabilistic*: an outcome that is preordained or strictly predictable with probability of exactly 1 or 0.

Deterrence (game theory): Preventing aggression from your opponent through the threat of escalation, e.g., by credibly threatening to go all-in in poker or launch a retaliatory nuclear strike.

DFS: Daily Fantasy Sports, a game where you select a lineup of players on a fixed budget and accumulate points based on their real-life statistics. DFS preceded legal sports wagering in most U.S. states but has since been eclipsed by it.

Diminishing returns: The tendency for further amounts of the same good to have progressively lower marginal utility: the fiftieth Oreo you consume doesn't taste as good as the first. Financial gains generally have diminishing returns too: the first dollar you make has more marginal utility than the billionth one.

Directionally correct: Pointing in the right direction relative to the consensus. If your model predicts the Detroit Lions will win by 10 points and the point spread has them favored by 3, it made a directionally correct bet even if the Lions win by only 4.

Dirty Diaper: Three-deuce offsuit, the worst hand in poker, a complete load of crap—and therefore a fun hand to bluff with.

Discount rate: The penalty assigned to future time periods when calculating utility or the EV of an investment. More precisely, it refers to the percentage rate used to devalue future benefits or costs to their *present value*. A higher discount rate implies a shorter time horizon.

Domain knowledge: Expertise in a particular subfield.

Dominant strategy: In game theory, a move that is always the best play no matter what your opponent does; the opposite is a *dominated strategy*.

DonBest: The most well-reputed supplier of real-time sports betting odds. A DonBest screen is the sign of a serious bettor, the industry's equivalent to a Bloomberg Terminal.

Donkbet: A bet made unexpectedly when a player is out of position in poker and has behaved passively so far. *Donk*, short for *donkey*, is another of the many terms for a bad poker player. A donkbet, therefore, was classically seen as a losing tactic by a poor player—but ironically, solvers have since found that donkbetting is sometimes +EV.

Doomer: Someone with a high p(doom) who is extremely worried about existential risk from AI.

Doomsday machine: A device that automatically retaliates if it detects a nuclear strike, deterring a decapitating first strike.

Double down: In blackjack, doubling your initial bet and receiving only one more card; this is a +EV tactic when the dealer is likely to bust (for instance if you have a 10 against her 6). When speaking Riverian, avoid "double down" outside of this context: it is clichéd and we'll size you up for being a fish.

Downriver*: The region of the River focused on casino gambling.

Drawing dead: A situation wherein there is literally no chance to win even if everything goes perfectly from there forward. If the last flight of the evening from Phoenix to Chicago gets canceled and you have a 7:00 a.m. meeting in Chicago the next morning, you're drawing dead to make it on time unless you have a friend with a private jet.

Drowning child: A parable proposed by Peter Singer that asks us to consider whether we would get our suit dirty to save a drowning child in a shallow pond. Since it's obvious that the answer is yes—the child's life is more valuable than our suit—Singer uses it to encourage altruistic thinking under the construct of utilitarianism.

Dystopia: The opposite of a utopia, a profoundly bad world.

EA: See: effective altruism.

E/acc: Effective accelerationism, a loosely defined and sometimes trollish movement (the name is a play on effective altruism) that advocates for pushing forward on AI because the risks are either overstated or outweighed by the benefits. See also: techno-optimist.

Economist brain*: The tendency to think all decisions can be resolved through cost-benefit analysis.

Edge: Having a persistent advantage or being +EV over the long run. The casino has a house edge in roulette, for instance, because players will inevitably lose if they take enough spins.

Edge case: An example occurring in extreme or unusual circumstances that might not be suitable for generalization.

Effective altruism: A movement founded by Will MacAskill and Toby Ord that advocates for using rigorous analysis to determine how to do the most good. Originally focused on charitable giving, EA now extends these principles to evaluate other issues, like existential risk. EA has origins in utilitarian philosophy, although not all EAs are utilitarians.

Effective hedonism*: Applying data-driven methods to optimize fun stuff, like your sex life.

Empirical: Knowledge or conclusions derived from data and observation rather than theory or pure reasoning.

(The) Enlightenment: An eighteenth-century philosophical movement championing individualistic liberal principles such as liberty, equal rights, and the separation of church and state. These principles greatly influenced the U.S. Constitution and continue to shape Western liberal democracies and were pivotal to the Industrial Revolution, capitalism, and the rise of the market economy.

Envy-based economy*: A term coined by *New York* magazine critic Jerry Saltz to refer to the top-heavy art market in which some small percentage of works become focal points for envy and command much higher prices; these characteristics have carried over to the NFT space.

Epistemic humility: The recognition of the limits of one's knowledge and the ability to acknowledge uncertainty in understanding the truth, rooted in the study of epistemology, the philosophy of knowledge acquisition.

Equilibrium: See: game-theory equilibrium.

Equity (poker): Your share of the pot in expected-value terms, e.g., a player with a flush draw after the flop has roughly 35 percent equity since that's how often she'll improve her hand.

Error bar: A graphical representation of a confidence interval or margin of error, indicating a range of uncertainty around a data point.

ETH, Eth, Ethereum: Respectively, the ticker symbol (ETH) and colloquial term (Eth) for Ether, the native cryptocurrency of the Ethereum blockchain, which was developed by Vitalik Buterin to allow for smart contracts and other improvements over Bitcoin.

EV: See: expected value.

EV maximizer*: A typical citizen of the River: the type of person who always likes to crunch the numbers to figure out the most profitable "play." EV maximizers are sometimes accused of taking this too far, e.g., by building an algorithm to determine when they should leave their partner.

Excess returns: In finance, persistently higher returns on investment than the market consensus, adjusted for the level of risk. See also: alpha.

Existential risk: In the strictest sense, an outcome that would kill all humans—but some scholars also use it to refer to outcomes in which humanity's potential for flourishing would be permanently impaired. Use "existential" cautiously; *catastrophic risk* is a more nimble term.

Expected value: The result you expect to wind up with on average after many "spins of the wheel," given your knowledge of the odds when you place a bet or choose a course of action. The term strongly implies that you're facing a tractable problem with a quantifiable answer.

Exploitative strategy: An approach designed to take advantage of an opponent who isn't playing a game-theory optimal strategy. Be careful, because exploitative strategies can be counterexploited and open you up to EV loss.

Externality: A cost imposed on others that you don't pay for (as in a *negative externality* such as pollution) or a benefit that accrues to others (as in a *positive externality* such as technological progress) that you don't directly profit from.

Fade: To bet against certain outcomes or hope they do not happen, e.g., if you bet on the Celtics to win the Eastern Conference, you're fading rival teams like the Bucks and 76ers. In poker, a player fades cards that could make her opponent a better hand.

Feedback loop: A process wherein outcomes recursively affect the future behavior of the system. For instance, increased global warming causes more glaciers to melt, which causes further warming by reducing the reflectivity of the Earth's surface. A feedback loop can also be called a *virtuous cycle* or a *negative cycle* depending on whether the effects are seen as positive or negative.

Fermi paradox: The question of why humans have not yet detected extraterrestrial life despite the vastness of the universe. Under some interpretations, it suggests civilizations may not endure long enough to be detectable across space. Named after the Italian physicist Enrico Fermi, who famously inquired, "Where are they?" referring to the expected presence of alien civilizations.

First strike: A disabling nuclear attack that eliminates the opponent's ability to retaliate.

Fish (poker): A -EV, typically inexperienced player who you want in your game. Possibly derived in opposition to *shark*, i.e., a skilled player. The term is insulting and players are advised not to "tap the glass" of the aquarium by questioning a fish's skills. A rich fish who plays poker at high stakes is a whale.

Flip: After "coin flip," a poker situation where the odds are about 50-50, e.g., getting all-in with AK against pocket queens. Also called a *race*.

Flop: The first three of five community cards dealt face up in Hold'em. Because three cards are dealt simultaneously, the flop can dramatically change the equities in a hand.

Flush (poker): Five cards of the same suit.

Focal point: A place, idea, or object that gains significance through collective recognition, enabling coordinated decision-making. A focal point can become a *self-fulfilling prophecy*, i.e., everyone wants to go to Harvard because everyone else wants to go to Harvard.

Fold (poker): Giving up on your hand and pitching it to the dealer, losing any investment you've made in the pot.

FOMO: An acronym for "fear of missing out," the attitude of many participants during a market bubble.

Foom: An onomatopoeic word—imagine the sound of some server powering on in an OpenAI back office at a volume barely more than a whisper—to refer to a very fast AI takeoff.

Fox: Along with a hedgehog, one of two decision-making personality typologies proposed by Phil Tetlock. Per the Greek poet Archilochus—"The fox knows many things, but the hedgehog knows one big thing"—foxes tend to be incrementalist, probabilistic jacks-of-all-trades, and are often willing to compromise or defer to the wisdom of crowds.

Freeroll: A gambling situation in which you can't lose money but have a chance of winning something, occasionally colorfully extended by Riverians to real-life situations: "Come to the party. Maybe you'll meet someone—it's a freeroll!"

Friction: Constraints that make it harder for someone to exercise an option that is nominally available to them. Friction can be insidious, e.g., if a casino makes it hard to find the exit in an effort to have you continue gambling.

Fungible: The property of interchangeability: dollar bills are fungible—one is just as good as the next one—while fine works of art are not (if you buy a Picasso someone can't settle their bill with a Warhol).

Fun player: A bad amateur poker player. See also: fish.

Gambler's fallacy: The erroneous belief that outcomes of a randomly determined process will "balance out" over the short run, e.g., that if a coin has come up heads a number of times in a row, you should bet tails because it's "due." The *hot hand* is the opposite fallacy, e.g., the belief that you should bet on heads because heads are "hot," even though the process is random.

Game theory: The mathematical study of the strategic behavior of two or more agents in situations where their actions dynamically impact one another. It seeks to predict the outcome of those interactions, and to model what strategy each player should employ, to maximize their EV while accounting for the actions of the other players.

Game-theory optimal (GTO): In poker, play in accordance with that recommended by game theory, such as a Nash equilibrium derived by a solver. Informally, GTO refers to a style of play that is perceived as mathematically precise but rigid, in contrast to *feel players* who rely on intuition or *exploitative players* who rely on psychology and detecting flaws in their opponent. Sometimes extended by poker players to everyday decisions, e.g., "ordering from the app is GTO so you can skip the line at Chipotle."

Game tree: The exploding array of branches (outcomes) from different nodes (decision points) in a game. Chess has a much larger game tree than tic-tac-toe because there are far more possible actions.

Gaming: A euphemism for gambling used by industry professionals.

Genesis Block: The inaugural block in the Bitcoin blockchain, marking the beginning of its ledger. See chapter 6 for further context.

Getting (money) down: Placing bets; this term implies that you've had to overcome some friction to do this, such as because the sportsbook thinks you're sharp and wants to limit your action.

Gg: Internet slang (though sometimes spoken aloud as "gee-gee") for "good game;" used when a player is eliminated from a competition such as a poker tournament. Can be sympathetic, sarcastic, or self-deprecating.

Glgl: "Good luck" or "good luck, good luck"—a cheerful text message to send to your friend when she's just entered a poker tournament. If you're also in the tournament, her most appropriate reply is *LFG:* let's fucking go!

GPT: A series of large language models created by OpenAI; the most recent version is GPT-4. GPT stands for Generative Pretrained Transformer. "Generative" refers to how LLMs generate output (responses to user queries) rather than merely classifying data; see also: training and transformer.

GPU: Graphics processing unit, a chip originally designed for rendering graphics but which is highly efficient for general mathematical computations, making it the gold standard in AI research and applications. See also: compute.

Grand-world problem: An open-ended, complex, dynamic problem that doesn't lend itself to tractable answers through the use of algorithms or models. See also: small-world problem.

Ground truth: Unimpeachable facts that can be observed through sensory experience and that carry considerable weight in any model of the world; the loss of verifiable ground truth is one hazard of a more virtual world.

GTO: See: game-theory optimal.

Hallucination (AI): Often "creative" false information produced by LLMs when they don't know the answer but pretend they do.

Handicapper: Someone who forecasts the outcome of sporting events to place bets herself or to sell her odds publicly—as opposed to a bookmaker, who accepts wagers.

Head-fake (sports betting): A bet intended to deceive sportsbooks into moving their line, followed by a larger bet on the other side once they do. Essentially, a form of bluffing.

Heads up (poker): A poker game with only two players.

Hedge: To reduce variance by making a bet with a negative correlation with your overall position, e.g., if you bet way too much on the Lakers in a tilt-inspired moment, you might make a smaller bet on the Celtics to hedge your exposure.

Hedge fund: A private firm that makes complex financial bets, often based on proprietary knowledge or statistical models; hedge funds do not necessarily hedge their risk.

Hedgehog: Along with a fox, one of two decision-making personality typologies proposed by Phil Tetlock. Hedgehogs tend to be stubborn, ideological, and to go "all-in" on particular theories of the case. They may be less reliable at forecasting and incremental decision-making, but are more natural leaders since their resolve may compel others to join them.

Hero call, hero fold: In poker, being a "hero" by calling with a weak hand that you'd ordinarily be expected to fold, or folding a strong hand that you'd ordinarily be expected to call with. A hero play implies that your opponent is behaving predictably so you can deviate from game theory.

Heuristic: A simple, practicable rule of thumb that has proven reliable more often than not. For instance, my poker coach (Andrew Brokos) coined the heuristic "they always have it," which means most players don't bluff enough so you should fold if your opponents make a large bet (they probably "have it"—a good hand).

HODL: Hold On for Dear Life; in crypto, a rallying cry used to implore someone to hold on to their assets rather than selling.

Hold'em: The most popular form of poker, beloved because it encourages aggressive, risky play. In *Texas Hold'em*, each player is dealt two private cards (hole cards) followed by a sequence of five face-up community cards that are shared by all players. In the related Omaha Hold'em, four private cards are dealt to each player, who must use exactly two to form a hand. Colloquially, "Hold'em" alone nearly always refers to the two-card variant.

Hold percentage: The percentage of betting action that a casino retains. For instance, American roulette has a hold percentage of 5 percent; for every $100 wagered, the casino's EV is +$5.

Hole cards: Two cards dealt face down to each player in Hold'em, which they can use along with the five shared community cards to make a poker hand.

House edge: The casino's expected profit in a game that is -EV for players.

Hyper-Commodified Casino Capitalism*: A dystopian near-term future where the world becomes more casino-like and some small percentage of people use AI to exploit the masses.

If you can't spot the sucker: A reference to every poker player's favorite movie quote from Mike McDermott in *Rounders*: "Listen, here's the thing. If you can't spot the sucker in your first half hour at the table, then you are the sucker."

Impartiality: The ethical principle, associated with utilitarianism and effective altruism, that we should place no more weight on the lives of those who are close to us than those who are far away—e.g., that a child's life in Africa is just as valuable as the life of a child in your hometown, or even your own child's life.

Index fund: An investment vehicle that tracks a major stock index like the S&P 500. Often regarded as a canny investment because they have low transaction fees and it's hard to outthink Wall Street.

Indifferent (game theory): The condition of having two or more choices that have the same EV. Game theory dictates that you should randomize between them under a mixed strategy.

Inductive reasoning: Deriving broad generalizations from specific observations. For instance, studying patterns in human behavior to formulate overarching moral theories. See also: deductive reasoning.

Industrial Revolution: A transformative era starting in the late eighteenth century in England and Northern Europe, characterized by swift technological advancements, mechanical inventions, and the adoption of Enlightenment values. The Industrial Revolution marked an inflection point from centuries of economic stagnation to sustained growth and progress.

Infinite ethics: A branch of moral philosophy concerned with the problems of an infinite universe, which often gives rise to paradoxes or counterintuitive conclusions.

Inflection point: The point at which a curve sharply changes direction—or less formally, when the behavior of a system begins to radically change.

Innovator's dilemma: Clayton Christensen's theory for why leaner insurgent companies tend to displace more powerful incumbents. Christensen's thesis focused on companies being weighed down by too many commitments to existing customers, but the concept can be extended to other commitments, like those to shareholders and employees.

Interpretability (AI): The degree to which the behavior and inner workings of an AI system can be readily understood by humans.

Inside straight: See: straight.

Instrumental convergence: The hypothesis that a superintelligent machine will pursue its own goals to minimize its loss function and won't let humans stand in its way—even if the AI's goal isn't to kill humans, we'll be collateral damage as part of their game of Paper Clip Mogul.

IRR: Internal rate of return; the annualized growth rate of an investment.

Isothymia: A term adapted from Plato by Francis Fukuyama to refer to the profound desire to be seen as equal to others. See also: megalothymia.

Iteration: One cycle in a repetitive process in which a model's estimates are progressively improved by incorporating the results from the preceding cycle.

J-Curve: The tendency in venture capital for a fund's returns to initially dip into the negative before becoming positive, forming a J-shaped pattern. It occurs because underperforming investments are identified early on, while successful ones take longer to mature and yield returns.

Kelly criterion: A formula derived by John Kelly Jr. that calculates what percentage of your bankroll you should bet given the odds and your estimate of the probability the bet wins. It seeks to maximize expected value while minimizing risk of ruin. Mathematically, it can be expressed as edge/odds, indicating that you should bet more as your edge grows larger and less as the odds grow longer. Bettors also use the term as an adjective, e.g., *half-Kelly* refers to betting half the amount recommended by the formula.

Keynesian beauty contest: A hypothetical contest described by John Maynard Keynes in which participants win prizes by guessing how beautiful other participants will find the contestants. See also: focal point.

Large language model: An AI model that generates text replies to user prompts. Modern LLMs are trained using machine learning from a large corpus of text, using transformers to understand the semantic relationships between different tokens in the user's request. See also: GPT.

LessWrong: The rationalist blog founded by Eliezer Yudkowsky, known for vigorous debates on nerdy topics.

Leverage: A risky technique involving borrowing capital to make larger bets.

Liberalism: In this book, and often elsewhere in the River, the term refers to classical Enlightenment values such as free speech, individualism, and the market economy—rather than being a synonym for "left wing."

Liquid, liquidity: In markets, a condition in which there are many buyers and sellers, allowing for efficient on-demand trading.

Limited (sports betting): Having your maximum wager reduced by a sportsbook because they think you're a sharp bettor. In some cases, players are limited to betting dollars or pennies, and limits serve as a pretext for not inviting controversy by banning them outright.

Limit Hold'em: A variant of poker where betting increments are fixed, as opposed to no limit Hold'em, in which you may bet any amount up to your stack.

Line shopping: The process of searching for the most favorable betting line among many sportsbooks.

Liveread: In poker, the act of picking up a tell or sussing out your opponent's hand strength based on the vibes of the situation.

LLM: See: large language model.

Locals casino: A casino with limited amenities aimed at local residents. See also: slot barn.

Longtermism: A philosophy championed by Will MacAskill and other EAs that assigns low or zero discount rates to future utility, implying that we should care about the well-being of people living in the far future.

Los Alamos: The New Mexico site of the Manhattan Project.

Loss function: A measure of the difference between predicted and actual results, where there is a penalty for being further from the right answer. Models seek to minimize this discrepancy.

Machine Gods*: Superintelligent AIs that humans allow to take over our decision-making for us because we're so impressed by them.

Machine learning: An AI technique in which computers learn relationships and patterns autonomously by analyzing large data sets with little or no explicit guidance from humans.

MAD: See: mutually assured destruction.

Main Event: The most prestigious and lucrative event at the World Series of Poker, with a $10,000 entry fee; the 2023 Main Event generated more than $100 million in buy-ins.

Manhattan Project: The U.S.-government project (1942–45) that successfully designed and tested an atomic bomb.

Marginal utility, Marginal revolution: In economics, the "marginal revolution" was the rapid development of the theory of "marginal utility" in the nineteenth century, focusing on evaluating changes at the margin ("Having another slice of pizza is pretty marginal because I'm already feeling stuffed"). In the River, however, the phrase may also refer to *Marginal Revolution*, the popular blog by the economists Tyler Cowen and Alex Tabarrok.

Margin of error: When used precisely, a measure of *sampling error* that results from taking a random sample of data (e.g., eight hundred voters in a political survey) rather than the entire population. Often, there are sources of estimation error other than sampling error, such as the possibility of a biased sample. See also: confidence interval, a broader term that does not necessarily refer to sampling error.

Market-maker: In the stock market, a market-maker is a firm that buys and sells shares to provide liquidity, earning small profits on transactions without assessing the stock's fundamental value. In sports betting, a market-maker is a bookmaker that uses bets from experienced bettors to help establish accurate pricing, adjusting odds swiftly. A market-maker's prices are often copied by *retail* bookmakers that have large marketing budgets but limit bets from sharp bettors.

Martingale: A system in which you continually bet more until you win, e.g., doubling the size of your wager on every spin of the roulette wheel until the ball lands on red. Martingale bets are -EV; the problem is that while you'll usually win a small amount and then quit, you'll occasionally lose a huge amount when you go on a losing streak and bust your bankroll.

Mean: Average.

Mean-reversion: The principle that over time a data series tends to return to its long-term average or expected value. Unlike the gambler's fallacy, which mistakenly assumes outcomes must balance out immediately, mean-reversion suggests that empirical probabilities will gradually come into alignment with long-term averages as more data is accumulated.

Median: The middle value in a dataset, such that an equal number of values are above and below it. In the series [9, 2, -4, 7, 12], the median is 7.

Megalothymia: A term adapted from Plato by Francis Fukuyama to refer to the profound desire to be seen as superior to others. See also: isothymia.

Meme Creation of Value*: Matt Levine's term for distorted prices generated through spontaneous coordination in online communities, which make no pretense of caring about the fundamental value of the asset.

Meme stock: A stock such as GameStop driven up to irrational values due to viral enthusiasm on platforms like r/wallstreetbets, temporarily squeezing out short sellers.

Middle (sports betting): A form of arbitrage in which you bet both sides of a line, taking advantage of price discrepancies. For instance, if you bet Lakers +5 at DraftKings and Celtics -3 at FanDuel, you'll *hit the middle* and win both bets if the Celtics win by exactly 4 points. The equivalent of a middle involving moneylines rather than point spreads is a *scalp*.

Midriver*: The region of the River centered around finance and investing, particularly Wall Street.

Mimetic desire: The idea proposed by René Girard that people imitate what others covet. This can contribute to market instability because assets may become focal points due to collective coveting rather than their intrinsic worth. See also: envy-based economy.

Mining (crypto): The computationally intensive practice of solving cryptographic puzzles to verify transactions on the blockchain—as a reward, miners receive new Bitcoins (or other cryptocurrencies) on a quasi-random basis.

Misclick: To blunder by literally or figuratively pushing the wrong button; the term originated in online poker but is colorfully used elsewhere in the River, e.g., "I meant to order the $80 bottle of wine but I misclicked and pointed toward the $400 bottle instead."

Mixed strategy: In game theory, when two or more strategies (such as raising or calling in poker) have the same expected value and you should randomize between them. A Nash equilibrium often requires the use of mixed strategies.

Model: A simplified representation of a complex system designed to replicate its essential features accurately enough to make reliable inferences or predict outcomes. The term is versatile and can range from statistical models and computer programs, to "mental models," to even physical representations, such as a scale model of a ship. The art and science of modeling lies in determining the optimal balance between simplicity and complexity.

Model maverick, Model mediator*: My terms for contrasting styles of making predictions. "Model mavericks" treat a prediction as a hypothesis to be proven or disproven. "Model mediators" treat a prediction as a basis for making bets, blending their personal views with the market consensus. See also: fox, hedgehog.

Moneyball-ization*: The process of turning things over to data science and algorithms, especially in fields that previously relied on outmoded conventional wisdom.

Moneyline: A bet, made at odds, on which team will win the game—as opposed to the point spread, which is a bet on the margin of victory.

Moral hazard: A situation in which a person or firm taking a risk does not bear the full downside consequences—for instance, a bank that believes it will be bailed out if it fails—and therefore has an incentive for risky behavior.

Motte-and-bailey fallacy: A nerdy Riverian term for an argument in which someone advances a controversial position (the bailey or low ground) and, when challenged, retreats to an easier-to-defend position (the motte or high ground). For instance, the bailey might be "we should immediately ban the use of fossil fuels," and the motte might be "we all support a transition toward more sustainable sources of energy." Watch for this; you'll soon see it everywhere you look.

Move fast and break things: Mark Zuckerberg's iconic Silicon Valley attitude—strike at potential +EV opportunities when you can and worry about the consequences later.

Mutually assured destruction: A theory of nuclear deterrence that holds that nuclear states won't attack one another because they'd be assured of a devastating retaliatory strike if they did.

Nash equilibrium: After the Princeton mathematician John Nash, a game theory solution in which all participants have optimized their EV and there are no further gains from unilateral changes in strategy. Nash proved that all games satisfying certain conditions have at least one equilibrium, although some have more than one.

Nerd-snipe: The act of persuading a nerd to study a problem that is geeky or cool, perhaps out of proportion to its underlying importance.

Neural net: A machine learning framework consisting of interconnected nodes that mimic the structure of the human brain. These nodes or neurons process and transmit information, contributing to the network's ability to make decisions. The accuracy of this metaphor to describe human cognition is disrupted, however.

NFT: Formally, a non-fungible token, a certificate of ownership on the blockchain. Colloquially, it more often refers to a collection of digital art whose ownership is verified through NFTs.

Nit: A poker player who is conspicuously risk-averse. It can also convey cheapness or neuroticism, being a stickler for the rules. The term is sometimes extended to other situations; e.g., you're a nit if you go to bed at 9:00 p.m. instead of joining your friends at the club, or *nitty* if you demand an itemized accounting rather than just split the bill. The antonym is degen.

Node: A decision point in a game, with possibilities branching out from there. For instance, in poker, a node might be the decision to call, fold, or raise. In computer science, the term is a synonym for neuron.

Nonplayer character: Originating in video games, a person or character with little agency who predictably interacts with other characters and their environment. Can be applied insultingly to a person who isn't seen as capable of strategic thinking.

Normal distribution: Informally known as a bell curve for its characteristic shape, a probability distribution that results over a large sample of data when certain conditions are satisfied under the central limit theorem. Normal distributions are symmetrical, easy to work with, and empirically useful in many real-world situations; for instance, a probabilistic range for an NBA player's shooting percentage after one hundred shots should approximate a normal distribution. However, be careful when these assumptions are violated; some conditions instead give rise to *fat-tailed* distributions, where outlier or "black swan" outcomes are far more likely than the normal distribution predicts.

Nosebleed: Very high-stakes poker or gambling, i.e., high enough to cause your nose to bleed because the air is thin up there.

NOT INVESTMENT ADVICE: Investment advice. A Riverian trope for a legalistic disclaimer that means the opposite of what it says. The phrase was frequently employed by Sam Bankman-Fried in all caps before offering analysis that in fact provided actionable intelligence to investors.

NPC: See: non-player character.

Nuts (poker): A hand that is so strong that it will essentially never lose. Modifiers may clarify whether this refers to the very best hand or merely one of the best; for instance, *stone-cold nuts* refers to the exact best hand, like 8♣6♣ (the best available straight flush) on a board of 5♣ 7♣ A♦4♣A♥. *Nutted* is the adjectival form. Often extended outside of poker to refer to a best-in-class experience, e.g., "We took some edibles at the Sphere. So cool, man, it was the nuts."

Occam's razor: A heuristic, named after the fourteenth-century English philosopher William of Ockham, that simpler solutions are more likely to be true. Generally regarded highly in the River, because more complex solutions can give rise to p-hacking and overfitting, where the data is tortured to produce the desired conclusion. A related term is *parsimony*.

Odds: Sometimes a synonym for probability, but more precisely, odds refer to the likelihood of an event *not* occurring compared to it happening, expressed as a ratio. For instance, if you assign 5:1 odds against Elon Musk replying to your email, that means there are 5 times he won't reply for every time he does, so your chances of getting a reply are 1 in 6. Odds of 1:5, conversely, indicate that you're an *odds-on favorite*; there's a 5 in 6 chance that Elon will respond. *American odds*, favored by sportsbooks, are expressed in multiples of 100, where positive numbers indicate your bet is an underdog (+500 is equivalent to 5:1) and negative numbers mean you've bet on the favorite (-500 is equivalent to 1:5).

Old Man Coffee (OMC): An older poker player, stereotypically drinking a cup of Dunkin' Donuts coffee, who plays tight and predictably.

Optionality: EV derived from the prospect of being able to make choices later on as more information is revealed. Calling rather than raising all-in in poker, for instance, provides more optionality because you'll be able to decide what to do later based on which card comes next.

Order of magnitude: By a factor of 10.

Originate (sports betting): To bet with proprietary knowledge or models that are likely to be seen as valuable by bookmakers, potentially compelling them to adjust their odds.

Orthogonal: A nerdy synonym for perpendicular, meaning intersecting at right angles, conveying the idea that component parts of a system are independent and don't affect one another.

Orthogonality thesis: A controversial idea proposed by Nick Bostrom that "more or less any level of intelligence could be combined with more or less any final goal"; it implies that advanced AI can be dangerous because machines could be highly effective at pursuing goals that aren't aligned with human interests. See also: paper clip.

Outlier: Far removed from the rest of the data; by implication, either a one-of-a-kind phenomenon or some type of error.

Outs: In poker, cards that might come to make you a winning hand. For example, A♣T♣ has 15 outs against K♦9♦ on a board of K♥J♣3♣2♥: any ace, queen (making a straight), or club (making a flush) will win the hand. More colloquially, "having outs" means a situation in which you still have some hope of wriggling out of a bad predicament. See also: drawing dead, the opposite situation, in which you don't have any outs.

Outside view: A prediction made without domain knowledge or inside information, instead calculated using broadly applicable heuristics or long-term base rates. Despite its seeming naïveté, the outside view often proves more accurate than the *inside view*.

Overbet: In poker, betting more than the size of the pot, which typically indicates either a strong hand or a bluff. (See also: polarized.) The opposite of an overbet is an *underbet*.

Overdetermined: A phenomenon that has two or more plausible causes, but where there isn't a reliable way to distinguish between them. If a popular beach is deserted following a simultaneous shark attack, oil spill, and tsunami warning, the absence of beachgoers is overdetermined. The antonym, where there aren't any sufficient explanations for what you observe in the data, is *underdetermined*.

Overfitting: The tendency to overcomplicate when building a statistical model by too rigidly adhering to the "shape" of past data, such as by including too many parameters. An overfit model won't generalize well and can lead to overconfidence; performance will deteriorate when predictions are made on new data. The opposite is *underfitting*, a model that is too simplistic and doesn't fully capture robust relationships in the training data—but overfitting is the more common problem in most applied research.

Over-under: See: total.

Paper clip: An allusion to a thought experiment by Nick Bostrom that imagined an advanced AI, tasked with maximizing paper clip production, consuming all resources to achieve its goal, leading to civilization's downfall.

Parameter: This term has subtly different definitions in different subfields of the River, but it can loosely be thought of as a knob that can be tuned to affect the overall shape of the behavior of the system. For instance, a musical note has parameters like pitch, duration, and volume. AI models have billions of parameters, far more than in classical statistics, indicating their complexity.

Pareto optimal: The condition named after the Italian economist Vilfredo Pareto, in which you have multiple objectives and can't improve performance along one dimension without compromising the others. For instance, in the COVID-19 pandemic, countries faced trade-offs. The set of Pareto optimal solutions (also called the *Pareto frontier*) involved various combinations of "lives saved" and "freedom preserved," but it was hard to achieve gains along one dimension without sacrificing the other.

Parlay: As a verb, to take your winnings and make another bet with them. As a noun, a sports bet involving multiple legs (e.g., five different NFL point spreads), where you must win each leg to win the bet but the odds compound if you do. Parlays are popular with recreational bettors because of the possibility of a big payout.

Pascal's Mugging: Introduced by Eliezer Yudkowsky, a counterpart to Pascal's Wager, wherein you're asked to make a sacrifice to avoid some small and implausible probability of a catastrophic outcome— for instance, a mugger who says you should give him five dollars or otherwise there's a chance he'll trigger a chain reaction in a particle accelerator that will lead to the heat death of the universe. It is an example of the potential shortcomings of utilitarian reasoning when applied to everyday problems.

Pascal's Wager: The French mathematician Blaise Pascal's famous "wager" in which he contended that you should believe in God because if there's even a small chance that God is real, you'll get an infinite benefit (ascending to Heaven for eternity) by doing so.

Payoff matrix: In game theory, a typically 2x2 table listing the EV of each player given different combinations of strategic choices available to them.

p(doom): Short for "probability of doom," one's subjective estimate of existential risk, particularly existential risk from AI.

Pepe: A reference to Rare Pepe, a popular early NFT collection featuring Pepe the Frog, a much-memed green cartoon frog. Although co-opted by right-wing groups in the mid-2010s, the creator of Pepe the Frog has disavowed that connotation and the meme is typically apolitical today.

p-hacking: Any of a number of dubious methods to obtain an ostensibly statistically significant result to increase the chances for publication in an academic journal. The term is derived from the *p-value*, a measure of statistical significance in classical statistics.

Pip: The spots on a dice or a playing card.

Pit boss: A senior casino employee in charge of a section of gaming tables.

Pits: The parts of a casino with -EV table games like blackjack; where a degen goes when he busts out of the poker tournament but still wants more action.

Plurality: In statistics, the most commonly chosen option even if it's not the majority; Bill Clinton won the 1992 election with a 43 percent plurality against George Bush and Ross Perot. However, in this book I use plurality in the sense of *pluralism*, i.e., employing multiple approaches to a problem instead of one.

Plus EV: Having a positive expected value.

Pocket pair: In poker, two hole cards of the same rank, e.g. 7♦7♣ is "pocket 7s"; these are generally strong hands.

Poker Boom: The period beginning in 2003 of rapid expansion in poker because of the increasing availability of online games and Chris Moneymaker's win at the 2003 Main Event. The Poker Boom ended between 2006 and 2008 because of increasingly aggressive enforcement actions against on-line poker.

Point spread: A sports bet in which you predict the margin of victory. A positive number (Chiefs +3) means that you win the bet if the Chiefs either win the game outright or lose by fewer than 3 points; a negative number (Chiefs -3) means that you *lay* points and the Chiefs must win by at least that amount.

Polarized (poker): Having a range in poker consisting of very strong hands and very weak ones or bluffs, with little in between. The antonym is *condensed*. Sometimes extended by Riverians to non-poker situations; your boss calling you in for an unexpected meeting is polarized because you're either getting promoted or fired.

Polymath: A jack-of-all-trades with strong-to-genius-level aptitude in several fields. A complimentary term in the River, which prizes general intelligence over domain knowledge. See also: fox.

Ponzi scheme: First "invented" by Italian "businessman" Charles Ponzi, a con that promises high investment returns but achieves these by paying existing investors with funds obtained from new investors. A related category is a *pyramid scheme*. Ponzis and pyramids may work fine until they run out of new suckers.

Position (poker): In poker, the order in which players must make decisions; the action rotates clockwise around the table. Being *in position* is a major strategic advantage because *out-of-position* players will have revealed information to you by the time it's your turn to act.

Pot-committed: In poker, a situation where you can't fold because you'll have the right odds to call no matter what your opponent does. This is often a more precise metaphor than "all-in" to indicate a situation where you can't back down. You may not have committed all your resources yet and may hope to avoid doing so—but if your opponent forces you to make a decision, you'll have to see the bet.

Pot-Limit Omaha (PLO): The second-most popular form of poker. Otherwise similar to Hold'em, it's distinguishing features are that (1) each player is dealt four hole cards rather than two, exactly two of which must be used in the final hand at showdown; and (2) bets may not exceed the size of the pot. PLO is known for wild swings; it's a favorite game of degens. Sometimes known as *four card*.

Precautionary principle: A heuristic that one ought to be risk-averse because of the potential for un-known harms. Avoid this term. It's often vague, perceived by Riverians as indicating an interloper from the Village who hasn't engaged in more rigorous cost-benefit analysis—although Riverians do have some similar ideas of their own. See also: Chesterton's fence.

Prediction market: A platform where people may bet on the outcome of real-world events, from presidential elections to personal occurrences. Prediction markets are highly regarded in the River because they are seen as promoting epistemic rationality, i.e., giving people an incentive to see whether their perceptions of the world are aligned with reality.

Preflop: The betting round in poker where each player has two private hole cards but the flop and other community cards have not yet been dealt.

Price discovery: The process of establishing a market price by letting people make bets or trades.

Prior: In Bayesian reasoning, an initial belief that you're prepared to revise as more information is revealed. Under Bayes' theorem proper, a prior takes the form of a statistical estimate of the probability of an event. However, the term is now used widely in the River as an approximate synonym for "assumption."

Prisoner's dilemma: A famous and broadly useful application of game theory, first described in 1950 by Melvin Dresher and Merrill Flood to refer to two members of a criminal gang who were arrested and imprisoned and independently had to decide whether to cooperate with the other prisoner or defect and stick their accomplice with a long sentence. The prisoner's dilemma predicts that both prisoners will defect, acting in their narrow self-interest, but leaving them collectively worse off than if they'd cooperated.

Probability distribution: The set of all possible outcomes in an uncertain situation, typically represented as a graph, where some regions reflect relatively more likely outcomes and therefore are denser in the graph. See also: normal distribution.

Progress studies: A term proposed by Patrick Collison and Tyler Cowen for a multidisciplinary field to study improvement in the human condition.

Prop bet: A sports bet on anything other than the winner of the game, the margin of victory, or the total number of points—such as which team will kick the first field goal or the length of the national anthem in the Super Bowl. Degens also take pride in making ridiculous prop bets against one another, like whether one tennis player can win a match against a less skilled one using a frying pan rather than a racket.

Prospect theory: An empirical tendency first described by Daniel Kahneman and Amos Tversky for people to be risk-averse when faced with the loss of something they already have. For instance, they might prefer a guaranteed $300 to a coin flip where they either win $1,000 or lose $100, even though the coin flip has a higher EV.

Provenance: The prestige, origin, and chain of custody of an object; collectibles like NFTs with well-established provenance are more valuable because they're more irreplaceable and less likely to be fakes.

Public (sports betting): The sum total of action from unskilled, recreational bettors; it is often advisable to *fade the public* (i.e., bet against the popular pick).

Pump-and-dump: Disingenuously hyping up an asset, and then selling once the price goes up.

Punt: In poker, a poor, -EV play that may have resulted from impatience or tilt ("I punted off my stack on a hopeless bluff"); *punter* (n.) is also a British term for a typically recreational gambling patron.

Pure strategy: Where game theory recommends taking an action 100 percent of the time instead of using a mixed strategy. In football, for example, a team facing third and long might always pass rather than run because passing is higher EV despite the lack of deception value.

Push (sports betting): A tie, e.g., you bet the Michigan Wolverines -3 and they win by exactly 3 points (see also: point spread); you get your wager back but don't make any profit.

Push the button*: As employed in this book, deciding to undertake a high-risk, high-reward action that could pose an existential risk.

Quant: A Riverian archetype who makes bets or decisions using statistical analysis.

Raise-or-fold situation: A circumstance in which you should either act aggressively or retreat, and the middle ground (equivalent to calling in poker) is worse than either. Although the term originates in poker, it can be applied to other contexts: for instance, the world arguably should have pursued a raise-or-fold strategy on COVID instead of the half measures we undertook.

Rake: A portion of a poker pot taken by the casino to secure itself a profit.

Randomize (poker or game theory): To make a decision at random because you're literally indifferent between two or more options. A player who decides in this fashion may say he *rolled* a certain strategy, alluding to rolling a physical or virtual die. See also: mixed strategy.

Range (poker): The set of all hands you could plausibly have given your play thus far. A wide range means you can have many hands and your range can't yet be narrowed down. This is a foundational concept in modern, probabilistic poker thinking; you should assign your opponent a range of hands and not guess her exact cards.

Rational: When defined by philosophers, not merely a synonym for "reasonable" but refers to either *instrumental rationality* (undertaking means that achieve one's ends) or *epistemic rationality* (having views grounded in reality). See chapter 7 for a more complete definition.

Rationalism: A loosely defined intellectual movement associated with Eliezer Yudkowsky and Robin Hanson with a broad goal of promoting more rational, less biased decision-making. Like effective altruism, rationalism often advocates for the use of quantitative methods, but applied to lots of problems and not just charitable giving. It is often more contrarian than EA, with less regard for social conventions. An adherent of rationalism is a *rat*.

Reciprocity: In game theory, responding to an action with an action that mirrors it—tit for tat or an eye for an eye. Or when used more broadly, recognizing that different players in the game occupy symmetrical strategic positions and each have agency to form appropriate strategic responses.

Rec player: A recreational gambler, typically -EV.

Reference class: The set of historical precedents one deems relevant when making a prediction.

Regression analysis: A statistical method used to determine the relationship between an *independent variable* and one or more *dependent variables*. For example, regression analysis can analyze how weather conditions and days of the week influence sales at a BBQ restaurant.

Regulatory capture: The tendency for entrenched companies to benefit when new regulation is crafted ostensibly in the public interest, such as because of successful lobbying.

Reinforcement Learning from Human Feedback (RLHF): A late stage of training a large language model in which human evaluators give it thumbs-up or thumbs-down based on subjective criteria to make the LLM more aligned with human values. Colloquially referred to by Stuart Russell as "spanking."

Repugnant Conclusion: Formulated by the philosopher Derek Parfit, the proposition that any amount of positive utility multiplied by a sufficiently large number of people—infinity people eating one stale batch of Arby's curly fries before dying—has higher utility than some smaller number of people living in abundance. The finding is counterintuitive. Depending on who you ask, it either speaks to the shortcomings of conventional morality or the shortcomings of utilitarianism.

Results-oriented: Judging the wisdom of an action by the result—like whether a bet won or lost—disregarding the role of luck and the process behind the action. Results-oriented thinking predominates outside the River, whereas Riverians strive to focus on process.

Return on investment: Your profits divided by your stake or investment. If you invest $10,000 in Krispy Kreme stock and its value increases to $12,000, your ROI is 20 percent.

Revealed preference: Behavior as indicated by actions rather than words; if you show up at the Bellagio $5/$10 game three hundred days a year, your revealed preference is that you like poker whether you admit it or not.

Risk-averse, Risk-loving, Risk-neutral: Various dispositions toward risk-taking; "risk-averse" means you'd decline a bet with zero expected value, "risk-loving" means you'd happily take it, and "risk-neutral" means you'd be indifferent.

Risk of ruin: The probability of losing so much money that your ability to make further bets is severely impaired.

River (poker): The fifth and last community card dealt face up in Hold'em, followed by a final round of betting and a showdown. The term possibly derives from poker's Mississippi riverboat origins, where if the dealer was suspected of cheating, he'd be thrown into the river.

(The) River: A geographical metaphor for the territory covered in this book, a sprawling ecosystem of like-minded, highly analytical, and competitive people that includes everything from poker to Wall Street to AI. The demonym is *Riverian*.

RLHF: See: Reinforcement Learning from Human Feedback.

Robust: In philosophy or statistical inference, reliable across many conditions or changes in parameters. A highly desirable property.

ROI: See: Return on Investment.

Rug pull: Hyping up a crypto project to attract investors, and then pulling a disappearing act before bringing the idea to fruition. An investor who fell for such a scam was *rugged*.

Running good/rungood: Achieving results in excess of one's EV because of good luck. The antonym is *running bad* or *runbad*. A *sunrun* is an extended period of rungood—running hotter than the Sun.

Russian roulette: A "game" in which you spin the chambers of a revolver, one of which is loaded with a bullet, then put the gun to your temple and pull the trigger; it implies a 1-in-6 chance that you'll shoot yourself dead.

r/wallstreetbets: A Reddit forum (subreddit) popular among amateur day traders and instrumental in facilitating meme stock bubbles like GameStop; known for trolling with adolescent humor and egging on degen behavior.

Sample size: The number of *data points* or *observations* collected in a study or analysis. There are no hard-and-fast rules for what makes an adequate sample size, but more data is strictly better than less.

Satoshi: Either a reference to Satoshi Nakamoto, the pseudonymous creator of Bitcoin, or a satoshi, the smallest denomination of Bitcoin, equal to 0.00000001 BTC.

SBF: Felonious FTX founder Sam Bankman-Fried.

Scaling (AI): The tendency in machine learning for capabilities to scale upward with the amount of compute. The scaling is typically not linear; instead, capabilities increase as some logarithmic function of compute. Sometimes referred to as *scaling laws* for the seeming inevitability of capabilities growth.

Secular stagnation: As originally defined, a prolonged period of little to no economic growth, often accompanied by low interest rates. Informally, the sense that technological and economic progress isn't happening as fast as it should be and that society faces many headwinds.

Selection bias: The tendency for members of a population with certain traits to be weeded out, resulting in a biased sample. For instance, the population of NFL quarterbacks suffers from selection bias with respect to arm strength because quarterbacks below a certain threshold will never make the pros. See also: survivorship bias.

Semantic: Interpretation, meaning, and context in the study of language.

Semi-bluff: In poker, raising with a hand like a flush draw that can either win by bluffing or by making the draw if called.

Set (poker): Three of a kind using a pocket pair; a pair of aces make a set if a third ace comes on the flop. Three of a kind using only one hole card (e.g., if you have one king and two kings come on the flop) is instead called *trips*.

Shape of things to come: A phrase used by Richard Rhodes in *The Making of the Atomic Bomb* to imagine the inner monologue of the Hungarian physicist Leo Szilard when he realized his ideas could lead to the creation of nuclear weapons. It refers to a science-fiction novel of the same name published by H. G. Wells the same year as Szilard's insight.

Sharp: Smart, winning, +EV; the highest compliment that a Riverian can pay to another Riverian. Usually used as an adjective ("a sharp betting line"; "She's sharp"). Avoid "sharp" as in *card sharp* to describe a skilled gambler because it can imply cheating. The homonym *card shark* has less of this connotation but is becoming archaic.

Shitcoin: As defined by Investopedia, "a cryptocurrency with little to no value or no immediate, discernible purpose." The line between shitcoins and more widely adopted cryptocurrencies can be blurry, however.

Shove (poker): A synonym for going all in, i.e., shoving all your chips into the pot.

Showdown (poker): When cards are exposed after all betting action and the best hand wins.

Shut Up and Multiply: An admonition, first coined by Eliezer Yudkowsky, to commit to the process of rigorous calculation—you shouldn't trust your gut if you can't translate your intuitions to mathematical form.

Signal-to-noise ratio: The quotient of meaningful to meaningless information.

Silicon Valley: As used in this book—other definitions will vary—the ecosystem of technology companies, largely backed by venture capital, focused in the San Francisco Bay Area or with close ties to it.

Singularity: A hypothesized future period of exceptionally rapid technological advancement. The term is sometimes capitalized, as by the AI researcher Ray Kurzweil, to refer to a predicted Singularity in the near future triggered by self-improving AI.

Skill game: A form of gambling in which at least some players can be +EV over the long run without cheating or advantage play. Poker and sports betting are examples.

Skin in the game: A term popularized by Warren Buffett (and later Nassim Nicholas Taleb, who used it as a book title) to refer to bearing the consequences of one's actions. Someone who bets $50,000 a pop on NFL games has skin in the game; an academic who publishes an NFL computer model but never bets with it doesn't.

Slot barn: A dingy casino with poor sight lines and wall-to-wall slot machines.

Slowplay: In poker, to just call rather than raise with a strong hand to induce your opponent to bluff or overplay a weaker hand.

Small ball: In poker tournaments, a tactical approach oriented around cautious play to avoid busting your stack while inducing mistakes from your opponents.

Small-world problem: A tractable problem in a closed system, like predicting the outcome of NFL games, that lends itself well to modeling. See also: grand-world problem.

Smart contract: A program stored on the blockchain to automatically execute contractual instructions, first associated with the Ethereum blockchain. NFTs and *DAOs* (decentralized autonomous organizations, a form of self-governance structure) are examples of smart contracts.

Solver: A poker computer program that calculates an approximation of the Nash equilibrium and thereby can advise you on the correct play.

Spectrumy: On the autism spectrum.

Splash zone*: My term for the vicinity near whales or degens where +EV gambling opportunities are likely to present themselves. It's always good to hang out in the splash zone.

Spread: See: point spread.

Stability-instability paradox: The tendency toward an increase in proxy wars (e.g., Vietnam or Ukraine) in states that aren't protected by superpower alliances and nuclear umbrellas, even as wars between nuclear states are less likely because of mutually assured destruction.

Stack (poker): The chips you have in front of you (n); to relieve your opponent of their chips ("I *stacked* Hellmuth") because they lost an all-in (v).

Stake: As a noun, the amount of money put at risk; as a verb, backing another player by providing him a bankroll in exchange for a share of his profits.

Standard deviation: A way to quantify the spread of data around the mean. In a normal distribution, 68 percent, 95 percent, and 99.7 percent of the data, respectively, is within one, two and three standard deviations of the mean, so someone whose IQ is said to be three standard deviations above the mean is very smart indeed.

Statistically significant: Unlikely to be due to chance. In classical statistics, it means that the null hypothesis can be rejected with a specified probability, usually 95 percent. The term is falling out of favor in the River as a result of the adaptation of Bayesian statistics and the *replication crisis*, the failure of many published academic findings using classical statistics to be verified by other researchers.

Steam chasing: In sports betting, the practice of following *steam*—changes in betting prices at bookmakers that you believe reflect the action of sharp bettors but which have not yet been incorporated by other bookmakers. Sportsbooks strongly dislike this practice and may limit you for it.

Steelman: The opposite of a *strawman*, a robust representation of an opponent's argument or the strongest articulation of a position. Seen as an honorable practice by EAs and rationalists as it aims for constructive debate.

St. Petersburg paradox: The observation, originally by the mathematician Nicolaus Bernoulli, that repeatedly making coin flips with positive expected value (e.g., the coin is weighted and you win 51 percent of the time) but a risk of ruin will inevitably result in ruin, even though the sequence of bets ostensibly has an expected value of positive infinity. Understood by everybody but Sam Bankman-Fried as a shortcoming of strict utilitarianism.

Straight (poker): Five consecutive cards of the same rank, e.g., 8♣7♦6♥5♥4♣. *Drawing to an inside straight* means you need one of the cards in the middle to complete your hand, e.g., if you have an 8, 7, 6, and 4 but not a 5, the odds of completing your straight on the river are about 10 percent.

Straight flush: Both a straight and a flush, the highest-ranking poker hand.

Strategic empathy: Coined by military historian Zachary Shore, the ability to put yourself in your opponent's shoes to make better decisions.

Street (poker): A round of betting following new cards being dealt. In Hold'em, the streets are pre-flop, the flop, the turn, and the river.

Suited (poker): Two starting cards of the same suit; suited hands make flushes more often and have a surprisingly large advantage over *offsuit* cards.

Superforecaster: A term used by Phil Tetlock for people who have demonstrated an ability to make well-calibrated probabilistic forecasts across many domains. See also: fox.

Superintelligent: Artificial intelligence with capabilities considerably surpassing those of humans, popularized by the Nick Bostrom book *Superintelligence*.

Survivorship bias: The tendency for a statistical sample to be biased or corrupted because some examples are more likely to survive into the "fossil record," possibly leading to incorrect inferences. This book potentially suffers from survivorship bias because it focuses more on successful risk-takers than failed ones who have faded into obscurity.

Syndicate: In sports betting, a group of skilled bettors who work in a coordinated fashion.

System 1, System 2: Daniel Kahneman's terms for, respectively, intuitive "fast" thinking (System 1) and more deliberative "slow" thinking (System 2). See chapter 2 for an extensive discussion.

Table stakes: In poker, your liability is limited to the chips you have in front of you on the table; metaphorically, the term implies that you should stop being a nit because you haven't been asked to put all that much at risk ("C'mon, these are just table stakes").

Tactic: A "play" executed to achieve a short-term goal (e.g., advancing your rook in chess to put your opponent in check), as opposed to a long-term *strategy*. Effective players ensure their tactics support their overall strategy.

Tail risk: A low-probability outcome, referring to the thin *tails* at either end of a bell curve.

Takeoff (AI): The speed at which AI progress is achieved; doomers fear a *fast takeoff* in which there won't be time to pull the plug if something goes wrong.

Technological Richter Scale (TRS)*: My term, modeled after the Richter scale for measuring earthquake magnitudes, for the amount of seismic disruption caused by an invention. As with the classic Richter scale, it is logarithmic (a TRS 8 technology is ten times more disruptive than a TRS 7), and the frequency of inventions is inversely related to their TRS magnitude (there are ten TRS 7s for every TRS 8).

Techno-optimist: After Marc Andreessen's "Techno-Optimist Manifesto," someone who believes that technological growth furthers human interests and should proceed apace with few constraints.

Tell (poker): A verbal or physical tic that gives away information about the strength of a player's hand—but be careful, because skilled players may deliberately give off *fake tells*.

Threat that leaves something to chance: In nuclear deterrence theory, Thomas Schelling's idea that escalation contains an intrinsic risk of provoking nuclear retaliation because accidents or impulsive decisions could happen in the fog of war.

Tight-aggressive (TAG): A poker strategy, advocated for by Doyle Brunson and others, of playing relatively few hands but playing them aggressively. Players who play a lot of hands and play them aggressively are instead known as *LAG* or *loose-aggressive*.

Tilt: In poker and other gambling, an emotional state that results in suboptimal play. The archetypal form is overly aggressive play following a bad beat or a losing streak as a player seeks to chase her losses, but tilt takes on many shapes; overly tight play because you're scared of losing is also tilt. Tilt often takes on modifiers, e.g., *monkey tilt, tilting one's face off.*

Time horizon: The duration of the window into the future that you deem relevant for evaluating your actions. A longer time horizon implies having more patience and a lower discount rate.

Token (AI): A unit of text used as a building block in large language models. A token is roughly equivalent to a word, but punctuation marks are also treated as tokens, and compound words like superhighway may be split into multiple tokens.

Token (crypto): A digital asset such as smart contract or NFT stored on a blockchain that is not the native cryptocurrency of the blockchain—although practical usage often blurs this distinction.

Total (sports betting): The combined number of points scored by both teams: you can bet over or under the total.

Training: In machine learning, the process of giving a model a large data set that it will learn and make inferences from. The term is sometimes also used in classical statistics, such as for the process of choosing the parameters in a regression analysis, but techniques like these involve far more human intervention than machine learning.

Traitorous Eight: Eight engineers who quit Shockley Semiconductor in 1957 to found a rival firm, Fairchild Semiconductor—a pivot point in Silicon Valley for initiating a legacy of entrepreneurship among technical professionals.

Transformer (AI): An architecture employed in large language models to transform text inputs by the user into vector mathematics and back again. Transformers operate by parsing all tokens in the user query simultaneously rather than sequentially, looking for complex semantic relationships. There is an extensive description of transformers in chapter ∞.

Transhumanism: The position that humans should be encouraged to use technological augmentation to enhance their capabilities. The term is vague, insofar as a technology as simple as eyeglasses might qualify as augmentation, though it usually refers to more advanced technologies like AI and cryonics. Distinguished from *posthumanism*, which goes further by arguing that *Homo sapiens* ought to welcome a transition into being a new species.

Trimmed mean: The mean after a specified proportion of the highest and lowest values are clipped off. A good working compromise between the mean and the median.

Trinity or Trinity test: The code name for the test that resulted in the first successful detonation of an atomic bomb during the Manhattan Project.

Trolley problem: A moral dilemma first proposed by the philosopher Philippa Foot. The original version involved a trolley that had lost its brakes and was on a collision course to kill some number of track workers, but that could be diverted to a different track to kill some smaller number of workers. Many creative variations have followed, serving as thought experiments to explore different precepts of moral reasoning.

TRS*: See: Technological Richter Scale.

Turing test: A litmus test proposed by the British mathematician Alan Turing in which a machine is deemed to possess practical intelligence if a third-party observer can't distinguish its responses to text queries from those of a human. AI researchers debate whether the Turing test is in fact a good measure of intelligence and whether models like ChatGPT have passed the test.

Turn (poker): The fourth of five community cards dealt face up in Hold'em.

Unit (sports betting): A betting increment with the cash value not specified, sometimes used to create ambiguity about how much someone is actually wagering: a unit might be $5 to one bettor and $50,000 to Billy Walters.

Update (Bayes' theorem): In line with Bayes' theorem, to revise your views after considering new evidence. Often used colloquially in the River as a somewhat pretentious way to refer to changing one's mind.

Upriver*: A more intellectual part of the River focused around the raw production of Riverian ideas, such as those expressed in the EA and rationalist movements or in the development of AI for non-commercial uses. Silicon Valley is influenced by Upriver but sits closer to Midriver.

Util, utility: A quantifiable but dimensionless unit of "goodness." Utilitarians seek to maximize the amount of utility in the universe. Utility also features prominently in economics, although economists usually do not advocate for strict utilitarianism; rather, utility serves as a conceptual measure of overall well-being.

Utilitarianism: A branch of consequentialism that argues that the morality of an action is based on its utility, sometimes stated as "the greatest good for the greatest number." Utilitarianism implies that utility can be quantified, appealing to the effective altruists and other quant types in the River. There are many variants of utilitarianism; e.g., *rule utilitarianism* holds that we should act such as if our behavior were universalized, it would maximize utility.

Value of a statistical life (VSL): An empirical estimate derived from people's revealed preferences for how much they're willing to trade the risk of death for financial gains; used in cost-benefit analysis to quantify the worth of lifesaving measures. As of 2024, the U.S. government values the VSL at approximately $10 million.

Variance: Statistical fluctuations resulting from randomness. It is defined mathematically as the square root of the standard deviation, though the term isn't usually used so precisely.

VC: See: venture capital.

Vector: In mathematics, a quantity with a specified magnitude and direction; think of an arrow pointing 5 paces east and 6 paces north on a graph. In AI, the term refers to information encoded with directionality. For instance, the word "Paris" in a large language model can be represented as a vector in multidimensional semantic space, with dimensions like latitude and longitude but also more subjective qualities like "fashionability" and "Europeanness."

Venture capital: The industry of private firms, most prominently in Silicon Valley, that provide capital to early-stage startup businesses.

Vig or Vigorish: In sports betting, the house edge implicitly built into betting lines, typically 4 to 5 percent of a wager. *Juice* and *hold* are synonyms.

(The) Village*: The rival community to the River, reflected most clearly in intellectual occupations with progressive politics, such as the media, academia, and government (especially when a Democrat is in the White House). To Riverians, the Village is parochial, excessively "political," and suffers from various cognitive biases. However, the Village has any number of cogent objections to the River, as outlined in the introduction. My coinage is not entirely original and bears some similarity to terms like "professional-managerial class." Both the Village and the River consist overwhelmingly of "elites"; the vast majority of the population doesn't fall into either group.

VIP (gambling): A degenerate gambler who gets the VIP treatment because he's expected to lose a lot of money. See also: whale.

Virtuous cycle: See: feedback loop.

VSL: See: value of a statistical life.

Whale: In poker and casino gambling, a relatively poor player who gives action and gambles at high stakes (see also: fish, VIP). In crypto, however, the term has a positive connotation to refer to a large holder of tokens or NFTs.

Where the action is: A reference to the Erving Goffman essay that created a romantic division of the world into people who play it safe and risk-takers who go where the action is.

White magic: Phil Hellmuth's self-aggrandizing term for his ability to intuitively pick up reads on other players.

Wisdom of crowds: In betting, investing, and forecasting, the tendency for the average estimate of all members of the group to be relatively accurate, often more accurate than the forecasts of even the sharpest individuals.

WPT: World Poker Tour, the main North American competitor of the WSOP, which typically holds around a dozen events per year.

Wordcel: A meme, popularized by **roon**, that plays on "incel" to refer to people who are "good with words" but bad at abstract mathematics. The term is often pejorative, used to describe people like journalists (and writers of nonfiction books), whose skills are becoming less valuable. The more left-brained counterpart to a wordcel is a *shape rotator*.

World Series of Poker: An annual poker festival held since 1970 in Las Vegas—though the owner of the WSOP brand, Caesars Entertainment, has extended the franchise to include online events and poker series in other countries.

Wrong on the internet: A reference to an xkcd cartoon in which a man stayed up all night because it was his duty to argue with idiots who were wrong on the internet.

WSOP: See: World Series of Poker.

X-risk: See: existential risk.

YOLO: An acronym for "you only live once." An argument for being a degen or an effective hedonist.

Zero-sum game: A situation in which one participant's gain is exactly balanced by another's loss, with the total utility remaining constant. Although zero-sum games were the original basis for game theory, many real-world scenarios like nuclear deterrence involve *mixed motives* blending elements of competition and cooperation.

NOTES

Chapter 0: Introduction

5 **Seminole Hard Rock:** David Lyons, "Guitar Hotel to Make Its Bow as Seminole Hard Rock Flexes Financial Might," *South Florida Sun Sentinel*, October 19, 2019, sun-sentinel.com/business/fl-bz-hard-rock-guitar-hotel-peek-20191018-xhnj3qwkv5fhbjtdgrrhkjtbxa-story.html.

6 **casino gaming revenues:** "United States Commercial Casino Gaming: Monthly Revenues," UNLV Center for Gaming Research, April 2022, web.archive.org/web/20220425090331/gaming.library.unlv.edu/reports/national_monthly.pdf.

6 **to traffic accidents:** "During COVID-19, Road Fatalities Increased and Transit Ridership Dipped," *GAO WatchBlog* (blog), January 25, 2022, gao.gov/blog/during-covid-19-road-fatalities-increased-and-transit-ridership-dipped.

7 **named Brek Schutten:** Sean Chaffin, "ICU Nurse Brek Schutten Claims Record-Breaking WPT Win—World Poker Tour," World Poker Tour, May 20, 2021, worldpokertour.com/news/icu-nurse-brek-schutten-claims-record-breaking-wpt-winc.

8 **I eventually finished:** Most tournaments let you enter multiple times and there are also "side events," or smaller tournaments. So even if you're fortunate enough to finish in the money, you still might come home with less money than you started with.

9 **expert guidance that changed:** Jack Brewster, "Is Trump Right That Fauci Discouraged Wearing Masks? Yes—But Early On and Not for Long," *Forbes*, October 20, 2020, forbes.com/sites/jackbrewster/2020/10/20/is-trump-right-that-fauci-discouraged-wearing-masks.

9 **within specific domains:** Ann-Renee Blais and Elke U. Weber, "The Domain-Specific Risk Taking Scale for Adult Populations: Item Selection and Preliminary Psychometric Properties," Defence R&D Canada, December 2009, apps.dtic.mil/sti/pdfs/ADA535440.pdf.

9 **riding a motorcycle:** Ezekiel J. Emanuel, "Stop Dismissing the Risk of Long Covid," *The Washington Post*, May 12, 2022, sec. Opinion, washingtonpost.com/opinions/2022/05/12/stop-dismissing-long-covid-pandemic-symptoms.

9 **Motorcycles are about thirty times:** "Facts + Statistics: Motorcycle Crashes," Insurance Information Institute, iii.org/fact-statistic/facts-statistics-motorcycle-crashes.

9 **younger people take on:** Wai Him Crystal Law et al., "Younger Adults Tolerate More Relational Risks in Everyday Life as Revealed by the General Risk-Taking Questionnaire," *Scientific Reports* 12, no. 1 (July 16, 2022): 12184, doi.org/10.1038/s41598-022-16438-2.

9 **far less risky behavior:** Jude Ball et al., "The Great Decline in Adolescent Risk Behaviours: Unitary Trend, Separate Trends, or Cascade?," *Social Science & Medicine* 317 (January 2023): 115616, doi.org/10.1016/j.socscimed.2022.115616.

10 **Americans lost around:** American Gaming Association, "2022 Commercial Gaming Revenue Tops $60B, Breaking Annual Record for Second Consecutive Year," February 15, 2023, prnewswire.com/news-releases/2022-commercial-gaming-revenue-tops-60b-breaking-annual-record-for-second-consecutive-year-301747087.html.

10 **unlicensed, gray-market:** "New AGA Report Shows Americans Gamble More Than Half a Trillion Dollars Illegally Each Year," American Gaming Association, November 30, 2022, americangaming.org/new/new-aga-report-shows-americans-gamble-more-than-half-a-trillion-dollars-illegally-each-year.

10 **about $30 billion:** "Lotteries, Casinos, Sports Betting, and Other Types of State-Sanctioned Gambling," Urban Institute, April 21, 2023, urban.org/policy-centers/cross-center-initiatives/state-and-local -finance-initiative/state-and-local-backgrounders/lotteries-casinos-sports-betting-and-other -types-state-sanctioned-gambling.

10 **amount they *wagered*:** Jonathan Chang and Meghna Chakrabarti, "The Real Winners and Losers in America's Lottery Obsession," WBUR, January 4, 2023, wbur.org/onpoint/2023/01/04/the-real-win ners-and-losers-in-americas-lottery-obsession.

10 **American life expectancy:** Elizabeth Arias et al., "Provisional Life Expectancy Estimates for 2021," NVSS Vital Statistics Rapid Release, no. 23, August 2022, cdc.gov/nchs/data/vsrr/vsrr023.pdf.

10 **have begun rebounding:** "Life Expectancy Increases, However Suicides Up in 2022," November 29, 2023, National Center for Health Statistics, cdc.gov/nchs/pressroom/nchs_press_releases/2023/20231129 .htm.

11 **being more risk-taking:** Max Roser, "Why Is Life Expectancy in the US Lower Than in Other Rich Countries?," Our World in Data, December 28, 2023, ourworldindata.org/us-life-expectancy-low.

12 **Ferdinand Thrun, was:** wiclarkcountyhistory.org/4data/87/87056.htm.

13 **underage male pages:** Peter Lee, "The Worldwide Gambling Storm," *China Matters* (blog), February 8, 2007, chinamatters.blogspot.com/2007/02/worldwide-gambling-storm.html.

13 **Jim Leach of Iowa:** David S. Broder, "A Veteran Moderate Moves On," *The Washington Post*, November 30, 2006, washingtonpost.com/archive/opinions/2006/11/30/a-veteran-moderate-moves-on/faade03e -2bd4-4be4-ab05-c068995f3622.

14 **analytics service Chartbeat:** Specifically, by total engaged minutes. Terri Walter, "The Results Are In: 2016's Most Engaging Stories," Chartbeat, January 24, 2017, blog.chartbeat.com/2017/01/24/the-re sults-are-in-2016s-most-engaging-stories.

14 **estimate of Trump's chances:** Matthew Yglesias, "Why I Think Nate Silver's Model Underrates Clinton's Odds," *Vox*, November 7, 2016, vox.com/policy-and-politics/2016/11/7/13550068/nate-silver-forecast -wrong.

14 **less than 1 percent:** Josh Katz, "Who Will Be President?," *The New York Times*, July 19, 2016, sec. The Up-shot, nytimes.com/interactive/2016/upshot/presidential-polls-forecast.html.

14 **around 1 chance in 6:** Matt Lott and John Stossel, "Election Betting Odds," Election Betting Odds, No-vember 7, 2016, web.archive.org/web/20161108000856/electionbettingodds.com.

15 **make billions of dollars:** Alfred Charles and Joan Murray, "Seminole Tribe Announces Expanded Gam-bling Options—Craps, Roulette, Sports Betting—at All Florida Locations," CBS News Miami, November 1, 2023, cbsnews.com/miami/news/seminole-tribe-announces-expanded-gambling-options-craps-rou lette-sports-betting-at-all-florida-locations.

16 **2000 presidential election:** Jonathan N. Wand, Kenneth W. Shotts, Jasjeet S. Sekhon, et al., "The Butter-fly Did It: The Aberrant Vote for Buchanan in Palm Beach County, Florida," *The American Political Science Review* 95, no. 4 (2001): 793–810, jstor.org/stable/3117714.

16 **over COVID-19 vaccines:** "See How Vaccinations Are Going in Your County and State," *The New York Times*, December 17, 2020, sec. U.S., nytimes.com/interactive/2020/us/covid-19-vaccine-doses.html.

17 **even God's will:** Steven Waldman, "Heaven Sent," *Slate*, September 13, 2004, slate.com/human-in terest/2004/09/does-god-endorse-bush.html.

17 ***betting* on politics:** For a variety of reasons—my employers wouldn't have liked it, I already have a lot of professional risk tied up in the outcomes, and I sometimes have inside knowledge or information—I haven't bet on elections myself. But I certainly don't have any moral qualms with doing so.

18 **a knotty problem:** According to scientists I spoke with for this book, the vast majority of activity in the human brain is directed toward movement. So this is probably a good idea: when you're moving around you're literally jogging your memory.

18 **gamblers love metaphors:** Although "river" is a gambling term too. The river is the last card that's dealt in a game of Texas Hold'em, following the flop (first three cards) and turn (penultimate card).

20 **promised to commit:** Mat Di Salvo, "FTX Pledges up to $1 Billion for Philanthropic Fund to 'Improve Humanity,'" Decrypt, February 28, 2022, decrypt.co/94045/ftx-1-billion-philanthropic-future-fund -improve-humanity.

20 **cost-effective intervention:** "Malaria," Effective Altruism Forum, forum.effectivealtruism.org/topics /malaria.

20 **One friend calls:** Matt Glassman, a government professor at Georgetown University.

21 **"Should ChatGPT make":** splinter, "Should ChatGPT Make Us Downweight Our Belief in the Conscious-ness of Non-Human Animals?," EA Forum, February 18, 2023, forum.effectivealtruism.org/posts/Bi 8av6iknHFXkSxnS/should-chatgpt-make-us-downweight-our-belief-in-the.

21 **ultraviolet germicidal irradiation:** Jam Kraprayoon, "Does the US Public Support Ultraviolet Germi-cidal Irradiation Technology for Reducing Risks from Pathogens?," EA Forum, February 2, 2023, forum .effectivealtruism.org/posts/2rD6nLqw5Z3dyD5me/does-the-us-public-support-ultraviolet -germicidal.

21 **well predicted by some EAs:** Scott Alexander, "Grading My 2018 Predictions for 2023," *Astral Codex Ten* (blog), February 20, 2023, astralcodexten.substack.com/p/grading-my-2018-predictions-for-2023.

22 **developed probability theory:** Thomas DeMichele, "Probability Theory Was Invented to Solve a Gambling Problem—Fact or Myth?," Fact/Myth, June 29, 2021, factmyth.com/factoids/probability-theory -was-invented-to-solve-a-gambling-problem.

22 **Signal-processing algorithms:** William Poundstone, *Fortune's Formula: The Untold Story of the Scientific Betting System That Beat the Casinos and Wall Street*, Kindle ed. (New York: Hill and Wang, 2006).

24 **The final term:** I first encountered the term "decoupling" through the work of John Nerst; everything studies.com/2018/05/25/decoupling-revisited/.

24 **As Sarah Constantin puts it:** Sarah Constantin, "Do Rational People Exist?," *Otium* (blog), June 9, 2014, srconstantin.wordpress.com/2014/06/09/do-rationalists-exist.

24 **logical and statistical reasoning:** Constantin, "Do Rational People Exist?"

24 **Imagine someone saying:** Or if you prefer to imagine a comment from a conservative speaker, replace "Chick-fil-A," "gay marriage," and "chicken sandwich" with "Nike," "Black Lives Matter," and "sneakers."

24 **"on gay marriage":** Grace Schneider and Cameron Knight, "Years Later, Chick-fil-A Still Feels Heat from LGBTQ Groups over Anti-Gay Marriage Remarks," *USA Today*, March 26, 2019, usatoday.com/story /news/2019/03/26/chickfila-ceo-gay-marriage-comments-still-impact-reputation-lgbtq-com munity/3279206002.

25 **the historical provenance:** John Nerst, "A Deep Dive into the Harris-Klein Controversy," *Everything Studies* (blog), April 26, 2018, everythingstudies.com/2018/04/26/a-deep-dive-into-the-harris-klein -controversy.

25 **"juicy collection":** Ben Smith, "An Arrest in Canada Casts a Shadow on a New York Times Star, and The Times," *The New York Times*, October 11, 2020, sec. The Media Equation, nytimes.com/2020/10/11/busi ness/media/new-york-times-rukmini-callimachi-caliphate.html.

26 **its most admired:** Jeffrey M. Jones, "Donald Trump, Michelle Obama Most Admired in 2020," Gallup, December 29, 2020, news.gallup.com/poll/328193/donald-trump-michelle-obama-admired-2020.aspx.

26 **flooded with dopamine:** John Coates, *The Hour Between Dog and Wolf: How Risk Taking Transforms Us, Body and Mind*, Kindle ed. (New York: Penguin Books, 2013), 8.

26 **Entrepreneurs usually have:** Jessica Elliott, "Traits Successful Entrepreneurs Have in Common," US Chamber of Commerce, April 13, 2022, uschamber.com/co/grow/thrive/successful-entrepreneu r-traits.

26 **I call it the Village:** Although I came up with "the Village" on my own, I've seen similar coinages to refer to similar groups of people elsewhere, for example from Freddie deBoer: freddiedeboer.substack.com /p/these-rules-about-platforming-nazis.

26 **adversarial toward the tech sector:** Kelsey Piper (@KelseyTuoc), "People might think Matt is overstating this but I literally heard it from NYT reporters at the time. There was a top-down decision that tech could not be covered positively, even when there was a true, newsworthy and positive story. I'd never heard anything like it," Twitter, November 3, 2022, twitter.com/KelseyTuoc/status/1588231892792328192.

26 **skeptical of movements such as EA:** Robby Soave, "What *The New York Times*' Hit Piece on *Slate Star Codex* Says About Media Gatekeeping," Reason, February 15, 2021, reason.com/2021/02/15/what-the -new-york-times-hit-piece-on-slate-star-codex-says-about-media-gatekeeping.

26 **major political player:** Bankman-Fried confirmed this in my interviews with him. Also see Nik Popli, "Sam Bankman-Fried's Political Donations: What We Know," *Time*, December 14, 2022, time.com /6241262/sam-bankman-fried-political-donations.

27 **the Village's claims:** Nate Silver, "Twitter, Elon and the Indigo Blob," *Silver Bulletin* (blog), October 1, 2023, natesilver.net/p/twitter-elon-and-the-indigo-blob.

28 **nakedly partisan positions:** Dan Diamond, "Suddenly, Public Health Officials Say Social Justice Matters More Than Social Distance," *Politico*, June 4, 2020, politico.com/news/magazine/2020/06/04/public -health-protests-301534.

28 **discourage Pfizer from making:** Keith A. Reynolds, "Coronavirus: Pfizer CEO Says Company to Seek EUA for Vaccine After Election," Medical Economics, October 16, 2020, medicaleconomics.com/view /coronavirus-pfizer-ceo-says-company-to-seek-eua-for-vaccine-after-election.

28 **most-educated counties in:** Based on counties with at least ten thousand people.

28 **17-point margin:** Author's calculations.

29 **standardized test scores:** Freddie deBoer, "Please, Think Critically About College Admissions," *Freddie DeBoer* (blog), May 27, 2021, freddiedeboer.substack.com/p/please-think-critically-about-college.

29 **disruptions to education:** Sarah Mervosh, "The Pandemic Erased Two Decades of Progress in Math and Reading," *The New York Times*, September 1, 2022, sec. U.S., nytimes.com/2022/09/01/us/national-test -scores-math-reading-pandemic.html.

29 **a plurality identify:** In a user survey for *Astral Codex Ten*, the influential rationalist blog by Scott Alexander that attracts a cross section of River types, 42 percent of American respondents said they were

registered as Democrats compared to just 10 percent as Republicans. Another 4 percent were registered with third parties, while the rest weren't registered with a party. Scott Alexander, "ACX Survey Results 2022," *Astral Codex Ten* (blog), January 20, 2023, astralcodexten.substack.com/p/acx-survey-results -2022.

29 **the River is very white:** In the *Astral Codex Ten* survey, 88 percent of readers identified as white and 88 percent as male. Other parts of The River are more racially and ethnically diverse—poker, for instance— but nearly all of it is quite male. Alexander, "ACX Survey Results 2022."

30 **cofounder of WeWork:** Andrew Ross Sorkin et al., "Adam Neumann Gets a New Backer," *The New York Times*, August 15, 2022, sec. Business, nytimes.com/2022/08/15/business/dealbook/adam-neumann -flow-new-company-wework-real-estate.html.

30 **revival of nationalist governments:** Sabina Mihelj and César Jiménez-Martínez, "Digital Nationalism: Understanding the Role of Digital Media in the Rise of 'New' Nationalism," *Nations and Nationalism* 27, no. 2 (April 2021): 331–46, doi.org/10.1111/nana.12685.

30 **depression among adolescents:** Jonathan Haidt and Jean M. Twenge, "This Is Our Chance to Pull Teen- agers Out of the Smartphone Trap," *The New York Times*, July 31, 2021, sec. Opinion, nytimes.com/2021 /07/31/opinion/smartphone-iphone-social-media-isolation.html.

30 **time for moral clarity:** Wesley Lowery, "A Reckoning Over Objectivity, Led by Black Journalists," *The New York Times*, June 23, 2020, sec. Opinion, nytimes.com/2020/06/23/opinion/objectivity-black-jour nalists-coronavirus.html.

31 **creates dumb rules:** Daniel Carpenter and David A. Moss, eds., *Preventing Regulatory Capture: Special Interest Influence and How to Limit It*, 1st ed. (New York: Cambridge University Press, 2013), doi.org /10.1017/CBO9781139565875.

Chapter 1: Optimization

39 **a people game:** Doyle Brunson, *Doyle Brunson's Super/System: A Course in Power Poker*, 3rd ed. (New York: Cardoza Publishing, 2002).

39 *Super System,* **a 608-page behemoth:** Brunson won the Main Event at the World Series of Poker twice, and had ten overall WSOP bracelets—a bracelet is awarded for winning any of the many tournaments that are part of the WSOP's annual schedule.

39 **"Timid players** *don't***":** Brunson, *Doyle Brunson's Super/System*, 21. Emphasis in original.

39 **"he becomes aggressive":** Brunson, *Doyle Brunson's Super/System*, 20.

39 **"how much bluffing":** Brunson, *Doyle Brunson's Super/System*, 29.

40 **French game** *poque***:** Most of this section is per conversation with James McManus and his book on poker history. James McManus, *Cowboys Full: The Story of Poker*, 1st Picador ed. (New York: Picador, 2010).

40 **six-time cancer survivor:** Pauly McGuire, "Doyle Brunson Beats Cancer for the Sixth Time," Club Poker, April 21, 2016, en.clubpoker.net/doyle-brunson-beats-cancer-for-the-sixth-time/n-215.

40 **gastric bypass surgery:** cardplayer.com/poker-blogs/30-doyle-brunson/entries/2902-do-as-i-say-8230 -not-as-i-do.

40 **cash out his chips:** Doyle Brunson Legacy (@TexDolly), "Just cashed in my chips but before I walk out that door one last time, I just wanted to tell you all how much I loved this poker world. I didn't want to go yet, was actually planning to play some events this summer . . . ," Twitter, May 19, 2023, twitter.com /TexDolly/status/1659456928945410048.

41 **accident unloading sheetrock:** Earl Burton, "Doyle Brunson Inducted into Hardin-Simmons University Athletic Hall of Fame," Poker News Daily, October 14, 2009, pokernewsdaily.com/doyle-brunson -inducted-into-hardin-simmons-university-athletic-hall-of-fame-5589.

43 **22 actually beats AK:** Combining the results for AK suited and AK offsuit.

43 **a substantial winner:** At least based on hands that were shown on the broadcast. High Stakes Poker is an edited show. HSP Stats Database, Two Plus Two Forums, forumserver.twoplustwo.com/27/casino-amp -cardroom-poker/hsp-stats-database-747892/index17.html.

43 **modern poker software:** Interview with Doyle Brunson.

45 **strong means weak:** This phrase is generally attributed to Mike Caro. See, for example: Mike Caro, *Ca- ro's Book of Poker Tells: The Psychology and Body Language of Poker* (New York: Cardoza Publishing, 2003).

45 **usually betting again:** Brunson, *Doyle Brunson's Super/System*, 422.

46 **program named Polaris:** Robert Blincoe, "Computers Tell a Poker Strategy," *The Guardian*, September 24, 2008, sec. Technology, theguardian.com/technology/2008/sep/25/computing.research.

46 **descendant of Polaris:** Oliver Roeder, "The Machines Are Coming for Poker," FiveThirtyEight, January 19, 2017, fivethirtyeight.com/features/the-machines-are-coming-for-poker.

46 **sibling called Pluribus:** James Vincent, "Facebook and CMU's 'Superhuman' Poker AI Beats Human Pros," *The Verge*, July 11, 2019, theverge.com/2019/7/11/20690078/ai-poker-pluribus-facebook-cmu -texas-hold-em-six-player-no-limit.

47 **another potential defense:** Brunson, *Doyle Brunson's Super/System*, 18.

48 aren't any insurmountable barriers: See for instance the responses in this Twitter thread, which drew replies from various people with expertise in robotics. Nate Silver (@NateSilver538), "Weird question for my book. Given current tech, could a robot physically play in a poker game? It would need to e.g.:—Handle poker chips—Lift up its cards to read them without revealing to other players—Visually recognize action without verbal cues (e.g. Player X bet \$200)," Twitter, March 31, 2023, twitter.com/NateSilver538/status/1641909746201493506.

48 their facial expression: Yilun Wang and Michal Kosinski, "Deep Neural Networks Are More Accurate Than Humans at Detecting Sexual Orientation from Facial Images," *Journal of Personality and Social Psychology* 114, no. 2 (February 2018): 246–57, doi.org/10.1037/pspa0000098.

48 third-best player: Barry Carter, "Polk Crowns the Greatest Poker Player of All Time," PokerStrategy .com, March 16, 2022, pokerstrategy.com/news/world-of-poker/Polk-crowns-the-greatest-poker-player -of-all-time_121951.

48 a "calling station": Daniel Negreanu (@RealKidPoker), "'Fundamentally sloppy, loose, passive, sticky, calling station.' That's me describing my poker style lol. #DontTryThisAtHomeKids," Twitter, February 9, 2014, twitter.com/RealKidPoker/status/432348562064564224.

48 who lost money: Andrew Burnett, "Daniel Negreanu Reveals His Last Decade of Poker Profit and Loss," HighStakesDB, August 3, 2021, highstakesdb.com/news/high-stakes-reports/daniel-negreanu-reveals -his-last-decade-of-poker-profit-and-loss.

49 From July 2021: Unless otherwise cited, tournament results are taken from the Hendon Mob Poker Database and are current as of January 5, 2024. See, e.g.: pokerdb.thehendonmob.com/player.php?a=r&n= 181&sort=place&dir=asc.

50 a child prodigy: Ananyo Bhattacharya, *The Man from the Future: The Visionary Life of John von Neumann*, Kindle ed. (New York: W. W. Norton & Company, 2021), 3; Harry Henderson, *Mathematics: Powerful Patterns into Nature and Society*, Milestones in Discovery and Invention (New York: Chelsea House Publishers, 2007), 30.

50 first computerized weather forecast: Jonathan Hill, *Weather Architecture* (London, New York: Routledge, 2012), 216.

50 a terrible driver: Bhattacharya, *The Man from the Future*, 66.

50 "cigarette-fueled discussions": Bhattacharya, *The Man from the Future*, 84–85.

50 "Chess is not a game": Jacob Bronowski, *The Ascent of Man*, 1st American ed. (Boston: Little, Brown, 1974).

51 a good hand: John von Neumann and Oskar Morgenstern, *Theory of Games and Economic Behavior*, Princeton Classic Editions, Kindle ed. (Princeton, N.J., Woodstock: Princeton University Press, 2007), 361.

51 modern economic theory: Robert Hanson, "What Are Reasonable AI Fears?," *Quillette*, April 14, 2023, quillette.com/2023/04/14/what-are-reasonable-ai-fears.

51 Let me try my hand: This definition was refined after a back-and-forth discussion with ChatGPT.

51 "Robinson Crusoe model": Von Neumann and Morgenstern, *Theory of Games and Economic Behavior*, 61.

52 nonplayer characters: Credit for this idea to Oliver Habryka. There is more about it in chapter 7.

52 prisoner's dilemma, first described in 1950: "Prisoner's Dilemma," ScienceDirect, sciencedirect.com /topics/social-sciences/prisoners-dilemma.

52 siblings, Isabella and Wyatt Blackwood: I chose these names from a set of ChatGPT suggestions for villainous-sounding names; they are not meant to allude to any specific people.

54 as a paradox: The Investopedia Team, Charles Potters, and Pete Rathburn, "What Is the Prisoner's Dilemma and How Does It Work?," Investopedia, March 31, 2023, investopedia.com/terms/p/prisoners -dilemma.asp.

54 human beings cooperate: Leonie Heuer and Andreas Orland, "Cooperation in the Prisoner's Dilemma: An Experimental Comparison Between Pure and Mixed Strategies," *Royal Society Open Science* 6, no. 7 (July 2019): 182142, doi.org/10.1098/rsos.182142.

54 Kant's Golden Rule: Janet Chen, Su-I Lu, and Dan Vekhter, "Applications of Game Theory," Game Theory, cs.stanford.edu/people/eroberts/courses/soco/projects/1998-99/game-theory/applications.html.

55 a nightly profit: That is, 2,000 slices times a \$1.50 profit per slice.

55 the average restaurant: Jessica Reimer and Sarah Zorn, "What Is the Average Restaurant Profit Margin?," Toast, January 21, 2021, pos.toasttab.com/blog/on-the-line/average-restaurant-profit-margin.

56 unable to cooperate: To be more precise, for a situation to be a prisoner's dilemma, people would have to be better off *individually* by cooperating and not just collectively. This point is frequently missed in popular mentions of the prisoner's dilemma. A 2020 *New York Times* article, for instance, citing the work of a pair of Canadian researchers, likened the failure to take COVID-19 precautions to a prisoner's dilemma. But even if you grant that society is collectively better off if people take more COVID precautions, that doesn't hold at an individual level. An extremely healthy eighteen-year-old student who had already recovered from a bout of COVID probably wouldn't be better off from a university lockdown requiring her to stay in her dorm room, for instance. If she snuck out one night to go to a party, you could say she was being selfish, but that probably suits her individual needs better than the university's one-size-fits-all policy. It's only a prisoner's dilemma when *every* participant in the "game" would be better off by cooperating. Siobhan Roberts, "'The Pandemic Is a Prisoner's Dilemma Game,'" *The New York Times*, December 20, 2020, sec. Health, nytimes.com/2020/12/20/health/virus-vaccine-game-the ory.html.

56 **when OPEC colludes to set:** "OPEC (Cartel)," Energy Education, energyeducation.ca/encyclopedia /OPEC_(cartel).

56 **avoid confrontations with each other:** Technically, these players *are* playing a zero-sum game, but it's a zero-sum game between *all players at the table.* When two players with big chip stacks collide, they're costing themselves money and transferring it to the table that's just sitting idly by.

56 **call him Holden:** I know the player's real name but I'm not going to use it because I don't want to make it seem as though I'm accusing him of misconduct—it was a highly ambiguous situation.

57 **Holden later told me:** He said he had A5s (ace-five suited). Although players sometimes lie about their hands.

58 **rotation of their poker chips:** YaGirlfriendsSidePc, "Can Anyone Help Me Find a Way to Randomize in a Live Cash Game?," Reddit post, R/Poker, January 26, 2022, www.reddit.com/r/poker/comments /scxzes/can_anyone_help_me_find_a_way_to_randomize_in_a.

58 **the economist Thomas Schelling:** Thomas Schelling, "The Threat That Leaves Something to Chance," RAND, rand.org/pubs/historical_documents/HDA1631-1.html.

58 **Nash's most famous paper:** John F. Nash, "Equilibrium Points in N-Person Games," *Proceedings of the National Academy of Sciences* 36, no. 1 (January 1950): 48–49, doi.org/10.1073/pnas.36.1.48.

58 **subject to a few other conditions:** The most important of which is that the players are acting independently rather than forming coalitions.

59 **should guess fastball:** There's nothing particularly special about these numbers: if you plugged in different numbers into the 2 × 2 matrix above, you'd come up with a different mix for both players.

60 **what pitch to throw:** Sean Braswell, "Should Baseball Pitchers Choose Their Pitches at Random?," Ozy, October 22, 2018, web.archive.org/web/20201030142411/ozy.com/the-new-and-the-next/should -baseball-pitchers-choose-their-pitches-at-random/88802.

60 **Maddux is a highly proficient:** William Gildea, "Mind over Battle," *The Washington Post*, October 13, 1995, washingtonpost.com/archive/sports/1995/10/13/mind-over-batter/06d2226e-82cd-49c5-b903-5ff 28a669f2e.

60 **chess engines that played:** "FRITZ 7 Making New Friends," ChessBase, web.archive.org/web/20020 806084641/http://www.chessbase.com/catalog/product.asp?pid=85.

60 **University of Alberta's AI work:** "Cepheus," Cepheus Poker Project, poker.srv.ualberta.ca/about.

61 **no two decks:** Matt Glassman (@MattGlassman312), "If you thoroughly shuffle a deck of cards, the odds than [*sic*] any deck in the history of the world has been in the same order is essentially zero," Twitter, August 3, 2020, twitter.com/MattGlassman312/status/1290409817727733762.

61 **two-card starting hands:** Assuming that suits matter, which they often don't. If you don't care about suits—that is, you treat A♦K♦ as equivalent to A♥K♥—there are 169 starting hands.

61 **possible sequences of:** This assumes that the order of the three cards on the flop doesn't matter since they're all dealt at once, but the order of the turn and river cards does.

61 **possible combinations of cards:** Michael Johanson, "Measuring the Size of Large No-Limit Poker Games" arXiv, March 7, 2013, arxiv.org/abs/1302.7008.

61 **process called "iteration":** Tom Boshoff, "How Solvers Work," *GTO Wizard* (blog), January 23, 2023, blog .gtowizard.com/how-solvers-work.

64 **prototype of PioSOLVER:** The first commercial version was available a year later, in 2015.

64 **a small species of oak tree:** "Post oak bluff," Urban Dictionary, urbandictionary.com/define.php?term= post%20oak%20bluff.

64 **Brunson considered these bets:** Brunson, *Doyle Brunson's Super/System*, 338.

66 **a mostly online:** The first two hundred hands were played live in the PokerGO studio, mostly as a way to build publicity for the match.

66 **quickly established Polk:** Will Shillibier, "We Take a Look at the Polk vs. Negreanu Betting Odds," November 2, 2020, PokerNews, pokernews.com/news/2020/11/negreanu-polk-match-betting-odds-38168.htm.

66 **to promote himself:** Negreanu is an ambassador for the online poker site GGPoker and had been hoping the match would be played there, but instead it was played on an unrelated site, WSOP.com.

66 **"Polk exploit ranges":** For instance, Negreanu told me that Polk three-bet with KJ (king-jack) too often, and as a result, he was able to four-bet more often with hands such as AJ and KQ that perform well against KJ. But a player only gets dealt KJ 1.2 percent of the time, and of those times, Negreanu will only rarely have a hand like KQ that can take advantage and make the exploit.

67 **significant side bets:** Mary Ortiz, "Polk vs. Negreanu: Doug Polk's Insane Side Bets," Ace Poker Solutions, February 1, 2021, web.archive.org/web/20210201234931/acepokersolutions.com/poker-blog/po kerarticles/polk-vs-negreanu-doug-polks-insane-side-bets.

68 **an unexpected move:** Steve Friess, "From the Poker Table to Wall Street," *The New York Times*, July 27, 2018, sec. Business, nytimes.com/2018/07/27/business/vanessa-selbst-poker-bridgewater.html.

68 Selbst discovered poker: Tim Struby, "Her Poker Face," *ESPN The Magazine*, June 27, 2013, espn.com /poker/story/_/page/Selbst/how-vanessa-selbst-became-best-female-poker-player-all-espn-magazine.

68 fame and fortune: Daniel G. Habib, "Online and Obsessed," *Sports Illustrated*, May 30, 2005, vault .si.com/vault/2005/05/30/online-and-obsessed.

69 one of the ESPN announcers: "$2K No-Limit Hold'em," WSOP 2006 Bracelet Events, PokerGO, 2006, pokergo.com/videos/0d82e9c0-ca54-4b08-8bd5-d8466d6ee54f.

70 Selbst's favorite example: The hand begins at approximately 10:35 in this video: "PCA 10 2013—$25,000 High Roller, Final Table," PokerStars, 2019, dailymotion.com/video/x6ai4k9.

72 one of the commentators said: The commentator in this hand was Joe "Stapes" Stapleton, a favorite of many players including myself. But Stapleton's approach is that he reflects the voice of the everyday poker player, and not a solver-trained whiz kid. So to the extent he's critical of Selbst, he's reflecting how most players would have viewed the play at the time.

72 journalist H. L. Mencken: It's unclear if Mencken said this directly or if it's a paraphrase of something else he wrote. Quote Investigator, March 1, 2020, quoteinvestigator.com/2020/03/01/underestimate.

73 poker hands I'm best known for: "America's Top Statistician Nate Silver Runs Epic Bluff in $10,000 Poker Tournament," PokerGO, 2022, youtube.com/watch?v=9cVrlVzoh48.

74 1 million in chips: This calculation is complicated to make when there are still multiple players in the tournament, but it's simple when there are just two left. You can simply divide the additional amount of money that goes to first place (in this case, $51,800) by the number of chips still in play between both players.

74 the Dirty Diaper: Jon Sofen, "Nick Rigby Plays the 2-3 'Dirty Diaper' in 2021 WSOP Main Event," PokerNews, November 14, 2021, pokernews.com/news/2021/11/nicholas-rigby-wsop-main-23-dirty -diaper-40241.htm.

75 play the solver likes: The solver I used to evaluate this hand is GTOx; app.gtox.io/app. Note that a raise is used as part of a mixed strategy; calling is also used as part of the mix.

75 solver would have recommended: The solver would have bet again with a slightly better hand, 92o.

77 we'd played earlier: In the earlier hand, the flop was an A, K, and a small card. I'd raised before the flop with a suited connector (two cards of the same suit and roughly the same rank) and had missed the board. Nevertheless, I'd bet the flop and Hendrix had called. The turn was another small card and we both checked—I was waving the white flag and giving up on the hand. The turn was a Q, making the final board AKQxx with two small cards. Hendrix checked and I bet, hoping to represent QQ, KQ or JT (which made a straight). Hendrix took a long time before calling with AT for top pair. For a solver, this is typically an easy call because the fact that he has a T—one of the cards I need for my straight—makes it less likely that I actually have one.

78 a $20,000 mistake: Per GTOx.

78 Hendrix could beat: Although this isn't quite true. The solver does have me betting a smattering of worse flushes, although it checks with some of them also. It's generally a mistake to fold if your opponent can sometimes be betting a worse hand for value.

Chapter 2: Perception

80 Garret Adelstein looked: Bart Hanson also used this phrase on the livestream.

80 former pharmaceutical marketing executive: This was reported by the *Los Angeles Times*, although I've been unable to confirm it independently.

80 "fake Hollywood way": Andrea Chang, "An Afternoon with Robbi Jade Lew, the Woman at the Center of the Poker Cheating Scandal," *Los Angeles Times*, October 7, 2022, sec. Business, latimes.com/business /story/2022-10-07/poker-cheating-scandal-robbi-jade-lew.

80 contestant on *Survivor*: Chang, "An Afternoon with Robbi Jade Lew."

81 Adelstein had significant say: Per interviews on the *Doug Polk Podcast* with Garrett Adelstein and Nik Airball.

81 the biggest winner: "*Hustler Casino Live* Poker Tracker," Tracking Poker, June 1, 2023, trackingpoker .com/playersprofile/Garrett-Adelstein/HCL-poker-results/all.

81 additional undisclosed amount: Once the show finishes recording, the games often continue and sometimes become even wilder because the players aren't risking public embarrassment with a misplay.

81 recently been voted: Barry Carter, "Polk Crowns the Greatest Poker Player of All Time," PokerStrategy .com, March 16, 2022, pokerstrategy.com/news/world-of-poker/Polk-crowns-the-greatest-poker -player-of-all-time_121951.

82 struggles with depression: Eric Mertens, "Garrett Adelstein Opens Up About Depression on Ingram's Poker Life Podcast," PokerNews, April 15, 2019, pokernews.com/news/2019/04/garrett-adelstein-talks -about-depression-poker-life-podcast-33883.htm.

84 chess player Magnus Carlsen: Bill Chappell, "Chess World Champion Magnus Carlsen Accuses Hans Niemann of Cheating," NPR, September 27, 2022, npr.org/2022/09/27/1125316142/chess-magnus -carlsen-hans-niemann-cheating.

84 **is extremely litigious:** Haley Hintze, "Veronica Brill Wins $27K Frivolous-Lawsuit Judgment Against Mike Postle," CardsChat, June 17, 2021, cardschat.com/news/veronica-brill-wins-27k-frivolous-law suit-judgment-against-mike-postle-101479.

84 **named Mike Postle:** Philip Conneller, "Poker Players Sue Stones Gambling Hall, Mike Postle for $30 Million," Casino.org, October 9, 2019, casino.org/news/poker-players-sue-stones-gambling-hall-mike -postle-for-30-million.

84 **treatment of women:** David Schoen, "Garrett Adelstein-Robbi Jade Lew Poker Hand Sparks Cheating Scandal," *Las Vegas Review-Journal*, October 7, 2022, sec. Sports, reviewjournal.com/sports/poker /poker-cheating-scandal-sparks-debate-about-math-sexism-2653637.

85 **explanation that Lew:** "(DAY 2) Garrett vs Robbi Investigation into Cheating Allegations. . . . ," 2022, youtube.com/watch?v=EwsXTcZnPn8.

85 **She'd received coaching:** Connor Richards, "Robbi Lew's Poker Coach Faraz Jaka Offers Thoughts on HCL Controversy," PokerNews, October 1, 2022, pokernews.com/news/2022/10/robbi-lew-s-poker -coach-faraz-jaka-offers-thoughts-on-hcl-co-42201.htm.

86 **$250,000 bounty out:** "$250,000 Bounty Award for Whistleblower in Robbi-Garrett Case," PokerPro, October 10, 2022, en.pokerpro.cc//news/250-000-bounty-award-for-whistleblower-in-robbi-garrett -case-568.html.

87 **poker essay contest:** Haley Hintze, "Matt Glassman Wins PokerStars Platinum Pass in 'Memorable Hand' Contest," Poker.org, January 5, 2023, poker.org/matt-glassman-wins-pokerstars-platinum-pass -in-memorable-hand-contest.

89 **Coates instead went:** "John M Coates," Edge, edge.org/memberbio/john_m_coates.

89 **the twilight hour:** Mark Macrides, "*Entre Chien et Loup* (Between Dog and Wolf)," Loft Artists Association, January 18, 2020, loftartists.org/archives/entre-chien-et-loup.

89 **"this primitive part":** John Coates, *The Hour Between the Dog and the Wolf* (New York: Penguin Books, 2013), 7.

90 **that their testosterone:** Coates, *The Hour Between the Dog and the Wolf*, 186.

90 **Steven Levitt, for example:** Annie Duke, *Quit: The Power of Knowing When to Walk Away*, Kindle ed. (New York: Portfolio/Penguin, 2022), 41.

91 **these biological factors:** Coates, *The Hour Between the Dog and the Wolf*, 22.

91 **"no other job":** Coates, *The Hour Between the Dog and the Wolf*, 10.

93 **Iowa Gambling Task:** Antoine Bechara et al., "Insensitivity to Future Consequences Following Damage to Human Prefrontal Cortex," *Cognition* 50, no. 1–3 (April 1994): 7–15, doi.org/10.1016/0010-0277(94) 90018-3.

93 **the risky decks:** Christian A. Webb, Sophie DelDonno, and William D. S. Killgore, "The Role of Cognitive Versus Emotional Intelligence in Iowa Gambling Task Performance: What's Emotion Got to Do with It?," *Intelligence* 44 (2014): 112–19, doi.org/10.1016/j.intell.2014.03.008.

94 **at the Masters:** "How Important Is Experience at Augusta National?," *Analytics Blog* (blog), Data Golf, April 8, 2019, datagolf.ca/does-experience-matter-at-augusta.

94 **the NBA playoffs:** Nate Silver, "Why the Warriors and Cavs Are Still Big Favorites," FiveThirtyEight, October 13, 2017, fivethirtyeight.com/features/why-the-warriors-and-cavs-are-still-big-favorites.

94 **from Michael Jordan:** David, "Michael Jordan's 1992 Playboy Magazine Interview: Jealously, Racism & Fear," Ballislife, September 28, 2017, ballislife.com/michael-jordans-1992-playboy-magazine-interview -jealously-racism-fear.

94 **goalie Ken Dryden:** Coates, *The Hour Between Dog and Wolf*, 78.

95 **national news coverage:** Ryan Glasspiegel, "Nate Silver Made Brutal All-in Call at WSOP: 'F—King Poker,'" *New York Post*, July 13, 2023, nypost.com/2023/07/13/nate-silver-made-brutal-all-in-call-at -wsop-f-king-poker.

95 **playing to survive:** This was not the exact phrasing, but it was the gist of the question.

95 **a $500,000 tournament:** The average prize awarded to players who finished in the top 100 was about $520,000; pokerdb.thehendonmob.com/event.php?a=r&n=909123.

95 **a big call:** The key sequence of hands begins at 4:30 in this video: "WSOP 2023 Main Event | Day 6 (Part 1)," PokerGO, pokergo.com/videos/d3643be8-68ac-43ca-adbf-1bbe58b1bf6d.

96 **never won more:** "Stephen Friedrich," Hendon Mob Poker Database, pokerdb.thehendonmob.com /player.php?a=r&n=1088643.

96 **the equivalent of around:** Derek Wolters (@derek_wolters), "ICM for WSOP Main Day 7 T.Co/mTOY9e 5Fwh," Twitter, July 13, 2023, twitter.com/derek_wolters/status/1679527855577766145.

97 **for a split second:** Chan called my all-in and flipped over his hand almost immediately, so there wasn't much time to relish the moment.

97 **nicknamed "Poker Brat":** Jon Sofen, "The Muck: Did Phil Hellmuth's F-Bomb Rant Cross the Line?," PokerNews, October 12, 2021, pokernews.com/news/2021/10/the-muck-did-phil-hellmuth-s-f-bomb -rant-cross-the-line-40034.htm.

98 **"grades were bad":** For clarity, this snippet is from my interview with Hellmuth where he was recalling what he wrote in his book—not a quote from the book itself.

99 **"best exploitative player"**: "Daniel Negreanu Explains Poker to Phil Hellmuth," 2021, youtube.com /watch?v=oa6NNI4SCh0.

102 **Seiver recalled a hand**: "Dumbest Fold Ever with Pocket Aces 2014," youtube.com/watch?v=ikkGB 3pQgA0.

108 **taxes poker players**: In the U.S., players are taxed on gambling winnings but generally aren't allowed to write off gambling losses. "Topic No. 419, Gambling Income and Losses," Internal Revenue Service, April 4, 2023, irs.gov/taxtopics/tc419.

109 **her remaining bankroll**: Except the cheapest, $1,000 buy-in events. I assume she'll play those until she's totally broke.

109 **a representative set**: I chose simulations at the fifth, fifteenth, twenty-fifth, thirty-fifth, forty-fifth, fifty-fifth, sixty-fifth, seventy-fifth, eighty-fifth, and ninety-fifth percentiles.

110 **Penelope will lose**: And that assumes she could magically replenish her bankroll to $500,000 at the start of each year. In real life, she'll go very long stretches where she won't have the money left to play the buy-ins that could return her to profitability.

111 **$100,000 per year**: Nathan Williams, "Good Poker Win Rate for Small Stakes (2023 Update)," *BlackRain79— Elite Poker Strategy* (blog), blackrain79.com/2014/06/good-win-rates-for-micro-and-small_6.html.

113 **He was raised in poverty**: Material in this section reflects a combination of my conversation with Koon and this story: Lee Davy, "Going Through Walls: The Jason Koon Poker Story," Triton Poker, September 9, 2020, triton-series.com/going-through-walls-the-jason-koon-poker-story.

113 **"proper" cowboy hat**: Dan Smith (@DanSmithHolla), "Important 🖐clarification: Jason Koon gave me my first proper cowboy hat. I am a bad friend and left this one on a plane in Macau[.] Doyle gave me one of his old hats, which I've been wearing this week," Twitter, July 17, 2018, twitter.com/DanSmithHolla /status/1019313267871645696.

113 **battles with depression**: Dan Smith, *Burning Man Blog* (blog), October 13, 2015, dansmithholla.com /burning-man-blog.

114 **a claim that checks out**: Gabriele Bellucci, Thomas F. Münte, and Soyoung Q. Park, "Influences of So-cial Uncertainty and Serotonin on Gambling Decisions," *Scientific Reports* 12, no. 1 (June 17, 2022): 10220, doi.org/10.1038/s41598-022-13778-x; Robert D. Rogers et al., "Tryptophan Depletion Alters the Decision-Making of Healthy Volunteers Through Altered Processing of Reward Cues," *Neuropsycho-pharmacology* 28, no. 1 (January 2003): 153–62, doi.org/10.1038/sj.npp.1300001; Michael L. Platt and Scott A. Huettel, "Risky Business: The Neuroeconomics of Decision Making Under Uncertainty," *Nature Neuroscience* 11, no. 4 (April 2008): 398–403, doi.org/10.1038/nn2062.

114 **a million views**: "I Buy In for $40,000 and Opponent Tries to Put ME All-In Immediately!," Poker Vlog #487, 2022, youtube.com/watch?v=zGQM-Oee6nI.

114 **as little as $200**: "All-In Flush over Flush!," Poker Vlog #1, 2018, youtube.com/watch?v=ZAD1fBHzuJ4.

114 **Rhode Island casinos**: At least based on Yelp reviews! "Bally's Twin River Lincoln—Lincoln, RI," Yelp, yelp.com/biz/ballys-twin-river-lincoln-lincoln.

115 **more than $500,000**: "Hustler Casino Live Stream," Tracking Poker, March 17, 2023, web.archive.org /web/20231108052335/https://trackingpoker.com/user-info/Rampage.

116 **here's a version**: Richard Wiseman, *The Luck Factor: Changing Your Luck, Changing Your Life: The Four Essential Principles* (New York: Miramax/Hyperion, 2003), 32.

117 **He admitted to losing**: youtube.com/watch?v=Q1U31NN_kXE.

117 **Eugene Calden, who**: Lee Jones, "Eugene Calden—the 100-Year-Old Poker Player," Poker.org, May 11, 2023, poker.org/eugene-calden-the-100-year-old-poker-player.

118 **empathy and emotional intelligence**: Agneta H. Fischer, Mariska E. Kret, and Joost Broekens, "Gender Differences in Emotion Perception and Self-Reported Emotional Intelligence: A Test of the Emotion Sensitivity Hypothesis," ed. Gilles Van Luijtelaar, *PLOS ONE* 13, no. 1 (January 25, 2018): e0190712, doi .org/10.1371/journal.pone.0190712.

118 **inferring someone's emotional state**: "Females Score Higher Than Males on the Widely Used 'Reading the Mind in the Eyes' Test, Study Shows," *Medical News*, December 27, 2022, news-medical.net/news /20221227/Females-score-higher-than-males-on-the-widely-used-Reading-the-Mind-in-the-Eyes -Test-study-shows.aspx.

118 **burn the Rio**: Jon Sofen, "The Muck: Did Phil Hellmuth's F-Bomb Rant Cross the Line?"

118 **a women's tournament**: Jeanette Settembre, "Florida Man Wins Women's Poker Tournament: 'Insan-ity,'" *New York Post*, May 3, 2023, nypost.com/2023/05/03/florida-man-wins-womens-poker-tournament -insanity.

118 **make them uncomfortable**: "Episode 407: Women's Events," Thinking Poker, 2023, thinkingpoker.net /2023/05/episode-406-womens-events.

119 **here's one stereotype**: For instance, in the American Time Use Survey in 2019, women spent more time "socializing and communicating" (0.66 hours per day vs. 0.62 hours per day for men) and on telephone calls (0.19 hours per day vs. 0.12) while men spent more time on sports (0.42 hours per day vs. 0.25) and games (0.36 hours per day vs. 0.16). "American Time Use Survey—2019 Results," Bureau of Labor Statis-tics, June 25, 2020, bls.gov/news.release/archives/atus_06252020.pdf.

119 **fewer close friends:** Daniel A. Cox, "Men's Social Circles Are Shrinking," The Survey Center on American Life, June 29, 2021, americansurveycenter.org/why-mens-social-circles-are-shrinking.

120 **American Time Use Survey:** "American Time Use Survey—2019 Results."

120 **less risk-averse than women:** Christine R. Harris and Michael Jenkins, "Gender Differences in Risk Assessment: Why Do Women Take Fewer Risks than Men?," *Judgment and Decision Making* 1, no. 1 (July 2006): 48–63, doi.org/10.1017/S1930297500000346.

120 **Current Population Survey:** "Current Population Survey," U.S. Bureau of Labor Statistics, bls.gov/cps/data.htm.

121 **Carlos Welch:** Chad Holloway and Jon Sofen, "Beating the Odds: Carlos Welch Went from Poverty to WSOP Online Champ," PokerNews, September 29, 2021, pokernews.com/news/2021/09/carlos-welch-interview-wsop-online-bracelet-champ-talks-39906.htm.

121 **often slept in his car:** Lee Jones, "Carlos Welch Doesn't Live in a Prius Anymore," Poker.org, June 23, 2023, poker.org/carlos-welch-doesnt-live-in-a-prius-anymore.

124 **Why did Sam Bankman-Fried:** Kate Gibson, "Sam Bankman-Fried Stole at Least $10 Billion, Prosecutors Say in Fraud Trial," CBS News, October 5, 2023, cbsnews.com/news/sam-bankman-fried-fraud-trial-crypto.

125 **also strongly disliked:** GTOx, gtox.io.

126 **altered sense of time:** Scott Sinnett et al., "Flow States and Associated Changes in Spatial and Temporal Processing," *Frontiers in Psychology* 11 (March 12, 2020): 381, doi.org/10.3389/fpsyg.2020.00381.

126 **experiencing the rush:** Lew had won $100K in her previous session of *Hustler Casino Live* and was also winning in this session at the time of the J4 hand.

126 **Hustler's security procedures:** "Report of the Independent Investigation of Alleged Wrongdoing in Lew-Adelstein Hand and Audit of Security of 'Hustler Casino Live' Stream, Commissioned by High Stakes Poker Productions, LLC," *Hustler Casino Live*, December 14, 2022, hustlercasinolive.com/j4report.

126 **throughout poker history:** Nate Meyvis, "Notes on the Garrett Adelstein-Robbi Jade Lew Hand," *Nate Meyvis* (blog), web.archive.org/web/20230326045329/https://natemeyvis.com/why-my-priors-about-cheating-at-poker-are-so-high.html.

126 **Chavez's motivations are:** Lew and Chavez were later spotted together at a Las Vegas Raiders game, leading to speculation that they were cheating; twitter.com/jesselonis/status/1584319495643926528?s=46&t=0lws6WvW7Ygn3FrfsPaSZg.

126 **the unfavorable terms:** According to Adelstein, Chavez gave Lew a freeroll, keeping 50 percent of any profit she made but getting nothing back if she lost; gman06, "Garrett Adelstein Report on Likely Cheating on Hustler Casino Live," Two Plus Two Forums, October 7, 2022, forumserver.twoplustwo.com/29/news-views-gossip/garrett-adelstein-report-likely-cheating-hustler-casino-live-1813491.

127 **access to view:** Andrew Burnett, "Hustler Casino Chip Thief Bryan Sagbigsal Speaks Out from Hiding," HighStakesDB, February 15, 2023, highstakesdb.com/news/high-stakes-reports/hustler-casino-chip-thief-bryan-sagbigsal-speaks-out-from-hiding.

127 **had taken $15,000:** *Hustler Casino Live* (@HCLPokerShow), "An Update T.Co/217duC33xJ," Twitter, October 6, 2022, twitter.com/HCLPokerShow/status/1578169889788862464.

127 **a sympathetic message:** Jon Sofen, "The Muck: Poker Twitter Questions Authenticity of Thief's Alleged DM to Robbi Jade Lew," PokerNews, October 7, 2022, pokernews.com/news/2022/10/muck-robbi-jade-lew-poker-twitter-dm-hustler-casino-live-42249.htm.

127 **stylistic tics similar:** "Robbi Jade Lew vs. Bryan Sagbigsal Text Comparison," 2022, youtube.com/watch?v=c8GiBAq5qHg.

127 **went into hiding:** Jon Sofen, "Cops Can't Locate Bryan Sagbigsal; Robbi-Garrett Saga Remains Unsolved," PokerNews, October 28, 2022, pokernews.com/news/2022/10/robbi-garrett-bryan-sagbigsal-42388.htm.

127 **benefited from cheating:** genobeam, "Part 3: All Robbi's Hands from the Sep 29th Stream (w/ THE Hand)," Reddit post, R/Poker, October 3, 2022, www.reddit.com/r/poker/comments/xur0l1/part_3_all_robbis_hands_from_the_sep_29th_stream.

128 **only around +$18,000:** This calculation is derived from the on-screen graphics on the Hustler livestream, which showed that Adelstein would win the hand 53 percent of the time and Lew 47 percent. This system has important information that would usually be lacking to the players: which other cards had been dealt to and folded by the other players. (In general, these were favorable cards for Adelstein: the cards he wanted were still alive in the deck.) However, if Lew was part of a cheating ring and had access to backstage hole-card information, she would have known this.

128 **easily wait for:** Remember, in GTO poker, many hands are indifferent—on the river, for instance, the expected value of calling and folding is sometimes exactly the same. If you just waited for a couple of these spots per session and always made the perfect decision, you'd be an incredibly profitable player and it would be very hard to detect cheating.

129 **somewhat falsely implied:** Both Adelstein and Lew agreed this was implied. Instead, however, Adelstein racked up his chips and left. Adelstein told me he wasn't sure what he wanted to do, but then Chavez was extremely angry and it would be uncomfortable to continue playing.

129 **resume playing poker:** Jeff Walsh, "Garrett Adelstein Ready for Livestream Return, 'I'm Built for This,'" December 2, 2023, World Poker Tour, worldpokertour.com/news/garrett-adelstein-ready-for-livestream -return-im-built-for-this.

130 **bothered by hypocrisy:** Daniel Cates, "Hidden Hypocrisies and the Futility of Judgment," Medium, May 8, 2020, medium.com/@jungleman12/hidden-hypocrisies-and-the-futility-of-judgment-c13dd3d1570f.

Chapter 3: Consumption

131 **hour of practice:** On my own, not with Ma's guidance.

132 **just 0.18 percent:** Michael Shackleford, "Blackjack Survey," The Wizard of Vegas, July 24, 2023, wizard ofvegas.com/guides/blackjack-survey.

132 **a 0.5 percent house advantage:** Audrey Weston, "Six and Eight Deck Blackjack in Vegas 2023," Gam blingSites.com, November 18, 2022, gamblingsites.com/las-vegas/blackjack/6-8-deck.

132 **make more blackjacks:** Michael Shackleford, "Card Counting," The Wizard of Odds, January 21, 2019, wizardofodds.com/games/blackjack/card-counting/introduction.

133 **offers a table:** Shackleford, "Blackjack Survey."

134 **casino can decline:** And if they can't decline your action, they can take other countermeasures, like requiring the deck to continually be shuffled after every hand. That resets the count to zero.

134 **notice of trespass:** Des Bieler, "O. J. Simpson Banned from Las Vegas Hotel Bar," *The Washington Post,* November 9, 2017, washingtonpost.com/news/early-lead/wp/2017/11/09/o-j-simpson-banned-from-las -vegas-hotel-bar.

134 **easy in tournament poker:** In a tournament, you're competing against other players rather than the house, which takes a fixed percentage of every entry. And while some of those other players are -EV, they may not realize it or they may find tournaments so fun that they don't care.

135 **"You were, like":** Note that this is the only Ma quote taken from a third-party source; all other lines were said directly to me. Eric Harrison, "Jeff Ma: Smart Enough to Bring Down the House," Chron, March 27, 2008, chron.com/entertainment/movies_tv/article/jeff-ma-smart-enough-to-bring-down -the-house-1769491.php.

136 **action from Asian players:** This is often pretty explicit, both from my conversations with casino executives and in other media coverage. See, for example: "Connecticut's Casinos Target Chinese Gamblers," Legit Productions, March 5, 2011, legitprod.com/blog/2018/7/5/connecticuts-casinos-target-chinese -gamblers.

136 **Whether or not the stereotype:** Samson Tse et al., "Examination of Chinese Gambling Problems Through a Socio-Historical-Cultural Perspective," *The Scientific World Journal* 10 (2010): 1694–704, doi.org/10 .1100/tsw.2010.167.

136 **point-shaving scandal:** "1978–79 Boston College Basketball Point-Shaving Scandal," Wikipedia, August 17, 2023, en.wikipedia.org/w/index.php?title=1978%E2%80%9379_Boston_College_basketball_point -shaving_scandal&oldid=1170906310.

136 **about 60 cents:** Stanford Wong, *Professional Blackjack* (Las Vegas: Pi Yee Press, 2011), Kindle ed., 33.

138 **record corporate profits:** U.S. Bureau of Economic Analysis, "Corporate Profits After Tax (without IVA and CCAdj)," FRED, Federal Reserve Bank of St. Louis, January 1, 1946), fred.stlouisfed.org/series/CP.

138 **fast food delivery:** Nate Silver, "The McDonald's Theory of Why Everyone Thinks the Economy Sucks," *Silver Bulletin* (blog), October 1, 2023, natesilver.net/p/the-mcdonalds-theory-of-why-everyone.

138 **fifty bucks in profit:** "Monthly Revenue Report," https://gaming.nv.gov/uploadedFiles/gamingnvgov /content/about/gaming-revenue/2022Dec-gri.pdf, Nevada Gaming Control Board, December 2022, gaming.nv.gov/modules/showdocument.aspx?documentid=19393.

139 **the Gold Rush:** Clare Sears, *Arresting Dress: Cross-Dressing, Law, and Fascination in Nineteenth-Century San Francisco,* Perverse Modernities (Durham, NC: Duke University Press, 2015), 24.

140 **gambling per capita:** David G. Schwartz, *Roll the Bones: The History of Gambling,* Kindle ed. (Las Vegas, NV: Winchester, 2013), 145.

140 **which it outlawed:** Martin Green, "California Online Casinos: Legal California Online Gambling," *The Sacramento Bee,* May 8, 2023, sacbee.com/betting/casinos/article270289967.html.

140 **Nevada's land is:** "Federal Land Ownership by State," Ballotpedia, ballotpedia.org/Federal_land_own ership_by_state.

140 **all but two years:** Schwartz, *Roll the Bones,* 198.

140 **"money talked":** Schwartz, *Roll the Bones,* 201.

141 **first gambling licenses:** Schwartz, *Roll the Bones,* 212-13.

141 **it's an attitude:** Schwartz, *Roll the Bones,* 211.

141 **71 percent of Americans:** "Gallup: Gambling as Morally Acceptable as Pot, Premarital Sex," Casino.org, June 28, 2020, casino.org/news/gallup-gambling-as-morally-acceptable-as-pot-premarital-sex.

142 **"the wherewithal financially":** John L. Smith, "From Busboy to the Gaming Hall of Fame: A Conversation with Mike Rumbolz," CDC Gaming Reports, September 22, 2022, cdcgaming.com/from-busboy -to-the-gaming-hall-of-fame-a-conversation-with-mike-rumbolz.

142 at that time: Trump later built a hotel in Vegas, but it doesn't have a gaming floor.

142 the race wire: Allan May, "The History of the Race Wire Service," *Crime Magazine*, October 14, 2009, crimemagazine.com/history-race-wire-service.

142 the Kefauver Committee: David G. Schwartz, "The Kefauver Hearing in Las Vegas," The Mob Museum, November 10, 2020, themobmuseum.org/blog/the-kefauver-hearing-in-las-vegas.

142 Stardust was involved: Wallace Turner, "Reputed Organized Crime Heads Named in Casino Skimming Case," *The New York Times*, October 12, 1983.

142 substantially toughen regulations: Schwartz, *Roll the Bones*, 256.

143 establishments were crooked: Schwartz, *Roll the Bones*, 100.

143 six-deck blackjack shoe: A blackjack shoe is shuffled long before all of the cards are dealt out, so you could never determine this through strict enumeration. You'd have to use statistical inference over a large sample of hands.

143 unlikely to be cheated: Dealers sometimes make mistakes, but they're generally honest ones—and sometimes they're mistakes in your favor.

144 most expensive building projects: "The 15 Most Expensive Buildings in the World," Luxury Columnist, February 26, 2023, luxurycolumnist.com/the-most-expensive-buildings-in-the-world.

144 seven thousand hotel rooms: "The Venetian Resort Las Vegas—Hotel Meeting Space—Event Facilities," Teneo Hospitality Group, teneohg.com/member-hotel/the-venetian-the-palazzo.

146 Trump's inauguration committee: "Adelson, Wynn among Trump's Inaugural Committee," KTNV 13 Action News Las Vegas, November 16, 2016, ktnv.com/news/political/adelson-wynn-among-trumps-inaugural-committee.

146 along with frenemy: Kimberly Pierceall, "Sheldon Adelson, Las Vegas Sands Founder and GOP Power Broker, Dies," *The Philadelphia Inquirer*, January 12, 2021, inquircr.com/obituaries/sheldon-adelson-dies-obituary-las-vegas-sands-gop-20210112.html.

146 Wynn took over: Schwartz, *Roll the Bones*, 253.

146 soon becoming president: Schwartz, *Roll the Bones*, 253.

146 a four-diamond rating: Galen R. Frysinger, "Golden Nugget," GalenFrysinger.com, galenfrysinger.com/las_vegas_golden_nugget.htm.

146 most ambitious project: Ken Adams, "Out with the Mirage and Volcano and in with a Rock and Guitar," CDC Gaming Reports, April 2, 2023, cdcgaming.com/commentary/out-with-the-mirage-and-volcano-and-in-with-a-rock-and-guitar.

147 a second life: "Hard Rock® Completes Acquisition of The Mirage Hotel & Casino®," Hard Rock Hotel & Casino, January 16, 2023, hardrockhotels.com/news/hard-rock-completes-acquisition-of-the-mirage-hotel-and-casino.

147 first new property: Brock Radke, "Las Vegas' First Modern Megaresort the Mirage Reopens This Week—Las Vegas Sun Newspaper," *Las Vegas Sun*, August 24, 2020, lasvegassun.com/news/2020/aug/24/mgm-resorts-mirage-reopens-las-vegas-strip.

147 number of attractions: Hubble Smith, "The Mirage Was for Real," *Las Vegas Review-Journal*, November 22, 1999, web.archive.org/web/20021220024833/http://www.lvrj.com/lvrj_home/1999/Nov-22-Mon-1999/business/12387993.html.

148 The large majority of: "Nevada Casinos: Departmental Revenues, 1984-2022," UNLV Center for Gaming Research, February 2023, gaming.library.unlv.edu/reports/NV_departments_historic.pdf.

149 had sexually harassed: Alexandra Berzon et al., "Dozens of People Recount Pattern of Sexual Misconduct by Las Vegas Mogul Steve Wynn," *The Wall Street Journal*, January 26, 2018, sec. Business, wsj.com/articles/dozens-of-people-recount-pattern-of-sexual-misconduct-by-las-vegas-mogul-steve-wynn-1516985953.

149 damages, fines: Julia Malleck, "Casino King Steve Wynn Was Banned from Nevada's Gambling Industry," Quartz, July 28, 2023, qz.com/steve-wynn-casino-king-ban-nevada-gaming-sexual-miscond-1850685469.

149 a proposed resort: Howard Stutz, "Wynn Unveils Plans and Renderings for a 1,000-Foot-Tall Hotel-Casino in UAE," *The Nevada Independent*, April 28, 2023, thenevadaindependent.com/article/wynn-unveils-plans-and-renderings-for-a-1000-foot-tall-hotel-casino-in-uae.

149 rapes were reported: "2019 Crime in the United States: Nevada," FBI, 2019, ucr.fbi.gov/crime-in-the-u.s/2019/crime-in-the-u.s.-2019/tables/table-8/table-8-state-cuts/nevada.xls; "2019 Crime in the United States: Rate: Number of Crimes per 100,000 Inhabitants," FBI, 2019, ucr.fbi.gov/crime-in-the-u.s/2019/crime-in-the-u.s.-2019/tables/table-16/table-16.xls.

150 Trump Entertainment Resorts: Associated Press, "Trump Casinos File for Bankruptcy," NBC News, November 22, 2004, nbcnews.com/id/wbna6556470; Michelle Lee, "Fact Check: Has Trump Declared Bankruptcy Four or Six Times?," *The Washington Post*, September 26, 2016, washingtonpost.com/politics/2016/live-updates/general-election/real-time-fact-checking-and-analysis-of-the-first-presidential-debate/fact-check-has-trump-declared-bankruptcy-four-or-six-times; Associated Press, "Trump Entertainment Resorts File for Bankruptcy in Blow to Atlantic City," *The Guardian*, September 9, 2014, sec. World News, theguardian.com/world/2014/sep/09/trump-casinos-atlantic-city-bankruptcy; Wayne Perry, "Trump's Bankrupt Taj Mahal Casino Now Owned by Carl Icahn," *The Spokesman-Review*, February 26, 2016, spokesman.com/stories/2016/feb/26/trumps-bankrupt-taj-mahal-casino-now-owned-by-carl.

150 **considerably enrich himself:** Russ Buettner and Charles V. Bagli, "How Donald Trump Bankrupted His Atlantic City Casinos, but Still Earned Millions," *The New York Times*, June 11, 2016, sec. New York, nytimes.com/2016/06/12/nyregion/donald-trump-atlantic-city.html.

150 **Michael Jackson:** "1990 Michael Jackson Attends the Grand Opening of Trump Taj Mahal Casino Resort," 2013, youtube.com/watch?v=GGWjUYWatTo.

150 **dressed in turbans:** Howard Kurtz, "Donald Trump's Big Bet," *The Washington Post*, March 25, 1990, washingtonpost.com/archive/lifestyle/1990/03/25/donald-trumps-big-bet/0c149273-3752-4f6f-96bf-432457039eb7.

150 **critic Paul Goldberger:** Paul Goldberger, "It's 'Themed,' It's Kitschy, It's Trump's Taj," *The New York Times*, April 6, 1990, sec. New York, nytimes.com/1990/04/06/nyregion/it-s-themed-it-s-kitschy-it-s-trump-s-taj.html.

151 **filed for bankruptcy:** Reuters, "Chapter 11 for Taj Mahal," *The New York Times*, July 18, 1991, sec. Business, nytimes.com/1991/07/18/business/chapter-11-for-taj-mahal.html.

151 **through junk bonds:** Robert O'Harrow Jr., "Trump's Bad Bet: How Too Much Debt Drove His Biggest Casino Aground," *The Washington Post*, May 24, 2023, washingtonpost.com/investigations/trumps-bad-bet-how-too-much-debt-drove-his-biggest-casino-aground/2016/01/18/f67cedc2-9ac8-11e5-8917-653b65c809eb_story.html.

151 **seeing a decline:** Lenny Glynn, "Trump's Taj—Open at Last, with a Scary Appetite," *The New York Times*, April 8, 1990, sec. Business, nytimes.com/1990/04/08/business/trump-s-taj-open-at-last-with-a-scary-appetite.html.

151 **pressured Roffman's firm:** Joel Rose, "The Analyst Who Gambled and Took on Trump," NPR, October 10, 2016, sec. Business, npr.org/2016/10/10/497087643/the-analyst-who-gambled-and-took-on-trump.

151 **the Taj's opening:** Glynn, "Trump's Taj—Open at Last."

151 **regulations, corrupt officials:** Inside Jersey Staff, "In Atlantic City, a Long History of Corruption," NJ.com, February 16, 2010, nj.com/insidejersey/2010/02/atlantic_citys_tradition_of_co.html.

151 **slot machines mysteriously:** Tim Golden, "Taj Mahal's Slot Machines Halt, Overcome by Success," *The New York Times*, April 9, 1990, sec. New York, nytimes.com/1990/04/09/nyregion/taj-mahal-s-slot-machines-halt-overcome-by-success.html.

151 **a helicopter crash:** Robert Hanley, "Copter Crash Kills 3 Aides of Trump," *The New York Times*, October 11, 1989, sec. New York, nytimes.com/1989/10/11/nyregion/copter-crash-kills-3-aides-of-trump.html.

151 **named Akio Kashiwagi:** Diana B. Henriques with M. A. Farber, "An Empire at Risk—Trump's Atlantic City; Debt Forcing Trump to Play for Higher Stakes," *The New York Times*, June 7, 1990, sec. Business, nytimes.com/1990/06/07/business/empire-risk-trump-s-atlantic-city-debt-forcing-trump-play-for-higher-stakes.html.

152 **but then declined:** After adjusting for inflation. Unadjusted figures can be found here: "Atlantic City Gaming Revenue," UNLV Center for Gaming Research, February 2023, gaming.library.unlv.edu/reports/ac_hist.pdf.

152 **Taj's gross revenues:** "Annual Report 1990," Trump Taj Mahal Associates, 1990, washingtonpost.com/wp-stat/graphics/politics/trump-archive/docs/trump-taj-mahal-associates-annual-report-1990.pdf.

152 **Nevada gaming revenues:** "Casinos: Gross Gaming Revenue by State US 2022," Statista, May 2023, statista.com/statistics/187926/gross-gaming-revenue-by-state-us.

156 **Disneyworld is famous:** Florencia Muther, "The Happiest Place on Earth: The Magic Recipe Behind Disney Parks 70% Return Rate," *HBS: Technology and Operations Management* (blog), December 7, 2015, d3.harvard.edu/platform-rctom/submission/the-happiest-place-on-earth-the-magic-recipe-behind-disney-parks-70-return-rate.

156 **about *80 percent*:** Heart+Mind Strategies, "2022 Las Vegas Visitor Profile Study," Las Vegas Convention and Visitors Authority, 2022, assets.simpleviewcms.com/simpleview/image/upload/v1/clients/lasvegas/2022_Las_Vegas_Visitor_Profile_Study_8a25c904-37b4-42d0-af4d-8d8f04af9ecf.pdf.

156 **are repeat customers:** Technically, this is not quite an apples-to-apples comparison—the percentage of visitors who return at some point is not the same as the percentage of visitors at any given time who are repeat customers—but there's no doubt both Disneyworld and Las Vegas create a lot of customer loyalty.

157 **Caesars Seven Stars:** "Caesars Rewards Benefits Overview," Caesars, caesars.com/myrewards/benefits-overview.

157 **even private jets:** Mark Saunokonoko, "Private Jets, Big Bets and Beautiful Women: Inside the Secret World of Las Vegas High-Rollers," October 14, 2017, 9news.com.au/world/rj-cipriani-inside-the-secret-world-of-las-vegas-high-rollers-whales-gamblers/4fb3275a-7b43-47a6-8d98-df09161ef011.

158 opened in 2005: zedthedeadpoet, "Consolidated 'Wynn' Thread," FlyerTalk, April 12, 2005, flyertalk .com/forum/3928690-post51.html.

160 Ivey return more: Mo Nuwwarah, "Phil Ivey Reportedly Settles with Borgata, Ending 6-Year Legal War," PokerNews, July 8, 2020, pokernews.com/news/2020/07/phil-ivey-borgata-settlement-37591 .htm.

161 every human society: Per interview with Per Binde.

161 hunter-gatherer cultures: Schwartz, *Roll the Bones*, 1-2.

162 "VACANT AND SPACIOUS": Bill Friedman, *Designing Casinos to Dominate the Competition: The Friedman International Standards of Casino Design* (Reno, NV: Institute for the Study of Gambling and Commercial Gaming, 2000), 16-17.

163 Casino Revenue Breakdown: "Monthly Revenue Report," Nevada Gaming Control Board, December 2022.

164 Slot machines first: Per interview with Mike Rumbolz.

164 around 11 percent: "Monthly Revenue Report," Nevada Gaming Control Board, June 2023, gaming .nv.gov/modules/showdocument.aspx?documentid=19988.

164 the government keeps: Sandra Grauschopf, "Which States Have the Biggest Lottery Payouts?," Live-About, October 29, 2022, liveabout.com/which-states-have-the-biggest-lottery-payouts-4684743.

164 purchased disproportionately by: John Wihbey, "Who Plays the Lottery, and Why: Updated Collection of Research," *The Journalist's Resource*, July 27, 2016, journalistsresource.org/economics/research-re view-lotteries-demographics.

164 Comparison of Odds: Adam Volz, "Why Horse Bettors Need to Know About Takeout Rates," *Casino.org* (blog), January 2, 2023, casino.org/blog/takeout-rates/; Michael Shackleford, "What Is the House Edge?," The Wizard of Odds, September 6, 2023, wizardofodds.com/gambling/house-edge/; Grauschopf, "Which States Have the Biggest Lottery Payouts?"; "Monthly Revenue Report," Nevada Gaming Control Board, June 2023; Michael Shackleford, "Blackjack Survey," The Wizard of Vegas, July 24, 2023, wizardofvegas .com/guides/blackjack-survey.

164 can be highly addictive: Robert B. Breen and Mark Zimmerman, "Rapid Onset of Pathological Gambling in Machine Gamblers," *Journal of Gambling Studies* 18, no. 1 (March 1, 2002): 31-43, doi.org/10.1023 /A:1014580112648.

165 become problem gamblers: Natasha Dow Schüll, "Slot Machines Are Designed to Addict," *The New York Times*, October 10, 2013, nytimes.com/roomfordebate/2013/10/09/are-casinos-too-much-of-a-gamble /slot-machines-are-designed-to-addict.

165 sociologist Erving Goffman: David G. Schwartz, "Erving Goffman's Las Vegas: From Jungle to Board-room," *UNLV Gaming Research & Review Journal* 20, no. 1 (May 23, 2016), digitalscholarship.unlv.edu /grrj/vol20/iss1/2.

166 "facing the excitement": Erving Goffman, *Interaction Ritual: Essays on Face-to-Face Behavior*, 1st Pan-theon Books ed. (New York: Pantheon Books, 1982), 203.

167 a continuous flow: Michelle Goldberg, "Here's Hoping Elon Musk Destroys Twitter," *The New York Times*, October 6, 2022, sec. Opinion, nytimes.com/2022/10/06/opinion/elon-musk-twitter.html.

167 spin the reels: Kevin A. Harrigan and Mike Dixon, "PAR Sheets, Probabilities, and Slot Machine Play: Implications for Problem and Non-Problem Gambling," *Journal of Gambling Issues* no. 23 (June 1, 2009): 81, doi.org/10.4309/jgi.2009.23.5.

168 $300 per trip: "Las Vegas Visitor Statistics," Las Vegas Convention and Visitors Authority, June 2023, assets.simpleviewcms.com/simpleview/image/upload/v1/clients/lasvegas/ES_Jun_2023_8bfa98de -9c13-439d-96e5-516621dc2146.pdf.

Chapter 4: Competition

170 met with Kyrollos: David Hill, "The Rise and Fall of the Professional Sports Bettor," The Ringer, June 5, 2019, theringer.com/2019/6/5/18644504/sports-betting-bettors-sharps-kicked-out-spanky-william -hill-new-jersey.

171 Bottom-up bettors: spanky (@spanky), "A bottom up approach is creating your own line using data sta-tistics analytics models etc. A top down approach assumes the line is correct and you find value looking for off numbers between bookmakers and information not reflected in the line such as injuries[.] I'm a top down guy," Twitter, December 12, 2019, twitter.com/spanky/status/1205265182664134657.

171 "information not reflected": spanky, "A bottom up approach."

172 one site limited me: Resorts World Bet limited me after only six games, even though I was very slightly in the red (-$66) on my betting there. Resorts World was using odds provided by PointsBet, which had already limited me—it may have been that they were also sharing customer information.

172 for Deutsche Bank: Hill, "The Rise and Fall of the Professional Sports Bettor."

172 about as close: A related technique called "scalping," in which you're betting moneylines instead of point spreads, *is* completely risk-free. For example, if I bet the Eagles moneyline at -110 at one site and the Chiefs at +120 at another site, I am guaranteed to make a small profit.

173 **equivalent to winning:** If you're betting point spreads.
174 **doesn't drive revenues:** "Monthly Revenue Report," Nevada Gaming Control Board, June 2023, gaming
.nv.gov/modules/showdocument.aspx?documentid=19988.
174 **world's largest sportsbook:** Circa also makes this claim. Having been to both venues, I think Circa is
probably right.
175 **4,250 square feet:** "Westgate Superbook: A Total WOW Factor," 2021, youtube.com/watch?v=jXstOz
Qj9mk.
175 **margin on sports betting:** Compare, for example, Nevada sports betting hold percentages in 2023
(around 5 percent) to 1993 (around 3 percent). The 2023 data: "Monthly Revenue Report," Nevada Gaming Control Board, June 2023; 1993 data: "Monthly Revenue Report," Nevada Gaming Control Board,
December 1993, gaming.nv.gov/modules/showdocument.aspx?documentid=3755.
176 **and repeatedly defeated it:** Richard Waters, "Man Beats Machine at Go in Human Victory Over AI," *Financial Times*, https://archive.is/tDYsY.
178 **Las Vegas Sports Consultants:** David Hill, "The King of Super Bowl Props, Part 1," The Ringer, September 21, 2022, theringer.com/2022/9/21/23363621/gamblers-super-bowl-props-rufus-peabody-nfl.
178 **"L.L.Bean catalog":** Hill, "The King of Super Bowl Props, Part 1."
178 **"that paid nothing":** Technically, Peabody wasn't making nothing. He was paid a starting salary of
$25,000.
178 **Peabody wrote his senior thesis:** Rufus Peabody, "Fundamentals or Noise? Analyzing the Efficiency of a
Prediction Market" (senior thesis, Yale University, 2008), drive.google.com/drive/folders/1DnApx0q
5W2YpRxuwhaZG6QzTbVuXyZte.
179 **the majority of results:** John P. A. Ioannidis, "Why Most Published Research Findings Are False," *PLOS
Medicine* 2, no. 8 (August 30, 2005): e124, doi.org/10.1371/journal.pmed.0020124.
179 **"tax on bullshit":** Alex Tabarrok, "A Bet Is a Tax on Bullshit," *Marginal Revolution* (blog), November 2,
2012, marginalrevolution.com/marginalrevolution/2012/11/a-bet-is-a-tax-on-bullshit.html.
179 **"Art Howes":** Alex Gleeman, "Art Howe Is Angry About How He Was Portrayed in 'Moneyball,'" NBC
Sports, September 27, 2011, nbcsports.com/mlb/news/art-howe-is-angry-about-how-he-was-portrayed
-in-moneyball.
180 **Peabody does pick:** David Hill, "Looking for an Edge, and Some Fun, Bettors Favor Super Bowl Props,"
The New York Times, February 7, 2023, sec. Sports, nytimes.com/2023/02/07/sports/football/super-bowl
-bets-props-odds.html.
180 **Plot the popularity:** These rankings are a bit subjective and combine my general knowledge about the
industry with data on the domestic and international popularity of each sport and their betting handles
in Colorado and Nevada. Some sports, for example major UFC bouts, tend to be especially popular
among bettors relative to their popularity with the general public.
180 **Russian ping-pong became:** Andrew Keh, "Think Americans Wouldn't Wager on Russian Table Tennis?
Care to Bet?," *The New York Times*, January 25, 2021, sec. Sports, nytimes.com/2021/01/25/sports/ping
-pong-sports-betting.html.
181 **second-highest grossing UFC fight:** Ben Davies, "UFC: Top 10 Biggest Earning PPV Events in History
(Ranked)," GiveMeSport, October 17, 2023, givemesport.com/biggest-earning-ufc-ppv-events-in-his
tory-ranked/#ufc-264-poirier-v-mcgregor-3-1-800-000-ppv-buys—-120-million.
182 **makes a pilgrimage:** Hill, "The King of Super Bowl Props, Part 1."
182 **literally thirty-eight pages:** "SB LVII Props-Westgate," Scribd, scribd.com/document/623527060/Sb
-LVII-Props-westgate.
182 **Kornegay is one:** Matt Jacob, "Super Bowl Props: How These Side Bets Became So Popular," Props, February 7, 2022, props.com/super-bowl-props-how-these-side-bets-became-so-popular.
182 **props make up:** Patrick Everson, "Sharp Bettors Fire Early, File Away for Later as Super Bowl Proposition Bets Hit Odds Board," Covers.com, January 23, 2020, covers.com/industry/sharp-bettors-fire
-early.
184 **Jason Robins rang:** "DraftKings Inc. Rings the Opening Bell," Nasdaq, June 11, 2021, nasdaq.com/events
/draftkings-inc.-rings-the-opening-bell.
184 **the largest state:** Weston Blasi, "New York Officially Approves Legal Online Sports Betting," Market-
Watch, April 10, 2021, marketwatch.com/story/new-york-approves-legal-online-sports-betting-1161
7744458.
185 **$1 billion on customer acquisition:** Brad Allen, "Can Caesars Sportsbook Make Its Mark with $1 Billion
in Spending?," Legal Sports Report, August 4, 2021, legalsportsreport.com/54987/caesars-sportsbook-
one-billion-us-sports-betting.
185 **DraftKings and FanDuel were complaining:** Robert Harding, "DraftKings, FanDuel Warn High Tax Rate
Could Threaten NY Mobile Sports Betting Success," *The Citizen* (Auburn), February 1, 2023, auburnpub
.com/news/local/govt-and-politics/draftkings-fanduel-warn-high-tax-rate-could-threaten-ny
-mobile-sports-betting-success/article_f775b29d-3dd4-5fb8-ba12-39eaf7abe8f6.html.
185 **high tax rate:** New York keeps 51 percent of the profits, much more than the average state. It earned almost $700 million in sports-betting tax revenues in 2022.

185 **Gibson was referring:** Oregon, Delaware, and Nevada were also allowed to continue operating sports-betting-themed lotteries. Troy Lambert, "Supreme Gamble: The Professional and Amateur Sports Protection Act," *HuffPost*, July 18, 2017, huffpost.com/entry/supreme-gamble-the-professional-and-amateur-sports_b_596e31b6e4b05561da5a5ae6.

185 **racebooks make up:** Closer to 3 percent if you count online wagering.

186 **about $7.5 billion:** Geoff Zochodne, "US Sports Betting Revenue and Handle Tracker," Covers.com, covers.com/betting/betting-revenue-tracker.

186 **frozen pizza market:** "Frozen Pizza Market Size USD 29.8 Billion by 2030," Vantage Market Research, vantagemarketresearch.com/industry-report/frozen-pizza-market-2179.

186 **Colorado *lost* nearly:** "Colorado Sports Betting Proceeds," Colorado Department of Revenue, June 2023, sbg.colorado.gov/sites/sbg/files/documents/38%20Monthly%20Summary%20%20%28June%20%2723%29.pdf.

186 **"eliminating the sharp action":** Brad Allen, "DraftKings CEO Jason Robins Wants Higher Hold, Fewer Sharps," Legal Sports Report, June 6, 2022, legalsportsreport.com/71027/draftkings-ceo-wants-higher-hold-less-sharp-betting.

187 **Miller's book calls:** Ed Miller and Matthew Davidow, *The Logic of Sports Betting*, Kindle ed. (self-pub., 2019), 57.

187 **a gargantuan sum:** "Form 10-K," DraftKings, Inc., February 17, 2023, draftkings.gcs-web.com/static-files/6aa9158d-fd23-4ea1-ad7e-48a1f79e37da.

188 **I bet $1,100:** Typically NBA lines are listed no more than about thirty-six hours in advance, but this was an unusual situation because of the All-Star break; there were no games for the next couple of days and sportsbooks were eager to give bettors something to gamble on.

188 **BOSS was willing:** Market-making books often have default limits that apply to all players. Others allow for a bit of wiggle room, though far less than the retail books do.

189 **"since that trade":** "Raptors Get Jakob Poeltl in Trade from Spurs," NBA.com, February 9, 2023, nba.com/news/spurs-trade-jakob-poeltl-raptors.

190 **That's still cheap:** Everson, "Sharp Bettors Fire Early."

192 **a $12,500-a-month home:** Scott Eden, "Meet the World's Top NBA Gambler," *ESPN The Magazine*, February 21, 2013, espn.com/blog/playbook/dollars/post/_/id/2935/meet-the-worlds-top-nba-gambler.

192 **internal power struggle:** Kevin Sherrington, "Titanic, Meet Iceberg: Bob Voulgaris' Mavs Exit Was Result of a Petty Clash of Egos," *The Dallas Morning News*, October 22, 2021, dallasnews.com/sports/mavericks/2021/10/22/titanic-meet-iceberg-haralabos-voulgaris-mavs-exit-was-result-of-a-petty-clash-of-egos.

192 **Voulgaris purchased a:** Jon Sofen, "Haralabos Voulgaris Purchasing a Spanish Soccer Club," PokerNews, July 24, 2022, pokernews.com/news/2022/07/haralabos-voulgaris-soccer-club-41739.htm.

192 **As of March 2024:** Note that Transfermarkt's calculations account for the resale value of the players on the roster only. The *franchise* values will be higher, potentially several times higher in the case of top La Liga teams, since they may also include stadiums, intangibles, etc.

192 **players on Castellón are valued:** "CD Castellón—Club Profile," Transfermarkt, transfermarkt.us/cd-castellon/startseite/verein/2502.

192 **La Liga, where:** "La Liga," Transfermarkt, transfermarkt.com/primera-division/startseite/wettbewerb/ES1.

192 **Brentford FC moved:** "Brentford Fans Set to Sell Shares," BBC Sport, June 20, 2012, bbc.com/sport/football/18519031.

192 **typically higher scoring:** "NBA Team 1st Half Points per Game," TeamRankings, teamrankings.com/nba/stat/1st-half-points-per-game.

193 **bookmakers did not realize:** Eden, "Meet the World's Top NBA Gambler."

193 **almost thirty thousand fans:** Counting people in the US Open grounds, even if not in Arthur Ashe Stadium itself; nytimes.com/2022/08/31/sports/tennis/serena-williams-kontaveit-crowd-us-open.html#:-:text=But%20Kontaveit%20did%20not%20go,a%20U.S.%20Open%20night%20session.

194 **never anything reported:** A Google search for "Federer" "Nobu" reveals nothing useful, for instance.

194 **his bottom teeth:** Billy Walters, *Gambler: Secrets from a Life at Risk*, Kindle ed. (New York: Simon & Schuster, 2023), 26.

194 **came to Vegas in debt:** Ian Thomsen, "The Gang That Beat Vegas," *The National Sports Daily*, June 6, 1990, ianthomsen.com/features.html#vegas.

195 **so-called Computer Group:** Walters, *Gambler: Secrets from a Life at Risk*, 88.

195 **Mindlin began experimenting:** Robert H. Boyle, "Using Your Computer for Fun and Profit," *Sports Illustrated*, March 10, 1986, vault.si.com/vault/1986/03/10/using-your-computer-for-fun-and-profit.

195 **its charismatic front man:** Thomsen, "The Gang That Beat Vegas."

195 **socially awkward mathematician:** Walters, *Gambler: Secrets from a Life at Risk*, 118.

195 **Westinghouse's high-speed computers:** Thomsen, "The Gang That Beat Vegas."

195 **Kent soon adapted:** Thomsen, "The Gang That Beat Vegas."

195 **Kent's records showed:** Thomsen, "The Gang That Beat Vegas."

196 **once betting $1.5 million:** Walters, *Gambler: Secrets from a Life at Risk*, 95.

196 **entire net worth:** Thomsen, "The Gang That Beat Vegas."

196 **"my boom-and-bust existence":** Walters, *Gambler: Secrets from a Life at Risk*, 5.

196 **Wirfs' backup was:** Although the backup was forced to play in the game.

196 **worth as many as 6 points:** Walters, *Gambler: Secrets from a Life at Risk*, 251.

197 **sentenced to five:** "William T. 'Billy' Walters Sentenced in Manhattan Federal Court for $43 Million Insider Trading Scheme," U.S. Attorney's Office, Southern District of New York, July 27, 2017, justice.gov/usao -sdny/pr/william-t-billy-walters-sentenced-manhattan-federal-court-43-million-insider-trading.

197 **ever since Mindlin:** Thomsen, "The Gang That Beat Vegas."

197 **wisdom of crowds:** James Surowiecki, *The Wisdom of Crowds* (New York: Anchor Books, 2005).

198 **deluged the airwaves:** Peter Kafka, "DraftKings and FanDuel Look Wobbly, and So Does $220 Million in TV Ads," *Vox*, November 11, 2015, vox.com/2015/11/11/11620574/draftkings-and-fanduel-look-wobbly -and-so-do-220-million-in-tv-ads.

198 **one typical DraftKings script:** "Welcome to the Big Time," DraftKings Fantasy Football TV commercial, 2015, youtube.com/watch?v=AIGap9cvu34.

198 **run the numbers:** "The Sleeper," DraftKings TV commercial, 2015, youtube.com/watch?v=QTfeK3L GpB0.

198 **outsmart your friends:** "Only One Bull," DraftKings TV commercial, 2015, youtube.com/watch?v =NvilKKbLUH4.

198 **"with bikini models":** Draft Kings TV commercial, 2013, youtube.com/watch?v=soniQkpTLhE.

198 **or show celebrities:** "DraftKings TV Commercials," iSpot.tv, ispot.tv/brands/IEY/draftkings.

198 **long-term winners helped:** "DraftKings, FanDuel Spar Over Ad Claim," Truth in Advertising, November 10, 2016, truthinadvertising.org/articles/draftkings-fanduel-spar-over-ad-claim.

199 **a carve-out for:** Ryan Rodenberg, "The True Congressional Origin of Daily Fantasy Sports," ESPN, October 28, 2015, espn.com/chalk/story/_/id/13993288/daily-fantasy-investigating-where-fantasy-carve -daily-fantasy-sports-actually-came-congress.

200 **notoriously big bettor:** Paul Conolly, "Floyd Mayweather Biggest Bets: How Much Money Has He Made Betting on Sport?," GiveMeSport, May 16, 2022, givemesport.com/88008783-floyd-mayweather-big gest-bets-how-much-money-has-he-made-betting-on-sport.

200 **call themselves "entertainment products":** "Q&A with Jason Robins of DraftKings," Public, June 9, 2021, public.com/town-hall/jasonrobins.

200 **matched my experience:** Danny Funt, "Sportsbooks Say You Can Win Big. Then They Try to Limit Winners," *The Washington Post*, November 17, 2022, washingtonpost.com/sports/2022/11/17/betting-limits -draft-kings-betmgm-caesars-circa/.

201 **Paddy Power Betfair:** "Paddy Power Betfair Buys Fantasy Sports Site Fan Duel," May 23, 2018, bbc.com /news/business-44227222.

202 **moneylines at the largest:** "Kansas City Chiefs vs. Philadelphia Eagles Line Movement," Covers.com, covers.com/sport/football/nfl/linemovement/kc-at-phi/281806.

203 **"MAX WAGER $2,475.37":** Generally speaking, sportsbooks decide by hand whether to limit players, but once they do, the amount you'll be allowed to bet on any particular event may be determined algorithmically. So if you're limited, the limit won't necessarily end in a round number.

204 **around $50 million:** This estimate is extrapolated from data published by the state of Colorado, which represents less than 5 percent of the legal U.S. market. It does not include parlay bets, which would significantly increase the total. "Colorado Sports Betting Proceeds May 2020–April 2023," Colorado Department of Revenue, sbg.colorado.gov/sites/sbg/files/documents/Top%2010%20Sports%20by%20Total %20Wagers%20May%202020%20to%20Present.pdf.

204 **amount so robust:** According to Farren, FanDuel will let you bet $30,000 on NFL game-time lines no matter how much they've limited you otherwise.

205 **Raptors at -3.5:** "New Orleans vs. Toronto Stats & Past Results—NBA Game on February 23, 2023," Covers.com, December 31, 2023, covers.com/sport/basketball/nba/matchup/270914.

208 **almost definitely violate:** "Can Someone Make Bets for Me? (US)," DraftKings Help Center (US), help .draftkings.com/hc/en-us/articles/17138205116691-Can-someone-make-bets-for-me-US-.

208 **so-called messenger betting:** Jeff German, "Messenger Betting Case Nets Probation, Fine in Plea Deal," *Las Vegas Review-Journal*, February 8, 2013, reviewjournal.com/crime/courts/messenger-betting-case -nets-probation-fine-in-plea-deal.

208 **charged with bookmaking:** "Twenty-Five Individuals Indicted in Multi-Million-Dollar Illegal Nationwide Sports Betting Ring," FBI, October 25, 2012, fbi.gov/newyork/press-releases/2012/twenty-five -individuals-indicted-in-multi-million-dollar-illegal-nationwide-sports-betting-ring.

208 **series of raids:** Mike Fish, "Meet the World's Most Successful Gambler," *ESPN The Magazine*, February 6, 2015, espn.com/espn/feature/story/_/id/12280555/how-billy-walters-became-sports-most-successful -controversial-bettor.

208 **typically combat bookmaking:** David Hill, "Requiem for a Sports Bettor," The Ringer, June 5, 2019, theringer.com/2019/6/5/18644504/sports-betting-bettors-sharps-kicked-out-spanky-william-hill -new-jersey.

208 **was eventually acquitted:** Fish, "Meet the World's Most Successful Gambler."

208 **Spanky pled guilty:** Hill, "Requiem for a Sports Bettor."

209 **bill of sportsbook health:** BetMGM had limited me before the 2022–23 season began, but I was still able to bet up to $1,001. Eventually, they limited me further to only $100.

210 **same amount outlayed:** In the NBA, sportsbooks typically don't take bets for games played more than a day in advance.

212 **Importance of Every Point:** Data is from TeamRankings.com—here for the Brooklyn Nets, for example: teamrankings.com/nba/team/brooklyn-nets.

213 **60 to 65 percent:** This calculation is based on getting 3 to 4 points of closing line value.

214 **some vicious winning:** Dom Luszczyszyn, "NHL Betting Guide: Daily Picks, Odds, Win Probabilities and Advice," *The Athletic*, July 26, 2022, theathletic.com/2884733/2022/06/26/nhl-betting-guide-daily -picks-odds-win-probabilities-and-advice.

214 **the well-known sociologist:** Erving Goffman, *Interaction Ritual: Essays on Face-to-Face Behavior*, 1st Pantheon Books ed. (New York: Pantheon Books, 1982), 179.

Chapter 13: Inspiration

219 **she immigrated to:** Joe Walker, "#147: Katalin Karikó—Forging the mRNA Revolution," *The Joe Walker Podcast*, August 2, 2023, josephnoelwalker.com/147-katalin-kariko.

219 **the Nobel Prize:** Karikó won the Nobel jointly with Drew Weissman.

219 **challenged an extradition order:** Gregory Zuckerman, *A Shot to Save the World: The Inside Story of the Life-or-Death Race for a COVID-19 Vaccine* (New York: Penguin Books, 2021).

219 **instead had to "run away":** "Run away" was Karikó's term in my interview with her.

219 **was repeatedly demoted:** Aditi Shrikant, "Nobel Prize Winner Katalin Karikó Was 'Demoted 4 Times' at Her Old Job. How She Persisted: 'You Have to Focus on What's Next,'" CNBC, October 6, 2023, cnbc .com/2023/10/06/nobel-prize-winner-katalin-karik-on-being-demoted-perseverance-.html.

219 **2 percent of NFL players:** Hunter S. Angileri et al., "Association of Injury Rates Among Players in the National Football League with Playoff Qualification, Travel Distance, Game Timing, and the Addition of Another Game: Data from the 2017 to 2022 Seasons," *Orthopaedic Journal of Sports Medicine* 11, no. 8 (August 1, 2023): 23259671231177633, doi.org/10.1177/23259671231177633.

220 **Trump both before:** Mark Landler and Eric Schmitt, "H. R. McMaster Breaks with Administration on Views of Islam," *The New York Times*, February 25, 2017, sec. U.S., nytimes.com/2017/02/24/us/politics /hr-mcmaster-trump-islam.html.

220 **after being fired:** Martin Pengelly, "HR McMaster on Serving Trump: 'If You're Not on the Pitch, You're Going to Get Your Ass Kicked,'" *The Guardian*, October 3, 2020, sec. US News, theguardian.com/us -news/2020/oct/03/hr-mcmaster-donald-trump-national-security-adviser-battlegrounds-book.

220 **a Silver Star:** Peter Baker and Michael R. Gordon, "Trump Chooses H. R. McMaster as National Security Adviser," *The New York Times*, February 20, 2017, sec. U.S., nytimes.com/2017/02/20/us/politics/mc master-national-security-adviser-trump.html.

220 **aggressive surprise maneuver:** Matthew Cox, "McMaster's Tank Battle in Iraq May Shape Advice in New Role," Military.com, October 31, 2017, military.com/daily-news/2017/02/23/mcmasters-tank-battle-in -iraq-may-shape-advice-in-new-role.html.

220 **bottom of each of the world's oceans:** Victor Vescovo, "The Final Frontier: How Victor Vescovo Became the First Person to Visit the Deepest Part of Every Ocean," *Oceanographic*, September 17, 2019, oceano graphicmagazine.com/features/victor-vescovo-five-deeps.

220 **Explorer's Grand Slam:** Vanessa O'Brien, "Explorers Grand Slam," Explorers Grand Slam, explorers grandslam.com.

224 **negative correlation between:** Simon Baron-Cohen, "Autism: The Empathizing-Systemizing (E-S) Theory," *Annals of the New York Academy of Sciences* 1156, no. 1 (March 2009): 68–80, doi.org/10.1111/j .1749-6632.2009.04467.x.

224 **Zachary Shore's book:** Zachary Shore, "A Sense of the Enemy," Zachary Shore, zacharyshore.com/a -sense-of-the-enemy.html.

224 **an army colleague:** The former U.S. Army officer Joel Rayburn.

225 **diagnosed with autism:** Rick Maese, "How to Win at Cards and Life, According to Poker's Autistic Superstar," *The Washington Post*, May 3, 2023, washingtonpost.com/sports/2023/05/02/jungleman-poker -dan-cates-autisic.

225 **"a bit aloof":** Jay Caspian Kang, "Online Poker's Big Winner," *The New York Times*, March 25, 2011, sec. Magazine, nytimes.com/2011/03/27/magazine/mag-27Poker-t.html.

225 **often dress up:** Jim Barnes, "High-Stakes Standout Dan 'Jungleman' Cates Wins 1st WSOP Bracelet,"

Las Vegas Review-Journal, November 6, 2021, reviewjournal.com/sports/poker/high-stakes-standout
-dan-jungleman-cates-wins-1st-wsop-bracelet-2473223.

226 **one of the biggest winners:** Brian Pempus, "Phil Galfond Returns to Online Poker," Card Player, July 27,
2011, cardplayer.com/poker-news/11752-phil-galfond-returns-to-online-poker.

226 **a "washed-up ex-pro":** Phil Galfond, "Heads Up Battle," Run It Once, November 19, 2019, runitonce.eu
/news/heads-up-battle.

227 **blacked out after:** Matt Goodman, "Into the Deep," *D Magazine*, February 4, 2020, dmagazine.com
/publications/d-magazine/2020/february/victor-vescovo-five-deeps-expedition-dallas-mariana
-trench.

227 **the fatality rate:** "The World's 15 Most Dangerous Mountains to Climb (by Fatality Rate)," Ultimate Kili-
manjaro, July 21, 2023, ultimatekilimanjaro.com/the-worlds-most-dangerous-mountains.

228 **his native India:** Though Khosla told me he thinks this is starting to change in India.

229 **only one more SpaceX launch:** Walter Isaacson, *Elon Musk*, Kindle ed. (New York: Simon & Schuster,
2023), 186.

231 **a compromise approach:** Between 2020 and 2022, Sweden had the lowest all-cause excess mortality in the
OECD. And New Zealand, although it had some problems once it opened up, had about one-third of the
COVID death rate of the United States. See Eugene Volokh, "No-Lockdown Sweden Seemingly Tied for
Lowest All-Causes Mortality in OECD Since COVID Arrived," Reason.com, January 10, 2023, reason.com
/volokh/2023/01/10/no-lockdown-sweden-seemingly-tied-for-lowest-all-causes-mortality-in-oecd
-since-covid-arrived/; "COVID—Coronavirus Statistics," Worldometer, worldometers.info/coronavirus.

232 **Still, Luck had earned:** Seth Wickersham, "Andrew Luck Finally Reveals Why He Walked Away from
the NFL," ESPN, December 6, 2022, espn.com/nfl/insider/insider/story/_/id/35163936/andrew-luck
-reveals-why-walked-away-nfl.

233 **2023 blog post:** Phil Galfond, "Simplify Your Strategy," Philgalfond.com, August 8, 2023, philgalfond
.com/articles/simplify-your-strategy.

234 **also been applied:** Alan Stern and David Grinspoon, *Chasing New Horizons: Inside the Epic First Mission to
Pluto* (New York: Picador, 2018).

235 **I reintroduced you:** Voulgaris was also featured prominently in *The Signal and The Noise*.

236 **on a yacht:** Haralabos Voulgaris (@haralabob), "Jellyfish no longer a problem," Twitter, June 21, 2022,
twitter.com/haralabob/status/1539269014928621569.

237 **second-biggest winner:** As of February 14, 2024; "All-Time TV Cash Game List," Highroll Poker, high
rollpoker.com/tracker/players.

237 **rather important hand:** "Exposed Cards Drama: The $3,100,000 Poker Pot," 2023, youtube.com/watch
?v=QWhJiRK5OC4.

239 **"was a moron":** Pat Jordan, "Card Stud," *The New York Times*, May 29, 2005, sec. Magazine, nytimes
.com/2005/05/29/magazine/card-stud.html.

241 **World Backgammon Championship:** Jeff Walsh, "Galen Hall Shows 'Guts and Brains' at Backgammon
World Championship," World Poker Tour, August 14, 2023, worldpokertour.com/news/galen-hall-shows
-guts-and-brains-at-backgammon-world-championship.

241 **he broke through:** Galen Hall (@galenhall), "I went out the back, tried two doors both locked, third
door also locked, said fuck it, kicked it in. Went in, was a no outlet murder room. . . . ," Twitter, July 17,
2022, twitter.com/galenhall/status/1548599432983166983.

Chapter 5: Acceleration

247 **"The reasonable man":** George Bernard Shaw, *Man and Superman*, Gutenberg.org, gutenberg.org/files
/3328/3328-h/3328-h.htm.

247 **"become spoiled brats":** "Young Elon Musk: 'There Are 62 McLarens in the World and I Will Own One of
Them!' | 1999 Interview," 2019, youtube.com/watch?v=pAt5OVl0mnA.

248 **eventually parlay his $22 million:** Adam Clark, "Musk Is World's Richest Person Again After Tesla Stock
Surge," *Barrons*, February 28, 2023, barrons.com/articles/elon-musk-net-worth-tesla-stock-price-7e
44bcee.

248 **case of opposites:** Dorothy Cucci, "Peter Thiel Thinks Elon Musk Is a 'Fraud,' and 6 Other Unexpected
Details About the Billionaires' Love-Hate Relationship," Business Insider, December 2, 2022, business
insider.com/peter-thiel-elon-musk-relationship-contrarian-book-max-chafkin-2021-9.

248 **flooring the accelerator:** "Elon Musk: How I Wrecked An Uninsured McClaren F1," 2012, youtube.com
/watch?v=mOI8GWoMF4M.

248 **all these stories:** For example, Dennis Barnhardt of Eagle Computer, who lost control of his Ferrari in
Los Gatos, California; web.stanford.edu/class/e145/2007_fall/materials/noyce.html.

249 **2023 "Techno-Optimist Manifesto":** Marc Andreessen, "The Techno-Optimist Manifesto," Andreessen
Horowitz, October 16, 2023, a16z.com/the-techno-optimist-manifesto.

250 **"being uniquely careful":** Vitalik Buterin, "My Techno-Optimism," *Vitalik Buterin's Website* (blog), November 27, 2023, vitalik.eth.limo/general/2023/11/27/techno_optimism.html#ai.

251 a given fund: Per interview with Marc Andreessen.

251 sworn to secrecy: Chamath Palihapitiya et al., "#AIS: FiveThirtyEight's Nate Silver on How Gamblers Think," *All-In with Chamath, Jason, Sacks & Friedberg*, 2022, podcasts.apple.com/ie/podcast/ais -fivethirtyeights-nate-silver-on-how-gamblers-think/id1502871393?i=1000564483582.

252 aggressive compensation deal: Walter Isaacson, *Elon Musk*, Kindle ed. (New York: Simon & Schuster, 2023), 408.

252 Founders Fund: Connie Loizos, "Founders Fund Talks Space, Robots, Elon Musk and Why It Didn't Back Tesla Motors," *Venture Capital Journal*, July 27, 2010, venturecapitaljournal.com/founders-fund-talks -space-robots-elon-musk-and-why-the-team-didnt-back-tesla-motors.

252 a relieved Musk: Stephen Clark, "Sweet Success at Last for Falcon 1 Rocket," Spaceflight Now, September 28, 2008, spaceflightnow.com/falcon/004.

252 "rocket company failed": Isaacson, *Elon Musk*, 186.

253 strongly religious upbringing: Max Chafkin, *The Contrarian: Peter Thiel and Silicon Valley's Pursuit of Power*, Kindle ed. (New York: Penguin Press, 2021), 2.

253 "graven in imperishable": From Conrad's *Lord Jim*. Thiel's recollection of the passage was not quite verbatim, but this was clearly the passage he was referring to; gutenberg.org/cache/epub/5658/pg5658 -images.html.

254 rationalize risky trades: Ian Stewart, "The Mathematical Equation That Caused the Banks to Crash," *The Guardian*, February 12, 2012, sec. Science, theguardian.com/science/2012/feb/12/black-scholes -equation-credit-crunch.

254 famously contrarian: Jennifer Szalai, "'The Contrarian' Goes Searching for Peter Thiel's Elusive Core," *The New York Times*, September 13, 2021, sec. Books, nytimes.com/2021/09/13/books/review-contrarian -peter-thiel-silicon-valley-max chafkin.html.

256 world's unicorn companies: "The Complete List of Unicorn Companies," CB Insights, instapage.cbin sights.com/research-unicorn-companies.

256 nerds rebelling against: Sebastian Mallaby, *The Power Law: Venture Capital and the Making of the New Future*, Kindle ed. (New York: Penguin Press, 2022), 17.

256 a semiconductor facility: David Leonhardt, "Holding On," *The New York Times*, April 6, 2008, sec. Real Estate, nytimes.com/2008/04/06/realestate/keymagazine/406Lede-t.html.

257 He recorded their: Joel Shurkin, *Broken Genius: The Rise and Fall of William Shockley, Creator of the Electronic Age* (London: Macmillan, 2008).

257 take lie-detector tests: Tom Wolfe, "The Tinkerings of Robert Noyce," web.stanford.edu/class/e145 /2007_fall/materials/noyce.html.

257 paying them particularly well: Bo Lojek, *History of Semiconductor Engineering* (Berlin, Heidelberg: Springer-Verlag Berlin Heidelberg, 2007), 75.

257 of "adventure capital": Mallaby, *The Power Law*, 17.

257 got substantial raises: Lojek, *History of Semiconductor Engineering*, 88.

257 about $4 million: Shurkin, *Broken Genius*, 182.

257 "known as burnout": Wolfe, "The Tinkerings of Robert Noyce."

260 took six years: Mohammed Saeed Al Hasan, PMP, "Is SpaceX Profitable? With $150 Billion Net Worth—$4.6 Billion in Revenue?," LinkedIn, August 25, 2023, linkedin.com/pulse/spacex-profitable -150-billion-net-worth-46-revenue-al-hasan-pmp-.

261 tricking cryptocurrency holders: Larry Neumeister, "FTX Founder Sam Bankman-Fried Convicted of Stealing Billions from Customers and Investors," *USA Today*, November 2, 2023, usatoday.com/story /money/2023/11/02/sam-bankman-fried-convicted-fraud/71429793007/.

262 psychedelic drug use: Kirsten Grind and Katherine Bindley, "Magic Mushrooms. LSD. Ketamine. The Drugs That Power Silicon Valley," *The Wall Street Journal*, June 27, 2023, sec. Tech, wsj.com/articles/sil icon-valley-microdosing-ketamine-lsd-magic-mushrooms-d381e214.

263 the polymathic Collison: Tyler Cowen and Patrick Collison, "Patrick Collison Has a Few Questions for Tyler (Ep. 21—Live at Stripe)," *Conversations with Tyler*, 2017, conversationswithtyler.com/episodes/pat rick-collison.

265 cut off communication: Andy Hertzfeld, "The Little Kingdom," Folklore.org, December 1982, folklore .org/The_Little_Kingdom.html?sort=date.

266 Moritz twice made: Dave Kellogg, "Moritz Tops Forbes Midas List," *Kellblog* (blog), January 30, 2007, kellblog.com/2007/01/30/moritz-tops-forbes-midas-list.

267 cofounder Chris Hughes: Ellen McGirt, "How Chris Hughes Helped Launch Facebook and the Barack Obama Campaign," *Fast Company*, April 1, 2009, fastcompany.com/1207594/how-chris-hughes-helped -launch-facebook-and-barack-obama-campaign.

267 underlying trends may: Jonathan Haidt, for instance, attributes changes in Village culture—such as its increasing willingness to trade off free speech with other values—to roughly 2015 instead. Julie Beck, "The Coddling of the American Mind 'Is Speeding Up,'" *The Atlantic*, September 18, 2018, theatlantic .com/education/archive/2018/09/the-coddling-of-the-american-mind-is-speeding-up/570505.

267 **Andreessen, who had:** Dawn Chmielewski, "Asked Why He Supports Clinton over Trump, Marc Andreessen Responds: 'Is That a Serious Question?,'" *Vox*, June 14, 2016, vox.com/2016/6/14/11940052/marc-andreessen-donald-trump-hillary-clinton.

268 **the "cross hairs":** Mike Isaac, "Facebook, in Cross Hairs After Election, Is Said to Question Its Influence," *The New York Times*, November 12, 2016, nytimes.com/2016/11/14/technology/facebook-is-said-to-question-its-influence-in-election.html.

268 **Russian hackers bought:** Scott Shane and Vindu Goel, "Fake Russian Facebook Accounts Bought $100,000 in Political Ads," *The New York Times*, September 6, 2017, sec. Technology, nytimes.com/2017/09/06/technology/facebook-russian-political-ads.html.

268 **this was a tiny fraction:** "Clinton Crushes Trump 3:1 in Air War," Wesleyan Media Project, November 3, 2016, mediaproject.wesleyan.edu/nov-2016.

268 **Clinton email scandal:** Nate Silver, "The Real Story of 2016," FiveThirtyEight, January 19, 2017, fivethirtyeight.com/features/the-real-story-of-2016.

269 **amid sometimes violent:** Brakkton Booker et al., "Violence Erupts as Outrage over George Floyd's Death Spills into a New Week," NPR, June 1, 2020, sec. National, npr.org/2020/06/01/866472832/violence-escalates-as-protests-over-george-floyd-death-continue.

269 **over the murder:** The police officer Derek Chauvin, who knelt on Floyd's neck for nine minutes, asphyxiating him, was convicted of murder. Amy Forliti, Steve Karnowski, and Tammy Webber, "Chauvin Guilty of Murder and Manslaughter in Floyd's Death," AP News, April 21, 2021, apnews.com/article/derek-chauvin-trial-live-updates-04-20-2021-955a78df9a7a51835ad63afb8ce9b5c1.

269 **Democratic data firm:** Matthew Yglesias, "The Real Stakes in the David Shor Saga," *Vox*, July 29, 2020, vox.com/2020/7/29/21340308/david-shor-omar-wasow-speech.

269 **race riots had tended to reduce:** Omar Wasow, "Agenda Seeding: How 1960s Black Protests Moved Elites, Public Opinion and Voting," *American Political Science Review* 114, no. 3 (August 2020): 638–59, doi.org/10.1017/S000305542000009X.

269 **as "2,851 Miles":** "All-In Summit: Bill Gurley Presents 2,851 Miles," 2023, youtube.com/watch?v=F9cO3-MLHOM.

269 **bringing lawsuits against:** Dara Kerr, "Lina Khan Is Taking Swings at Big Tech as FTC Chair, and Changing How It Does Business," NPR, March 9, 2023, sec. Technology, npr.org/2023/03/07/1161312602/lina-khan-ftc-tech.

269 **thesis is well regarded:** George J. Stigler, "The Theory of Economic Regulation," *The Bell Journal of Economics and Management Science* 2, no. 1 (1971): 3, doi.org/10.2307/3003160.

270 **legal gray area:** Harry Davies et al., "Uber Broke Laws, Duped Police and Secretly Lobbied Governments, Leak Reveals," *The Guardian*, July 11, 2022, sec. News, theguardian.com/news/2022/jul/10/uber-files-leak-reveals-global-lobbying-campaign.

271 **a political cudgel:** Nate Silver, "Twitter, Elon and the Indigo Blob," *Silver Bulletin* (blog), October 1, 2023, natesilver.net/p/twitter-elon-and-the-indigo-blob.

272 **bigger swings in:** Jed Kolko and Toni Monkovic, "The Places That Had the Biggest Swings Toward and Against Trump," *The New York Times*, December 7, 2020, sec. The Upshot, nytimes.com/2020/12/07/upshot/trump-election-vote-shift.html.

272 **contributions are disproportionately:** Krystal Hur, "Big Tech Employees Rally Behind Biden Campaign," OpenSecrets, January 12, 2021, opensecrets.org/news/2021/01/big-tech-employees-rally-biden.

272 **extremely conservative views:** Max Chafkin's biography of Thiel, *The Contrarian*—although it takes a Villagey perspective by putting Thiel's politics at the front and center of the story—is nevertheless convincing that Thiel is quite conservative along a number of dimensions, more so than he is libertarian.

273 **James Damore circulated:** Kate Conger, "Exclusive: Here's the Full 10-Page Anti-Diversity Screed Circulating Internally at Google," *Gizmodo*, August 5, 2017, gizmodo.com/exclusive-heres-the-full-10-page-anti-diversity-screed-1797564320.

273 **Google fired him:** Aja Romano, "Google Has Fired the Engineer Whose Anti-Diversity Memo Reflects a Divided Tech Culture," *Vox*, August 8, 2017, vox.com/identities/2017/8/8/16106728/google-fired-engineer-anti-diversity-memo.

273 **relatively mainstream positions:** Kim Parker, Juliana Menasce Horowitz, and Renee Stepler, "On Gender Differences, No Consensus on Nature vs. Nurture," Pew Research Center's Social & Demographic Trends Project, December 5, 2017, pewresearch.org/social-trends/2017/12/05/on-gender-differences-no-consensus-on-nature-vs-nurture.

273 **an anonymous survey:** Romano, "Google Has Fired the Engineer Whose Anti-Diversity Memo Reflects a Divided Tech Culture."

273 **nothing of the sort:** Silver Bulletin, natesilver.net/p/google-abandoned-dont-be-evil-and.

274 **awarded $140 million:** Bill Chappell, "Gawker Files for Bankruptcy as It Faces $140 Million Court Penalty," NPR, June 10, 2016, sec. America, npr.org/sections/thetwo-way/2016/06/10/481565188/gawker-files-for-bankruptcy-it-faces-140-million-court-penalty.

274 **secretly been funded:** Andrew Ross Sorkin, "Peter Thiel, Tech Billionaire, Reveals Secret War with Gawker," *The New York Times*, May 26, 2016, sec. Business, nytimes.com/2016/05/26/business/deal book/peter-thiel-tech-billionaire-reveals-secret-war-with-gawker.html.

274 **which outed him:** Ryan Holiday, *Conspiracy: Peter Thiel, Hulk Hogan, Gawker, and the Anatomy of Intrigue* (New York: Portfolio, 2018).

274 **forced into bankruptcy:** Although, the outcome was appealed and the case was later settled for $31 million. Robert W. Wood, "Hulk Hogan Settles $140 Million Gawker Verdict for $31 Million, IRS Collects Big," *Forbes*, November 3, 2016, forbes.com/sites/robertwood/2016/11/03/hulk-hogan-settles-140-million-gawker-verdict-for-31-million-irs-collects-big.

274 **"the human drama":** Peter A. Thiel and Blake Masters, *Zero to One: Notes on Startups, or How to Build the Future*, Kindle ed. (New York: Crown Business, 2014), 38.

274 **have hot spouses:** Emily Chang, "'Oh My God, This Is So F—ed Up': Inside Silicon Valley's Secretive, Orgiastic Dark Side," *Vanity Fair*, January 2, 2018, vanityfair.com/news/2018/01/brotopia-silicon-valley-secretive-orgiastic-inner-sanctum.

275 **basically self-made:** Gigi Zamora, "The 2023 Forbes 400 Self-Made Score: From Silver Spooners to Boot-strappers," *Forbes*, October 2, 2023, forbes.com/sites/gigizamora/2023/10/03/the-2023-forbes-400-self-made-score-from-silver-spooners-to-bootstrappers.

276 **simply scions of:** Vanessa Sumo, "Most Billionaires Are Self-Made, Not Heirs," *Chicago Booth Review*, August 22, 2014, chicagobooth.edu/review/billionaires-self-made.

276 **Chetty, overall income:** Raj Chetty et al., "The Fading American Dream: Trends in Absolute Income Mobility Since 1940," *Science* 356, no. 6336 (April 28, 2017): 398–406, doi.org/10.1126/science.aal4617.

276 **and wealth mobility:** Raj Chetty et al., "The Opportunity Atlas: Mapping the Childhood Roots of Social Mobility," working paper 25147, National Bureau of Economic Research, October 2018, doi.org/10.3386/w25147.

276 **Forbes 400 list:** "Forbes 400 2023," *Forbes*, forbes.com/forbes-400.

276 **new businesses founded:** Commerce Institute, "How Many New Businesses Are Started Each Year? (2023 Data)," Commerce Institute, March 27, 2023, commerceinstitute.com/new-businesses-started-every-year.

277 **a Burger King:** Drake Bennett, "Social+Capital, the League of Extraordinarily Rich Gentlemen," Bloomberg, July 27, 2012, bloomberg.com/news/articles/2012-07-26/social-plus-capital-the-league-of-extraordinarily-rich-gentlemen.

277 **"chips on shoulders":** Josh Wolfe (@wolfejosh), "Chips on shoulders put chips in pockets," Twitter, July 17, 2020, twitter.com/wolfejosh/status/1284108444656717825.

277 **gritty Coney Island:** Sheelah Kolhatkar, "Power Punk: Josh Wolfe," *Observer*, December 15, 2003, observer.com/2003/12/power-punk-josh-wolfe.

277 **a difficult childhood:** Isaacson, *Elon Musk*, 7.

277 **became estranged from:** Isaacson, *Elon Musk*, 469.

277 **gay and closeted:** Chafkin, *The Contrarian*, 30.

278 **childhood trauma:** Although the scope and extent of these effects are debated; thelancet.com/article /S2468-2667(19)30145-8/fulltext.

280 **an uncanny ability:** Scott Alexander, *Astral Codex Ten*, "Book Review: Elon Musk."

281 **put $350 million:** Andrew Ross Sorkin et al., "Adam Neumann Gets a New Backer," *The New York Times*, August 15, 2022, sec. Business, nytimes.com/2022/08/15/business/dealbook/adam-neumann-flow-new-company-wework-real-estate.html.

281 **"superior living environment":** "Senior Accountant," Flow, jobs.lever.co/flowlife/687db5e3-c2a4-484b-a818-a9f7b3ae71e4.

281 **before imploding spectacularly:** Gennaro Cuofano, "How WeWork's Implosion Turned It into a Shell of Its Initial $47 Billion Promise," HackerNoon, March 11, 2022, hackernoon.com/how-weworks-implosion-turned-it-into-a-shell-of-its-initial-$47-billion-promise.

281 **a pregnant employee:** Brendan Pierson, "WeWork, Former CEO Adam Neumann Accused of Pregnancy Discrimination," Reuters, November 1, 2019, sec. Technology, reuters.com/article/idUSKBN1XA2OA.

281 **expanded far too quickly:** Amy Chozick, "Adam Neumann and the Art of Failing Up," *The New York Times*, November 2, 2019, sec. Business, nytimes.com/2019/11/02/business/adam-neumann-wework-exit-package.html.

281 **enormous annual losses:** Rani Molla, "The WeWork Mess, Explained," *Vox*, September 23, 2019, vox.com/recode/2019/9/23/20879656/wework-mess-explained-ipo-softbank.

282 **reported on elsewhere:** Kate Clark, "Andreessen Horowitz's AI Crusader Emerges as a Confidant of the Founders," The Information, June 3, 2023, theinformation.com/articles/andreessen-horowitzs-ai-crusader.

282 **common to find:** "Elon Musk Reveals He Has Asperger's on Saturday Night Live," May 9, 2021, bbc.com /news/world-us-canada-57045770.

282 **Daniel "Jungleman" Cates:** Rick Maese, "How to Win at Cards and Life, According to Poker's Autistic Superstar," *The Washington Post*, May 3, 2023, washingtonpost.com/sports/2023/05/02/jungleman-poker-dan-cates-autisic.

282 **Asperger's is sometimes:** Isaacson, *Elon Musk*, 120–21.

282 **lack of adherence:** Drake Baer, "Peter Thiel: Asperger's Can Be a Big Advantage in Silicon Valley," Business Insider, April 8, 2015, businessinsider.com/peter-thiel-aspergers-is-an-advantage-2015-4.

283 **prevalence of autism:** In a survey of readers of Scott Alexander's rationalist blog *Astral Codex Ten*, 5 percent of people said they had a formal autism diagnosis but another 17 percent said they think they might have the condition. Scott Alexander, "ACX Survey Results 2022," *Astral Codex Ten* (blog), January 20, 2023, astralcodexten.substack.com/p/acx-survey-results-2022. By contrast, the prevalence in the general U.S. adult population is about 2 percent, according to the CDC. "CDC Releases First Estimates of the Number of Adults Living with ASD," Centers for Disease Control and Prevention, April 27, 2020, cdc .gov/ncbddd/autism/features/adults-living-with-autism-spectrum-disorder.html.

283 **based on post-facto diagnoses:** Michael Fitzgerald, "John von Neumann was on the autism spectrum," ResearchGate, researchgate.net/publication/369141516_John_von_Neumann_was_on_the_autism _spectrum.

283 **classification scheme DSM-5:** "What Is Asperger Syndrome?," Autism Speaks, autismspeaks.org/types -autism-what-asperger-syndrome.

283 **moderately correlated personality:** Lars-Olov Lundqvist and Helen Lindner, "Is the Autism-Spectrum Quotient a Valid Measure of Traits Associated with the Autism Spectrum? A Rasch Validation in Adults with and Without Autism Spectrum Disorders," *Journal of Autism and Developmental Disorders* 47, no. 7 (July 2017): 2080–91, doi.org/10.1007/s10803-017-3128-y.

283 **The Autism-Spectrum Quotient:** Simon Baron-Cohen et al., "The Autism-Spectrum Quotient (AQ): Evidence from Asperger Syndrome/High-Functioning Autism, Males and Females, Scientists and Mathematicians," *Journal of Autism and Developmental Disorders* 31, no. 1 (2001): 5–17, doi.org/10.1023/A:1005 653411471.

283 **into five subcategories:** Although these category headings appear in the Baron-Cohen et. al. paper, ChatGPT helped me to formulate these definitions.

284 **moved to Miami:** Kara Swisher, "Is Tech's Love Affair with Miami About Taxes, or Something Else?," *The New York Times*, February 17, 2022, sec. Opinion, nytimes.com/2022/02/17/opinion/sway-kara -swisher-keith-rabois.html.

284 **a Barry's Bootcamp:** Candy Cheng, "VC Keith Rabois Has a New Side Hustle in Miami as a Barry's Bootcamp Instructor," Business Insider, March 31, 2021, businessinsider.com/why-vc-keith-rabois-new -side-hustle-at-barrys-bootcamp-2021-3.

285 **founders and hedge-funders:** Ashley Portero, "11 Notable Techies Who Moved to South Florida in 2021," *South Florida Business Journal*, December 22, 2021, bizjournals.com/southflorida/news/2021/12/22/tech ies-who-moved-to-miami-in-2021.html.

285 **Keynesian beauty contest:** John Maynard Keynes, *The General Theory of Employment, Interest, and Money* (New York: Harcourt, Brace & World, 1935), archive.org/details/generaltheoryofe00keyn.

287 **to female-only founders:** Sarah Silano, "Women Founders Get 2% of Venture Capital Funding in U.S.," *Morningstar*, March 6, 2023, morningstar.com/alternative-investments/women-founders-get-2-ven ture-capital-funding-us.

287 **Black founders typically:** Dominic-Madori Davis, "Black Founders Still Raised Just 1% of All VC Funds in 2022," TechCrunch, January 6, 2023, techcrunch.com/2023/01/06/black-founders-still-raised-just -1-of-all-vc-funds-in-2022.

287 **2 percent goes:** Arielle Pardes, "Latino Founders Have a Hard Time Raising Money from VCs," *Wired*, January 26, 2022, wired.com/story/latino-founders-hard-raising-money-vcs.

287 **going to immigrants:** Steven Overly, "Study: Venture-Backed Companies with Immigrant Founders Contribute to Economy," *The Washington Post*, May 18, 2023, washingtonpost.com/business/capital business/study-venture-backed-companies-with-immigrant-founders-contribute-to-economy /2013/06/25/b3689ac6-dce4-11e2-85de-c03ca84cb4ef_story.html.

287 **of Asian ancestry:** Mary Ann Azevedo, "Untapped Opportunity: Minority Founders Still Being Overlooked," *Crunchbase News*, February 27, 2019, news.crunchbase.com/venture/untapped-opportunity -minority-founders-still-being-overlooked.

288 **more than 250:** Kimberly Weisul, "After Meeting with 257 Investors, This Founder Realized That Authenticity Is Everything," *Inc.*, November 15, 2019, inc.com/kimberly-weisul/jean-brownhill -sweeten-authenticity-founders-project.html.

290 **Stanford and Harvard:** "U.S. News Rankings for 57 Leading Universities, 1983–2007," September 13, 2017, Public University Honors, publicuniversityhonors.com/2017/09/13/u-s-news-rankings-for-57 -leading-universities-1983-2007.

290 **Harvard was also:** Irwin Collier, "Economics Departments and University Rankings by Chair men. Hughes (1925) and Keniston (1957)," *Economics in the Rear-View Mirror* (blog), April 9, 2019, irwin collier.com/economics-departments-and-university-rankings-by-chairmen-hughes-1925-and -keniston-1957.

291 **in Andreessen's Netscape:** "Netscape: Bringing the Internet to the World Through the Web Browser," Kleiner Perkins, kleinerperkins.com/case-study/netscape.

291 **in Thiel's PayPal:** "PayPal," Sequoia Capital, sequoiacap.com/companies/paypal.

291 **list in 1972:** "Fortune 500: 1972 Archive Full List 1–100," CNN Money, money.cnn.com/magazines/fortune/fortune500_archive/full/1972.

291 **list in 2022:** "Fortune 500 2022," *Fortune*, fortune.com/ranking/fortune500/2022.

291 **have yield rates:** Andrew Belasco, "How to Get Into Stanford: Data & Acceptance Rate & Strategies," College Transitions, May 31, 2023, collegetransitions.com/blog/how-to-get-into-stanford-data-admissions-strategies.

292 **durable excess returns:** Robert S. Harris et al., "Has Persistence Persisted in Private Equity? Evidence from Buyout and Venture Capital Funds," *Journal of Corporate Finance* 81 (August 2023): 102361, doi.org/10.1016/j.jcorpfin.2023.102361.

292 **top VC firm:** "Top 66 Venture Capital Firm Managers by Managed AUM," SWIFI, accessed December 31, 2023, swfinstitute.org/fund-manager-rankings/venture-capital-firm.

292 **confirmed by email:** Andreessen declined to provide more specific documentation, citing the proprietary nature of the data.

292 **The industry as a whole:** Diane Mulcahy, "Six Myths About Venture Capitalists," *Harvard Business Review*, May 1, 2013, hbr.org/2013/05/six-myths-about-venture-capitalists.

293 **20 percent IRR:** The Regents of the University of California, "Private Equity Investments as of June 30, 2023," University of California, 2023, ucop.edu/investment-office/_files/updates/pe_irr_06-30-21.pdf; theinformation.com/articles/andreessen-horowitz-returns-slip-according-to-internal-data.

293 **for the endnotes:** For the simulations, I created a set of one hundred hypothetical companies with returns corresponding to Andreessen's data. More specifically, the first twenty-five companies returned 0x, the next twenty-five returned amounts on a sliding scale between 0.01x and 0.99x, the next twenty-five returned amounts on a sliding scale between 1x and 3x, the next fifteen returned amounts on a sliding scale between 3.4x and 10x, and the final ten returned the following: 15x, 20x, 25x, 30x, 40x, 50x, 75x, 100x, 250x, and 500x. These large payoffs are necessary to achieve an IRR in the 20s, as top-decile firms target. The same return could be drawn more than once for a given fund (essentially, the ping-pong ball was returned to the tumbler after it was picked). I then took the total return and calculated the IRR, assuming the fund was held for ten years. To account for cyclical volatility, I randomly chose a ten-year stretch of Nasdaq returns for each fund, and added it to the IRR from the fund, then subtracted the long-run average Nasdaq return. For instance, say the companies in a particular simulation initially returned an IRR of 22 percent, but for the Nasdaq ball I drew a 3 percent, meaning it was a poor cycle for the sector (the long-run average Nasdaq return since 1972 is 13 percent). The IRR would be adjusted to 22% + 3% – 13% = 12%.

294 **jobs at Google had a college degree:** Steve Lohr, "A 4-Year Degree Isn't Quite the Job Requirement It Used to Be," *The New York Times*, April 8, 2023, nytimes.com/2022/04/08/business/hiring-without-college-degree.html.

294 **congressional hearing featuring:** Nate Silver, "Why Liberalism and Leftism Are Increasingly at Odds," *Silver Bulletin* (blog), December 12, 2023, natesilver.net/p/why-liberalism-and-leftism-are-increasingly.

295 **several credible accusations:** Sally E. Edwards and Asher J. Montgomery, "Harvard President Claudine Gay Plagued by Plagiarism Allegations in the Tumultuous Final Weeks of Tenure," *The Harvard Crimson*, January 3, 2024, thecrimson.com/article/2024/1/3/plagiarism-allegations-gay-resigns.

295 **panned the performance:** Kyla Guilfoil, "White House Condemns University Presidents after Contentious Congressional Hearing on Antisemitism," NBC News, December 7, 2023, nbcnews.com/politics/white-house/white-house-condemns-university-presidents-contentious-congressional-h-rcna128373.

295 **to its motto:** Eliot A. Cohen, "Harvard Has a Veritas Problem," *The Atlantic*, December 22, 2023, theatlantic.com/ideas/archive/2023/12/harvard-gay-plagarism-standards/676948.

295 **confidence in higher ed:** Megan Brenan, "Americans' Confidence in Higher Education Down Sharply," Gallup, July 11, 2023, news.gallup.com/poll/508352/americans-confidence-higher-education-down-sharply.aspx.

295 **canonical Village institution:** Megan Brenan, "Media Confidence in U.S. Matches 2016 Record Low," Gallup, October 19, 2023, news.gallup.com/poll/512861/media-confidence-matches-2016-record-low.aspx.

295 **trust in Big Tech:** Megan Brenan, "Views of Big Tech Worsen; Public Wants More Regulation," Gallup, February 18, 2021, news.gallup.com/poll/329666/views-big-tech-worsen-public-wants-regulation.aspx.

297 **in a simulation:** Rounak Jain, "Are We Living in a Multiverse or a Simulation? Depends on Who You Ask, Says Peter Thiel," *Benzinga*, October 5, 2023, benzinga.com/news/23/10/35111877/are-we-living-in-a-multiverse-or-a-simulation-depends-on-who-you-ask-says-peter-thiel.

297 **roughly 120 billion:** Ted Kaneda and Carl Haub, "How Many People Have Ever Lived on Earth?," PRB, prb.org/articles/how-many-people-have-ever-lived-on-earth.

297 **the chosen ones:** This idea was inspired by a conversation with Nick Bostrom.

297 **"curing" death:** Tad Friend, "Silicon Valley's Quest to Live Forever," *The New Yorker*, March 27, 2017, newyorker.com/magazine/2017/04/03/silicon-valleys-quest-to-live-forever.

Chapter 6: Illusion

298 **once $32 billion:** Jamie Redman, "From a $32 Billion Valuation to Financial Troubles: An In-Depth Look at the Rise and Fall of FTX," Bitcoin News, November 10, 2022, news.bitcoin.com/from-a-32-billion -valuation-to-financial-troubles-an-in-depth-look-at-the-rise-and-fall-of-ftx.

298 **FTX had defrauded:** Nikhilesh De and Sam Kessler, "Sam Bankman-Fried Guilty on All 7 Counts in FTX Fraud Trial," November 2, 2023, coindesk.com/policy/2023/11/02/sam-bankman-fried-guilty-on-all-7 -counts-in-ftx-fraud-trial.

298 **worth $26.5 billion:** "Sam Bankman-Fried," *Forbes*, forbes.com/profile/sam-bankman-fried.

299 **the Met Gala:** Michael Lewis, *Going Infinite: The Rise and Fall of a New Tycoon*, Kindle ed. (New York: W. W. Norton & Company, 2023), 19–20.

299 **$35 million apartment:** MacKenzie Sigalos, "Inside Sam Bankman-Fried's $35 Million Crypto Frat House in the Bahamas," CNBC, October 10, 2023, cnbc.com/2023/10/10/inside-sam-bankman-frieds -35-million-crypto-frat-house-in-bahamas.html.

299 **the AI company Anthropic:** Decrypt / Andrew Asmakov, "US Prosecutors Calls SBF's $500 Million Investment in AI Firm Anthropic 'Wholly Irrelevant,'" Decrypt, October 9, 2023, decrypt.co/200649/u-s -prosecutors-say-sbf-500-million-investment-ai-firm-anthropic-wholly-irrelevant.

299 **a category FTX:** Andrew Cohen, "Crypto Exchange FTX Has Tried Buying Sports Betting App PlayUp for $450 Million," *Sports Business Journal*, December 14, 2021, sportsbusinessjournal.com/Daily/Issues /2021/12/14/Technology/crypto-exchange-ftx-has-tried-buying-sports-betting-app-playup-for -450-million.aspx.

299 **surreptitiously in the latter case:** Bankman-Fried confirmed this to me, but it's also been reported elsewhere; see, for example: Brian Schwartz, "Sam Bankman-Fried, FTX Allies Secretly Poured $50 Million into 'Dark Money' Groups, Evidence Shows," CNBC, October 20, 2023, cnbc.com/2023/10/20/sam -bankman-fried-ftx-allies-donated-millions-in-dark-money.html.

300 **played video games:** David Gura, "What to Know About Sam Bankman-Fried and FTX Before His Crypto Financial Fraud Trial," NPR, October 2, 2023, sec. Business, npr.org/2023/10/02/1203097238 /what-to-know-about-sam-bankman-fried-and-ftx-before-his-crypto-financial-fraud-t.

301 **a flight risk:** Rohan Goswami, "Sam Bankman-Fried Denied Bail in Bahamas on FTX Fraud Charges, Judge Cites Flight Risk," CNBC, December 13, 2022, cnbc.com/2022/12/13/sam-bankman-fried -denied-bail-in-bahamas-on-ftx-fraud-charges-judge-cites-flight-risk.html.

301 **veteran of Enron:** Richard Lawler, "FTX Files for Chapter 11 Bankruptcy as CEO Sam Bankman-Fried Resigns," *The Verge*, November 11, 2022, theverge.com/2022/11/11/23453164/ftx-bankruptcy-filing-sam -bankman-fried-resigns.

301 **with Kevin O'Leary:** Sam Reynolds, "TV's Kevin O'Leary: 'All the Crypto Cowboys Are Going to Be Gone Soon,'" October 3, 2023, coindesk.com/business/2023/10/03/tvs-kevin-oleary-all-the-crypto -cowboys-are-going-to-be-gone-soon.

303 **$477 million hack:** Elliptic Research, "The $477 Million FTX Hack: A New Blockchain Trail," *Elliptic* (blog), October 12, 2023, elliptic.co/blog/the-477-million-ftx-hack-following-the-blockchain-trail.

303 **FTX had made:** Hannah Miller, "FTX's Plan to Potentially Reopen Is a New Sign of Crypto Arrogance," Bloomberg, November 17, 2023, bloomberg.com/news/newsletters/2023-11-17/when-did-ftx-collapse -sbf-s-former-crypto-exchange-could-return.

303 **Ray later discussed:** Nelson Wang, "New FTX Head Says Crypto Exchange Could Be Revived: *The Wall Street Journal*," CoinDesk, January 19, 2023, coindesk.com/business/2023/01/19/new-ftx-head-says -crypto-exchange-could-be-revived-wall-st-journal.

304 **one of FTX's subsidiaries:** "FTX Digital Markets Ltd. (In Liquidation)," PricewaterhouseCoopers, accessed December 31, 2023, pwc.com/bs/en/services/business-restructuring-ftx-digital-markets.html.

304 **resigned as CEO:** MacKenzie Sigalos, "Sam Bankman-Fried Steps down as FTX CEO as His Crypto Exchange Files for Bankruptcy," CNBC, November 11, 2022, cnbc.com/2022/11/11/sam-bankman-frieds -cryptocurrency-exchange-ftx-files-for-bankruptcy.html.

305 **nerdy, overconfident, Adderall-popping:** William Skipworth, "SBF's Lawyers Are Asking the Judge for More Adderall," *Forbes*, October 16, 2023, forbes.com/sites/willskipworth/2023/10/16/sbfs-lawyers-are -asking-the-judge-for-more-adderall.

305 **on the autism spectrum:** SBF's lawyers asked for a shorter prison sentence due to what they said was his autism spectrum disorder. *Wall Street Journal*, wsj.com/finance/currencies/sam-bankman-fried -suggests-shorter-sentence-for-fraud-conviction-citing-autism-e8481876.

306 **Bitcoin had achieved:** "Bitcoin Price Today, BTC to USD Live Price, Marketcap and Chart," CoinMarketCap, coinmarketcap.com/currencies/bitcoin/historical-data.

306 **the average annual:** Afifa Mushtaque, "Average Salary in Each State in US," Yahoo Finance, July 26, 2023, finance.yahoo.com/news/average-salary-state-us-152311356.html.

306 Bitcoins were first: Bernard Marr, "A Short History of Bitcoin and Crypto Currency Everyone Should Read," Bernard Marr & Co., July 2, 2021, bernardmarr.com/a-short-history-of-bitcoin-and-crypto-currency-everyone-should-read.

306 Heat's basketball arena: Lora Kelley, "FTX Spent Big on Sports Sponsorships. What Happens Now?," *The New York Times*, November 11, 2022, sec. Business, nytimes.com/2022/11/10/business/ftx-sports-sponsorships.html.

307 join a DAO: Kevin Roose, "What Are DAOs?," *The New York Times*, March 18, 2022, sec. Technology, nytimes.com/interactive/2022/03/18/technology/what-are-daos.html.

307 Art Basel weekend: "NFTs Took Over Art Basel," Coinbase, December 8, 2021, coinbase.com/bytes/archive/nfts-took-over-art-basel-miami.

307 meet Alex Mashinsky: John Mccrank and Hannah Lang, "Who Is Alex Mashinsky, the Man Behind the Alleged Celsius Crypto Fraud?," Reuters, January 5, 2023, sec. Technology, reuters.com/technology/who-is-alex-mashinsky-man-behind-alleged-celsius-crypto-fraud-2023-01-05.

307 Mashinsky claimed: "About," Alex Mashinsky, mashinsky.com/about.

307 role is disputed: Jeff Wilser, "Sky-High Yields and Bright Red Flags: How Alex Mashinsky Went from Bashing Banks to Bankrupting Celsius," CoinDesk, July 27, 2022, coindesk.com/layer2/2022/07/27/sky-high-yields-and-bright-red-flags-how-alex-mashinsky-went-from-bashing-banks-to-bankrupting-celsius.

307 regarded as dubious: "A Pattern of Deception, Part 1: Arbinet," Dirty Bubble Media, November 4, 2022, dirtybubblemedia.com/p/a-pattern-of-deception-part-1-arbinet.

308 later go bankrupt: "Celsius Network LLC, et al.," Stretto, cases.stretto.com/celsius.

308 charged with fraud: "Alex Mashinsky's Jury Trial Scheduled for September 2024," Cointelegraph, October 3, 2023, cointelegraph.com/news/alex-mashinsky-trial-september-2024.

308 Mashinsky had sent: Zeke Faux, *Number Go Up: Inside Crypto's Wild Rise and Staggering Fall*, Kindle ed. (New York: Currency, 2023), 316–17.

308 halt customer withdrawals: Brian Quarmby, "10 Crypto Tweets That Aged Like Milk: 2022 Edition," *Cointelegraph*, December 30, 2022, cointelegraph.com/news/10-crypto-tweets-that-aged-like-milk-2022-edition.

309 sometimes borrowed it: Lewis, *Going Infinite*, 144.

309 even SBF refused: Faux, *Number Go Up*, 216.

309 as high as 18 percent: Zeke Faux and Joe Light, "Celsius's 18% Yields on Crypto Are Tempting—and Drawing Scrutiny," Bloomberg, January 27, 2022, bloomberg.com/news/articles/2022-01-27/celsius-s-18-yields-on-crypto-are-tempting-and-drawing-scrutiny.

309 "amounted to a Ponzi scheme": Shoba Pillay, "Final Report of Shoba Pillay, Examiner, in re: Celsius Network LLC, et al.," January 30, 2023, cases.stretto.com/public/x191/11749/PLEADINGS/1174901312380000000039.pdf.

310 "boredom markets hypothesis": Matt Levine, "The Bad Stocks Are the Most Fun," Bloomberg, June 9, 2020, bloomberg.com/opinion/articles/2020-06-09/the-bad-stocks-are-the-most-fun.

310 peak in newly diagnosed: "COVID—Coronavirus Statistics," Worldometer, accessed December 31, 2023, worldometers.info/coronavirus.

311 South Sea Bubble: Terry Stewart, "The South Sea Bubble of 1720," Historic UK, December 23, 2021, historic-uk.com/HistoryUK/HistoryofEngland/South-Sea-Bubble.

311 tech bubble in the early 2000s: Adam Hayes, "Dotcom Bubble Definition," Investopedia, June 12, 2023, investopedia.com/terms/d/dotcom-bubble.asp.

311 for a CryptoPunk: "CryptoPunks NFT Floor Price Chart," CoinGecko, coingecko.com/en/nft/cryptopunks.

311 a.k.a. Gary Vee: Gary Vaynerchuk, "Road to Twelve and a Half: Self-Awareness," Gary Vaynerchuk, September 28, 2021, garyvaynerchuk.com/road-to-twelve-and-a-half-self-awareness.

312 majority of NFTs: Steve Randall, "Hero to Zero: Most NFTs Are Now Worthless Says New Report," *InvestmentNews*, September 25, 2023, investmentnews.com/alternatives/news/hero-to-zero-most-nfts-are-now-worthless-says-new-report-243795.

312 dominated by men: Jon Cohen and Laura Wronski, "Cryptocurrency Investing Has a Big Gender Problem," CNBC, August 30, 2021, cnbc.com/2021/08/30/cryptocurrency-has-a-big-gender-problem.html.

312 tumbled even further: Estimates are derived from combining these two sources: U.S. Bureau of Labor Statistics, "Employment Level—20-24 Yrs., Men," FRED, Federal Reserve Bank of St. Louis, January 1, 1948, fred.stlouisfed.org/series/LNS12000037; "Population Pyramids of the World from 1950 to 2100," PopulationPyramid.net, populationpyramid.net/united-states-of-america/1979.

312 who complete college: Richard V. Reeves and Ember Smith, "The Male College Crisis Is Not Just in Enrollment, but Completion," Brookings, October 8, 2021, brookings.edu/articles/the-male-college-crisis-is-not-just-in-enrollment-but-completion.

313 another $10 million: Joseph Gibson, "We Now Know (Allegedly) How Much Sam Bankman-Fried Paid Tom Brady, Steph Curry and Larry David for Their FTX Endorsements," Celebrity Net Worth, October 4,

2023, celebritynetworth.com/articles/celebrity/we-now-know-allegedly-how-much-sam-bankman-fried-paid-tom-brady-steph-curry-and-larry-david-for-their-ftx-endorsements.

313 **who scoffed at:** "FTX Super Bowl Don't Miss out with Larry David," 2022, youtube.com/watch?v=hWMnbJJpeZc.

314 **several thousand retail locations:** "Form 10K," GameStop, March 28, 2023, news.gamestop.com/static-files/f4494fbe-9752-4056-a3c7-451f0cf9a668.

314 **its market capitalization:** "GameStop Market Cap," Ycharts, ycharts.com/companies/GME/market_cap.

314 **most video game sales:** Richard Breslin, "90% of Video Game Sales in 2022 Were Digital," GameByte, January 11, 2023, gamebyte.com/90-of-video-game-sales-in-2022-were-digital.

314 **net loss every year:** "Form 10K," GameStop, March 23, 2021, news.gamestop.com/node/18661/html.

314 **day traders wanted:** Matt Phillips and Taylor Lorenz, "'Dumb Money' Is on GameStop, and It's Beating Wall Street at Its Own Game," *The New York Times*, January 27, 2021, sec. Business, nytimes.com/2021/01/27/business/gamestop-wall-street-bets.html.

314 **Blockbuster Video dinosaur:** Daniel Howley, "Why GameStop Is Destined to Become Another Blockbuster Video," Yahoo Finance, January 27, 2021, finance.yahoo.com/news/why-game-stop-is-destined-to-become-another-blockbuster-video-221243155.html.

315 **shortly after its creation:** Andrew Couts, "Dogecoin Fetches 300 Percent Jump in Value in 24 Hours," Digital Trends, December 19, 2013, digitaltrends.com/cool-tech/dogecoin-price-value-jump-bitcoin.

315 **of cryptocurrency users:** "Crypto Users Worldwide 2016–2023," Statista, December 1, 2023, statista.com/statistics/1202503/global-cryptocurrency-user-base.

318 **so-called tech wreck:** Paul R. La Monica, "A New Bubble Bursting? Tech Stocks Plunge," CNNMoney, June 9, 2017, money.cnn.com/2017/06/09/investing/tech-stocks-goldman-sachs/index.html.

318 **Li is obviously:** "Runbo Li," LinkedIn, linkedin.com/in/runboli.

319 **stock market increases:** "S&P 500 Historical Annual Returns," MacroTrends, macrotrends.net/2526/sp-500-historical-annual-returns.

320 **directly from Robinhood:** "What's Margin Investing?," Robinhood, robinhood.com/us/en/support/articles/margin-overview.

321 **some of these animations:** Maggie Fitzgerald, "Robinhood Gets Rid of Confetti Feature amid Scrutiny over Gamification of Investing," CNBC, March 31, 2021, cnbc.com/2021/03/31/robinhood-gets-rid-of-confetti-feature-amid-scrutiny-over-gamification.html.

321 **much higher volumes:** Nathaniel Popper, "Robinhood Has Lured Young Traders, Sometimes with Devastating Results," *The New York Times*, July 8, 2020, sec. Technology, nytimes.com/2020/07/08/technology/robinhood-risky-trading.html.

322 **the first Bitcoins:** Though due to a quirk in the code, these particular BTC can't be spent or traded. "Genesis Block," Bitcoin Wiki, en.bitcoin.it/wiki/Genesis_block.

322 *Times* **of London:** Benedict George, "The Genesis Block: The First Bitcoin Block," CoinDesk, January 3, 2023, coindesk.com/tech/2023/01/03/the-genesis-block-the-first-bitcoin-block.

322 **had inspired Nakamoto:** Alan Feuer, "The Bitcoin Ideology," *The New York Times*, December 14, 2013, sec. Sunday Review, nytimes.com/2013/12/15/sunday-review/the-bitcoin-ideology.html.

322 **"with conventional currency":** Satoshi Nakamoto, "Bitcoin Open Source Implementation of P2P Currency," Satoshi Nakamoto Institute, February 11, 2009, satoshi.nakamotoinstitute.org/posts/p2pfoundation/1/#selection-45.

322 **digital ledger of every transaction:** Antony Lewis, *The Basics of Bitcoins and Blockchains: An Introduction to Cryptocurrencies and the Technology that Powers Them*, Kindle ed. (Coral Gables, FL: Mango Publishing, 2018), p. 15.

323 **first digital asset:** Lewis, *The Basics of Bitcoins and Blockchains*, 23.

323 **his white paper:** Satoshi Nakamoto, "Bitcoin: A Peer-to-Peer Electronic Cash System," October 31, 2008, bitcoin.org/bitcoin.pdf.

323 **has been likened:** Lewis, *The Basics of Bitcoins and Blockchains*, 132.

323 **process is random:** Jake Frankenfield, "What Is Bitcoin Mining?," Investopedia, October 11, 2023, investopedia.com/terms/b/bitcoin-mining.asp.

324 **makes julienne fries:** "Slices, Dices, and Makes Julienne Fries," TV Tropes, tvtropes.org/pmwiki/pmwiki.php/Main/SlicesDicesAndMakesJulienneFries.

324 **"fully fledged Turing-complete":** Vitalik Buterin, "Ethereum: A Next-Generation Smart Contract and Decentralized Application Platform," 2014, https://blockchainlab.com/pdf/Ethereum_white_paper-a_next_generation_smart_contract_and_decentralized_application_platform-vitalik-buterin.pdf.

324 **an award-winning programmer:** "IOI 2012: Results," International Olympiad in Informatics Statistics, stats.ioinformatics.org/results/2012.

324 **was just nineteen:** Michael Adams and Benjamin Curry, "Who Is Vitalik Buterin?," *Forbes Advisor*, April 20, 2023, forbes.com/advisor/investing/cryptocurrency/who-is-vitalik-buterin.

324 **capitalization of gold:** "Market Capitalization of Gold and Bitcoin Chart," In Gold We Trust, December 9, 2021, ingoldwetrust.report/chart-gold-bitcoin-marketcap/?lang=en.

324 **to drop out:** Pete Rizzo, "$100k Peter Thiel Fellowship Awarded to Ethereum's Vitalik Buterin," CoinDesk, June 5, 2014, coindesk.com/markets/2014/06/05/100k-peter-thiel-fellowship-awarded-to -ethereums-vitalik-buterin.

324 **or decentralized finance:** "What Is DeFi? A Beginner's Guide to Decentralized Finance," Cointelegraph, cointelegraph.com/learn/defi-a-comprehensive-guide-to-decentralized-finance.

325 **decentralized autonomous organizations:** "What Is DAO and How Do They Work?," Simplilearn, August 12, 2022, simplilearn.com/what-is-dao-how-do-they-work-article.

325 **usually isn't stored:** "What Does 'On-Chain' Really Mean?," Right Click Save, June 23, 2023, rightclick save.com/article/what-does-on-chain-really-mean.

325 **information disclosed within:** "How to Create ERC-721 NFT Token?," SoluLab, solulab.com/how-to -create-erc-721-token/?utm_source=SoluLabBlogs&utm_medium=FractionalNFTOwnershipBegin nersGuide.

325 **or even kidnapped:** Rob Price, "Kidnapped for Crypto: Criminals See Flashy Crypto Owners as Easy Targets, and It Has Led to a Disturbing String of Violent Robberies," Business Insider, February 9, 2022, businessinsider.com/crypto-nft-owners-targeted-kidnaps-home-invasions-robberies-2022-2.

326 **evolves, or regenerates:** Tyler Hobbs, tylerxhobbs.com.

326 **shirtless Trump with:** Scott Chipolina, "Legendary NFT Artwork Gets Resold for $6.6 Million," Decrypt, February 25, 2021, decrypt.co/59405/legendary-nft-artwork-gets-resold-for-6-6-million.

326 **another Beeple NFT:** Jonathan Heaf, "Beeple: The Wild, Wild Tale of How One Man Made $69 Million from a Single NFT," *British GQ*, September 4, 2021, gq-magazine.co.uk/culture/article/beeple-nft-interview.

327 **that wokeness is:** Zaid Jilani, "John McWhorter Argues That Antiracism Has Become a Religion of the Left," *The New York Times*, October 26, 2021, sec. Books, nytimes.com/2021/10/26/books/review/john -mcwhorter-woke-racism.html.

327 **that effective altruism is one:** Dominic Roser and Stefan Riedener, "Effective Altruism and Religion: Synergies, Tensions, Dialogue," *Canopy Forum*, September 30, 2022, canopyforum.org/2022/09/30/ef fective-altruism-and-religion-synergies-tensions-dialogue.

327 **a famous conundrum:** Thomas C. Schelling, *The Strategy of Conflict*, Kindle ed. (Cambridge, MA: Harvard University Press, 2016), 56.

328 **He theorized this:** Schelling, *The Strategy of Conflict*, 80.

329 **being first counts:** Schelling, *The Strategy of Conflict*, 56.

329 **a fixed number:** "How Many Bitcoins Are There and How Many Are Left to Mine?," Blockchain Council, February 15, 2024, blockchain-council.org/cryptocurrency/how-many-bitcoins-are-left.

329 **Bitcoin's protocols are:** Per interview with Vitalik Buterin.

329 **Andy Warhol silkscreen:** Robin Pogrebin, "Warhol's 'Marilyn,' at $195 Million, Shatters Auction Record for an American Artist," *The New York Times*, May 10, 2022, sec. Arts, nytimes.com/2022/05/09/arts /design/warhol-auction-marilyn-monroe.html.

329 **auction houses often:** "How Do Art Auctions Really Work," USA Art News, July 28, 2022, usaartnews .com/art-market/how-do-art-auctions-really-work.

329 **said Amy Cappellazzo:** "Most Powerful Women 2019: Amy Cappellazzo," Crain's New York Business, June 3, 2019, crainsnewyork.com/awards/most-powerful-women-2019-amy-cappellazzo.

330 **Cappellazzo doesn't see:** Melanie Gerlis, "Amy Cappellazzo: 'I Feel Like I've Been in the Crypto Business for 20 Years,'" *Financial Times*, May 31, 2021, sec. Collecting, ft.com/content/502815cd-ec7b-40a5 -a072-714f99523ccd.

330 **CryptoPunks to Warhols:** Sandra Upson, "The 10,000 Faces That Launched an NFT Revolution," *Wired*, November 11, 2021, wired.com/story/the-10000-faces-that-launched-an-nft-revolution.

330 **Peter Thiel's favorite philosopher:** "Rene Girard," Memo'd, October 9, 2021, memod.com/jashdholani /peter-thiel-s-favorite-philosopher-rene-girard-3359.

331 **very heart of the human condition:** "Who Is René Girard?," *Mimetic Theory* (blog), mimetictheory.com /who-is-rene-girard.

331 **"mime" and "mimetic":** Kara Rogers, "Meme," Britannica, November 13, 2023, britannica.com/topic /meme.

331 **behavior of leaderless mobs:** Schelling, *The Strategy of Conflict*, 90.

331 **the $69 million:** It was $55 million after various fees and commissions, Winklemann told me.

332 **first NFT projects:** "CryptoPunks: A Short History," Public, public.com/learn/cryptopunks-short-history.

336 **Einhorn and I:** Paul Amin, "Hedge Fund Billionaire Einhorn Places Sixth in Major Poker Tournament," CNBC, July 18, 2018, cnbc.com/2018/07/18/hedge-fund-billionaire-einhorn-places-sixth-in-major -poker-tournament.html.

336 **an infamous hand:** Paul Oresteen, "Vanessa Selbst Eliminated from Feature Table in Blockbuster Hand," PokerGO Tour, July 9, 2017, pgt.com/news/vanessa-selbst-eliminated-on-day-1b-of-main-event.

336 **Bloomberg *Odd Lots*:** Matt Levine, "Transcript: Sam Bankman-Fried and Matt Levine on How to Make Money in Crypto," taizihuang.github.io, April 25, 2022, taizihuang.github.io/OddLots/html/odd-lots -full-transcript-sam-bankman-fried-and-matt-levine-on-crypto.html.

336 Celsius had employed: Faux, *Number Go Up*, 176.

337 own dubious token: David Gura, "FTX Made a Cryptocurrency That Brought in Millions. Then It Brought Down the Company," *NPR, November* 15, 2022, sec. Business, npr.org/2022/11/15/1136641651/ftx-bank ruptcy-sam-bankman-fried-ftt-crypto-cryptocurrency-binance.

337 of nearly $2 billion: Erin Griffith and David Yaffe-Bellany, "Investors Who Put $2 Billion into FTX Face Scrutiny, Too," *The New York Times*, November 11, 2022, sec. Technology, nytimes.com/2022/11/11 /technology/ftx-investors-venture-capital.html.

337 quasi-journalistic profile: Adam Fisher, "Sam Bankman-Fried Has a Savior Complex—And Maybe You Should Too," Sequoia Capital, September 22, 2022, web.archive.org/web/20221027181005/sequoiacap .com/article/sam-bankman-fried-spotlight.

337 partner Alfred Lin: Ana Paula Pereira, "Sequoia Partner Says Investing in FTX Was the Right Move: Report," Cointelegraph, June 23, 2023, cointelegraph.com/news/sequoia-partner-says-investing-ftx-was -right-move.

338 told me that: Email to Nate Silver, January 8, 2024.

338 by SBF nemesis: David Marsanic, "CZ and SBF Twitter Fight Reveals How They Became Rivals," Daily-Coin, December 9, 2022, dailycoin.com/cz-and-sbf-twitter-fight-reveals-how-they-became-rivals.

339 Former U.S. presidents: Lewis Pennock, "Bahamas Crypto Festival Where FTX Boss Welcomed Clinton and Katy Perry," *Mail Online*, November 14, 2022, dailymail.co.uk/news/article-11426949/Inside -Bahamas-crypto-festival-FTX-CEO-Bankman-Fried-welcomed-Bill-Clinton-Katy-Perry.html.

339 misled by SBF: https://twitter.com/sequoia/status/1590522718650499073 https://www.wsj.com/articles/sequoia-capital-apologizes-to-limited-partners-for-ftx-investment-11669144914

Chapter 7: Quantification

340 first three-Michelin-star vegan: "Eleven Madison Park: First Vegan Restaurant Awarded Three Michelin Stars," Falstaff, July 10, 2022, falstaff.com/en/news/eleven-madison-park-first-vegan-res taurant-awarded-three-michelin-stars.

340 "using evidence and": "CEA's Guiding Principles," Centre for Effective Altruism, centreforeffectiveal truism.org/ceas-guiding-principles.

340 $335 a person: The $335 price is for the full tasting menu; we had a more abbreviated version. Pete Wells, "Eleven Madison Park Explores the Plant Kingdom's Uncanny Valley," *The New York Times*, September 28, 2021, sec. Food, nytimes.com/2021/09/28/dining/eleven-madison-park-restaurant-review -plant-based.html.

340 off about $30,000: Nanina Bajekal, "Inside the Growing Movement to Do the Most Good Possible," *Time*, August 10, 2022, time.com/6204627/effective-altruism-longtermism-william-macaskill-interview.

340 hosted by Sam Bankman-Fried: SBF was described as the host in the invitation that MacAskill emailed to me. When I later asked SBF about the choice of venue, he told me he didn't know who had selected it, which I took to mean that someone else on his staff had.

341 the FTX foundation, which: "Announcing the Future Fund," FTX Future Fund, February 28, 2022, web .archive.org/web/20220301010944/ftxfuturefund.org/announcing-the-future-fund.

341 The actual amount: Thalia Beaty and Glenn Gamboa, "Facebook Cofounder Blames SBF's 'Effective Altruism' Mindset for FTX Troubles," *Fortune*, November 14, 2022, fortune.com/2022/11/14/ftx-bank ruptcy-puts-charitable-donations-in-doubt-and-some-blame-sam-bankman-frieds-effective -altruism-mindset-for-troubles.

341 SBF thought this: Kelsey Piper, "Sam Bankman-Fried Tries to Explain Himself," *Vox*, November 16, 2022, vox.com/future-perfect/23462333/sam-bankman-fried-ftx-cryptocurrency-effective-altruism -crypto-bahamas-philanthropy.

341 Bankman-Fried had worked: Benjamin Wallace, "The Mysterious Cryptocurrency Magnate Who Became One of Biden's Biggest Donors," Intelligencer, February 2, 2021, nymag.com/intelligencer/2021 /02/sam-bankman-fried-biden-donor.html.

342 6th Congressional District: Per interview with Carrick Flynn.

342 backing Carrick Flynn: Daniel Strauss, "The Crypto Kings Are Making Big Political Donations. What Could Go Wrong?," *The New Republic*, May 24, 2022, newrepublic.com/article/166584/sam-bankman -fried-crypto-kings-political-donations.

342 EA-friendly political neophyte: Miranda Dixon-Luinenburg, "Carrick Flynn May Be 2022's Unlikeliest Congressional Candidate. Here's Why He's Running," *Vox*, May 14, 2022, vox.com/23066877/carrick -flynn-effective-altruism-sam-bankman-fried-congress-house-election-2022.

342 Flynn had never: Coordinating with a super PAC would have been illegal anyway under campaign finance laws. "Super PACs Can't Coordinate with Candidates—Here's What Happened When One Did," Campaign Legal Center, January 30, 2023, campaignlegal.org/update/super-pacs-cant-coordinate -candidates-heres-what-happened-when-one-did.

342 **Ahead in the polls:** Rachel Monahan, "Cryptocurrency-Backed Democratic Congressional Candidate Carrick Flynn Leads Race, Opposing Campaign Poll Found," *Willamette Week*, April 24, 2022, wweek .com/news/state/2022/04/24/cryptocurrency-backed-democratic-congressional-candidate-carrick -flynn-leads-race-opposing-campaign-poll-found.

342 **Flynn eventually lost:** "Carrick Flynn," Ballotpedia, ballotpedia.org/Carrick_Flynn.

343 **call "small-world problems":** Miloud Belkoniene and Patryk Dziurosz-Serafinowicz, "Acting upon Uncertain Beliefs," *Acta Analytica* 35, no. 2 (June 2020): 253–71, doi.org/10.1007/s12136-019-00403-2.

343 **around $2 billion:** Dylan Matthews, "Congress's Epic Pandemic Funding Failure," *Vox*, March 22, 2022, vox.com/future-perfect/22983046/congress-covid-pandemic-prevention.

343 **2022–23 budget deal:** Kavya Sekar, "PREVENT Pandemics Act (P.L. 117-328, Division FF, Title II)," Congressional Research Service, August 15, 2023, crsreports.congress.gov/product/pdf/R/R47649.

343 **estimated $14 trillion:** Jakub Hlávka, "COVID-19's Total Cost to the U.S. Economy Will Reach $14 Trillion by End of 2023," *The Evidence Base*, https://healthpolicy.usc.edu/blogs (blog), May 16, 2023, health policy.usc.edu/article/covid-19s-total-cost-to-the-economy-in-us-will-reach-14-trillion-by-end -of-2023-new-research.

344 **to Bill Gates:** Catherine Cheney, "Can This Movement Get More Donors to Maximize Their Impact?," *Devex*, November 27, 2018, devex.com/news/sponsored/can-this-movement-get-more-donors-to-max imize-their-impact-90903.

344 **Great Man Theory:** Will Oremus, "Analysis: Elon Musk and Tech's 'Great Man' Fallacy," *The Washington Post*, April 27, 2022, washingtonpost.com/technology/2022/04/27/jack-dorsey-elon-musk-singular -solution.

344 **endorsed MacAskill's book:** Nicholas Kulish, "How a Scottish Moral Philosopher Got Elon Musk's Number," *The New York Times*, October 8, 2022, sec. Business, nytimes.com/2022/10/08/business/effective -altruism-elon-musk.html.

344 **player Igor Kurganov:** Rob Copeland, "Elon Musk's Inner Circle Rocked by Fight over His $230 Billion Fortune," *The Wall Street Journal*, July 16, 2022, sec. Tech, wsj.com/articles/elon-musk-fortune-fight -jared-birchall-igor-kurganov-11657308426.

345 **a well-groomed poodle:** Andy Newman, "The Dog Was Running, So the Subway Was Not," *The New York Times*, February 17, 2018, sec. New York, nytimes.com/2018/02/16/nyregion/dog-subway-tracks.html.

345 **a trolley problem:** Judith Jarvis Thomson, "The Trolley Problem," *The Yale Law Journal* 94, no. 6 (May 1985): 1395, doi.org/10.2307/796133.

346 **relatively dangerous occupation:** Steven Markowitz et al., "The Health Impact of Urban Mass Transportation Work in New York City," July 2005, nycosh.org/wp-content/uploads/2014/10/TWU_Report_Final -8-4-05.pdf.

346 **something like $40:** "Occupational Employment and Wages in New York–Newark–Jersey City—May 2022," U.S. Bureau of Labor Statistics, bls.gov/regions/northeast/news-release/occupationalemploy mentandwages_newyork.htm.

348 **"Elephants have more neurons":** Suzana Herculano-Houzel et al., "The Elephant Brain in Numbers," *Frontiers in Neuroanatomy* 8 (June 12, 2014), doi.org/10.3389/fnana.2014.00046.

348 **drew tremendous criticism:** Abigail Cartus and Justin Feldman, "Motivated Reasoning: Emily Oster's COVID Narratives and the Attack on Public Education," *Protean*, March 22, 2022, proteanmag.com /2022/03/22/motivated-reasoning-emily-osters-covid-narratives-and-the-attack-on-public -education.

348 **whose parents were:** Sam Roberts, "Sharon Oster, Barrier-Breaking Economist, Dies at 73," *The New York Times*, June 14, 2022, sec. Business, nytimes.com/2022/06/14/business/sharon-oster-dead.html.

349 **their advanced age:** Karla Romero Starke et al., "The Age-Related Risk of Severe Outcomes Due to COVID-19 Infection: A Rapid Review, Meta-Analysis, and Meta-Regression," *International Journal of Environmental Research and Public Health* 17, no. 16 (August 17, 2020): 5974, doi.org/10.3390/ijerph17165974.

349 **Oster wrote in May:** Emily Oster, "How to Think Through Choices About Grandparents, Day Care, Summer Camp, and More," *Slate*, May 20, 2020, slate.com/technology/2020/05/coronavirus-family -choices-grandparents-day-care-summer-camp.html.

349 **costs of lockdowns:** Philippe Lemoine, "The Case Against Lockdowns," Center for the Study of Partisanship and Ideology, October 11, 2022, cspicenter.com/p/the-case-against-lockdowns.

349 **It's also disputed:** Dyani Lewis, "What Scientists Have Learnt from COVID Lockdowns," *Nature* 609, no. 7926 (September 7, 2022): 236–39, doi.org/10.1038/d41586-022-02823-4; Leonidas Spiliopoulos, "On the Effectiveness of COVID-19 Restrictions and Lockdowns: Pan Metron Ariston," *BMC Public Health* 22, no. 1 (October 1, 2022): 1842, doi.org/10.1186/s12889-022-14177-7.

350 **about $10 million:** Sarah Gonzalez, "How Government Agencies Determine the Dollar Value of Human Life," NPR, April 23, 2020, sec. National, npr.org/2020/04/23/843310123/how-government-agencies -determine-the-dollar-value-of-human-life.

351 **warring federal agencies:** W. Kip Viscusi and Joseph E. Aldy, "The Value of a Statistical Life: A Critical Review of Market Estimates Throughout the World," *Journal of Risk and Uncertainty* 27, no. 1 (2003): 5–76, doi.org/10.1023/A:1025598106257.

352 **"Definition of Effective Altruism"**: William MacAskill, "The Definition of Effective Altruism," in *Effective Altruism*, ed. Hilary Greaves and Theron Pummer (Oxford: Oxford University Press, 2019), 10–28, doi.org/10.1093/oso/9780198841364.003.0001.

352 **rationalism originally referred**: Peter Markie and M. Folescu, "Rationalism vs. Empiricism," in *The Stanford Encyclopedia of Philosophy*, ed. Edward N. Zalta and Uri Nodelman (Stanford, CA: Metaphysics Research Lab, Stanford University, 2021), plato.stanford.edu/archives/spr2023/entries/rationalism -empiricism.

352 **called "The Sequences"**: Eliezer Yudkowsky, "Original Sequences," LessWrong, 2023, lesswrong.com /tag/original-sequences.

353 **his Harry Potter fanfic**: Eliezer Yudkowsky, *Harry Potter and the Methods of Rationality*, hpmor.com.

353 **felt burned by**: Cade Metz, "Silicon Valley's Safe Space," *The New York Times*, February 13, 2021, sec. Technology, nytimes.com/2021/02/13/technology/slate-star-codex-rationalists.html.

353 **The Rationalists saw**: Metz, "Silicon Valley's Safe Space."

354 **don't neatly fall**: Scott Alexander, "I Can Tolerate Anything Except the Outgroup," *Slate Star Codex* (blog), October 1, 2014, slatestarcodex.com/2014/09/30/i-can-tolerate-anything-except-the-outgroup.

354 **an xkcd cartoon**: Randall Munroe, "Duty Calls," xkcd, xkcd.com/386.

354 **most popular stories**: As of December 21, 2023; Nate Silver, "Fine, I'll Run a Regression Analysis. But It Won't Make You Happy," *Silver Bulletin* (blog), October 1, 2023, natesilver.net/p/fine-ill-run-a-re gression-analysis.

355 **Even public figures**: Peter Hartree, "Tyler Cowen on Effective Altruism," EA Forum, January 13, 2023, forum.effectivealtruism.org/posts/NdZPQxc74zNdg8Mvm/tyler-cowen-on-effective-altruism -december-2022.

356 **is more radical**: The Yuskowdsky-Hanson stream is also quite radical, but in ways that are more self-evident, with people and ideas that are often unapologetically weird.

356 **Usually but not always**: In Scott Alexander's survey of *Astral Codex Ten* readers, 74 percent of people who identify as EAs say they lean toward consequentialism—the branch of philosophy from which utilitarianism derives—versus just 26 percent of non-EAs.

357 **"Famine, Affluence and Morality"**: Peter Singer, "Famine, Affluence, and Morality," *Philosophy & Public Affairs* 1, no. 3 (1972): 229–43, jstor.org/stable/2265052.

357 **a drowning child**: dphilo, "Peter Singer's Drowning Child," *Daily Philosophy*, November 24, 2020, daily -philosophy.com/peter-singers-drowning-child.

357 **his later writings**: Peter Singer, *The Life You Can Save: Acting Now to End World Poverty* (New York: Random House, 2009).

357 **the Harvard endowment**: "Financial Report Fiscal Year 2022," Harvard University, October 2022, fi nance.harvard.edu/files/fad/files/fy22_harvard_financial_report.pdf.

358 **more than $50 billion**: Krishi Kishore and Rohan Rajeev, "Harvard Endowment Value Falls for Second Consecutive Year, Records Modest 2.9% Return During FY2023," *The Harvard Crimson*, October 20, 2023, thecrimson.com/article/2023/10/20/endowment-returns-fy23.

358 **how effective charities**: Nico Pitney, "That Time a Hedge Funder Quit His Job and Then Raised $60 Million for Charity," *HuffPost*, March 26, 2015, huffpost.com/entry/elie-hassenfeld-givewell_n_69 27320.

358 **"The uncontroversial appearance"**: Singer, "Famine, Affluence, and Morality."

358 **principle of impartiality**: Troy Jollimore, "Impartiality," in *The Stanford Encyclopedia of Philosophy*, ed. Edward N. Zalta and Uri Nodelman (Stanford, CA: Metaphysics Research Lab, Stanford University, 2021), plato.stanford.edu/archives/win2023/entries/impartiality.

358 **our own children**: Peter Singer, *The Life You Can Save: Acting Now to End World Poverty* (New York: Random House, 2009), 151.

359 **$3,000 to 5,000**: Based on a GiveWell estimate of the impact of donations to anti-malaria nets in Guinea; "How Much Does It Cost To Save a Life?," GiveWell, September 2022, givewell.org/how-much-does -it-cost-to-save-a-life.

359 **refuses to save**: In *The Life You Can Save*, for instance, Singer writes about how you're not off the hook just because you've given some money to effective charity. "You must keep cutting back on unnecessary spending, and donating what you save, until you have reduced yourself to the point where if you give any more, you will be sacrificing something nearly as important as preventing malaria," 38–39.

359 **all sentient animals**: "Peter Singer, 'Equality for Animals,'" hettingern.people.cofc.edu/Environmen tal_Ethics_Fall_07/Singer_Equality_For_Animals.htm.

359 **"longtermism," is controversial**: Richard Fisher, "What Is Longtermism and Why Do Its Critics Think It Is Dangerous?," *New Scientist*, May 10, 2023, newscientist.com/article/mg25834382-400-what-is -longtermism-and-why-do-its-critics-think-it-is-dangerous.

359 **artificial intelligences that achieve**: Michael Dahlstrom, "Peter Singer: Can We Morally Kill AI If It Becomes Self-Aware?," Yahoo News, May 5, 2023, au.news.yahoo.com/peter-singer-can-we-morally -kill-ai-if-it-becomes-self-aware-022630798.html.

359 **for Singer's utilitarianism:** Will MacAskill, Dirk Meissner, and Richard Yetter Chappell, "Elements and Types of Utilitarianism," in *An Introduction to Utilitarianism*, ed. Richard Yetter Chappell, Dirk Meissner, and Will MacAskill, 2023, utilitarianism.net/types-of-utilitarianism.

359 **Greek prefix *deon*-:** "Deontology," Online Etymology Dictionary, etymonline.com/word/deontology.

359 **Singer is suspicious:** Singer, "Famine, Affluence, and Morality."

359 **"the greatest amount":** Julia Driver, "The History of Utilitarianism," in *The Stanford Encyclopedia of Philosophy*, ed. Edward N. Zalta and Uri Nodelman (Stanford, CA: Metaphysics Research Lab, Stanford University, 2014), plato.stanford.edu/archives/win2022/entries/utilitarianism-history.

360 **when a subcommittee:** Kathleen Dooling, "Phased Allocation of COVID-19 Vaccines," ACIP COVID-19 Vaccines Work Group, November 23, 2020, cdc.gov/vaccines/acip/meetings/downloads/slides-2020-11/COVID-04-Dooling.pdf.

360 **significant public outcry:** Kelsey Piper, "Who Should Get the Vaccine First? The Debate over a CDC Panel's Guidelines, Explained," *Vox*, December 22, 2020, vox.com/future-perfect/22193679/who-should-get-covid-19-vaccine-first-debate-explained.

360 **been playing favorites:** Americans preferred prioritizing health-care workers, nursing-home residents, and people with comorbidities rather than "people of color and other communities with higher COVID-19 burden." Govind Persad et al., "Public Perspectives on COVID-19 Vaccine Prioritization," *JAMA Network Open* 4, no. 4 (April 9, 2021): e217943, doi.org/10.1001/jamanetworkopen.2021.7943.

360 **Sam Bankman-Fried's conclusion:** James Fanelli, "Sam Bankman-Fried's Moral Thinking," *The Wall Street Journal*, October 11, 2023, wsj.com/livecoverage/sam-bankman-fried-ftx-trial-caroline-ellison/card/sam-bankman-fried-s-moral-thinking-FbKBJQkdl83SlNEUWwiT.

360 **as "infinite ethics.":** Joe Carlsmith, "Infinite Ethics and the Utilitarian Dream," September 2022, jc.gatspress.com/pdf/infinite_ethics_revised.pdf.

361 **as high as people:** "GRE Scores by Major," Educational Testing Service, 2011, umsl.edu/~philo/files/pdfs/ETS%20LINK.pdf.

362 **same for dogs:** "List of Animals by Number of Neurons," Wikipedia, en.wikipedia.org/w/index.php?title=List_of_animals_by_number_of_neurons&oldid=1192618831.

362 **defense of bestiality:** Peter Singer (@PeterSinger), "Another thought-provoking article is 'Zoophilia Is Morally Permissible' by Fira Bensto (Pseudonym), which is just out in the current issue of @JConIdeas . . . ," X, November 8, 2023, twitter.com/PeterSinger/status/1722440246972018857.

362 **animals are kept:** "How Are Factory Farms Cruel to Animals?," The Humane League, January 6, 2021, thehumaneleague.org/article/factory-farming-animal-cruelty.

362 **player Dan Smith:** "About Double Up Drive," Double Up Drive, doubleupdrive.org/about.

363 **emotionally laden societal conventions:** Peter Singer, *The Most Good You Can Do: How Effective Altruism Is Changing Ideas About Living Ethically*, Castle Lectures in Ethics, Politics, and Economics, Kindle ed. (New Haven, CT, London: Yale University Press, 2015), 78.

363 **produced through inbreeding:** Shirley Davis, "Incest and Genetic Disorders," *Trauma-Informed Blog*, https://cptsdfoundation.org/trauma-informed-blog (blog), April 4, 2022, cptsdfoundation.org/2022/04/18/incest-and-genetic-disorders.

363 **actually relatively unpopular:** Per conversation with Kevin Zollman.

363 **Kevin Zollman:** "Kevin J. S. Zollman," kevinzollman.com.

364 **the Repugnant Conclusion:** Gustaf Arrhenius, Jesper Ryberg, and Torbjörn Tännsjö, "The Repugnant Conclusion," in *The Stanford Encyclopedia of Philosophy*, ed. Edward N. Zalta and Uri Nodelman (Stanford, CA: Metaphysics Research Lab, Stanford University, 2017), plato.stanford.edu/archives/win2022/entries/repugnant-conclusion.

366 **as Singer has pointed out:** Singer, *The Life You Can Save*, 25.

366 **people a thousand years:** Hartree, "Tyler Cowen on Effective Altruism."

366 **MacAskill have answers:** Will MacAskill, Toby Ord, and Krister Bykvist, "About the Book: *Moral Uncertainty*," William MacAskill, williammacaskill.com/info-moral-uncertainty.

367 **"essentially back-of-the-napkin":** David Kinney, "Longtermism and Computational Complexity," EA Forum, August 31, 2022, forum.effectivealtruism.org/posts/RRyHcupuDafFNXt6p/longtermism-and-computational-complexity.

367 **Kant's categorical imperative:** Immanuel Kant, *Grounding for the Metaphysics of Morals; with, On a Supposed Right to Lie Because of Philanthropic Concerns*, trans. James W. Ellington (Indianapolis, IN: Hackett Publishing Company, 1993), archive.org/details/groundingformet000kant.

367 **analogized to the prisoner's dilemma:** Janet Chen, Su-I Lu, and Dan Vekhter, "Applications of Game Theory," Game Theory, cs.stanford.edu/people/eroberts/courses/soco/projects/1998-99/game-theory/applications.html.

368 **called "rule utilitarianism":** Stephen Nathanson, "Utilitarianism, Act and Rule," Internet Encyclopedia of Philosophy, iep.utm.edu/util-a-r.

368 **even their planet:** Tyler Cowen and Will MacAskill, "William MacAskill on Effective Altruism, Moral Progress, and Cultural Innovation (Ep. 156)," *Conversations with Tyler*, July 7, 2018, conversationswithtyler.com/episodes/william-macaskill.

369 **"gathering of forecasting nerds":** Manifest 2023, 2023, manifestconference.net.

370 **will irrecoverably collapse:** Toby Ord, *The Precipice: Existential Risk and the Future of Humanity*, Kindle ed. (New York: Hachette Books, 2020), 30.

370 **than a supervolcano:** Joel Day, "Experts Explain How Humanity Is Most Likely to Be Wiped Out," Express.co.uk, August 13, 2023, express.co.uk/news/world/1801233/supervolcanoes-climate-change-nuclear-war-end-of-humanity-spt.

370 **play money dollars:** Although Mana can be donated to charity, at a rate of $1 per 100 Mana, and there is something of a gray market for converting Mana to U.S. dollars; "About," Manifold, manifold.markets /about.

370 **Israel Defense Forces:** "Was an IDF Strike Responsible for the Al-Ahli Hospital Explosion?," Manifold, manifold.markets/MilfordHammerschmidt/did-the-idf-just-now-blow-up-a-hosp.

370 **whether Austin Chen:** As of December 27, 2023; "Will @Austin Chen Still Believe in God at the End of 2026?," Manifold, manifold.markets/WilliamEhlhardt/will-austin-chen-still-believe-in-g.

370 **an orgy at Manifest:** Kevin Roose, "The Wager That Betting Can Change the World," *The New York Times*, October 8, 2023, sec. Technology, nytimes.com/2023/10/08/technology/prediction-markets-manifold -manifest.html.

370 **Magic: The Gathering:** "Zvi Mowshowitz," MTG Wiki, December 30, 2023, mtg.fandom.com/wiki/Zvi _Mowshowitz.

372 **such poor forecasts:** Philip E. Tetlock and J. Peter Scoblic, "The Power of Precise Predictions," *The New York Times*, October 2, 2015, sec. Opinion, nytimes.com/2015/10/04/opinion/the-power-of-precise -predictions.html.

372 **close to 100 percent:** Gary Marcus, "p(doom)," *Marcus on AI* (blog), August 27, 2023, garymarcus.sub stack.com/p/d28.

372 **many paper clips:** Joshua Gans, "AI and the Paperclip Problem," Centre for Economic Policy Research, June 10, 2018, cepr.org/voxeu/columns/ai-and-paperclip-problem.

372 **adopt means suitable:** Niko Kolodny and John Brunero, "Instrumental Rationality," in *The Stanford Encyclopedia of Philosophy*, ed. Edward N. Zalta and Uri Nodelman (Stanford, CA: Metaphysics Research Lab, Stanford University, 2023), plato.stanford.edu/archives/sum2023/entries/rationality-instrumental.

372 **thirty thousand Big Macs:** Alex Portée, "Man Has Eaten a Big Mac a Day for 50 Years, Attributes Good Health to Walking," Today.com, May 24, 2022, today.com/food/people/don-gorske-eaten-big-mac -every-day-50-years-rcna30157.

373 **FiveThirtyEight forecasts have:** Jay Boice and Gus Wezerek, "How Good Are FiveThirtyEight Forecasts?," FiveThirtyEight, April 4, 2019, projects.fivethirtyeight.com/checking-our-work.

373 **scrambled to correct:** "Editors' Note: Gaza Hospital Coverage," *The New York Times*, October 23, 2023, sec. Corrections, nytimes.com/2023/10/23/pageoneplus/editors-note-gaza-hospital-coverage.html.

374 **But one person:** I spoke with Habryka in an interview we arranged after Manifest, not during the event.

375 **prices that implied:** Vitalik Buterin, "Prediction Markets: Tales from the Election," *Vitalik Buterin's Website* (blog), February 18, 2021, vitalik.eth.limo/general/2021/02/18/election.html.

375 **"exactly zero chance":** Different markets had different resolution criteria, so if Trump had won by extralegal means, such as the January 6 insurrection having been successful, it might or might not still have counted as a Biden win. It's always important to check the fine print to see how a bet is resolved in the event something unusual happens.

375 **people's favorite fetishes:** Aella, "Fetish Tabooness vs. Popularity," *Knowingless* (blog), September 23, 2022, aella.substack.com/p/fetish-tabooness-vs-popularity.

375 **off-again sex worker:** "Aella—Why I Became an Escort," 2023, youtube.com/watch?v=shB6ovnjYEs.

375 **former OnlyFans star:** Aella, "Readjusting to Porn," *Knowingless* (blog), May 25, 2020, knowingless .com/2020/05/25/readjusting-to-porn.

376 **about becoming addicted:** Aella, "You Will Forget, You Have Forgotten," *Knowingless* (blog), August 17, 2019, aella.substack.com/p/you-will-forget-you-have-forgotten.

376 **his future wife:** Scott Alexander, "There's a Time for Everyone," *Astral Codex Ten* (blog), November 17, 2021, astralcodexten.com/p/theres-a-time-for-everyone.

376 **"Everyone here thinks":** Scott Alexander, "Half an Hour Before Dawn in San Francisco," *Astral Codex Ten* (blog), November 17, 2021, astralcodexten.com/p/half-an-hour-before-dawn-in-san-francisco.

377 **have sometimes complained:** Scott Alexander, "In Continued Defense of Effective Altruism," *Astral Codex Ten* (blog), November 17, 2021, astralcodexten.com/p/in-continued-defense-of-effective.

377 **among non-EA rationalists:** Scott Alexander, "ACX Survey Results 2022," *Astral Codex Ten* (blog), November 17, 2021, astralcodexten.com/p/acx-survey-results-2022.

377 **a 2018 blog post:** Robin Hanson, "Two Types of Envy," *Overcoming Bias* (blog), July 22, 2023, overcom ingbias.com/p/two-types-of-envyhtml.

377 **posted racist comments:** Christopher Mathias, "This Man Has the Ear of Billionaires—And a White Supremacist Past He Kept a Secret," *HuffPost*, August 4, 2023, huffpost.com/entry/richard-hanania -white-supremacist-pseudonym-richard-hoste_n_64c93928e4b021e2f295e817.

378 **critical of the movement:** Alexander, "In Continued Defense of Effective Altruism."

378 didn't think EAs: Cowen and MacAskill, "William MacAskill on Effective Altruism, Moral Progress, and Cultural Innovation."

378 rationalists like Hanson: Robin Hanson, "16 Fertility Scenarios," *Overcoming Bias* (blog), July 22, 2023, overcomingbias.com/p/13-fertility-scenarios.

379 like in Hanson's book: Robin Hanson, *The Age of Em: Work, Love and Life When Robots Rule the Earth* (New York: Oxford University Press, 2016), 21.

379 "While some ems": Hanson, *The Age of Em*, 23.

379 often surprisingly hard: Holden Karnofsky, "Why Describing Utopia Goes Badly," *Cold Takes* (blog), December 7, 2021, cold-takes.com/why-describing-utopia-goes-badly.

380 provocative or offensive: Nick Bostrom, "Apology for Old Email," Nick Bostrom's Home Page, January 9, 2023, nickbostrom.com/oldemail.pdf.

380 Hanson founded his blog: Robin Hanson, "How to Join," *Overcoming Bias* (blog), July 22, 2023, overcomingbias.com/p/introductionhtml.

380 Hanson and Yudkowsky: Per interview with Robin Hanson.

380 risk at Jane Street Capital: "The Hanson-Yudkowsky AI-Foom Debate," LessWrong, accessed January 2, 2024, lesswrong.com/tag/the-hanson-yudkowsky-ai-foom-debate.

380 support for futarchy: Robin Hanson, "Futarchy: Vote Values, but Bet Beliefs," accessed January 2, 2024, mason.gmu.edu/~rhanson/futarchy.html.

381 Marxism is one: Per interview with Émile Torres, although Torres attributed the idea to Peter Singer.

Chapter 8: Miscalculation

382 trials at random: "The Assignment of Judges in the Criminal Term of the Supreme Court in New York County," New York City Bar, July 1, 2002, nycbar.org/member-and career-services/committees/reports-listing/reports/detail/the-assignment-of-judges-in-the-criminal-term-of-the-supreme-court-in-new-york-county.

382 "call out bingo": Benjamin Weiser, "Spin of Wheel May Determine Judge in 9/11 Case," *The New York Times*, November 27, 2009, sec. New York, nytimes.com/2009/11/28/nyregion/28judge.html.

382 name of Lewis Kaplan: Tom Hals, Jonathan Stempel, "Bankman-Fried's Criminal Case Assigned to Judge in Trump, Prince Andrew Cases," Reuters, December 27, 2022, sec. Legal, reuters.com/legal/bankman-frieds-criminal-case-assigned-judge-lewis-kaplan-court-filing-2022-12-27.

382 Prince Andrew and Kevin Spacey: Associated Press, "Trump and Prince Andrew Judge Will Preside over SBF Cryptocurrency Case," *The Guardian*, December 27, 2022, sec. Business, theguardian.com/business/2022/dec/27/judge-trump-prince-andrew-trials-sbf-sam-bankman-fried-ftx-cryptocurrency.

383 $4 million gray: Sophie Mann, "SBF Arrives at $4m Family Home for Christmas Under House Arrest," *Daily Mail*, December 23, 2022, dailymail.co.uk/news/article-11569591/Sam-Bankman-Fried-arrives-4m-family-home-California-Christmas-house-arrest.html.

383 lived in Stanford: The Bankman-Fried home is sometimes described as being in Palo Alto, but there are some addresses in the area, including the SBF house, that are technically in the unincorporated town of Stanford. I'm sensitive to this because the condo building where I lived for that year was also in Stanford.

383 tough terms that Kaplan: Rebecca Davis O'Brien and David Yaffe-Bellany, "Judge Signals Jail Time If Bankman-Fried's Internet Access Is Not Curbed," *The New York Times*, February 16, 2023, sec. Business, nytimes.com/2023/02/16/business/bankman-fried-crypto-fraud-bail.html.

384 back door between FTX: Jamie Crawley, "FTX Employees Knew About the Backdoor to Alameda Months Before Collapse: WSJ," CoinDesk, October 5, 2023, coindesk.com/policy/2023/10/05/ftx-employees-knew-about-the-backdoor-to-alameda-months-before-collapse-wsj.

385 71 percent chance: "Does SBF Get a Sentence of 20 Years or More?," Manifold, manifold.markets/BenjaminIkuta/does-sbf-get-a-sentence-of-20-years.

385 Ellison pled guilty: MacKenzie Sigalos and Rohan Goswami, "FTX's Gary Wang, Alameda's Caroline Ellison Plead Guilty to Federal Charges, Cooperating with Prosecutors," CNBC, December 2022, cnbc.com/2022/12/22/ftxs-gary-wang-alamedas-caroline-ellison-plead-guilty-to-federal-charges-cooperating-with-prosecutors.html.

385 on conflict-of-interest grounds: Justin Wise, "Paul Weiss Drops Ex-FTX CEO Bankman-Fried on Conflicts (Correct)," Bloomberg Law, November 18, 2023, news.bloomberglaw.com/business-and-practice/paul-weiss-drops-ex-ftx-ceo-bankman-fried-as-client-on-conflicts.

385 SBF couldn't afford: Per a background source.

387 Ellison warned SBF: Elizabeth Lopatto, "Sam Bankman-Fried Was a Terrible Boyfriend," *The Verge*, October 10, 2023, theverge.com/2023/10/10/23912036/sam-bankman-fried-ftx-caroline-ellison-alameda-research.

387 transcript I obtained: I obtained it for a fee.

387 **"thought 10 percent"**: Caroline Ellison testimony, October 10, 2023, U.S. District Court, Southern District, *United States of America vs. Samuel Bankman-Fried*, as prepared by Southern District Reporters, P.C., 698.

387 **additional $3 billion**: Caroline Ellison testimony, October 10, 2023, 703.

387 **didn't dispute the risks**: Caroline Ellison testimony, October 10, 2023, 704–5.

387 **repay Alameda's loans**: Caroline Ellison testimony, October 11, 2023, U.S. District Court, Southern District, *United States of America vs. Samuel Bankman-Fried*, as prepared by Southern District Reporters, P.C., 765.

387 **he frequently checked**: Caroline Ellison testimony, October 11, 2023, 753.

388 **substantial market downturn**: Caroline Ellison testimony, October 10, 2023, 725.

388 **summer or fall 2021**: Caroline Ellison testimony, October 10, 2023, 698.

388 **once between April and July**: "Bitcoin USD (BTC-USD) Stock Historical Prices & Data," Yahoo Finance, finance.yahoo.com/quote/BTC-USD/history.

390 **about sleep deprivation**: Kari McMahon and Vicky Ge Huang, "4 Hours of Sleep a Night in a Bean Bag Chair: Inside the Hectic Life of Crypto Titan Sam Bankman-Fried, the World's Youngest Mega-Billionaire," Business Insider, December 17, 2021, businessinsider.in/cryptocurrency/news/4-hours-of-sleep-a-night-in-a-bean-bag-chair-inside-the-hectic-life-of-crypto-titan-sam-bankman-fried-the-worlds-youngest-mega-billionaire/articleshow/88338455.cms.

390 **carefully manipulated press image**: Maggie Harrison, "Sam Bankman-Fried's Friend Says He Was Exaggerating How Much He Slept on His Bean Bag Chair," Futurism, October 6, 2023, futurism.com/the-byte/sam-bankman-fried-exaggerating-bean-bag.

390 **an Adderall prescription**: Per interview with Sam Bankman-Fried.

390 **popular theories online**: Scott Alexander, "The Psychopharmacology of the FTX Crash," *Astral Codex Ten* (blog), November 17, 2021, astralcodexten.com/p/the-psychopharmacology-of-the-ftx.

391 **on the payroll**: David Yaffe-Bellany, Lora Kelley, and Kenneth P. Vogel, "The Parents in the Middle of FTX's Collapse," *The New York Times*, December 13, 2022, sec. Technology, nytimes.com/2022/12/12/technology/sbf-parents-ftx-collapse.html.

392 **amount of rainfall**: "List of Countries by Average Annual Precipitation," Wikipedia, en.wikipedia.org/w/index.php?title=List_of_countries_by_average_annual_precipitation&oldid=1192465548.

392 **poor soil quality**: Per interview with Jacklyn Chapsky.

392 **world's highest rates**: "List of Sovereign States by Wealth Inequality," Wikipedia, en.wikipedia.org/w/index.php?title=List_of_sovereign_states_by_wealth_inequality&oldid=1190195353.

392 **GDPs per capita**: "GDP per Capita (Current US$)—Latin America & Caribbean," World Bank Open Data, data.worldbank.org/indicator/NY.GDP.PCAP.CD?locations=ZJ.

393 **tightened anti-money-laundering statutes**: Nicole M. Healy, "Impact of September 11th on Anti-Money Laundering Efforts, and the European Union and Commonwealth Gatekeeper Initiatives," *International Lawyer* 36, no. 2 (2002), scholar.smu.edu/cgi/viewcontent.cgi?article=2148&context=til.

393 **its economy dependent**: "Bahamas—Country Commercial Guide," International Trade Administration, trade.gov/country-commercial-guides/bahamas-market-overview.

393 **places like Margaritaville**: Yuheng Zhan, "FTX's Margaritaville Tab Swells to $600K," *New York Post*, March 17, 2023, nypost.com/2023/03/17/ftxs-margaritaville-tab-swells-to-600k.

394 **for his anhedonia**: Spencer Greenberg, "Who Is Sam Bankman-Fried (SBF) Really, and How Could He Have Done What He Did?—Three Theories and a Lot of Evidence," *Optimize Everything* (blog), November 10, 2023, spencergreenberg.com/2023/11/who-is-sam-bankman-fried-sbf-really-and-how-could-he-have-done-what-he-did-three-theories-and-a-lot-of-evidence.

394 **"was a utilitarian"**: Caroline Ellison testimony, October 11, 2023, 807.

395 **BTC crossed over**: "Bitcoin USD (BTC-USD) Stock Historical Prices & Data," Yahoo Finance.

396 **signal processing algorithms**: William Poundstone, *Fortune's Formula: The Untold Story of the Scientific Betting System That Beat the Casinos and Wall Street*, Kindle ed. (New York: Hill and Wang, 2006), 69.

396 **drinker and smoker**: Poundstone, *Fortune's Formula*, 63.

396 **outcome of football**: Poundstone, *Fortune's Formula*, 63.

397 **16 percent of your bankroll**: Assuming industry standard odds of -110.

397 **minimizing your risk**: Jeremy Olson, "Kelly Criterion Gambling Explained—What Is Kelly Criterion Betting?," *Techopedia*, October 13, 2023, techopedia.com/gambling-guides/kelly-criterion-gambling.

397 **go *completely* broke**: Assuming you're estimating your edge correctly. If you aren't, it could have you wager 100 percent of a bankroll on a bet you think is a sure thing that isn't.

397 **2020 Twitter thread**: SBF (@SBF_FTX), "1) Better is Bigger," Twitter, December 11, 2020, twitter.com/SBF_FTX/status/1337250686870831107.

397 **could become president**: Aaron Katersky, "Sam Bankman-Fried Thought He Had 5% Chance of Becoming President, Ex-Girlfriend Says," ABC News, October 10, 2023, abcnews.go.com/US/sam-bankman-fried-thought-5-chance-becoming-president/story?id=103870644.

397 **"closer to linear"**: SBF (@SBF_FTX), "12) In many cases I think $10k is a reasonable bet. But I, personally, would do more. I'd probably do more like $50k. Why? Because ultimately my utility function isn't

really logarithmic. It's closer to linear," Twitter, December 11, 2020, twitter.com/SBF_FTX/status /1337250704075833347.

398 actually a misconception: Brad DeLong, "There Are Complex-Number One-Norm Square-Root of Probability Amplitudes of 0.006 in Which Sam Bankman-Fried Is Happy," *Brad DeLong's Grasping Reality* (blog), October 5, 2023, braddelong.substack.com/p/there-are-complex-number-one-norm.

398 further technical details: A full week's NFL schedule has sixteen games. I assumed that in an average week, the model spits out six bets that win 50 percent of the time (which you don't bet since they're they're not +EV after considering the vig), four bets that win at 53 percent (this and all subsequent bets are +EV so you bet these games), three bets that win at 55 percent, two bets that win at 57 percent, and one bet that wins at 60 percent. However, the bets are chosen at random for each game, meaning that in some weeks you might have more strong bets than in others.

398 played one at a time: This is a simplification, since usually there are several NFL games simultaneously.

400 Sam's potential emotional deficits: Greenberg, "Who Is Sam Bankman-Fried (SBF) Really, and How Could He Have Done What He Did?"

401 government's incisive prosecutor: Caroline Ellison testimony, October 10, 2023, 694–95.

402 *"enormously* valuable existence": Emphasis in original.

402 St. Petersburg paradox: Martin Peterson, "The St. Petersburg Paradox," in *The Stanford Encyclopedia of Philosophy*, ed. Edward N. Zalta and Uri Nodelman (Stanford, CA: Metaphysics Research Lab, Stanford University, 2023), plato.stanford.edu/archives/fall2023/entries/paradox-stpetersburg.

403 combined $452 billion: "The World's Billionaires 2013," Wikipedia, March 17, 2023, en.wikipedia.org /w/index.php?title=The_World%27s_Billionaires_2013&oldid=1145222845.

403 shot up to $1.17 trillion: "Forbes Billionaires 2023: The Richest People in the World," *Forbes*, forbes.com /billionaires.

Chapter ∞: Termination

405 "Looking for where the action is": Erving Goffman, *Interaction Ritual: Essays on Face-to-Face Behavior* (New York: Pantheon Books, 1982), 268.

405 said Paul Graham: My interview with Graham was conducted by email.

405 of YC companies:: Y Combinator, ycombinator.com.

406 frenetic minutes to pitch: Antonio García Martínez, *Chaos Monkeys: Obscene Fortune and Random Failure in Silicon Valley*, Kindle ed. (New York: Harper, 2016), 104–5.

406 his company Loopt: Liz Games, "Loopt's Sam Altman on Why He Sold to Green Dot for $43.4M," AllThingsD, March 9, 2012, allthingsd.com/20120309/green-dot-buys-location-app-loopt-for-43-4m.

406 most interesting founders: Paul Graham, "Five Founders," April 2009, paulgraham.com/5founders .html.

406 later handpicked Altman: Paul Graham, "Sam Altman for President," Y Combinator, February 21, 2014, ycombinator.com/blog/sam-altman-for-president.

406 he was fired: Elizabeth Dwoskin and Nitasha Tiku, "Altman's Polarizing Past Hints at OpenAI Board's Reason for Firing Him," *The Washington Post*, November 22, 2023, washingtonpost.com/technology /2023/11/22/sam-altman-fired-y-combinator-paul-graham.

407 "Technology happens because": Cade Metz, "The ChatGPT King Isn't Worried, but He Knows You Might Be," *The New York Times*, March 31, 2023, sec. Technology, nytimes.com/2023/03/31/technology/sam -altman-open-ai-chatgpt.html.

407 that Altman knew: Per email to Nate Silver, January 19, 2024.

408 taking a shot: Sam Altman (@sama), "i've been stopping myself from sending my EA tweetstorm for a week but idk how much more self-restraint i have," Twitter, November 17, 2022, twitter.com/sama/sta tus/1593046158527836160.

408 rejected Peter Singer's rigid utilitarianism: In a 2016 *New Yorker* profile, Altman said that he cared much more about his family and friends than other human beings—a commonsensical moral sentiment, but one that goes strongly against Singer's notion of impartiality. Tad Friend, "Sam Altman's Manifest Destiny," *The New Yorker*, October 3, 2016, newyorker.com/magazine/2016/10/10/sam-altmans-manifest -destiny.

408 like Emmett Shear: When I asked Shear if he had formally become the OpenAI CEO, he said, "That's a very, very good complicated question that has no linear correct answer." But he also said, "I accepted a job. I got paid for that job. My title for the duration of that job was CEO." That sounds like a yes to me.

408 a chain reaction: Toby Ord, *The Precipice: Existential Risk and the Future of Humanity*, Kindle ed. (New York: Hachette Books, 2020), 91–92.

409 President Harry Truman: Raymond H. Geselbracht, "Harry Truman, Poker Player," *Prologue*, Spring 2003, archives.gov/publications/prologue/2003/spring/truman-poker.html.

409 addressing the world: "Statement by the President Announcing the Use of the A-Bomb at Hiroshima," Harry S. Truman Museum, August 6, 1945, trumanlibrary.gov/library/public-papers/93/statement -president-announcing-use-bomb-hiroshima.

409 simple, one-sentence statement: "Statement on AI Risk," Center for AI Safety, 2023, safe.ai/statement -on-ai-risk.

409 highly-regarded AI companies: This is not my personal opinion but my interpretation of the Silicon Valley consensus after extensive reporting. Other companies such as Meta are considered a step or two behind. Interestingly, far fewer Meta employees signed the one-sentence statement than those at OpenAI, Google and Anthropic; the company may take more of an acceleratonist stance since it feels as though it's behind.

409 the eye-rolling treatment: "Stop Talking About Tomorrow's AI Doomsday When AI Poses Risks Today," *Nature* 618, no. 7967 (June 29, 2023): 885–86, doi.org/10.1038/d41586-023-02094-7.

409 no clear exceptions: Per a background source, genetic engineering and nuclear power are arguable exceptions, technologies where humanity has progressed cautiously.

409 lacking in humans: Joy Wiltermuth, "San Francisco Office Buildings Have 53% Less Foot Traffic Than Four Years Ago," MarketWatch, January 8, 2024, marketwatch.com/story/san-francisco-office-buildings -have-53-less-foot-traffic-than-four-years-ago-199a7eb5.

410 echoing Goffman's phrase: Though the phrase didn't originate with Goffman. It was a somewhat common phrase at the time Goffman wrote *Interaction Ritual* in 1967, such as being the name of a variety TV show.

410 will be obliged: Goffman, *Interaction Ritual*, 269.

410 played poker on the evening before Trinity: Richard Rhodes, *The Making of the Atomic Bomb*, Kindle ed. (New York: Simon & Schuster Paperbacks, 2012), 971.

410 *Post* describes him: Nitasha Tiku, "OpenAI Leaders Warned of Abusive Behavior before Sam Altman's Ouster," *The Washington Post*, December 8, 2023, washingtonpost.com/technology/2023/12/08/open -ai-sam-altman-complaints.

411 companies like OpenAI and Anthropic: "Google Brain Drain: Where are the Authors of 'Attention Is All You Need' Now?" *AIChat*, aichat.blog/google-exodus-where-are-the-authors-of-attention-is-all-you -need-now.

411 Altman has tipped his hat: @SamA, https://twitter.com/sama/status/1540227243368058880?lang=en.

412 thinks the "schtick": roon (@tszzl), "e/acc's are both dangerous and cringe and cribbed half my schtick. disavow!," Twitter, August 7, 2022, twitter.com/tszzl/status/1556344673681059840.

412 5 billion years: Ali Sundermier, "The Sun Will Destroy Earth a Lot Sooner Than You Might Think," Business Insider, September 18, 2016, businessinsider.com/sun-destroy-earth-red-giant-white-dwarf -2016-9.

413 Aztecs had achieved: roon (@tszzl), "what we've done is trapped our current moral standards in amber and amplified their effectiveness manyfold. if the Aztecs had AGI they would be slaughtering simulated human children by trillions to keep the proverbial sun from going out," Twitter, December 16, 2022, twitter.com/tszzl/status/1603633113006952449.

413 optimistic about them: Paul Graham (@paulg), "How can one become more optimistic? It seems hard to cultivate directly. But optimism is contagious, so you can do it by surrounding yourself with optimistic people. This is one of the big forces driving Y Combinator, and Silicon Valley in general," Twitter, May 23, 2019, twitter.com/paulg/status/1131490092110012417.

413 has testified about his concerns: Cat Zakrzewski, Cristiano Lima-Strong, and Will Oremus, "CEO Behind ChatGPT Warns Congress AI Could Cause 'Harm to the World,'" *The Washington Post*, May 17, 2023, washingtonpost.com/technology/2023/05/16/sam-altman-open-ai-congress-hearing.

414 "Attention Is All": Ashish Vaswani et al., "Attention Is All You Need," arXiv, August 1, 2023, arxiv.org /abs/1706.03762.

415 most rapidly adopted technologies: Krystal Hu, "ChatGPT Sets Record for Fastest-Growing User Base— Analyst Note," Reuters, February 2, 2023, sec. Technology, reuters.com/technology/chatgpt-sets -record-fastest-growing-user-base-analyst-note-2023-02-01.

415 "all our woe": Rhodes, *The Making of the Atomic Bomb*, 23.

416 "I beseech you": Sometimes also called Cromwell's rule. "Cromwell's Rule," Wiktionary, February 4, 2024, en.wiktionary.org/w/index.php?title=Cromwell%27s_rule&oldid=77945222.

416 What about the Sentinelese: "Sentinelese," Survival International, survivalinternational.org/tribes /sentinelese.

416 Yudkowsky's stylized version: Although the conversation has been reported on, I can find no reference online to these precise words. So I'd treat this as Yudkowsky's takeaway impression of the conversation and certainly not a verbatim account. Michael Lee, "Elon Musk Was Warned That AI Could Destroy Human Colony on Mars: Report," Fox News, December 4, 2023, foxnews.com/us/elon-musk-was -warned-that-ai-could-destroy-a-human-colony-on-mars-report.

417 "all biological life": Eliezer Yudkowsky, "The Open Letter on AI Doesn't Go Far Enough," *Time*, March 29, 2023, time.com/6266923/ai-eliezer-yudkowsky-open-letter-not-enough.

417 incorrect, overconfident predictions: bgarfinkel, "On Deference and Yudkowsky's AI Risk Estimates," EA Forum, June 19, 2022, forum.effectivealtruism.org/posts/NBgpPaz5vYe3tH4ga/on-deference-and -yudkowsky-s-ai-risk-estimates.

417 he posed for: Sam Altman (@sama), Twitter, February 24, 2023, twitter.com/sama/status/162897416 5335379973.

418 "any final goal": Nick Bostrom, *Superintelligence: Paths, Dangers, Strategies*, Kindle ed. (Oxford: Oxford University Press, 2017), 127.

419 IQ of 145: IQ is defined as having an average of 100 and a standard deviation of 15. So three standard deviations higher would mean an average IQ of 145.

419 von Neumann's estimated 190: "IQ Estimates of Geniuses," *Jan Bryxí* (blog), janbryxi.com/iq-john-von-neumann-albert-einstein-mark-zuckerberg-elon-musk-stephen-hawking-kevin-mitnick-cardinal-richelieu-warren-buffett-george-soros-steve-jobs-isaac-new.

419 "transformations are not": John von Neumann, "Can We Survive Technology?," sseh.uchicago.edu/doc/von_Neumann_1955.pdf.

420 at Bikini Atoll: "John von Neumann," Von Neumann and the Development of Game Theory, cs.stanford.edu/people/eroberts/courses/soco/projects/1998-99/game-theory/neumann.html.

420 about global warming: Von Neumann, "Can We Survive Technology?"

420 "might not survive": Marina von Neumann Whitman, *The Martian's Daughter: A Memoir*, Kindle ed. (Ann Arbor: University of Michigan Press, 2013), 25.

420 bombing not Hiroshima: Alan Bollard, *Economists at War: How a Handful of Economists Helped Win and Lose the World Wars*, Kindle ed. (Oxford: Oxford University Press, 2020), 228.

420 three times the population: "Largest Cities in Japan: Population from 1890," Demographia, demographia.com/db-jp-city1940.htm.

420 bomb's horrifying effects: Bollard, *Economists at War*, 229.

421 considered so valuable: Ashutosh Jogalekar, "What John von Neumann Really Did at Los Alamos," 3 Quarks Daily, October 26, 2020, 3quarksdaily.com/3quarksdaily/2020/10/what-john-von-neumann-really-did-at-los-alamos.html.

421 of nuclear deterrence: Andrew Brown and Lorna Arnold, "The Quirks of Nuclear Deterrence," *International Relations* 24, no. 3 (September 2010): 293–312, doi.org/10.1177/0047117810377278.

421 number of nuclear states: The five signatories to the Nuclear Non-Proliferation Treaty—the U.S., Russia, China, France, and the UK—plus India, Pakistan, North Korea (which declared itself a nuclear weapon state in September 2022), and Israel (which officially follows a policy of strategic ambiguity but is widely believed to possess nuclear weapons).

422 next twenty years: This can be calculated as $1 - (1 - 0.037)^{20}$, which equals a 53 percent chance that nuclear weapons *would* be used at least once in the next 20 years.

424 John F. Kennedy: Ord, *The Precipice*, 26.

424 Stanislav Petrov: Dylan Matthews, "40 Years Ago Today, One Man Saved Us from World-Ending Nuclear War," *Vox*, September 26, 2018, vox.com/2018/9/26/17905796/nuclear-war-1983-stanislav-petrov-soviet-union.

425 "bomb is shit": Rhodes, *The Making of the Atomic Bomb*, 938.

426 "just announce to the enemy": T. C. Schelling, "The Threat That Leaves Something to Chance," RAND Corporation, 1959, doi.org/10.7249/HDA1631-1.

427 about 90 percent of you: At twenty-eight minutes in this video: "Tick, Tick, Boom? Presidential Decision-Making in a Nuclear Attack," 2022, youtube.com/watch?v=S6r3A2mSNlU.

428 in evolutionary psychology: McDermott has an MA in experimental social psychology in addition to her PhD in political science.

429 made us human: Francis Fukuyama, *The End of History and the Last Man*, Kindle ed. (New York: Free Press, 2006), 151.

429 exhibit revenge-seeking traits: Rose McDermott, Anthony C. Lopez, and Peter K. Hatemi, "'Blunt Not the Heart, Enrage It': The Psychology of Revenge and Deterrence," *Texas National Security Review* 1, no. 1 (November 24, 2017), tnsr.org/2017/11/blunt-not-heart-enrage-psychology-revenge-deterrence.

430 about three hundred thousand years: Gil Oliveira, "Earth History in Your Hand," Carnegie Museum of Natural History, carnegiemnh.org/earth-history-in-your-hand.

430 a "proud co-parent": "Nick Ryder," LinkedIn, linkedin.com/in/nick-ryder-84774117b.

431 hundreds of billions: Tom B. Brown et al., "Language Models Are Few-Shot Learners," arXiv, July 22, 2020, arxiv.org/abs/2005.14165.

431 most similar word: "Semantically Related Words for 'roadrunner_NOUN,'" vectors.nlpl.eu/explore/embeddings/en/#.

433 pioneering chess computer: Murray Campbell, "Knowledge Discovery in Deep Blue," *Communications of the ACM* 42, no. 11 (November 1999): 65–67, doi.org/10.1145/319382.319396.

433 playing against themselves: David Silver et al., "Mastering Chess and Shogi by Self-Play with a General Reinforcement Learning Algorithm," arXiv, December 5, 2017, arxiv.org/abs/1712.01815.

435 ChatGPT said verbatim: With some minor cuts for length.

438 some deliberate randomization: Eric Glover, "Controlled Randomness in LLMs/ChatGPT with Zero Temperature: A Game Changer for Prompt Engineering," *AppliedIngenuity.ai: Practical AI Solutions* (blog), May 12, 2023, appliedingenuity.substack.com/p/controlled-randomness-in-llmschatgpt.

439 it's come closer: Per conversation with Stuart Russell.

445 Participants were asked: Ezra Karger et al., "Forecasting Existential Risks: Evidence from a Long-Run Forecasting Tournament," Forecasting Research Institute, July 10, 2023, static1.squarespace.com /static/635693acf15a3e2a14a56a4a/t/64f0a7838ccbf43b6b5ee40c/1693493128111/XPT.pdf.

446 "Math doesn't WANT": Marc Andreessen (@pmarca), "The obvious counterargument to AI foom et al arguments is that they are category error. Math doesn't WANT things. It doesn't have GOALS. It's just math," Twitter, March 5, 2023, twitter.com/pmarca/status/1632237452571312128.

447 the "blind empiricism": Eliezer Yudkowsky, "Blind Empiricism," LessWrong, November 12, 2017, less wrong.com/posts/6n9aKApfLre5WWvpG/blind-empiricism.

449 some mundane utility: The phrase "mundane utility" is frequently used by Zvi Mowshowitz.

449 "be irreversibly transformed": Ray Kurzweil, *The Singularity Is Near: When Humans Transcend Biology*, Kindle ed. (New York: Viking, 2005), 7.

450 Melanie Mitchell: *The Hub* Staff, "Is AI an Existential Threat? Yann LeCun, Max Tegmark, Melanie Mitchell, and Yoshua Bengio Make Their Case," *The Hub*, July 4, 2023, thehub.ca/2023-07-04/is-ai-an -existential-threat-yann-lecun-max-tegmark-melanie-mitchell-and-yoshua-bengio-make-their -case.

450 development of bioweapons: Zvi Mowshowitz, "AI #49: Bioweapon Testing Begins," *Don't Worry About the Vase* (blog), February 1, 2024, thezvi.substack.com/p/ai-49-bioweapon-testing-begins.

452 futures from a Reddit post: Xisuthrus, "The Only 16 Ideologies That Exist in My World," Reddit post, R/Worldjerking, August 12, 2019, reddit.com/r/worldjerking/comments/cphds9/the_only_16_ideologies _that_exist_in_my_world.

452 OpenAI is nominally: Alnoor Ebrahim, "OpenAI Is a Nonprofit-Corporate Hybrid: A Management Expert Explains How This Model Works—And How It Fueled the Tumult Around CEO Sam Altman's Short-Lived Ouster," The Conversation, November 30, 2023, http://theconversation.com/openai-is-a-non profit-corporate-hybrid-a-management-expert-explains-how-this-model-works-and-how -it-fueled-the-tumult-around-ceo-sam-altmans-short-lived-ouster-218340.

453 like fast food: Nate Silver, "The McDonald's Theory of Why Everyone Thinks the Economy Sucks," *Silver Bulletin* (blog), October 1, 2023, natesilver.net/p/the-mcdonalds-theory-of-why-everyone.

453 "The rationalist utopia": Ursula K. Le Guin, "A Non-Euclidean View of California as a Cold Place to Be," 1982, bpb-us-e1.wpmucdn.com/sites.ucsc.edu/dist/9/20/files/2019/07/1989a_Le-Guin_non-Euclidean -view-California.pdf.

454 "peninsula sticking out": Ursula K. Le Guin, *Always Coming Home*, Kindle ed. (Berkeley: University of California Press, 2001), 170.

454 but not all that many: This is not stated explicitly, but it is clearly implied; the cover of *Always Coming Home* depicts an empty landscape.

454 questions of you: Le Guin, *Always Coming Home*, 167.

454 benevolently seen to it: Le Guin, *Always Coming Home*, 438.

456 Altman reportedly wants: wsj.com/tech/ai/sam-altman-seeks-trillions-of-dollars-to-reshape-business -of-chips-and-ai-89ab3db0.

457 the broader population: This paragraph was shaped by a conversation with Paul Christiano.

457 Existential risk itself: Ord, *The Precipice*, 62.

458 already worried about AI doomsday: Taylor Orth and Carl Bialik, "AI Doomsday Worries Many Americans. So Does Apocalypse from Climate Change, Nukes, War, and More," YouGov, April 14, 2023, today .yougov.com/technology/articles/45565-ai-nuclear-weapons-world-war-humanity-poll.

458 January 2024 poll: Daniel Colson (@DanielColson6), "@TheAIPI's latest polling featured in @Politico today. We found people prefer political candidates that take strong pro-regulation stances on AI. (We did not reveal to respondents the source of the quotes below.)," Twitter, January 24, 2024, twitter.com /DanielColson6/status/1750026192982593794.

458 the religious share: Pew Research Center, "The Changing Global Religious Landscape," Pew Research Center, April 5, 2017, pewresearch.org/religion/2017/04/05/the-changing-global-religious-landscape.

459 "for real, killed": Jack Clark (@jackclarkSF), "People don't take guillotines seriously. Historically, when a tiny group gains a huge amount of power and makes life-altering decisions for a vast number of people, the minority gets actually, for real, killed. People feel like this can't happen anymore," Twitter, August 6, 2022, twitter.com/jackclarkSF/status/1555992785768984576.

459 no economic growth: Lawrence H. Summers, "Harvard's Larry H. Summers on Secular Stagnation," IMF, March 2020, imf.org/en/Publications/fandd/issues/2020/03/larry-summers-on-secular-stagnation.

459 GDP has grown: Based on real GDP through the third quarter of 2023.

460 considered extreme poverty: Max Roser, "Extreme Poverty: How Far Have We Come, and How Far Do We Still Have to Go?," Our World in Data, December 28, 2023, ourworldindata.org/extreme-poverty -in-brief.

Chapter 1776: Foundation

461 **"as radical and as revolutionary"**: Gordon S. Wood, *The Radicalism of the American Revolution*, Kindle ed. (New York: Vintage Books, 1993), 5.

461 **rule of law**: Nate Silver, "Why Liberalism and Leftism Are Increasingly at Odds," *Silver Bulletin* (blog), December 12, 2023, natesilver.net/p/why-liberalism-and-leftism-are-increasingly.

461 **was vastly larger**: "How Were the Colonies Able to Win Independence?," Digital History, digitalhistory .uh.edu/disp_textbook.cfm?smtID=2&psid=3220.

461 **had been stagnant**: "Global GDP over the Long Run," Our World in Data, 2017, ourworldindata.org /grapher/world-gdp-over-the-last-two-millennia.

461 **progress was foreign**: David Simpson, "The Idea of Progress," condor.depaul.edu/~dsimpson/awtech /progress.html.

462 **England GDP, 1270**: Yes, England specifically and not the United Kingdom. The principal data source is the Bank of England's "millennium of macroeconomic data," which covers years through 2016; bankofengland.co.uk/statistics/research-datasets. For more recent years, I used data from the UK Office for National Statistics. For 2022 and 2023, I estimated growth rates using the United Kingdom overall rather than England specifically.

462 **the social safety net**: Donald N. McCloskey, "New Perspectives on the Old Poor Law," *Explorations in Economic History* 10, no. 4 (June 1973): 419–36, doi.org/10.1016/0014-4983(73)90025-9.

463 **"soon starve to death"**: Paul R. Ehrlich, *The Population Bomb* (Cutchogue, NY: Buccaneer Books, 1971), xi.

463 **"through the mob"**: Ehrlich, *The Population Bomb*, 1.

463 **in extreme poverty**: Population data: "India Population 1950–2024," MacroTrends, macrotrends.net /countries/IND/india/population. Data on extreme poverty: Michail Moatsos, "Global Extreme Poverty: Present and Past since 1820," in *How Was Life?*, vol. 2, *New Perspectives on Well-Being and Global Inequality since 1820* (Paris: OECD, 2021), doi.org/10.1787/3d96efc5-enmacrotrends.net/countries/IND /india/population.

464 **denying billions of people**: Ehrlich believes that the optimal global population is 1.5 to 2 billion rather than the actual 8 billion. Damian Carrington, "Paul Ehrlich: 'Collapse of Civilisation Is a Near Certainty Within Decades,'" *The Guardian*, March 22, 2018, sec. Cities, theguardian.com/cities/2018/mar/22/col lapse-civilisation-near-certain-decades-population-bomb-paul-ehrlich.

464 **Global GDP growth**: "GDP growth (annual %)," World Bank Open Data, data.worldbank.org/indicator /NY.GDP.MKTP.KD.ZG.

465 **considered more autocratic**: Bastian Herre and Max Roser, "The World Has Recently Become Less Democratic," Our World in Data, December 28, 2023, ourworldindata.org/less-democratic.

465 **subtract an estimated**: Christopher Flavelle, "Climate Change Could Cut World Economy by $23 Trillion in 2050, Insurance Giant Warns," *The New York Times*, April 22, 2021, sec. Climate, nytimes.com/2021 /04/22/climate/climate-change-economy.html.

465 **decline in IQ**: Elizabeth M. Dworak, William Revelle, and David M. Condon, "Looking for Flynn Effects in a Recent Online U.S. Adult Sample: Examining Shifts Within the SAPA Project," *Intelligence* 98 (May 2023): 101734, doi.org/10.1016/j.intell.2023.101734.

465 **going to college**: "What Percentage of US High School Graduates Enroll in College?," USAFacts, usafa cts.org/data/topics/people-society/education/higher-education/college-enrollment-rate.

465 **suffer from depression**: Dan Witters, "U.S. Depression Rates Reach New Highs," Gallup, May 17, 2023, news.gallup.com/poll/505745/depression-rates-reach-new-highs.aspx.

465 **large language models**: ChatGPT, Claude, and Google Bard.

465 **my Twitter followers**: Nate Silver (@NateSilver588), "The most important inventions of the decade of the 1900s vs the decade of the 2000s. Pretty good evidence for secular stagnation," Twitter, x.com/Nate Silver538/status/1753433550148206696?s=20.

465 **Top Technological Inventions**: Many inventions are hard to date specifically, but here is more detail on some of the more controversial cases. Radio broadcasting refers to first transmission involving full voice and sound. Vacuum cleaner refers to the modern vacuum cleaner using power and suction. Electrocardiograph refers to the first practical version of the technology. The hamburger is a notoriously disputed example; 1904 is the date when the hamburger became famous at the St. Louis World's Fair, but other sources date its origins to 1885 or 1900. mRNA vaccines are another ambiguous case. But the seminal paper cited to Katalin Karikó and Drew Weissman in their award of the Nobel Prize dates to 2005. Cloud computing refers to commercial application with Amazon Web Services. Human genome project refers to the completion of the project in 2003. And Tesla's 2008 date refers to the first commercial sales.

466 **Barzun used "decadent"**: Jacques Barzun, *From Dawn to Decadence: 500 Years of Western Cultural Life 1500 to the Present* (New York: HarperCollins, 2000), xvi.

467 **Some scholars tie this feeling**: *The Decadent Society: How We Became the Victims of Our Own Success* Kindle Edition (New York: Avid Reader Press / Simon & Schuster), 1.

468 **he calls "*thymos*"**: Francis Fukuyama, *The End of History and the Last Man*, Kindle ed. (New York: Free Press, 2006), location 118.

469 **an unofficial slogan**: Ministry for Europe and Foreign Affairs, "Liberty, Equality, Fraternity," France Diplomacy, diplomatie.gouv.fr/en/coming-to-france/france-facts/symbols-of-the-republic/article/liberty-equality-fraternity.

469 **an *agentic* AI**: "Research into Agentic AI Systems," OpenAI, openai.smapply.org/prog/agentic-ai-research-grants.

471 **Avoid "noble lies"**: Kerrington Powell and Vinay Prasad, "The Noble Lies of COVID-19," *Slate*, July 28, 2021, slate.com/technology/2021/07/noble-lies-covid-fauci-cdc-masks.html.

INDEX

Page numbers in italics refer to illustrations.